◇ THIRD EDITION

Introduction to Physical Anthropology

◇ THIRD EDITION

Introduction to Physical Anthropology

HARRY NELSON
Department of Anthropology
Foothill College
Los Altos, California

ROBERT JURMAIN
Department of Anthropology
San Jose State University
San Jose, California

WEST PUBLISHING COMPANY
St. Paul   New York   Los Angeles   San Francisco

Library of Congress Cataloging in Publication Data

Nelson, Harry.
    Introduction to physical anthropology.

    Bibliography: p.
    Includes index.
    1. Physical anthropology.   I. Jurmain, Robert.
II. Title.
GN60.N44   1985   573   84–25671
ISBN 0–314–85282–4

Design: Janet Bollow
Copy editor: Stuart Kenter
Illustrations: Brenda Booth, Sue Sellars, Evanell Towne
Cover: A partial reproduction of the Mtoko Cave frieze, Zimbabwe. The cover is a photograph of a painting by Elizabeth Goodall, done as part of her work with Leo Frobenius in 1929. Courtesy of the Frobenius Institute, Frankfurt, Germany
Composition: Hansen & Associates Graphics

Credits

CHAPTER 1:   5 (top) Public Relations, San Francisco State University; bottom) H. Nelson. 8 Courtesy of Frank Spenser. 13 R. Jurmain. 16 Diana L. Davis, University of Oklahoma. 17 Wayne Fogle.

CHAPTER 2:   25, 27, 29, 32, 33, 35 Courtesy of the American Museum of Natural History. 37 Courtesy Library of the New York Academy of Medicine. 41 M.W.F. Tweedie, Photo Researchers, Inc.

CHAPTER 3:   48 Dr. Linus Pauling, Institute of Orthomolecular Medicine. 49 From J. D. Watson, *The Double Helix*, Atheneum, New York, 1968, p. 215. © 1968 by J. D. Watson. 52 Prenatal Diagnosis and Cytogenetics Laboratory, University of California, San Francisco.

CHAPTER 4:   80 Adapted from M. E. Challinor/*Science 82* Magazine. 83 Courtesy of the American Museum of Natural History. 85, 86 Malcolm Gutter. 100 Courtesy of *Annual Reviews of Genetics*.

CHAPTER 5:   130 Courtesy of D. E. Schreiber, IBM Research Laboratory, San Jose. 139 From: A. E. Mourant, et al., *The Distribution of the Human Blood Groups and Other Polymorphisms*, Oxford University Press, © 1976. By permission of the publisher. 142 From Edward Novitski, *Human Genetics*, Macmillan Publishing Co., Inc., © 1977. Reprinted with permission of the publisher. 145 From: A. E. Mourant, et al., *The Distribution of the Human Blood Groups and Other Polymorphisms*, Oxford University Press, © 1976. By permission of the publisher.

CHAPTER 6:   161 Wide World Photos. 163 From C. S. Coon and E. E. Hunt, *The Living Races of Man* © 1965 Alfred A. Knopf, Inc. 168 Courtesy of the American Museum of Natural History. 170 Courtesy of Dr. Richard Ingraham. 171 Reprinted with permission from *Man in the Andes: A Multidisciplinary Study of High-Altitude Quechia*, edited by Baker and Little © 1976 by Dowden, Hutchinson & Ross, Inc., Stroudsburg, Pa. 175 Courtesy of UNICEF, photo by P. Grant. 180 Wide World Photos. 182 United Press International. 185 Wide World Photos.

CHAPTER 7:   195 Courtesy of R. Heglar; photo by H. Nelson. 197 (top) Courtesy of the New York Academy of Medicine; (bottom) H. Nelson.

CHAPTER 8:   222 Courtesy of Biological Sciences Curriculum Study. Permission to use this figure does not consistute an endorsement. 223 Courtesy of the American Museum of Natural History. 228 Reprinted by permission of *American Scientist*. 231 Courtesy of Biological Sciences Study. Permission to use this figure does not constitute an endorsement. 232 (top) San Diego Zoo photo; (bottom) New York Zoological Society photo. Drawing: From *Life: An Introduction to Biology* by Simpson, Pittendrigh, and Tiffany. Copyright © 1957 by Harcourt Brace Jovanovich, Inc. Redrawn by permission of the publishers. Redrawn from Romer, *The Vertebrate Body*, W. B. Saunders.

CHAPTER 9:   241 © National Geographic Society. Courtesy Dr. Dian Fossey. 245 Redrawn with permission of Quadrangle/The New York Times Book Co. from *The Antecedents of Man* by W. E. Le Gros Clark. Also redrawn by permission of Edinburgh University Press, Edinburgh, Scotland. 248, 250 San Diego Zoo photo. 251 (a) Ron Garrison, San Diego Zoo; (b) R. D. Schmidt, San Diego Zoo photo. 252, 253 San Diego Zoo photo. 254 H. Nelson. 258 Ron Garrison, San Diego Zoo photo. 259 (left) Ron Garrison, San Diego Zoo; (right) Courtesy of Dr. Faren Akins, National Aeronautics and Space Administration, Ames Research Center. 260 San Diego Zoo photo. 261 (top) H. Nelson; (bottom) Ron Garrison, San Diego Zoo. 262 H. Nelson.

CHAPTER 10:   270 David Bygott, © National Geographic Society. 276 (top) T. W. Ranson; (right) San Diego Zoo photo. 277 (top right) H. Nelson; (bottom left) courtesy of Masao Kawai; (bottom right) Gladys Porter Zoo, Brownsville, Texas. 278 (top left) Ron Garrison, San Diego Zoo; (a) San Diego Zoo photo; (b) H. Nelson. 279 H. Nelson. 280 H. F. Harlow, University of Wisconsin Primate Laboratory. 282 Courtesy of Hans Kummer. 284 Photograph courtesy of T. W. Ransom. 288, 290 Baron Hugo van Lawick © National Geographic Society. 295 Geza Teleki. 298 Phyllis Dolinhow. 299 Courtesy of Beatrice Gardner. 306 Courtesy of Masao Kawai. 309, 311, 312 From George Schaller, *The Serengeti Lion*, University of Chicago Press, © 1972 by the University of Chicago. 316, 317, 318, 319 Courtesy of Jon Yellen.

CHAPTER 11:   331 Redrawn with permission of Quadrangle/The New York Times Book Co. from *The Antecedents of Man* by W. E. Le Gros Clark. Also redrawn by permission of Edinburgh University Press, Edinburgh, Scotland. 336 Courtesy of Dr. E. L. Simons. 341 (top) Courtesy the British Museum; (bottom) R. Jurmain. 345 Courtesy David Pilbeam. 348 Courtesy of Dr. David Pilbeam. 349 The Bettmann Archive. 350 R. Jurmain. 356 From *Populations, Species and Evolution* by Ernest Mayr, Harvard University Press. Copyright © 1963, 1970 by the President and Fellows of Harvard College.

CHAPTER 12:   364 R. Jurmain. 368 M. D. Leakey, *Olduvai Gorge*, Vol. III. Cambridge University Press, 1971. 370 David Siddon, L. S. B. Leakey Foundation. 371, 373 R. Jurmain. 375 H. Nelson. 382, 383 R. Jurmain.

CHAPTER 13:   394 R. Jurmain. 395 Courtesy of the Geological Society of London, British Museum. 396 Courtesy of Dr. Raymond Dart, photo by Alun R. Hughes. 397 Photo by Alun R. Hughes; reproduced by permission of Professor P. V. Tobias. 399 San Diego Zoo photo. 400 Courtesy of the American Museum of Natural History. 402 Photo provided courtesy of Transvaal Museum, South Africa (also source of specimen). 403 The Bettmann Archive. 404 R. Jurmain. 405 H. Nelson. 406 (top) H. Nelson; (bottom) Photo provided courtesy of the Transvaal Museum, South Africa (also source of the specimen). 408 Ron Garrison, San Diego Zoo.

CHAPTER 14:   418 From C. K. Brain, "New Finds at the Swartkrans Australopithecine Site," *Nature*, Vol. 225:1112-1119. Redrawn with per-

(continued following Index)

◇ CONTENTS

◇ CHAPTER FOUR
Issue: The Gene Makers 80

Genetics and Evolution   79

Living Primates

Models for Human Behavior

◇ CHAPTER ELEVEN

Issue: Is There a Bigfoot?   326

Primate Evolution   **325**

◇ CHAPTER FIFTEEN
Issue: Man, the Hunter; Woman, the
Gatherer 446

Plio-Pleistocene Hominids: Organization and Interpretation 445

◇ CHAPTER SIXTEEN
Issue: Seeking the Peking
Bones 464

Homo Erectus   463

Homo Sapiens 505 ◇ CHAPTER SEVENTEEN
ISSUE: The Frozen Neandertal 506

◇ PREFACE

Anthropologists and other researchers continue to discover more fossils, to study more primates, to theorize about problems of human evolution, and to ponder the significance of all this material. In this third edition of our text, we have tried to keep up with these extensive recent developments.

Besides updating, we have employed several pedagogical devices to help the diverse students enrolled in introductory physical anthropology classes, to assist them in understanding unfamiliar subject matter. For example, the writing style is geared to the level of students; a running glossary in the page margins defines difficult or unfamiliar terms, often with phonetic spelling; we have increased the number of maps which, we believe, help students to fix in their minds the sites and events discussed in the text; and frequent charts, tables, and photographs are used to aid in visualizing and organizing text material. We have continued with the "Issues" at the beginning of each chapter. These provide a popular introduction to the chapters and are intended to catch the students' interest and motivate their reading.

We believe this approach is suitable for both students who do, and those who do not, plan to major in anthropology.

The text is divided into three fundamental areas: evolution and genetics, primates, and hominids. Following the Introduction, Chapter 2 takes up the concept of evolution and Chapter 3 introduces the cell. Continuing with genetics, Chapter 4 deals with Mendel and his experiments, and Chapters 5 and 6 are devoted to modern populations from a genetic point of view. Chapter 7 concludes this "genetic unit" with a discussion of human diversity.

The next four chapters treat the subject of primates. Chapter 8 provides an overview of vertebrate evolution with special emphasis on mammals. Chapter 9 deals with living primates, Chapter 10 with primate behavior, and Chapter 11 with primate evolution. This leads to hominid evolution, the main focus of the course and the subject of chapters 12 through 17.

As an introduction to hominid evolution, the various aspects of paleoanthropology are discussed in Chapter 12, early hominids from South Africa in Chapter 13 and from East Africa in Chapter 14. The evolutionary significance of australopithecines is the topic of Chapter 15. From here, we move on to the genus *Homo*: *H. erectus* in Chapter 16 and *H. sapiens* in Chapter 17.

There are instructors who may prefer to present modern populations following the discussion of human evolution. For those who wish to do so, or to rearrange chapters to suit their own sequence, it is an easy matter to adjust chapters to a variety of approaches.

For their assistance in this revision, we wish to thank the following reviewers for their constructive critiques:

Norm Alger, Moorpark College

Gail Kennedy, University of California, Los Angeles

Henry M. McHenry, University of California, Davis

Larry Mai, University of California, Los Angeles

Robert J. Meier, Indiana University

Edward Myers, Chaffey College

Judy Regensteiner, University of Colorado

Irin Rovner, North Carolina State University

Sam Sandt, Pierce College

Our special thanks also to: Wayne Fogel for photography, Phillip Tobias and Alun Hughes for providing unpublished data and photographs, Sandra Reed for her work on the index, and Lynn Kilgore and C. Loring Brace for their assistance and comments.

Harry Nelson
Robert Jurmain

We are physical anthropologists. In this text, we introduce you to our discipline, the study of human evolution.

Evolution is a biological process and must therefore be understood from a biological perspective. Accordingly, the early chapters acquaint you with several broad principles of the evolutionary process, as well as with genetics and cell biology.

Unavoidably, a scientific discipline like ours uses many terms which students feel compelled to memorize, and on which instructors feel equally compelled to test. For some of you—particularly those with little or no high school biology—understanding these terms may take some extra effort. Thus, to aid you in learning the basics of physical anthropology, we have set off and clearly defined many of the more important terms and concepts. Studying these (even memorizing them) will help you understand the fundamentals of physical anthropology.

Following the suggestion of students, a further study aid has been incorporated into this edition. Those boxes that are tinted are, for the most part, somewhat extraneous items concerning the history of discoveries, famous personalities, and so on. They are included for your interest, but it is unlikely you would be responsible for such material on exams. On the other hand, those boxes that are not tinted are more integral to the text and may, in fact, be included as exam material. For further clarification concerning specific items, consult your instructor.

Those of you who have had advanced high school or even college biology courses may find that you are already familiar with much of the introductory material. We suggest that you review this material so that, along with others exposed to it for the first time, you will leave the text with a basic understanding of evolution and how it has affected our ancestors and continues to act on our species.

As a scientific discipline, physical anthropology is an ongoing pursuit of knowledge. Throughout the world today research projects continue and data accumulate at a fantastic rate. We have made this text as "up-to-date" as possible; however, there will doubtless be new information known by the time you read this book. New data may produce new hypotheses. In any case, your basic understanding should not necessarily be about the minute details of human evolution, but rather about the principles involved in the interpretation of our evolution.

For example, discoveries of a vast new array of 8 to 10 million-year-old fossils have caused dramatic revisions of our ideas concerning this stage of evolution. A partial skull found in Pakistan (during the 1979–1980 field season) and discussed in print in 1982 has had particularly important impact. However, the Second Edition of this text—published in early 1982—came our just prior to this crucial publication and, consequently, did not incorporate some of these new developments.

We have modernized this edition considerably, expanding the relevant portions in Chapter 11 and elsewhere. Still, no book can be completely up-to-date. As a case in point, further discoveries of related fossil material to the Pakistani skull just mentioned have recently come to light in China—in fact, up to 1000 new specimens! Unfortunately, almost none of these new fossils have been described. Some preliminary findings (not yet published) suggest that these Chinese fossils are quite different from those in Pakistan (data not discussed in this edition). Thus, further revisions of our text are, no doubt, on the way.

New discoveries are always just around the corner. As members of an educated public, you will be able to understand and perhaps even participate in the development of a more complete comprehension of *Homo sapiens*, the animal, as well as *Homo sapiens*, the human being.

Robert Jurmain
Harry Nelson

◇ THIRD EDITION

Introduction
to Physical
Anthropology

Introduction

CONTENTS

◇ ISSUE Fact, Fantasy, and Anthropology

At the beginning of each chapter throughout this book you will find brief discussions of an assortment of contemporary issues. Some of these—for example, the existence and implications of such phenomena as Bigfoot, extraterrestrials, and frozen Neandertals—may seem too bizarre to be discussed in a scholarly textbook. However, scientists and scholars cannot make these issues disappear by ignoring them. Someone in the scientific community must deal with them, hopefully in a rational way. This task often falls to the physical anthropologist.

Since the public is concerned about these topics, we shall address them. You may not always agree with our conclusions (you may notice, by the way, that our own personal biases occasionally emerge), but to induce you to agree or disagree with us is not the point. What you should do, is think seriously and rationally about these issues. In light of all the bizarre and ridiculous claims floating around today in pseudoscientific guise, you will do best by adopting the cautious "show me" approach attributed to inhabitants of Missouri. Without hard evidence, no distinction may be made between fiction, fantasy, and fact. Judge for yourself!

◇ What Is Anthropology?

Anthropology is the study of human beings. As a scientific discipline, anthropology is concerned with all aspects of humankind: social behavior, language, attitudes, values, personality, government, kinship, history, prehistory, art, illness, healing, religion, economics, technology, and clothing, to name just a few. Furthermore, anthropology is concerned with such biological aspects of humans as body build, pigmentation, blood types and other biochemical traits, our ancestry and ancestors, and the evolutionary processes involved in our physical development.

Anthropology, therefore, is a **holistic** science, with the entire gamut of humankind as the focus of study. Other disciplines that deal with people—sociology, psychology, economics, political science, history, and others—tend to specialize in single aspects of human activity. Economists, for example, study the production, distribution, and consumption of goods; the market system; and systems of exchange; but they would rarely consider the effect of religion or kinship on the economic system. Anthropology, however, takes a broader, holistic approach and considers the findings of all academic fields pertaining to humans; in fact, anything associated with humankind is considered within the scope of our discipline.

The division of anthropology into two* broad categories—cultural and physical—illustrates its breadth. Cultural anthropology, often divided into sociocultural anthropology, **archeology**, and linguistics, is involved with the **culture** of peoples, both past and present. The sociocultural anthropologist concentrates on the culture of existing peoples, traditionally focusing on the less technologically complex societies of the world. Studying, say, the Yurok, a California Indian society, the sociocultural anthropologist would not restrict investigation to clothing, food, and religious practices, but would include the entire range of Yurok behavior.

An archeologist would be concerned with the same society through attempting to reconstruct its ancient culture. By studying the **artifacts** obtained by excavation, the archeologist could learn the kinds of food the Yurok once gathered, hunted, and ate; what kinds of tools and weapons they made and used; what sort of housing they had erected and clothing they had worn; how they disposed of the dead and, perhaps, their attitudes toward death; what goods they traded with neighbors, etc. The archeologist would, in a sense, do what the sociocultural anthropologist does, but data would come mainly from artifacts rather than from informants and actual observation of the people.

As a focus of culture, the linguist would take the description and history of language. Anthropological linguistics is considered a part of cultural anthropology because language is such an integral part of culture. Language is

Anthropology
anthropos: man
logos: science or study of

Holism
Viewing the whole in terms of an integrated system; cultural and ecological systems as wholes.

Archeology
(ar-kee-ol'-o-jee)
arche: beginning, ancient
logos: discourse, science or study of
The study of material things (artifacts) of past human life and activities; reconstruction of culture of peoples no longer in existence.

Culture
The set of rules, standards, and norms shared by members of a society; transmitted by learning, and responsible for the behavior of those members.

Artifact
artis: art
fact: make
Any object made or modified by humans.

---

*Anthropology is sometimes divided into four branches: physical anthropology, cultural anthropology, archeology, and linguistics.

Biocultural
A combination of the biological, cultural, and ecological. An approach to the study of human evolution and behavior that stresses the influence of each of these three clusters and their reciprocating effects on one another.

Primates
(pry'-mates; also, pry-may'-tees) The order of mammals to which humans, apes, monkeys, and prosimians belong.

the basic means by which humans communicate, organize themselves, and transmit their culture from one generation to the next. In investigating the Yurok, the linguist would probably look at the entire culture, but would concentrate, perhaps, on the relationship of the Yurok language to the languages of neighboring societies, would analyze the structure of the language, or would trace the history of the language or the relationship of the language to the culture.

Unlike anthropologists whose main concern is culture, the physical anthropologist, in a comprehensive study of the Yurok, would collect data on all aspects of inherited physical characteristics, such as body build, blood types, pigmentation, ability to tolerate cold, and susceptibility to various diseases. The physical anthropologist would also include notes on such cultural behavior as marriage and kinship, population patterns, migrations, dietary practices, and other cultural behavior that may affect Yurok biology.

In order to understand the human condition, anthropologists believe it necessary to investigate human biological *and* cultural behavior. Since we are both animal and human, such a broad perspective—what is known as a **biocultural approach**—makes sense. Examining only cultural behavior fails to consider our animal capabilities and limitations, and concentrating on our biology omits the single most important attribute of humans: culture.

This biocultural approach to the study of human beings makes anthropology a unique discipline. As a social science, cultural anthropology is the study of culture—that broad area of learned behavior that humans have developed as their basic strategy for survival. As a biological science, physical anthropology is the study of the biological aspects of humans. Combining the biological and social aspects, we have a comprehensive view of the animal *Homo sapiens*, which we call human.

◇ What Is Physical Anthropology?

As already indicated, anthropology may be divided into cultural and physical approaches to the study of human beings. Whereas it is possible to emphasize one or the other, it is impossible to separate completely the subject matter of these two branches.

In order to understand the physical human being, we must of necessity consider the special way of life of this organism. Unlike all other creatures in the Animal Kingdom, we human beings have developed a strategy of adaptation (obtaining food, producing the next generation, protecting the group against enemies and the elements, developing concepts of life's meaning) that is learned, not biologically inherited. Although other animals, especially mammals, may learn some things, most of their behavior is built into their nervous system from birth. **Primates** are capable of much more learning, and the learning ability of the great apes is now well recognized; nevertheless, no other mammal is as dependent on learning as are humans. While possessing a biologically based capacity for culture, we humans must learn behavior anew every generation. We must learn what, when, where, and with whom to obtain food, eat, marry, associate, etc. We must learn what is right and

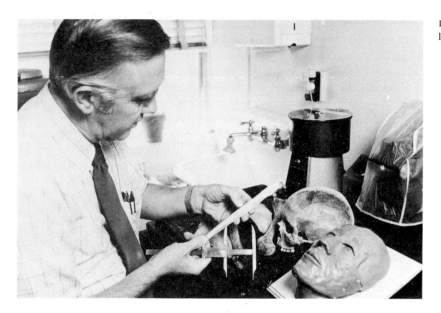

Figure 1-1 Physical anthropologist in his lab.

wrong, what to wear and not wear; what weapons and utensils to use and when, and how to relate to parents, cousins, and friends. All of this learning process comes under the heading of culture.

Culture, then, is the way humans discover, invent, and develop in order to survive; that is to say, adapt to the environments in which they live. One cannot imagine humans today surviving without culture. Indeed, such a case is very likely impossible. Obtaining and preparing food, coping with severe climatic conditions, trying to understand the world around us, cooperating with others—all of these normal and daily activities require cultural solutions. Our bodies alone are not adequate for the task of living. We must have material

Figure 1-2 Humans are biocultural animals who developed culture as an adaptive strategy for survival and thus became human. Note the many items of material culture and social behavior that make the human way possible.

Human Variation
Physical differences among humans.

Human Evolution
Physical changes over time leading to anatomically modern human beings.

items to help us acquire what we need and ideas to help us communicate
with one another.

Cultural anthropology is the comprehensive study of what humans have
learned to do, and are doing, in order to survive and adapt. What is the
connection between these learned processes and our biological constitution?
Was our evolutionary development dependent on culture? Was the development of culture dependent on our biological constitution?

In the biocultural view, culture and our biological structure are critically
related. Had we not come from primate beginnings, culture would never have
developed, and had our ancestors not developed culture, we would not have
evolved our present physical form. The two are inextricably related, and if we
wish to learn something of physical anthropology, we *must* understand the
role culture has played in the process of human evolution. As one anthropologist has stated it:

> Our present biological makeup is a consequence among other things of cultural
> selection pressures. We are, therefore, biologically constituted to produce culture,
> not simply because by some accident we got a brain that could do cultural things,
> but because the cultural things themselves propelled us into getting a larger brain.
> We are not simply the *producers* of institutions like the family, science, language,
> religion, . . . we are the product of them (Fox, 1971, p. 59).

Figure 1-3 An early multipurpose tool.
Here being used for digging edible roots.

Figure 1-4 Early humans possessed a small and simple tool kit. At a modern hardware store, an overwhelming variety of tools, utensils, and weapons is available.

With this introduction, let us examine more closely the field of physical anthropology, the concern of this book. Although physical anthropologists are not in complete agreement on precisely what is to be included within their field, they do generally agree that two areas are basic: **human variation** and **human evolution**.

Human variation (the subject of Chapters 5, 6, and 7) examines the differences within and between human populations. Within a population such as the Eskimos* or San, variation occurs in body shapes and sizes; in anatomical structures, organs, and tissues; and in physiological responses to heat, cold, humidity, and exercise. Physical anthropologists are interested in the environmental and hereditary bases of this diversity and attempt to make evolutionary explanations of it.

As human biologists, physical anthropologists in the field or laboratory collect such data as susceptibility and immunity to disease, the effects of malnutrition, and patterns of human growth. These data may be used by medical scientists, physicians, and government agencies in their efforts to combat disease and improve the health of peoples around the world.

While all human beings belong to the same genus and species (*Homo sapiens*) and can interbreed and produce fertile offspring, there is a wide variation within the species. Physical anthropologists study these variations to learn how humans have biologically and culturally adapted to the stressful conditions of heat, humidity, altitude, working conditions, and other human activities. As evolutionary biologists, anthropologists are interested in microevolution, small-scale biological modifications that can accumulate and make for large-scale evolutionary changes (see Microevolution, p. 108). More recently, anthropologists have considered the probability of rapid evolution that produces new species more quickly than small-scale modifications. Such rapid evolutionary change has been called *punctuated equilibrium* (see p. 109).

*Some Eskimos are now referred to as Inuit.

◇ Box 1-1   The Founding and Growth of a Profession*

Aleš Hrdlička (1869–1943)

Aleš Hrdlička, Curator of the Division of Physical Anthropology from 1902 to 1942 at the U.S. National Museum of Natural History, Washington, D.C., had waged an unremitting campaign for the recognition of physical anthropology as a legitimate and independent scientific profession for nearly three decades. This campaign, however, was essentially brought to an end on the afternoon of December 28, 1928, when he persuaded a group of sympathetic scientists assembled at the Section H meeting of the American Association for the Advancement of Science in New York City that the time had come to

*Contributed by Frank Spencer, Queens College, The City University of New York.

found the American Association of Physical Anthropologists (AAPA). Following the adoption of this proposal, a "committee of organization" was formed. This committee consisted of Fay-Cooper Cole (ethnologist), Charles H. Danforth (anatomist), George A. Dorsey (archeologist), William K. Gregory (paleontologist), Earnest A. Hooton (physical anthropologist), Aleš Hrdlička (physical anthropologist), and Robert J. Terry (anatomist). During the next year, Hrdlička (assisted by this committee) worked diligently to enlist members to this new professional body.

When the AAPA held its inaugural meeting at Charlottesville, Virginia, in April, 1930, it had a total membership of 83, which was comprised of 49 anatomists, 18 anthropologists (of which only 8 were full-time professional physical anthropologists), 8 zoologists, and 8 others whose professional affiliation is not known. As this indicates, the main strength of the discipline was in anatomy rather than anthropology, as it is today. This situation is hardly surprising when one considers that most of the academic institutions of the period with programs in anthropology tended to stress either ethnology or archeology. By and large, physical anthropology was either neglected or inadequately taught. In fact, in 1930, Harvard University was the only school in the United States that offered a program leading to the doctorate in physical anthropology. Furthermore, this program, developed under the aegis of Earnest A. Hooton (1887–1954), produced its first Ph.D. only four years prior to the Charlottesville meeting. However, between 1926 and 1954, Hooton was to produce some thirty or more Ph.D.s, many of whom were to play an important role in the subsequent development of academic physical anthropology following World War II.

Although the AAPA's membership continued to grow annually at a steady rate after 1930 (reaching a figure of 285 in 1943), the ratio of anatomists to academically trained physical anthropologists did not change appreciably until well after the war.

Beginning in the early 1950s, higher education in the United States entered a period of unprecedented growth. Among the many factors contributing to this were: the passage of the GI Bill, which guaranteed free tuition and a living stipend to all veterans of military service; the post-war "baby-boom"; and the creation of research funding organizations, such as the National Science Foundation.

From all appearances, the development of academic programs in physical anthropology in the 1950s was confined to those universities that already had established departments of anthropology namely, Arizona, Berkeley, Chicago, Columbia, UCLA, Michigan, Pennsylvania, and Wisconsin. Almost without exception these programs were organized either by former students of Hooton or by a student of a Hooton student. After 1960, there was a rapid proliferation of programs in physical anthropology, which continued well into the first half of the 1970s. Consequently, there is now hardly a college or university in the United States that does not offer well-taught undergraduate courses in physical anthropology. Similarly, most of the schools that presently grant a doctorate in anthropology also offer the degree in physical (sometimes called "biological") anthropology.

The impact of this growth of the discipline in academe is clearly reflected in the AAPA's membership and its journal, the *American Journal of Physical Anthropology*, which, incidentally, was founded by Hrdlička in 1918. Prior to 1964, this journal was limited to one volume per year (usually consisting of 500 pages), but since then it has expanded to two volumes per year (ranging up to 1,000 pages). More recently, it has become a monthly, rather than a bimonthly, journal. As for the AAPA's membership, it grew at an exponential rate between 1950 and 1980, and is now clearly dominanted by academically trained physical anthropologists. Today, its membership is well in excess of 1,500, and represents the largest community of its kind in the world.

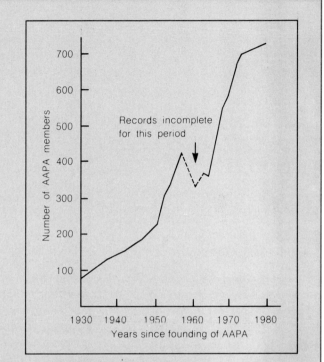

This graph shows the increase in membership in the American Association of Physical Anthropologists (AAPA) from the time of its founding in 1930 to the present.

SOURCES:

Comas, J. *Historia Sumaria de la Asociación Americana de Antropológos Fisicos* (1928–1968). Mexico: Instituto Nacional de Antropologia y Historia, 1969.

Hrdlička, A. *Physical Anthropology: Its Scope and Aims; Its History and Present Status in the United States.* Philadelphia: Wister Institute of Anatomy and Biology, 1919.

Hrdlička, A. "American Association of Physical Anthropologists." *American Journal of Physical Anthropology*, 12: 519–521, 1929.

Races
Breed or variety; subdivisions of a species. Large divisions of humans, based on physical traits. As it applies to humans, the term is not favored by many anthropologists.

Osteology
(os-tee-ol'-o-jee)
osteon: bone
The study of bones.

Prosimians
(pro-sim'-ee-ens)
pro: before
simian: ape or monkey
Common form of Prosimii, a suborder of primates, composed of small primates such as lemurs and tarsiers.

Forensic
(from forum)
Pertaining to courts of law. In anthropology, the use of anthropology in questions of law.

Paleopathology
(pay'-lee-o-path-ol'-o-jee)
pathos: suffering
The study of ancient diseases.

As comparative human geneticists, physical anthropologists have studied variations among humans and, in the past, have classified the world's population into physical types called **races**, a practice seldom followed in recent years.

The second focus of physical anthropology, human evolution, may itself be subdivided into two areas: paleoanthropology and primatology.

Paleoanthropology is the study of the fossil remains of our ancestors. Physical anthropologists, together with archeologists, geologists, and other scientists, have unearthed fossil remains in many parts of the world. With their knowledge of **osteology**, paleoanthropologists examine, measure, and reconstruct these remains, often from mere fragments. This has enabled physical anthropologists to propose possible lines of descent from our ancient ancestors to our present form, *Homo sapiens.*

Primatology, as the word suggests, is the study of nonhuman primates, the group (*order* is the technical term) of the Animal Kingdom to which humans, apes, monkeys, and **prosimians** belong. The anatomy of nonhuman primates, especially monkeys and apes, has been studied to ascertain the similarities and differences between these primates and humans. This kind of study helps trace the evolutionary relationships of human and nonhuman primates. Because of the remarkable similarities among monkeys, apes, and humans, researchers have been able, through laboratory experiments with monkeys and apes, to learn what effects certain diseases, stresses, and other conditions might have on humans. Work with the rhesus monkey, for example, led to the discovery of the Rh blood factor which, due to incompatibility between mother and fetus, may cause a disease fatal to human infants. Because of the similarity in blood types and physiological responses of chimpanzees and humans, the space program, in 1961, selected a chimpanzee by the name of Ham to be a passenger in a space capsule launched into suborbital flight. Scientists believed that Ham's reactions would be very similar to human reactions under the same conditions.

A fascinating area of primate investigation concerns observing primates in their natural habitat. This kind of investigation, often difficult and dangerous, has been practiced for many years; only recently, however, have primate field studies become so frequent. Perhaps the best-known program is Jane Goodall's work in East Africa, but a number of others bear mention: Phyllis Dolhinow's work with langurs in India; Dian Fossey's study of gorillas in Rwanda; Biruté Galdikas' work with orangutans in Borneo; the extensive research on baboons in Africa and macaques at the Japanese Monkey Centers.

Such studies have uncovered important patterns of social interactions, such as the relationships between dominant and subordinate males, mothers and offspring, and the young and old. In addition, toolmaking and the ability to learn complex tasks (behaviors until recently hardly believed possible) have also been discovered with surprising frequency among certain species of primates.

Physical anthropologists hope that this current, rapidly accumulating data will help trace human evolution from our primate ancestors, as well as aid in understanding the behavior of humans today.

We have been discussing what might be termed *academic anthropology*. There are, however, physical anthropologists who pursue their work outside of (or in addition to) academe in a branch called *applied anthropology*. In this field, the principles and data of anthropology are related to practical situations. Many years ago, for example, physical anthropologists were already applying their knowledge by developing standard sizes for the clothing industry and the military, and more comfortable seats for automobiles and airplanes. Space requirements for industrial workers were also analyzed, and mechanical problems associated with the body, such as the placement of foot pedals and hand controls for machine operators, were studied.

Physical anthropologists sometimes also assist judicial and law enforcement agencies. Practitioners of **forensic** anthropology, as the field is called, may be asked to ascertain the age and sex of a corpse, and how long it has been buried; they may, in some cases, assist the coroner in determining the cause of death.

For many years, physical anthropology has had application in the field of medicine. The relationship between body build and disease, and the question of whether a particular disease is hereditary or social, have been among those investigated by physical anthropologists. Data on diseases have been collected from many countries in an effort to determine what special social conditions might be involved in the causes and cures.

A final area of physical anthropology that has been a central focus since the beginnings of the discipline in this country might be termed *skeletal biology*. Over the years, archeologists have excavated thousands of human burials from sites all around the world. As the most durable parts of the human organism, the hard tissues (bones and teeth) may endure for centuries (and, if fossilized, perhaps for millions of years).

As experts in the anatomical structure of these hard tissues, physical anthropologists (here usually called osteologists) can, by using techniques similar to those of forensic anthropologists, often determine the sex and the age-at-death of the individual from which the specimen came. In addition, osteologists can, with the aid of specialized instruments, exactly measure hundreds of different dimensions regarding size and shape variation. Finally, osteologists carefully inspect the skeletal material for indications of such diseases as tuberculosis, healed fractures, arthritis, and rickets. This approach, called **paleopathology**, can inform us not only about the history of human disease, but can also occasionally help elucidate the causes of certain diseases as well.

All the areas of physical anthropology discussed here give only the barest outlines of the fascinating topics investigated by our discipline. In a recent professional meeting of the American Association of Physical Anthropologists, more than 300 academic papers were read, covering a vast array of subjects. Box 1-2 presents a sampling.

◇ Paleoanthropology and Other Disciplines

Searching for ancient human remains—organic and cultural—is the work of *paleoanthropologists* (see Chapter 10). Organic material, such as bones and teeth, is examined and analyzed by physical anthropologists; cultural material, such as tools, weapons, shelters, and so forth, by archeologists.

◇ Box 1-2   Research in Physical Anthropology

Interests of physical anthropologists range far and wide. Reflecting this scope are titles of some of the papers presented at the 1984 meeting of the American Association of Physical Anthropologists:

New findings on incest among free-ranging rhesus monkeys

The impact of evolution on the biology of the human female

Researching human exposure to hazardous waste: some ethical dilemmas in field research

Reconstructed hand posture in *Proconsul africanus*

The evolutionary and functional significance of the "extensor digitorum profundus" muscle in human and nonhuman primates

Albumin clocks and the evolutionary divergence of apes and humans

Experiment in human growth response to improving diet and disease control

Physique and age at menarche of Maharastrian girls of Bombay

The morphological basis of hominid manipulatory behavior

Anthropometric analysis of Huntington disease families

Dietary pattern of body fatness among young Samoan men

Bone strontium levels in modern animals and strontium isotopic evidence for diagenetic alteration of bone: consequence for diet reconstructions

Socio-economic, population structure, and migration effects on the epidemiology of malarial infection in an ethnically stratified relocation center near Lahore, Pakistan

Polygyny vs. polyandry: why the bias?

Phylogenetic analysis of Plio-Pleistocene hominids

Seasonality of marriages and conceptions on Carriacou, Grenada

The anterior dentition of *Notharctus*: implications for the origin of anthropoids

Size and shape of the hominoid foot: implications for function and evolution

Birth-spacing, lactation and effective fecundability: models and estimates from highland New Guinea

Experimental fracturing of antelope limb bones: a taphonomic perspective

Forensic anthropological research in military identification laboratories: an update

Frequencies of spondylopathy and caries during the early Middle Ages in Southwest Germany

Blood pressure in blacks and whites and its relationship to dietary sodium and potassium intake

Nutritional stress and health in ancient Egypt

Phylogeny
(fy-loj'-en-ee)
phylon: tribe or race
The evolutionary history of a species; evolutionary relationships of organisms; a "family tree."

Geochemistry
(jee-o)
ge: earth
The study of the chemical composition of the earth's crust.

However, as our discussion suggests, paleoanthropology is quite closely associated with other disciplines. In fact, a paleoanthropologist could not function without cooperation from a host of other scientists. For example, in working out the **phylogeny** of our species, one must have the vital knowledge (as accurately as possible) concerning the dates of fossil remains. To obtain this crucial information, the paleoanthropologist consults the **geochemist** for a **chronometric dating** of the fossils themselves, or of the matrix containing the fossil material.

If these facts are unobtainable, then a **geologist** may be able to give some idea of the dating from an analysis of the rock strata holding the material, and may also be able to reconstruct the physical landscape of the period in which these ancient creatures were living. Thus, armed with such information, the physical anthropologist may justifiably speculate about the environment of the now-fossilized creatures, how they lived, how they obtained their food, how they used their bodies, and, to some extent, what kind of stone was available for tools.

For purposes of searching for fossils, the actual excavation is usually the responsibility of the archeologist, who studies the material remains—tools, indications of clothing, shelters, fire, etc.—and attempts to reconstruct the culture of that period.

Recently, primatologists have studied the same group of primates for years, and these longitudinal studies have given them insights into the way of life of **hominid** ancestors. Feeding practices, age and sex relationships, **agonistic** behavior, and other nonhuman primate behavior offer suggestive clues to the transitional period of prehominid to hominid. Paleoanthropologists utilize data from primatologists and archeologists in constructing models for hominid origins (see Chapter 10 for examples of one of these models).

Also of assistance to paleoanthropologists have been the increasing contributions of a fairly new science, **taphonomy**, defined as "the laws of burial" (Olson, 1980). Taphonomists analyze fossil assemblages and "hope to find the means for reconstructing animals in their community context" (Behrensmeyer, 1980, p. 2). Through their analysis of animal bones found at ancient sites, taphonomists can offer information on: the paleoecology of the early hominid period; the relationship of hominids to the animals they hunted (or scavenged); the possible dates of mammalian bones found in the fossil assemblages; the changes that occur to bones after death, and whether these changes are due to chemical, carnivore, or hominid activity. This information may give paleoanthropologists a better picture of the early hominid environment. It thus extends the ability of paleoanthropologists to understand the behavior, as well as the physical structure, of the hominid remains they discover.

In reconstructing the way of life of our ancient ancestors, one must have certain important knowledge concerning what other animals and plants were living at the same time. Such information would suggest clues to kinds of food eaten, the hunting and gathering techniques, the possible materials for clothing and shelter and, in general, considerable other anthropological data about how these ancient peoples adapted to their environment. For this, the physical anthropologist looks to the **paleontologist** and **palynologist** (who identifies plants by pollen samples taken from the soil) to identify the remains of these materials.

Much of physical anthropology deals with evolution, including physical changes within a species and the transmission of physical characteristics from one generation to the next. Scientists from all the biological sciences have contributed insights to evolutionary theory, and geneticists, in recent years, have greatly expanded their understanding of the processes of biological heredity. This knowledge has been of considerable theoretical assistance to physical anthropologists as they speculate about how the transition from prehuman to human may have occurred.

Since cultural information would shed light on the evolution of the human form, physical anthropologists have currently become increasingly interested in how our early ancestors lived. Necessarily, then, we have come to rely on

Chronometric Dating
Dating by methods that give time in years, also known as absolute dating (compared with relative dating). It includes radiometric techniques (carbon 14 and potassium-argon) and dendrochronology (tree-ring dating).

Geology
The study of the history and structure of the earth, as recorded in rocks.

Hominid
The common term for Hominidae, the family to which humans belong.

Agonistic
Agones: ancient
Greek contests; therefore, combative. Used by primatologists to describe aggressive, hostile, or threatening behavior.

Taphonomy
(taf-on'-o-mee)
taphe: grave or burial
nomy: rules or laws of

Paleontology
(pay'-lee-on-tol'-o-jee)
onta: existing things
The study of ancient forms of life based on fossil bones.

Palynology
Identifying ancient plants by examining pollen from archeological sites.

Figure 1-5 Paleopathology. The infectious reaction on the frontal part of this twelfth-century Pueblo Indian skull suggests syphilis. Other diseases are also a possibility.

Hominidae
The family, of the order Primates, to which humans belong.

Australopithecines
(os-tray-lo-pith'-e-seens)
australo: southern
pithecus: ape
The earliest hominids known; located in South and East Africa.

Ecological Niche
(econiche)
The life style of an organism or species in relation to its habitat; the habitat of an organism or species that makes life possible; the feeding habits of an organism or species.

Estrus
(also oestrus)
oistros: sting, frenzy
Period of sexual heat of female mammals; receptive period.

the findings of those cultural anthropologists who work with less technologically complex societies. Living patterns seen today, such as family structure, division of labor, and hunting techniques, suggest ideas and concepts to physical anthropologists in their reconstructions of the life of early humans and the evolution of physical form.

Similarly, primate anatomy and behavior studies done by zoologists, psychologists, psychiatrists, medical scientists, linguists, and others have contributed to the physical anthropologist's exploration of human evolution.

◇ What Is Human?

Two terms already introduced—"human" and "hominid"—require some clarification. The word hominid comes from *homo*, the Latin word for man:

> From its use in Latin works on logic [and] scholastic language, in the sense "human being" (Oxford English Dictionary).

Whatever its origin, hominid is used by anthropologists as an abbreviated or popular form of **Hominidae**, the family to which we belong, as opposed to, say, Pongidae, the ape family. Hominid is a useful term since it is neutral, unaffiliated with gender, time, or superiority. The family Hominidae includes the genus *Australopithecus* (the earliest hominids we know of), who emerged somewhere around 4 m.y.a.* Hominidae also includes the genus *Homo*, with several species (see chart on p. 220 for details). Because **australopithecines**, the early hominids, did not possess all the criteria we assign to humans, especially a complex brain, we are reluctant to place them in the category of humans.

The concept "human" is more difficult to clarify. What makes human beings unique and thereby different from all other animals is a perplexing and age-old question that has been the subject of religious, philosophical, and sociological inquiry. Human uniqueness is based on two general classes of criteria: the biological and the behavioral.

From the biological view, the differences between humans and other animals are quantitative. The difficulty is not that we possess physical characteristics lacking in, or radically different from, other animals, but that we possess the same attributes to a greater or lesser degree. We are larger than most animals, but have less hair; our brain is not the largest in relative or absolute size, but it is very large according to the standards of both these categories. We are not the only animal that is bipedal (birds are, too), but we have a skeleton adapted for standing upright and walking, which leaves the hands free for purposes other than locomotion. All these traits, elaborated and coordinated under the control of a brain capable of abstract thought, give us our remarkable physical uniqueness.

In the behavioral area, human uniqueness is even more noteworthy. Every species, in adapting to its **ecological niche** (econiche), has developed its own distinct behavior, but human uniqueness is revealed in behaviors absent in

*The abbreviation m.y.a. indicates "million years ago."

Bird   Human   Gorilla

Figure 1-6 Bipedal vertebrates. An upright (orthograde) posture evolving from an
apelike structure explains the short, wide
human pelvis.

other animals. For example, our sexual behavior does not include a mating
season or **estrus** for females. Or, as another example, most animals build
shelters for themselves and eat in ways particular to their species; but among
humans, activities like the building of shelters and preparing of food are
learned, vary in each society, and can be successfully accomplished only
with the assistance of tools. Without tools, even people with the most unso-
phisticated culture could not survive.

Our social relationships are not only learned but also vary from society to
society. Cultural anthropologists have routinely observed societal differences
in marriage, residence, and kinship patterns, in attitudes toward the elderly
and the young, and in behavior between the sexes. This diversity is unlike other

Bipedalism
(by-pee'-dal-ism)
bi: two
ped: feet
Walking on two feet as among hominids
and some other animals.

Hypothesis
Unproved theory. A theory is a statement
with some confirmation.

Cosmology
kosmos: world
The study of the creation of the universe
and the laws that govern it.

World View
A literal translation from the German, Weltanschauung (Welt: world; anschauung:
view).
A personal or group philosophy explaining
history; a way of looking at the world.

Empirical
(em-pir'-i-kal)
empirikos: experienced
Derived from or depending on experience
or experiment.

animal species, where very little flexibility occurs in the behavior of individuals. Within species, members of a particular category (such as sex or age) behave similarly. Mammals exhibit more flexibility than other vertebrates, with primates displaying the most of all. Recent observations of the variety of behavior among chimpanzees in the wild, along with the apparent ability of captive chimpanzees to learn sign language in a number of experiments, have astonished scientists. Nevertheless, no troop of chimpanzees displays the degree of variety in behavior found in *any* human society.

One of the most important factors that differentiates humans from other species is our ability to communicate symbolically through language, an activity that, as far as we know, is specific to humans. Chimpanzee achievements with sign language (discussed in Chapter 10) *taught them by humans* are truly remarkable. Even when these intelligent apes do occasionally sign to other chimps, such a display in no way compares to the crucial reliance humans place on symbolic communication. Furthermore, what chimpanzees or any other animals achieve with *human assistance* is quite different from what humans, as a species, developed by themselves.

What then is "human"? There may well be as many definitions as there are human beings! We suggest, however, that a sound explanation of the term be based on the two criteria previously mentioned: first, a body structured for standing upright and walking on two legs (**bipedalism**), thus leaving the arms free for functions other than locomotion; second, a complex brain that provides the abilities for abstract thought, symbolic communication, and the development of culture as a way of life. With this dual emphasis on biology and culture, our definition once again underlines the biocultural view of human evolution.

◇ The Scientific Approach

Physical anthropology is a scientific discipline and, more precisely, a *biological science*. Physical anthropologists, therefore, employ an empirical/scientific approach to understanding the universe.

What do we mean by "scientific"? The scientific approach is still very much surrounded by popular misunderstanding. First of all, scientists do *not* seek to disprove religious doctrine but, rather, attempt to understand the universe through direct *observation*, generating **hypotheses** to explain these observations, and then continually testing their results against further information. As new evidence accumulates, hypotheses are modified.

Strict theologians, on the other hand, understand the universe through faith, not through physical evidence. The written documents of the Eastern and Western religions reveal the universe through the direct word of an all-knowing spiritual power. Such a **cosmology** is intended to explain systematically and completely the nature of the universe, our planet, and ourselves. Since the Truth is known absolutely, there is little room for argument. In the furthest extension of this world view, it is not even necessary or desirable to gather further information about our universe.

Figure 1-7   Jesabel, a 6-year-old chimp
signing "drink."

Figure 1-8 Observation is a scientific approach.

In the last 400 to 500 years, however, a different **world view** has come to predominate in the Western world. This view entails what we have called the "**empirical/scientific approach.**" Since theological and scientific approaches consist of entirely different ways of understanding the universe, no reasonable means exist for arguing one versus the other. We simply start with alternate assumptions: either we understand the universe by divine revelation, or we comprehend it by observation. In the former, we can find absolute Truth (large "T"); in the latter, we merely make the most reasonable hypothesis, and in a sense, know only relative truth (small "t"). All of our understanding, religious and scientific, is based on *some* kind of theory.

Because scientists must theorize does not mean, however, that we cannot come to grips with the physical universe and the organisms within it. Scientific theories are only as good as their capacity to explain comprehensively natural and experimental observations, both those already gathered and those that may be made in the future. Some hypotheses, "theories," or "laws" are powerful explanatory principles, indeed: that the sun is the center of the solar system with the earth rotating around it; that our universe is not fixed but in constant motion; that heredity is transmitted from one generation to the next by cells, not blood, to name a few. Organic evolution (discussed in the next chapter) is also a theory; but like those just noted, it has tremendous explanatory value, and has been confirmed by millions of independent observations.

Must science and religion conflict? Certainly not. It is possible for scientists to accept some form of supernatural doctrine and, at the same time, believe in evolution. Unfortunately, science in our society today has become a kind of religion for many people. We often think of scientific principles as unalterable dogma based on faith. However, from an empirical point of view, our understanding of the universe is never absolute; it is gained by human beings slowly piecing together bits of evidence gathered through observations that explain the universe. We certainly do not know everything. But we do know enormously more than we did a century, a decade, or even a year ago. Every day our data increase, and, consequently, our understanding increases as well. This book attempts to tell the dramatic and continually unfolding story of human evolution.

◇ Summary

Anthropology is the study of human beings and their primate ancestors. It is a holistic science divided into two main branches: cultural and physical. Cultural anthropology is the study of what humans have learned to do in order to adapt to their environment; physical anthropology, the study of man as animal, is mainly concerned with human variation and human evolution.

Specialized fields within physical anthropology include comparative human genetics, growth and development, paleoanthropology, human osteology, and primatology. Some physical anthropologists have specialized in applied anthropology, forensic anthropology, and human paleopathology. For assistance in their research physical anthropologists work closely with a variety of biological, social, and physical scientists.

Two terms of similar meaning—hominid and human—have been defined. "Hominid," the more inclusive term, embraces australopithecines, which the term "human" does not. Human includes those hominids who display the phenomenon of a complex brain capable of abstract thought, symbolic communication, and culture.

Physical anthropologists, in order to understand the universe, employ an empirical/scientific approach, one based on observation and physical evidence. This method of understanding is opposed to a religionist approach, which is based on faith. Since these are alternative ways of comprehending the universe, there is no necessary conflict between them.

◇ Questions for Review

1. What is meant by "holistic," and why is anthropology a holistic science?
2. Explain the biocultural approach in anthropology.
3. What are the two main branches of anthropology?
4. What are the two main areas of physical anthropology?
5. How do other disciplines assist physical anthropological research?

6. What are the fields of specialization within physical anthropology?
7. How does the concept "hominid" differ from the concept "human"?
8. In what ways are humans unique from other animals?
9. What role does culture play in human uniqueness?
10. Explain why there is no necessary conflict between the scientific and religionist approach to understanding the universe.

◇ Suggested Further Reading

Beals, Ralph L., Harry Hoijer, and Alan R. Beals. *An Introduction to Anthropology* (5th Ed.), New York: Macmillan Publishing Co., 1977.

An introductory textbook in anthropology covering all aspects of the discipline. Comprehensive and traditional in approach, the work is useful for quick reference to the wide variety of anthropological areas.

Eiseley, Loren. *The Immense Journey*, New York: Random House, 1957.

This book is also cited in Chapter 2, but it is recommended here as an extended view of human evolution, the main concern of our textbook. Eiseley is well known for his literary and almost mystical style of writing, and The Immense Journey *has enjoyed much success among college students.*

Johnson, Francis E. and Henry Selby. *Anthropology: The Biocultural View*, Dubuque: Wm. C. Brown Co., 1978.

Another introductory textbook in both physical and cultural anthropology. The coverage in physical anthropology is greater and the approach more dynamic than in many other general anthropology texts.

Napier, John. *Monkeys Without Tails: The Story of Man's Evolution.* New York: Taplinger, 1976.

A light, witty, and brief review of human evolution. The reading is pleasant and the book recommended as an overview of physical anthropology.

Sagan, Carl. *The Dragons of Eden*, New York: Random House, 1977.

This book has also been recommended in another chapter where, perhaps, it may be more appropriate. Since Sagan raises and discusses a number of questions basic to anthropology, his book might be considered as an introduction to the introduction of anthropology.

Washburn, S. L. and Elizabeth R. McCown (eds.). *Human Evolution: Biosocial Perspectives*, Menlo Park, California: The Benjamin/Cummings Publishing Co., 1978.

A collection of articles that deal particularly with the interphase between behavior and biological evolution. Some of the material is fairly advanced, but will nevertheless be of topical interest to the introductory student.

Principles of Evolution

CONTENTS

That it shall be unlawful for any teacher in any of the universities, normals and all other public schools of the State ... to teach any theory that denies the story of the Divine Creation of man as taught in the Bible, and to teach instead that man has descended from a lower order of animals (Section 1 of the Butler Act, March 21, 1925, State of Tennessee).

In May, 1925, several leading citizens of Dayton, Tennessee (population 1,800) were sitting around Doc Robinson's drug store, the town's social center, discussing various and sundry topics of great import. To settle an argument, they sent for John T. Scopes, a local high school coach and teacher of algebra, physics, and chemistry. Scopes came over from his tennis game not realizing that he was about to enter the most dramatic period of his life, one he would never forget.

One of the men, a local businessman, said, "John, we've been arguing, and I said that nobody could teach biology without teaching evolution."

"That's right," said Scopes, and showed them the biology textbook that had been adopted by the state of Tennessee.

"Then," said Doc Robinson, "you've been violating the law."

Although he did not teach biology, Scopes had, one day in April, substituted for the principal, who did. Technically, therefore, it could be said that he had taught biology and had thus violated the newly passed law.

As the discussion continued, and it became clear that Scopes felt strongly on the matter of academic freedom, Robinson asked him whether he would stand for a test case. Scopes said he would, whereupon Robinson called the *Chattanooga News* and reported, "This is

F. E. Robinson in Dayton. I'm chairman of the school board here. We've just arrested a man for teaching evolution." The man who had been "arrested" finished his soft drink and returned to his tennis game. (Writing forty years later in 1967, Scopes suggested that the trial was deliberately planned by Dayton businessmen to put that town on the map and bring in business, which is precisely what happened.)

The "arrest" made front page news across the country. William Jennings Bryan—three times Democratic nominee for President, Secretary of State under Woodrow Wilson, famous for his Cross of Gold speech at the Democratic convention of 1896, and acknowledged leader of the crusade against Darwinism—offered his services to the prosecution as the representative of the World's Christian Fundamentals Association.

With Bryan's entry into the fray, Clarence Darrow, nationally known labor and criminal lawyer, offered his services to the defense without fee or expense. The American Civil Liberties Union was in charge of the case for the defense and provided other well-known lawyers: John Randolph Neal, Arthur Garfield Hayes, and Dudley Field Malone.

In the weeks before the trial, the town of Dayton took on the atmosphere of a circus. The trial was referred to as "the monkey business." Merchants used monkey motifs in their advertising: little cotton apes were featured in store windows; pins that read "Your Old Man's a Monkey" could be purchased; and at Doc Robinson's drug store, a monkey fizz was available for refreshment from the summer heat. Hot dog stands, lemonade peddlers, booths selling books on biology or religion, and Bryan's truck, equipped with loud-

speaker touting Florida real estate, all added spice and noise to the carnival.

The trial began on Friday, July 10, 1925, with Judge John T. Raulston on the bench, and ended on Tuesday, July 21. It was clear from the start that Scopes would be convicted. The court, strongly religious, consistently favored the prosecution and forbade the testimony of expert defense witnesses—scientists—who were prepared to prove that evolution was a valid scientific concept. The prosecution insisted that the trial was not about the validity of evolution but that the real issue was simply whether or not Scopes had violated the law.

There were magnificent speeches. On Monday, July 13, in his support of the motion to squash the indictment against Scopes, Darrow displayed his famous forensic ability, and the crowded courthouse hung on every word. If the teaching of evolution is outlawed, he argued, then:

After a while, Your Honor, it is the setting of man against man and creed against creed until with flying banners and beating drums we are marching backward to the glorious age of the sixteenth century when bigots lighted faggots to burn the men who dared to bring any intelligence and enlightenment and culture to the human mind.

On Thursday, Bryan stood up to speak against the admissibility of scientific testimony. The crowd had been waiting for this moment, but they were to be disappointed. Bryan was an old man, not the man he once was; the fire was missing. H. L. Mencken, the acidulous reporter from the *Baltimore Sun*, attended the trial and wrote:

His ... speech was a grotesque performance and downright touching in its imbecility. Its climax came when he launched into a furious denunciation of the doctrine that man is a mammal. It seemed a sheer impossibility that any literate man should stand up in public and discharge any such nonsense. Yet the poor old fellow did it. . . . To call man mammal, it appeared, was to flout the revelation of God (Tompkins, 1965, p. 48).

Malone replied to Bryan, his former superior officer at the State Department, and his eloquence carried the day even among the spectators who fully supported Bryan. Bryan himself recognized this when he told Malone afterwards, "Dudley, that was the greatest speech I have ever heard."

The climax of the trial came on Monday afternoon, July 20, when the defense called Bryan as an expert witness on the Bible. The prosecutors immediately jumped to their feet protesting, aware of the danger inherent in the questions that might be asked and the answers that might be given. However, Bryan himself insisted on testifying, perhaps because he felt compelled to defend the Bible and "show up" the evolutionists. It was an opportunity not to be missed.

Darrow's strategy was to question Bryan about his literal interpretation of the Bible. The Bible, Bryan held, was true, every word of it, every comma. Every miracle recorded in the Bible actually happened. And it was on these points that Darrow broke Bryan, made him appear foolish, unthinking, and even a "traitor" to the cause of fundamentalism. At one point Darrow asked, "Do you think the earth was made in six days?"

"Not in six days of twenty-four hours," Bryan replied.

The crowd gasped at this heresy.

The Bible read six days, and a day was obviously twenty-four hours. What was Bryan thinking of? Toward the end of the afternoon Darrow brought up the Bible story of Adam and Eve and the serpent. Had God punished the serpent by making him crawl on his belly? Bryan said he believed that. Then, Darrow asked, "Have you any idea how the snake went before that time?"

"No, sir."

"Do you know whether he walked on his tail or not?"

"No, sir, I have no way to know."

The crowd laughed and Bryan's hands nervously trembled and his lips quivered.*

The trial ended the next day. The jury (excused for most of the trial) was called back and charged to decide whether Scopes had violated the law; no other question was to be considered. The jury took but a short time and returned with their verdict—guilty! Judge Raulston fined Scopes $100 and the trial closed.

The case was appealed to the Tennessee Supreme Court, which handed down its decision on January 15, 1927. The Court upheld the Butler Act and also recommended that the State drop the indictment against Scopes on the technicality that the judge had imposed the fine, instead of the jury, as Tennessee law required. The Court thus made it impossible to appeal the case before the United States Supreme Court.

Update

In the sixty years since the Scopes trial, religious fundamentalists have not ceased their attempts to remove the teaching of evolution from the

public schools of the nation. Known as "creationists" because they explain the existence of the universe, energy, and life as a result of sudden creation, they are determined either to eliminate the teaching of evolution or to introduce antievolutionary subject matter. In a ploy developed in recent years, creationists have insisted that "creation-science" is just as much science as what they term "evolution science." Therefore, they claim, in the interest of fair play, a balanced view should be offered to students—if evolution is taught as science, then creationism should also be taught as science.

So-called "creation-science" is not science as we know it.† Far from the spirit of science, creationists, for instance, assert that their position is absolute and not subject to error. Therefore, it is impossible for any sort of evidence to alter their position, for anything that might modify creationism is automatically rejected.

Creationists have been active in state legislatures, promoting the passage of laws mandating the inclusion of creationism in school curricula wherever evolution is taught. To this effect, creationists successfully lobbied the legislature of the State of Arkansas, which passed Act 590 in March of 1981.

As used in the Act, "creation-science" means the scientific "evidence" for creation, as well as inferences based on such evidence, including:

1. sudden creation of the universe, energy, and life, from nothing
2. inadequacy of mutation and natural selection to explain how all liv-

*A diabetic and in ill health, Bryan died on Sunday, July 26, five days after the trial ended.

†See Eldridge, Niles, "Creationism Isn't Science," *The New Republic*, Apr. 14, 1981, pp. 15–20.

ing kinds developed from a single organism

3. changes of forms of life only within fixed limits of originally created kinds of plants and animals

4. idea of a separate ancestry for man and apes

5. explanation of the earth's geology by catastrophism

6. concept of a relatively recent inception of the earth and living kinds

The American Civil Liberties Union (ACLU) challenged Act 590 (also known as the "Balanced Treatment for Creation-Science and Evolution-Science Act") in the case of McLean vs. Arkansas State Board of Education. The case came to trial in federal district court in December, 1981. ACLU contended that Act 590 infringed on three separate rights guaranteed under the United States Constitution:

1. separation of church and state, guaranteed by the First Amendment

2. academic freedom, guaranteed by the First Amendment

3. the right to due process under the Fourteenth Amendment: the act was vague, and teachers could be placed in jeopardy since it would be easy to misinterpret such phrases as "fixed limits" and "kinds of plants and animals," these being too unclear for identification

On January 5, 1982, Judge William Ray Overton ruled against the State of Arkansas. He found that "creation science has no scientific merit or education value," that "a theory that is by its own terms dogmatic, absolutist and never subject to revision is not a scientific theory," and that "since creation is not science, the conclusion is inescapable that the only real effect of Act 590 is the advancement of religion."

Judge Overton declared that the Act violated the Constitution's guarantees of separation of church and state, and he accompanied his decision with an injunction against the enforcement of the Act.

This was not, by the way, the first Arkansas attempt to introduce anti-evolution legislation. In 1928, just three years after the Scopes trial ended, the Arkansas legislature passed a law that forbade

any teacher or other instructor in any university, college, normal, public or any other institution of the state . . . to teach the theory or doctrine that mankind ascended or descended from a lower order of animals.

The law was finally challenged in 1965 by Susan Epperson, a high-school biology teacher. Trial was held on April 1, 1966, and the court found the 1928 statute unconstitutional because it violated the First and Fourteenth Amendments. On appeal, the Arkansas Supreme Court overturned the lower court decision, but, on fur-

ther appeal, the U.S. Supreme Court decided that the 1928 law violated the First Amendment, and was an intrusion of religion into the state schools.

A similar Louisiana law was scheduled for court action sometime in 1984.

Although Act 590 was declared unconstitutional, creationists continue their efforts. In Texas, California, Kentucky, and other states, creationist legislation and biology textbook censorship remain as goals of the religious fundamentalists.

SOURCES FOR ISSUE:

Ginger, Ray. *Six Days or Forever?*, Boston: Beacon Press, 1958.

Scopes, John T. and James Presley. *Center of the Storm*, New York: Holt, Rinehart and Winston, 1967.

Tompkins, Jerry R. (ed.). *D-Days at Dayton*, Baton Rouge: Louisiana State University Press, 1965.

SOURCES FOR UPDATE:

New York Times, Jan. 6, 1982.

New York Times, Jan. 12, 1982.

Science. 215 (4531) pp. 381–384, Jan. 22, 1982.

◇ CHAPTER TWO

◇ Introduction

As a concept, evolution, during the Middle Ages, was not a view seriously considered by medieval philosophers. Scholarly interpretations of the Bible, especially Genesis, had given European philosophers a *Weltanschauung* (world view) in which change had no place. Evolution, therefore, is an idea that would not only have been considered heretical, but "common sense" of the era would have labeled it ridiculous.

Nevertheless, scholars of the fifteenth, sixteenth, and seventeenth centuries demonstrated that the universe—planets (including the earth) and stars (including the sun)—was not rigidly fixed, and the belief that organic beings were similarly not fixed was being entertained. Attempts to explain how the process of evolution worked failed until Charles Darwin, in the nineteenth century, succeeded with his theory of natural selection.

How we understand evolution today is drawn directly from Darwin's work, as well as from contributions, mainly from the field of genetics, made during the twentieth century. Our focus throughout this text is *human evolution*, but, in this chapter, we discuss the general evolutionary principles applicable to all organisms. The evolutionary process is a unified one, and the principles are the same for all life forms, including humans. We will examine the changes in intellectual thought that led to the theory of natural selection, acclaimed as the most important scientific contribution of the nineteenth century. First, though, let's take a brief look at the man responsible for this theory: Charles Darwin.

◇ Darwin's Life

Charles Darwin (1809–1882) was the son of Dr. Robert and Susannah Darwin and grandson of the eminent Dr. Erasmus Darwin. Charles, one of six children, was thought by his family and by himself to be a "very ordinary boy." As an ordinary boy, he did the usual things (collecting shells, stamps, coins) and, at school, he displayed no special inclination for scholarship.

Because he showed little interest in, or aptitude for, anything particular (with the possible exception of science), Dr. Darwin decided that Charles should study medicine at Edinburgh. After two years, Charles conceded medicine was not for him, and instead turned to hunting and fishing, which he thoroughly enjoyed. His father complained that Charles was only interested in "shooting, dogs and rat-catching."

For sons who had no discernible academic leanings, parents could, as a last refuge, turn them to the church. Although indifferent to religion, Charles dutifully took up residence at Christ's College, Cambridge, in 1828, at the age of 19. While ostensibly enrolled in theology, Charles became interested in what we today call natural science. He became a constant companion of the

Figure 2-1 Charles Darwin (at age 32).

Figure 2-2 Examples of some of Darwin's finches. Note the similarities and differences in beak structure.

Reverend John Stevens Henslow, professor of botany, and often joined his classes in their botanical excursions.

Darwin was graduated in 1831, at the age of 22, not with a distinguished record, but one good enough to satisfy his family, and he could look forward to a serene future as a country cleric. However, that was not to be, for something happened that summer that Darwin referred to as "the most important event of my life."

He received a letter from his friend, Professor Henslow, informing him that he had recommended Darwin as the best-qualified person he knew for the position as naturalist on a scientific expedition that would circle the globe. (See Box 2-1.) Darwin was willing, even eager, for this opportunity to combine travel with the pursuit of botany, zoology, and geology, but his father objected and Charles regretfully declined. However, Charles found a champion in his uncle, Josiah Wedgewood, who persuaded Dr. Darwin that the voyage would be desirable. Dr. Darwin reluctantly gave his consent. With mixed feelings of elation and dismay, Charles set sail on board the H.M.S. *Beagle*, December 27, 1831, on a voyage where attacks of seasickness would place him in his hammock for days on end. Having begun the voyage as a clergyman (at least such had been his intent) with hobbies of zoology, botany, and geology, Darwin found, within a short time, that his true calling was natural science. Through his industrious and diligent work of collecting, arranging, and dissecting specimens, Darwin matured from an amateur observer into a professional naturalist.

Darwin went aboard the *Beagle* not as an evolutionist but as a believer in the fixity of species. His observations, however, quickly raised evolutionary suspicions in his mind. As early as 1832, for example, he noted in his diary that a snake with rudimentary hind limbs marked "the passage by which Nature joins the lizards to the snakes." He came across fossils of ancient giant animals that looked, except for size, very much like forms living in the same vicinity, and wondered whether the fossils were the ancestors of those forms. He observed that the Andean Mountain Range constituted a natural barrier to life and, as might be expected according to geologists, flora and fauna on opposite sides of the range differed.

The stopover at the Galapagos Islands profoundly impressed Darwin. He noted that the flora and fauna of South America were very similar—yet dissimilar—to those of the Galapagos. Even more surprising, the inhabitants of the various islands differed slightly. The thirteen kinds of finches resembled one another in the structure of their beaks, body forms, and plumage, and yet each constituted a separate species despite the fact that few geographic differences existed among the islands. What, he asked himself, could cause this modification if the physical geography and climate were not responsible? These observations, and the questions they raised, caused Darwin to wonder whether the theory of fixity of species was a valid one after all.

This abbreviated account of Darwin and his research on the *Beagle* does not do justice to the significant role the voyage played in Darwin's intellectual growth. He returned to England on board the *Beagle* on October 2, 1836, just short of five years from the date he sailed.

In 1842, Darwin wrote a short summary of his views on natural selection and revised it in 1844. The 1844 sketch was surprisingly similar to the

◇ Box 2-1 Darwin: Naturalist or Companion?

Robert Fitzroy, Captain of the *Beagle*.

Was Darwin invited to sail aboard the H.M.S. *Beagle* as a naturalist or as a companion to **Captain Fitzroy?*** Since Darwin had been recommended as a naturalist, and had acted in that capacity throughout the *Beagle*'s five-year voyage (during which he developed ideas that ultimately led to his concept of natural selection), the answer has always seemed obvious.

However, Dr. Stephen Jay Gould (1976) has suggested that Darwin was invited to be Fitzroy's companion, and that the position of naturalist was an enticement to that end. The reasons, says Gould, were that a captain in the

*The captain's name is spelled variously as Fitz-Roy, FitzRoy, and Fitzroy.

British navy was not permitted to speak to members of his crew except on ship's business; that Fitzroy was aware of the awful loneliness of a captain who had to dine by himself in his own cabin; and that he, Fitzroy, was not too stable. Therefore, someone to share his cabin, meals, and conversation was absolutely mandatory. For this, Fitzroy required someone of the proper social rank—a gentleman—and in order to persuade such a person, the captain offered the position of naturalist.

The interesting and important aspect of this, according to Gould, is that Darwin's view of evolution may have grown out of the strained relationship that developed between the two men. They argued on several subjects: slavery, for one; God and nature, for another. Fitzroy's dogmatic assertions about the universe, suggests Gould, acted as the catalyst that drove Darwin to an opposite view, leading to "an evolutionary theory based on chance variation and natural selection by a largely external environment: a rigidly materialistic (and basically atheistic) version of evolution."

Today it is difficult to know why Fitzroy wanted a naturalist on board. He has been described as "a public spirited and zealous officer." Since the purpose of the *Beagle's* voyage was entirely scientific, it is certainly possible that Fitzroy may have been serious in his search for a naturalist who might also — as a subordinate function — serve as companion.

Darwin's correspondence to his friend and professor Dr. Henslow (who first recommended him for the position), and to his father, seems to leave no doubt about why he thought he was sailing: to work as a naturalist. Darwin was aware that he was expected to be a companion to Captain Fitzroy (Henslow mentioned it in his letter to Darwin), but this function must have impressed him very little. He never referred to it in his correspondence.

Figure 2-3a The route of the H.M.S.
Beagle.

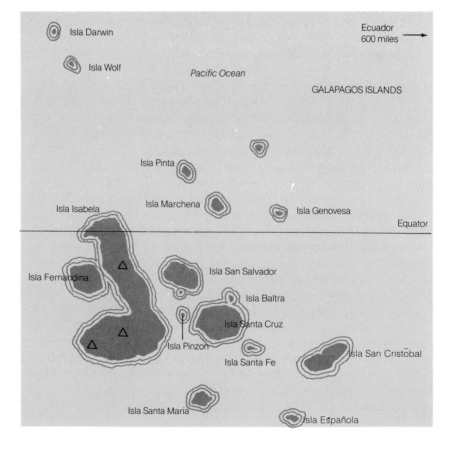

Figure 2-3b The Galapagos Islands.
Finches (because of their variety) and tor-
toises (because each island was inhabited
by its own variety) influenced Darwin's
thinking about evolution.

argument he presented fifteen years later in *Origin of Species*, but Darwin did not feel he had sufficient data to support his views, and he continued to accumulate facts.

Time passed. In 1855, an article by Alfred Russel Wallace on the succession of species impressed Darwin because it supported his views on species' mutability. Darwin was not disturbed at this time by the possibility that the publication of his own theory might be anticipated. Darwin had been encouraged by his close friends, especially Lyell (see p. 36) and Hooker (a well-known botanist) to publish his "theory," but he declined because he felt there was much more evidence to collect. His friends cautioned him that someone else might publish before he did, and, indeed, his friends' warning was realized in June, 1858, when Wallace sent him his paper on natural selection.

Alfred Russel Wallace (1828–1913) was born in a small English village into a family of modest means. He went to work at 14 and, without any special talent, moved from one job to the next. He became interested in collecting, and joined an expedition to the Amazon Valley in 1848, at the age of 25. After four happy years of collecting specimens in South America, Wallace returned to England and two years later, in 1854, he sailed to the Malayan Archipelago to continue his study and collection of bird and insect specimens. He remained there eight years, collected 125,660 specimens, and often thought about the problem of the succession of species.

Figure 2-4   Alfred Russel Wallace.

In 1858, on the island of Ternate, just off the coast of the Celebes Islands, Wallace was in bed suffering from one of his periodic attacks of fever. Suddenly, the solution to the problem he had so long thought about flashed through his mind. Recalling the phrase, "the positive checks to increase," from Malthus' *Essay* (p. 37), he immediately realized that this phenomenon could apply to animals as well as to human beings. If there were no checks, the earth would quickly be overrun by the most prolific breeders. Why, then, did some species of plants or animals perish while others survived? The answer came at once: the best adapted survived; the less well adapted perished. Wallace at once set his thoughts down on paper and sent Darwin his essay, "On the Tendency of Varieties to Depart Indefinitely from the Original Type" (Löwenberg, 1959).

When Darwin read Wallace's paper he was thoroughly depressed. He wrote Lyell, "Your words have come true with a vengeance—that I should be forestalled" (F. Darwin, 1950, p. 199). With the publication of Wallace's paper, Wallace would be given credit for a theory that Darwin felt belonged to him, since he had thought of it at least twenty years before. What to do? Darwin considered publishing a resumé of his own work but wondered whether it would be honorable to do so. He told Lyell, "I would far rather burn my whole book, than that he [Wallace] or any other man should think I have behaved in a paltry spirit" (F. Darwin, 1950, p. 201). After much indecision, Darwin finally decided to let his close friends, Lyell and Joseph Hooker, devise a formula that would be fair to both Wallace and himself.

This difficult task was achieved by his friends, who decided that joint papers by Wallace and Darwin would be read before a meeting of the Linnaean Society. The Society agreed, and the papers were read on the evening of July 1, 1858, with Darwin ill in bed and Wallace in the Far East. What is remarkable is that the papers did not create a furor at the meeting, since most members of the Society disagreed with the concepts of natural selection.

The solution to the problem of Wallace's paper pleased Darwin, and Wallace was delighted that he had been so fairly treated. After the presentation of the two papers, the trustees of the Linnaean Society brought urgent pressure on Darwin to publish as speedily as possible a full account of his "theory." Darwin returned to his work with exemplary energy and, within a year, in 1859, had completed and published his great work, *On the Origin of Species*.*

With publication, the storm broke, and has not abated even to this day. While there was much praise for the book from many quarters, the gist of opinion was negative. Scientific opinion gradually came to Darwin's support, assisted especially by Darwin's able friend, Thomas Huxley (known as "Darwin's bulldog"), who for years wrote and spoke in favor of natural selection. The riddle of species was now explained: species were not fixed, but mutable; they evolved from other species through the mechanism of natural selection. Science was never to be the same again.

◇ Darwin's Theory of Evolution

Darwin did not originate the idea of evolution, which had been suggested (or at least hinted at) 200 years previously—and much longer, if we include Greek thought of 2000 years ago. Darwin's grandfather, Erasmus Darwin, had written in defense of evolution before Charles was born, and Lamarck, a French scientist, had drawn up a schema trying to explain how new species were formed. However, his explanation met with unfavorable criticism and, in fact, did not accurately explain how the evolutionary process functioned.

Nor were the basic ideas used by Darwin completely of his own invention. Struggle for existence, extinction of species, variation, adaptation—these were all known and discussed for years by many European scientists. Darwin's great contribution was to bring these divergent ideas together and add the key: natural selection.

In his book, *On the Origin of Species*, published in 1859, Darwin explained his concept of evolution:

1. All species are capable of producing offspring faster than the food supply increases (see Malthus, p. 37)
2. All living things show variations; no two individuals of a species are exactly alike
3. Because there are more individuals than can possibly survive, there is a fierce struggle for existence and those with a favorable variation in size, strength, running ability, or whatever characteristics are necessary for survival, will possess an advantage over others (see Malthus, p. 37)
4. These favorable variations are inherited and passed on to the next generation
5. Over long periods of geologic time, these successful variations produce great differences that result in new species

*The complete title of Darwin's book is *On The Origin of Species by Means of Natural Selection, or the Preservation of Favoured Races in the Struggle for Life*.

Darwin called this process "natural selection." He did not believe in creation by design; that is, that life forms were placed on earth by creation, that variation in plants and animals was part of a grand divine design, or that the inorganic and the organic could be viewed as a progression from inferior to superior types, with humans at the top.

Darwin did not arrive at natural selection—his solution to the process of evolution—without assistance. When we look at the intellectual climate of Europe of the Middle Ages, we find that Christianity was associated with certain views of the universe. Since the time of Ptolemy, a Greco-Egyptian mathematician, geographer, and astronomer of the second century A.D., the earth was considered to be fixed at the center of a universe of spheres that revolved with perfect regularity around it. Not only was the inorganic world fixed and unchanging, but the organic world was believed to be equally static. It was believed that all species of the earth had been created (according to Genesis of the Old Testament) on a progression from the simplest forms to the most complex—humans. This progression was not evolutionary; that is, one species did not lead to or evolve into the next. The forms and sequence were fixed, no new ones had appeared since creation, and none had disappeared.

This progression was known as the Great Scale of Being, and the plan of the entire universe was seen as the Grand Design, that is, God's Design. The limbs of men and animals seemed designed to meet the purpose for which they are required. The wings of birds, eyes, etc., all of these structures were interpreted as neatly fitting the functions they performed. It was considered to be a deliberate plan, a design of the Grand Designer. Furthermore, it had all occurred in quite a short time, since creation was dated at 4004 B.C. by Archbishop James Ussher (1581–1656), an Irish prelate and scholar, who worked out the date by analyzing the "begat" chapter of Genesis.

Until these concepts of fixity and time were changed, it would be very unlikely that the idea of natural selection could even be conceived. What, then, upset the medieval belief in a rigid universe of planets, stars, plants, and animals? What scientific philosophy would, within the following 150 years, strike a death blow to the whole medieval system of thought? How would the scientific method as we know it today develop and, especially with Newton and Galileo in the seventeenth century, demonstrate a moving, not unchanging, universe?

The man who began this revolution was Copernicus (1473–1543), a Polish mathematician and astrologer, who simplified the Ptolemaic system by placing the sun at the center of the universe and the earth as one of the planets revolving around it. "The Copernican Revolution," as it is sometimes called, "is the supreme symbol of the passage from the medieval to the modern world, from an outlook which now seems like that of fairyland to the matter-of-fact outlook of the present day" (Dingle, 1959, p. 18).

Copernicus may not have realized the far-reaching effects of his new celestial system, but scientists of the seventeenth century—Bacon (inductive method), Harvey (circulation of the blood), Galileo (experimental science, central position of the sun, gravity, etc.), Newton (laws of motion and gravity)— gave the intellectual thought of their era a definite naturalistic basis. Although scientists remained religiously oriented, their observations and experiments

Figure 2-5 Linnaeus.

provoked notions of the universe that were new, exciting, and challenging, although sometimes condemned as heretical, Darwin, in the nineteenth century, was heir to the thinking and ideas of these seventeenth-century giants. At Cambridge, Darwin associated with professors (all churchmen) who were anti-evolutionists, but the radical change in intellectual thought of the seventeenth century enabled scientists of the eighteenth to think about the universe in a manner that made the idea of evolution possible, and paved the way for Darwin.

By the early decades of the 1700s, motion, not fixity, had become accepted for the physical universe, but most biological scientists held that change was unacceptable for living forms. Species had been fixed at creation, they still insisted, and since then there had been no new species formed or old species driven to extinction—there had simply been no change. Without change there cannot, of course, be evolution, and until it was recognized that species could alter, evolution and Darwin's natural selection could not be considered. This view of fixity of species was solidly held by one of the leading naturalists of his day, **Carolus Linnaeus**, who believed that "There are just as many species as there were created in the beginning," and again, "There is no such thing as a new species" (quoted in Singer, 1959, 379–380).

The son of a Lutheran pastor, Linnaeus (1707–1778) was born at Roeshult, Sweden. He is best known for developing a classification system for plants and animals, first published in 1835, which he called *Systema Naturae*. Linnaeus isolated those particular physical traits that best characterized a particular group of organisms. In plants, for instance, he used blossoms; in insects, wings; and in fish, scales. He even included humans in his classification of animals, thus defying the then-contemporary thought that humans, made in God's image, should be considered separately and outside the Animal Kingdom.

Linnaeus' scheme was well received throughout Europe, and, when applied to collections in museums and botanical gardens, it worked. He then proceeded to assign names to the animals and plants. Linnaeus hit upon the simple but effective idea of assigning two Latin names to each organism. The first word would be the generic term—the genus—for the organism and the second word, the specific term—the species. Thus, the two words together would become a unit internationally recognized as the name for that particular form. This system of binomial (or binominal) nomenclature was widely accepted, and is still used today.

We are concerned not so much with the problems and solutions that resulted in Linnaeus' *Systema Naturae* as we are in his ideas about evolution, which reflected the scientific thought of his time. Linnaeus saw nature as a "rationally ordained system of means and ends"; that is, every living thing is created perfectly adapted to the environment in which it lives, making further change unnecessary. According to Linnaeus (and many other scientists as well as laymen), this natural relationship did not exist for its own sake, but for the glory of God. It is, they believed, the duty of humans to study nature diligently, so that God might be glorified. Although some scientists had abandoned the age-old notion that nature was fixed, Linnaeus still adhered to the idea that species, once divinely created, had never changed, and "to study nature diligently" meant assigning to every living thing its proper name.

This Linnaean emphasis on classification, and his concept of the perfection of nature once fixed by creation and never altered, neatly delineated the views of the opponents of evolutionary thought. However, there were other voices, especially in France, raised loudly and clearly in favor of a universe based on change, and much more to the point, of the relationship between similar forms based on descent from a common ancestor.

The leading advocate of this point of view was Georges Louis Leclerc, who came from an old noble family in Burgundy and was later raised to the rank of Count, under the name of Buffon by Louis XV. **Buffon** (1707–1788), as he is known, was born the same year as Linnaeus. He knew of his contemporary and disagreed with him on most points. Buffon's writings made natural science popular drawing-room conversation, in which he himself excelled with sly wit. Talking one day with his female visitors, he said, "Nothing stands still. Everything moves. Even the seed of man does so, otherwise it would never reach its goal. May I show it to you under the microscope?" (Wendt, 1963, p. 83).

Figure 2-6 Buffon.

Buffon believed neither in the perfection of nature nor in the idea that nature had purpose. He stressed again and again the importance of change in the universe, and he underlined the changing nature, or mutability, of species.

In contrast to Linnaeus' static "rationally ordained system of means and ends," Buffon emphasized the variety and minute gradations of nature, which he explained in terms of "a system of laws, elements and forces." Thus, nature could be seen as functioning by natural means rather than through a divine mind. Buffon considered it important to see life as a dynamic system of processes instead of a static pattern of structure. He felt that the true aim of natural history was to discover and understand these processes, not simply to classify their result. Buffon

> put the hypothesis of organic evolution . . . in clear and definite form. He called . . . attention to the facts of comparative anatomy which constitute one of the principal evidences for that hypothesis. . . . He, finally, did more than any one else to habituate the mind of his time to a vastly (though not yet sufficiently) enlarged time-scale in connection with the history of organic nature, a necessary prerequisite to the establishment of transformation (Lovejoy, 1959, pp. 111–112).

The contrast between the thinking of Linnaeus and that of Buffon reflects not merely the old and the new, but also the response of many scientists and clergymen to the publication of Darwin's *Origin*. Although Linnaeus appeared to have changed his mind about fixity late in life, the concept of immutability of species continued to be the dominant theme among most scientists. Darwin was familiar with the writings of Buffon, which helped to make a belief in evolution acceptable. With the voluminous publications of Buffon and others, it is not at all surprising that when we arrive at the latter portion of the eighteenth century, the ideas of mutability of species and the possibility of unlimited organic change were well known throughout Europe. This doctrine of organic change was not widely accepted, but at least it was being discussed at length in intellectual circles.

In this enlightened era of the popularization of science (which saw the beginnings of archeology and the recognition that fossil bones belonged to

Figure 2-7 Erasmus Darwin.

Figure 2-8 Lamarck.

species of animals since perished), we must take notice of a most interesting figure who saw clearly the force of evolutionary ideas. Charles Darwin was well aware of the writings of this man, his grandfather, **Erasmus Darwin** (1731–1802), who was a country physician, poet, and versatile and eccentric scientist. More than fifty years before his grandson was to startle the world with his views on natural selection, Erasmus had expressed such ideas as "evolution by natural and sexual selection, protective adaptation, inheritance of acquired characteristics, and even the evolution of mankind" (Francoeur, 1965, p. 68). In fact, one biographer wrote of Erasmus Darwin, "the theory of natural selection was the only cardinal one in the evolution system on which Erasmus Darwin did not actually forestall his more famous and greater namesake" (Clodd, 1897, p. 114).

Although Charles Darwin had read his grandfather's writings, it is not possible to say what influence these had on his views. Erasmus had not solved the problem of the evolutionary process, but it is likely that his discussion of evolution made it easier for Charles to approach it. Erasmus Darwin had little influence on the scientific thought of his day, which is not difficult to understand, since he described his scientific ideas in ambiguous verse. For example, he expressed his thoughts on the struggle for existence thus:

Where milder skies protect the nascent brood
And earth's warm bosom yields salubrious food,
Each new descendant with superior powers
Of sense and motion speeds the transient hours;
Braves every season, tenants every clime,
And nature rises on the wings of Time.
(Wendt, 1955, p. 138)

During the eighteenth century, Erasmus Darwin wrote about and believed in evolution, but was never able to explain the process. He came close but, as Buffon before him and Lamarck afterwards, he relied on the concept of acquired characteristics to indicate how species were transformed: "'All animals undergo perpetual transformations; which are in part produced by their own exertions . . . and many of these acquired forms or propensities are transmitted to their posterity'" (E. Darwin, quoted in Singer, 1959, p. 505). However, neither Buffon nor E. Darwin codified their beliefs into a comprehensive system. The first European scientist to do this was Jean Baptiste Pierre Antoine de Monet de **Lamarck** (1744–1829).

Like Erasmus Darwin and Buffon, Lamarck also developed most of the ingredients of the concept of evolution, but he went beyond these men by organizing his ideas. Ernst Heinrich Haeckel, the well-known scientist of the late nineteenth century, said that to Lamarck "will always belong the immortal glory of having for the first time worked out the Theory of Descent as an independent scientific theory of the first order, and as the philosophical foundation of the whole science of Biology" (Clodd, 1897, p. 115).

One of the points stressed by Lamarck was the interaction of organic forms with their environment. He believed the stability of organic forms was directly proportionate to the stability of the conditions of life, and, as the conditions of life changed, organic forms were altered.

The alterations were caused by the *effort* the form makes in using those parts of its body that are most adaptive under given environmental conditions. Little by little, as time goes on, these changes result in new organs that are passed on through heredity. What is the mechanism that induces change?

If a particular part of the body feels a certain need, "fluids and forces" would be directed toward that point and a new organ would be slowly produced to satisfy that need. That the environment affects and can eventually induce change in organic forms is commonplace knowledge today, but that felt needs are the mechanism, while an intriguing idea, is not true.

Lamarck also believed that a characteristic acquired in the manner described above for a new organ could be passed on through heredity to the next generation. This theory of acquired characteristics, or Lamarckism, had already been suggested by Erasmus Darwin, but was not really questioned until it was carefully scrutinized by one of the leading scientists of France, Georges Cuvier, whose ideas we shall discuss shortly.

It should be stressed, on the other hand, that many of Lamarck's views of nature and evolution are as valid today as they were 150 years ago. His emphasis on the dynamic interaction of organic forms with the environment and the consequent adaptation is well placed. He brought together vast quantities of materials to support his evolutionary ideas, carrying them beyond those of Buffon. The world of science, especially biology, owes him a great debt.

However, like E. Darwin, he failed to solve the riddle of "how it works." It is true enough that all living forms may acquire characteristics during their lifetime. We know, for example, that a man may develop large muscles simply through exercise, but we also know that the physical characteristics we acquire in our lifetime (with the possible exception of mutations) are not transmitted to our offspring. Our highly muscled man does not pass on his overdeveloped muscles to his children. It is interesting to note that Charles Darwin, while he used natural selection as the mechanism for evolution, also used, at times, the belief that acquired characteristics could be inherited.

Lamarck, we might say, popularized the idea of evolution, but there remained vehement opposition to the notion that species may change and develop into new species. The outstanding opponent of evolution at this time was one of the great scientists of his day. He was not only a contemporary of Lamarck, but a man to whom Lamarck had given a position at the Jardin des Plantes, the institution where Buffon had worked for so many years. This was **Georges Cuvier** (1769–1832), who was to become famous as the "Pope of Bones," the father of zoology, paleontology, and comparative anatomy.

Our interest in Cuvier resides mainly in his unwavering, obstinate, and at times nasty criticism of Lamarck's views on evolution. Although not an especially religious person, Cuvier insisted upon the fixity of species with almost religious fervor, refusing to believe that a new species could evolve from an old one. By this time, most scientists thought it quite obvious that new species of animals and plants had come into existence, and, if Cuvier was to successfully counteract the growing interest in evolution, he had to offer an alternative explanation about how new species could appear. He did so by proposing a theory of catastrophism.

Figure 2-9   Cuvier.

This theory was based on the assumption of a series of violent and sudden catastrophes.* These catastrophes were produced by natural, not divine,† means, such as the formation of the Alps, and were responsible for ending each major stratigraphical sequence (see geologic table, p. 220). All creatures living in those parts of the world where "revolutions" or catastrophes took place were destroyed. Then, after things settled down, these areas were restocked with new forms, different from those previously living there. These new forms came from neighboring areas unaffected by the catastrophes. Cuvier's representation thus avoided the idea of evolution to explain the appearance of new forms.

Cuvier was an antievolutionist and one of the most brilliant scientists of his time. Did his antievolutionary views retard the development of evolutionary ideas? As we have seen, they did not affect Lamarck, who developed his evolutionary scheme despite Cuvier. Oldroyd (1980) suggests that, on the contrary, Cuvier's work led to Darwin!

Cuvier divided the Animal Kingdom into four divisions or embranchements: vertebrates, molluscs, jointed or segmented animals, and zoophytes (no special nervous system or sense organs). Each of these major groupings was seen as a separate organizational type, and each one had its particular anatomical and physiological characteristics functionally adaptive for the conditions of its environment. Thus, each of these divisions, one separate from the other, was not rigidly set in an inseparable Chain of Being, as was the Linnaean arrangement. Although separate, Cuvier believed these divisions fixed and not subject to change. However, since Cuvier separated these four divisions, thus eliminating the Chain of Being concept, he also opened the way for someone else to explain the appearance and disappearance of forms by an evolutionary theory.

Changes necessary from Cuvier's representation had to suggest mutability instead of fixity and to link species with their environments. Darwin did this, and added natural selection to complete the scheme. Thus, as Oldroyd suggests (1980, p. 43), "the route from Linnaeus to Darwin lay through the antievolutionist Cuvier, as much as the evolutionist Lamarck."

Cuvier's influence on Darwin was indirect, since his ideas did not act specifically on matters discussed by Darwin. Still, it may have made it easier for Darwin to argue (and others to accept) the notion that the Chain of Being concept was inadequate. On the other hand, Cuvier's catastrophism was of no help to Darwin; it is quite likely that, early in his thinking, Darwin rejected catastrophism because of the influence of Lyell, the period's most influential opponent of Cuvier's view.

Charles Lyell (1797–1875) was a lawyer by training and geologist by choice. When Darwin returned to England in 1836, he became Lyell's close friend and confidant, a relationship that was to last a lifetime despite differences on a number of intellectual points.

*A recent school of thought suggests that evolution can occur with sudden and rapid change. This idea (quite different from catastrophism) is known as "punctuated equilibrium" and is discussed on page 109.

†Cuvier's catastrophism had no religious basis, and he was careful to separate his religious beliefs from his scientific work. Creationists mistakenly use Cuvier's views to support their position.

Lyell's important contribution to science was his popular three-volume work, *Principles of Geology* (1830–1833), in which he rejected the catastrophism of Cuvier. Lyell reaffirmed the principle of **uniformitarianism**; that is, no forces had been active in the past history of the earth that are not also working today—an idea introduced into European thought in 1785 by James Hutton. Lyell showed, through the process of uniformitarianism, that the earth's crust was formed via a series of slow and gradual changes. Mountains, rivers, valleys, lakes, deserts, and coastlines were not the sudden result of cataclysms, but rather the result of purely natural forces, such as erosion by land, water, frost, ice, and rain. These forces, which could be seen operating in the present, could (assuming sufficient time) have caused all geological events of the past.

When he embarked on the *Beagle*, Darwin was more interested in geology than in any other science. In 1832, while in South America, Darwin received the second volume of Lyell's *Principles* (Professor Henslow had presented Darwin with the first volume just before the *Beagle* sailed, but cautioned Darwin not to believe everything Lyell had written). Lyell's work immediately struck a responsive chord as Darwin observed the mountains, rocks, and coastline of South America. From Lyell, Darwin learned first of all about the development of the earth's crust, the environmental conditions that, through the struggle for existence, could modify living forms, and, secondly, about the immense age of the earth, far beyond Archbishop Ussher's 4004 B.C.

Two important points in Darwin's explanation of evolution are the struggle for existence and descent with modification. The principle of struggle for existence was basic to Darwin's evolutionary theory, and this he credits to Lyell, though the idea was not original with him. Descent with modification Darwin saw as a slow and gradual process and, for this to work, time would be necessary. Lyell believed the earth was extremely old, on the order of hundreds or thousands of million years (much older than Buffon had suggested in the previous century), thus giving to Darwin a notion of time that would have made the gradual process of evolution possible.

Shortly after his return to England, Darwin opened his first notebook in July, 1837. He planned to collect evidence on the subject of the gradual modification of species since, as he said ". . . the subject haunted me" (F. Darwin, 1950, p. 15). As he worked, he came to realize that "selection was the keystone of man's success in making useful races of animals and plants. But how selection could be applied to organisms living in a state of nature remained for some time a mystery to me" (F. Darwin, 1950, p. 53). The mystery was solved for Darwin in October, 1838, fifteen months after he had begun his systematic enquiry, when he happened "'to read for amusement" Malthus' essay on the principle of population.

Thomas Robert Malthus (1766–1834) was an English clergyman, political economist, and devotee of the natural sciences. His work was to become a standard consulted by politicians dealing with population problems and a source of inspiration to both Charles Darwin and Alfred Wallace in their separate discoveries of the principle of natural selection.

In his *Essay*, Malthus pointed out that if human population growth is unrestrained by natural causes, it will double every twenty-five years, but that the capacity for food production increases only in a straight arithmetic

Uniformitarianism
The thesis that geological processes have always been the same as they are today.

Figure 2-10 Lyell.

progression. In nature, Malthus noted, this impulse to multiply was *checked by the struggle for existence*, but humans had to apply artificial restraints. Malthus emphasized two facts: the infinite fertility of humankind, and the limited size and resources of the earth.

Upon reading this, Darwin wrote:

> . . . it at once struck me that under these circumstances favourable variations would tend to be preserved, and unfavourable ones to be destroyed. The result of this would be the formation of a new species. *Here then I had at last got a theory by which to work* (F. Darwin, 1950, pp. 53–54). (Emphasis added.)

While Darwin had already realized that selection was the key to evolution, it was due to Malthus that he saw how selection in nature could be explained. In the struggle for existence, those *individuals* with favorable variations would survive; those with unfavorable variations would not. The significance here is that Darwin was thinking in terms of individuals (not species) that interact with one another. This was quite different from the nineteenth-century philosophy prevalent in Europe since the time of Plato. It was the significance of individuals in the struggle for existence that led Darwin to his concept of natural selection.

Before Darwin, scientists (Linnaeus and Lyell, for example) thought of species as an entity that could not change, and, if species changed, they were not species. It was species that were at the basis of the discussions of plants and animals. Individuals within the species did not appear to be significant and, therefore, it was difficult for many scientists to imagine how change could occur. Darwin, as we have pointed out, saw that variation of individuals could explain how selection occurred. Favorable variations were selected by nature for survival; unfavorable ones eliminated (Malthus, of course, believed God did the selecting, not nature). Thus, "Population thinkers stress the uniqueness of everything in the organic world. What is important for them is the individual, not the type. They emphasize that every individual in sexually reproducing species is uniquely different from all others. . . . There is no 'typical' individual, . . ." (Mayr, 1982, p. 46).

This emphasis on the uniqueness of the individual (the variation that occurs in all populations—that a population is a group of interacting individuals and not a type) led Darwin to natural selection as the mechanism that made evolution work. Natural selection operates on individuals, favorably or unfavorably, but it is the population that evolves. As pointed out on p. 106, the unit of natural selection is the individual; the unit of evolution is the population.

DARWIN'S EVIDENCE

By 1859, Darwin had accumulated a tremendous amount of data. In addition to the thousands of observations made during his five-year voyage on the *Beagle*, Darwin read voluminously in geology, paleontology, and related disciplines, and meticulously collected observations on domesticated plants and animals. Darwin had originally planned to detail all this information in a huge multivolume treatise. But when Wallace forced his hand, Darwin—in *Origin*—summarized his conclusions in what he modestly called an "abstract."

Domesticated Plants and Animals   Through what Darwin called "uncon-scious selection," animal and plant breeders had greatly modified varities of domestic species during historic times. Darwin believed such observations provided strong support for the process of natural selection, and was partic-ularly impressed with pigeons (which he had studied and bred for years):

> Altogether at least a score of pigeons might be chosen, which if shown to an ornithologist, and he were told that they were wild birds, would certainly, I think, be ranked by him as well-defined species. Moreover, I do not believe that any ornithologist would place the English carrier, the short-faced tumbler, the runt, the barb, pouter, and fantail in the same genus; more especially as in each of these breeds several truly-inherited sub-breeds, or species as he might have called them, could be shown him.
>
> Great as the differences are between the breeds of pigeons, I am fully convinced that the common opinion of naturalists is correct, namely, that all have descended from the rock-pigeon (*Columbia livia*) including under this term several geograph-ical races or sub-species, which differ from each other in the most trifling respects (Darwin, 1859, pp. 22–23).

Geographic Distribution of Life Forms   Darwin drew widely upon his expe-rience from the *Beagle* voyage, as well as an intimate knowledge of the flora and fauna of his native England, to argue further for the role of natural selection:

> Isolation, also, is an important element in the process of natural selection. In a continued or isolated area, if not very large, the organic and inorganic conditions of life will generally be in a great degree uniform; so that natural selection will tend to modify all the individuals of a varying species throughout the area in the same manner in relation to the same conditions. Intercrosses, also, with the individuals of the same species, which otherwise would have inhabited the sur-rounding and differently circumstanced districts, will be prevented (Darwin, 1859, p. 104).

The Geological and Paleontological Record   Darwin clearly understood that the major verification for his theory of slow and gradual evolutionary modi-fication must come from fossil evidence embedded within the earth's strata. He also recognized that the paleontological record could never be complete (much less, of course, was known about this record at that time). Even given these limitations, Darwin's perceptive use of paleontological examples strengthened his argument and provided a great stimulus for future research:

> We can understand how it is that all the forms of life, ancient and recent, make together one grand system; for all are connected by generation. We can understand, from the continued tendency to divergence of character, why the more ancient a form is, the more it generally differs from those now living. Why ancient and extinct forms often tend to fill up gaps between existing forms, sometimes blending two groups previously classed as distinct into one; but more commonly only bringing them a little closer together. The more ancient a form is, the more often, apparently, it displays characters in some degree intermediate between groups now distinct; for the more ancient a form is, the more nearly it will be related to, and consequently resemble, the common progenitor of groups since become widely divergent (Dar-win, 1859, pp. 344–345).

Comparative Anatomy   A basic element of biological interpretation in Darwin's time (as well as our own) involves anatomical comparison. How do we know whether two living forms are really related to each other, or to whom a fossil form is related?

> We have seen that the members of the same class, independently of their habits of life, resemble each other in the general plan of their organisation. This resemblance is often expressed by the term "unity of type," or by saying that the several parts and organs in the different species of the class are homologous. The whole subject is included under the general name of Morphology. This is the most interesting department of natural history, and may be said to be its very soul. What can be more curious than that the hand of a man, formed for grasping, that of a mole for digging, the leg of the horse, the paddle of the porpoise, and the wing of the bat, should all be constructed on the same pattern, and should include the same bones, in the same relative positions? (Darwin, 1859, p. 434).

Embryology   It has long been known that the immature stages organisms pass through during development can give important clues concerning evolutionary relationships—a fact that did not escape Darwin's attention.

> The embryos, also, of distinct animals within the same class are often strikingly similar; a better proof of this cannot be given, than a circumstance mentioned by Agassiz, namely, that having forgotten to ticket the embryo of some vertebrate animal he cannot now tell whether it be that of a mammal, bird, or reptile. The vermiform larvae of moths, flies, beetles, &c., resemble each other much more closely than do the mature insects (Darwin, 1859, p. 439).

Vestigial Organs   A final line of evidence presented by Darwin concerned those "rudimentary, atrophied, or aborted" organs that appeared to no longer perform any apparent function. If life had not evolved, what possible "Design" could explain their presence?

> Rudimentary organs may be compared with the letters in a word, still retained in the spelling, but become useless in the pronunciation, but which serve as a clue in seeking for its derivation. On the view of descent with modification, we may conclude that the existence of organs in a rudimentary, imperfect, and useless condition, or quite aborted, far from presenting a strange difficulty, as they assuredly do on the ordinary doctrine of creation, might even have been anticipated, and can be accounted for by the laws of inheritance (Darwin, 1859, pp. 455–456).

NATURAL SELECTION IN ACTION

A modern example of natural selection can be shown through research on the process in operation. The best historically documented case of natural selection acting in modern populations deals with changes in pigmentation among peppered moths near Manchester, England. Before the nineteenth century, the common variety of moth was a mottled gray color that provided extremely effective camouflage against lichen-covered tree trunks. Also present, though in much lower frequency, was a dark variety of moth. While resting on such trees, the dark, uncamouflaged moths against the light tree trunks were more visible to birds, and were therefore eaten more often. Thus, in the end, they produced fewer offspring than the light, camouflaged moths. Yet, in fifty years, by the end of the nineteenth century, the common gray, camouflaged form had been almost completely replaced by the black variety.

What had brought about this rapid change? The answer lies in the rapidly changing environment of industrialized nineteenth-century England. Pollutants released in the area settled on trees, killing the lichen and turning the bark a dark color. Moths living in the area continued to rest on trees, but the gray (or light) variety was increasingly conspicuous as the trees became darker. Consequently, they began to be preyed upon more frequently by birds and contributed fewer genes to the next generation. This process caused the gene for gray-colored moths to decrease in frequency. On the other hand, the black variety had greater reproductive success, and the gene for black increased from one generation to the next.

In the twentieth century, increasing control of pollutants has allowed some forested areas to return to their lighter, preindustrial conditions with lichen growing again on the trees. As would be expected, in these areas the black variety is now being supplanted by the gray.

The substance that produces pigmentation is called *melanin* and the evolutionary shift in the peppered moth, as well as many other moth species, is termed *industrial melanism*. Such an evolutionary shift in response to environmental change is called **adaptation**.

This example provides numerous insights into the mechanism of evolutionary change by natural selection:

1. A trait must be inherited to have importance in natural selection. A characteristic that is not hereditary (such as a change in hair pigmentation brought about by dye) will not be passed on to succeeding generations. Therefore, gene frequencies will not change and evolution will not occur. In moths, pigmentation is a demonstrated hereditary trait.

2. Natural selection cannot occur without variation in inherited characteristics. If all the moths had initially been gray (you will recall some dark forms were present) and the trees became darker, the survival and reproduction of all moths may have been so low that the population would have become extinct. Such an event is not unusual in evolution and, without variation, would nearly always occur. *Selection can only work with variation already present.*

3. "Fitness" is a relative measure that will change as the environment changes. Fitness is simply reproductive success. In the initial stage, the gray moth was the most-fit variety, but as the environment changed, the black moth became more fit, and a further change reversed the adaptive pattern. It should be obvious that statements regarding the "most-fit" life form mean nothing without reference to specific environments.

The example of peppered moths shows how different death rates influence natural selection, for moths that die early tend to leave fewer offspring. But mortality is not the entire picture. Another important aspect of natural selection is fertility, for an animal that gives birth to more young would pass its genes on at a faster rate than those who bear fewer offspring. However, fertility is not the whole picture either, for the crucial element is the number of young raised successfully to the point where they reproduce themselves. We may

Adaptation
An evolutionary shift in a population in response to environmental change; the result of natural selection.

(a)

(b)

Figure 2-11 Variation in the peppered moth. In (*a*), the dark form is more visible to bird predators on the light (unpolluted) trees. In (*b*), the light form is more visible: trees are darker due to pollution.

state this simply as *differential net reproductive success*. The way this mechanism works can be demonstrated through another example.

In a common variety of small birds called swifts, data show that giving birth to more offspring does not necessarily guarantee that more young will be successfully raised. The number of eggs hatched in a breeding season is a measure of fertility. The number of birds that mature and are eventually able to leave the nest is a measure of net reproductive success, or offspring successfully raised. The following tabulation shows the correlation between the number of eggs hatched (fertility) and the number of young that leave the nest (reproductive success) averaged over four breeding seasons (Lack, 1966).

Number of eggs hatched (fertility)	2 eggs	3 eggs	4 eggs
Average number of young raised (reproductive success)	1.92	2.54	1.76
Sample size	72	20	16

As the tabulation shows, the most efficient fertility number is three eggs, for that yields the highest reproductive success. Raising two is less beneficial to the parents since the *end result* is not as successful as with three eggs. Trying to raise more than three young is actually detrimental, since the parents may not be able to provide adequate nourishment for any of the offspring. An offspring that dies before reaching reproductive age is, in evolutionary terms, an equivalent of never having been born in the first place. Actually, such a result may be an evolutionary minus to the parents, for this offspring will drain their resources and may inhibit their ability to raise other offspring, thereby lowering their reproductive success even further. Selection will favor those genetic traits that yield the maximum net reproductive success. If the number of eggs laid* is a genetic trait in birds (and it seems to be), natural selection in swifts should act to favor the laying of three eggs as opposed to two or four.

DARWIN'S FAILURES

Darwin argued eloquently for the notion of evolution in general and the role of natural selection in particular, but he did not entirely comprehend the exact mechanisms of evolutionary change.

As we have seen, natural selection acts on *variation* within species. Neither Darwin, nor anyone else in the nineteenth century, understood the source of all this variation. Consequently, Darwin speculated about variation arising from "use"—an idea similar to Lamarck's. Darwin, however, was not as dogmatic in his views as Lamarck, and most emphatically argued against inner "needs" or "effort." Darwin had to confess that when it came to explaining variation, he simply did not know.

> Our ignorance of the laws of variation is profound. Not in one case out of a hundred can we pretend to assign any reason why this or that part differs, more or less, from the same part in the parents. But whenever we have the means of instituting a comparison, the same laws appear to have acted in producing the lesser differ-

*The number of eggs hatched is directly related to the number of eggs laid.

ences between varieties of the same species, and the greater differences between species of the same genus. The external conditions of life, as climate and food, &c., seem to have induced some slight modifications. Habit in producing constitutional differences, and use in strengthening, and disuse in weakening and diminishing organs, seem to have been more potent in their effects (Darwin, 1859, pp. 167–168).

In addition to his inability to explain the origins of variation, Darwin also did not completely understand the mechanism by which parents transmitted traits to offspring. Almost without exception, nineteenth-century scholars were confused about the laws of heredity, and the popular consensus was that inheritance was *blending* by nature. In other words, offspring were always expected to express intermediate traits as a result of a blending of their parents' contributions. Given this view, we can see why the actual nature of genes was thus unimaginable. Without any viable alternatives, Darwin accepted this popular misconception. As it turned out, a contemporary of Darwin had systematically worked out the rules of heredity. However, the work of this obscure Augustinian monk, Gregor Mendel (whom you shall meet in Chapter 4), was not recognized until the beginning of the twentieth century.

◇ Summary

The concept of evolution as we know it today is directly traceable to developments in intellectual thought in Western Europe over the last 300 years. In particular, the contributions of Linnaeus, Lamarck, Buffon, Lyell, and Malthus all had significant impact upon Darwin. The year 1859 marks a watershed in evolutionary theory for, in that year, the publication of Darwin's *On the Origin of Species* crystallized the evolutionary process (particularly the crucial role of natural selection) and, for the first time, thrust evolutionary theory into the consciousness of the common person. Debates both inside and outside the sciences continued for several decades (and in some corners persist today), but the theory of evolution irrevocably changed the tide of intellectual thought. Gradually Darwin's formulation of the evolutionary process became accepted almost universally by scientists as the very foundation of all the biological sciences, physical anthropology included. In this, the twentieth century, contributions from genetics allow us to demonstrate the mechanics of evolution in a way unknown to Darwin and his contemporaries.

Natural selection is the central determining factor influencing the long-term direction of evolutionary change. How natural selection works can best be explained as differential reproductive success, meaning, in other words, how successful individuals are in leaving offspring to succeeding generations.

◇ Questions for Review

1. Trace the history of evolutionary ideas from Copernicus to the time of Darwin.
2. In what ways do Linnaeus and Buffon differ in their approach to the concept of evolution?

3. What are the bases of Lamarck's theory of acquired characteristics? Why is this theory unacceptable?
4. What was Lamarck's contribution to nineteenth-century evolutionary ideas?
5. Explain Cuvier's catastrophism.
6. What did Malthus and Lyell contribute to Darwin's thinking on evolution?
7. What major areas of evidence did Darwin use to strengthen his argument concerning evolution?
8. How did Darwin's explanation of the source of variation compare with that of Lamarck?
9. What hereditary mechanism did Darwin utilize to explain transmission of traits from parents to offspring?
10. What is meant by adaptation? Illustrate through the example of industrial melanism.

◇ Suggested Further Reading

Barash, David. *Sociobiology and Behavior* (2nd Ed.), New York: Elsevier, 1982.
   A sociobiological survey of the ways natural selection causes behavior to evolve. Many interesting examples from the field of behavior (ethology) are included. While this book is clearly slanted toward a sociobiological orientation, the explanations of how natural selection operates are clear and concise.

Darwin, Charles. *Voyage of the Beagle*, New York: Doubleday, 1962.
   Darwin's own account of his historic five-year journey as naturalist on board the Beagle. *Highly recommended for its insight into Darwin's changing views toward evolution.*

————. *On the Origin of Species*, New York: Mentor Books, 1958.
   A book to be read by all students of evolution. This is considered to be one of the most influential books written in the nineteenth century.

————. *The Illustrated Origin of Species*, New York: Hill and Wang, 1979.
   Abridged and introduced by Richard E. Leakey. A handsomely illustrated version of Darwin's 6th edition, with excellent running commentary. This version is often re-worded from Darwin's original text. Such abridgement may occasionally aid reada-bility, but the reader should refer to Darwin's original for a more accurate historical document.

Eiseley, Loren. *The Immense Journey*, New York: Random House, 1958, 1961.
   A fascinating story of evolution told by a physical anthropologist who became well known for his writings on nature. Every student should read this most interesting book.

Futuyma, Douglas J. *Science on Trial*, New York: Pantheon Books, 1983.
   Futuyma (who has subtitled this book "The Case for Evolution") presents a clear and readable discussion of evolution, as well as the fallacies of creationism. Recom-mended for beginning students.

Gillespie, Neal C. *Charles Darwin and the Problem of Creation*, Chicago: University of Chicago Press, 1979.
   Intellectual thought of the last century from a philosophical point of view. One of the questions the author attempts to answer is why Darwin pursued so assiduously the idea of natural selection. For the more serious student.

Godfrey, Laurie R. (ed.). *Scientists Confront Creationism*, New York: W. W. Norton & Co., Inc., 1983.

This work contains an introduction by Richard Lewontin and articles by fifteen different scientists—anthropologists, geologists, astronomers, biochemists, etc.— who refute creationist arguments. For a well-rounded view of the weaknesses of the creationist viewpoint, this book is excellent.

Huxley, Julian and H.B.D. Kettlewell. *Charles Darwin and His World*, New York: The Viking Press, 1965.

An interesting biography of Darwin by Julian Huxley, noted biologist and grandson of T. H. Huxley, Darwin's most powerful supporter; also by Bernard Kettlewell, well-known geneticist. Many excellent illustrations.

Irvine, William. *Apes, Angels and Victorians*, New York: McGraw-Hill Book Co., 1955.

A readable story of Darwin, Huxley, and evolution. It is told in detail, with skill and imagination.

Keynes, Richard Darwin. *The Beagle Record*, New York: Cambridge University Press, 1979.

A splendidly illustrated book worthwhile for the beautiful drawings and photographs alone. Selections from Darwin's journal. Highly recommended.

Löwenberg, Bert James. *Darwin, Wallace, and the Theory of Natural Selection*, Cambridge: Arlington Books, 1959.

A brief review of the developments leading to Darwin's and Wallace's concept of natural selection. Interesting and dramatic story.

Mayr, Ernst. *Population, Species, and Evolution*, Cambridge: Harvard University Press, 1970.

A thorough and quite technical exposition on the processes of evolution, particularly the mechanics of speciation. Highly recommended for the advanced student.

Miller, Jonathan and Borin Van Loon. *Darwin for Beginners*, New York: Pantheon Books, 1982.

An amusing account of Darwin, natural selection, and evolution, or, as the authors say, "The Strange Case of Charles Darwin and Evolution." There are many drawings in cartoon style; nevertheless, evolution is well discussed, and students without a background in Darwin and evolution are encouraged to read this small book.

Rose, Michael. *The Darwinian Revolution*, Chicago: University of Chicago Press, 1979.

A historian discusses the intellectual climate of Darwin's time and its influence on Darwin's study of evolution. For the more serious student.

Scientific American, September 1978.

An up-to-date survey of evolution by specialists (Mayr, Washburn, Lewontin, and others) in their field. The entire issue is devoted to evolution.

Simpson, George Gaylord. *The Meaning of Evolution* (Revised Ed.), New Haven: Yale University Press, 1967.

An authoritative account of the evolutionary process by the leading evolutionary biologist of this century. After reviewing the fossil record, Simpson succinctly discusses the mechanics of the evolutionary process.

Stebbins, G. Ledyard. *Processes of Evolution* (2nd Ed.), Englewood Cliffs: Prentice-Hall, Inc., 1971.

A straightforward discussion of the modern, synthetic theory of evolution. Very well organized and presented with many excellent illustrations. Highly recommended for the beginning or moderately advanced student.

Stone, Irving. *The Origin: A Biographical Novel of Charles Darwin*, New York: Doubleday and Co., 1980.

Although a somewhat fictional account, this massive work gives a detailed background of Darwin's childhood, education, family life, scientific experiences, and personal concerns. Written by a leading historical biographer, this book is entertaining.

Biological Basis of Life

CONTENTS

Linus Pauling.

At Cambridge University's Cavendish Laboratory, from 1951 to 1953, a brash young American scientist from Chicago, **James D. Watson** and a garrulous Englishman from Northampton, **Francis H. C. Crick**, worked more or less together (with the assistance of English physicist Maurice Wilkins and others) to solve the puzzle of DNA structure.

Watson should have been hard at work in Copenhagen learning chemistry to help him in his postdoctoral biological research, and Crick, already at Cambridge, should have been busily engaged researching hemoglobin crystals for his Ph.D. Neither should have been involved in DNA research, but, as a matter of fact, both men were very much involved, and they hoped not only to discover the structure of DNA and win a Nobel Prize, but to beat **Linus Pauling** who, they were quite sure, was close to success on the same project at California Institute of Technology.

But Pauling was not as close to success as Crick and Watson believed. In November, 1951, Pauling started working on a triple helix and thought he succeeded, "although the structure was described as 'an extraordinarily tight one, with little opportunity for change in positions of the atoms'" (Pauling, 1974). A copy of the paper on his experiment was sent to Crick and Watson, who had themselves built an unsuccessful triple helix model a year earlier. They had considered their model a failure, and, after reading Pauling's paper (and catching an error in basic chemistry), knew his to be a failure also.

As Watson tells the story, he knew that Pauling was wrong, and that the earlier model he and Crick had constructed was also wrong, and now he was stumped. It was not until Wilkins showed him an X-ray diffraction photograph of DNA (taken by Cavendish scientist Rosalind Franklin) early in 1953, that Watson thought he saw a bit of light. The X-ray indicated that a helix was the correct structure, which he had been sure of anyway, and, further, that a 2-chain model—a double helix rather than a triple helix—might possibly be the answer. Watson and Crick deliberately kept the X-ray photograph from Pauling, since they feared that if he saw the X-ray, he would solve the problem before they did.

Watson designed a 2-chain metal helical model of DNA for experimental purposes to be built by the Cavendish Laboratory. The key to the mystery occurred abruptly to Watson while he was impatiently waiting for the Lab machine shop to complete the model. He had cut accurate representations of the four bases from stiff cardboard and was shifting them around trying out various pairing possibilities when:

Suddenly I became aware that an adenine-thymine pair held together by two hydrogen bonds was identical in shape to a guanine-cytosine pair held together by at least two hydrogen bonds. All the hydrogen bonds seemed to form naturally; no fudging was required to make the two types of base pairs identical in shape (Watson, 1968, p. 194).

The enigma of the basic DNA structure was solved and the race won. In 1962, the Nobel Prize for Medicine and Physiology was awarded to Crick, Watson, and Wilkins.

Actually, Watson and Crick need not have worried about Pauling's beating them to the DNA solution since Pauling did not consider this research a race (Pauling, personal communication); however, Pauling does believe there was a chance, had he seen the X-ray photograph,

. . . that I would have thought of the Watson-Crick structure during the next few weeks. . . . Nevertheless, I myself think that the chance is rather small that I would have thought of the double helix in 1952, before Watson and Crick made their great discovery (Pauling, 1974, p. 771).

SOURCES:

Pauling, Linus. "Molecular Basis of Biological Specificity," *Nature*, **248** (no. 5451):769, 771, April 26, 1974.

Olby, Robert. *The Path to the Double Helix*, Seattle: University of Washington Press, 1974.

Watson, James D. *The Double Helix*, New York: Atheneum, 1968.

James Watson and Francis Crick.

◇ CHAPTER THREE

◇ Introduction

In the preceding chapter, evolution was discussed from a conceptual point of view, but the mechanics of evolution—how hereditary characteristics are actually passed on from one generation to the next—were not included in that generalized presentation. In the body, what physiological processes operate to produce and distribute variation, and enable natural selection to function? In this chapter, we shall examine the specifics, beginning with the nature of the cell, since that is where, in a sense, the evolutionary process begins. The basic evolutionary process applies to all forms of life—to plants as well as to animals; however, our interest is mainly humankind, and cells and genetics will be discussed for the most part from the point of view of human beings. Nevertheless, we should keep in mind that the cell is basic to all forms of life, and that cellular characteristics (such as genes, chromosomes, and DNA) are found in the cells of all animals and plants. Finally, we should remember that the process of heredity is essentially similar in all species of life. Heredity, as we deal with it here, refers simply to the passage of genetic information from the cells of one generation to those of the next.

◇ The Cell

SOMATIC AND SEX CELLS

Basically, two kinds of cells are directly involved with heredity: **somatic cells** and **sex cells**. The body is composed of various kinds of specialized tissues (blood, liver, muscle, skin, nerve) consisting of billions of somatic cells continually being manufactured to replace those that have died. Indeed, one estimate has it that the cells of the human body are replaced every seven years.

Sex cells are similar to somatic cells but play no part in the structural composition of the body. They originate in the testes of males and ovaries of females, and their only function is to transmit life and hereditary information from parents to offspring.

CELL STRUCTURE

Cells (Fig. 3-1) are composed of four major types of organic materials: carbohydrates, lipids, nucleic acids, and especially **proteins**.

The structure of a cell is best described as a small unit consisting of a **nucleus** and **cytoplasm**. Within the cytoplasm are various substances and structures only a few of which (ribosomes, RNA, amino acids) are important to us in tracing how hereditary information from the nucleus is processed.

The focal point of heredity is the nucleus, usually located in the center of

Somatic cells
soma: body
Cells that do not divide by meiosis and do not become gametes.

Sex cells
Cells that divide by meiosis and become gametes.

Protein
Proteins are composed of amino acids. A single protein molecule contains nitrogen, oxygen, hydrogen, carbon, and, usually, sulfur.

Nucleus
A body, present in most types of cells, containing chromosomes.

Cytoplasm
That portion of the cell except the nucleus.

Figure 3-1   Generalized diagram of a cell.

the cell and separated from the cytoplasm by a thin nuclear membrane. Within the nucleus are two nucleic acids central to understanding the hereditary process: ribonucleic acid (RNA) and deoxyribonucleic acid (DNA). Just outside the nucleus and associated with its function, are two small cylindrical bodies called *centrioles*.

Chromosomes   During division of the cell, **chromosomes** become readily visible within the nucleus. The structure of a chromosome may be portrayed as two arms held together by a circle (**centromere**). (See Fig. 3-2 and Fig. 3-3.) The number of chromosomes in different plant and animal species varies, but normally all the members of a single species possess the same number of chromosomes (46 for humans).

The 46 chromosomes found in the somatic cells of all human beings are more accurately considered as 23 pairs, since there are two sets of 23 different chromosomes (Fig. 3-4). The first 22 pairs of chromosomes are known as *autosomes*; the 23rd pair (or *sex chromosomes*) is known alphabetically as XX or XY. (A female carries two X chromosomes and a male one X and one Y. We will discuss these later in the chapter.) Each pair of chromosomes has been identified by the size of the arms on each side of the centromere (the small, circular clear area joining the arms). Generally speaking, chromosome pair 1 is the largest, with gradual shortening of each succeeding chromosome pair through 22. However, X is quite a large chromosome and Y is one of the smallest. Figure 3-4 illustrates the gradation from large to small.

Chromosome
chrome: color
soma: body
Threadlike, gene-containing body found in the nucleus.

Centromere
centro: central
mere: part
That part of the chromosome to which spindle fibers are attached during mitosis and meiosis.

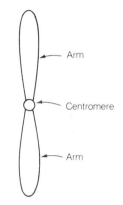

Figure 3-2   A normal chromosome.

Figure 3-3   Types of chromosomes.

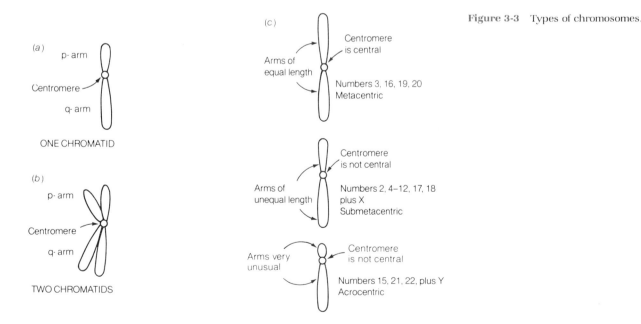

Figure 3-4   Human chromosomes: a male
karyotype.

◇ Cell Division: Mitosis

The nature of cells is to divide. Since division of the two kinds of cells differs, let us first take the less complex somatic cell division, called **mitosis**.

In mitosis, cell division passes through four basic phases: *prophase*, *metaphase*, *anaphase*, and *telophase*. For our present purposes, we need not describe division in complex detail. For those whose interests lie in that direction, Figure 3-5 separates mitosis into its basic phases, and even greater detail may be found in any college introductory biology or genetics textbook.

Somatic cell division serves several functions. As cells divide, they multiply, thus aiding in the growth of the organism. Cell division is also a means by which old cells are replaced by new ones. What is of interest to us is the part

Karyotype
(care'-ee-o-type)
karyo: nut, kernel
In biology, refers to the nucleus—a description or illustration of the number, size, and shapes of the chromosomes in the cells of an organism.

Mitosis
(my-toe'-sis)
mit: thread
osis: process or state
Somatic cell division producing two daughter cells identical to the parental cell.

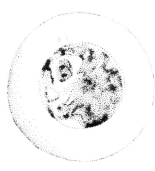

Interphase: Growth phase; synthesis; chromosome duplication.

Prophase: Chromosomes visible; spindle and asters form.

Metaphase: Centromere joined to spindle fibers. Alignment of centromeres along equatorial plane.

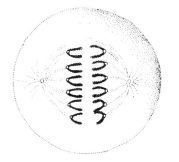

Anaphase: Each (doubled) chromosome divides and chromatids move to opposite poles.

Late Telophase: Spindles and asters disappear; two sets of daughter chromosomes organize into nucleus of two identical daughter cells.

Figure 3-5   Basic phases of mitosis.

Meiosis
(my-oh'-sis)
meioun: to make smaller
osis: process or state
Reduction division; sex cell division; reduction of a diploid cell, through two divisions, to a haploid (gamete) cell.

Gamete
A haploid cell (sperm or ovum) that may combine with a haploid cell of the other sex to form a fertilized cell.

Anomaly
Different, irregular deviation.

of this process of cell division resulting in the development of two daughter cells identical to the mother cell. In this way, as new body cells are produced they are exactly the same as those they replace, and the body, except for maturation and degeneration, remains essentially the same throughout life.

Mitosis operates in ingenious fashion in order to produce these two identical daughter cells (Fig. 3-6). A cell with 46 chromosomes must divide into two daughter cells, each containing the exact number of chromosomes as the mother cell. This is accomplished in the following manner:

1. At the beginning of the division process, each chromosome duplicates itself and actually consists of two longitudinal components called *chromatids*. There are now 46 doubled chromosomes, or 92 chromatids.
2. The doubled chromosomes position themselves along the equator of the nucleus and, as the cell divides, the chromatids separate.
3. As the cell continues to divide, the chromatids move away from each other in opposite directions. When the cell completes its division, there are two daughter cells, each with a complete set of 46 chromosomes.

The result of this division is the production of two daughter cells, each identical to the other and to the mother cell. Each daughter cell contains the same 46 chromosomes; that is, the same genetic material as the mother cell.

◇ Cell Division: Meiosis

We have seen how mitosis produces two daughter cells with the same number of chromosomes and genetic material as the mother cell. Reproduction, however, is quite another matter, requiring a specialized division process called **meiosis**.

The function of meiosis also appears simple—the production of cells with 23 chromosomes by dividing a cell of 46 chromosomes. However, it is not merely a matter of dividing 46 by 2, since that could result in cells with a random collection of any 23 chromosomes. The problem is to produce cells (called **gametes**) containing one of each of the 23 different kinds of chromosomes, no more and no less. If, for example, there were an additional chromosome number 21 and an absence of number 19, even though there would be 23 chromosomes in the gamete, it would probably not function in fertilization. If it did, the chances are it would produce a lethal **anomaly**. A normal gamete, following the meiotic process, will have a complete set of 23 chromosomes, one of each pair.

The process of reducing the number of chromosomes from 46, the *diploid* number (the full complement of chromosomes) to 23, the *haploid* number (exactly half the full complement), is the reason why meiosis is known as reduction division.

Meiosis is perhaps even more ingenious than mitosis, and requires not one but *two* divisions. As in mitosis, the parent cell (the sex cell in meiosis) before division contains 46 chromosomes, and again as in mitosis, a number of phases occur during the division process. For our purposes, an abbreviated account of the meiotic process will suffice. Those who wish to study meiosis

Somatic cell with 46 chromosomes in nucleus

Cell divides; the nucleus of each daughter cell contains 46 chromosomes

Figure 3-6 Mitosis. An "ingenious" method of dividing a cell with 46 chromosomes and producing two daughter cells with 46 chromosomes identical to each other and to the mother cell.

in greater detail are again encouraged to refer to a college introductory biology or genetics textbook.

FIRST DIVISION

1. Before the process of meiosis actually begins, the 46 chromosomes have arranged themselves in 23 homologous pairs.
2. The 23 doubled pairs of chromosomes are positioned along the equator of the nucleus. Spindle fibers are attached to both centromeres of each doubled chromosome, and, as the fibers shorten, the centromeres lead their doubled chromosomes away from each other toward opposite poles. The cytoplasm divides, and the result is two daughter cells.

Examine Figure 3-7 and you will see that meiotic and mitotic daughter cells are quite different from each other. In mitosis, each daughter cell contains 46 chromosomes, the diploid number; in meiosis, after first division, each daughter cell contains not 46, but 23 chromosomes. Each cell contains only one of the homologous pairs (see Box 3-1), but in a doubled state. A doubled chromosome of a homologous pair is known as a **homologue**.

When the cell divides (see Fig. 3-8), the tetrad (see Box 3-1) is separated. The homologue on the left moves to one daughter cell, and the homologue on the right moves to the other daughter cell. Each of the two daughter cells now contains one of each of the 23 different homologues. Figure 3-7 illustrates the differences of mitotic and meiotic division.

Homologue
(hom'-a-log)
Occurs in meiosis when a chromosome duplicates itself. The double-strand chromosome is a homologue.

Homologue   Homologue

Homologous pair

GENERAL PLAN OF MITOSIS
OF A HUMAN CELL

46 — 46 chromosomes (23 pairs)

Duplication

First cell division

46 chromosomes
(23 pairs in each
daughter cell)

GENERAL PLAN OF MEIOSIS
OF A HUMAN CELL

46 — 46 chromosomes (23 pairs)

Duplication

First cell division

Each cell now has
23 chromosomes
(one member of
each pair in
doubled strands).

Second division

Each cell has
23 chromosomes
(one member of
each pair in
single strands).

Figure 3-7 During mitosis, each parent cell gives rise to two daughter cells genetically identical to the parent; that is, with the same complement of chromosomes as the parent cell. During meiosis, which is completed in two consecutive cell divisions, four daughter cells are produced, and the chromosome complement is reduced from the diploid to the haploid number.

◇ Box 3-1 Terms Used in Discussion of Chromosomes

Diploid (*dipl*: double; *oid*: resembling, similar to). The full set of chromosomes, 46 in humans. Since there are 23 different chromosomes, doubling that makes 46, the diploid number. There are two (a pair) of each kind of chromosome.

Haploid (*hapl*: single, simple; *oid*: resembling, similar to). Simple here means uncomplicated, the basic number, referring to the 23 different chromosomes found in the gamete after the second division. There is a single representative, not a pair, of each kind of chromosome.

Tetrad (*tetr*: four). A structure of four—refers here to the 4 chromatids of a pair of homologous chromosomes—the 4-strand stage.

Locus (pl. *loci*, pronounced lo-sigh). The place of a gene on a chromosome.

Autosomes   In humans, the first 22 pairs of chromosomes; not sex chromosomes.

Homologous chromosomes   A matched pair of chromosomes.

SECOND DIVISION

We stated earlier that the function of meiosis was to produce cells with 23 chromosomes. When we left our daughter cells after first division, they had not yet reached that goal, since the chromosomes in each daughter cell were still doubled. In order to produce a cell with 23 single-stranded chromosomes, another division becomes necessary to separate the doubled chromosomes, and that is exactly what second division does.

The two daughter cells now pass through the already familiar process of division. The 23 homologues position themselves again along the equator of the cell, the single centromere joining the two chromatids is doubled, spindle fibers are again attached to each centromere and lead their respective chromatids to opposite poles. The cytoplasm of each daughter cell divides, and now each gamete finally contains one of each of the 23 different chromosomes, the haploid number. The meiotic function, to produce cells with one set of 23 chromosomes, has been achieved.

Reduction of the number of chromosomes from the diploid to the haploid number (46 to 23) is basic to the process of heredity, as a glance at the simple arithmetic involved clearly demonstrates. In bisexual reproduction, each parent contributes half the genetic information. Each parent through sexual intercourse contributes one gamete, and, if fertilization occurs, a child normally will be produced. Since the child's cells must have 46 chromosomes, it is clear that each parent cannot transmit a cell with 46 chromosomes because that would produce a cell with 92 chromosomes. Therefore, the number of chromosomes of each parental cell must be reduced to half the diploid number, or 23.

If the paternal and maternal gametes combine in the female, the result is one fertilized cell, called a **zygote**, which carries the full complement of 23 pairs, one member of each pair coming from the father and one from the mother (Fig. 3-8). The zygote divides by mitosis and develops into an embryo, and then a fetus.

This description outlines the essentials of meiosis, how parents produce cells that contain the blueprint for the next generation. But in order to understand the process of heredity, we must necessarily examine chromosomes more carefully.

We have mentioned a number of times that there are 23 pairs of homologous chromosomes. The question then arises: What is meant by homologous? In attempting to answer, we shall have to take a moment with the concept of the gene. What is called a gene is that segment of a chromosome that carries the hereditary code for a particular protein; that is, the gene is the unit of inheritance. This is not, strictly speaking, a completely accurate statement, but it will suffice for the present. We shall discuss genes in more detail later in the chapter.

On a chromosome, a gene occupies a position (its "street address" as it were) called a *locus*, and there are thousands (perhaps millions) of loci (pronounced lo'-sigh), each one occupied by a gene (Fig. 3-10). Among the 46 chromosomes there are 22 matching pairs; that is, with genes influencing the same trait. The gene at a particular locus on one chromosome codes for the same hereditary characteristic as the gene at that particular locus on the matching chromosome. This holds for every gene and every locus on these two particular chromosomes (except X and Y, as we shall see). For this reason,

Zygote
(yoked)
A fertilized cell formed by the union of a male gamete and a female gamete.

Gene
A segment of a DNA molecule with a detectable function; sometimes used synonymously with locus and allele.

Figure 3-8 Simplified diagram of spermatogenesis and oögenesis. (See Fig. 3-9 for more detailed diagram.)

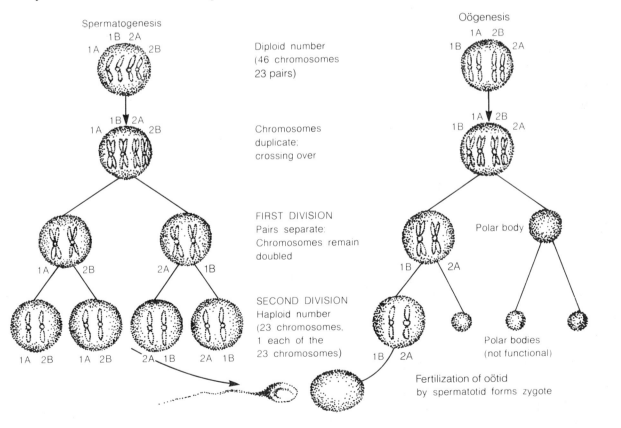

Spermatogenesis
1B 2A
1A   2B

Diploid number
(46 chromosomes
23 pairs)

Oögenesis
1A 2B
1B   2A

1B 2A
1A   2B

Chromosomes
duplicate:
crossing over

1A 2B
1B   2A

1A   2B
2A   1B

FIRST DIVISION
Pairs separate:
Chromosomes remain
doubled

Polar body
1B   2A

1A 2B   1A 2B   2A 1B   2A 1B

SECOND DIVISION
Haploid number
(23 chromosomes,
1 each of the
23 chromosomes)

1B 2A

Polar bodies
(not functional)

Fertilization of oötid
by spermatotid forms zygote

Figure 3-9   Meiotic cell division.

FIRST DIVISION

Prophase I

Double-stranded chromosomes appear; homologous chromosomes come together in pairs (*synapse*); each *homologue* consists of two identical chromatids, and the pairing involves four chromatids, a *tetrad;* crossing-over occurs at synapse. *Diploid* number of chromosomes.

Metaphase I

Spindle forms; chromosomes move to equator; spindle fibers attach to centromeres of each homologue; nuclear envelope begins to disappear.

Anaphase I

Homologues move away from each other toward opposite poles; cell begins to divide.

Telophase I

Nuclear envelope reappears; cell divides; each homologue of chromosome pair in separate cell. End of first division.

SECOND DIVISION

Prophase II

Chromosomes condense; *haploid* number of *two-stranded* chromosomes present.

Metaphase II

Spindles form; chromatids move to equator; fibers attach to centromeres.

Anaphase II

Centromeres divide; sister chromatids (now single chromosomes) separate and move toward opposite poles.

Telophase II

Each cell divides, resulting in four cells (spermatids); each cell with haploid number of single-stranded chromosomes. Spermatids will become spermatocytes.

the two chromosomes whose loci share corresponding genes are called an *homologous pair* (Fig. 3-10). On another pair of *homologous chromosomes*, the loci will not be occupied by the particular corresponding genes found in our example, but the loci on that pair will share their own specific genes. The chromosome of one pair will not share the same corresponding genes at the same loci with any other chromosome except its homologous partner.

Sex Chromosomes A further point of interest concerning chromosomes involves the 23rd pair, known as the sex chromosomes. Earlier, we noted that in females the 23rd pair consists of two X chromosomes, whereas in males there is one X and one Y. These are called the sex chromosomes because they are the determiners of sex in offspring. As we have seen, each parent contributes 23 chromosomes. The mother can only contribute an X, since she has two Xs for her 23rd pair. There can be no alternative in her contribution. In the case of the father, however, an alternative is possible since his 23rd pair consists of one X and one Y, and he contributes one or the other. There is a fifty-fifty chance that the father's sperm (which fertilizes the ovum of the mother) will carry an X, and an equal chance it will carry a Y. If the sperm carries an X, the child will be female, since she will have received an X from both father and mother. If, on the other hand, the sperm carries a Y, then the offspring will have, as its 23rd pair, an X from the mother and a Y from the father, and it will be male. (Actually, for reasons not clearly understood, the probability of forming a male zygote is about 110 to 100 in humans.)

Two functions of meiosis have now been discussed: (1) the reduction of the number of chromosomes in a sex cell from 46, the diploid number, to 23, the haploid number; and (2) separation of X and Y chromosomes in the male sex cells so that sex determination of the offspring becomes possible.

Variation There is another function of great significance, especially in terms of natural selection and evolution: The production of *variation* (discussed in Chapter 4). Without variation, natural selection would be impossible; without natural selection, adaptation would be impossible; without adaptation, evolution would be impossible; and without evolution, life as we know it on earth would be impossible.

Recombination In addition to mutation (also discussed in Chapter 4), variation is produced in at least two other ways. First, a child is the result of a recombination of genes derived from the father *and* mother; therefore, an individual is always different, to a greater or lesser degree, from either parent. Furthermore, each time a sex cell divides, the 23 chromosome pairs position themselves differently, so that when first division occurs, a new alignment of chromosomes takes place.

Figure 3-11 shows two sex cells with alternate positioning of the same chromosomes when they align along the cell's equator. After first division, when the chromosomes have separated, the daughter cells contain a different combination of genes. Since chromosomes carry genes, the varying combinations of chromosomes result in the recombination of genes. Cell 1a, for example, combines chromosomes 1A, 2B, 9A, and X. Cell 1b combines the other members of the pairs: 1B, 2A, 9B, and Y.

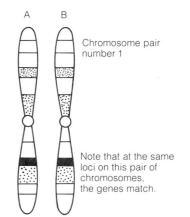

A   B

Chromosome pair number 1

Note that at the same loci on this pair of chromosomes, the genes match.

Figure 3-10 Idealized chromosome form. Each space represents a locus; 12 are shown here. Actually, there are thousands, perhaps several million, loci on a chromosome. The figure is a diagrammatic representation of a pair of chromosomes with matching genes: a homologous pair.

Figure 3-11 At alignment before division, chromosomes assort themselves randomly (but always in homologous pairs). Each different alignment produces a different random assortment of chromosomes in the daughter cells after first division. In the two daughter cells of cell 1, for example, cell 1a carries an X, and cell 1b a Y. Since chromosomes carry genes, the varying combinations of chromosomes result in the recombination of genes. In cell 1a, genes on X chromosomes are combined with those on 1A, 2B, and 9A. In cell 2b, Y is combined with the opposite members of those chromosomes. This particular combination of chromosomes and genes (if all 23 were considered) is unique. It probably never occurred before and will probably never occur again.

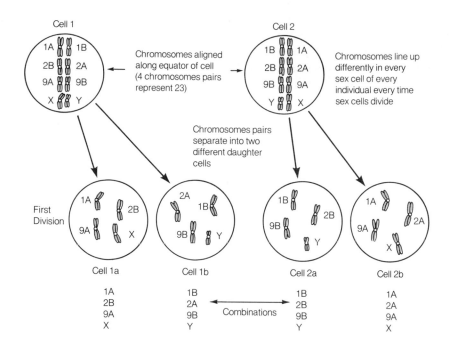

If cell 2a were to fertilize the ovum, the offspring would be different than if cell 1b had performed the action. In the case of 1a, the offspring would be female; in 1b, a male. But the difference goes beyond that. Let us return to cell 1 at alignment and take one chromosome pair, 9A/B. Let us say that on a locus on 9A is the gene for blood type A and on the same locus on 9B is the gene for blood type O. After division, cell 1a combines a gene for blood type A with the X chromosome, while cell 1b combines blood type O with the Y. If cell 2a and 2b were to fertilize the ovum, still different combinations of genes would occur.

Let us continue with our hypothetical situation. Look at the chromosome pair 9A/B (Fig. 3-12). Genes are indicated for several loci, and we emphasize that the actual location of all these genes is not yet known.

We know that the chromosome pair will be separated, with A of the pair going to one daughter cell and B to the other. (After second division in a male there would be four sperm produced from each sex cell, with two sperm containing A and two containing B. Review the preceding discussion for sex cell division, if necessary.) If the sperm carrying the 9A chromosome achieves fertilization, then the combination would include genes coding for blood type A, blood type M, hemoglobin A, attached ear lobes, and ability to taste. The actual characteristics of the offspring would depend on the female's contribution as well.

Since there are 23 pairs of chromosomes instead of just one pair, the number of different possible combinations is staggering. Imagine Figure 3-11 with cell 1a containing 23 pairs (instead of 4 pairs) of chromosomes all randomly aligned independently of one another. The number of different possible combinations for any given gamete is then about 8 million. This

Figure 3-12 Idealized diagram of chromosome pair. (This illustration is not intended as an accurate representation of the genes on chromosome 9.)

number represents the possibility of only one gamete: the sperm, for example. An equal number of possibilities (8 million) exists for the gamete of the other parent, so the possible different kinds of individuals that could result from one human mating is about 70 trillion. This number is mind-boggling. It is more than all the human beings who have ever lived or are ever likely to live.

Another way of looking at this process is to consider that a human male can produce several hundred million sperm a day from puberty until death, and the chances are that no two of those sperm will be identical.

These endless recombinations of genes provide variation which, in terms of natural selection, is extremely significant. They assure the availability to a population of genetic alternatives that may be adaptive in a changing environment. With less variation, natural selection would have less to choose from, perhaps even leading to extinction of the group.

Crossing-Over   Variation occurs in yet another way. Known as **crossing-over**, this process occurs at the tetrad stage of the chromosomes, during first division. The chromosomes are arranged in pairs that have duplicated themselves, resulting in 4 chromatids. Before division, sections of each of the chromatids may exchange with other chromatids. The right-hand side of Figure 3-13(a) shows the exchange of corresponding parts of sister chromatids. At crossing-over, a section of an M^2 chromatid has crossed-over with a section of P^1. (M stands for the maternal chromosome; P, for the paternal chromosome.) When the chromatids "straighten out," a section of M^2 chromatid has become part of P^1 chromatid.

Figure 3-13(b) depicts further examples of crossing-over. These illustrate the extent to which an "original" M chromatid takes on portions of P, and vice versa.

A brief examination of the recombination possibilities (Fig. 3-13) that may occur in the sex cell before division will help us understand the incredibly tremendous range of variation that can result from crossing-over. Let us assume that the chromatids marked A (in black) represent the father's contribution and those marked B (in color) the mother's.

At cross-over, the chromatids exchange sections with other chromatids. We see in example 4 of Figure 3-13 that, after two divisions, each chromosome carries paternal and maternal genetic material, and the genes on each of the 4 chromosomes are combined differently. These chromosomes no longer are the same as this person inherited from his parents, but are a mixture of the father's and mother's genes. The offspring who inherits any one of these chromosomes will inherit a combination of genes that probably never before existed exactly in that sequence and will probably never occur again.

When we consider the random assortment of chromosomes and crossing-over, we are struck with the truly infinite number of recombination possibilities. And when we add mutation to these, we realize the unbelievable potential for variation that occurs during the meiotic process. This process is the raw material that natural selection acts on.

Interestingly, Darwin, who knew the significance of variation, was unable to explain how it was produced. The answers to this puzzle came only with the modern development of the sciences of biology and genetics.

Crossing-over
Exchange of genetic material between chromatids of homologous chromosomes.

Figure 3-13 (a) Recombination of genes at cross-over. (b) Four examples of crossing-over. An infinite number of gene combinations may easily be imagined. The single chromosomes show how the genes contributed by parents may be recombined.

◇ DNA: Structure

We have now seen how heredity is influenced through what might be called mechanical processes. Sex cells divide, chromosomes cross-over, and genes recombine. These mechanical processes do not, however, transmit actual characteristics; in fact, parents do not pass on physical traits, they pass on information. Cell division, crossing-over, and gene recombination do not explain how the information passes from parents to offspring. For that, we must turn to the chemical nature of the phenomena involved.

Heredity is transmitted through information chemically coded in deoxyribonucleic acid (DNA), which is usually referred to as the carrier of the genetic code. An examination of the structure and process of DNA will help us understand how the information carried in chemically coded form is transformed from a code to actual physical characteristics of the body.

DNA is a large molecule consisting of four (among other) chemical substances that are its building blocks, or *bases*: *adenine*, *guanine*, *cytosine*, and *thymine*. Adenine (A) and guanine (G) belong to the class of substances known as **purines**; cytosine (C) and thymine (T) are **pyrimidines**. Each base is combined with a sugar (deoxyribose) and a phosphate residue which, all together, are called a *nucleotide* (Fig. 3-14). The DNA molecule is formed by linking many nucleotides into a long chain (Fig. 3-14). The sugar and phosphate alternate to form a backbone of the molecule, and the base sticks out from

Purines
A class of organic compounds to which adenine and guanine bases belong.

Pyrimidines
A class of organic compounds to which cytosine, thymine, and uracil belong.

Figure 3-14   Part of a DNA molecule.

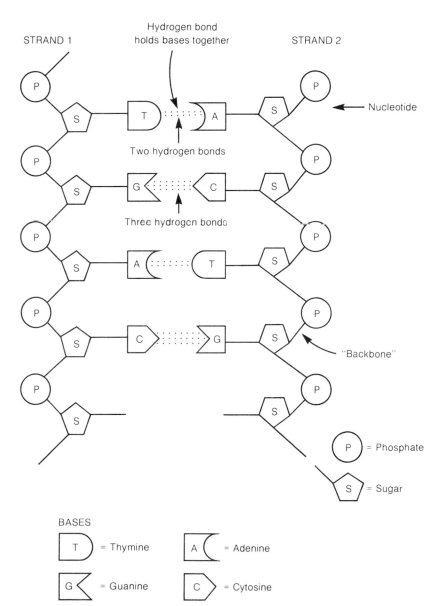

the sugar. The base attached to the sugar may be any one of four (A, G, C, T) mentioned above.

Each base of this long chain is attached to another base (shown in Fig. 3-14), so that the DNA molecule is actually composed of two long chains, or strands, of nucleotides. The bonding of the pairs follows a pattern called the *base pairing rule*, which states that one of the purines—adenine (A) and guanine (G)—must pair with one of the pyrimidines—cytosine (C) and thymine (T). In other words, A, a purine, must pair with T, a pyrimidine; and C must pair with G. The purine A does not pair with C or G, and C and G do not pair with T. Figure 3-14 illustrates the base pair rule.

In Figure 3-15(*a*), the DNA molecule is represented as a flat structure, which might be compared to a ladder. The alternating sugar and phosphates represent the sidepieces of the ladder and the bases represent the rungs. Actually, the two chains twist around each other to form a loose spiral called a **helix**. Since there are two strands, and each one forms a helix, DNA is referred to as a **double helix**. If the ladder in Figure 3-15(*a*) were twisted to form a double helix, the representation would be more accurate, as in Figure 3-15(*b*). The discovery of the DNA molecule structure as a double helix was made by James Watson and Francis Crick, an American and English team. Their work, which earned them a Nobel Prize, sparked a phenomenal period of research in molecular biology. (See Issue, this chapter.)

Figure 3-14 illustrates the double helix nature of the DNA molecule. Alter-

Figure 3-15 (*a*) DNA molecule resembles a ladder. (*b*) Ladder twisted into a helix.

(*a*)

DNA molecule resembles a ladder

(*b*)

Ladder twisted into helix

nating sugar and phosphates represent the backbone of the DNA chain, and the bases are paired according to rule. For our purposes, the significance of the DNA structure lies in the bases, especially in the sequence of the bases, because this location is where the hereditary information is stored. In the following sections on DNA *process*, note carefully the role of the bases in transmitting the genetic message.

Helix
A spiral or anything having a spiral form.

Double helix
The structure of DNA, composed of a pair of matching helices.

◇ DNA: The Genetic Code

We have mentioned that the genetic information is contained within the DNA molecule, and it is this information that is passed on from parent to offspring. The first requirement of the genetic material (DNA) is, then, that it have some efficient means of *self-replication*, so that hereditary information can be accurately reproduced and passed on to succeeding generations of individuals (or, even more basically, to succeeding generations of cells). Replication is essential because it enables parents to retain the master copy, so to speak, of the genetic information and send the duplicate copy to offspring. Without replication, the only set parents possessed would be transmitted to offspring, and parents would then be left without genetic material for future transmissions.

The way replication is accomplished is revealed directly in the beautifully simple structure of the DNA molecule itself. Figure 3-15(*a*) shows the DNA molecule simplified as a ladderlike structure. As we can easily see, the molecule has two sides, with each base on one side paired with a specific base on the other side. In other words, T only pairs with A; G with C; A with T; and C with G. In this way, one entire side of one strand of the molecule is *complementary* to the other side. To put it even more simply, one side of the molecule forms a complementary pairing of the opposite side.

In order for the DNA to replicate, the two strands must first unwind—much in the manner of a zipper unzipping—and separate, as indicated in Figure 3-16. The two single strands then attract free DNA nucleotides (bases, phosphates, and sugars), thus forming a complementary strand. The result is that where we started with one double-stranded molecule, we now have two identical double-stranded molecules. The genetic information has been completely replicated.

We have already discussed, earlier in this chapter, the mechanics of cell division (mitosis, meiosis), working through the duplication and distribution of chromosomes. These processes take place at a fairly gross level, and are clearly visible through a light microscope. What goes on in the DNA operates at the *molecular* level. While not visible by current methods, the process can be detected by biochemical methods and radioactive labeling. However, we can observe a direct association between the replication of DNA at the molecular level and the duplication of chromosomes. In fact, current thinking considers a chromosome as one giant DNA molecule. When a single-stranded chromosome duplicates to become a double-stranded (two chromatids) chromosome in the late interphase of both mitosis and meiosis, what we are actually seeing is the result of the DNA molecules unwinding and replicating their complementary strands. And, for example, when the chromosomes dur-

◇ Box 3-2   Terms Used in Discussion of DNA

Base   One of the four chemicals attached to a sugar molecule and a phosphate to make up a nucleotide; in DNA and RNA, a base is always paired with another base.

Adenine   } The four chemical bases.
Guanine   { Adenine and thymine are
Cytosine   { paired; cytosine and guanine
Thymine   } are paired.

Uracil   A chemical base found in RNA in the same position as thymine in DNA.

Amino acids   Small molecules that are the building blocks of protein.

Codon   A triplet sequence of bases on DNA and mRNA.

Anticodon   A triplet sequence of bases on tRNA.

DNA   Deoxyribonucleic acid; a large molecule composed of adenine, guanine, cytosine, and thymine plus phosphate and sugar; carries the genetic code.

RNA   Ribonucleic acid; slightly different chemically from DNA; found in the nucleus and the cytoplasm.

mRNA   Messenger RNA; carries genetic information from DNA in the nucleus to the ribosomes in the cytoplasm.

tRNA   Transfer RNA; brings an amino acid to match the mRNA bases.

rRNA   Ribosomal RNA; a major constituent of ribosomes.

Molecule   Smallest portion of a substance (element or compound) that acts like that substance and is capable of existing independently. Several to many atoms constitute a molecule.

Nucleotide   A base attached to a sugar and a phosphate group; a subunit of DNA and RNA.

Peptide   A compound of two or more amino acids joined by peptide bonds. Linked peptides form polypeptides which, in turn, join to form proteins.

Polypeptide   A group of peptides linked together.

Protein   A macromolecule, composed of one or more polypeptide chains of amino acids, responsible for carrying out most of the cell's metabolic activities; also contributes to cell structure.

Ribosomes   Small, minute bodies found in the cytoplasm of the cell; composed of rRNA and proteins; site of protein synthesis.

Protein synthesis   The manufacture of a protein. The process by which amino acids are linked (by a peptide bond) to form a polypeptide chain. The completed chain or chains form a protein.

ing mitosis are later distributed to respective daughter cells, they carry the same genetic information. Each has equal and identical amounts of DNA produced by simple replication.

◇ DNA: Process

Hereditary information, we know, is transmitted from parents to children through the process of meiosis. Once the father and mother contribute a sex cell each with 23 chromosomes, the result (if fertilization occurs) is a cell with 46 chromosomes called a zygote. The zygote acts as a body cell and passes through the stages of embryo, fetus, and birth. During this period of growth, and for the rest of the individual's life, the hereditary information (coded in the DNA of the nucleus) is taken from the DNA by RNA out into the cytoplasm. Here, it is converted into proteins, which build and maintain the body according to that hereditary information. The information is coded in the *sequence of bases*, and the student is again asked to bear in mind the significant role of the sequence.

How is the information taken out of the nucleus? How is it decoded? And how is it converted into protein? The process begins when a gene receives the stimulus to send out information.

1. The two strands of DNA separate (unzip) at a point along the helix. One of the DNA strands assembles a strand of RNA by attracting RNA nucleotides that match the DNA bases (Fig. 3-17a).

   DNA adenine (A), for example, will attract RNA uracil since RNA does not contain thymine, and DNA guanine (G) will attract RNA cytosine (C), etc.

   The formation of the RNA strand is one of the critical steps in transmitting hereditary information from the nucleus to the cytoplasm. It is in the cytoplasm where protein synthesis takes place.

   Transcription. RNA copies the sequence of DNA bases, but in complementary form. Our example in Figure 3-17a) illustrates an RNA strand being formed by RNA nucleotides that match the DNA bases. DNA serves as a template from which RNA is manufactured.

Cytosine
Thymine
Adenine
Guanine

Original material

From nucleoplasm

Original material

Figure 3-16 The replication of a DNA molecule. The double helix uncoils and then unzips, separating base pairs. Complementary base pairs are attracted and attach to the exposed nucleotides. When replication is completed, each daughter strand is composed of one strand of the parent DNA and one new strand.

Figure 3-17 Formation of mRNA strand. (a) DNA has separated. One DNA strand attracts complementary RNA nucleotide (uracil in RNA replaces thymine). A basic step in the transmission of genetic information. (b) RNA strand completed. Note that RNA bases are exact complements of DNA bases. The sequence of the bases is important.

Strands separate

Free nucleotides attracted to DNA bases

(a) Transcription

(b) Completed mRNA strand; mRNA will leave nucleus and migrate to cytoplasm

Upon completion of transcription (Fig. 3-17b), the RNA strand will be an exact copy of the DNA sequence, but with the corresponding bases. The genetic message is coded in the sequence of bases, and, as we follow the DNA/RNA process, we shall see why the sequence of bases is so significant in the translation of genetic information into physical characteristics.

2. When the DNA/RNA matching is completed, the single strand of RNA disengages from the DNA, and the separated DNA strands rejoin.

3. The RNA strand is now prepared to migrate out of the nucleus into the cytoplasm of the cell, carrying the genetic code in the sequence of bases (UUUCCG in the illustration). Because this RNA is carrying the hereditary message, it is known as *messenger RNA*, or mRNA.

4. mRNA leaves the nucleus and enters the cytoplasm of the cell; here it is attracted to a string of ribosomes that are located in the cytoplasm.

5. *Translation.* A ribosome (or several ribosomes) move along the mRNA strand "reading" the message (Fig. 3-19). The message is located in the bases with every three bases forming a "word" called a *codon*. (See Fig. 3-18.)

   UUU, for example, forms one "word" (it is the symbol for phenylalanine) and is different from UUA (the symbol for leucine) and from AUU (the symbol for isoleucine). These 3-letter codons are symbols for the 20 common amino acids, the building blocks of proteins. (See Fig. 3-18.)

   By translating the message in the mRNA, the ribosomes activate the next step: building a chain of amino acids.

6. As the ribosome reads the mRNA message of the 3-base codon, another kind of RNA is attracted to the ribosome. This is *transfer RNA*, or tRNA, and it brings with it an amino acid. Transfer RNA is a small molecule with

several loops and an open end (receptor arm) on which a specific amino acid can attach (Fig. 3-20). The molecule resembles a highway cloverleaf, and one of the loops is known as the *anticodon* loop. The anticodon, like the mRNA codon, consists of a sequence of three chemicals that are the same as those found in mRNA: adenine, guanine, cytosine, and uracil.

The amino acid on the receptor arm is keyed to the sequence of chemicals of the anticodon. A tRNA with an anticodon of AAA would carry the amino acid phenylalanine at the receptor end. During translation, the anticodon, AAA, would engage the codon, UUU, on the mRNA.

7. When the ribosome has translated the entire mRNA message, and tRNA molecules have brought the appropriate amino acids to the ribosome site, a chain of amino acids, called a *polypeptide chain*, has been formed. The completed polypeptide chain of amino acids is a protein or part of one, and the process of converting the DNA genetic code for this particular protein has ended.

Proteins are the basic structural and functional compounds of the cell; they are responsible for carrying out most of the metabolic functions of the cell, as well as making up most of the cell structure. The structural components of tissue, hormones, enzymes, hemoglobins, etc., are proteins. In turn, the kind of protein that is synthesized depends upon the information that comes from the DNA. The result is that the kind of body the proteins build (pigmentation, blood type, body build, etc.) is largely determined by the sequence of bases found in DNA.

Figure 3-18   The genetic code.

Amino Acid Symbol	Amino Acid	DNA Codon	mRNA Codon
ALA	ALANINE	CGA, CGG, CGT, CGC	GCU, GCC, GCA, GCG
ARG	ARGININE	GCA, GCG, GCT, GCC, TCT, TCC	CGU, CGC, CGA, CGG, AGA, AGG
ASN	ASPARAGINE	TTA, TTG	AAU, AAC
ASP	ASPARTIC ACID	CTA, CTG	GAU, GAC
CYS	CYSTEINE	ACA, ACG	UGU, UGC
GLN	GLUTAMINE	GTT, GTC	CAA, CAG
GLU	GLUTAMIC ACID	CTT, CTC	GAA, GAG
GLY	GLYCINE	CCA, CCG, CCT, CCC	GGU, GGC, GGA, GGG
HIS	HISTIDINE	GTA, GTG	CAU, CAC
ILE	ISOLEUCINE	TAA, TAG, TAT	AUU, AUC, AUA
LEU	LEUCINE	AAT, AAG, GAA, GAG, GAT, GAC	UUA, UUG, CUU, CUC, CUA, CUG
LYS	LYSINE	TTT, TTC	AAA, AAG
MET	METHIONINE	TAC	AUG
PHE	PHENYLALANINE	AAA, AAG	UUU, UUC
PRO	PROLINE	GGA, GGG, GGT, GGC	CCU, CCC, CCA, CCG
SER	SERINE	AGA, AGG, AGT, AGC, TCA, TCG	UCU, UCC, UCA, UCG, AGU, AGC
THR	THREONINE	TGA, TGG, TGT, TGC	ACU, ACC, ACA, ACG
TRP	TRYPTOPHAN	ACC	UGG
TYR	TYROSINE	ATA, ATG	UAU, UAC
VAL	VALINE	CAA, CAG, CAT, CAC	GUU, GUC, GUA, GUG
Terminating triplets		ATT, ATC, ACT	UAA, UAG, UGA

Figure 3-19 Translation of the genetic code into strings of amino acids and finally into polypeptides and proteins.

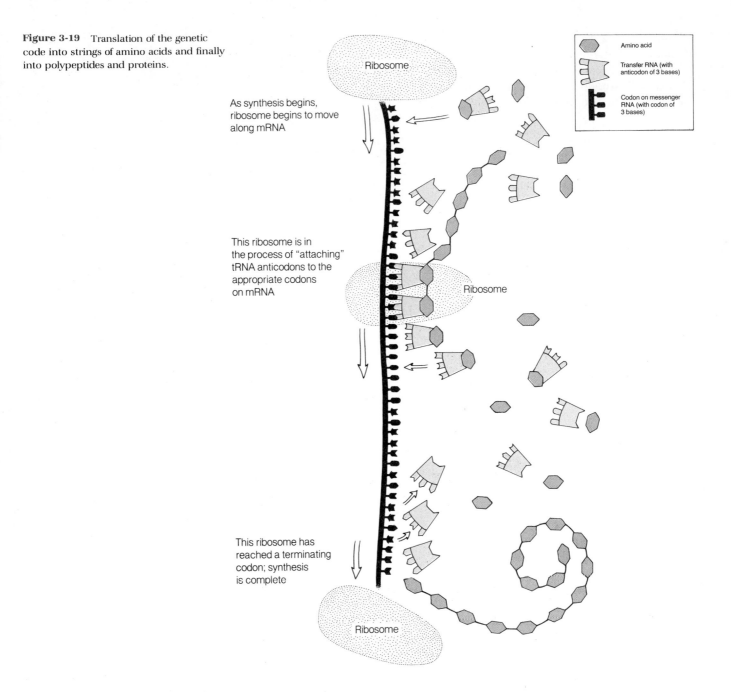

As synthesis begins, ribosome begins to move along mRNA

This ribosome is in the process of "attaching" tRNA anticodons to the appropriate codons on mRNA

This ribosome has reached a terminating codon; synthesis is complete

Amino acid

Transfer RNA (with anticodon of 3 bases)

Codon on messenger RNA (with codon of 3 bases)

Ribosome

Ribosome

Ribosome

The preceding discussion may appear quite involved, and the biochemical process of DNA is, of course, complicated. However, the basic process is quite simple, so let us review the steps briefly:

1. A segment of DNA, which we may refer to as a gene, is copied by a strand of mRNA.
2. mRNA carries this sequence of bases—coded genetic information—from the nucleus into the cytoplasm.

3. An mRNA strand is attached to ribosomes, which read and translate the code.
4. Appropriate tRNA (anticodon triplet complements mRNA codon triplet) is attracted to the ribosome side of mRNA; for example, UUU codon attracts its complement, AAA. At the same time, tRNA transports to the mRNA an amino acid associated with its anticodon triplet (AAA anticodon carries the amino acid phenylalanine).
5. As each mRNA triplet is read, tRNA carries in another amino acid, thus forming a chain of amino acids.
6. When the entire mRNA strand is read, and all appropriate amino acids assembled, the chain is complete. A functional protein, or part of a protein, is formed.

The discovery of the structure of DNA and how it functions (although the entire story is still unknown) resolves a number of questions about heredity. We now know that what children inherit from their parents is not actual traits, such as hair color or stature, but a genetic blueprint—DNA. We also know that the information is stored in the nucleus and, when required, is taken from the nucleus and brought into the cytoplasm of the cell. And we know further that this information is instrumental in building or synthesizing proteins which will, in turn, build and maintain the body according to that information.

(a)

(b)

Figure 3-20 tRNA The cloverleaf molecular configuration of tRNA. (a) The open end is the end that attaches to free amino acids. (b) the anticodon loop attaches to a codon on mRNA.

Sickle-cell anemia
A disease caused by a mutant form of hemoglobin (when inherited in double dose).

Intron
Within a genetic locus, a section of DNA that is not coded.

Point mutation
The change in a single base in the DNA molecule.

◇ Theory of the Gene

DNA structure and function are directly related to what we have called genes. An understanding of a gene may be gained through a demonstration of the way it changes, or mutates. The best-known example of a mutation in humans concerns the gene that produces adult hemoglobin, a globular molecule found in red blood cells.

POINT MUTATION

Normal adult hemoglobin is made up of protein chains that are direct products of gene action. One of these chains, called the *beta chain*, is in turn made up of 146 amino acids. Individuals with **sickle-cell anemia** inherit from *both* their parents mutant genes that produce a different type of hemoglobin. As a result, these individuals usually have major circulatory disturbances, destruction of red blood cells, and severe anemia often resulting in early death. Individuals who inherit this gene from only one of their parents are much less severely affected and usually have a normal life span.

The cause of all these dramatic changes in the individual's health is a seemingly minute change in the gene that produces hemoglobin. Both normal adult hemoglobin and the sickle-cell variety have 146 amino acids and, of these, 145 are identical. A substitution of only one amino acid (at position #6—see Fig. 3-21) causes all the problems.

We know, of course, that it is the sequence of bases in the DNA that codes for the sequence of amino acids in the final protein product. We also know that 3 bases (1 codon) code for one amino acid. Therefore, it takes 438 bases (146 × 3) to produce the chain of 146 amino acids seen in the adult hemoglobin beta chain.

Recent research has shown that, within the DNA, there are considerably more nucleotides than just those that are eventually translated into amino acid sequences. In fact, in human DNA (and other organisms with nucleated cells, but *not* bacteria) most genes are fragmented. Between those sections that are eventually coded there are often long intervening sequences called **introns**, which do not contribute information for protein synthesis. For example, for the hemoglobin beta locus we have seen there is a total of 438 nucleotides, which code for the eventual polypeptide chain. However, when one also counts those sections at the beginning and end of the locus (promoter and termination regions), as well as two long introns, the entire locus is 1,652 nucleotides long.

While all this genetic information is not utilized directly in protein synthesis, it may serve some function. The entire locus is transcribed onto mRNA. However, before the molecule leaves the nucleus, the intervening sequences are excised and the coded regions are spliced precisely back together. Such apparent DNA superfluity may provide an evolutionary basis for flexible recombination of genetic components. Another possible role in *direct* cell metabolism might operate through the excised sequences being used as "messages" sent to other genes—informing them that the synthesis of a particular polypeptide chain is taking place (Lewin, 1981).

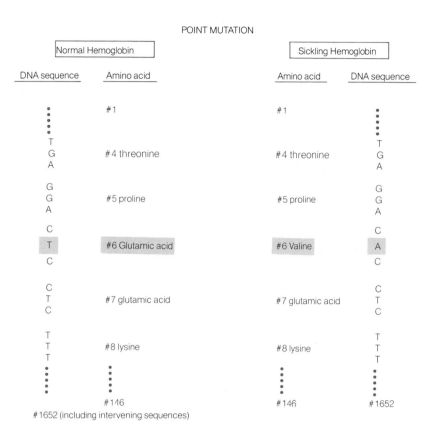

POINT MUTATION

Figure 3-21 Substitution of one base at position #6 produces a sickling hemoglobin.

Bear in mind that whereas DNA replication is highly efficient and accurate, it is not perfect—mistakes can and *do* occur. The difference between normal and sickling hemoglobin, however, concerns a change at only one point in the hemoglobin gene. The first 5 and the last 140 amino acids in the protein chains of both varieties of hemoglobin are identical. Only at position #6 (Fig. 3-21) is there an alteration.

Figure 3-21 shows a possible DNA base sequence and the resulting amino acid products for both normal and sickling hemoglobin. As can be seen, a single base substitution (from CTC to CAC) could result in an altered amino acid sequence (... proline–*glutamic acid*–glutamic acid ... to ... proline–*valine*–glutamic acid ...). This, in turn, would alter the properties of the whole protein (hemoglobin), resulting in differently shaped red blood cells, oxygen-bonding properties, etc. In other words, the only difference between normal hemoglobin and sickling hemoglobin is a change in *one base* out of the 438 bases that make up the coded portion of this gene. Such an alteration is called a **point mutation** and, in evolution, is probably the most common and most important source of new variation.

Point mutations probably occur relatively frequently during cell division, but a new mutation will have evolutionary significance only if it is passed on to offspring through the gametes. Once such a new mutation has occurred, its fate in the population will depend on the other evolutionary forces, especially natural selection. Sickle-cell, in fact, is the best-demonstrated example of natural selection acting in human beings, and we will take this point up in considerably more detail in Chapter 5.

DEFINITION OF THE GENE

Although not all biologists agree on the definition, we have defined the gene as that section of DNA—a sequence of codons on the DNA template—responsible for the ultimate synthesis of a specific polypeptide chain of amino acids. To put it another way, a gene is that portion of a DNA molecule that specifies the manufacture (synthesis) of a protein (hemoglobin, say) that will produce, or assist in the production of, one or more physical traits. A gene, then, is not a discrete unit operating in the nucleus or the cell; it is part of a large DNA molecule.

HEREDITY AND ENVIRONMENT

For years scientists, debating societies, philosophers, writers, preachers and others have debated, often acrimoniously, the question of what is more important: heredity or environment, nature or nurture. The question is whether human beings—physically, behaviorally, and psychically—are the result of their heredity or are fashioned and molded by their environment. Or, if both, which is more influential? Differences of opinion on this subject have been bitter.

The English philosopher John Locke (1632–1704) believed that, at birth, the mind of the human being is a blank slate (*tabula rasa*), and all differences are environmentally produced. On the other hand, the French writer Count Joseph Arthur de Gobineau (1816–1882), notorious for his belief in the inequality of races, held that differences in ability are inherited. The behavioral psychologist, J. B. Watson, left no doubt of his position:

> Give me a dozen healthy infants, well-formed, and my own specified world to bring them up, and I'll guarantee to take any one at random and train him to become any type of specialist I might select—doctor, lawyer, artist, merchant and yes, even beggar and thief, regardless of the talents, penchants, tendencies, abilities, vocations, and race . . . (Watson, 1924, p. 42).

To demonstrate whether hereditary or environment is the primary factor responsible for human development is very difficult. Genetics teaches that it is not an either-or proposition, since both factors contribute to what we are physically and behaviorally. From our discussion of genes, we might infer that heredity determines exactly what the nature of a physical trait will be. This circumstance may be so with some genes, but probably not so with most. In the case of the ABO blood system mentioned above, the genes do determine blood type, and, as far as we know, the environment has no effect on the expression of the blood-group genes. If both parents are O, then all their children will be O, regardless of environmental conditions.

Genotypes and Phenotypes   The underlying basis of what we have called heredity in the preceding discussion is known as the *genotype*—"the sum total of the hereditary materials received by an individual from its parents and other ancestors" (Dobzhansky, 1979, p. 32).

An individual's genotype does not change during his or her lifetime—with the exception of some cells in aberrant tissue lines that arise from what are called *somatic mutations*. The consequences may be quite significant for the individual, since experimental work with animals suggests some cancers may well arise from somatic mutations. However, in no case are these somatic mutations passed to offspring. Moreover, for the vast majority of genes in the vast majority of one's cells, we could say the genotype is "fixed" at birth and does not change.

When we observe, probe, or measure people, what we see is their *phenotypes*; for example, a person's skin color, stature, blood type, etc. The phenotype is the *ascertainable* aspect of an organism (see p. 87 for a more complete definition). Phenotypes, as such, are partly products of the genotype, but, because of their plasticity, they *also* can be modified by the environment. However, other more complex traits, such as stature, weight, personality, or intelligence, are often modified dramatically by the environment (see pp. 160–172). In these cases, a person's phenotype could be said to result from an interaction of the genotype with the environment.

Diet, good or poor, may affect stature and weight; sun exposure may affect skin pigmentation; phenotypes of monozygotic twins, genetically identical individuals, may vary if the twins are raised in different environments. Thus, it is obvious that an individual's phenotype changes continuously from birth to death as glandular and maturation effects occur.

What we are, then, for the most part, is the result of the interaction of hereditary material and environmental conditions. As the well-known geneticist Theodosius Dobzhansky wrote,

> Between the genes ... and the adult phenotypes [observable characteristics] ... there intervenes a set of developmental processes, which ... may be exceedingly long and elaborate. This leaves ample opportunity for the uniform primary action of a gene to yield a variety of manifestations in the developing phenotypes. ... Which potentialities will in fact be realized in a given individual at a certain stage of his development is decided by the sequence of the environments in which the development takes place (Dobzhansky, 1970, p. 33).

A gene may be perceived as potentiality. What potentiality will actually be realized, after an "exceedingly long and elaborate" developmental process, depends upon the environmental conditions. It is this interaction between biology and environment, nature and nurture, which makes us the kind of individuals we are—physically, behaviorally, and psychically. This interaction also emphasizes the point already made in the first chapter: That humans are biocultural beings.

With this introduction to the biological basis of life in mind, let us now, in the next chapter, examine how the genetic process can be applied to the process of evolution.

◇ Summary

We have dealt with two kinds of cells in this chapter—somatic cells, of which our bodies are composed, and sex cells, which are used only in the transmission of hereditary information.

Somatic cells divide by mitosis, producing two daughter cells identical to each other and to the mother cell. Sex cells divide twice by meiosis and produce four gametes. Meiosis is known as reduction division because the diploid number of chromosomes (46) is reduced to the haploid number (a complete set of 23).

There are 23 pairs of chromosomes in a human cell. Two chromosomes with similar loci, of which there are 22 pairs, are called homologous. The 23rd pair is the sex chromosomes.

Genetic information is contained in the DNA double helix. Information is taken from nucleus to cytoplasm by mRNA. Ribosomes in the cell translate the mRNA message and attract tRNA molecules. The tRNA molecules transport amino acids to the ribosomes forming a polypeptide chain. A polypeptide chain (or chains) of amino acids is a protein that makes up most of the cell structure and carries out most of the cell's metabolic functions.

A gene is not a discrete unit but is an orderly sequence of DNA codons that designates a specific chain of amino acids. The equation, one gene equals one polypeptide chain, is sometimes used as a definition of a gene.

Genes do not necessarily determine the precise nature of a physical characteristic. Genes are potentials modified by the environment, and it is the interaction of genes and environmental conditions that produces physical traits.

◇ Questions for Review

1. Name the parts of a cell discussed in the chapter.
2. List the differences between mitosis and meiosis.
3. List the steps in mitosis; in meiosis.
4. Name two important functions of meiosis.
5. Why is a pair of homologous chromosomes homologous?
6. What is a locus?
7. What is the difference between a locus and a gene?
8. Define DNA.
9. What different kinds of RNA are there?
10. What is the function of mRNA?
11. What is the function of ribosomes?
12. What is a nucleotide?
13. Name the four bases. Which bases complement each other in DNA?
14. What base is found in RNA but not in DNA?
15. What are the building blocks of a protein?
16. How is a chain of amino acids formed?
17. How are tRNA and mRNA matched?

18. What is the difference between codon and anticodon?
19. What is the difference between diploid and haploid?
20. Why do gametes contain the haploid instead of the diploid number?
21. What is the function of cross-over?
22. Why is variation important in the evolutionary process?
23. What is meant by recombination of genes?
24. How would you answer the question of nature versus nurture?
25. Give an example of how the effect of a gene may be modified by the environment.

◇ Suggested Further Reading

American Institute of Biological Sciences. Biological Sciences Curriculum Study. *Molecules to Man*, Boston: Houghton Mifflin, 1968.

A very useful reference book. Although written for high school students, it can be used for reviews and for the study aids at the end of the chapters.

Beadle, George and Muriel Beadle. *The Language of Life*, New York: Doubleday and Co., 1966.

An interesting and popular account of genetics written in nontechnical language by a Nobel Prize winner in genetics and his wife. Well worth reading.

Bodmer, W. F. and L. L. Cavalli-Sforza. *Genetics, Evolution, and Man*. San Francisco: W. H. Freeman and Co., 1976.

A thorough discussion of genetics, with an emphasis on human genetics. An excellent reference work, with many illustrations.

Dobzhansky, Theodosius. *Genetics of the Evolutionary Process*, New York: Columbia University Press, 1970.

An excellent book written by a distinguished geneticist. It is not written as a textbook and covers evolution from a genetics point of view.

Goldstein, Philip. *Genetics Is Easy* (4th Ed.), New York: Lantern Press, 1967.

The title is the clue. Genetics is discussed completely and in uncomplicated fashion. Plenty of illustrations make the text even more understandable. Recommended for students with little or no genetics background.

Lerner, I. Michael and William J. Libby. *Heredity, Evolution and Society* (2nd Ed.), San Francisco: W. H. Freeman and Co., 1976.

Evolution with a genetics emphasis. A thorough treatment of the subjects of the title. The emphasis is on genetics and its relationship to evolution, and how genetics and evolution affect society. Written for advanced students but very useful for additional reading.

Villee, Claude A. *Biology* (6th Ed.), Philadelphia: W. B. Saunders Co., 1972.

A biology textbook with several excellent chapters on cells, chromosomes, DNA, and population genetics.

Ward, Jack A. and Howard R. Hetzel. *Biology*, St. Paul: West Publishing Co., 1979.

An up-to-date biology text. Clearly written and recommended for the student with little biology background.

Winchester, A. M. *Biology and Its Relation to Mankind* (5th Ed.), New York: D. Van Nostrand Co., 1972.

A biology textbook. Chapters on genetics emphasize human genetics. Excellent and useful illustrations.

Genetics and Evolution

CONTENTS

Automated genetic engineering

1. UNKNOWN PROTEIN

2. AMINO ACID SEQUENCER

lysine leucine proline

proline lysine leucine

cytosine guanine adenine thymine

Synthetic gene

4. PROTEIN FACTORY

5. HARVESTED PROTEIN

In the first edition of this textbook, we took note of a new biological practice known as *recombinant DNA* (gene-splicing or genetic engineering). We pointed out that scientists themselves were asking questions about the danger of such laboratory experiments. Journalists wondered whether scientists were trying to play God, and some biologists questioned the necessity or desirability of continuing experiments that could "counteract irreversibly the evolutionary wisdom of millions of years." One well-known scientist, profoundly disturbed by the implications of these experiments, warned:

This world is given to us on loan. We come and we go; and after a time we leave earth and air and water to others who come after us. My generation, or perhaps the one preceding mine, has been the first to engage, under the leadership of the exact sciences, in a destructive colonial warfare against nature. The future will curse us for it (Chargaff, 1976).

There were those, of course, in favor of recombinant genetics, and the National Institutes of Health established guidelines to prevent disastrous accidents. Those who favored research in this area predicted that it would be possible to form a bacterial DNA molecule capable of directing the formation of insulin and other proteins, and insulin was, in fact, manufactured in 1978.

Despite the concerns of many people—scientists, public officials, and others—laboratory work on recombinant DNA has not only flourished in the past few years but multiplied in astonishing fashion. Profitable corporations have been formed to produce different kinds of proteins, and industrialization rushes on with ever-increasing improvements in technology.

One development is the gene machine (Menosky, 1981). This is "an automated genetic engineering laboratory, a desktop set of boxes that can synthesize a fully workable gene segment in a day." Until now, this same job took months of painstaking and tedious laboratory routine. Several kinds of gene, or DNA, synthesizers are already on the market, or ready to be introduced. The user simply types the genetic code for the desired gene on the machine's keyboard. Hours later, the machine delivers a number of synthetic gene fragments that can then be spliced together and placed into the DNA of living organisms. The machine is so cheap that just about every biologist can own one.

As if this were not enough, another machine—a protein sequencer—is now available. This machine will tell you the sequence of amino acids making up any protein. It was barely thirty years ago that Crick and Watson discovered the structure of DNA, and now it is merely necessary to put a sample of protein in one end, and, in a few hours, the kinds of amino acids and their sequence come out the other end. Then, with this amino acid sequence, the gene machine can be programmed to synthesize a gene that, when put into bacteria, will manufacture virtually unlimited quantities of the protein for research or therapy. The possibilities are astonishing.

Update

The first-generation gene machines, plagued by mechanical problems, were not successful. Second-genera-tion DNA synthesizers, however, have been improved in speed, efficiency, and reliability. In 1984, there were seven fully automated DNA synthesizers on the market, ranging in price from $20,000 to $70,000. Customers for these machines are university research labs, large chemical and drug companies, and genetic-engineering firms. At the present time, about 60% of the machines are used in the United States.

One of the most common uses of the synthesizer is to make "probes" to "help locate a natural gene of scientific or commercial interest—human growth hormone, insulin, or interferon—among thousands of different genes in the DNA of a cell" (Tucker, 1984, p. 52).

Another contemplated use of the probes is to improve and expedite medical diagnosis. The probes should be able to identify the source of life-threatening infections much faster than methods now used. Also, inherited diseases, such as cystic fibrosis, hemophilia, and phenylketonuria (PKU), could be detected by probes during prenatal screening or routine blood tests. The practical use of probes has already been demonstrated for sickle-cell anemia and other inherited blood diseases (Tucker, 1984). Curing diseases, however, has lagged far behind. It appears that the hope of inserting a gene in an individual to replace a defective gene is not even close to fulfillment.

The fears associated with recombinant genetics continue. Religious and ecology groups have raised ethical questions about recombinant genetic experiments, and a congressional report suggests that regulation should be turned over from the Recombinant DNA Advisory Committee (RAC) of the National Institutes of Health to the Environmental Protection Agency. A number of lawsuits have been initiated against the RAC actions. Nevertheless, RAC continues to monitor recombinant research, and, in 1983, for the first time, gave its permission to release genetic-engineered material in test fields outside of research laboratories. As of late 1984, court action has stalled these tests.

The research continues rapidly, and so do the ethical and regulatory problems involved.

SOURCES FOR ISSUE:

Chargaff, Ervin. "On the Dangers of Genetic Meddling," *Science*, 192:938, 940, June 4, 1976.

Menosky, Joseph A. "The Gene Machine," *Science 81*, 38–41, July/August, 1981.

SOURCES FOR UPDATE:

Judson, H. F. "Thumbprints in Our Clay," *The New Republic*, 12–17, September 19 and 26, 1983.

Tucker, Jonathon B. "Gene Machines: The Second Wave," *High Technology*, 50–59, March, 1984.

Note: Articles on genetic engineering appear frequently in *Science* (weekly journal of the American Association for the Advancement of Science).

◇ CHAPTER FOUR

◇ Introduction

In Chapter 3, we have seen in some detail how, within the cell, genetic material is organized, packaged, distributed, and passed on to succeeding generations of cells. But when we look at the world of organisms, we see individuals who are in most cases composed of billions of cells, and our focus of organization must be shifted to a different level. In this chapter, we shall investigate the processes that allow us not only to understand, but also to predict, how genes are passed from parent to offspring. This process is the basis of the science of genetics, and its modern beginnings date to Gregor Mendel's work in the 1850s and 1860s.

◇ Early Theories of Inheritance

For ages man has been interested in the rules of heredity. We can easily imagine the early farmers of 10,000 years ago wondering how tiny grains produced wheat. Already in the fourth century B.C., Theophrastus, a Greek, had carefully studied seed germination and written a book on the subject. Some early Greeks believed that heredity among humans was a question of which sex dominated in the sex act. In the eighteenth century, Linnaeus suggested a two-layer theory, which held that "the outer layer including the vascular system is derived from the father, the inner layer including the nervous system comes from the mother."

An interesting theory dating as far back as Aristotle developed further in the seventeenth century (E. Gardner, 1965, p. 275). This theory was based on the belief, called *preformation*, that "the development of an organism is no more than the unfolding of that which is already present in miniature [Fig. 4-1]. Every organism must therefore contain in its reproductive organs an infinite series representing all of its future descendants." Ovists believed the female possessed this future of the series, and the spermists insisted it was the male.

While there were differences of opinion about the role of sex, and ignorance of the laws of animal heredity, plants were not generally discussed in these terms. That plants lacked sexuality was the conventional wisdom of the day. Not until the end of the seventeenth century was the presence of sex organs in plants demonstrated in the experiments performed in Germany by Rudolph Camerarius.

The notion that plants consisted of male and female parts came as a shock to many people. " 'What man,' exclaimed J. G. Siegesbeck, Professor of Botany at St. Petersburg, 'will ever believe that God Almighty should have introduced such confusion, or rather such shameful whoredom, for the propagation of the reign of plants. Who will instruct young students in such a voluptuous system without scandal?' " (Olby, 1966, pp. 18–19).

Figure 4-1 Some early investigators thought that they could see tiny human embryos within the sperm.

The discovery of sexual reproduction in plants was a notable achievement not simply because it added to our knowledge of plants, but also because it makes possible an experimental approach to plant hybridization. Once begun by Camerarius, crossing hybrids and observing what regularities might occur among the offspring became one of the most popular methods of investigating the laws of heredity.

Hybridization experiments continued in the eighteenth and nineteenth centuries. Hybrids offered an opportunity, it was believed, to work out the rules of heredity. Purebred plants produced purebreds, and there was little to learn about heredity from that kind of experiment. Among the offspring of hybrids, on the other hand, some resembled the parents, but others were quite different. If, in this apparent confusion of offspring, there were regularities of such traits as form, color, or germination patterns, they would serve as clues to the principles of heredity.

Or so it seemed. Many investigators worked on plant hybrids, but the secrets of heredity eluded them. Experimenters demonstrated, for example, that neither sex was entirely responsible for offspring but both parents contributed equally. They also demonstrated that hybrids did not breed true (as Linneaus believed they did), yet the laws of heredity remained undiscovered.

Figure 4-2   Gregor Mendel.

There were several reasons for this failure. The plants used were not the proper ones for the study of heredity—they were genetically too complex for the kind of observations possible at that time. Experimenters did not work with enough plants, or through sufficient generations, to find regularities. And, finally, they did not count the offspring of hybrids; that is, they failed to examine the results of their experiments from a statistical point of view. What the early experimenters saw were offspring in a confusing variety of forms and colors, which they were unable to clarify. Their conclusion was that clarification was imposible, that there probably were no universal laws of heredity.

Thus matters stood, more or less at a standstill as far as the laws of heredity were concerned, until Gregor Mendel solved the riddle in the 1860s.

◇ Mendel's Life

Gregor Mendel (1822–1884), shown in Figure 4-2, was born into a family of peasant farmers, in the small Silesian village of Heinzendorf in what we now Czechoslovakia. At school, he did so well in his academic studies that his teachers recommended he be transferred to a high school in a nearby town. Within a year, he had moved on to the Gymnasium (an advanced high school) at Troppau where, in 1840, he received a certificate which recognized his "great industry and all-round ability."

To continue his studies, he enrolled in the University Philosophical Institute of Olmutz. Because of lack of funds, Mendel had a difficult time, and his attempts to earn money as a private tutor failed. He wrote of this period of his life (in the third person): "The sorrow over these disappointed hopes and the anxious, sad outlook which the future offered him, affected him so powerfully at that time that he fell sick and was compelled to spend a year with his parents to recover!" (in Olby, 1966, p. 106).

Figure 4-3   Central Europe during Mendel's lifetime.

In 1841, Mendel returned to the university, and this time succeeded in finding part-time tutorial work, but he worked so hard his health failed again. In 1843, he discussed his future with one of his professors, Friedrich Franz, who suggested a monastery as a place that would provide the quiet kind of life Mendel required. He encouraged Mendel to apply to the monastery at Brünn and recommended him as "a young man of very solid character. In my own branch [physics] he is almost the best" (in Olby, 1966, p. 107). Mendel followed Franz' advice, was admitted as a novice on October 9, 1843, and took the name of Gregor.

Early on, it became clear that Mendel was not temperamentally suited to serve as a parish priest, since he could not witness suffering without falling ill himself. The understanding abbot of the monastery assigned him as a substitute teacher to a high school in a nearby town, and Mendel soon became known as an excellent teacher. He could not be given a permanent appointment because he lacked a teacher's certificate, and for him to obtain this document, he had to take courses at the University of Vienna.

It was at Vienna, where he came into contact with leading professors in botany, physics, and mathematics, that Mendel acquired his scientific education. His studies there helped him in his later experiments, especially in his mathematical approach, which was so different from that of other plant experimenters.

Upon completing his studies at Vienna, Mendel returned to the monastery and resumed his teaching career, as well as his work in the monastery garden. He had been experimenting for some time with the fertilization of flowers, attempting to develop new variations in colors. What impressed Mendel was the "striking regularity with which the same hybrid forms always reappeared when fertilization took place between the same species," which induced him "to follow up the development of the hybrids in their progeny."

◇ Mendel's Experiments

Mendel was well aware that no laws governing the formation and development of hybrids had yet been formulated, and he was also aware that hybridization experiments were very difficult. Nevertheless, he decided to proceed with his experiments and had definite ideas of how to go about it. He pointed out that not one experiment

Figure 4-4 The monastery at Brünn (as it looks today), where Mendel spent much of his life.

had been carried out to such an extent and in such a way as to make it possible to determine the number of different forms under which the offspring of hybrids appear, or to arrange these forms with certainty according to their separate generations, or definitely to ascertain their statistical relation (Mendel, 1965, pp. 1–2).

What Mendel decided to do apparently even before he began his experiments on hybrids was: (a) to determine the number of different forms of hybrids produced; (b) to arrange the forms according to generations—F_2, F_3, etc. (see terms in Box 4-1 for definitions); and (c) to attempt to evaluate the statistical relations (the proportions) of the various forms.

These three points, wrote the eminent geneticist of the early twentieth century, William Bateson, led to "the whole success of Mendel's work. . . . So far as I know this conception was absolutely new in his day" (Mendel, 1965, p. 2n) and is the basis of modern biological research.

Selection of Plants   Before discussing Mendel's actual experiments and his conclusions, one more point should be considered, for it illustrates Mendel's genius compared to other plant hybridizers. This point concerns the *kind* of plant to be used. "The value and utility of any experiment," Mendel noted in the paper he read at a meeting of the Natural History Society of Brünn in February, 1865, "are determined by the fitness of the material to the purpose for which it is used, and thus in the case before us it cannot be immaterial what plants are subjected to experiment and in what manner such experiments are conducted" (Mendel, 1965, p. 2). He went on to say that the selection of the plant "must be made with all possible care" and two qualifying conditions *must* be met: That the plant (1) possess constant differentiating characters; and (2) the hybrids of such plants be protected from foreign pollen.

Figure 4-5   Mendel's "plantation," where he conducted his genetic experiments. The garden is presently ornamental. Mendel's statue can be seen in the background.

◇ Box 4-1   Terms Used in Discussion of Genetics

Alleles   Alternative forms of the same gene. (In the ABO blood system, A, B, and O are alternative forms found at the same locus. In a population where alternative forms are available at a particular locus, they are called alleles. The gene for round seeds and the gene for wrinkled seeds are such alternative forms.)

Dominant   A trait determined by a dominant allele. A trait that is visible or measurable and which prevents the appearance of the recessive. The allele for round seeds is dominant and when present "prevents" the appearance of wrinkled seeds.

Recessive   A trait determined by the recessive allele. A trait is not visible or measurable when paired with the dominant allele. The heterozygote Rr possesses both the dominant and recessive allele, but the wrinkling is not expressed phenotypically. (R = upper case of first letter of dominant trait; used as symbol for dominant trait. r = lower case of dominant symbol, used as a symbol for recessive trait.)

Generation
P_1 The parental generation in which homozygous dominants and recessives are crossed. Parents pure or homozygous for round seeds and parents homozygous for wrinkled represent such a parental cross.

F_1 First filial generation. The offspring resulting from a parental cross of homozygotes for different alleles.

F_2 Second filial generation. The offspring resulting from a cross of F_1 individuals (or self-fertilization of F_1 individuals, where this is possible).

Genotype   The genetic makeup of a particular organism. The genes at a particular locus. The genotype for a person with A blood type may be AA or AO. The genotype of a person with O blood type is OO. The genotype for homozygous round seeds is RR, and for heterozygous round seeds it is Rr (R = round; r = wrinkled). The DNA sequence is the genotype, which is not directly ascertainable, at least at the present time.

Phenotype   The observable or measurable characteristics of an organism. Roundness in a seed is a phenotype, as is wrinkledness. These are observable. In blood types, A, B, and O are also phenotypes; they are not observable to the naked eye but they are measurable. The phenotype is an observable expression of the genotype.

Heterozygous   Having different alleles at a given locus on a pair of homologous chromosomes.

Heterozygote   A cell or individual that is heterozygous. (A hybrid is heterozygous for a particular trait.) A person who is AO is heterozygous for ABO; an F_1 round pea (Rr) is heterozygous for form.

Homozygous   Having the same allele at a given locus on a pair of homologous chromosomes.

Homozygote   A cell or individual that is homozygous. (A purebred is homozygous for a particular trait.) A pea that is RR or rr is a homozygote.

Hybrid   The progeny resulting from a cross of different parental stock.

By constant differentiating characters—a most important point—Mendel meant that the plant must possess two contrasting characters of the same trait. If color were the trait, then the plant should possess two contrasting colors; if stature, then tall and short. These conditions led Mendel to devote his attention to legumes, and experiments with several members of this group led him to the genus *Pisum*, the common garden pea.

Clearly, Mendel knew what he was doing from the very beginning. Unlike those who preceded him, he concentrated on the underlying genetic factors, what we today call genes. He proposed to follow the progress of the hybrids through a number of generations, counting the number of different types of

Terminal flowers   Axial flowers

Round seed   Wrinkled seed

Figure 4-6   Contrasting characters.

Figure 4-7   Mendel cross-fertilizing his plants by hand.

hybrid progeny. He would carefully select the kind of plant that possessed the traits he considered necessary for the experiment, contrasting characters and fertility for a number of successive generations. Finally, he planned to use a large number of plants, so that the uniqueness of a small number of seeds would not bias the results.

From several nurserymen, Mendel obtained thirty-four varieties of peas, and, after checking them during a two-year trial, he selected twenty-two varieties for fertilization. Most of them belonged to the species *Pisum sativum*. As already noted, Mendel deliberately planned to use a plant that possessed at least one set of contrasting characters. With the pea he selected seven:

1. Form of the ripe seed: round/wrinkled
2. Difference in color of the seed: yellow/green
3. Difference in color of seed coat: white/gray
4. Form of the ripe pods: inflated/constricted
5. Color of unripe pods: green/yellow
6. Position of flowers: axial/terminal
7. Length of stem: tall/dwarf

THE PEA EXPERIMENTS—P GENERATION

Mendel launched his experiment in the spring of 1856. He divided the garden into sections, one for each of the seven characters of the pea. He placed contrasting characters next to each other so they would be easier to compare. Round seeds went next to wrinkled; yellow next to green; tall next to dwarf.

When the plants were ready to blossom, Mendel opened the flower buds of each plant and performed the surgery necessary to prevent the peas from fertilizing themselves in the normal manner. He then proceeded to do the cross-fertilizing himself (Fig. 4-7). Altogether, Mendel made 287 cross-fertilizations on 70 plants and then waited for the plants to mature in what the other monks called "Mendel's pea plantation."

F_1 *Generation*   The offspring of the P_1 cross (Fig. 4-8a) are designated as the F_1 generation, and when the F_1 generation matured, Mendel observed the seeds. They were all round (as in Fig. 4-8a). He then grew plants from these F_1 round seeds and, when the plants matured, allowed them to self-fertilize (Fig. 4-8b). Mendel then examined the offspring of the F_1 generation of round peas and found that in this generation (F_2) there were both round seeds *and* wrinkled seeds (Fig. 4-8c). When he carefully counted the numbers of each, they added up to 5,474 round seeds and 1,850 wrinkled, a ratio of 2.96 to 1. Among the other traits, the ratios were slightly over or under 3:1, and the average ratio of all the seeds of all the traits in the F_2 generation was 3:1 (Fig. 4-8). Mendel now saw clearly that when F_1 hybrids are bred, three offspring are produced that resemble one P_1 grandparent for every one offspring that resembles the other P_1 grandparent. The character that appeared three times, Mendel called *dominant*, and that which appeared once, *recessive*. (A list of definitions of terms used throughout this discussion may be found in Box 4-1).

F₂ Generation The experiment continued through another (F₃) generation. The plants of the F₂ generation were allowed to self-fertilize, and once more Mendel carefully counted the results. He found that one-half of the F₂ plants produced round and wrinkled seeds at a ratio of 3:1; one-fourth produced only round seeds; and one-fourth produced only wrinkled seeds. Since the one-half that produced a 3:1 ratio of round to wrinkled seeds behaved in exactly the same way as the F₁ hybrids, Mendel reasoned that these must also be *hybrids*, or *heterozygotes* (Fig. 4-7).

"... it is now clear," said Mendel, "that the hybrids form seeds having one or the other of the two differentiating characters, and of these one-half develop again the hybrid form, while the other half yield plants which remain constant and receive the dominant or the recessive characters in equal numbers" (Mendel, 1965, p. 13).

Figure 4-8 Gregor Mendel's logic. Mendel concluded: (1) the ½ of F₂ plants that produced a 3:1 ratio of round to wrinkled were the same as the F₁ rounds that produced a 3:1 ratio—therefore ½ of the F₂ plants *must be hybrids* (heterozygous); (2) the ¼ of the F₂ plants that produced only round seeds must be homozygous for round; (3) the ¼ of the F₂ plants that produced only wrinkled must be homozygous for wrinkled; (4) hybrid forms yield a genotypic ratio of 1:2:1 (that is, 1:homozygous dominant to 2:heterozygous dominant to 1:homozygous recessive).

P1 generation
(a)

Plant producing only round peas; homozygous

Plant producing only wrinkled peas; homozygous

F1 generation
(b)

All seeds are round

Plants allowed to self-fertilize and when mature seeds are counted

F2 generation
(c)

RESULT

5,474 Round to 1,850 wrinkled
A phenotypic ratio of 3:1

The round resembled P1 round
The wrinkled resembled P1 wrinkled

F1

F2   Self-fertilized produced

1/4 of F2 produced 1/4 only round

1/2 of F2 produced 3:1 ratio of round to wrinkled

1/4 of F2 produced only wrinkled

F3
(d)

Figure 4-9   Dominance.

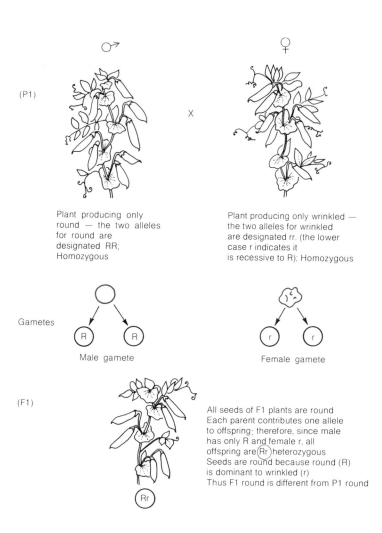

EXPERIMENT RESULTS—THE RIDDLE SOLVED

Using current terminology, we would say that one-half of the F_2 generation plants must be heterozygous, since they produced a 3:1 ratio just as the F_1 hybrids did. One-fourth of the F_2 plants produced only round seeds; therefore, they must be *homozygous* dominant. The remaining one-fourth produced only wrinkled seeds; therefore, they must be homozygous recessive. This led to Mendel's conclusion that the genotypic ratio is 1:2:1 for the F_2 generation:

¼   homozygous dominant
½   heterozygous dominant   =   1   : 2   : 1
¼   homozygous recessive   RR   : Rr   : rr

Mendel continued his experiments through several succeeding generations, and the results reinforced conclusions already reached. He had succeeded brilliantly where others had failed. By carefully selecting the proper experimental plant, by using a large number of plants, and—perhaps, most importantly—by carefully counting the numbers and kinds of offspring, Mendel had accomplished two goals: (1) he clarified the confusion surrounding the reproduction of hybrids; and (2) he had discovered the laws of heredity. For a modest, unknown amateur this achievement was indeed remarkable.

We should point out that this method of experimental breeding was simple, but original and unique. Moreover, the experiments were *deliberately designed to test a theory*, a new idea in biology (Dunn, 1965, p. 193).

Mendel's Report   After eight years of constant work, Mendel was at long last prepared to report on his findings, and, at the February, 1865, meeting of the Natural History Society of Brünn, Mendel read his paper. Members of the society, familiar with the methodology of more traditional botanists, were confused by his ideas. The next month, when Mendel presented his algebraic equations, the lack of understanding was even greater. The idea that "heredity was the giant shuffling and reshuffling of separate and invisible hereditary factors" was so different from what had been taught that it was probably incomprehensible. When Mendel finished his report, no one rose to ask a question, and the minutes of the society record no discussion.

The society published the monograph Mendel had prepared and copies were sent, as was the custom, to cities throughout Europe, but it attracted no attention. Mendel was disappointed. He was aware of the significance of his work and decided to send his report to one of Europe's outstanding botanists, Karl von Naegeli of Munich. Naegeli obviously failed to understand the experiment and replied in a condescending letter that Mendel's work was "far from being finished." Thus, a second opportunity for science to learn the rules of heredity was lost, not to be rediscovered until 1900.

In 1868, at the age of 46, Mendel was elected abbot of the monastery and, because of heavy administrative duties, he was unable to continue his scientific work. He died January 6, 1884, a beloved figure in the town of Brünn but unknown to the world of science.

GENES, CHROMOSOMES, AND MENDEL

With this brief survey, let us now examine more systematically the rules of heredity Mendel discovered. First, it may be useful to summarize pertinent information regarding genes and chromosomes already presented in Chapter 3.

Sex cells carry two sets of chromosomes to make up a full complement (46 in humans), the diploid number. On a pair of homologous chromosomes there is a number of loci, and at each locus on the pair is genetic material (a segment of DNA—a gene) that affects a particular trait. Thus, in any individual there are two genes for each trait. There may be several loci, by the way, that affect the same trait (stature, say), but, for our purpose, it is sufficient to deal with only one locus at a time. These are called simple or Mendelian traits and follow Mendelian ratios. If at a locus there is a gene, let us say, for round seeds or a gene for wrinkled seeds, then these different forms of the gene are known as *alleles*. Alleles are similar, but slightly different, sequences of DNA that control the same trait. Normal hemoglobin and sickling hemoglobin discussed in the preceding chapter are examples of alleles for the same trait. With this review, we return to Mendel's rules.

PRINCIPLE OF SEGREGATION

Dominant and Recessive Cross   In his experiment with peas, Mendel obtained seeds that were homozygous. He tested them by planting to make sure that those intended to produce round seeds did so, and those for wrinkled seeds produced only wrinkled. The second step was to cross the plants producing only round seeds with plants producing only wrinkled seeds.* The offspring of this cross were all round even though the sex cells of the plant contained an allele for wrinkled (Fig. 4-10). They were all round, as we know, because round is dominant to wrinkled. Please note that, phenotypically, the seeds are round, but, genotypically, both alleles are present, Rr, or heterozygous. The F_1 round (Rr) are genotypically different from their P_1 round (RR) parent (Fig. 4-10).

How is the difference between the F_1 and P_1 round seeds to be explained? Both seeds are phenotypically round, but the genotypes are different. Recalling the meiotic process, we know that after cell division a gamete contains one set of chromosomes, the haploid number. Therefore, the gamete contains only one of the alleles for a particular trait. To take Mendel's example, the parent plants each contained two genes for either roundness or wrinkledness. Because of meiotic division, each parent contributes only one. Since both parents are homozygous—one for round and the other for wrinkled—one parent would have to contribute an R allele and the other an r allele (Fig. 4-10).

The offspring in the F_1 generation possess both alleles, the big R from one parent and the small r from the other. Thus, the offspring are hybrid, or heterozygous.

Heterozygous Cross—3:1 Phenotypic Ratio   In the next step of the experiment, Mendel allowed these F_1 heterozygotes to fertilize themselves (pea plants contain both male and female parts). Although fertilization occurs within one plant, the male and female sex cells may be diagrammed thus:

$$Rr \times Rr$$

The result of this self-fertilization, as we have seen, was the production of three round seeds for every wrinkled. What happened in the F_1 cross to produce a 3:1 ratio? Bearing in mind what we know of meiosis, homologous chromosomes, and alleles, it is only necessary to add one point, the element of chance.

We know that as a result of meiosis a parent can contribute, at any one time, only one of a pair of chromosomes and therefore only one of two alleles for a trait. In this case, each parent will contribute either R *or* r. There is an even chance that the male R will combine with the female R or with the female r. Similarly, the odds are even that the male r will combine with the female R or r. In other words, there are four, and only four, possible combinations. Each combination has an equal chance, a one out of four (or 25%) chance of occurring (Fig. 4-11).

---

*In our discussion, we shall use the round and wrinkled traits. Mendel, of course, experimented with all seven traits, and the results in every case were similar.

Figure 4-10 Segregation of gametes.

Since round, R, is dominant, a round seed must contain at least one gene for round, R. In the F$_2$ generation, Mendel counted three round seeds for every wrinkled, which means that three-fourths (or 75%) of the seeds contained at least one gene for round, R. A glance at Figure 4-10 indicates that this percentage is exactly correct. The fourth combination, rr, does not contain a big R; therefore, that seed cannot be round. A seed with two alleles for wrinkled—rr—must be phenotypically wrinkled.

An illustration using heads and tails of two coins might possibly let us see the situation more clearly. Let us say we have a dime and a quarter, both of which are tossed in the air simultaneously. What possible combinations will come up, and what are the chances of these combinations? The possibilities, as we see in Figure 4-12, are two heads, two tails, and one heads and one

Figure 4-11 Gametic combinations.

(R)(R) Male gamete with R may fertilize female gamete with R = (RR)	
(R)(r) Male gamete with R may fertilize female gamete with r = (Rr)	
(r)(R) Male gamete with r may fertilize female gamete with R = (rR)	
(r)(r) Male gamete with r may fertilize female gamete with r = (rr)	

Figure 4-12 Possible combinations of coins. If any two coins are tossed many times, the probability is that each combination would come up the same number of times. Since there are four combinations, each combination will turn up 25% of the time. Or, in other words, there is a 25% chance of any one combination coming up. If you were betting on the toss, which combination would be your best bet? Heads/tails, of course, because there are two ways in which this combination could turn up. Therefore, there is a two out of four, or 50%, chance of its success, whereas there is only a 25% chance of two heads or two tails coming up.

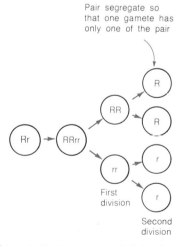

Pair segregate so that one gamete has only one of the pair

First division

Second division

Figure 4-13 Segregation of alleles during meiosis. This illustration represents an idealized division. If male, all gametes would be sperm; if female, one ovum and three polar bodies.

tails. The latter combination can occur in two ways: quarter heads and dime tails, or dime heads and quarter tails. Thus, there are four possible combinations.

What are the chances of any one of these combinations coming up? Well, if you were to wager on the toss of one coin, you would have a 50% chance of calling the right combination. You have as much chance of winning the bet as your partner. In our illustration, however, you are betting on the simultaneous toss of *two* coins, so the chances of calling the correct combination are cut to 25%, exactly half of the first. Since there are four possible combinations, you have one chance in four of any one combination turning up.

Statistically, that is precisely the situation with the round and wrinkled peas, and it was Mendel's insight that perceived this when none of his predecessors had done so. Perhaps it was Mendel's training in mathematics at the University that enabled him to approach his experiments from a statistical point of view.

Mendel could not have worked the statistics out had he used only a few plants. To flip a coin ten times and expect it to come up heads five times and tails five times is unreasonable. A thousand flips might average 500 heads and 500 tails. Similarly, Mendel was aware, as we have seen, that a large number of plants are required to achieve a complete random assortment. When Mendel counted all the dominant and recessive characters of the seven traits, he found an average **phenotypic ratio** of 2.98 to 1, which he considered to be a 3:1 ratio.

Mendel's explanation for the 3:1 ratio solved the riddle of heredity. He suggested that the characters (genes) are paired and *segregated* when they are passed on from one generation to the next. That is, the gene on one chromosome does not normally affect the gene at the same locus on the paired chromosome. We might say each gene goes its own way. Therefore, the capital R in the male influences inheritance separately from the influence of the lower-case r, and similarly with the female. (We have seen how this separation operated during meiosis.) This is Mendel's first law, called the **principle of segregation**, which states that genes, the units of heredity, exist within individuals in pairs. The pairs are segregated during the production of gametes, so that a gamete has only one of each kind.

Interestingly, Mendel was not the first to observe this 3:1 ratio. In 1820, an Englishman named John Goss carried out an experiment very similar to Mendel's, even to the extent of using peas. When the hybrids produced a mixture of dominants and recessives, he merely pointed out the facts but did not count the numbers of each. He failed to see the significance of the ratio of dominants to recessives. Perhaps even more curious is Darwin's experience with snapdragons. Darwin crossed normal and irregular snapdragons and in the F_1 generation all the offspring were normal. When he bred the F_1 normal snapdragons, the offspring were normal to irregular at roughly a 3:1 ratio. Darwin noted the F_1 uniformity and the mixture of the F_2 generation, but the significance of the 3:1 proportion escaped him also (Iltis, 1966, pp. 118–127).

Having solved the problem of the 3:1 ratio, Mendel's next task was to determine whether what he called "the law of development" also applied to a cross of two different traits (a dihybrid cross). For this experiment he used the traits of form, round/wrinkled—Rr—and color, yellow/green—Yy. He crossed round and wrinkled peas with yellow and green peas, and he found the results were the same as in the first experiment. The proportions in the F_2 generation for color and form of seeds were:

9 round and yellow—both traits dominant

3 round and green—round dominant, green recessive

3 wrinkled and yellow—wrinkled recessive, yellow dominant

1 wrinkled and green—both traits recessive

When the numbers of round and wrinkled seeds are totaled, a proportion of 12 round to 4 wrinkled, or a 3:1 phenotypic ratio, emerges. When the number of yellow (dominant) and green seeds are totaled, we find 12 yellow to 4 green, also a 3:1 phenotypic ratio.

Conclusion: Gene pairs on one set of homologous chromosomes do not influence the distribution of gene pairs on other chromosomes; they separate independently from one another during meiosis, and are randomly assorted in the gametes. This phenomenon is known as Mendel's second law, the **principle of independent assortment** (Figs. 4-14, 4-16).

PRINCIPLE OF INDEPENDENT ASSORTMENT

Random Assortment   Mendel was not aware of the precise cellular mechanism that caused this random assortment of one trait with respect to another. However, a brief glance at our earlier discussion of meiosis (p. 54) quickly solves the mystery. As you will recall, when homologous pairs of chromosomes align along the equator of a cell, the relative positions of one homologous pair are independent of all other pairs.

Simply stated, this is the process of *random assortment*. The independent

Phenotypic ratio
The ratio of phenotypes, especially from a hybrid cross. Mendel's famous F_1 hybrid cross of peas produced a 3:1 phenotypic ratio.

Principle of Segregation
Genes occur in pairs. In the production of a gamete, the pair is separated so that each gamete contains only one of the pair.

Principle of Independent Assortment
The separation of one pair of genes does not influence the separation of other pairs of genes.

Figure 4-14 Mendel's Law of Independent Assortment.

CHROMOSOME ALIGNMENT
(all equally probable)

GAMETES PRODUCED

Pair # 1   Pair # 2   Possiblity 1   Possibility 2   Possibility 3   Possibility 4

assortment of traits observed by Mendel is the direct result of the random assortment of chromosomes that respectively carry those traits.

Figure 4-14 shows two pairs of chromosomes in an F_1 (heterozygous) pea plant, each containing one of the two traits discussed above (color of seed, shape of seed). As can be seen, the way the chromosomes align during meiosis directly affects the combination of alleles in the resulting gametes, which, in turn, combine to produce individuals exhibiting the phenotypic ratios of observed traits (round and yellow, round and green, etc.).

Possible Alignments   There are four equally possible ways the chromosomes can align, and four different kinds of gametes that can be produced in this manner in each parent. This recombination of genes—by random assortment of chromosomes—leads to all the combinations of traits we observe in different individuals in the next generation.

If Mendel had used just *any* two traits for recombination, the phenotypic ratios would quite possibly not have conformed to those expected by independent assortment (9:3:3:1). The ratio came out as he predicted, because the traits Mendel chose to observe were carried on different chromosomes. Had the two traits *both* been carried on the *same* chromosome, the alleles for the two traits would not have assorted independently but would have been transmitted together.

An exception may be produced by the process of crossing-over (see p. 61). Even if carried on the same chromosome, genes can and usually do cross-over independently of each other *if* they are not located too closely together. In this case, all four possible recombinations of alleles (CD, Cd, cD, cd) may be produced, and the expected ratios of independent assortment (9:3:3:1) may be approached (Fig. 4-15).

Figure 4-15 Crossing-over in chromosomes. Genes are more likely to cross-over and recombine when they are far apart (right) than when they are close together (left).

Genotypic Ratio   Going one step further, Mendel also demonstrated that the genotypic ratio for form and color remained the same as it did in his first experiment with the contrasting characters of only one trait. The ratio of homozygous dominant, RR, to heterozygous, Rr, to homozygous recessive, rr, is 1:2:1. (The entire process from the parental generation to the F₂ generation is shown schematically in Fig. 4-16.) The proportions for color, YY, Yy, yy, are of course the same, 1:2:1.

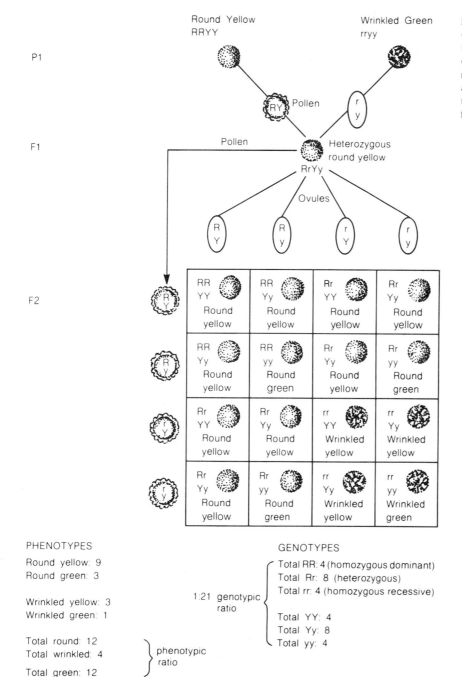

Figure 4-16 Dihybrid cross; Principle of Independent Assortment. Shape (round and wrinkled) has no effect on color (yellow and green). The phenotypic ratios for both shape and color are 3:1, as in the cross of a single trait. Similarly, the genotypic ratio—1:2:1—is the same for both traits.

PHENOTYPES

Round yellow: 9
Round green: 3

Wrinkled yellow: 3
Wrinkled green: 1

Total round: 12
Total wrinkled: 4

Total green: 12
Total green: 4

GENOTYPES

Total RR: 4 (homozygous dominant)
Total Rr: 8 (heterozygous)
Total rr: 4 (homozygous recessive)

Total YY: 4
Total Yy: 8
Total yy: 4

1:21 genotypic ratio

phenotypic ratio

In summary, Mendel demonstrated, and cellular biology has confirmed, that there are regularities or laws of heredity. The laws may be explained in the following manner:

1. Each individual possesses two genes for a particular trait.
2. During meiosis, the two genes from each parent segregate into different gametes (principle of segregation). This means that a parent contributes only one of the two genes to an offspring.
3. If each parent contributes a different allele for a particular trait (such as R or r), a hybrid (heterozygote) results.
4. When the two heterozygotes are crossed, or self-fertilized, there is an even chance that each of the two genes from one parent will combine with each of the two genes from the other parent. A male Rr and a female Rr can combine in four ways: RR, Rr, rR, rr. (In a large population, the result of such a hybrid cross would produce 25% RR, 25% Rr, 25% rR, and 25% rr. If we combine the two Rr, then the genotypic ratio would be 25% RR, 50% Rr, 25% rr, or 1:2:1.)
5. When two traits are crossed, each pair assorts independently of the other (principle of independent assortment).

The concept of two genes for each trait—that the two genes segregate independently of one another, that a parent contributes one of the two, that genes from parents enter into all possible combinations with each other, that genes during meiosis segregate into separate gametes—all of these made sense of what appeared to be unintelligible confusion in the process of heredity.

Professor L. C. Dunn has nicely summed up Mendel's contribution:

> . . . his work has served as a kind of constructional keystone upon which subsequent developments of genetics have rested. The discovery of the statistical unit of heredity has turned out to be the spearhead of a changing conception of living matter which has penetrated and illuminated all of the major questions of biology (Dunn, 1965, p. 197).

It would be pleasing to report that Mendel's experiments and conclusions were swiftly accepted by an eager community of scientists that immediately applied his conclusions to the development of genetic research. Unfortunately, the case was otherwise. Mendel's methods were ahead of his time. It was not until 1900, thirty-five years after he read his paper before the Natural History Society of Brünn, that three geneticists—Hugo de Vries in Holland, Erich von Tschermak in Austria, and Carl Correns in Germany—working independently of one another, discovered for themselves the laws Mendel had already formulated. Genetics had lost thirty-five years.

◇ Modern Theory of Evolution

Following the rediscovery of Mendel's work in 1900, attention quickly turned to the study of genetics in animals, particularly humans. In 1902, Archibald Garrod identified the pattern of incidence in a metabolic disorder called *alkaptonuria* as a clear example of Mendelian inheritance in humans. Since that time the catalog of human traits known to operate in simple Mendelian fashion has grown steadily. Recent advances in biochemical techniques have greatly aided this research; the list now includes more than 3,300 such traits (McKusick, 1983). In addition, great advances have been made in chromosome mapping, and more than 500 genes have been pinpointed to specific human chromosomes (McKusick, 1983).

By the beginning of the twentieth century, the essential foundations for evolutionary theory had already been developed. Darwin and Wallace had articulated the key principle of natural selection forty years earlier, and the rediscovery of Mendelian genetics contributed the other major component— a mechanism for inheritance. We might expect that these two basic contributions would have been joined rather quickly into a consistent theory of evolution. However, such was not the case. For the first thirty years of this century, geneticists (working with experimental animals, such as fruit flies) emphasized sharp contrasts within particular characteristics of organisms. As such, evolution was seen as a process of fairly large radical "jumps," and this "mutationist" view came to be seen as an alternative to the "selectionist" tradition.

A *synthesis* of these two views was not achieved until the mid-1930s, and we owe much of our current view of the evolutionary process to this intellectual development. (See Box 4-2.)

The Modern Synthesis

Biologists working on mathematical models of evolutionary change in the late 1920s and early 1930s came to realize that genetic and selective processes were not opposing themes, but that a comprehensive explanation of organic evolution required *both*. Small new changes in the genetic material—transmitted from parent to offspring by strict Mendelian principles—are, in fact, the fuel for natural selection. The two major foundations of the biological sciences had thus been brought together in what Julian Huxley termed the "modern synthesis."

From such a "modern" (that is, the middle of the twentieth century onwards) perspective we define evolution as a two-stage process:

1. Production and redistribution of **variation** (inherited differences between individuals).
2. **Natural selection** acts on this variation (inherited differences, or variation, among individuals differentially affect their ability to reproduce successfully).

Definition of Evolution

Darwin saw evolution as the gradual unfolding of new varieties of life from previous forms over long periods of time. This depiction is what most of us think of as "evolution," and it is indeed the end result of the evolutionary process. But these long-term effects can only come about by the accumulation of many small evolutionary changes occurring every generation. In order to understand how the process of evolution works, we must necessarily study

Variation (genetic)
Inherited differences between individuals. The basis of all evolutionary change.

Natural selection
The evolutionary factor (first articulated by Charles Darwin) that causes changes in gene frequencies in populations due to differential net reproductive success of individuals.

◇ Box 4-2   Development of Modern Evolutionary Theory

Theodosius Dobzhansky.

Our modern understanding of the evolutionary process came about through contributions of biologists in the United States, Great Britain, and the Soviet Union.

While "mutationists" were arguing with "selectionists" about the single primary mechanism in evolution, several population geneticists began to realize that both small genetic changes and natural selection were necessary ingredients in the evolutionary formula.

These population geneticists were largely concerned with mathematical reconstructions of evolution—in particular, measuring those small accumulations of genetic changes in populations over just a few generations. Central figures in these early theoretical developments included Ronald Fisher and J.B.S. Haldane in Great Britain, Sewall Wright in the United States, and Sergei Chetverikov in the Soviet Union.

While the work of these scientists often produced brilliant insights (see particularly Fisher's *The Genetical Theory of Natural Selection*, 1930) their conclusions were largely unknown to most evolutionary biologists, especially in North America. It remained, therefore, for an individual to transcend these two worlds: the mathematical jargon of the population geneticists and the general constructs of theoretical evolutionary biologists. The scientist who performed this task (and to whom we owe the most credit as the first true synthesizer) was **Theodosius Dobzhansky**. In his *Genetics and the Origin of Species* (1937), Dobzhansky skillfully integrated the mathematics of population genetics with overall evolutionary theory. His insights then became the basis for a period of tremendous activity in evolutionary thinking that directly led to major contributions by George Gaylord Simpson (who brought paleontology into the synthesis), Ernst Mayr,[*] and others. In fact the "Modern Synthesis" produced by these scientists stood basically unchallenged for an entire generation as *the* explanation of the evolutionary process. In recent years, however, some aspects of this theory have been brought under serious question. (See the section "Recent Challenges to the Modern Synthesis," this chapter.)

[*]For an interesting discussion of the intellectual developments concerning the formulation of modern evolutionary theory see: Ernst Mayr and William B. Provine (eds.), *The Evolutionary Synthesis*, Cambridge, Mass.: Harvard University Press, 1980.

these short-term events. Darwin attempted this kind of study in his breeding experiments, but because the science of genetics was still in its infancy, he was not able to comprehend fully the mechanics of evolutionary change. Today, we study in various organisms (including humans) evolutionary changes occurring between generations, and are able to demonstrate how evolution works. From such a modern genetics perspective, we define evolution as *a change in gene frequency from one generation to the next.*

Gene frequencies are numerical indicators of the genetic makeup of an interbreeding group of individuals known as a **population**. (We will return to this topic in more detail in Chapter 5.) Here, let us illustrate the way gene frequencies change (that is, how evolution occurs) through a simplified example. First of all, we must look at a physical trait that is inherited, in this case human blood type. The best known of the human blood-type traits is ABO. There are, however, many similar blood-type systems controlled by different genes, which determine genetically transmitted properties of the red blood cells.

An inherited trait, such as human blood type, may be of slightly different form in different individuals. We call the variant genes that underlie these different forms of an inherited trait, **alleles**. The best-known blood-type alleles are A, B, and O. These different expressions of inherited traits constitute genetic variation within a population.

Let us assume that your present class of 100 members represents a population, an interbreeding group of individuals, and that we have ascertained the blood type of each member for the MN trait, a blood-group system similar to ABO (but with only two alternatives or alleles, M and N). To be a population, individuals in your class must choose mates more often from *within* the group than from outside it. Of course, the individuals in your class will not meet this requirement, but for this example's sake we will make the assumption that they do. The proportions of each of the M and N alleles are the gene frequencies for this trait. For example, suppose we find that the proportion of gene combinations in your class (population) is as follows:*

Blood Type	Number of Individuals		Percent
M	35	=	35
MN	50	=	50
N	15	=	15
	100		100%

Since the frequencies for combinations of these genes represent only proportions of a total, it is obvious that gene frequencies can refer only to whole groups of individuals; that is, populations. Individuals do not have a gene frequency, they have either M or N. Nor can individuals change gene frequency. From conception onward, the genetic composition of an individual is fixed. If you start out with blood type M, you will remain type M. Therefore, an individual cannot evolve: Only a group of individuals—a population—can evolve over time.

*This simplified example shows frequencies for the various gene combinations, what are called genotypes. The way gene (allele) frequencies are calculated will be shown in Chapter 5.

Population
Within a species, a community of individuals where mates are usually found.

Allele
A variant form of a gene.

What happens when a population evolves? Evolution is not an unusual or a mysterious process. In fact, it is incredibly commonplace, and may occur between every generation for every group of organisms in the world, including humans. Assume we measure the gene combination frequencies for the MN blood trait twenty-five years later in the children of our classroom population and find the following:

Blood Type	Number of Individuals		Percent
M	20	=	20
MN	50	=	50
N	30	=	30
	100		100%

We can see that the relative proportions have changed: M has decreased, N has increased, while MN has remained the same in frequency. Such a simple, apparently minor, change is what we call evolution. Over the short run of just a few generations, such changes in inherited traits may be only very small, but if further continued and elaborated, the results can and do produce spectacular kinds of adaptation and whole new varieties of life.

Whether we are talking about such short-term effects as our classroom population from one generation to the next, which is sometimes called **microevolution**, or the long-term effects through fossil history, sometimes called **macroevolution**, the basic evolutionary mechanisms are similar. As we will discuss below, however, they are not necessarily identical.

The question may be asked: How do gene frequencies change? Or, to put it another way, what causes evolution? The modern theory of evolution isolates general factors that can produce alterations in gene frequencies. As we have noted, evolution is a two-stage process. Genetic variation must be first produced and distributed before it can be acted upon by natural selection.

FACTORS THAT PRODUCE AND REDISTRIBUTE VARIATION

Mutation   An actual alteration in genetic material is called **mutation**. A genetic trait may take one of several alternative forms, which we have defined as alleles (M or N, for example). If one allele changes to another—that is, if the gene itself is altered—a mutation has occurred. As we have seen, a mutation is a molecular alteration—a change in the base sequence of DNA. For such changes to have evolutionary significance, they must occur in the sex cells, which are passed between generations. Evolution is a change in gene frequencies *between* generations. If mutations do not occur in sex cells (either the egg or sperm), they will not be passed to the next generation, and no evolutionary change can result. If, however, a genetic change does occur in the sperm or egg of one of the 100 individuals in our classroom (M mutates to N, for instance) the offspring's blood type also will be altered, causing a change in gene frequencies of that generation. Evolution would have occurred by mutation.

Actually, it would be rare to see evolution occurring by mutation *alone*. Mutation rates for any given trait are quite low, and, thus, their effects would rarely be seen in such a small population as our class. In larger populations mutations might be observed (one individual in 10,000, say), but would, by themselves, have very little impact on shifting gene frequencies. However, when mutation is coupled with natural selection, evolutionary changes are quite possible.

Mutation is the basic creative force in evolution, and in fact is the only way to produce "new" variation. Its key role in the production of variation represents the first stage of the evolutionary process. Darwin was not aware of the nature of mutation. Only in the twentieth century, with the spectacular development of molecular biology, have the secrets of genetic structure been revealed.

Migration The movement of genes from one population to another is called **migration**. If all individuals in our classroom population do not choose their mates from within the group, significant changes in gene frequencies could occur. For example, if four of the people who were type M married and settled outside the population, and four new individuals who were type N moved in and interbred with classroom individuals, the gene frequencies would be altered. If a change in gene frequency does take place, evolution will have occurred, this time by migration.

In humans, social rules, more than any other factor, determine mating patterns, and cultural anthropologists must work closely with physical anthropologists in order to isolate and measure this aspect of evolutionary change.

Genetic Drift The random factor in evolution is called **genetic drift**, and is due primarily to sampling error. Since evolution occurs in populations, it is directly tied not only to the nature of the initial gene freqencies of the population, but to the size of the group as well. If, in our parent population of 100 individuals, two type M individuals had been killed in an auto accident before completing reproduction, their genes would have been removed from the population. The frequency of the M gene would have been reduced in the next generation, and evolution would have occurred. In this case, with only 100 individuals in the population, the change due to the accident would have altered the M frequency from 60% to 59%, a noticeable change. If, however, our initial population had been very large (10,000 people), then the effect of removing a few individuals would be very small indeed. In fact, in a population of large size, random effects, such as traffic accidents, would be balanced out by the equal probabilities of such events affecting N and MN individuals as well. As you can see, evolutionary change due to genetic drift is directly related to population size.

When considering genetic drift, we must remember that the genetic makeup of individuals is in no way related to the chance happenings that affect their lives. When applied to our example, this fact means that the genetic makeup of individuals has absolutely nothing to do with their being involved in automobile accidents. This is what is meant by a random event and why this factor is usually called *random genetic drift*. If, for example, a person had died in an auto accident caused by hereditary poor eyesight, such an event would not be genetic drift. If the individual, because of some such hereditary trait, dies early and produces fewer offspring than other individuals, this is not random genetic drift, it is natural selection.

Microevolution
Small, short-term changes occurring over just a few generations.

Macroevolution
Large changes produced only after many generations.

Mutation
An alteration in the genetic material (a change in the base sequence of DNA).

Migration
Movement of genes between populations.

Genetic Drift
Evolutionary changes produced by random factors.

◇ Box 4-3   Models of Natural Selection

Directional Selection   As environmental pressures change gradually, selection pressures should also shift. If the environmental pressure is directional, selection should also be directional (see Fig. 1). For example, in the last one million years, there have been long periods of gradual cooling in the earth's climate. One means of coping with cold among mammals has been increase in body size (see p. 168). If we assume animals, such as mammoths, are descendants from

Figure 1   Directional selection.

smaller ancestors, how did they gradually get bigger? The answer lies in understanding natural selection. Those animals with genotypes for larger overall size perhaps resisted cold better, lived longer, mated more often, cared better for their young offspring, and so forth. In any case, the result was that they reproduced more successfully than other (smaller) individuals. Gradually, then, gene frequencies shifted. As the climate continued to grow progressively colder, gene frequencies also continued to shift, and average mammoth size gradually increased.

Stabilizing Selection   If, on the other hand, environments remain relatively stable, there should be selection for those genotypes already established within an "adaptive plateau" (see Fig. 2). In other words, those phenotypes (which are influenced by genotypes) in the center of the populational distribution ("modal" varieties) should have higher reproductive success, and those at either extreme will be selected against (as long as the environment remains stable).

If we again choose size as a characteristic, we can note that some varieties of turtle have changed little in millions of years. In any given generation, the environment of turtles has not changed much from that of previous generations. Therefore, the "optimal" phenotype is probably an average-sized turtle, and

Recombination   Since in any sexually reproducing species both parents contribute genes to offspring, the genetic information is inevitably reshuffled every generation. Such recombination does not in itself change gene frequencies (i.e., cause evolution). However, it does produce the whole array of genetic combinations, which natural selection can then act upon. In fact, we have shown how the reshuffling of chromosomes during meiosis can produce literally trillions of gene combinations, making every human being genetically unique.

NATURAL SELECTION ACTS ON VARIATION

The evolutionary factors just discussed—mutation, migration, genetic drift, and recombination—act to produce variation and to distribute genes within and between populations. But there is no long-term *direction* to any of these

Figure 2 Stabilizing selection.

those much larger or much smaller should be selected against.

Diversifying Selection In this type of selection, phenotypic variants at *both* extremes are favored, and those in the center of the distribution (closer to the mean) are selected against. For example, in the case of baboon size relative to predation pressure, it may be advantageous to be small (less conspicuous) or very large (for active defense).

Over time, such selection pressure would act to create a twin-peak (bimodal) phenotypic distribution as shown in Figure 3.

In fact, such a process would not have long-term effects in a *fully* reproductive population, since individuals of all sizes would be mating with each other, thus producing individuals of intermediate body size. In order for the diversifying selection pressures to be maintained, some degree of reproductive isolation between segments of the population would be required. Another possibility is that phenotypic variation can be partitioned and maintained by other genetic differences—sex, for example. In fact, baboons do differ markedly in size, with males averaging about twice the size of females.

Figure 3 Diversifying selection.

factors. What then does enable populations to adapt to changing environments? The answer is, of course, natural selection—the process so well elucidated by Darwin more than 125 years ago. Given that there is genetic variation among individuals within a population, some of these variations *may* influence reproductive success (numbers of offspring successfully raised). If, as a result of genetic variation, some individuals contribute more offspring to succeeding generations, this is natural selection. In fact, we have defined natural selection as *differential net reproductive success* (see p. 42).

How then do populations adapt? A result of natural selection is a change in gene frequency relative to specific environmental factors. If the environment changes, then the selection pressures change as well. Such a functional shift in gene frequencies is what we mean by *adaptation*. If there are long-term environmental changes in a consistent direction, then gene frequencies should also shift gradually each generation. If sustained for many generations, the results may be quite dramatic. (See Box 4-3.)

Speciation
The evolutionary process that produces new species from previous ones.

The Unit of Selection   Selection acts on the individual. It is individuals who reproduce or do not reproduce and who continually attempt to maximize their own reproductive success. Thus, statements such as "The group was undergoing selection in order to survive" have no meaning. *The individual, not the group, is the unit of selection.* If the total reproductive success of all members of a population continuously falls below replacement value (where more individuals die than are born in a generation), the population will become extinct. Individuals will attempt to maximize their own reproductive success even in the face of such impending extinction.

Overpopulation is the result of individuals maximizing their reproductive success. Even if such behavior means the whole group will perish, no evolutionary mechanisms exist to keep individuals from reproducing at their greatest capacity. Of course, humans have the potential to manipulate their numbers, and the entire world now faces the problem of controlling an exploding population. Evolution, therefore, has no built-in mechanism to guard against extinction. Indeed, extinction is actually the rule—not the exception—in evolution. Of all the species that have ever lived on earth, less than .1% (one-tenth of one percent) are now currently living; the remaining 99.9% met their almost inevitable evolutionary fate.

The Unit of Evolution   While selection acts on the individual, changes in gene frequency occur *between* generations for an entire population; that is, an interbreeding group of organisms. The net result of all individuals' reproductive success (natural selection)—in addition to the possible effects of mutation, migration, and genetic drift—will affect the entire population. *The population, then, is the unit of evolution*, and it is the population that changes (as measured by gene frequencies) from generation to generation.

EVOLUTION AT THE SPECIES LEVEL

A species is defined as a group of interbreeding organisms that are *reproductively isolated* and, therefore, cannot successfully interbreed with other groups. The capacity to reproduce is the critical factor in defining species. Theoretically, one can test whether two kinds of organisms are members of different species by observing their reproductive behavior under natural conditions (who mates with whom), and by observing the results (are the offspring fertile?).

Actually, a species is composed of subunits that are the breeding communities we have called populations. All members of a species can potentially interbreed, and some degree of interbreeding (migration) is theoretically possible between all populations.

The net result of all the forces of evolution (mutation, migration, genetic drift, recombination, and natural selection) acting on all populations determines the fate of the species as a whole. If sustained over a long period of time, gradual changes in gene frequencies between member populations can eventually lead to sufficient genetic differences, so that fertile reproduction is no longer possible. We then may recognize a new form of life having arisen from one species "splitting" and producing new species, a process called **speciation**. (See Box 4-4.) This level of evolutionary change was the one

◇ Box 4-4 Speciation

According to the biological species concept (Mayr, 1970), the way new species are first produced involves some form of isolation. Picture a single species of some organism (baboons, say) composed of several populations distributed over a wide geographic area. Gene exchange (migration) will be limited if a geographic barrier, such as a river, lake, ocean, or mountain range, separates these populations. This extremely important form of isolating mechanism is called *geographic isolation*.

Now, if one population (A) is separated from another population (B) by a mountain range, individual baboons of A will not be able to mate with baboons from B. As time passes (several generations), genetic differences will accumulate in both populations. If group size is small, we can predict that drift will cause gene frequency changes in both population A and population B. Since drift is *random* in nature, we would not expect the effects to be the same. Thus, the two populations would begin to diverge.

As long as gene exchange is limited, the populations can only become more divergent with time. Moreover, further genetic difference would be expected if the baboon groups are occupying somewhat different habitats. (Ecological conditions usually do vary from one area to another within a species' range.) These additional genetic differences would arise through the process of natural selection. Certain individuals in population A may be most reproductively fit in their own environment, but may be less fit in the environment occupied by population B. Consequently, gene frequencies will change, and the pattern will be dissimilar in the two populations.

Again, as time passes, and perhaps as environments change further, the populations will become still more divergent.

With the cumulative effects of drift and natural selection acting over many generations, the result will be two populations which—even if they were to come back into geographic contact—could no longer interbreed fertilely.

More than just geographic isolation would now apply; there may, for instance, be behavioral differences interfering with courtship—what we call *behavioral isolation*. There may even be sufficient differences in body size and proportions to make copulation physiologically impossible.

Using our *biological* definition of species, we now would recognize two distinct species, where initially only one existed.

Some isolation — B A — A and B Not yet diverged

More isolation — B A — A and B Just beginning to diverge

Complete isolation — B A — A and B Diverged to point where no longer able to reproduce; speciation complete

This model of speciation is called branching evolution or cladogenesis described by Darwin and Wallace. If, on the other hand, total reproductive success is so low that all, or even most, populations become extinct, the whole species will be doomed and will disappear from the earth forever. The gross interference of natural habitats by modern industrial society has pushed numerous "endangered species" to this crucial juncture.

◇ Recent Challenges to the Modern Synthesis

In the last decade, serious reexamination has stimulated ongoing debate concerning some aspects of modern evolutionary theory.

NEUTRAL MUTATIONS

One of the premises postulated by traditional evolutionists is that natural selection is the major factor explaining most of the variation found in contemporary organisms. There is general agreement that significant aspects of variation are channeled by selection, thus leading to adaptation. But is all (or even most) of the "genetic baggage" that a species carries understandable strictly in terms of natural selection? Some scientists believe it is not. Pointing to the vast amount of variation seen in all organisms (28% of all human genes are estimated to exhibit significant population variation), these researchers argue that *much* of variation seen in natural populations is due to neutral mutations and chance factors (i.e., genetic drift).

A major aspect of this argument is that many mutations are neutral; in other words, they have no impact on reproductive success in any conceivable environment. We know, of course, that there is considerable redundancy in the DNA code, so that many point mutations will not alter the amino acid sequence whatsoever. In such a case, the phenotype is not affected at all, and selection cannot act on what it cannot see. Or as King and Jukes have put it, "Natural selection is the editor, rather than the composer of the genetic message" (King and Jukes, 1969, p. 788). These researchers, however, go far beyond postulating strictly synonymous mutations as neutral—they claim a large majority of other genetic changes are completely neutral to selective action, and are established in populations by random genetic drift.

This controversy has not yet been resolved. There is a vast store of genetic variation in all interbreeding populations. Certainly, both selection and drift have contributed, but what has been the primary architect? The consensus among most evolutionary biologists still is that natural selection is the most significant factor in explaining evolutionary change. A recent reveiw of genetic variation among humans concludes that "there is little doubt that many amino acid substitutions appear to be neutral or quasi-neutral, but neutral models do not seem to fit the distribution of most loci in the human species" (Livingstone, 1980, p. 39).

MODES OF EVOLUTIONARY CHANGE

The modern synthesis primarily explains those gene frequency changes seen over just a few generations—what is called *microevolution*. Until recently, the general consensus among evolutionary biologists was that these microevolutionary mechanisms could be translated directly into larger-scale evolutionary changes—what is called *macroevolution*, or transspecific evolution. These major evolutionary events involve the appearance of new species (i.e., speciation) as well as higher taxonomic categories (for example, genera, families, orders, etc.). A smooth gradation of changes was postulated to run directly from microevolution into macroevolution. A representative view was expressed by a leading synthesist, Ernst Mayr:

> The proponents of the synthetic theory maintain that all evolution is due to the accumulation of small genetic changes, guided by natural selection, and that transspecific evolution is nothing but an extrapolation and magnification of the events that take place within populations and species (Mayr, 1970, p. 351).

In the last decade, however, this view has been seriously challenged. Many theorists now believe that macroevolution cannot be explained *solely* in terms of accumulated microevolutionary changes. Many current researchers are now convinced that macroevolution is only partly understandable through microevolutionary models, as recently stated by two proponents of this revised view:

> We recognize that the within-population concept of adaptation via natural selection is a viable hypothesis accounting for the deterministic part of much genetic, behavioral, and morphological change in evolution. However, we strongly disagree that a smooth extrapolation of within-population (microevolutionary) processes is a logical or effective integration of such within-population mechanisms with among-species phenomena (macroevolution) (Eldredge and Cracraft, 1980).

Gradualism vs. Punctuationalism   The traditional view of evolution has emphasized that change accumulates gradually in evolving lineages—the idea of "phyletic gradualism." Accordingly, the complete fossil record of an evolving group (if it could be recovered) would display a series of forms with finely graded transitional differences between each ancestor and its descendant. The fact that such transitional forms are only rarely found is attributed to the incompleteness of the fossil record, or, as Darwin called it, "a history of the world, imperfectly kept, and written in changing dialect."

For more than a century, this perspective dominated evolutionary biology. Paleontologists searched diligently to find evidence of these gradual changes. So strong was this notion of gradualism (Darwin called it "descent with modification") that when little evidence was found to support it, researchers assumed there must be something wrong with their data—either their geological beds were inadequately dated or the paleontological record was yet too incomplete to allow a firm conclusion. Rarely did anyone suspect that the premise of gradualism itself might be flawed.

In the last decade, some evolutionary biologists have called this notion into serious question. The evolutionary mechanisms operating on species over the long run are often not continuously gradual. In a great many cases, species persist for thousands of generations basically unchanged. Then, rather suddenly—at least in evolutionary terms—a "spurt" of speciation occurs. This nongradual process of long stasis and quick spurts has been termed **punctuated equilibrium** (Gould and Eldredge, 1977).

Punctuated equilibrium
The view that evolutionary rates are not constant, but proceed slowly (equilibria) until "punctuated" by rather sudden spurts.

From a comprehensive survey of well-documented and long-ranging fossil series (including especially marine invertebrates), paleontologists Stephen Gould and Niles Eldredge conclude that:

> Most species during their evolutionary history, either do not change in any appreciable way, or else they fluctuate mildly in morphology, with no apparent change in any direction. Phyletic gradualism is very rare and too slow, in any case, to produce the major events of evolution. Evolutionary trends are not the product of slow, directional transformation within lineages; they represent the differential success of certain species . . . speciation may be random with respect to the direction of a trend (Gould and Eldredge, 1977, p. 115).

What the punctuationalists are disputing concerns the "tempo" and "mode" of evolutionary change comonly understood since Darwin's time. Rather than a slow steady tempo, this new view postulates long periods of no change interspersed only occasionally by sudden bursts. From this observation, punctuationalists concluded that the mode of evolution, too, must be different from that suggested by classical Darwinists. Rather than gradual accumulation of small changes within a single lineage, advocates of punctuated equilibrium believe an additional evolutionary mechanism is required to push the process along. Accordingly, *speciation* (see Box 4-4) is seen to be the major influence in bringing about rapid evolutionary change. Given new environmental opportunities, speciation events could occur in a sudden flurry—a whole array of new, fairly isolated and small incipient species would then possess a great deal of evolutionary potential. Of these, probably only a small minority would survive—through a "higher" evoltuionary process sometimes called *species selection*.

How well does the paleontological record agree with this new theory? Indeed, a tremendous amount of fossil data shows long periods of stasis punctuated by occasional quite rapid changes (the transformation taking perhaps on the order of 10,000 to 50,000 years). Intermediate forms are rare, not because the record is so poor, but because the speciation events and longevity of these transitional species were so short we should not expect to find them very often.

The best supporting evidence for punctuated equilibrium has come from the fossilized remains of a variety of invertebrates, the paleontological specialty of both Gould and Eldredge. How well, then, does the human fossil record fit a punctuationalist model? Gould and Eldredge (1977, p. 115) believe, "the record of human evolution seems to provide a particularly good example." When it comes to the evolution of our family, other researchers, however, are still not as convinced. Many believe punctuationalism is not all that apparent in the human evolutionary record and, alternatively, that gradualism fits the facts better (Cronin et al., 1981). Others (e.g., Tobias, 1983) believe human evolution displays periods of both punctuated *and* gradualistic changes.

It would be unreasonable to expect a single mode of evolutionary change to characterize all lineages at all times. Clearly, the rigid Darwinian belief that evolutionary change must *always* be gradual in nature is improbable. Abundant evidence shows that, in many evolutionary lines, this has not been the case. Punctuated equilibrium with change brought about by rapid speciation is another mode that now must be considered. Regarding human evolution, it is still not clear which of the two models (gradualism or punctuational-ism)—or a combination of the two—provides the best approximation. As we will be discussing in great detail later in this text (Chapters 14–18), speciation was probably never very common within our particular evolutionary line since the time we diverged from other primates. As such, our lineage may not be typical, and is thus not a good example on which to base general theories of evolutionary change.

Microevolution and Macroevolution   As we have seen, gene frequencies over the span of a few generations seem to change in gradual fashion. Thus, microevolution, as conceived within the modern synthesis, conforms to the gradualistic model.

We have also seen that long-term changes (i.e., macroevolution) are not always gradual in nature; in fact, in many evolutionary lineages, the rate of change is manifestly sporadic. Are, then, microevolution and macroevolution really quite different phenomena?

While the mechanisms of microevolution and macroevolution may be partially "decoupled," that is not to say that they are unrelated. In fact, speciation can be understood as the result of accumulated genetic changes, particularly when facilitated by geographic isolation. This does not imply that the process is always gradual. Indeed, since processes affecting isolating mechanisms (for instance, mountain building, formation of island chains, etc.) are themselves irregular, we should expect speciation rates to vary as well. Species, once they have formed, are real entities. Categories of higher rank (genera, families, and so on) are merely human abstractions; they do not exist in nature. Populations evolve; species may eventually diverge and, once distinct, can only become more genetically separate. All the rest of evolutionary change is basically an extension of this process.

◇ Review, Genetics and Evolutionary Factors

Starting in Chapter 2 with a discussion of natural selection, we proceeded in Chapter 3 to show the molecular and cellular bases of heredity, and to illustrate in this chapter how such genetic information is passed from individuals in one generation to those in the next. It may seem that these different levels, molecular, cellular, individual, and populational, are different aspects of evolution, but they are all related and highly integrated in a way that can eventually produce evolutionary change. A step-by-step example will make this clear.

In our earlier discussion of sickle-cell hemoglobin (see p. 73), you will recall that the actual genetic information was coded in the sequence of bases in the DNA molecule. We started out with a situation where everyone in the population has the same hemoglobin type; therefore, initially no variation for this trait exists, and without some source of new variation evolution is not possible. How does this gene change? We have seen that a substitution of a single base in the DNA sequence can alter the code significantly enough to alter the protein product and ultimately the whole phenotype of the individ-

Table 4-1   Levels of Organization in the Evolutionary Process

Evolutionary Factor	Level	Evolutionary Process	Science	Technique of Study
Mutation	DNA	Storage of genetic information; ability to replicate; influences phenotype by production of proteins	Molecular biology	Theoretical: from evidence of spectrophotometry, biochemistry, electron microscopy
Mutation	Chromosomes	A vehicle for packaging and transmitting genetic material (DNA)	Cytogenetics	Light, electron microscope
Recombination (sex cells only)	Cell	The basic unit of life that contains the chromosomes and divides for growth and for production of sex cells	Cytogenetics	Light, electron microscope
Natural selection	Organism	The unit, composed of cells, that reproduces and which we observe for phenotypic traits	Genetics	Visual, biochemical
Drift, migration	Population	A group of interbreeding organisms. We look at changes in gene frequencies between generations; it is the population that evolves	Population genetics	Statistical

ual. Imagine that, several generations ago, just such an "accident" occurred in a single individual. For this mutated gene to be passed on to succeeding offspring, the gametes must carry the alteration. Any new mutation, therefore, must be transmitted during sex cell formation.

Once the mutation has occurred in the DNA, it will be packaged into chromosomes, and these chromosomes in turn will assort during meiosis to be passed to offspring. The results of this process are seen by looking at phenotypes (traits) in individuals, and the mode of inheritance is described simply by Mendel's principle of segregation. In other words, if our initial individual has a mutation in only one paired allele on a set of homologous chromosomes, there will be a 50% chance of passing this chromosome (with the new mutation) to an offspring.

Thus far, we have seen what a gene is, how it can change, and how it is passed on to offspring. But what does all this activity have to do with *evolution*? To repeat an earlier definition, evolution is a change in gene frequency in a *population* from one generation to the next. The key point here is that we are now looking at a whole group of individuals, a population, and it is the population that will or will not change over time.

We know whether gene frequencies have changed in a population where sickle-cell anemia is found by ascertaining the percentage of individuals with the sickling allele (Hb^S) versus those with the normal allele (Hb^A). If the relative proportions of these alleles alter with time, evolution has occurred. In addition to discovering that evolution has occurred, it is important to know why. Several possibilities arise. First, we know that the only way the new allele Hb^S could have arisen is by mutation, and we have shown how this process might happen in a single individual. This change, however, is not yet really an evolutionary one, for in a relatively large population the alteration of one individual's genes will not significantly alter gene frequencies of the entire population. Somehow, this new allele must spread in the population.

One way this could happen is in a small population where mutations in one of just a few individuals and their offspring may indeed alter the overall frequency quite quickly. This case would be representative of genetic drift. As discussed above, drift acts in small populations where random factors may cause significant changes in gene frequency. Due to small population size, there is not likely to be a balance of factors affecting individual survival, reproduction, etc. Consequently, some alleles may be completely removed from the population, while others may become established as the only allele present at that particular locus (and are said to be "fixed" in the population).

In the course of human evolution, drift may have played a significant role at times, but long-term evolutionary trends could only have been sustained by *natural selection*. The way this has worked in the past and still operates today (as in sickle-cell) is through differential reproduction. That is, individuals who carry a particular gene produce more offspring. By producing more offspring than other individuals with alternative alleles, such individuals cause the frequency of the new allele in the population to increase slowly in proportion from generation to generation. When this process is compounded over hundreds of generations for numerous genes, the result is significant evolutionary change.

◇ Summary

We have now come full circle. We started our discussions of evolution (Chapter 2) talking about populations and, indeed, this is where evolution occurs. But populations are made up of individual organisms, organisms are made up of cells, cells contain chromosomes, and chromosomes are composed of DNA. Understanding the actual mechanics of the evolutionary process comes *only* from considering all these various levels of organization.

◇ Questions for Review

1. Explain why botanists before Mendel failed to solve the problem of heredity.
2. How was Mendel's approach to the study of heredity different from those of his predecessors?
3. Why did the pea plant suit Mendel's experimental model?
4. What is the significance of contrasting characters?
5. What are the differences between P_1 and F_1 crosses?
6. Explain the principle of segregation.
7. Explain the principle of independent assortment.
8. How do these principles help us to understand evolution?
9. How is a mutation—a change in the DNA genetic code—transmitted into an actual physical change? Use sickle-cell hemoglobin as an example.
10. What are the major elements of the modern synthesis? What earlier dispute did the modern synthesis resolve?

11. Discuss two recent challenges to the modern synthetic theory of evolution.
12. Assume a mutation occurs in a small human population. What does this mutation have to do with evolution? In other words, how might gene frequencies be changed?

◇ Suggested Further Reading

(Many of the reading suggestions for Chapter 3 are recommended for this chapter as well.)

Bodmer, W. F. and L. L. Cavalli-Sforza. *Genetics, Evolution, and Man*, San Francisco: W. H. Freeman & Co., 1976.

An excellent authoritative discussion of the hereditary mechanism and specific genetic traits seen in human populations. With its emphasis on medical genetics, this work is a superb source for premedical students.

Cavalli-Sforza, L. L. *Elements of Human Genetics* (2nd Ed.), Menlo Park, Ca.: W. A. Benjamin, Inc., 1977.

A relatively simplified discussion of genetics that should be useful for an introductory student who wishes to refer to an expanded discussion of genetics. Recommended especially for students with little or no background in biology.

Dunn, Leslie C. and Th. Dobzhansky. *Heredity, Race and Society*, New York: Mentor Books, 1953.

Although somewhat dated, this work is still a classic for the subjects mentioned in the title. The book is written in layman's language and aimed at the beginning student. (Try a used book store if otherwise unavailable.)

Eldredge, Niles and Joel Cracraft. *Phylogenetic Patterns and the Evolutionary Process*, New York: Columbia University Press, 1980.

A straightforward introduction to cladistic analysis in evolution written in a non-technical fashion. Also included is a thought-provoking discussion of microevolution and macroevolution.

Hartl, Daniel L. *Human Genetics*, New York: Harper and Row, 1983.

An excellent, up-to-date textbook on human genetics, primarily for premedical courses. Detailed and well written. Recommended for advanced students.

Novitski, Edward. *Human Genetics* (2nd Ed.), New York: Macmillan Publishing Co., 1982.

Like dozens of other texts, this book is designed for a college level course in human genetics. Recommended for moderately advanced students. It is quite well written.

Scheinfeld, Amram. *The Basic Facts of Human Heredity*, New York: Washington Square Press, Inc., 1961.

Written in simple language, this book provides excellent background for students lacking knowledge in biology or genetics. In addition to basic genetics, there is also material on "racial" characteristics such as pigment, hair-form, etc.

Sciulli, Paul W. *Introduction to Mendelian Genetics and Gene Action*, Minneapolis: Burgess Publishing Co., 1978.

This short paperback (sixty-three pages) is intended as a supplement for students who feel their background in genetics is inadequate. The bulk of the book deals with Mendel's laws and molecular genetics.

Evolution in Modern Populations

CONTENTS

Twins have been objects of fascination for centuries. In our own time biologists, anthropologists, and psychologists have tested, bled, and probed them in the hope of better understanding hereditary/environmental influences on humankind. There are two varieties of twins: (1) fraternal—those conceived from two separate eggs (dizygotic)—related to each other to the same degree as siblings; and (2) identical—those conceived from a single egg (monozygotic)—and genetically identical to each other (a naturally formed clone).

Identical twins, especially, have attracted considerable interest from researchers in recent years. In an ongoing project at the University of Minnesota scientists are reuniting pairs of identical twins who were separated soon after birth. For an exhaustive week psychological, physical, and physiological testing is performed on these twins. Thus far, upwards of fifteen pairs have been studied, but the researchers hope to increase the sample to fifty pairs before completely publishing their results.

Despite this understandable caution of the researchers, a few "tidbits" of their data have leaked into the popular press. In particular, several remarkable behavioral similarities between twins have been observed. For example, the "Jim" twins (both named Jim) had been adopted into different middle-class Ohio families

Chromosome 1

Wife-naming loci. These are obviously different loci, perhaps acting in a time-sequential developmental pathway. Earlier in life the "Linda" allele is switched on, but later in life is supplanted by the "Betty" allele.

Chromosome 2

Son-naming locus. There are at least two alleles, James and Alan — which are codominant (Alan/Allan allele seems to have some slight variability in expression)

Chromosome 12

Dog-naming locus (Only one allele here; are the twins homozygous for "Toy"?)

Chromosome 15

Occupational preference locus; expression of sheriff allele must be dominant. If the brothers are heterozygous (other genes coding for ballet dancing?), these other alleles are most obviously recessive.

at four weeks of age and had not met again until they were 39 years old. A string of amazing coincidences, however, marked both their lives. Both had law enforcement training and worked part-time as deputy sheriffs; both married and divorced women named Linda and remarried women named Betty; both had dogs named Toy; both had sons respectively named James Allan and James Alan; both drove Chevrolets; and both vacationed on exactly the same stretch of beach in Florida!

The Minnesota scientists have not yet commented comprehensively on

Chromosome 19

Vacation preference loci. This must be a very large region of several closely-linked genes. A particular combination of genes coding for region of country, state, beach preference, and individual locality are being expressed identically in the two brothers.

Chromosome 20

Automobile preference locus. In American populations this is highly polymorphic — with many fairly common alleles (Buick, Ford, Plymouth, and, of course, Chevrolet). Recent massive migration has introduced an entirely new array from different populations (Datsun, Toyota, Volkswagon, etc.).

Chromosome 21

Gullibility locus. Obviously homozygous for anyone who believes this chromosome map.

these observations, but the popular press has made a great fuss over them. What exactly is being intimated? These twins were separated soon after birth, so similarities are strictly coincidental. Or are they *genetic?*

Coincidental circumstances are not all that intriguing, so the usual implication is that the similarities are somehow genetic in origin. How could this be? What genetic mechanism could possibly underlie these behavioral observations?

As we discussed earlier in the text, great progress has been made in re-cent years identifying particular genetic loci on individual chromosomes. If these behaviors seen in twins are genetic, it stands to reason that some genetic loci should exert specific influence. Perhaps in the not-too-distant future we may be able to find particular gene combinations that influence these behavioral patterns. A map of the Jim Twins' chromosomes might be imagined as shown in the accompanying figure.

SOURCE:

Holden, Constance, "Twins Reunited," *Science 80*, 1:55–59, (1980).

◇ Introduction

The process of evolution acts on all species, including *Homo sapiens*. In modern populations, recombination and mutation continue to produce variation, the fuel for natural selection. Can we then see these ongoing evolutionary processes at work in human populations?

Today we find only one species of hominid represented by 4½ billion individuals widely scattered over most of the earth. However, the distribution is by no means even, since both geographical and social factors influence where people live, how many individuals collect to form a group, and who mates with whom. Moreover, there are obvious visible physical differences as well as numerous biochemically detectable variations among groups of modern human beings. How do we explain these differences?

The branch of physical anthropology dealing with modern human variation is centrally concerned with answering such questions in *evolutionary* terms. As discussed throughout this text, physical anthropology is the study of human evolution, not just in the past but the present as well.

Human populations continue to be influenced by the forces of evolution, continue to adapt to their biocultural environments, and thus continue to evolve. Investigating the dynamic processes that mold our species is the domain of **microevolutionary** studies. From such work we not only develop a fuller understanding of why *Homo sapiens* varies from area to area (as well as from individual to individual), but we also can more fully comprehend how *Homo sapiens* came to be in the first place.

The following chapters tell the tale of a long succession of hominid fossils, but these are simply luckily preserved bits and pieces of earlier populations who were subject to the same dynamic evolutionary processes influencing humankind today. Over the space of several tens of thousands or millions of years small microevolutionary changes can be modified into **macroevolutionary** ones. Given the process of punctuated equilibrium (see pp. 108–111), macroevolutionary changes of course do not translate *completely* from microevolutionary changes.

In this chapter we will discuss some of the ways modern human beings vary from one another as well as the evolutionary interpretations of this variation. Bear in mind that the continuing saga of humankind evolving is but the most recent chapter in a very long tale indeed.

◇ The Population

The unit of evolutionary change is the *population*, which we defined in Chapter 4 as a group of interbreeding individuals. More precisely, the population is the group within which one is most likely to find a mate. As such, a population is a genetic unit marked by a degree of genetic relatedness and sharing in a common **gene pool**. In theory, this concept is not particularly difficult. Picture a kind of giant blender into which every generation's genes are mixed (by recombination). What comes out the next generation is a direct product of the genes going into the pool, which in turn is a direct result of who is mating with whom.

In practice, however, isolating and describing actual human populations is a sticky business. The largest population of *Homo sapiens* that can be described is the entire species, all of whose members are at least potentially capable of interbreeding (but are incapable of interbreeding, fertilely, with members of other species). Our species is thus a *genetically closed system* (human/nonhuman hybrids are not known). The problem arises not in describing who potentially can interbreed, but in isolating exactly the patterns of those individuals who are doing so.

Factors that determine mate choice are geographical, ecological, and social. If individuals are isolated into groups in an Alpine village or on an island in the middle of the Pacific, there is not much possibility of finding a mate outside the immediate vicinity. Such **breeding isolates** are fairly easily defined and are a favorite target of microevolutionary studies. Geography plays a dominant role within these isolates through influencing the range of available mates. But even within these limits cultural prescriptions can still play a powerful part in deciding who is most proper among those potentially available.

Since social factors usually play such a crucial role in human mating patterns, a cultural anthropologist is an invaluable aid to population studies in helping to decipher what is going on in the complex world of real human beings. Additional complexity (sometimes found in other cultures) is introduced when biological and social paternity are defined differently. Moreover, the physical anthropologist must always be aware of the possibility of illegitimacy; whereas marriage patterns are useful indicators, what we are ultimately after is the pattern of actual matings.

Smaller human population segments within the species are defined as groups with relative degrees of **endogamy** (marrying/mating within the group). They are not, however, totally closed systems. Migration often occurs between groups, and individuals may choose mates from distant localities. The advent of modern means of rapid transportation has greatly accelerated **exogamy** (marrying/mating outside the group), a process which always has characterized human society to some degree.

It is obvious that most humans today are not clearly members of specific breeding populations as they would be in breeding isolates. Inhabitants of large cities may seem to be members of a single population, but actually within the city borders social, ethnic, and religious boundaries crosscut in a complex fashion to form smaller population groupings. In addition to being members of these highly open local population segments, we are simultaneously members of overlapping gradations of larger populations—the immediate geographical region (a metropolitan area or perhaps a whole state), a region of the country, the whole nation, the Western world, and ultimately again, the whole species.

In all this confusion how do anthropologists locate a population? Since most humans today live in densely inhabited, socially complex areas, a population must be isolated arbitrarily. Usually the population is defined with a particular research goal in mind.

Microevolutionary
Small-scale evolutionary changes (shifts in gene frequency) that can occur over the span of just a few generations and can, therefore, be seen in living populations.

Macroevolutionary
Large-scale evolutionary changes that require many hundreds of generations and can, therefore, usually be only seen paleontologically (that is, in the fossil record).

Gene pool
The total complement of genes in a population.

Breeding isolates
Populations geographically (and/or socially) separate and, therefore, easy to define.

Endogamy
Mating within a social unit.

Exogamy
Mating outside a social unit.

Hardy-Weinberg equilibrium
The mathematical relationship expressing—under ideal conditions—the predicted distribution of genes in populations; the central theorem of population genetics.

For example, the Jewish inhabitants of New York City form a *partially* closed population defined by socioreligious affiliation—an example of religious endogamy. Certainly, considerable migration occurs both in and out of this group, and degree of genetic relatedness is therefore probably not all that significant. However, for some purposes it is useful to treat this group as a population. The incidence of Tay-Sachs disease (see p. 134) is known to be considerably higher in descendants of Eastern European Jewish populations than in other groups. In order to ascertain the frequency of this tragic disease in New York City and to target prevention programs, it is useful to contrast parents of Jewish and non-Jewish heritage. In addition, studies of changes in gene frequency (evolution) in this or any other population can be facilitated in the same manner. Of course, the definition of this population does not refer directly to the socioreligious makeup of this group, but only to a degree of shared relationship dating back to earlier generations in Eastern Europe. For that matter, the whole Jewish "population" could be broken down further into smaller populations, those with Eastern European ancestry and all others. In fact, this has been done, and Jewish descendants of non-Eastern European populations have about the same low incidence of Tay-Sachs disease as that of the overall United States population.

Several other social/ethnic subpopulations are treated in this manner for particular microevolutionary studies. Please remember that none of these populations is a completely closed system and, indeed, most of them are quite open.

◇ Population Genetics

Once the microevolutionist has isolated a specific human population, the next step is to ascertain what evolutionary forces, if any, are operating on this group. In order to determine whether evolution is taking place, we measure gene frequencies for specific traits and compare the observed frequencies with a set predicted by a mathematical model: the **Hardy-Weinberg equilibrium** equation. This model provides us with a baseline set of evolutionary expectations under *known* conditions.

More precisely, Hardy-Weinberg equilibrium postulates a set of conditions where *no* evolution occurs. In other words, none of the forces of evolution is acting, and all genes have an equal chance of recombining in each generation (that is, random mating of individuals):

1. The *population* is assumed to be *infinitely large* (therefore no sampling error—*no random genetic drift*)
2. *No mutation* (no new genes are added by molecular alterations within gametes)
3. *No migration* (no new genes added by influx from outside our target population)
4. *No selection* (genes have no differential advantage relative to reproductive success)
5. *Random mating* (panmixia—no bias in who mates with whom; any female is assumed to have an equal chance of mating with any male)

If all these conditions are satisfied, gene frequencies will not change (that is, no evolution will take place) and a permanent equilibrium will be maintained as long as these conditions prevail. An evolutionary "barometer" is thus provided which may be used as a standard against which actual circumstances are compared. Similar to the way a typical barometer is standardized under known temperature and altitude conditions, the Hardy-Weinberg equilibrium is standardized under known evolutionary conditions.

The relationship of the gene frequencies in populations to Mendelian genotypic proportions is a straightforward extension of simple Mendelian genetics. In fact, in 1903, soon after the rediscovery of Mendel's work, the American geneticist and animal breeder W. E. Castle developed a model showing the relationship of genes to populations. However, Castle felt the results were so obvious that he did not take the trouble to state unequivocally the conditions for genetic equilibrium nor did he actively push for acceptance of his views.

However, within just five years the English mathematician G. H. Hardy (1877–1947) and the German physician W. Weinberg (1862–1937) independently reached the same conclusion, and their formulation eventually won wide acceptance. The mathematical relationship of gene and genotype frequencies in populations is therefore usually called the Hardy-Weinberg formula or "law."

Interestingly, we note once again that the science of genetics was advancing intellectually along a broad international front. At the turn of the century three scientists in three different countries discovered Mendel's initial contribution and realized its implications. Within just another eight years the application of these principles to populations was again independently reached in three separate countries, and the discipline of population genetics was born.

Under the idealized conditions of Hardy-Weinberg equilibrium no new alleles are added and no alleles removed from the population. Morever, every allele for a given locus has an equal chance of combining with any other allele at that locus within the gene pool.

The simplest situation applicable to a microevolutionary study is a genetic trait that follows a simple Mendelian pattern and has only two alleles (A, a). As you recall from earlier discussions, there are then only three possible genotypes: AA, Aa, aa. Proportions of these genotypes (AA:Aa:aa) are a function of the allele frequencies themselves (percentage of A; percentage of a). In order to provide uniformity for all genetic loci, a standard notation is employed to refer to these frequencies:

Gene frequency of first allele (A) = p (p = dominant allele—if there is dominance)

Gene frequency of second allele (a) = q (q = recessive allele)

Since in this case there are only two alleles, their combined total frequency must represent all possibilities. In other words:

$$p + q = 1 \text{ (unity; that is, 100\% of alleles in the gene pool)}$$

(Proportion of A alleles) (Proportion of a alleles)

To ascertain the expected proportions of genotypes, we simply compute the chances of the alleles combining with one another into all possible combinations. Remember, they all have an equal chance of combining and no new alleles are being added.

These probabilities are a direct function of the gene frequency of the two alleles. The chances of all possible combinations occurring randomly can be simply shown as:

$$
\begin{array}{r}
p + q \\
\times \quad p + q \\
\hline
pq + q^2 \\
p^2 + \quad pq \\
\hline
p^2 + 2pq + q^2
\end{array}
$$

(Mathematically, this is known as a binomial expansion)

What we have just calculated is simply:

Allele Combination	Genotype Produced	Expected Proportion in Population
Chances of:		
A combining with A	AA	$p \times p = p^2$
Chances of:		
A combining with a a combining with A	Aa	$\begin{array}{l} p \times q \\ p \times q \end{array} = 2pq$
Chances of:		
a combining with a	aa	$q \times q = q^2$
Proportions of		
genotypes AA: Aa: aa p^2 2pq q^2		

where p = frequency of dominant allele and q = frequency of recessive allele in a population.

CALCULATING GENE FREQUENCIES: AN EXAMPLE

How microevolutionists use the Hardy-Weinberg formula is best demonstrated through an example. Let us return to the classroom "population" of 100 individuals we discussed in Chapter 4. Now that you are aware of the precise definition of a breeding population you can see that a classroom group does not meet the key prerequisite of social and/or geographic isolation. But once again let us assume that it does and thus represents a good biological population.

In addition, we will once again use the MN blood group locus as the gene to be measured. You will recall that this gene produces a blood group antigen—similar to ABO—located on red blood cells. We therefore can fairly quickly ascertain everyone's phenotype by taking blood samples and observing reactions with specially prepared antisera. From the phenotypes we can then directly calculate the gene frequencies. So let us proceed.

◇ Box 5-1   Calculating Gene Frequencies in a Hypothetical Population

Observed Data:

GENOTYPE	NUMBER OF INDIVIDUALS*	PERCENTAGE	NUMBER OF ALLELES	
			M	N
MM	40	(40%)	80	
MN	40	(40%)	40	40
NN	20	(20%)		40
Totals	100	(100%)	120 + 80 = 200	
		Proportion:	.6 + .4 = 1	

Observed allele frequencies:

M = .6(p)
          p + q should = 1 (and they do)
N = .4(q)

Expected Frequencies   What are the predicted genotype proportions if genetic equilibrium (no evolution) applies to our population? We simply apply the Hardy-Weinberg formula:

$p^2 + 2pq + q^2$

p^2	= (.6) × (.6)	=	.36
2pq	= 2(.6)(.4) = 2(.24)	=	.48
q^2	= (.4) × (.4)	=	.16
Total			1.00

There are only three possible genotypes (MM:MN:NN) so the total of the relative proportions should equal 1.00; as you can see, they do.

How do these expected frequencies compare with the observed frequencies in our population?

	Expected Frequency	Observed Frequency
MM	.36	.40
MN	.48	.40
NN	.16	.20

*Each individual has two alleles; thus a person who is MM contributes two M alleles to the total gene pool. A person who is MN contributes one M and one N. One hundred individuals, then, have 200 alleles for the MN locus.

All 100 individuals are tested and the results are shown in Box 5-1. Although the match between observed and expected frequencies is not perfect, it is close enough statistically to satisfy equilibrium conditions. Since our population is not a large one, sampling may easily account for the small observed deviations. Our population is therefore probably in equilibrium (that is, it is not evolving).

◇ Evolution in Modern Populations

DEVIATIONS FROM HARDY-WEINBERG EXPECTATIONS

Our small population is seemingly in evolutionary equilibrium, but in many modern human populations we can find examples where this is not the case. In other words, we can discover populations that are evolving.

What causes evolution in human populations? Evolution operates in our species through the same factors as in any other species: mutation, migration, genetic drift, and natural selection. In addition, nonrandom mating—while it does not change gene frequencies by itself—may create the conditions for evolutionary change.

MUTATION

Mutation is one way that new alleles can be introduced into a population. Effects on any given gene should be minor, however, since mutation rates at a single locus are quite low (estimated at about 100 per million gametes per generation). In fact, because mutation occurs so infrequently at any particular locus it would rarely have any significant effect on Hardy-Weinberg equilibrium comparisons. Certainly, mutations occur every generation, but unless we sample a huge number of subjects we are unlikely to detect any effects.

However, because we each have many genes (estimated between 100,000 and 2.5 million), we all possess numerous mutations that have appeared over recent generations. Most of these are not expressed in the phenotypes and are "hidden" as recessive genes. (See Chapter 4 for a discussion of the mechanics of inheritance for such traits.) This situation is fortunate because most mutations are likely to be harmful, just as any random altering would mess up a finely tuned machine. One of the more common variant alleles (which probably arose by a mutation) found in white American populations produces a genetic disease called PKU (phenylketonuria). When a recessive allele is inherited in double dose, it leads to a metabolic block in the conversion of the amino acid phenylalanine into the amino acid tyrosine. As a result, phenylalanine accumulates and eventually leads in an unknown manner to severe mental retardation. It is estimated that about 500 babies per year are born in the United States with this disease and another 1,000 individuals newly appear with the mutation in heterozygous and therefore unexpressed form.

Fortunately, this disease can be effectively treated if diagnosed early and the infant is placed on a special diet. As of 1976, thirty-seven states required a compulsory test of all newborns for PKU. Such testing is part of a **genetic screening** program which in many states has been extended to include several other genetic diseases. In addition, subcommittees within the United States Congress have considered adoption of a national genetic screening program requiring mandatory testing of newborns for PKU and other inherited diseases.

Another fairly common variant allele leads to what is called *familial hypercholesterolemia*. Here, however, individuals can be affected when they carry the genes in *single* dose (that is, a dominant gene). (See p. 88 for a discussion of dominance.) In individuals who carry this gene the risk of coronary disease is five times that of the general population (Kane et al., 1981). In fact, for untreated heterozygotes, males often display cardiovascular problems before age 50, and females before they reach 60. Those unfortunate individuals who inherit the defective allele in double dose usually develop severe problems in childhood, and death commonly occurs before age 20.

This genetic condition is particularly significant, as it occurs frequently: $\frac{1}{500}$ individuals have the heterozygous condition and $\frac{1}{3,500}$ display the more severe homozygous condition. The situation, however, is not hopeless. Drug therapy is making progress in alleviating some of the potentially disastrous effects.

Another kind of mutation that affects several loci simultaneously is caused by chromosomal rearrangements. These result mainly from mistakes during meiosis when chromosomes come apart, attach incorrectly, and lose pieces, or when distribution to the gametes is unequal (producing sperm or egg cells with too many or too few chromosomes).

Some chromosomal aberrations are probably quite common. Because they are so deleterious, most of them remain undetected as very early and unnoticed spontaneous abortions. Lerner and Libby estimate that between 25 and 50% of all **spontaneous abortions**—totaling several hundred thousand per year in the United States—are due to chromosomal rearrangements (1976, p. 285).

NONRANDOM MATING

Although sexual recombination does not itself alter *gene frequencies*, any consistent bias in mating patterns can alter the *genotypic proportions*. By affecting the combination frequencies of genotypes, nonrandom mating causes deviations from Hardy-Weinberg expectations of the proportions: p^2, $2pq$, and q^2. It, therefore, sets the stage for action of other evolutionary factors, particularly natural selection.

One such variety of nonrandom mating is called **positive assortative mating**, and occurs when individuals of like phenotype mate more often than expected by random mating predictions. Because individuals with like phenotypes are also similar to some degree in genotypes as well, the result of positive assortative mating increases the amount of homozygosity in the population and reduces heterozygosity (p^2 and q^2 greater than expected; $2pq$ less than expected).

The most consistent mating biases documented in the United States deal with stature and IQ. Of course both these traits are influenced by environment as well as heredity (see Box 5-4), and observed correlations also reflect socioeconomic status (generating like environments). Eye color in a Swedish population and hair color in a Lapp group have shown significant degrees of correlation among married couples. Moreover, several studies in the United States and Britain have shown significant correlations for several other phenotypic traits (see Table 5-1).

The other side of the coin of positive assortative mating is **negative assortative mating** or mating with an individual who is phenotypically dissimilar. Theoretically, if this occurs more than expected by random mating predictions, it should increase the amount of heterozygosity in the population while correspondingly reducing homozygosity. Curt Stern (1973) has suggested that red-headed persons marry each other less often than would be expected, but this has not been substantiated; nor has any other instance of negative assortative mating been conclusively demonstrated in human populations.

Genetic screening
Testing programs to ascertain individuals with genetic diseases or carriers of deleterious genes.

Spontaneous abortion
Occurs naturally and is not induced by artificial means. Geneticists now suspect a large proportion, perhaps a majority, of conceptions end this way.

Positive assortative mating
A type of nonrandom mating in which individuals of like-phenotype mate more often than predicted under random mating conditions.

Negative assortative mating
A type of nonrandom mating in which individuals of unlike-phenotype mate more often than predicted under random mating conditions.

Table 5-1 Positive Correlations between Husbands and Wives in the United States and Britain

IQ	.47
Ear lobe length*	.40
Waist circumference	.38
Stature	.28
Hip circumference	.22
Weight	.21
Neck circumference	.20

*This is not to say that prospective mates go around measuring or even paying particular attention to each other's ear lobes. Correlation for this trait may be residual of assortative mating for overall size or for certain head dimensions. It also may mean absolutely nothing. If one measures enough traits, statistically some will appear associated strictly on the basis of chance.

Source: Lerner and Libby, 1976, p. 369.

◇ Box 5-2   Inbreeding Coefficients

Inbreeding coefficient (F) measures the increased chance of inheriting an allele in double dose (homozygous) from a common ancestor. For an entire population, estimates are for the average amount of inbreeding ($\propto$).

Values of 0	= no inbreeding—mates unrelated
Values of 1.0	= total inbreeding—on average mating with identical twin (all members of population = genetically identical)

Values of .5	= on the average mating with full sib
Values of .063	= on the average mating with first cousin
Values of .016	= on the average mating with second cousin

A third type of nonrandom mating in humans which can disrupt expected genotype proportions occurs when relatives mate more often than expected. Called **inbreeding** or consanguinity, such mating will increase the amount of homozygosity, since relatives who share close ancestors will more than likely also share similar genes.

All societies have some sort of incest taboo banning matings between very close blood relatives such as parent/child or brother/sister. Therefore, such matings usually occur less frequently than predicted under random mating conditions (which postulates that these matings, like all others, have a certain probability of occurring).

Whether incest is prohibited strictly by social proscriptions or whether biological factors also interact to condition against such behavior has long been a topic of heated debate among anthropologists. For numerous social, economic, and ecological reasons exogamy is an advantageous strategy for hunting-gathering bands. Moreover, selective pressures may also play a part, since highly inbred offspring have a greater chance of expressing a genetic disorder and thereby lowering their reproductive fitness. In addition, inbreeding reduces variability among offspring thereby also potentially reducing reproductive success (Murray, 1980). In this regard, an interesting note is that incest avoidance is widespread among vertebrates (Parker, 1976). Moreover, detailed studies of free-ranging chimpanzees indicate they avoid incestuous matings within their family group (Goodall, 1968b), and savanna baboon males consistently establish themselves, and then mate, within groups other than the one in which they were reared (Parker, 1976). Apparently, both biological factors also interact to condition against such behavior has long cultural factors have interacted during hominid evolution to produce this universal behavior pattern among contemporary societies.

Conversely, in certain societies inbreeding among fairly close relations such as cousins is actively encouraged or is unavoidable due to the small number of potential mates available. A famous case of the latter situation occurred in Pitcairn Island among descendants of the mutineers of the *Bounty* and their

Tahitian wives. Only a small founding population (23 or 24) initially settled this tiny island, and this group was still further reduced by intragroup violence. As a result, young men and women of the ensuing generations usually chose spouses with whom they shared several common ancestors. On Pitcairn there was no choice but to partake in considerable inbreeding.

On the other hand, there are some areas where, although inbreeding is avoidable, it is still actively encouraged. In some parts of Japan, among certain social classes, first cousin marriages make up almost 10% of all marriages, and in the Andhra Pradesh area of India, among certain castes, uncle/niece unions also make up about 10% of marriages.

It must be kept in mind, however, that such considerable inbreeding is the exception rather than the rule among human populations. In fact, most groups seem to work very hard at maintaining exogamy, actively promoting exchange of marriage partners between groups. For example, many polar Eskimo groups live in small geographically separate isolates. Despite this, through socially established rules, very little inbreeding occurs.

As a general rule, then, most human populations do not inbreed if they can at all help it. A measure of the relative degree of inbreeding, the inbreeding coefficient of .04 (4 per hundred), which is between the average for first and group so far studied. The highest inbreeding coefficient yet observed is among Samaritans of Israel and Jordan, a small socially isolated religious sect today consisting of only about 350 individuals. This group has an average inbreeding coefficient of .04 (4 per hundred) which is between the average for first and second cousin matings. The vast majority of human groups, however, are characterized by values of less than .001 (1 per 1,000).

Inbreeding has important medical consequences in addition to its influence on genetic equilibrium. When relatives mate, their offspring have increased probability of inheriting an allele in homozygous dose. Many potentially deleterious genes normally "masked" in heterozygous carriers may be expressed in offspring of consanguineous matings and thereby "exposed" to the action of natural selection. Among offspring of first cousin matings in the United States the risk of congenital disorders is 2.3 times greater than it is for the overall population. Matings between especially close relatives—incest—often lead to multiple congenital defects.

Migration (Gene Flow)

A factor more significant than nonrandom mating in human evolutionary history is *migration* (also known as *gene flow*), the exchange of genes between populations. Population movements (particularly in the last 500 years) have reached enormous proportions, and few breeding isolates remain. It should not, however, be assumed that significant population movements did not occur prior to modern times. Our hunting and gathering ancestors throughout the Paleolithic probably lived in small groups which were both mobile and flexible in membership. Early farmers also were probably highly mobile, moving from area to area as the land wore out. Intensive, highly sedentary agricultural communities came later, but even then significant migration was still possible. From the Near East, one of the early farming centers, populations

Inbreeding
A type of nonrandom mating in which relatives mate more often than predicted under random mating conditions.

spread very gradually in a "creeping occupation of Europe, India, and northern and eastern Africa" (Bodmer and Cavalli-Sforza, 1976, p. 563).

Migration between populations has been a consistent feature of hominid evolution since the first dispersal of our genus, and explains why speciation has not occurred in human evolution for at least the last million years.

An interesting application of how migration influences microevolutionary changes in modern human populations is seen in the admixture of parental groups among American blacks over the last three centuries. Blacks in the United States are largely of West African descent, but there has also been considerable influx of genes from European stock. By measuring gene frequencies for specific genetic loci (for example, Rh and Duffy blood groups—discussed subsequently) we can estimate the amount of migration: European genes → Afro-American gene pool. By using different methods, migration rate estimates have varied considerably, but one of the most comprehensive studies has suggested for northern cities a figure close to 20% (22% in Oakland, California but much lower in the deep South: 4% in Charleston, South Carolina and 11% in rural Georgia).

It would be a misconception to think that migration can occur only through such large-scale movements of whole groups. In fact, significant alterations in genotype frequencies can come about through long-term patterns of mate selection. If exchange of mates were consistently in one direction over a long period of time, ultimately genotype frequencies would be altered. Due to demographic, economic, and social pressures, individuals must often choose mates from outside the immediate vicinity. For example, exogamy rates (percent marrying outside village or parish) for English villages were 40% in the early seventeenth century, increasing to about 64% in the last fifty years.

Transportation factors play a crucial role in determining the potential radius for finding mates. Limited to walking or use of the horse, transportation ranges were restricted to around 10 miles. With the advent and spread of railway transportation into the rural areas of England in the nineteenth century, a dramatic increase in mean marital distance* (20–30 miles) is seen. Today, highly efficient mechanized forms of transportation make the potential radius of mate choice worldwide, but actual patterns are obviously somewhat more restricted. For example, data from Ann Arbor, Michigan, indicate marital distance of about 160 miles, which obviously includes a tremendous number of potential marriage partners.

Genetic Drift

As discussed earlier, random genetic drift is the chance factor in evolution and is hence tied to population size. More important than overall population size, drift is directly related to the size of the *effective breeding population*, those individuals actually producing offspring. Since other individuals are not contributing to the gene pool of the next generation, they are not considered. Thus, the effective breeding population is usually considerably smaller than the overall population, usually representing about one-third of the total.

An example of a particular kind of drift seen in modern populations is

*The average distance between husband's and wife's birthplaces.

called the **founder effect**, or after its formulator, the *Sewall Wright effect*. Founder effect operates when only an exceedingly small group of individuals contributes genes to the next generation, a kind of genetic bottleneck. This phenomenon can occur when a small migrant band of "founders" colonizes a new and separate area away from the parent group. Small founding populations may also be left as remnants when famine, plague, or war ravage a normally larger group. Actually, each generation is the founder of all succeeding generations in any population.

The cases of founder effect producing noticeable microevolutionary changes are necessarily in small groups. For example, several small and isolated Alpine villages have unusually high frequencies of albinism, and an island in the South Atlantic, Tristan da Cunha, has unusually high frequencies of an hereditary eye disorder. First settled in 1817 by one Scottish family, this isolated island's native inhabitants include only descendants of this one family and a few other individuals, such as shipwrecked sailors. All in all, only about two dozen individuals constituted the founding population of this island. In 1961, the 264 inhabitants were evacuated because of an impending volcanic eruption and removed to England. Extensive medical tests were performed, which revealed four individuals with the very rare recessive disease, retinitis pigmentosa. The gene frequency for the allele causing this disease was abnormally high in this population* and a considerable portion of the group were no doubt carriers.

How did this circumstance come about? Apparently, just by chance, one of the initial founders carried the gene in heterozygous form and later passed it on to offspring who through inbreeding occasionally produced affected individuals. Since so few individuals founded this population, the fact that one carried the allele for this disease made a disproportionate contribution to succeeding generations (Bodmer and Cavalli-Sforza, 1976).

Genetic drift has probably played an important role in human evolution, influencing genetic changes in small isolated groups. From studies of recent hunter-gatherers in Australia the range of potential mates is limited to the linguistic tribe usually consisting of around 500 members. Hence, the effective breeding population is less than 170, allowing for significant effects of genetic drift, particularly if drought, disease, etc., should reduce the population even further.

Much insight concerning the evolutionary factors that have acted in the past can be gained by understanding how such factors continue to operate on human populations today. In small populations like Pitcairn or Tristan da Cunha, drift plays a major evolutionary role. Fairly sudden fluctuations in gene frequency can and do occur owing to the small population size. Likewise, throughout a good deal of human evolution (at least the last 4–5 m.y.) hominids probably lived in small groups, and drift, therefore, would have had significant impact.

Joseph Birdsell, a physical anthropologist who has worked extensively in Australia, has postulated general models for human evolution from his Australian data. He suggests population size during most of the Pleistocene was

Founder effect
Also called the *Sewall Wright effect*. A type of genetic drift in which gene frequencies are altered in small populations which are nonrandom samples of larger ones.

---

*See if you can calculate the gene frequencies and the expected percent of carriers in the population. Hint: $q^2 = \frac{1}{264}$.

comparable to the 500 "magic number" seen in Australia. Moreover, when agriculturists became sedentary and isolated in small villages, the effects of drift may have been even greater. Indications of such a phenomenon are still operative in Melanesia, where individuals often spend their entire lives within just a few miles of their birthplace.

While drift has been a factor in human evolution from the start, the effects have been irregular and nondirectional (for drift is *random* in nature). Certainly the pace of evolution could have been accelerated if many small populations became isolated and thus subject to drift. However, by producing populations with varying evolutionary potential, drift only provides fodder for the truly directional force of evolution, natural selection.

NATURAL SELECTION

Over the long run of evolution in hominids or any other organism, the most important factor influencing the direction of evolutionary change is natural selection.

Controlled observations on several experimental animals and natural populations of quickly reproducing organisms such as bacteria, fruit flies, and moths (industrial melanism, for example—see Chapter 2) have repeatedly

Figure 5-1 The sickle-cell allele distribution in the Old World.

Allele Frequencies of Hb^S Allele

Greater than 0.140	From 0.080 to 0.100	From 0.020 to 0.040
From 0.120 to 0.140	From 0.060 to 0.080	From 0.000 to 0.020
From 0.100 to 0.120	From 0.040 to 0.060	

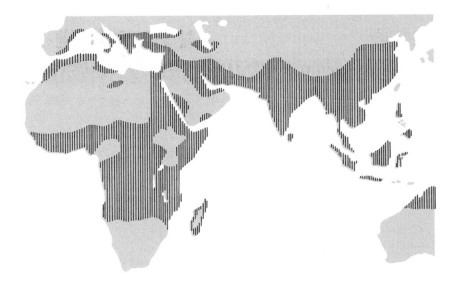

Figure 5-2   Malaria distribution in the Old World.

demonstrated how differential reproductive success eventually leads to adaptive shifts.

Human beings are neither quickly reproducing nor are they amenable to controlled laboratory manipulations. Therefore, unambiguous examples of natural selection in action among contemporary human populations are extremely difficult to demonstrate.

The best documented case deals with the *sickle-cell trait* which, as discussed earlier, is the result of point mutation within the gene producing the hemoglobin beta chain. If inherited in double dose, this gene causes severe problems of anemia, circulatory disturbances, and usually early death. (See Table 5-2.) Even with aggressive medical intervention life expectancy in the United States today is less than twenty years for victims of sickle-cell anemia. Worldwide, sickle-cell anemia causes an estimated 100,000 deaths per year, and in the United States an estimated 40,000–50,000 individuals, mostly of African descent, suffer from this disease.

With such obviously harmful effects it is surprising to find the sickle-cell allele (Hb^s) so frequent in some populations. The highest allele frequencies are found in western and central African populations, reaching levels close to 20%; values are also moderately high in some Greek and Asiatic Indian populations. How do we explain such a phenomenon? Obviously the allele originated from a point mutation, but why did it spread?

The answer lies in yet another kind of disease producing enormous selective pressure. In those areas of the world where Hb^s is found in unusually high frequencies *falciparium malaria* is also found (see Fig. 5-2). Caused by a protozoan parasite (*Plasmodium*), this debilitating infectious disease is transmitted to humans by mosquitoes. In areas that are endemically affected, many individuals suffer sharp declines in reproductive success due to high infant mortality or lowered vitality as adults.

Such a geographic correlation between malarial incidence and sickle-cell distribution is an indirect suggestion of a biological relationship. More positive

Agricultural practices → Mosquitoes spread

Sickle-cell mutation ↑

Mosquitoes spread → Human malaria

Adaptation DDT-resistant strains

DDT spraying

Figure 5-3   Sickle-cell. An evolutionary dynamic system.

Table 5-2   Sickle-Cell Terminology

Sickle-cell allele in single dose:
Hb^{A}Hb^s
= carrier; called the sickle-cell trait (not much affected; functions normally in most environments)
Sickle-cell allele in double dose:
Hb^{s}Hb^s
= sickle-cell disease or sicklemia (very severe effects, usually lethal)

Balanced polymorphism
The maintenance of two or more alleles in a population due to a selective advantage of the heterozygote.

evidence comes from experimental work done by the British biologist A. C. Allison. Volunteers from the Luo population of East Africa with known genotypes were injected with malaria-causing agents. After a short time the results showed that heterozygous carriers were much more resistant to malarial infection compared to homozygous "normals." (Hb^{A}Hb^A: 15 injected—14 had malarial parasites; Hb^{A}Hb^S: 15 injected—only 2 had malarial parasites.) Carriers resist malarial infection because their red blood cells provide a less adequate environment for the *Plasmodium* parasite. Approximately 40% of a carrier's hemoglobin is Hb^S; some of their red blood cells should therefore show tendencies to sickle. Under normal circumstances only about 5% would be expected to sickle, but when infected by the parasite this is greatly increased. The presence of the parasite apparently stimulates greater sickling, disrupting the cell membrane, releasing intracellular potassium and thereby killing the host cell (*and* the parasite—before it can reproduce itself) (Friedman and Trager, 1981).

The sickle-cell trait apparently has not always been an important genetic factor in human populations. In fact, human cultural modification of environments provided the initial stimulus. Before agriculture humans rarely, if ever, lived close to mosquito breeding areas. With the development and spread to Africa of slash-and-burn agricultural practices, perhaps in just the last two thousand years, penetration and clearing of tropical rain forests occurred. As a result, open stagnant pools provided fertile mosquito breeding areas in close proximity to human settlements.

Malaria, for the first time, now struck human populations with its full impact, and as a selective force it was powerful indeed. No doubt, humans attempted to adjust culturally to these circumstances, and numerous biological adaptations also probably came into play. The sickle-cell trait is one of these, and the experimental evidence just cited demonstrates its biological value as a malarial resistant. However, there is a definite cost involved with such an adaptation. While carriers have more malarial resistance and presumably higher reproductive success, some of their offspring will be lost through the genetic disease, sickle-cell anemia. So there is a counterbalancing of selective forces with an advantage for carriers *only* in malarial environments.

Following World War II extensive DDT sprayings by the World Health Organization began systematically to wipe out mosquito breeding areas in the tropics. As would be expected, malaria decreased sharply, and also as expected Hb^S frequencies were apparently on the decline. The intertwined story of human cultural practices, mosquitoes, malarial parasites, and the sickle-cell trait is still not finished. Thirty years of DDT spraying killed many mosquitoes, but selection is acting on these insect populations also. Due to the tremendous amount of genetic diversity among insects as well as their short generation span, several DDT-resistant strains have arisen and spread over the last few years. As a result, malaria is again on the upswing, with several hundred thousand new cases reported in India, Africa, and Central America.

Recent advances in recombinant DNA technology have provided evidence suggesting the sickle-cell mutation arose independently in different parts of the world. The appearance of the sickle-cell mutation in West Africa was

◇ Box 5-3   Other Genetic Traits Possibly Associated with Malaria

In many parts of the world malaria has been an extremely important selective factor over the last several thousand years. Sickle-cell is probably only one of several inherited traits that have spread because they provide resistance. It must be noted, however, that none of these other traits have been documented as well as sickle-cell nor has there been conclusive experimental evidence comparable to the work of A. C. Allison. Concordance between higher incidence of these genetic traits with geographic areas exhibiting high malarial infection provides *indirect* evidence of possible association in the following:

1. Hemoglobin C—allele of the same gene producing Hb^A and Hb^s; distributed in Africa mainly in the west but a few pockets of high incidence in the south. Hb^c is found in many populations where Hb^s is also present. Possibly this allele provides resistance to another strain of malaria and *both* alleles occur in populations exposed to multiple varieties of malaria (Weiss and Mann, 1981).

2. Thalassemia—a general term for several inherited disorders. Rather than a defect in the hemoglobin molecule itself, thalassemias involve a block in hemoglobin production (absence of, or deficient production of, the alpha or beta globin molecules). There are probably a variety of genetic mechanisms (mutations) that can lead to thalassemia, including point mutations, deletions, and disruption of gene regulation. For example, one variety of thalassemia (β+) is caused by inadequate production of mRNA; consequently, protein synthesis of the beta hemoglobin chain is disrupted. The most harmful expression of this disease syndrome is seen in homozygous dose, producing severe anemia. In heterozygous dose there are little, if

any, harmful effects. Geographic evidence suggests a possible connection between thalassemia and malaria—with the highest frequencies of the disease found among populations around the Mediterranean. The severe form of beta-thalassemia (in homozygous dose called *Cooley's anemia*) affects as many as 1% of newborns in some parts of southern Europe. Tentative experimental evidence suggests that in heterozygous dose thalassemia—like sickle-cell—provides an inadequate environment for malarial infestation and proliferation (Friedman and Trager, 1981).

3. G-6-PD—glucose-6-phosphate dehydrogenase—an enzyme in red blood cells; individuals with a genetically caused deficiency do not produce this enzyme. The gene for this trait is on the X-chromosome (that is, X-linked) and some populations are up to 60% deficient (Bodmer and Cavalli-Sforza, 1976). First discovered by adverse reactions with severe anemia when individuals were given certain antimalarial drugs, anemia can also result from exposure to some foods (fava beans, for example). Distribution is again correlated with malarial areas, but apparently different alleles cause the deficiency in southern Europe from those in sub-Saharan Africa. At the biochemical level G-6-PD deficiency may act like thalassemia, producing a cellular environment not conducive to malarial infection. When exposed to certain drugs or foods (particularly fava beans), individuals with G-6-PD deficiency may have a severe anemic reaction. It is possible, however, that heterozygous carriers may actually increase malarial resistance by eating such foods—potentially an extremely important biocultural interaction (Friedman and Trager, 1981).

apparently of different origin from that in other parts of Africa or in Asia (Kan and Dozy, 1980).

A genetic trait like sickle-cell that provides a reproductive advantage in certain circumstances is a clear example of natural selection in action among human populations. The precise evolutionary mechanism in the sickle-cell example is usually called a **balanced polymorphism**.

A genetic trait is called a polymorphism "when two or more alleles at a given genetic locus occur with appreciable frequencies in a population" (Bodmer and Cavalli-Sforza, 1976, p. 308). How much is "appreciable" is a fairly arbitrary judgment, but is usually placed at around 1%.

In other words, if a population is sampled for a particular genetic trait and frequencies of more than one allele are higher than 1%, the trait is polymorphic.

The limit of 1% is an attempt to control for mutation effects, which should always be adding new alleles much less frequently than our 1% level (for example, mutations rates are probably more like $\frac{1}{10,000}$—or lower). So when a trait like sickle-cell is found in some populations in frequencies approaching 10%, this is clearly polymorphic. It is higher than can be accounted for by mutation *alone* and thus demands a fuller evolutionary explanation. In this case, the additional mechanism is natural selection.

This brings us back to the other part of the term, balanced polymorphism. By "balanced," we are referring to the interaction of selection pressures operating in malarial environments. Some individuals (mainly $Hb^A Hb^A$) will be removed by the infectious disease malaria and some ($Hb^S Hb^S$) will be eliminated by the inherited disease, sickle-cell anemia. Those with the highest fitness (that is, reproductive success) are the heterozygotes ($Hb^A Hb^S$), but what alleles do they carry? Obviously they are passing *both* Hb^A and Hb^S to offspring, and that explains why both alleles are maintained in the population—at least as long as malaria continues to be a selective factor.

◇ Interaction of Evolutionary Forces

Human populations usually evolve not simply through action of single evolutionary agents, but by a complex interplay of several forces. For example, the partially isolated population comprised of people of Eastern European Jewish descent previously discussed illustrates these processes. Tay-Sachs disease, a lethal degenerative disease of the nervous system, is caused by a mutant recessive allele. In descendants of Eastern European Jews the incidence of this disease is almost 100 times more frequent at $\frac{1}{4,000}$ ($q \cong .02$) compared to only $\frac{1}{500,000}$ ($q = .0014$) for the general United States population.

Where did this allele come from, and why is it so much more frequent in some populations, particularly considering its deleterious effects in the homozygote? Apparently, it first arose as a simple mutation and possibly spread initially through random genetic drift factors, such as founder effects in small migratory populations fleeing the persecutions of the Crusades six to seven centuries ago. Another possibility is that the allele spread because of some selective advantage of the heterozygote (that is, a balanced polymorphism), and some very tentative data suggest a possible greater resistance to pulmonary tuberculosis.

In any case, effects of nonrandom mating today certainly increase the likelihood of this allele being expressed in its lethal homozygous form. In fairly small socially isolated groups, individuals who mate may well share some fairly recent common ancestors. By inbreeding they have more chance of passing on the deleterious allele in double dose to an offspring.

What has probably happened with Tay-Sachs is an interaction of evolutionary factors. Mutation was the starting point, and further spread probably occurred through the combined effects of genetic drift and nonrandom mating. Moreover, possible intermittent selection effects to yet unknown factors in particular environments may also have acted to alter gene frequencies. A form of selection still obviously operates against the homozygous recessive, an inevitably lethal condition by age 5.

We can see that evolution in modern populations is a complex phenomenon. Simple models like the Hardy-Weinberg equilibrium give us a means of measuring the overall evolutionary effects, but are not really sufficient in sorting out the specific factors involved.

◇ Human Polymorphisms

Human geneticists study some human polymorphisms because, as we have seen in cases like sickle-cell and Tay-Sachs, these traits can be expressed as tragic, deadly diseases.

Other genetic polymorphisms are also medically important due to incompatibilities and clinical complications during pregnancies or following transfusions and organ transplants. In addition, there are several other genetic polymorphisms (mainly studied through biochemical analysis) that are interesting because they vary significantly from one human population to another. As we have seen, a genetic trait can be a polymorphism *only* if more than one allele exists in appreciable frequency. Therefore, new alleles must have somehow increased in frequency from initially very low mutation rates to those recognizable as "appreciable." In other words, some *additional* evolutionary factor must have been at work. Clearly, then, the understanding of human genetic polymorphisms demands evolutionary explanations. As students of human evolution, physical anthropologists use these polymorphisms as their principal tool to both measure and understand the dynamics of evolution in modern populations.

In particular, they employ *simple* genetic polymorphisms whose genetic mechanisms are known. Such *complex traits* as stature, IQ, etc. (see Box 5-4) are no doubt partly genetic, but we do not know which or even how many alleles are involved. On the other hand, simple polymorphisms are controlled by one genetic locus, and the different alleles are directly ascertainable at the phenotypic level.

By employing such simple polymorphisms, and by comparing gene frequencies in different human populations, we can reconstruct the evolutionary events that relate these groups with one another.

◇ Polymorphisms Found in Human Blood

In addition to the hemoglobin and other polymorphisms possibly related to malaria, there are a great many other polymorphisms known in human blood. Because samples can be easily obtained and transported, blood has long been the favorite tissue for studying human polymorphisms. Consequently, we know a good deal concerning a wide variety of polymorphisms in red

---

◇ Box 5-4   Complex Traits

Traits such as stature, weight, IQ, body proportions, skin color, and so on are controlled by several genetic loci and are thus termed **polygenic** traits. For simple, one-gene (Mendelian) traits the distribution of phenotypes is discontinuous with no overlap. For example, the gene for hemoglobin (beta chain) in some populations has two alleles (Hb^A, Hb^S) that combine to produce three and *only* three genotypes. These genotypes are in turn reflected in the phenotypes, so for a population we can ascertain the phenotypes of all individuals in a completely clearcut fashion.*

As can be seen, no overlap exists between phenotypes; in other words, they are discontinuous. All individuals are specifically one of the three phenotypes, and there is an observable *qualitative* difference in their hemoglobin.

On the other hand, polygenic traits are influenced by several loci, each perhaps with several alleles. The possible number of genotypes and corresponding phenotypes is therefore very large, and the gradation between them appears to overlap. In addition, the differences between individual phenotypes is further obscured by environ-

*In this case Hb^A and Hb^S are codominant, so there is no difficulty in directly relating the observed phenotypes to their underlying genotypes. However, in traits where there is *dominance*, it may be difficult or impossible to differentiate all the genotypes (in other words, AA and Aa would *appear*—at least as far as we can tell— phenotypically identical).

mental influence which, in traits like weight (due to excess food, dieting, starvation, etc.) or IQ (due to early schooling, family size, etc.), can greatly affect phenotypic expression. Because the relationship between the actual genotype and the eventual phenotypic expression in polygenic traits is so complexly determined, phenotypic variation can only be handled in a statistical manner. Contrary to simple traits, their distribution appears *continuous* with only *quantitative* phenotypic differences observable.

Since both genetic and environmental variability influence the expression of polygenic traits, it is often an interesting venture to try to partition this variation. As we have noted before, such an undertaking raises the age-old nature/nurture argument.

For domestic animals or crops, such a study can provide important economic information. For example, if a dairy farmer wants to improve the milk yield of his cows, should he invest his capital in better food or in upgrading his stock (buying a prize bull or sperm for artificial insemination)? Such a question can be answered by a *heritability* study, which will partition the variance between genetic and environmental components of this polygenic trait (milk yield in cows). In animals the methodology is fairly straightforward, where controls are possible such as deliberately randomizing environments or breeding-in genetic homogeneity (accomplished in

---

Polygenic
Poly: many
genic: genes
Traits controlled by several loci; for example, stature, weight, skin color. Also called complex traits.

blood cells, white blood cells, and in the blood serum. Other tissues are probably just as variable, but as you will see, most of our current information concerns traits found in human blood.

BLOOD GROUP ANTIGEN SYSTEMS

ABO   With the first use of transfusions as a medical practice around the turn of the century, serious problems were immediately recognized. Some patients had severe reactions, such as agglutination (clumping) of their blood cells, kidney failure, and even death. Very soon after transfusions became common, the underlying cause of these incompatibilities was shown by Karl Landsteiner, in 1900, to be due to a genetic trait. This trait, called the ABO blood group system, is expressed phenotypically in individuals as antigens* located on

*Antigens are large macromolecules, usually proteins, that react specifically with antibodies.

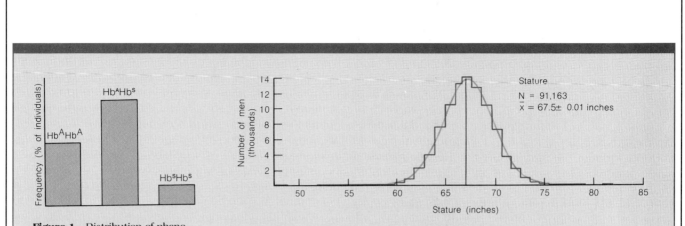

Figure 1 Distribution of phenotypes for adult hemoglobin (beta chain). Example: population living in malarial area.

Figure 2 Distribution of stature. The data shown are from a population of over 90,000 English military recruits (1939). The mean ($\overline{X}$) is shown by the solid line. Data from Martin, *Physique of Young Adult Males*, HMSO, 1949.

laboratory animals through successive close inbreeding).

However, humans present a much stickier problem, since we cannot artificially manipulate human beings in laboratories. We must therefore attack the genetic/environmental issue somewhat indirectly. Human heritability studies are accomplished through comparative studies of twins: monozygotic and dizygotic. From such investigations we can obtain crude approximations of genetic vs. environmental influence on the variance of polygenic traits in human groups (samples). However, many complexities remain that are difficult or impossible to control. For example, twins are not necessarily representative of whole populations, and even more significantly, studies done on one population under special environmental conditions do not apply to other populations.

The tremendous public furor over the genetic environmental contributions to IQ and variability in scores among human groups dramatizes many of the problems in our still very crude attempts at understanding polygenic inheritance in human beings. (See p. 203.)

the surface of their red blood cells. The blood group (that is, what antigens a person has) is directly determined by his/her genotype for the ABO locus. The complications sometimes resulting from transfusions are due to *antigen-antibody* reactions. In a manner still largely a mystery, the body can recognize foreign antigens (proteins) and combat their invasion by producing specific antibodies that deactivate the foreign substances. Such an *immune system* is normally beneficial, for it is the basis of fighting infections caused by a foreign bacteria or virus. (See pp. 177–178.)

Usually antibodies are produced "on the spot" when foreign antigens are introduced. However, in the case of ABO, naturally occurring antibodies are already present in the blood serum at birth. Actually, no antibodies are probably "natural," although they may be (as in ABO) stimulated early in fetal life. The genotypes, phenotypes, and antibody reactions in the ABO system are shown in Table 5-3.

The ABO system is most interesting from an anthropological perspective

Monozygotic

mono: one

zygote: fertilized egg

Twins derived from one zygote, genetically identical. Differences between the twins are caused solely by the environment.

Dizygotic

di: two

zygote: fertilized egg

Twins derived from two zygotes, genetically related the same as any full sibs, and differences between them are caused both by the environment and genetic variation.

Cline
A gradual change in distribution of gene frequencies over space.

because the frequencies of the three alleles (A, B, O) vary tremendously among human populations. As the distribution maps indicate (see Fig. 5-4), A or B is only rarely found in frequencies greater than 50%; usually frequencies for these two alleles are considerably below this figure. Most human groups, however, are polymorphic for all three alleles. Occasionally, as in native South American Indians, frequencies of O reach 100%, and this allele is said to be "fixed" in this population. Indeed, in most native New World populations, O is at least 80% and is usually considerably higher. Unusually high frequencies of O are also found in northern Australia, and some islands off the coast show frequencies of 90% and higher. Since these frequencies are considerably greater than presumably closely related mainland populations, founder effect is probably the evolutionary agent responsible.

In general, the lowest values for O found in the world are in eastern Europe and central Asia.

As you might expect, frequencies for A and B can only be relatively higher where O tends to be lower. Generally, B is the rarest of the three alleles and, except for Eskimos, it is completely absent in the pre-Columbian New World. Moreover, the allele has apparently been introduced into Australia only in recent times.

The B allele reaches its highest peak in Eurasia, where its distribution is the inverse of O. Values up to 20% and occasionally slightly higher are found in a broad area in central Asia, western Siberia, and central Mongolia. The highest reported frequencies for B are found in the Himalaya area, reaching a peak of 25–30%.

Generally, the frequency of B declines gradually in populations the further westward they are in Eurasia. Such a gradual distribution of allele frequencies over space is a good example of what is called a **cline**.

The A allele has two interesting peaks, one among Blackfoot Indians and surrounding groups of North America and the other distributed over almost the entire Australian continent. With frequencies greater than 50%, the Blackfoot display the highest frequencies of A anywhere in the world. Certainly they are divergent from other North American groups, who all have very high

Table 5-3   The ABO Blood Group System

Individual's Genotype	Phenotype (Blood Group)	Antibodies in Serum	Clumping* will Occur when Exposed (e.g., through Transfusion) to the Following Kinds of Blood:
OO	O	anti-A and anti-B	A, B, AB
AA AO	A	anti-B	B, AB
BB BO	B	anti-A	A, AB
AB	AB	neither	none

*In ABO antigen-antibody reactions, clumping, or agglutination, of cells occurs with some destruction of cells. In other immune responses, such as Rh, more complete destruction of cells takes place.

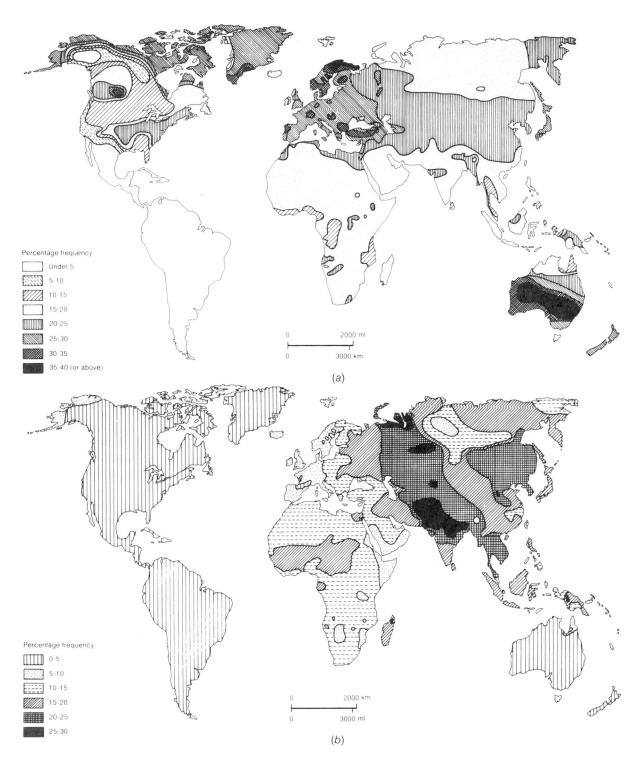

Figure 5-4 (a) ABO blood group system. Distribution of the A allele in the indigenous populations of the world. (b) ABO blood group system. Distribution of the B allele in the indigenous populations of the world. (After Mourant et al., 1976.)

frequencies of O (and, therefore, low frequencies of A). How did A increase so much among this one tribe and its close neighbors compared to surrounding populations? Possibly drift (founder effect) is the answer; possibly some unknown selective factor. No one knows.

In Australia, except for the northern part, frequencies of A are generally high—particularly in central Australia, where frequencies are 40% or higher. One tribe has especially high frequencies of A (53%), significantly higher than any surrounding group. Once again, is founder effect responsible? Over the rest of Australia, A frequencies are fairly even in distribution and are gradually decreasing as populations become further removed from the center of the continent.

We must point out that distributions of alleles for a single genetic trait like ABO do not conclusively demonstrate genetic relationships between populations. For example, the North American Blackfoot and central Australian Mandjiljara have similar frequencies of A, but are obviously not closely related. On the other hand, in South Africa, San have lower B frequencies than Hottentots, with whom they share fairly close genetic ties. In order to understand *patterns* of population relationships, it is absolutely necessary to consider gene frequency distributions for several traits simultaneously.

Why do frequencies of the ABO alleles vary so much in different populations? In some cases, as with the islands off northern Australia and perhaps with the Blackfoot, drift may be the key factor. However, the clinal distribution of alleles (as B in Eurasia; A in Australia) indicates selection may also be playing an important role, for the regularity in the frequency distributions is thought to mirror gradual changes in environments.

If, in fact, selection is operating, what are the specific factors involved? Unfortunately, unlike sickle-cell, there is not as yet any proven association between ABO frequencies and *any* selective agent (such as various diseases, etc.) There are, however, some suggestive clues. For example, A individuals have significantly more stomach cancer and pernicious anemia, while O individuals have more gastric and duodenal ulcers. Such chronic diseases as these are not at all that common, and they probably do not affect reproductive success very much, since they occur so late in life.

On the other hand, infectious diseases (as already shown for malaria) are potentially selective factors of enormous significance. Some interesting clinal association between ABO frequencies and incidence of smallpox, tuberculosis, syphilis, bubonic plague, and leprosy have been suggested. Moreover, it has also been suggested that O individuals are more attractive to mosquitoes and are thus bitten more often than A, B, or AB individuals (Wood et al., 1972). Here, too, could be an important influencing factor for an infectious disease, since many—malaria, yellow fever, typhus, etc.—are transmitted by insects (Brues, 1977). As yet none of these associations is well substantiated. Consequently, the evolutionary factors influencing the distribution of ABO alleles are still largely a mystery.

Rh   Another group of antigens found on red blood cells is called the *Rh system*, named after rhesus monkeys that initially provided the source of red blood cells to make antiserum. Discovered in 1940 by Wiener and Landsteiner (a full forty years after the latter's discovery of ABO!), this antiserum was then tested in a large sample of white Americans, in which 85% reacted positively.

The individuals showing such a positive agglutination reaction are usually called Rh positive (Rh$^+$) and those whose blood does not agglutinate with the antiserum are called Rh negative (Rh$^-$). These standardized designations refer to an apparently simple two-allele system with DD and Dd as Rh$^+$ and the recessive dd as Rh$^-$.

Clinically, the Rh factor—like ABO—can also lead to serious complications. However, the greatest problem is not so much incompatibilities following transfusions as those between a mother and her developing fetus. (See Box 5-5.) For most significant medical applications, Rh$^+$ compared to Rh$^-$ is accounted for by the three genotypes noted above (DD, Dd, dd). However, the actual genetics of the Rh system are a good deal more complex than explained by just two alleles at one locus. The famous English population geneticist Sir R. A. Fisher suggested that the Rh system is actually three closely linked loci with at least two alleles each (C and c, D and d, E and e).

The fact that the various antigens of the Rh system occur much more frequently only in a few combinations is of great interest to anthropologists. Of all the possible combinations in Fisher's three-locus system (eight of them), only three are commonly found. These eight combinations are called *haplotypes*, and their standard designations according to Fisher, with the common ones in boldface, are:

CDE   **CDe**   **cDE**   cDe   **cde**   Cde   cdE   CdE

The precise genetics of the Rh system remain a mystery. An alternative hypothesis to Fisher's three-locus system was suggested by Weiner and postulates one locus with at least eight alleles.

In either hypothesis there are numerous *possible* gene combinations; what is interesting is that only a minority of these are actually found in human populations. In a very large Swedish study (sample greater than 8,000) nine combinations (out of forty-five possibilities) were found in frequencies exceeding 1% (Heiken and Rasmuson, 1966).

The distribution of the various allele combinations within the Rh system (which may be pictured as large genes) varies considerably among human populations. Generally Rh$^-$ (d) is quite high in European groups, averaging around 40%. Of those Europeans who are Rh$^-$, the vast majority (more than 95%) have the haplotype cde. African populations also have a fair amount of polymorphism at the D locus, with frequencies of Rh$^-$ centering around 25%. American Indians and Australians, on the other hand, are almost 100% Rh$^+$.

An evolutionary explanation is demanded to account for this polymorphism. Why is Rh$^-$ so high only in certain populations, particularly those in Europe? Due to mother-fetus incompatibilities (see Box 5-5) heterozygotes (Dd) should be selected against. Theoretically then, whichever allele starts out in a population with a lower frequency should be gradually selected out. In all human populations except the Basques of the Pyrenees mountain area between Spain and France (where d = 53%), Rh$^-$ is lower in frequency than

◇ Box 5-5   Mother-Fetus Incompatibilities

A mother-fetus incompatibility occurs when the system of the mother is immunized by cells from a fetus and forms antibodies which then raise problems for that fetus, or future ones.

For the Rh trait, complications occur only when the mother is Rh⁻ (dd) and the father Rh⁺ (DD or Dd). Actually, the other loci (C, E) can also cause incompatibilities, but 95% of the problems are due to the D locus.

European populations are the most polymorphic for Rh, and about 13% of all matings are at risk. Not all those at risk, however, run into problems. Only about 6% of those potentially in danger have any complications. With new preventative treatment this figure can be expected to decline even further.

The problem of incompatibility arises only if the mother is Rh⁻ and her fetus is Rh⁺. Usually there are no serious effects in the first pregnancy, for the mother's system has not been immunized. Transfer along the placental boundary does not generally include blood cells, except in the case of rupture. Ruptures, however, do occur normally at birth so that fetal blood gets into the mother's system, stimulating the production of antibodies. Such antibodies do not occur naturally as in the ABO system, but they are produced "on the spot" quite quickly. About 70% of all Rh⁻ people have the capability of producing significant amounts of these antibodies, and it requires only one drop of Rh⁺ blood to stimulate the process!

When the next pregnancy occurs, transfer of the antibodies from the mother's system takes place across the placental boundary into the fetus. Here is the real problem: the anti-Rh⁺ antibodies react with the fetal blood, causing cell destruction. Consequently, the fetus will be born with a severe malady called *hemolytic disease of the newborn*, which produces severe anemia with accompanying "oxygen starvation." Because of the lack of oxygen,

Figure 1   Rh incompatibility matings.

such newborns are sometimes called "blue babies." In recent decades, doctors, prepared in advance for such complications, administered massive transfusions and often saved the infant. However, previous to modern medical treatment this disease was probably nearly always fatal. Such incompatibilities were thus fairly common in polymorphic populations and should have exerted a powerful selection pressure.

Quite recently physicians have sought to prevent incompatibilities by administering serum containing anti-Rh⁺ antibodies to women at risk after their first birth. These antibodies quickly destroy any fetal red blood cells as they enter the mother's circulation thereby preventing her from forming her own antibodies. Since the serum given the mother is a passive form of immunization (to her), it will shortly leave her bloodstream. She, therefore, does not produce any long-acting antibodies, and the quite low risk of first pregnancies should not be increased in the future.

It should also be mentioned that mother-fetus incompatibilities result from ABO as well. However, these are considerably rarer than Rh complications, with less than 0.1% of newborn affected. It is possible, though, that some ABO incompatibilities go undetected due to early fetal death.

Rh⁺. In all these populations, then, Rh⁻ theoretically should gradually be eliminated. Apparently, in European and African populations, this phenomenon has not happened. We are not sure why this case should be so, but a possible, totally unconfirmed, suggestion is that the Dd heterozygote has some sort of reproductive advantage later in life (another balanced polymorphism?).

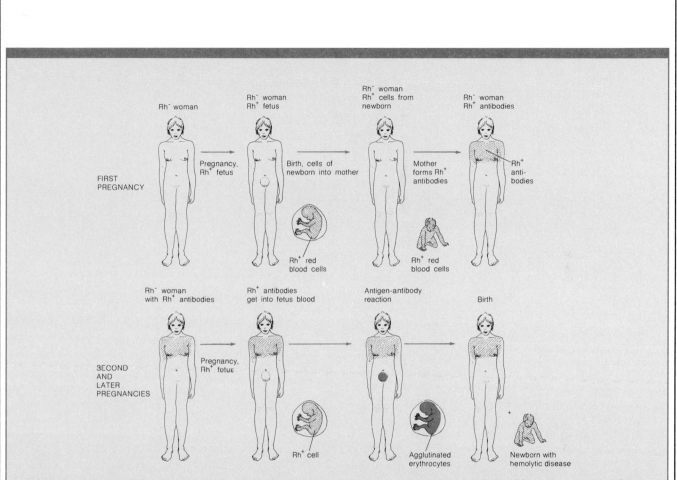

Figure 2   Rh incompatibility and hemolytic disease of the newborn. The series of events during first and later pregnancies. (After Novitski, 1977.)

A very interesting relationship appears to exist between Rh and ABO incompatibilities. Surprisingly, if the fetus is *both* ABO and RH incompatible with the mother, the effects are less than if the incompatibility were for only one trait. ABO incompatibility seems to buffer the potentially very serious effects of Rh immunization. How this occurs is still unknown, but possibly the naturally occurring anti-A and/or anti-B antibodies coat and inactivate incoming cells, thus preventing them from stimulating the Rh immune response in the mother's system.

OTHER RED BLOOD CELL ANTIGEN SYSTEMS

MN   The pattern of inheritance of the MN blood group that we have referred to a number of times is very straightforward and is thus a favorite tool in population genetics research. There are three genotypes—MM, MN, NN—all clearly ascertainable at the phenotypic level using antisera obtained from

Table 5-4 Other Blood Group Systems Used in Human Microevolutionary Studies

Major Systems	Number of Known Antigens
P	3
Lutheran	2
Kell-Cellano	5
Lewis	2
Duffy	2
Kidd	2
Diego	1
Auberger	1
Xg (sex-linked)	1
Dombrock	1
Stolzfus	1

Source: Lerner and Libby, 1976, p. 354.

rabbits. Clinically, no observable complications arise due to transfusions or mother-fetus incompatibilities; the MN system is anthropologically important because of its variable distribution among human populations.

Almost all human populations are polymorphic (that is, having both M and N in "appreciable" frequencies), but the relative frequency of the two alleles varies tremendously. In some areas of Australia, M is as low as 2% contrasted with many areas of the New World, where frequencies exceed 90%, even 100% in some areas. The allele M is also found in quite high frequency in Arabia, Siberia, and portions of Southeast Asia.

In addition to ABO, Rh, and MN, there are several other polymorphic red blood cell antigen systems. While not clinically significant like ABO or Rh, many of these are important for anthropological studies of population variation. Table 5-4 lists the currently known major antigen systems of human red blood cells.

POLYMORPHISMS IN WHITE BLOOD CELLS

An important polymorphic trait called the HLA system has recently been discovered on some white blood cells (lymphocytes). Of great medical importance, HLA affects histocompatibility or recognition and rejection of foreign tissues—the reason skin grafts and organ transplants are usually rejected. Genetically, the HLA system is exceedingly complex, and researchers are still discovering further subtleties within it. There are at least five closely linked loci on chromosome number six, making up the HLA system; presumptive evidence exists for at least three additional loci. Taken together, there are already almost 100 antigens known within the system, with a potential of at least 30,000,000 different genotypes (Amos and Kostyu, 1980). By far, this is the most polymorphic of any known human polymorphic system.

The component loci of the HLA system function together as a kind of "supergene." In addition to the components of the HLA loci themselves, many other components affecting immune response are known to exist in the same region of chromosome number six. Altogether, the whole system is called the *major histocompatibility complex* (MHC). (See pp. 177–178.)

Since this system has only recently been discovered, the geographic distribution of the various alleles is not yet well known. Some interesting patterns, however, are apparent. For example, Lapps, Sardinians, and Basques show deviations in frequencies of HLA alleles from other European populations, paralleling evidence for ABO, Rh, and MN. In addition, many areas in New Guinea and Australia are quite divergent, possibly suggesting the effects of drift. It is imperative, however, that care be taken in postulating genetic relatedness from restricted polymorphic information. Otherwise, such obviously ridiculous links as some of those proposed from HLA data (for example, Tibetans and Australian aborigines; Eskimos with some New Guineans) would obscure the evolutionary process in human populations (Livingstone, 1980). Since HLA is involved in the superfine detection and deactivation of foreign antigens, selection relative to infectious diseases (particularly those caused by viruses) may also play a significant role in the distribution of HLA alleles.

Evidence is still exceedingly tentative, but some HLA antigens are apparently associated with susceptibility to certain diseases. A disease of the spine called ankylosing spondylitis, the disease multiple sclerosis, and some varieties of hay fever may all result from individuals developing an autoimmune response to their own HLA antigens.

POLYMORPHISMS IN THE BLOOD SERUM

In addition to those found on the red and white blood cells, polymorphisms have also been discovered in the blood serum. The most important of these are the *immunoglobulins* and *haptoglobins.* Immunoglobulins are themselves antibody molecules made of long chains, which apparently have the capacity to change in response to foreign antigens. The best known of the immunoglobulins is called the *Gm system*, composed of several closely linked loci. Alleles for these loci are combined into haplotypes, which are of anthropological interest because of their variable occurrence among human populations. As has been suggested for ABO and HLA, the Gm system perhaps acts as part of the human immune response system and may therefore be distributed relative to particular infectious diseases.

Haptoglobins are serum proteins whose function is to bind with free hemoglobin and transport it to a site where it will be recycled. Haptoglobins are apparently determined by one locus with two common alleles (Hp¹, Hp²)

Figure 5-5 MN blood group system. Distribution of the M allele in the indigenous populations of the world. (After Mourant et al, 1976.)

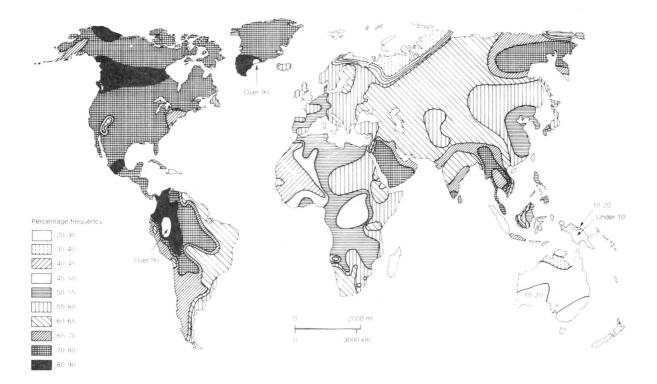

Percentage frequency

	20-30
	30-40
	40-45
	45-50
	50-55
	55-60
	60-65
	65-70
	70-80
	80-90

whose geographic distribution varies considerably. Frequencies of Hp¹ as low as .12 are found among Swedish gypsies, while frequencies as high as .90 are known in parts of Nigeria.

◇ Miscellaneous Polymorphisms

TASTERS AND NONTASTERS

An interesting genetically controlled variation in human populations was discovered by accident in 1931. When the artificially synthesized chemical phenylthiocarbamide (PTC) was dropped in a laboratory, some researchers were able to smell it, while others could not. It was later established that there is a dichotomy in human populations between individuals who can and cannot taste PTC (although tasters vary considerably in sensitivity). The pattern of inheritance appears to follow that of a simple Mendelian trait, with TT and Tt being the tasters and tt the nontasters. In most populations, a majority of individuals are tasters, but the frequency of nontasters varies considerably from as low as 5% in sub-Saharan Africa to as high as 40% in India.

It is an interesting fact that other primates show the PTC polymorphism, suggesting this trait is a long-standing one. What is its function? Obviously selection pressures were not operating in primate evolution relative to a synthesized substance. PTC-tasting variability, then, is probably an expression of a gene coding for taste discrimination for some naturally occurring substance(s). Chemically, PTC is similar to substances found in plants of the mustard family (cabbage, brussels sprouts, etc.), which, if overconsumed, can cause thyroid problems. Perhaps a selective mechanism allowing avoidance of these plants explains this mysterious polymorphism.

In any case, it is easy to postulate that genetically conditioned tasting variability among human populations could be an important adaptation. High taste discrimination could be of great selective advantage particularly to children who, uninitiated into the dietary rules of the group, may easily pick up and eat poisonous wild plants. The fact that tasting ability appears to vary with age may well indicate the importance of taste discrimination in early childhood.

EARWAX

Another puzzling human polymorphism is the genetic variability seen in earwax, or cerumen. Earwax is found in human groups in two basic varieties: (1) yellow, sticky, with a good deal of lipids (fats and fatlike substances); and (2) gray, dry, with less lipids.

Cerumen variation appears to be inherited as a simple Mendelian trait with two alleles (dry = homozygous recessive). Interestingly, frequencies of the two varieties of earwax vary considerably among human populations. In European populations, about 90% of the individuals have the sticky variety, while in northern China only about 4% are of this type.

How do we explain these differences? What selection pressures would act directly on earwax are difficult to imagine. Perhaps earwax variation is an incidental expression of a gene controlling something more adaptively significant. Production of earwax is apparently related to secretion in other glands, particularly the axillary glands under the arms. Odors produced by these glands may have importance for sexual behavior, as recent studies in nonhuman primates suggest. Moreover, human males produce characteristically different scents from females. It might be added that other animals also recognize differences in human scents, as shown by the particular aversion of Southeast Asian water buffaloes to the smell of Europeans.

Cladogram (tree diagram)
A diagrammatic presentation of population relationships using several genetic traits simultaneously.

◇ Human Polymorphisms: Anthropological Applications

All the patterns of variation in the diverse traits we have discussed may seem somewhat confusing. In fact, without the aid of computer technology it is difficult to gain a clear view of what is going on. More than looking at just one trait at a time, anthropologists seek to understand the *pattern* of several polymorphisms simultaneously. From an analysis of these patterns we hope to reconstruct the evolutionary events and population histories that have shaped the development of human variation observable today. In a sense, we are looking for the family tree of *Homo sapiens*.

With the assistance of computer analysis, we can construct trees, or **cladograms**, such as the one shown in Figure 5-6 based on fifteen different genetic polymorphisms (including ABO, MN, Rh, Gm, and HLA). The logic behind such a reconstruction is based on the assumption that populations more closely related should be more similar in gene frequencies. Many traits must be used together, since drift may cause wide and nonsystematic deviations in the pattern of only a few loci.

Anthropological studies of modern evolution seek to make these kinds of reconstructions, but even abundant gene frequency data do not provide clearcut solutions. The form of the tree varies considerably depending on which loci are employed. A vast variety of possible interpretations can be drawn from the same data. As a population geneticist has stated, "Phylogenetic trees are like flower arrangements: it is enough that they are pretty, without asking that they are meaningful" (N. E. Morton, quoted in Livingstone, 1980, p. 33). Still, such an approach is extremely helpful and provides an alternative to the traditional "racial" studies of the history of human population (see Chapter 7).

Yanomama (S. America)
Eskimo
Australian aborigines
New Guinean
Japanese
Chinese
Italian
English
San (Bushmen)
African pygmies

Figure 5-6 Cladogram. A "tree" of relationships among human populations derived from statistical analyses of fifteen human polymorphisms. (After Bodmer and Cavalli-Sforza, 1976.)

◇ Genetic Coadaptation

Throughout this chapter we have discussed evolutionary factors, such as selection and drift acting on single genetic loci. This device is a convenient way to picture evolution, but in natural populations the situation is not so simple. Genes are not floating around as isolated entities, but are "packaged"

Coadaptation
Interaction of genes to produce phenotypes which selection then acts upon.

into individuals who are composites of many (perhaps 100,000?) loci. Selection acts not on the genetic locus itself, but on the whole individual—the combined product of genes and environment.

Moreover, genes interact complexly with one another so that the gene frequency values observed in populations are more intricate than simple totals would indicate. Such interaction at the genotypic level is called **coadaptation**. The kinds of interactions are not simply additive because some genes are better "mixers" than others. For example, ABO and Rh appear to mix well, since incompatibility for both traits is less harmful than for one. (See p. 143.)

From the view of selection, the crucial bottom line is the most fit *total* genotype, and factors influencing this composite are complex and multiple. Consequently, simple evolutionary models cannot cope with such complexity, and computer generated multivariate ("many variables") simulations are required.

However, for the purposes of demonstration and to gain a basic understanding of the evolutionary process, it is still beneficial to conceptualize evolution as acting on single genes. We can then use relatively simple models, such as the Hardy-Weinberg formula, to ascertain crude approximations of evolutionary changes in populations.

◇ Understanding Human Polymorphisms

WHAT MAKES EVOLUTION TICK

From the discussion of numerous human polymorphisms in this chapter (Table 5-5), you may begin to feel there is a great deal of variability in human populations. Indeed there is. Research thus far has but scratched the surface of the vast store of genetic variation in our species. A random sample of various proteins indicates that approximately 28% of all loci in humans are polymorphic, and similar results in other animals suggest such a tremendous store of variation is typical. Where did all this variation come from?

Obviously any new allele must first be introduced through a mutation. But to be polymorphic this allele *must* somehow spread; in other words, gene frequencies must increase well above low mutation rates.

There are several possible explanations of the ways genes have spread in human populations. One possibility that comes to mind immediately concerns balancing selection, as demonstrated so well by the sickle-cell trait. Such a balanced polymorphism fully explains why more than one allele is maintained in relatively high frequency. This mechanism has also been suggested for other human polymorphisms such as ABO, MN, HLA, and so forth, but *none* of these has yet been demonstrated.

Whereas it is true that we rarely know how selection pressures directly influence human variation, we certainly can see the gross effects of natural selection at work. You will recall that selection is defined as "differential reproductive success." Clearly, not all humans reproduce equally, and some

Table 5-5 Human Polymorphisms of Anthropological Interest

In the Blood

Red blood cells:
　Hemoglobins (hemoglobin beta chain: Hb^A, Hb^S, Hb^C)
　G-6-PD and several other enzymes
　Thalassemia loci (suppress production of hemoglobin)

Antigen systems:
　ABO
　Rh
　MN
　Others (Kell, Diego, Duffy, for example)

White blood cells:
　HLA system

Blood serum:
　Immunoglobulins (Gm, for example)
　Haptoglobins

Miscellaneous Polymorphisms
PTC tasting
Cerumen (earwax)

---

of the reasons causing these disparities are genetic. Put quite simply, this is natural selection.

Even in our medically sophisticated culture, many individuals never pass on their genes. Of all the zygotes conceived today, it is estimated that the great majority never make it to reproduction. Approximately 50% are lost before birth, 3% are stillborn, 2% die shortly after birth, and another 3% die before maturity. Of those who survive into adulthood, approximately 20% never marry (and presumably do not mate) and 10% of those who marry are childless (Damon, 1977, p. 111). The cumulative result is that perhaps only about 10–15% of all zygotes conceived ever reproduce! Without modern medicine, the incidence of stillbirths and infant deaths would be considerably higher.

Reproductive rates in human populations are influenced by several complex factors, some biological/ecological, others cultural. Some populations, particularly in "open" environments, have shown high fertility rates, increasing extremely quickly in size. For example, the offspring of the *Bounty* mutineers and Tahitian women on Pitcairn Island increased fourfold in just forty years (Shapiro, 1936). The peopling of the New World may also have involved rapid expansion of an initially fairly small group.

The highest fertility rate known in recent human groups was recorded in the 1930s for Hutterites, an isolated religious sect living in the United States. The *average* number of children born per Hutterite woman was an incredible 10.4. Given the cooperative social structure of this group, sound medical treatment, and so on, this probably represents close to the maximum potential for human groups.

Fertility rates for the overall United States population are much lower, and social factors within the last century have seen them drop significantly further. In the middle of the nineteenth century, the average number of children per woman was somewhat over 5; in the period 1960 to 1964 this figure had fallen to approximately 3.5. Since the 1960s, fertility rates in the United States have shown an even steeper decline. Figures for 1973 indicate a rate of only 1.9, a full 45% drop from a decade before (Damon, 1977).

Obviously, social pressures of an urbanized, technological society have a great deal to do with this decline, but there may be a biological component as well. Are reduced fertility rates partly the product of altered selection pressures in crowded urban environments?

Selection pressures may go a long way toward explaining human polymorphisms, but they do not completely account for all the observed variation. Another significant factor, particularly in small populations, is *genetic drift*. Drift explains the spread of alleles due strictly to chance factors. As we discussed in Chapter 4, many biologists today argue for a primary role for random drift in the development of human variation and thereby dispute the role of selection (see, for example, King and Jukes, 1969).

In all probability, *both* natural selection and genetic drift acted significantly as factors influencing the spread of alleles in human populations. Selection certainly acts on genes causing severe inherited disorders such as sickle-cell anemia, Tay-Sachs, and cystic fibrosis. These are all very deleterious, causing early death. Therefore, the genes causing these diseases should gradually be reduced in frequency (or never have spread initially) in the absence of some special balancing mechanism.

Moreover, selection pressures no doubt also relate to such infectious diseases as malaria, smallpox, typhoid, and plague, which either kill or debilitate much larger numbers of people than the inherited disorders noted in the preceding paragraph. If there are genes that lead to some form of protection (those that build up immunity, for instance) from these infectious diseases, they should spread in human populations. Keep in mind that exposure of human populations to most infectious diseases is greatly influenced by

Figure 5-7 Natural selection today. Perhaps only about 15% of all zygotes conceived ever reproduce.

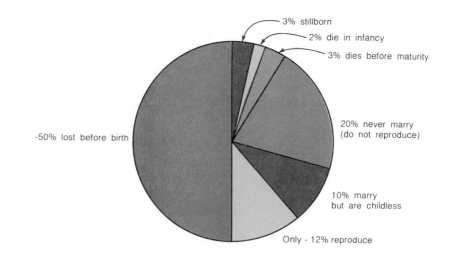

- 3% stillborn
- 2% die in infancy
- 3% dies before maturity
- 20% never marry (do not reproduce)
- 10% marry but are childless
- Only - 12% reproduce
- -50% lost before birth

cultural factors, such as settlement patterns, population size, and prevailing standards of sanitation. (See pp. 175–177.)

Drift too has been significant, particularly when small human populations become isolated—either socially or geographically. During most of human prehistory, hunting-gathering subsistence groups were probably fairly small, but their available range of mates was expanded considerably due to group exogamy and mobility. Drift may have played its most decisive role in early agricultural times when human groups were not only small but sedentary as well.

Today, facilitated by mechanized transportation, migration is breaking down genetic isolates throughout the world. As human groups become less and less isolated, we can expect the evolutionary effects of genetic drift to decrease. That does not mean our species has stopped evolving. On the contrary, our ever-increasing disruption of the earth's ecosystem, our over-crowded cities, our synthesized and often inadequate diets, and the manifold psychological stresses of complex society are all causing new kinds of selection pressures. The question is therefore not whether our species is still evolving, but in which direction, how rapidly, and is it evolving rapidly enough to prevent extinction?

◇ Summary

Physical anthropologists study evolution in human populations using the perspective of *population genetics*. In order to apply the principles of this perspective, we first must isolate actual human *populations*. As we have seen, in geographically and/or socially isolated situations, this process is relatively straightforward, but, in complex societies, it becomes quite arbitrary.

Once populations are defined, we can apply evolutionary models, such as the Hardy-Weinberg formula, to ascertain whether changes in gene frequency (that is, evolution) are occurring. In human populations, gene frequencies change through one or a combination of the four forces of evolution: mutaton, migration, random genetic drift, and natural selection.

The kinds of genetic traits measured in population genetics studies are called *polymorphisms*, traits with more than one allele in appreciable frequency. Some of these traits, particularly the *sickle-cell trait*, have a direct relation to potent selection pressures due to malaria.

In addition to hemoglobin, there are many other polymorphisms found in human blood that are of interest to anthropologists. On the red blood cells are several antigen systems, the most important of which are ABO, Rh, and MN. There are also polymorphisms on the white blood cells (HLA, for instance) and in the blood serum. Finally, two other rather puzzling polymorphisms—PTC-tasting and cerumen (earwax)—are also of anthropological significance.

All these traits vary considerably among modern human populations and thus demand evolutionary explanations. Such explanations are, however, necessarily complex and must account for interaction of genes (*coadaptation*) and interaction of evolutionary forces. For example, mutation is the usual starting point, but further spread of alleles must involve some combination of natural selection, drift, and migration.

We seek to understand human variation, but such an understanding is grounded in basic knowledge of the processes of human evolution.

◇ Questions for Review

1. Why is it so important to study human *populations* in order to understand human evolution?
2. Why is it difficult to isolate actual populations?
3. Under what conditions does the Hardy-Weinberg equilibrium model hold true? If a deviation from expected frequencies is found, what does that suggest?
4. What is nonrandom mating? Cite some suspected examples for human populations and explain how each will affect Hardy-Weinberg predictions.
5. What is meant by migration? Give examples of how migration has affected human evolution.
6. What is genetic drift and why are examples of drift in human populations usually found in small groups?
7. What is a polymorphism? Why are polymorphisms used in evolutionary studies?
8. How does the distribution of the sickle-cell trait indicate the action of natural selection? Describe the specific evolutionary mechanics involved in this "balanced polymorphism."
9. Why are so many polymorphisms known in human blood? Give several examples and discuss why they are of evolutionary interest.
10. Give a detailed account for a hypothetical human population: (a) How a mutation might arise; and (b) how it might then spread.

◇ Suggested Further Reading

Two other introductory physical anthropology texts cover the topics of this chapter in somewhat more depth, but at approximately the same level of difficulty.

Birdsell, Joseph. *Human Evolution* (3rd Ed.), Boston: Houghton Mifflin Co., 1981.
  Excellent review of human microevolution drawing particularly on the author's wide experience in Australia. (See Chaps. 14 through 16, especially.)
Weiss, Mark L. and Alan E. Mann. *Human Biology and Behavior* (3rd Ed.), Boston: Little, Brown, and Co., 1981.
  An up-to-date look at human biology from the perspective of human evolution with a strong emphasis on biocultural factors. (See Chaps. 8 through 12.)

Other, more specialized works:

Bodmer, W. F. and L. L. Cavalli-Sforza, *Genetics, Evolution, and Man*, San Francisco: W. H. Freeman & Co., 1976.

> *This work emphasizes medical genetics. Written by two leading population geneticists, discussions of this topic are authoritative and up-to-date.*

Cavalli-Sforza, L. L. and W. F. Bodmer. *The Genetics of Human Populations*, San Francisco: W. H. Freeman & Co., 1971.

> *The most authoritative recent synthesis of human population genetics. This highly technical work is recommended only for those students wishing to explore the detailed mathematics of population genetics.*

Damon, Albert. *Human Biology and Ecology*, New York: W. W. Norton and Company, 1977.

> *A straightforward approach to understanding human variation, adaptations, and disease from an evolutionary point of view. This work also contains a good review of population genetics.*

Garn, Stanley. *Human Races* (3rd Ed.), Springfield, Ill.: Charles C. Thomas, Inc., 1971.

> *Although concentrating primarily on patterns of geographic variation, this book is an excellent reference for discussions of the various polymorphisms discussed in this chapter.*

Lerner, I. M. and W. J. Libby. *Heredity, Evolution, and Society*, San Francisco: W. H. Freeman & Co., 1976.

> *Well written and up-to-date, this text contains a tremendous amount of information on human genetics and variation. Particularly useful are the discussions of the medical applications of this knowledge.*

Underwood, Jane. *Biocultural Interactions and Human Variation*, Dubuque, Iowa: Wm. C. Brown Co., 1975.

> *Brief but excellent introduction into how evolution is measured in human populations, particularly estimating the effects of natural selection. Especially helpful are the discussions of dietary adaptations and the influence of disease.*

Human Adaptability: Meeting the Challenge of the Environment

CONTENTS

About 12 million Americans have disabilities attributable to heredity, and such traits account for approximately one-third of admissions to pediatric wards. The estimates for 1980 suggested that out of 3½ million newborns in the United States, 96,075 would be afflicted with genetic disorders: 19,075 with chromosomal abnormalities; 35,000 with deleterious Mendelian traits; and 42,000 with multifactorial disorders (Miles, 1980).

Dramatic advances in human genetics, medicine, and the law now allow the detection of certain carriers of recessive mutations and chromosomal aberrations, prenatal diagnosis by amniocentesis, and safe, selective abortion to alleviate the personal and social burdens of the abovementioned hereditary disorders. The U.S. Supreme Court decision in Roe vs. Wade (1973) stipulates that a woman's right to privacy has precedence over the life of any embryo or fetus that is incapable of independent existence outside the womb. Consequently, in the United States, abortion is permitted in the first six months of a pregnancy.

Prenatal diagnosis becomes feasible after the sixteenth week of pregnancy when the uterus has enlarged above the pubic bone (allowing a needle to penetrate the abdominal wall and uterus) and there is sufficient amniotic fluid to withdraw 10 to 20 milliliters in a syringe without endangering the fetus. This procedure is termed *amniocentesis*.

Certain diagnostic tests can be made directly on the fluid, but the tests for most metabolic errors and the analysis of chromosomes require that fetal cells be cultured for a few

*This Issue was contributed by Richard L. Ingraham, Ph.D., Professor of Biology, San Jose State University, San Jose, California.

weeks to obtain a large enough population for making karyotype preparations and biochemical assays. Waiting for results can be disconcerting for participating couples since abortion is a more difficult procedure medically and psychologically the longer it is delayed. However, amniocentesis has proven to be "safe, highly reliable, and extremely accurate" (Golbus, et al, 1979). At present, any identifiable chromosomal anomaly and over 70 metabolic disorders can be ascertained *in utero*. A test result indicating the fetus is free from a suspected disorder allays the anxiety of those couples having a high risk of producing defective offspring. A recent government study indicates that prenatal diagnosis has led to a 10% increase in the child-bearing of such couples.

Down's syndrome (sometimes called "mongolism"—a disorder caused by presence of an extra chromosome number 21) increases in frequency with advanced maternal age. The risk of a woman bearing an affected baby is 1 out of 1,923 at 20 years and 1 out of 32 at 45 years. About one-half of all Down's infants are born to women 35 years or older. Although such children may be cheerful and affectionate, their mental handicap (usually severe mental retardation as well as physical disorders) and continued dependency can disrupt normal family life and make them a financial burden upon society. Since modern medicine has increased the life span of those affected with Down's syndrome, it is quite possible that an affected person will outlive his or her parents.

Inasmuch as the care of the 50,000 Down's individuals in the United States cost families and society about $250 million annually, some states have passed legislation that encour-

ages the expansion of prenatal diagnostic services to reduce the incidence of such traits. Considering the pluralistic character of American society and the social, ethical, and legal issues raised by advances in human genetics, controversy cannot be avoided.

Regardless of parental age, couples carrying recessive mutations for hereditary disease (for example, Tay-Sachs disease, hemophilia, and thalassemia major) and/or structural aberrations of chromosomes constitute a second group seeking prenatal diagnoses. Neural tube defects, involving the brain and spinal cord, may result in neonatal death, mental retardation, and paralysis. In Great Britain, neural tube defects are the most common of serious congenital malformations. Evidence suggests a multifactorial cause for this malady. The presence of abnormally high levels of a particular protein in the maternal blood serum (as well as in the amniotic fluid) is a good indication that the neural tube has not closed properly. Visual evidence of malformation can be corroborated by ultrasound techniques that use the same equipment employed to ascertain the position of the fetus in the womb prior to making a transabdominal tap by amniocentesis. Some families have an unusually high occurrence of chromosomal aberrations perhaps caused by a translocated chromosome. In fact, the probability that normal carriers of such translocated chromosomes will have affected offspring may be as high as one-in-three.

The analysis of chromosomal problems utilizes a now fairly standard technique; thus, most major hospitals provide such karyotyping service. However, detecting metabolic errors (most of which are individually

Needle withdraws
fluid containing cells

Wall of uterus

Placenta

Amniotic fluid

Cells shed by
growing
fetus

Laboratory separates
cells from fluid

Cells are grown in culture,
then tested for
chromosomal abnormalities

phisticated methods are in the offing: for example, new techniques arising from research with recombinant DNA are proving useful for the *in utero* diagnosis of sickle-cell anemia. In addition, diagnoses are being made on fetal cells present in maternal blood thus obviating the need for rare) requires a multiplicity of sophisticated procedures that differ among traits. Not every research laboratory can suitably handle such complex diagnoses.

Update

A method of prenatal diagnosis that can be performed as early as 10 weeks after conception will become more widely available in the United States in coming years. Known as *chorionic villi sampling*, the method involves the insertion of a plastic catheter (tube) through the cervix of the uterus. Chorinonic tissue, consisting of rapidly dividing fetal cells, is then removed for subsequent chromosomal and biochemical studies. It is often possible to obtain diagnostic information from chorionic cells within a day—instead of after a wait of several weeks. Consequently, a pregnancy that is diagnosed by this technique to have a major genetic problem can (at the discretion of parents and physician) be more safely terminated within the medically suggested period of the first trimester.

Since technical problems associated with chorionic villi sampling are greater than they are for amniocentesis, this newly developed technique is now available at only a few medical centers. Even though general adoption of the method will lead to a decline in the number of amniocentesis tests performed, amniocentesis itself will still be used for certain diagnostic purposes, such as ascertaining neural tube defects, a procedure that requires a sample of amniotic fluid.

Even more sophisticated techniques are on the drawing board. For example, a significant "fall-out" from genetic engineering research that utilizes recombinant DNA has allowed accurate diagnosis of a number of deleterious genetic traits. Such techniques have already made it possible to ascertain several medically important mutations (including sickle-cell), and are but a portent of the extraordinary array of tests that will be available in the future.

SOURCES:

"Cutting the Risk of Childbirth after 35," *Consumer Reports*, May 1979, pp. 302–306.

Emery, A.E.H. (ed.). *Antenatal Diagnosis of Genetic Disease*, Baltimore: The Williams and Wilkins Co., 1973.

"First-Trimester Prenatal Diagnostic Method Becoming Available in U.S.," Medi-cal News, *Journal of the American Medical Association*, 250:1249–1250, September 9, 1983.

Golbus, M. S., et al., "Prenatal Genetic Diagnosis in 3000 Amniocenteses," *New England J. of Medicine*, 300:157–163, January 25, 1979.

Harris, H. *Prenatal Diagnosis and Selective Abortion*, Cambridge, Mass.: Harvard University Press, 1975.

Miles, J. H. "Medical Genetics: Impact and Strategy," *Stadler Genetics Symposia*, 12:33–41, 1980.

"Recombinant DNA Methods for Prenatal Diagnosis," *Annuals of Internal Medicine*, 99:718–719, November, 1983.

◇ Introduction

In the previous chapter, we discussed several specific genetic traits that are known to vary among human populations. Some of these, particularly sickle-cell hemoglobin, are probably directly related to selection pressures. Most human variation, however, cannot yet be conclusively tied to any specific selection factor.

In this chapter, we will take up possible adaptive responses in human populations to more general kinds of selection pressures. For example, are there genetic differences in human populations allowing adaptation to heat stress, cold stress, high altitude, ultraviolet radiation, or specific dietary factors? Moreover, have the conditions of modern technological society presented new selection pressures such as crowding, artificial radiation, and noise?

Again, we must emphasize that demonstrating direct effects of natural selection on humans is extremely difficult. So many variables have to be considered simultaneously that clearly proven associations between specific phenotypes and specific environments are not usually possible. Rigorous experimental controls, practical for studies of other organisms, are not feasible for humans. Moreover, adaptations to general kinds of ecological conditions of heat, light, altitude, etc., are made through numerous complex physiological changes. Such adaptations involve several polygenic traits, none of which has a clearly understood hereditary basis.

Many different human populations today live under arduous environmental conditions. Some live in scalding temperatures averaging above 100°F in the summer and others survive through frigid winter months averaging − 50°F. Still others exist all year long at altitudes above 15,000 feet. In all these cases, the groups living under these severe environmental stresses have made adjustments, both cultural and physiological. Without culture (which *is* humankind's ecological niche), none of these demanding environments could ever have been conquered. If culture is the dominant means of human adaptation, are there also biological changes in populations that have been subjected for several generations to severe stresses?

Certainly, general climatic/ecological conditions exert strong selection pressures, and human populations do show differences in their average physiological responses to certain environmental conditions. The question then becomes: *Are these populations more adapted through natural selection (differential success of certain genotypes), or are they just showing a physiological adjustment capacity common to all humans?*

◇ Adaptation and Acclimatization

The way in which humans and other organisms meet the challenges of the environment is through a general process called *adaptation*. This term has a wide variety of meanings, and in its broadest connotation can refer to any

159

Biological adaptation
Genetic changes within populations in response to selection (environmental) pressure; usually takes many generations.

Acclimatization
Physiological response within individuals to environmental pressure; usually takes a few weeks to a few months.

changes (genetic, environmental, physiological, or behavioral) by which organisms surmount the challenges to life (Lasker, 1969). In fact, archeologists and cultural anthropologists often refer to *cultural* adaptive responses of human societies, such as those dealing with the adjustments resulting from technological innovation.

Among physical anthropologists and other human biologists, however, a more restricted definition of **biological adaptation** is usually implied. From this perspective, adaptation is viewed as an *evolutionary* process and, even more precisely, as the result of natural selection. Consequently, biological adaptation works only on whole populations.

In terms of natural selection, individual organisms cannot adapt; they just produce offspring as well as they can under the circumstances. Biological adaptation occurs only *between* generations as the result of differential reproductive success among all the individuals of the population. Biological adaptations, then, *must* have a genetic basis. As environments change so do selection pressures and so also does the reproductive success of various genotypes. Groups of organisms can respond adaptively to changing environmental conditions only over the span of several generations. In quickly reproducing organisms, demonstrated by the adaptation of mosquito populations to DDT, this may appear rapid. However, for slowly reproducing organisms, such as *Homo sapiens*, at least a few thousand years are required for significant adaptive shifts. For example, the spread of the sickle-cell allele in the human populations of the western and central portions of Africa took at least 2,000 years and perhaps considerably longer (8,000–10,000 years?).

On the other hand, all *individual* organisms can respond to environmental changes by physiological adjustments, displaying their phenotypic plasticity. Called **acclimatization**, such responses can occur relatively quickly as in the physiological changes induced by high altitude stress.

For this reason, college football teams playing the Air Force Academy in Colorado Springs (elevation 6,008 ft.) like to arrive a day or two early to allow some time for some short-term physiological responses to occur. The same was true of athletes training for the 1968 Olympic Games in Mexico City (elevation 7,347 ft.), who began training months earlier at high-altitude locations to permit a more long-term physiological acclimatization.

◇ Light/Solar Radiation and Skin Color

One kind of environmental stress that varies considerably over the earth (and therefore differentially affects human populations) is the amount of solar radiation.

In response to this kind of environmental stress, the body uses a mechanism that alters the skin pigment. Actually, the color of the skin is influenced by three pigments: (1) carotene (yellow) derived from foods such as sweet potatoes and carrots, but not really important in determining skin color— the other two pigments are much more significant; (2) hemoglobin (red) in the red blood cells; and (3) melanin, a biochemically complex compound produced in the basal layers of the epidermis and secreted by specialized cells called *melanocytes*. Populations differ in skin color not so much because

Figure 6-1 Jimmy Hines (U.S.A.) winning 100-meter sprint, 1968 Olympic Games, Mexico City. Elevation 7,347 ft.

of the number of melanocytes, but in the way these cells are bunched, and the size and number of the melanin granules produced.

Of these pigments, only melanin absorbs ultraviolet light (the end of the spectrum causing radiation), so only melanin can protect against the really harmful effects of solar radiation.

Cells (melanocytes) of stratum granulosum

Cells of stratum spinosum with intercellular bridges

Stratum corneum
Duct of sweat gland
Stratum lucidum
Stratum granulosum
Stratum spinosum
Stratum basal

EPIDERMIS

Papillary layer

DERMIS

Reticular layer

SUBCUTANEOUS FASCIA

Figure 6-2 Diagrammatic section of human skin.

Figure 6-3 An African albino. (From *Genetics, Evolution, and Man* by W. H. Bodmer and L. L. Cavalli-Sforza. W. H. Freeman and Company. Copyright © 1976.)

One potentially and extremely hazardous result of overexposure to ultra-violet (u-v) solar radiation is skin cancer. An immediate way the body can respond (acclimate) is to increase the production of melanin granules, causing what we call a "tan." All human populations can tan in response to exposure to u-v light, but the effects are obviously more noticeable in those who are more fairskinned.

Individuals with albinism (Fig. 6-3), a rare inherited condition found in all human populations, produce no melanin, cannot tan, and in tropical populations often develop skin cancer early in life. For that matter, there is considerable variation in skin cancer incidence in the United States depending on the intensity of u-v light. Among United States whites, rates of skin cancer are five times higher in Texas than in Massachusetts (Damon, 1977, p. 216).

In the United States today, skin cancer afflicts people mostly late in life—after reproduction is completed; its role as a potent selective agent could thus be questioned. However, in considering the potentially harmful effects of u-v radiation from an *evolutionary* perspective, three points must be kept in mind: (1) Early on, hominids lived mostly in the tropics, where u-v is much more intense than in temperate areas like the United States; (2) unlike modern urban dwellers, most earlier hominids spent the majority of their time outside; and (3) they wore little or no clothing. As we will see below, however, adoption of clothing in temperate climes may have played a role in influencing depigmentation. Thus, it is reasonable to consider protection against skin cancer and severe sunburn as *potentially* important selective factors influencing the evolution of dark pigmentation.

Another physiological effect caused by sunlight, particularly u-v radiation, is the stimulation in the human body of the production of vitamin D, necessary for normal bone growth and maintenance. Individuals with insufficient vitamin D often develop such growth defects as rickets. Presumably, it would be harmful, particularly to children, to be too dark-skinned in areas where sunlight is low.

Dr. Peter Post has suggested an additional factor that may help explain the distribution of skin color. Epidemiological data from the Korean War (such as more frostbite occurring in black soldiers) as well as experimental evidence led Post to the conclusion that light skin is less susceptible to cold injury. Therefore, in northern latitudes—which not only get less u-v radiation but are also colder than tropical areas—light skin may provide protection against cold injury (Post et al., 1975).

So far we have established that: (1) solar radiation exerts potentially harmful environmental stress if too much is absorbed (possibly leading to skin cancer) or if too little is absorbed (leading to insufficient vitamin D production and/or cold injury); and (2) individual human beings can respond by tanning to increased amounts of u-v light.

The important question remains: Do populations that have long resided under widely varying u-v conditions show *biological adaptations* in skin color?

For a long time, data on skin color were inconsistent, but recent application of reflectance spectrophotometry has removed some of the earlier problems. Such observations of human skin color have shown that average readings vary considerably with latitude and, presumably, amount of u-v light (see map, Fig. 6-4). This association is, of course, inconclusive; we still do not know for

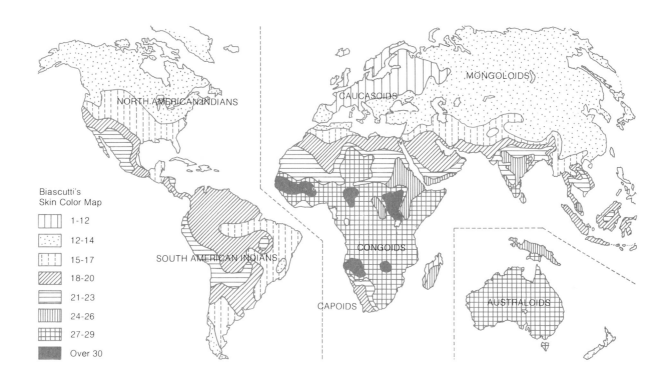

Biascutti's
Skin Color Map

⊞	1–12
⣿	12–14
⊞	15–17
⧄	18–20
☰	21–23
⦀	24–26
▦	27–29
■	Over 30

Figure 6-4 Distribution of skin color among the indigenous populations of the world. (After Coon and Hunt, 1965.)

certain the specific selection factors involved. Hypothetically, dark skin in areas with high u-v light protects against skin cancer. It has also been suggested that dark skin protects against overproduction of potentially toxic amounts of vitamin D. Another unconfirmed hypothesis postulates that dark skin is a concealment device developed in hominids evolving in tropical forests. Since hominid populations have probably only recently penetrated densely forested areas, this explanation seems unlikely.

Why skin on the average is dark in some areas may therefore be reasonably explained if we *assume* that sunburn, skin cancer, overproduction of vitamin D, or some other unknown consequence of overexposure to sunlight is an important selection factor. But then why, on the average, are some populations light-skinned? The popular hypothesis here runs as follows: In northern areas, dark skin would be selected against since it would cause underproduction of vitamin D, thereby resulting in growth defects (leading to lower reproductive success).

Another theory explaining why some humans have light skin has been proposed by anthropologists Loring Brace and Ashley Montagu (1977). As with the vitamin D hypothesis, the assumption here is that humans originated in the tropics, where darkly pigmented skin was a selective advantage. According to Brace and Montagu, permanent habitation of extreme northern temperate zones occurred only within the last 100,000 years, and was partly made possible by the cultural innovation of warm clothing. Once humans in these northerly areas began to wear full-body clothing, the selective advantage of dark skin was no longer in force; thus, through random mutation (and with no selective mechanism opposing it), depigmentation eventually took place.

All this conjecture concerning skin color as an adaptation to differential amounts of solar radiation remains open to question. No proven association exists, and the only tentative supporting evidence is the rough correlation with latitude. But even here some notable exceptions occur. In the New World, there is tremendous latitude variation encompassing almost the full range of u-v conditions; but, among native populations, only minor differences in skin color exist.

The smaller degree of geographic skin color variation in the New World may be explained by (1) the amount of time involved; and (2) the rates of evolutionary change postulated for skin color adaptations. In fact, computer simulations of evolutionary rates for skin pigmentation (Livingstone, 1969) suggest that as many as 30,000 years would be required to produce the magnitude of color variation seen in the Old World. If we further assume that New World population distribution (at least into the tropics) occurred in the last 10,000 to 20,000 years, we should not necessarily *expect* extremely marked pigmentation variation. Of course, the possibility also exists that New World populations have evolved some novel biological mechanism for coping with the effects of u-v light.

◇ The Thermal Environment

Homo sapiens is found in a great variety of habitats, with thermal environments differing from exceedingly hot deserts to the frigid tundra of the arctic circle. Human groups live through the winter in areas as cold as eastern Siberia, where January temperatures *average* an unbelievable −63°F. Such extreme environmental conditions place the human body under great stress.

Cold Stress

The way the human body copes with cold stress is mostly through those physiological adjustments we have termed acclimatization. Perhaps there are some differences between populations in the rate such adjustments occur; but the ability to adjust gradually to cold is a general capacity of all human beings.

The manner of studying human reaction to cold involves either controlled laboratory observations, such as taking skin temperatures of appendages immersed in cold water, or such overall tolerance measurements as the sleeping bag test. This latter method is a testimony to the dedication and foolhardiness of physical anthropologists. Using standardized sleeping bags, experimenters sleep out in the open and contrast the amount of sleep, comfort, and shivering between themselves and natives. Many a researcher has spent long, cold nights with chattering teeth and shivering bones!

In addition, inferential support for populational adjustment to cold stress has been obtained through the distributional method. In this kind of study, data are gathered from several populations on such physical characteristics as stature and nose shape and are then checked for any correspondence with environmental factors (for example, mean annual temperature, humidity).

From such observations, several mechanisms of physiological acclimatization to cold have been demonstrated in different human populations (after Damon, 1977, p. 222):

1. Redistribution of heat to extremities (shown in the Quechua of South America and Lapps of Scandinavia)
2. Overall metabolic rate increased (shown in Eskimos and Alacaluf of Tierra del Fuego—the high protein diet of Eskimos is an important contributing factor among this group)
3. Insulation acclimatization yielding cooler skin surface temperatures, but maintaining internal ones (shown in central Australians and Kalahari San). Such a physiological response may have originated in tropical areas where no real danger of frostbite prevails. However, in northern latitudes, it would be highly maladaptive, and physiological responses have apparently been modified (Steegman, 1975).

It is remarkable how well these physiological changes will eventually buffer the effects of cold. For example, Australian aborigines sleep in the nude with no covering in temperatures close to freezing! In sleeping bag tests in Scandinavia, Norwegian students gradually acclimatized and could sleep although they continued to shiver. An involuntary response, shivering is controlled by the hypothalamus mediated by cold receptors in the skin. By increasing the body's heat production up to three times that of resting temperatures, shivering is an effective response to cold.

Carleton Coon and his associates have proposed a cold stress hypothesis to explain facial shape variation among human populations (Coon et al., 1950). Since genetic shifts are seen here to have occurred as the result of evolution, this type of change would be an adaptation (not acclimatization, as in the adjustments discussed above). It is postulated that cold stress selective factors (particularly frostbite) have favored wider (less sharp) noses and larger, more protrusive cheekbones, thus accounting for the evolution of the "Asian face." However, recent experimental evidence (Steegman, 1970) appears to contradict this hypothesis. In fact, facial temperatures were colder in those individuals with more protrusive cheekbones. Moreover, no consistent correlations exist between temperature and nose shape, although the latter does appear to be influenced by humidity (see the following section).

All the means of tolerating cold stress just discussed are physiological responses seen to some degree in all populations, and not merely those most subject to cold conditions. While mechanisms of physiological response to cold may vary somewhat among human groups, as yet we cannot conclusively demonstrate any clear biological adaptations specific to certain populations.

HEAT AND HUMIDITY

While populations living in extremely cold climates face the problem of conserving heat, those groups living in hot environments face the opposite challenge, how to dissipate excess heat. In fact, the human body can adjust more easily to heat load than it can to extreme cold. Thus, cold is usually considered more of a serious threat to life than heat, unless the latter is accompanied by a lack of water. This greater tolerance of heat as opposed to cold might well reflect the tropical origins of our lineage.

Axillae
Armpits

Whereas body build, skin pigmentation (which protects against solar radiation), and the circulation of more blood close to the skin surface are all factors that help the human body adjust to heat stress, the most efficient means for humans is sweating. By cooling the surface of the skin, sweating causes heat to radiate to the surrounding air. In desert climates, individuals can lose up to one quart of water per hour; however, if such rates of water loss go unchecked, dangerous tissue dehydration and sodium loss will result. At maximum sweating capacity, the body can lose its entire sodium pool in just three hours—ultimately leading to death (Hanna and Brown, 1979).

The capacity to dissipate heat by sweating is seen in all populations to an almost equal degree. Interestingly, the average number of *sweat glands* does not vary between human populations. Each of us has approximately 1.6 million sweat (eccrine) glands. In addition, in the **axillae** and groin areas, apocrine glands are found; these, however, are not really involved in heat regulation but are more likely olfactory in nature (scent cues, particularly for sexual attraction?). While humans are not unique for the number or size of their eccrine sweat glands, these are remarkable for their high secretory level. "*Homo sapiens* has the greatest sweating capacity for a given surface area for any known animal" (Newman, 1970).

When introduced into very hot areas, humans acclimatize quite rapidly, the process taking just a few days. Such plasticity seems to characterize all human populations, and no heat adaptations have been found that differentiate one human group from others. "Indeed, the similarity in response of all acclimatized peoples is remarkable" (Hanna and Brown, 1979, p. 179). This physiological adjustment is accomplished through a faster response and increased output of the sweat glands (directed by the thyroid) and a general decrease in the pulse rate and heart output. Again, is it possible that such a rapid and efficient capacity to adjust to heat stress reflects our tropical hominid origins?

More than just temperature, rapid physiological adjustment is also dependent on humidity. All populations seem to be able to adjust quickly to hot, wet climates, but acclimatization to hot, dry areas takes longer. The most consistent data suggesting a connection between physical response and humidity concern nose shape (Weiner, 1954). Populations living in colder areas (where absolute humidity is lower) have narrower noses. Similarly, in deserts (where absolute humidity is also low), narrow noses also are the rule. The physiological explanation is not yet completely understood, but a narrow nose may act as a more efficient humidifier (Steegman, 1975). Such changes in nose shape would obviously be significantly influenced by genetic shifts; that is, this explanation emphasizes adaptation rather than acclimatization.

Clearly, all humans have inherited a genetically based plasticity to deal with heat stress. In this context, it may be said that we have been adapted for adaptability. Even given such a flexible physiological capacity there are limitations (such as the one just discussed concerning severe sodium loss). Consequently, humans also adjust to hot climates through a variety of cultural means (Hanna and Brown, 1983). Among the Tuareg people of the Sahara, clothing is worn loosely, thereby allowing sweat to evaporate and additionally providing an insulating layer of air next to the skin. Physical activities are usually performed during the cooler hours, and individuals stay in the shade whenever possible. In the Sahara, the air is hot and dry with solar radiation intense, posing the dual problems of excessive water loss and sunburn. On the other hand, in tropical humid rainforests, such as those occupied by the Semai of Malaya, the reverse is true—sweat evaporation is much slower. Accordingly, these people wear few clothes.

Likewise, human adjustments to cold also are mostly cultural in nature. As we will see later in the text, our ancestors long ago invaded temperate latitudes, and there is little doubt that it was primarily cultural innovation that allowed such a migration in the first place. Evidence of consistent use of fire is at least 500,000 years old. Artificial structures are also exceedingly ancient. Windbreaks may have been constructed in Africa almost 2 million years ago, and by 200,000 years ago more sophisticated structures were being erected in Europe.

There is little direct evidence for the earliest use of clothing. Long before garments were sewn, loose untailored skins, furs, etc. were certainly utilized. With the advent of sewn clothing 35,000 years ago, clear archeological evidence of needles has been discovered (Chard, 1975). After this, as Brace and Montagu have suggested (1977), *permanent* habitation of really cold areas became possible.

As we see, humans cope with environmental challenges by a *combination* of both biological and cultural strategies, which again underlines the essential biocultural nature of human existence.

Another feature of human physiological response to the thermal environment that has received considerable attention concerns body proportions. Data on heat-related deaths among World War II soldiers in the deserts of North Africa indicate excess quantities of fat or muscle are a hindrance in such an environment. A linear body build is apparently the most advantageous and is reflected in many groups who have been subject to heat stress for a long time: Arabs, Nilotic Africans (Watusi, Nuer, Dinka, etc.), and central Australians.

BODY SIZE AND SHAPE

Indeed, there seems to be a general relationship between climate and body size/shape within warm-blooded species (that is, both mammals and birds). In general, within a species, body size (weight) increases proportionately as distance from the equator increases. In humans, this relationship holds up fairly well, but there are numerous exceptions. For example, Polynesians basking in the sunny climes of the South Pacific are tall and heavy, whereas Scandinavian Lapps are short and slender.

Presumably, body size and proportion are strongly influenced by genetic mechanisms; thus, shifts in these dimensions should come about primarily as the result of adaptation. Yet, physiological response (that is, acclimatization) may also be playing an important role here. Body weight and limb length are both phenotypically plastic, with significant environmental influence upon them (Hanna and Brown, 1983). Even first generation migrants to tropical areas (American children reared in Brazil) show different body proportions (more linear than would be expected). Obviously, this response occurs too quickly to be explained by genetic adaptation. The body during development

(a)

(b)

Figure 6-5 Contrasting body sizes and proportions in modern *Homo sapiens*. (*a*) Masai (East Africa); (*b*) Eskimo.

is being influenced by environmental factors, such as heat, which in turn influences blood flow which, in turn, might well affect the differential growth of bone and other tissues.

Nevertheless, some general principles applicable to body size/shape variation seen in other warm-blooded species seem also to apply broadly to *Homo sapiens*:

1. *Bergmann's Rule* involves the relationship of body mass to surface area. As weight (mass) increases, the relative amount of surface area decreases proportionately. Therefore, large size with relatively less surface area for heat loss is an adaptation for more efficient heat maintenance. It is interesting to note that cold-adapted fauna during glacial peaks of the Pleistocene are generally larger than their modern descendants. Moreover, humans are almost certainly less robust than our ancestors during much of the last 1 million years. In humans today, there is also some correspondence of size with climate, since peoples living farther from the equator tend to be larger. Eskimos, who are stocky in physique, are one good example.

2. *Allen's Rule* involves the shape of the body, particularly the appendages. In colder climates, appendages should be short, thereby reducing the amount of surface area. In humans, this is seen as shorter arms and legs, but in other animals tails, ears, or beaks may be affected.

Considerable data gathered from several human populations generally conform to the above rules. In colder environments, body sizes are larger with broader, longer chests and shorter arms (Roberts, 1973). These relationships pertain most clearly to indigenous New World populations, but they do not apply to the populational distribution of body size and shape found in Africa (Hiernaux, 1968).

Another complication in attempting to apply these rules to humans is that of acclimatization. An individual's body size may reflect much more about short-term physiological adjustment to ecological/dietary conditions than about long-term biological adaptation. For example, an extensive study of more than 15,000 white males in the United States revealed as large a correspondence in body size and temperature (based on the State in which one was born) as that seen for indigenous North American populations (Newman and Munro, 1955). Since this entire group represented recent migrants from generally the same region (Europe), biological adaptation was ruled out (too little time). Acclimatization, therefore, was responsible for the tendency for larger males to predominate in colder parts of the United States. Colder weather may be a direct causative factor, stimulating more physical activity and appetite.

Body size and shape variation among human populations may also be influenced by cultural factors. Alice Brues in an article titled "The Spearman and the Archer," suggested that different body builds are better suited for use of different weapons (Brues, 1959). According to Brues, the most efficient body build for spear use is long and slender, but for using a bow the body should be short with thick muscles. Hypothetically, as bow technology spread several thousand years ago selection pressures would have shifted favoring a shorter, stockier build. A potential complication here is that most populations that use bows *also* use spears.

A similar scenario to the one above has been recently proposed by David Frayer (1980). In this theory, body size among our ancestors also changed as a result of cultural variables, but here the key was a shift in size of game animals. From 35,000 to 10,000 years ago, larger, more aggressive game was hunted less and less as our ancestors gradually adopted a more sedentary way of life. Thus, according to this view, the males (who, presumably, were doing most of the big game hunting) gradually became smaller, while female body size remained approximately the same. While biocultural factors have assuredly influenced human body size, these imaginative suggestions still remain unproven.

◇ High-Altitude Stress

Today perhaps as many as 25 million people live at altitudes above 10,000 ft. In Tibet, permanent settlements exist above 15,000 ft., and in the Andes they can be found at 17,500 ft. (with daily trips to mines at 19,000 ft.)!

At such high altitudes, multiple stresses act on the human body creating several physiological problems. Most pervasive is the low barometric pressure creating low oxygen pressure in inspired air. Consequently, oxygen diffuses less quickly into the lung membranes and less oxygen eventually reaches the body's tissues. All these problems become particularly critical during any kind of exercise.

High altitude, however, also involves cold stress. In Tibet, winter temperatures plunge to as low as $-27°F$. In addition, populations living in such environments must also cope with low humidity, high winds, high solar radiation, a limited nutritional base (generally poor agricultural land), and rough terrain.

Initially, human beings respond to high-altitude stress (primarily low oxygen pressure) through short-term compensation, but eventually a more permanent acclimatization develops. When freshly introduced into high altitude environments, we react by breathing faster and deeper. Gradually, our systems adjust so that respiration rates are permanently increased and the number of red blood cells is also increased. In the Peruvian Andes (from which our most comprehensive data come), natives have up to 30% more red blood cells than populations at sea level. Such an adjustment allows the blood to carry more oxygen. The right ventricle of the heart may also increase in size, pumping more blood to the lungs. Also, there are probably adjustments in the body tissues to function at lowered oxygen tension.

With the increased physiological demands of pregnancy, hypoxia (oxygen deficiency) could be expected to have negative effects on fertility. However, the data here are somewhat conflicting. A recent comparative study of Himalayan populations suggests that there is no evidence to support the popular conception that high-altitude stress reduces fertility (Goldstein et al., 1983). In fact, as this study points out, confounding cultural attitudes (such as those affecting the exposure of females to intercourse) must be considered.

On the other hand, high infant mortality has been reported for several groups living at high altitude, most of the problems resulting from respiratory infections. Many of these infant deaths are attributable to the generally poor

Figure 6-6   Andean Highlands. An Indian village with llamas to the right.

health care available, but once infants contract bronchitis, tuberculosis, etc., the low oxygen pressure, no doubt, causes further complications. Even in areas with good health care, infant mortality resulting from respiratory problems is greater at high altitudes. For example, in Colorado, infant deaths were nearly twice as common in areas above 8,200 ft. (2,500 m) as at lower elevations (Moore and Regensteiner, 1983).

Other physiological adjustments displayed by highland Andean peoples include lower birth weights, but relatively larger placentas—probably supplying more oxygen to the developing fetus. In addition, slower rates of maturation with delayed sexual maturity may provide more time to grow in an oxygen-poor and nutritionally deprived environment.

Most of the adjustments humans exhibit in response to high-altitude stress can be accounted for by physiological plasticity (acclimatization). However, some effects of natural selection may well cause differential spread of genotypes more adapted to high altitudes.

How do we sort out the possible effects due to adaptation from those due to acclimatization? Once again we are faced with a complex nature/nurture phenomenon and, once again, for humans the answers are far from clear. Laboratory tests may tell us something of the range of variation of human responses, and observations of other animals may tell us something about general physiological plasticity. However, for human populations, so complexly intertwined in a web of environmental/cultural/genetic factors, we require a special methodology. One helpful technique is called the *migrant model*, which compares genetically related populations living under very different environmental conditions. For example, investigations of lung function were done on the Aymara (highland natives) of northern Chile and compared with data from non-Aymara (Spanish) and a group termed "mixed" (Mueller et al., 1979). Upward migrants as well as downward migrants were contrasted with nonmigrants, controlling for age, sex, stature, ethnicity, occupation, and permanence (age at migration and length of stay). Even with all these controls, confounding factors obscure results from such cross-sectional studies. Long-term physiological data from individuals (longitudinal studies) are therefore also necessary to help untangle the web of genetic, physiological, ecological, and cultural variables.

High-altitude inhabitants may also meet the rigorous demands of their environment through nutritional adaptations. Some evidence points to differences among high-altitude populations in food utilization, particularly fat metabolism. Their typically low fat/low protein/high carbohydrate diet may possibly be a cultural adaptation to living under high altitude conditions. In addition, alcohol consumption and coca leaf chewing have also been suggested as cultural adjustments to high-altitude stress (particularly, cold).

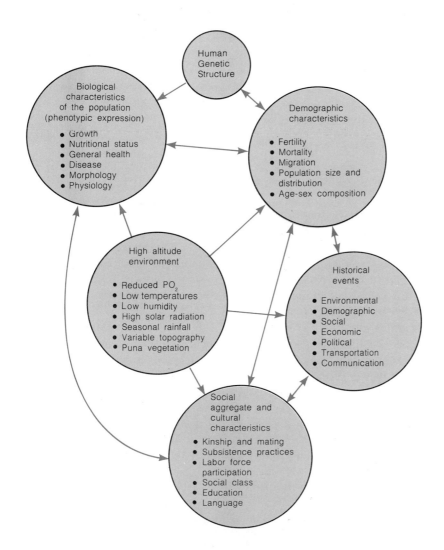

Figure 6-7 High altitude factors. (Baker and Little, 1976.)

Alcohol facilitates vasodilation making the skin surface feel warmer. Over the short run, alcohol consumption can thus increase comfort levels. If extended over long periods, however, it can be dangerous, causing greater heat loss and further contributing to possible frostbite.

Coca leaves contain cocaine and may also act to warm surface temperatures. Native chewers claim coca helps alleviate the symptoms of hunger, thirst, fatigue, cold, and pain (Fuchs, 1978). Controlled studies show, however, that when consumed in small amounts (as is typical), coca has no observed effect on metabolism or work performance.

◇ Dietary Adaptations

Nutritional behavior has long been a central element in human evolution. For at least the last 1 million years, meat has been an extremely important element in human diets; evidence from modern hunter-gatherers suggests perhaps only about one-third of all calories come from meat, but it still provides a crucial qualitative contribution in the form of essential amino acids. Adult humans can get by on a strictly vegetarian diet, but only with considerable effort. The increased demands of pregnancy, lactation, or disease make a wholly vegetarian diet even more marginal. For an infant, the protein sources from mother's milk are essential for normal development.

Beginning around 10,000 years ago, the agricultural revolution wrought a profound ecological impact on human evolution. Domestication of crops provided a larger and more geographically concentrated food resource, permitting both permanent settlements and population expansion, which in turn greatly increased the spread of infectious diseases in human populations.

Moreover, dietary habits shifted profoundly. The varied ecological base characteristic of Paleolithic hunter-gatherers gave way to the generally much more restrictive diets of settled agriculturists. Relying primarily on a few or perhaps just one staple crop, such diets can be exceedingly narrow, giving way easily to malnutrition. Did such massive shifts in human diets bring about any behavioral changes? Perhaps. Some recent evidence has suggested a possible relationship between a low calorie/high carbohydrate diet and increased aggressiveness (Bolton, 1973). When combined with intense physical activity, such diets lead to chronic lowering of blood sugar levels (hypoglycemia), which in turn may be reflected as behavioral alterations.

Such a diet is characteristic of the physically active Qolla Indians of the Andean Highlands. From a limited data base (one village of 1,200 individuals documented over about 15 years), the Qolla have been depicted as unusually aggressive on the basis of an apparently quite high homicide rate (Bolton, 1984). This is a position, however, that has not gone unchallenged (see Lewellen, 1981). In order to determine how characteristically aggressive the entire Qolla cultural group is, as well as the precise degree of their nutritional/metabolic difficulties, will require further research. In any case, many biologists and anthropologists believe there is sufficient data at hand at least to *suspect* a link between diet and behavior.

No Milk, Please!

Probably the best-known genetic adaptation to dietary factors is shown by the population distribution of the ability in adults to digest cow's milk. A main ingredient in milk is the sugar *lactose*, which the body normally breaks down by an enzyme called *lactase*.

In all human populations, infants and young children can digest milk, an obvious necessity to any young mammal. However, in many populations the gene coding for lactase production "switches off" by about four years of age. If too much milk is ingested, it ferments in the large intestine leading to diarrhea and severe gastrointestinal upset. Among many African and Asian populations—a majority of humankind today—most individuals are *intolerant* of milk (see Table 6-1). Contrary to popular advertising, every body does *not* need milk, at least not as adults. In fact, for billions of human beings, milk consumption leads to severe discomfort.

Unfortunately, this fact had been overlooked by United States foreign aid personnel who naively shipped huge quantities of powdered milk to Asia and Africa. Occasionally, a good deal of sickness resulted, but more usually the natives simply avoided drinking the milk. Some of it even ended up being used as whitewash!

Quite apparently, lactose intolerance is a hereditary trait, but the pattern of inheritance is not yet clearly established. Some familial data suggest that the trait operates as a simple dominant or, perhaps, is more complicated with three alleles.

The environment also plays a role in expression of the trait (that is, whether a person will show milk intolerance) since intestinal bacteria can somewhat buffer the adverse effects. Because these bacteria will increase with previous exposure to smaller quantities of milk, some acclimatized tolerance can be acquired even in individuals who are genetically lactase-deficient.

Why do such differences occur in lactose tolerance among human populations? Throughout the Paleolithic, no milk was generally available after weaning in hunting-gathering societies. Perhaps, in such circumstances, continued action of an unnecessary enzyme might get in the way of digesting other foods. Therefore, there *may* be a selective advantage for the gene, coding for lactase production, to switch off. The question then can be asked: Why can some adults (a majority in many populations) tolerate milk? The distribution of lactose-tolerant populations is very interesting, revealing the probable influence of cultural factors on this trait.

European groups, who are generally lactose-tolerant, are partially descendant from groups of the Middle East. Often economically dependent on pastoralism, these groups raised cows, goats, etc., and no doubt drank considerable milk. Strong selection pressures would act in such a *cultural* environment to shift gene frequencies in the direction of more lactose tolerance. Modern European descendants of these populations apparently retain this ancient ability.

Even more informative is the distribution of lactose tolerance in Africa. For example, groups such as the Fulani and Tutsi, who have been pastoralists probably for thousands of years, have much lower rates of lactose intolerance than nonpastoralists. Former hunters and gatherers, such as the Ibo and

Table 6-1   Frequencies of Lactose Intolerance

	Percent
U.S. whites	2–19%
Finnish	18
Swiss	12
Swedish	4
U.S. blacks	70–77
Ibos	99
Bantu	90
Fulani	22
Thais	99
U.S. Orientals	95–100
Australian aborigines	85

Source: Lerner and Libby, 1976, p. 327.

Undernutrition
A diet insufficient in quantity (calories) to support normal health.

Malnutrition
A diet insufficient in quality (i.e., lacking in some essential component) to support normal health.

Yoruba, are as much as 99% lactose-intolerant. More recently, these groups have abandoned their former subsistence pattern. They do not raise cattle, however, since they have settled in areas infested with tsetse flies.

As we have seen, the geographic distribution of lactose tolerance is related to a history of cultural dependence upon milk products. There are, however, some populations that culturally rely on dairying but are not characterized by high levels of lactose tolerance. It has been suggested that such populations have traditionally consumed their milk produce as cheese and other derivatives in which the lactose has been metabolized through bacterial action (Durham, 1981). In fact, peoples can be generally divided into lactose absorbers and nonabsorbers. Because lactose acts biochemically in a similar fashion to vitamin D (facilitating the absorption of calcium), we should expect the frequency of lactose absorption to increase directly with increasing distance from the equator—a prediction generally supported by the data (Durham, 1981).

The interaction of human cultural environments and changes in lactose tolerance in human populations is a clear example of biocultural evolution. In the last few thousand years, cultural factors have produced specific evolutionary changes in human groups.

Cultural factors no doubt have influenced the course of human evolution for at least the last 3 million years (probably much longer), and today they are of paramount importance.

Malnutrition

While the agricultural revolution brought about a restricted dietary base, most groups were probably able to supplement their diets adequately by hunting small mammals, raising domesticated animals, and so on. However, today the crush of billions of humans almost completely dependent on cereal grains has drastically altered the situation, so that millions face undernutrition, malnutrition, and even starvation.

By **undernutrition** we refer to an inadequate quantity of food. In other words, not enough calories are consumed to support normal health. Exactly what constitutes an "adequate" diet is difficult to ascertain, and estimates of minimum requirements vary widely—body size and activity level are important considerations.

Given these uncertainties there are no precise data on how many human beings are today undernourished, but estimates vary between 16 and 63% of the world's population.

Malnutrition refers to inadequacy of some key element in the diet, such as proteins, minerals, or vitamins. In underdeveloped countries, protein malnutrition is the most common variety, and probably one-fourth to one-third of individuals in the underdeveloped world are protein deficient (M. Newman, 1975). The hallmark of severe protein malnutrition is a generalized disease called *kwashiorkor*, showing typical symptoms of tissue swelling, anemia, loss of hair, and apathy. A related syndrome called *marasmus* is caused by the combined effects of protein *and* calorie deficiency.

More than causing discomfort, malnutrition greatly affects reproduction and infant survival. Malnourished mothers have more difficult labor, more premature births, more children born with birth defects, higher prenatal mortality, and generally lower birth weights of newborns. Given all these potential physiological difficulties, it is surprising that overall *fertility* among malnourished mothers is not disrupted more than it is. Moderate chronic malnutrition (unless it becomes exceedingly severe, approaching starvation) has only a small effect on the number of live births (Bogaarts, 1980).

MALNUTRITION AND DEVELOPMENT

Children born to malnourished mothers are already at a disadvantage: They are smaller and behind in most aspects of physical development. After birth, if malnourished conditions persist, such children fall further behind due to their mothers' generally poor lactation (the milk quantity may be cut by as much as one-half).

Growth processes often slow down greatly when environmental insults are severe (malnutrition and/or disease). Later on, a period of accelerated growth (called the "catch-up period") can make up some of the deficit. However, there are some critical periods in which growth in certain tissues is normally very rapid. If a severe interruption occurs during one of these periods, the individual may never catch up completely. For example, severe malnutrition during the last trimester of fetal life or during the first year of infancy can have marked effects on brain development. Children who had died from complications accompanying severe malnutrition and were subsequently autopsied showed reduced brain size and weight, as well as fewer numbers of brain cells (Frisancho, 1978).

Researchers estimate that in some countries one-half of all newborns die before the age of 5. Of the estimated 60 million deaths per year worldwide, perhaps as many as 20 million are due to dietary deprivation (Dumont and Rosier, 1969). Not all of these people "starve to death," but most die as a result of weakened resistance to a whole set of infectious and gastrointestinal diseases.

Infectious disease, in particular, seems to act in a feedback relationship with malnutrition. Inadequate nutrition can interrupt the normal functioning of the immune response system by reducing the number of active cells or antibodies available (see below). "In summary, a vicious cycle between malnutrition, infection, and immunodeficiencies is established, further intensifying malnutrition, facilitating new infection or permitting existing infection to become more severe" (Frisancho, 1978, p. 181).

Figure 6-8   Kwashiorkor. Bangladesh.

◇ Disease and Human Adaptation

Without question, one of the primary challenges to survival faced by all humans is that of disease. Diseases vary tremendously in their causes and their consequent effects on human health. For example, diseases may originate from any one, or a combination of, the following factors: hereditary (e.g., cystic fibrosis, sickle-cell anemia); metabolic (vitamin deficiencies, such as rickets); degenerative (e.g., heart disease); cell malignancy (e.g., many varieties of cancer); or infections (e.g., malaria).

Human disease does not only result from a complex set of physiological causes—cultural factors are also a crucial element. Settlement patterns and architectural style greatly influence the spread of disease-carrying pathogens (e.g., viruses and bacteria). In New Hebrides the typical Melanesian house is not only designed to be "ghost-tight" but also air-tight thereby greatly facilitating the spread of respiratory diseases among the occupants (Weiner, 1977). Settlement patterns and population density are also most important. Before urbanization (with its large permanent settlements) became characteristic (5,000–10,000 y.a.), airborne infections (influenza, common cold, measles, smallpox) were of less significance; in moderately small communities, there is insufficient quantity and variety of contacts among individuals to perpetuate these diseases (Weiner, 1977).

Domestication of animals also brought the risk of disease. Of course, the development of domesticated animal varieties initially was itself a culturally directed process. Mediating cultural factors further influencing disease are: which animals are kept; in how close proximity; and what (if any) sanitary practices are followed. In the arctic, for example, pathogens (tapeworm, rabies) carried by domestic dogs can be significant factors affecting human health. health.

Ritual, too, can be a contributing factor to the spread of disease. In Yemen, schistosomiasis (a fluke worm infection) is sometimes spread through communal use of ritual ablution pools, and the kuru viral infection was spread in some New Guinea highland groups by ritual cannibalism of the brains of one's dead relatives.

Finally, major ecological modifications usually have marked impacts on disease. As we discussed in Chapter 5, the spread of slash-and-burn agriculture cleared previously forested areas, created more stagnant pools, and consequently greatly stimulated mosquito breeding—a crucial vector in the spread of malaria. Likewise, unsanitary crowded urban conditions contribute to an increase in the rat population size, and these animals also act as a vector in exposing humans to a host of infectious diseases. The best known of these diseases is bubonic plague, which in the thirteenth century "Black Death" epidemic is estimated to have killed one-third the population of Europe.

For thousands of years, the interaction of biology and culture has produced fertile conditions for some diseases while limiting the spread of others. The great twentieth-century advances in controlling many infectious diseases have not, of course, eliminated human disease, but has simply shifted the focus. As average life span increased, degenerative syndromes, such as coronary artery disease, have become much more prevalent. Such crucial cultural factors as diet and psychological stress also have contributed to this increase. Moreover, the exposure to a host of natural and artificial substances has greatly increased the frequency of many varieties of cancer—benzo(a)pyrene in tobacco smoke is but one example. In fact, many cancer researchers now believe that 70 to 80% of all cancers originate primarily from exposure to environmental carcinogens (Hiatt, et al., 1977).

INFECTIOUS DISEASE

Those diseases, however, that have had the most dramatic and long-lasting impact on human populations are infectious in nature. We have seen the potent effect of malaria and the consequent spread of the sickle-cell allele (see pp. 131–134). Several other hereditary traits have also been suggested as possible biological mechanisms providing resistance against malarial infection (e.g., thalassemias, G-6-PD, and some alleles of the Duffy blood group system) (Livingstone, 1980).

Infection refers to the introduction into the body of foreign organic matter; these may include microbes (viruses, bacteria, protozoa), fungi, or even entire multicellular organisms (e.g., worms). Each of us is equipped with a genetically programmed defense apparatus—called the *immune response system*—which discriminates such foreign invaders from our own cells and attempts to isolate and deactivate them.

The Immune Response System   The immune response system is made up of several components, the primary one of which includes several linked loci on chromosome number 6. In addition to the five HLA loci (see p. 144), there are nearby a large number of additional loci. These code for specific proteins (antigens) characteristic of various cell populations that are integral parts of the immune system. The entire genetic region as a whole (HLA and associated regions) in humans is called the **major histocompatibility complex**.

What stimulates the immune system are antigens—the introduction into the body of proteins perceived as different from self. Actually, our bodies can recognize *any* foreign molecule, even nourishing ones that originate in other organisms. The only way to incorporate these vital nutritive materials is to have them first pass through the digestive tract where they are broken down by enzymes and then absorbed through the intestinal walls as amino acids.

Other foreign antigens that enter the body via the respiratory tract or through breaks in the skin surface elicit an immune response. It is this ability to recognize any foreign cell that causes a reaction in blood transfusions of unmatched type (see p. 137). Since red blood cells lack nuclei, blood matches are relatively easy to make. Most other tissues, however, contain nucleated cells, and proper matches are much more difficult to obtain, as in kidney or liver transplants.

Occasionally, the immune system fails to distinguish truly foreign materials from self, and one's own cells are attacked. Such a reaction is termed an *autoimmune response*. Medical research has recently implicated such a process as an important contributory agent in several human diseases: a severe form of paralyzing spinal arthritis (ankylosing spondylitis); psoriasis; and (as recent compelling evidence suggests) multiple sclerosis.

Another related function of the immune system is its ability to recognize and destroy our own cells that have gone awry. In this way, early cancerous cells are normally contained. Since cell mutations or viruses can often cause highly irregular cell development, we would be overwhelmed with cancerous tissues if we had no regulatory mechanism. In fact, some forms of cancer probably develop due to a failure in the immune system.

The immune response system has been adapted in a wide variety of

Major histocompatibility complex (MHC)
The large genetic complex (located in humans on chromosome number 6) that plays a central part in immune response—recognition of foreign antigens and production of specialized cells to deactivate them.

vertebrates; an apparatus similar to that of humans has been discovered in the mouse, pig, rabbit, rhesus monkey, and chimpanzee (Amos and Kostyu, 1980). We and other organisms are constantly exposed to possible danger by a variety of foreign antigens (e.g., insect or snake venom). Most especially, however, the immune system has evolved to protect against infection by microbes. Natural selection has thus endowed the entire human species with a finely tuned defense mechanism.

Although every individual has a unique tissue type and consequently varies in some genetic components of the immune response system, it remains to be determined whether *populations* differ in their immune response to specific diseases. The history of plague, measles, smallpox, influenza and other diseases suggests that natural selection could well have acted differentially on human populations. The questions remain: What diseases have average populational differences in immune response? What ecological/evolutionary factors brought them into being? How might individuals be ascertained for risk to specific diseases? What kinds of therapeutic intervention may mitigate or even prevent the development of a variety of human diseases? One of the great frontiers of medical and evolutionary research concerns the attempt to answer these questions.

◇The Hazards of Modern Life

The specter of tens of millions dying annually because of dietary deprivation is but one of the hazards humanity has created for itself. The cultural pace set by technological, urbanized humankind is radically altering our environments and presumably selection pressures as well. As yet, however, the specific adaptive responses are unknown.

ARTIFICIAL RADIATION

One of the potential perils receiving wide public attention is the danger of manmade radiation. We are all constantly subjected to natural forms of radiation (called background sources) as we are bombarded by cosmic rays from above and from below by radiation-emitting elements in the earth's crust (radium and thorium, for instance).

Worldwide, there is considerable variation in the amount of such background radiation (particularly correlated with altitude), but a typical natural dose for an individual (that is, a "whole body") over a thirty-year period is 3,000–5,000 mrems.*

We are concerned with radiation hazards because of their potentially harmful biological effects. In particular, radiation is a known cause of mutation (changes in DNA sequence).

Estimating possible genetic damages of increased radiation involves con-

---

*Radiation is measured in absorption units. A rem (radiation equivalent for man) is a unit expressing the biological effects of a standard dose (one roentgen) of radiation. 1,000 mrems = 1 rem.

◇ Box 6-1   Artificial Radiation

Dosage effects of radiation tend to accumulate through time, so that several small doses can eventually have biologically harmful ramifications. However, a single large dose will probably do more damage than several small ones, where cells at least have some opportunity for repair.

Accidental exposure to very large doses of radiation at one time will cause severe radiation sickness that especially affects areas of rapidly forming cells, such as the gastrointestinal tract, skin, and blood-forming marrow. A very large single dose of radiation usually causes irreparable damage and can be lethal. The long-term effects of smaller radiation exposure are not well known, but experimental evidence suggests increased incidence of cataracts (scarring of the cornea of the eye), increased frequency of several varieties of cancer, and accelerated aging (Gerson, 1977).

Radiation Exposure Levels*

Lethal dose (would kill 50% of population)	400,000 mrems/ single dose**
Maximum permissible to an individual without harmful effects	500 mrems/year
Exposure from background sources	120 mrems/year
Exposure from medical sources	70 mrems/year

*Extrapolated from experimental evidence and observations on humans who have been exposed.
**Note: A lethal dose is extremely large compared to dosages normally incurred.

siderable guess work, but the dangers are alarming. If there were an approximate tenfold increase in annual background radiation (from 500 to 5,000 mrems, say) by artificial sources (nuclear weapons, medical sources, nuclear power plants/waste), an estimated 50,000 new cases of inherited disease would appear worldwide in the first generation alone. Eventually the effects would translate into as many as 500,000 additional cases every generation (see Box 6-1).

SOURCES OF ARTIFICIAL RADIATION

Nuclear Weapons   Most of the evidence concerning the effects of nuclear explosions on humans comes from long-term studies of the survivors of Hiroshima and Nagasaki and their descendants.

Comparative studies conducted initially by the Atomic Bomb Casualty Commission and later by the Radiation Effects Research Foundation surprisingly have not demonstrated any proven association among survivors' offspring for congenital defects, stillbirth rate, newborn mortality, or childhood mortality. Among those who were themselves directly exposed to the explosion (including *in utero*) there is an increase in chromosomal abnormalities. Since these usually cause death or sterility, they are not generally passed on to the next generation. For those who were severely exposed, there is also a sharp increase in overall mortality rates. It would seem that the effects of radiation exposure of the magnitude of Hiroshima and Nagasaki cause severe biological effects in the first generation, but surprisingly few in future gener-

Figure 6-9 Hiroshima, several months after atomic bomb was dropped.

ations (Schull, et al., 1981). However, long-term effects may initially appear "masked" as recessive mutations that will express themselves as lethals somewhere down the road. We may well see some of these biological costs as the studies of the Japanese descendants continue. Much concern also surrounds the possible dangers of atmospheric nuclear testing. Prior to 1963, the United States and the Soviet Union exploded several large devices in the atmosphere. The total radiation produced, however, was not an important mutagenic factor, for a dosage less than 1% of background radiation was generated.

Medical Sources   The major source of biologically harmful radiation exposure from medical sources is X-rays, particularly if the gonads are exposed. As a diagnostic tool, X-rays are extremely helpful, but great caution must be used—particularly in individuals who have not completed reproduction. Even more hazardous is the X-ray exposure of a developing fetus, for an early somatic mutation may be ramified into major abnormalities.

Radiation is also used for therapeutic purposes in the treatment of some cancers. Such exposure, however, applies only to a tiny fraction of the population, and these few individuals are usually critically ill before exposure. Given the dire circumstance there is often little choice, but harmful side effects are significant. While the treatment is designed to slow down the progress of a lethal tumor, it can stimulate the onset of other cancers (in the skin, thyroid, and bone, for example).

Nuclear Power Plants   Hazards from conventional nuclear power plants (not breeder reactors) can potentially come from either release of radioactive elements in the fission process or release from waste material. Barring a

Figure 6-10   Three Mile Island.

major accident, the kinds of materials *likely* to escape from a nuclear power plant are not exceedingly radioactive. On the other hand, a major failure (that is, a "meltdown") of the plant's radioactive core could be catastrophic. The most serious accident at a nuclear power plant in the United States occurred at the Three Mile Island facility near Harrisburg, Pennsylvania, on March 28, 1979. Due to mechanical failure and human error the plant's cooling system failed to operate correctly, causing the nuclear reactor's fuel core to overheat, and bringing the plant dangerously close to a meltdown. In addition, a large (1,000 cubic foot) bubble of explosive hydrogen gas formed within the reactor building, and this potentially dangerous situation was only brought under control after five days.

Waste material (as a direct product of uranium fission) from nuclear power plants can be highly radioactive and must be disposed of with extreme caution. Usually, such material is buried in special underground containers hopefully far from dense population centers and active geological faults.

Careful monitoring around nuclear power plants has thus far shown little radiation pollution—well within minimum safety limits; potential dangers persist, however. The possibility of a major leak at a plant or waste site due to carelessness, sabotage, or earthquake continues to cause much apprehension.

Miscellaneous Sources   Most other sources of artificial radiation produce only small amounts of radioactivity. Potentially harmful effects are, however, possible from excessive exposure to television, particularly if watched at close distances (the radioactivity is inversely proportional to distance). If continued for several years, such exposure will accumulate, posing a possible hazard. Children who spend several hours every day planted directly in front of their radiation-emitting sets may be exposed to as much as 40 mrems/year— potentially a mutagenic factor (Lerner and Libby, 1976).

CHEMICALS AND MUTATIONS

Today, more significant than radiation as a mutagenic agent is the wide variety of synthesized chemicals we eat, breathe, and with which we come into physical contact. We might be startled to learn that few of these exotic chemicals so widely used in business, agriculture, food processing, and the drug industry have received adequate enough systematic testing to measure their mutagenic danger accurately.

Not only those chemicals produced by human innovation have mutagenic effects; some of those formed naturally also have striking mutagenic properties. For example, aflatoxin—a substance formed from mold on peanuts and other organic substances—is one of the strongest mutagens known. In addition, horseradish is also suspected of having mutagenic properties.

We often read of experimental evidence (on lab animals) pointing to possible harmful effects of cyclamates, saccharin, and so forth. After some public furor and industry protests, these substances are usually removed from the market—not so much because we understand their effects on humans, but because we fear their possibilities.

Cyclamate is apparently not a mutagen itself, but it can be converted into a substance that is. Caffeine may also increase the likelihood of mutation by interfering with DNA repair. In all these cases, however, the direct evidence obtained from laboratory organisms is still unclear when extrapolated to human beings.

CROWDING

Another human problem realized only since the advent of agricultural settlements is crowding. Today, the stresses of humanity pressing against humanity are becoming ever more apparent throughout most of the inhabited world.

Crowding is defined as a problem primarily in terms of population density—in other words, the numbers of people per unit area. Population densities alone, however, do not measure the human stress involved. More relevant here is the *quality* of life possible, which in turn is dependent on technological sophistication, architectural design, and prevailing cultural values.

What is most significant in determining whether an individual feels crowded is his/her microenvironment, or what is sometimes called "personal space." In some urban areas of the United States and many parts of the underdeveloped world, several families crowd into housing units designed for single families. The amount of personal space per individual is thus reduced to just a few dozen square feet. Experimental data support this aspect of immediate space, since the strongest density-dependent correlations with social pathologies concern the number of people per room (Altman, 1978).

How much space is required for individuals to feel comfortable and function normally depends on the individual and the situation. In addition to actual physical space, other important aspects include: cleanliness, heat, odor, ventilation, whether individuals can be mobile within the space provided, whether they are in the crowded conditions voluntarily or not, and most importantly, how long they are required to stay in such conditions (ranging from a few minutes to a lifetime). Individual tolerance of crowded

Figure 6-11   Hong Kong. A side alley packed with humanity.

conditions and ability to adjust to altered quantity and quality of social interactions also show marked variation.

While there are no *absolute* measures of minimum space requirements, a general standard of 38 sq. ft. per person has been recommended for United States penal institutions. If this is taken as a rough standard, the following extremely crowded conditions come into sharper focus:

	Sq. Ft./Person
crowded disco	10
nineteenth-century London slum	9
Nazi concentration camp at Belsen	3
New York subway at rush hour	2
Black Hole of Calcutta	2

As humans pack themselves in ever larger numbers into smaller areas, what effects can we expect? Numerous experimental studies have shown serious behavioral disturbances among overcrowded animals. Moreover, there are also physiological alterations, such as accelerated adrenocortical activity leading to increased production of glucocorticoids. The exact functions of these substances are still unclear, but they seem to be secreted in generally stressful situations (Weiss and Mann, 1975).

Observations of overcrowding in animals either in the laboratory (rats, mice) or in natural populations (among deer and lemmings for example) indicate three major kinds of behavioral and reproductive abnormalities (Damon, 1977).

1. Disruption of reproduction, ovulation, sperm function, mating, nest building, lactation
2. Increase in incidence of abortions, stillbirths, infant mortality
3. Increased aggression, particularly by males

The direct pathological associations of overcrowding in animals, however, are still far from clear. If growth is slow in mice populations, they generally will adjust, showing no more mortality than a control group. Moreover, definite associations of disease incidence and overcrowding are also not clearly established. Sometimes animals (normally social) have higher incidences of disease when they are isolated; other animals show more disease symptoms when crowded.

What does all this experimental evidence from animals mean for humans? Very few studies have been done on crowding using human data, but as yet no clearly harmful associations of overcrowding have been demonstrated.

We must point out that the concept of crowding is not strictly a biological one but has important cultural connotations as well. In fact, most researchers consider "crowding" as primarily a psychological subjective state. Typically, some sort of stress is implied. This is believed to be derived from individual perceptions of too little physical and/or psychological space (social overload theory) or from feelings of loss of personal control over interpersonal interactions ("thwarting" theory).

In many cultures close physical contact with other humans is seen as highly desirable, whereas in others it is avoided. For example, the !Kung San of the Kalahari Desert live in an environment with vast open space. In fact, their overall population density (approximately one person per ten square miles) is among the lowest in the world (Draper, 1973). However, San deliberately arrange their living space—huts in tight circles with few physical barriers—in order to provide maximum interpersonal contact. A possible explanation of this kind of behavior is that it is a cultural means of coping with the cold during the long, chilly Kalahari nights. Indeed, this arrangement creates the equivalent effect of thirty people living in a single room! The !Kung do not have to live closely together but clearly prefer to do so. How we then perceive their personal environment (as overcrowded or not) depends largely on what cultural definition we apply.

NOISE

One by-product of crowding in urban, heavily industrialized areas is noise. The largest contributor to noise pollution is made by mechanical devices. We are all constantly bombarded by the sounds of planes, buses, cars, construction equipment, and even music.

An obvious physical effect of excessive noise (high amplitude) is a deterioration of hearing ability. Urban dwellers on the average perform less well on hearing tests than rural folk. Such loss of hearing is seen particularly in airline workers, construction personnel, and rock band members. Just two hours in a disco can adversely affect one's hearing—even permanently! Noise-induced hearing loss may be quite common. Two different studies estimate the number of individuals in the United States suffering from such hearing loss at between 4.5 and 5 million people (Bugliarello, et al., 1976).

Clearly, extremely high levels of noise produce harmful effects, but what about moderate noise levels? Some evidence suggests such pollution can lead to a loss of sleep and reduced concentration (Damon, 1977). We all have experienced such noise levels (for example, with traffic or construction equipment) and obviously considerable adaptability is possible. Particularly if the noise is steady and predictable, we can learn to "phase it out." But are we really able to ignore it completely? Some extremely tentative data suggest that continuous noise pollution may produce harmful consequences in humans. For example, in the area around a London airport, admissions to mental hospitals are significantly higher than in less noisy areas (Damon, 1977).

In recognition of the harmful effects of noise pollution around airports, a California Superior Court decision in 1970 awarded $740,000 to 549 property owners around Los Angeles International Airport for "loss of full enjoyment of their property" (Anthrop, 1973). Debate concerning noise pollution from jet aircraft peaked in the early 1970s over the proposed development of a commercial supersonic transport (SST). Eventually, the U.S. Senate withdrew federal support for an American SST; the English/French-built supersonic *Concorde* began operation in the mid-1970s, but has been allowed only restricted access to a few United States airports.

◇ Summary

In this chapter, we have investigated human responses to a variety of environmental stresses: solar radiation, heat, cold, high altitude, malnutrition, disease, artificial radiation, crowding, and noise. We have seen that in most cases individual humans make physiological adjustments to such environmental stress—what we have termed *acclimatization*.

We have also posed the question of adaptation: Do human populations vary in the proportions of genotypes in response to general ecological stress? The answer to this last query is still open, since it necessitates a demonstration of specific selection pressures affecting differential reproductive success—a most tricky task for human data!

While still unproven, we may reasonably postulate that variable conditions of solar radiation, the thermal environment, nutrition, disease, and altitude have led to differential success of genotypes influencing body size/shape, skin pigmentation, the immune response system, and so forth.

We may also, with some reason, postulate that cultural environments of the technological, urban, overcrowded twentieth century are also acting to shift selection pressures. The real question is: How?

◇ Questions for Review

1. What are the differences between adaptation and acclimatization? Illustrate through the example of high altitude adjustments.
2. Under what conditions might light color skin be adaptive? Under what conditions might dark color skin be adaptive?
3. What physiological adjustments do humans show in coping with cold stress?
4. What physiological adjustments do humans show in coping with heat stress?
5. What does body size and shape have to do with climate adaptation?
6. How do humans cope with high altitude stress (both physiologically and culturally)?
7. Give an explanation for the distribution of lactose intolerance among the world's populations.
8. How might malnutrition cause changes in selection pressures? Describe what kinds of data would *test* for such changes.
9. Discuss how human disease is influenced by an interaction of biocultural factors.
10. A foreign antigen has just entered your body. Discuss how your body recognizes it as foreign and deals with it.
11. What are the various possible sources of artificial radiation? Why is there so much concern over radiation pollution?
12. Discuss how crowding and noise *might* affect selection pressures.

◇ Suggested Further Reading

Anthropological Aspects of Pigmentation. *American Journal of Physical Anthropology*, 43:387–443, November 1975.

> *A collection of seven articles providing an historical perspective and current hypotheses concerning the nature and evolution of human skin pigmentation.*

Baker, Paul T. and Michael A. Little (eds.). *Man in the Andes*, Stroudsburg, Penn.: Dowden, Hutchinson, & Ross, Inc., 1976.

> *This book is the report of seventeen scientists involved in the multidisciplinary study of highland Quechua Indians (part of the International Biological Program). The most thorough and systematic study of human adaptation/adaptability yet attempted, this work includes information on ecological conditions, physiological responses, diet, disease, and demographic patterns.*

Bier, O. G., W. D. da Silva, D. Götze, and I. Mota. *Fundamentals of Immunology*, New York: Springer-Verlag, 1981.

> *An up-to-date introduction to the complex and rapidly advancing field of immunology. Although this work is aimed at introductory students (in biology and medicine), the technical details of this complex field are still imposing.*

Bodley, John H. *Anthropology and Contemporary Human Problems*, Menlo Park, Ca.: Cummings Publishing Co., 1976.

> *A thorough review of the world's nutritional crisis and the related problem of overconsumption. Written from an evolutionary, cross-cultural perspective, this work makes extreme efforts to show the relevance of anthropology to contemporary problems.*

Damon, Albert (ed.). *Physiological Anthropology*, New York: Oxford University Press, 1975.

> *A superior set of articles with clear authoritative reviews of environmental stress resulting from solar radiation, heat, (and humidity), cold, high altitude, malnutrition, disease and noise. Every article is well written, and this work is highly recommended for any initial study of human adaptability.*

———. *Human Biology and Ecology*, New York: W. W. Norton and Company, 1977.

> *An up-to-date look at contemporary issues in human biology. Includes a good review of general evolutionary processes and excellent discussion of crowding, noise, and artificial radiation (the latter in a chapter by Donald F. Gerson).*

Harrison, G. A., J. S. Weiner, J. M. Tanner, and N. A. Barnicot. *Human Biology* (2nd Ed.), New York: Oxford University Press, 1977.

> *Written by leading human biologists, this work contains up-to-date authoritative discussions of human evolution, genetics, population genetics, growth and development, and ecology. Particularly relevant to topics relating to human adaptability is the section by J. S. Weiner on human ecology.*

Roberts, D. F. *Climate and Human Variability* (2nd Ed.) (An Addison-Wesley Module in Anthropology, No. 34), Reading, Mass.: Addison-Wesley, 1978.

> *Written by one of the leading authorities on human adaptability, this short discussion pulls together much of the current knowledge in this field, particularly relating to associations of body build and climatic factors. Also included is a good summary of skin pigmentation and climatic variables. Highly recommended for introductory students.*

Stini, William A. *Ecology and Human Adaptation*, Dubuque, Iowa: Wm. C. Brown Company, 1975.

> *A short but authoritative review of selective processes acting on human populations. Particularly recommended is the discussion of high-altitude stress.*

Human Diversity

CONTENTS

Note: Arthur R. Jensen is one of the leading proponents of the usefulness of IQ tests for measuring intelligence, a subject discussed in this chapter. To support his position, Jensen has cited evidence on twins gathered by British psychologist Sir Cyril Burt.

The Issue for this chapter recounts the story of Burt and his statistics. (Jensen has stated he can no longer accept Burt's evidence, but he continues to believe that IQ tests reflect intelligence.)

Did Sir Cyril cook the figures?

One of the most influential educational psychologists of this century, especially in the field of intelligence testing, was Sir Cyril Burt, who died in 1971.

Burt believed that heredity could explain the high scores achieved in intelligence tests, that mental abilities were inborn, and that intelligence was concentrated in the higher social classes. When he found an unusually high IQ among orphans or adopted children, he explained, "We commonly learned later on that the child was the illegitimate offspring of a father belonging to a superior social class." The class system, he firmly believed, was an economic reflection of a genetically determined order of human merit.

It is not surprising to learn that Burt was influenced by eugeni-

cists, and, as a matter of fact, was acquainted with Sir Francis Galton, the principal founder of eugenics, who believed that social controls could improve or impair the qualities of future generations. Burt's explanation of differences in intelligence was invariably associated with social class. In 1912, he coauthored a paper in which Liverpool slumboys were compared with Oxford preparatory boys. He claimed the results were consistent with investigations of savage and civilized races!

Burt also conducted studies of separated pairs of identical twins.* His results showed a high correlation in the IQs of the separated twins, thus effectively reducing the significance of the environment on intelligence scores.

Burt's work influenced educational legislation in England. The British Education Act of 1944 was based explicitly on his statistical reports, which established principles of educational selectivity and segregation: three types of schools established for different innate abilities—grammar schools, technical schools, and secondary schools.

In 1961, he published a major paper, "Intelligence and Social Mobility," which was a deadly attack against those who argued

*Monozygotic twins raised from birth in separate households.

that the environment could affect scores achieved in intelligence tests. This paper also demonstrated a remarkable correlation between intelligence and social class.

This work has been widely quoted by geneticists and psychologists, especially those involved in IQ testing, since it appeared to be the most comprehensive study ever performed in the relation of intelligence to social class and social mobility. Burt's publications had great impact on such men as Jensen, Eyesenck, and Herrnstein, staunch supporters of the importance of heredity on intelligence and intelligence scores. Burt was knighted in 1946 for his work on intelligence and his recommendations for educational reform.

Doubts about the validity and accuracy (as well as the honesty) of Burt's work surfaced just a few years after his death. Professor Leon Kamin (1971) of Princeton questioned Burt's studies of twins. Kamin pointed out that Burt's number of separated identical twin pairs increased from 15 in 1943 to 21 in 1955, to 30 in 1957, to 42 in 1958, and in 1966 reached 53, probably the world's largest sample of an extremely rare phenomenon. Yet the correlation of intelligence of the separated twin pairs remained constant to three decimal places over this period of twenty-five years, even though the number of pairs had increased almost four times. Such a stable correlation is so unlikely that statisticians consider it impossible unless the figures were deliberately fixed. ately fixed.

An English journalist, Oliver Gillie (1978, 1979), tried to find the women who had collaborated with Burt in his research and publications in order to learn more of Burt's unlikely statistics. Gillie searched records at universities and psychological societies for traces of these three women associates, and he also talked to friends and employees of Burt who should have known the women and something of their whereabouts. However, he found no trace of them with the possible exception of one—a Miss Howard—who, said Gillie, if she did exist, was not the person Burt said she was. It is difficult to know why Burt would fabricate such associates, or what purpose this might have served.

The most damaging report on Burt's work is probably Professor D. D. Dorfman's examination of the statistics given in Burt's 1961 report. Burt claimed he had studied 40,000 people over a period of fifty years, comparing the intelligence of children and their fathers. He illustrated his findings in tables that showed the intelligence of fathers of six social classes and, in another table, the intelligence of their children.

In results so perfect they are too good to be true, Burt found an almost perfect normal curve of intelligence among fathers and children, and the statistics for each group were almost identical. The probability of a normal curve for intelligence is highly unlikely. The U.S. Army, for example, in the Alpha test scores for intelligence given to draftees in World War I, found a skewed, not a normal, curve. Other summaries of intelligence scores show similarly skewed results. That children's intelligence scores would be identical with their fathers', over a period of fifty years, is equally unlikely.

Dorfman concluded that Burt's results were precisely what they should have been according to a theoretical formula for such work, but, he added, such results do not occur in nature. "The almost perfect fit of Burt's adult and child distributions to the normal curve suggests that his 'actual' distributions are not actual distributions." Furthermore, "we may now say that, beyond a reasonable doubt, the frequency distributions of Burt's tables . . . were carefully constructed so as to [be] in agreement with the normal curve." And, finally, "these findings show, beyond any reasonable doubt, that Burt fixed the row and column totals of the tables in his highly acclaimed 1961 study."

We might ask, along with Gillie, "Why did psychologists, educationalists, and civil servants let him get away with it for so long?—for any reasonably careful inspection shows Burt's work to be careless, riddled with implausibilities, and inadequately documented? . . . Sir Cyril Burt, the supposed guardian of intellectual rigour, the hero of the educational conservatives, the defender of a future which was to be given over to the genetically pure, was one of the most formidable confidence tricksters British society has produced. . . . Sir Cyril takes his place alongside the manufacturers of the Piltdown Skull."

SOURCES:

Dorfman, D. D., "The Cyril Burt Questions: New Findings," *Science*, 201:1177, September 29, 1978.

Gillie, Oliver, "Sir Cyril Burt and the Great IQ Fraud," *New Statesman*, 24, November, 1978.

———, "Burt's Missing Ladies," *Science*, 204:1035, June 8, 1979.

Jensen, Arthur R., *Bias in Mental Testing*, New York: Free Press, 1980.

Kamin, Leon, *The Science and Politics of IQ*, New York: John Wiley & Sons. 1974.

◇ Introduction

We examined human variation in Chapters 5 and 6 from an adaptive point of view, in which physical differences among populations were explained largely in terms of selection pressures leading to possible adaptive responses.

This emphasis on selection and adaptation is a recent approach to human variation. In the past, scholars busied themselves constructing racial typologies, seeking the origin of races, and attributing to races a variety of personality traits.

In this chapter, we shall briefly trace the history of the scholarly and scientific approaches to human diversity. We shall question the value of racial typologies and the concept of race itself. We shall also examine the relationship—if any—between human diversity and behavior. Do physical traits determine what people do? Does pigmentation, for example, limit or aid intelligence? Is intelligence, as reflected in IQ test achievements, the result of heredity or environment, or the interaction of both?

◇ Racial Classification

As early as 1350 B.C., Egyptians recognized physical differences of populations by using four colors to distinguish various groups: red for Egyptians, yellow for those to the east, white for people from the north, and black for Africans to the south (Gossett, 1963, p. 4). In more recent times, classification of populations has been based mainly on such physical traits as pigmentation of skin, eyes, and hair; hair form, body build, and nose form. Three hundred years ago, in 1684, François Bernier, a French physician, divided the world's populations into what we call races: Europeans, Far Easterners, Blacks, and Lapps. It was "probably the first attempt in history to classify all the races of mankind" (Gossett, 1963, p. 33).

From that time until the present, scientists, including such luminaries as Linnaeus, Buffon, Huxley, and others have constructed racial classifications. In Box 7-1 are examples of racial classifications, which range from the simple fourfold division of Linnaeus to the complex schemes of Deniker and Hooton.

During the sixteenth and seventeenth centuries, explorers returning from their travels to newly discovered continents brought back information about people unknown to Europeans. Scholars, like Linnaeus, attempted to fit this knowledge into an orderly arrangement, basing their classifications mainly on skin color and geography. Johann Blumenbach, a professor of medicine at the University of Göttingen in Germany, made a thorough study of numerous skulls and developed an influential racial classification. His 1781 division of

Caucasian,* Mongolian, Malay, Ethiopian, and American (which came to be popularly known as white, yellow, brown, black, and red) still persists to this day as one of the most common racial divisions of humankind. Blumenbach used the same criteria of skin color and geography as earlier scholars and added a number of others, such as shape of skull and face, hair color, nose and chin form.

Differences in races at this time were often explained by climate and environment. In the United States, the Reverend Mr. Samuel Stanhope Smith, a professor at the College of New Jersey (later Princeton) attributed color mainly to climate and believed dark skin could "be considered as a universal freckle" (Gossett, 1963, p. 39). He further believed that environment was "all that stood in the way of the advancement of Negroes and other non-white races . . ." (Gossett, 1963, p. 39).

In the latter half of the eighteenth and much of the nineteenth centuries, there was a continuing discussion of the origin of races: The **monogenists** believed all races were derived from a single pair, and credited Adam and Eve as the source. The multitudinous progeny of the original pair then spread over the world and assumed their present diversity in response to the climate and other conditions to which they were subjected. Monogenists also explained differences in human populations as deviant degeneration from the original stock.

Polygenists took the position of a multiple origin of races and ridiculed the idea that all people could have descended from Adam and Eve. In the nineteenth century, an American physician, Dr. Samuel George Morton (1799–1851), argued in favor of polygenism by pointing to his researches, which indicated that the offspring of a black and white cross, a mulatto, could bear children only with difficulty. If these women mated only with mulattoes, he maintained, their descendants would bear fewer and fewer children, and in time there would be no descendants at all! (Gossett, 1963).

In the latter part of the eighteenth century, researchers such as Blumenbach began what they considered a more scientific approach, and initiated the careful study and measurements of skulls. This practice was refined in the nineteenth century when Samuel Morton developed new ways of measuring crania by filling skulls with seed (and, later on, shot) and then weighing this material. This new science, called **anthropometry**, became the primary concern of physical anthropologists. In 1842, Anders Retzius, a Swedish anatomist, believed he had discovered a true scientific basis for racial classification: the shape of the head. This measurement, called the *cephalic index* and a refinement of Morton's technique, was a measure of the ratio of the breadth of the skull to its length. Retzius used the cephalic index to divide

Monogenists
Term applied to those who believe that all races derived from a single pair (Adam and Eve).

Polygenists
Term applied to those who believe in a multiple origin of races.

Anthropometry
anthropos: man
metric: measure
Measurement of the human body.

---

*Blumenbach was the first to use the term Caucasian for Europeans. Thomas Huxley commented that "A Georgian woman's skull was the handsomest in his collection. Hence it became his model exemplar of human skulls, from which all others might be regarded as deviations; and out of this, by some strange hocus-pocus, grew up the notion that the Caucasian man is the prototypic 'Adamic' man, and his country the primitive centre of our kind" (cited in Count, 1950, p. 119).

◇ Box 7-1   Racial Classifications

Linnaeus, 1758

Homo europaeus
Homo asiaticus
Homo afer
Homo americanus

Buffon, 1749

Lapland
Tartar
Southern Asiatic
European
American

Blumenbach, 1781

Caucasian
Mongolian
Malay
Ethiopian
American

Saint Hilaire, 1861

Caucasian	(Caucasian, Alleghenian)
Mongolian	(Hyperborean, Malay, American, Mongo-
Ethiopian	lian, Paraborean, Australian)
Hottentot	(Kaffir, Ethiopian, Negro, Melanesian)
	(Hottentot)

Thomas H. Huxley, 1870

Negroid	(Bushman, Negro, Papuan)
Australoid	(Australians, Dravidians, Ethiopian)
Mongoloid	(Mongol, Polynesian, American Eskimo, Malay)
Xanthochroid	(Xanthochroid of Northern Europe, Melanochroid of Southern Europe, Melanochroid of Asia—Arabs, Afghans, Hindus, etc.)

J. Deniker, 1900

Types	Examples
Wooly hair; broad nose:	Bushman, Negrito, Negro, Melanesian
Curly or wavy hair:	Ethiopian, Australian, Dravidian, Assyroid
Wavy brown or black hair; dark eyes:	Indo-Afghan, Arab or Semite, Berber, Littoral-European, Ibero-insular; Western European, Adriatic
Fair, wavy or straight hair; light eyes:	Northern European, Eastern European
Straight or wavy hair; dark, black eyes:	Ainu, Polynesian, Indonesian, South American
Straight hair:	Northern American, Central American, Patagonian, Eskimo, Lapp, Ugrian, Turkish, Mongol

E. A. Hooton, 1946

Primary Race	Primary Subrace	Composite Race*	Composite* Subrace	Residual Mixed* Types
White	Mediterranean	Australian	Armenoid	Nordic-Alpine
	Ainu	Indo-Dravidian	Dinaric	Nordic-
	Keltic	Polynesian		Mediterranean
	Nordic			
	Alpine			
	East Baltic			

Primary Race	Primary Subrace	Composite Race*	Composite Subrace*	Residual Mixed Types*
Negroid	African Negro	Bushman-Hottentot		
	Nilotic Negro			
	Negrito			
	Classic	Indonesian-		
Mongoloid	Mongoloid	Mongoloid		
	Arctic Mongoloid	American Indian		
	Secondary Subrace			
	Malay-Mongoloid			
	Indonesian			

Stanley M. Garn, 1965

Geographical Races: "A collection of race populations, separated from other such collections by major geographical barriers" (p. 14).

Amerindian
Polynesian
Micronesian
Melanesian-Papuan
Australian
Asiatic
Indian
European
African

Local Races: "A breeding population adapted to local selection pressures and maintained by either natural or social barriers to gene interchange" (p. 16).

Northwest European
Northeast European
Alpine
Mediterranean
East African   These are examples of local races; there are many, many more.
Bantu
Tibetan
North Chinese
Extreme Mongoloid
Hindu

Micro-Races: Not well defined but apparently refers to neighborhoods within a city or a city itself since "marriage or mating, is a mathematical function of distance. With millions of potential mates, the male ordinarily chooses one near at hand" (p. 19).

*Example of categories, not to be read across.

Dolichocephalic
dolicho: narrow
cephal: head
Narrow or long-headed; a skull in which
the width is less than 75 percent of the
length.

Brachycephalic
brachy: short, broad
Broad-headed; a skull in which the width is
80 percent or more of the length.

Typology
The science of dividing humankind into
discrete racial types.

Mongrelization
Racial mixture.

Europe into two types: a longheaded or **dolichocephalic** type and a round-headed or **brachycephalic** type.

Anthropometry was enthusiastically promoted by Paul Broca, French neurosurgeon and physical anthropologist, who, in 1859, founded The Anthropological Society of Paris, the first anthropological organization in Europe. He published statistical treatises with complicated diagrams and arranged his collection of 2,000 skulls into 60 different series (Gossett, 1963, p. 76). Broca was also a resourceful, ingenious inventor of measuring instruments and devised craniometers and other gadgetry in order to discover statistical relationships of the skull. Cranial measurements proceeded with enthusiastic zeal, and the peak of anthropometry was probably reached in 1900, when A. von Török took 5,000 measurements on a single skull (Barzun, 1965, p. 117).

Broca, as did many other anthropologists during this period, believed there was some connection between brain and race, and that measuring the shape of the skull was the best way to determine the content of the brain. He even believed it possible to identify the social class of the skulls he studied!

Despite the emphasis on anthropometry by these "scientific anthropologists," others were questioning the value of such measurements. Broca himself noted that two anthropologists rarely obtained the same figures when they measured the same skull. "The human head," he complained, "is too irregular ... to allow accurate comparison on a statistical basis" (Gossett, 1963, p. 76), a conclusion which nevertheless did not deter his anthropometric research.

With the publication of Darwin's *Origin of Species* in 1859, there was some attempt to take evolutionary principles into consideration for racial classifications. But the emphasis on typology continued, as we see (Box 7-1), in the racial types suggested by Deniker in 1900 and Hooten as late as 1946.

However, concern with the division of the earth's human population into races was the goal of many physical anthropologists during the latter half of the nineteenth century. The assumption throughout this period was that pure races existed (sometime in the past), and it was the responsibility of anthropologists to define them. To support such a position, it was necessary to believe that races had not basically changed from whatever they were at the time of origin. And if races were fixed—a conflict with evolutionary thought, which anthropologists accepted—then there must be physical traits that remain fixed. That is, those physical traits that did not adapt to environmental conditions could be used for racial classification; those that did adapt, could not. There was, therefore, constant effort to locate *nonadaptive* traits. It was believed that once races evolved, racial traits persisted even if the people moved to another environment. Since it was obvious that pure races did not exist, certainly not in Europe, physical differences in modern populations were said to be the result of a mixture of already formed races.

The search for nonadaptive traits to serve as a basis for the classification of racial types centered on the cephalic index, although hair form, eye form, and prominence of the nose were also considered nonadaptive. W. Z. Ripley, in a book published in 1899 and widely read in the United States, summarized much of the research of European scientists. Ripley relied heavily on headform as a basis for his racial classification of Europe into three types. Not everyone agreed with the emphasis on head measurements, and Franz Boas, early in this century, criticized Ripley for "treating the cephalic index as the 'primary principle of classification' " (Stocking, 1968, p. 181). As a result of his well-known study of body form of European immigrants and their children, Boas claimed that headform was a nonadaptive trait (Boas, 1940). Although Boas was influential in the area of cultural anthropology, his views in physical anthropology did not have the same impact, and interest in typing populations continued.

Typology presents problems not readily resolved. How many divisions are there? Estimates range from as few as 3 to more than 300. There are primary divisions, major subdivisions, minor subdivisions, composite subdivisions, and so on. What is the significance of these divisions of divisions, and what is their reality? Do they represent actual living populations, or merely ideal types? What criteria are used to separate one type from another, one subdivision from another? Is one trait more important than another? Skin pigmentation, for example, is the trait most people would consider as the basic classificatory criterion; should it carry more weight than, say, head shape, nose shape, body build, or stature? If so (or if not), why? For example, in his racial classification of 1900, Deniker typed northern Europeans as tall with wavy, reddish hair, reddish white skin, and dolichocephalic skulls. What, then, shall we do with a northern European answering this description whose brother is short, not tall, with straight rather than wavy hair, and a darkish rather than reddish white skin?

There is a basic assumption in typological classification (noted above) that races existed in a pure state at some time in the past, before migrations of recent times produced the mixtures of today. **Mongrelization** is the term often used by racists. But migration has always existed; with culture, humans are capable of taking a goodly portion of their environment with them, and as Hooten has succinctly aphorized, "when groups meet they may or may not bleed, but they always breed." As Mayr has said, "To speak of 'pure races' is sheer nonsense" (1970, p. 397).

Finally, typologies tell us little if anything of human evolution. Classification, as Washburn noted, is useful if we are concerned with anatomical, genetic, and structural differences between people, "but it is useful under no other circumstances, as far as I can see" (Washburn, 1963, p. 527).

For these and other reasons, many anthropologists no longer accept the assumption that races exist and have turned away from the racial concept as biologically unrealistic. Such studies are regarded as unrewarding. Those still concerned with classification have drawn upon population genetics and consider the breeding population "the basic unit of evolutionary change . . . the unit whose structure changes in response to the action of the mechanisms of evolution" (Kelso, 1974, p. 301).

It is difficult to escape the conclusion that as a concept, race, like quicksilver, is awkward to take hold of. Just when we think we have it in our grasp, it slips through our fingers. As French anthropologist Jean Hiernaux puts it:

> To dismember mankind into races as a convenient approximation requires such a distortion of the facts that any usefulness disappears; on the contrary, only the harm done by such practices remains (Hiernaux, 1964, p. 43).

Figure 7-1 Craniometer.

◇ Definitions of Race

To understand the difficulties the concept of race presents, it may help to review briefly the process of speciation (p. 107). Species is defined as "a group of interbreeding organisms that are reproductively isolated from other such groups" (p. 106), and biologists are agreed that species is an evolutionary unit. The definition of race is more elusive, and race is not an evolutionary unit, but an arbitrary one. We see this more clearly with the process of speciation.

As the populations within a species diverge, especially between isolated groups, differences arise. When the differences become detectable, taxonomists may classify the populations as races, or subspecies. With continued isolation and divergence, the groups are known as *incipient species* (or biological races), on their way to becoming species. However, ". . . the decisions about what characteristics to emphasize in describing differences between the populations are relatively arbitrary ones" (Bodmer and Cavalli-Sforza, 1976, p. 561).

The division of the populations of any species into biological "races" tends to be arbitrary to some degree, but when it comes to human races, the situation is a quagmire. The populations of *H. sapiens* are not on their way to becoming separate species, and the reasons for this are quite clear. Human groups have been isolated in the past but never long enough to speciate. As mentioned, humans take their culture with them when they migrate, and are not entirely dependent on their environment. They can and do migrate to a considerable extent. Consequently, there has been gene exchange between groups that has kept them interfertile and, therefore, members of the same species. As communication and the means of transportation improved, and as more efficient technology developed, humans became even more independent of the environment, and the chance of speciation has become remote.

Perhaps the basic problem in defining race is to decide on the criteria. As we see from the examples on pages 192–193, these are arbitrary. A recent definition demonstrates the dilemma: A race is ". . . a division of a species which differs from other divisions by the frequency with which certain hereditary traits appear among its members" (Brues, 1977, p. 1). Which hereditary traits? How are they selected? On what basis? Do the same traits apply in all cases? There is no agreement on the answers. Besides, no group classified as a race differs in all its traits from another race. ". . . the boundaries between the races drawn on the basis of one trait will not coincide with boundaries drawn on the basis of another trait" (Bodmer and Cavalli-Sforza, 1976, p. 562). If we cannot agree on racial criteria, then defining race and classifying populations into racial groups appears impossible.

Although we question the value of the racial concept, it may be instructive to list definitions of race, which may delineate even further the reasons why anthropologists are dissatisfied with the concept.

Already, in 1749, Buffon (see p. 33) was aware that humankind did not consist of separate species, but were varieties of the same species. This is not, strictly speaking, a definition, but it does recognize the separation of our species into subdivisions based upon the environment and interbreeding.

Upon the whole, every circumstance concurs in proving that mankind are [*sic*] not composed of species essentially different from each other; that, on the contrary, there was originally but one species, who, after multiplying and spreading over the whole surface of the earth, have undergone various changes by the influence of climate, food, mode of living, epidemic diseases, and the mixture of dissimilar individuals. . . . (Buffon, cited in Snyder, 1962, p. 102).

Rudolf Virchow (1896) also saw races as varieties originating from two factors, heredity and environment: ". . . there can be no doubt that *races are nothing more than hereditary variations* . . . we must derive races also from the influence of external causes, and we may define them as *acquired deviations from the original type*" (cited in Count, 1950, p. 193). Although not the first, Virchow's view of race as hereditary variations suggests an evolutionary orientation.

As time went on, anthropologists emphasized phenotypic traits as important in racial analysis. In 1926, Hooton offered the following definition:

A race is a great division of mankind, the members of which, though individually varying, are characterized as a group by a certain combination of morphological and metrical features, principally non-adaptive, which have been derived from their common descent.

Figure 7-2   Virchow.

In addition to emphasizing visible phenotypic traits (morphological features), Hooten included measurements of the body that had occupied so much of anthropological research in the latter half of the nineteenth century. He also made an attempt to construct a more precise definition by restricting it to traits that were presumably nonadaptive—that is, unaffected by the environment—since he considered these the most objective racial markers. Implicit in this approach is the belief that races do not change over time, that if it were possible somehow to find traits unaffected by the environment, true or pure races could be determined (see p. 194).

We now know the search for nonadaptive traits is a futile quest, that a phenotype is the result of the dynamic interaction of several genes *and* the environment.

As population genetics became important in biological research, the concept of population became part of the definition. In 1950, Boyd defined race "as a population which differs significantly from other human populations in regard to the frequency of one or more genes it possesses" (Boyd, 1950, p. 207).

Livingstone objects to the simplistic use of gene frequencies as a criterion for race, since such a position implies that each population—which probably differs in the frequency of some gene from other populations—would be a separate race (Livingstone, 1964, p. 49).

One of the most recent modifications of the definition of race adds the concept of a *breeding*, or Mendelian, population (Garn, 1969). Livingstone again objects since the concept of breeding population may be difficult to apply (see p. 119). Garn, however, views race "as a breeding population, neither more nor less" (1969, p. 6). One local race (see Box 7-1), ranging from Tangier to the Dardanelles and including the Arabian Peninsula, Garn calls Mediterranean. However, this is a very unlikely breeding population, containing, as it

Figure 7-3   E. A. Hooton.

does, wide differences in such factors as social class, religion, economy, and philosophy. Very few Christians interbreed with Muslims, or Arab Beduins with, say, Italian farmers. And even if it were possible to identify a local race, "The actual fabric of human mating behavior today is made of such a complicated and continually changing weave that not only is a simple count impossible, but even an estimate is a deception" (Kelso, 1974, p. 304).

The foregoing definitions of race and comments are not intended to discourage or confuse. The plain fact is that a great deal of confusion abounds among anthropologists, geneticists, and other researchers concerned with the concept of race. That there are physical differences among human beings is an obvious fact requiring no discussion. No one will mistake an indigenous resident of China for a European or African. But the matter is not that simple.

Topinard, writing almost 100 years ago, already recognized the problems still being discussed today:

> Races exist; it is undeniable; our intelligence comprehends them; our minds see them; our labors separate them out. If in thought we suppress the intermixtures of peoples, their interbreedings, in a flash we see them stand forth—simple, inevitable, with their trait-patterns and physiological systems—a compulsive consequence of collective heredity. *But nowhere can we put our fingers upon them* (emphasis ours, cited by Scheidt, 1924, p. 389).

To confuse the matter of race definition even further, the term "race," as it is popularly used, is more a sociocultural than biological concept. That is, a group of people may be designated as a race regardless of their genetic traits. Thus, children of mixed black and white parents are considered black, though genetically they are as much "white" as "black." Often designated as races are ethnic groups (Germans, French, Russians, etc.), religious groups (Muslims, Buddhists, Jews, etc.), political groups (communists, fascists). This also adds to the confusion. In wartime, when emotions run high, all manner of vices, based on "racial" traits, are attributed to the enemy (e.g., the Germans and Japanese in World War II and the Vietnamese in the Vietnam war.)

If we restrict the word "race," no matter how difficult it may be to define the term, to genetic traits, it may be possible to eliminate some of the misunderstanding associated with the concept of race. However, the prognosis is not optimistic.

What, then, are we to do about the concept of race? Is race a reality? Is a breeding population a race? Are races geographic isolates? Is it even possible to study races? Is the word "race" so loaded with misconception, misunderstanding, fallacy, prejudice, and bigotry that the term itself should be changed and its study limited? Or is Dunn more perceptive when he suggests, "It seems better to define and explain its use, and to free it from its bad and false meaning, than to give up the problem by excluding the word" (Dunn, 1951, p. 12).

The validity and utility of race, as a concept, is still debated by anthropologists. Typological divisions of humankind, however, which once occupied so much anthropological effort, appear to be a phenomenon of the past. As we have indicated, there are too many problems in the construction of racial typologies, and, once a typology is developed, the nagging question remains: So what?

Instead of placing an entire population in, as it were, a racial straightjacket, many anthropologists consider the study of the distribution of single traits to be more rewarding from the point of view of evolutionary theory. This is the clinal approach to human diversity.

◇ Clinal Distribution: One Genetic Trait

A relatively recent approach* to human variation is *clinal distribution*. Just as temperatures are plotted on a weather map by means of isotherms that join points with the same temperature, so also may gene frequencies be plotted. Thus, the distribution of a particular trait is indicated on a map by zones, known as clines (Fig. 7-4). This description simply reveals the variation of that trait over a geographic area, and by itself implies no explanation, racial or otherwise. Nor does such a distribution lead to racial typologies. A clinal distribution calls for an *evolutionary explanation* of the variation: Why does the frequency of allele B, in our figure, vary as we move from east to west across Europe? Evolutionary theory—mutation, genetic drift, natural selection, migration—is one way in which clinal variation may be explained.

Human variation is perceived quite differently when approached from a clinal point of view. No attempt is made to construct a typology of traits, but rather to apply the principles of evolution. Is the variation of gene frequency due to the advantage of one gene over another? Has there been migration to or from the clinal area that may have altered the gene frequency, or perhaps an accident known genetically as drift? An advantage of a clinal study is that gene and trait frequencies can be graphically represented as they are in Figures 7-4 and 7-5. They suggest "migratory patterns and other aspects of population history" and "observed clinal variation in a trait is particularly amenable to explanation by mathematical methods of population genetics. In this sense, there is probably no superior method by which the evolutionary mechanisms responsible for interpopulation variation in single traits can be identified" (Bennett, 1979, pp. 357–358).

An example of an evolutionary clinal approach may be seen in Dr. Joseph Birdsell's discussion of the distribution of tawny hair he found in his field work among Australian aborigines. The heaviest distribution of this blond hair is among several tribal groups in the Australian western desert (see Fig. 7-5), and the frequency then declines on a gradient outward from this center, although not uniformly in all directions. Professor Birdsell writes (1981, pp. 352–353):

> The evolutionary significance of this clinal distribution seems apparent, even though the exact genetic basis for its inheritance has not yet been unraveled. The trait acts as though it was determined by a single codominant gene. It would

---

*J. S. Huxley introduced the clinal concept, as it applied to plants, in 1938.

Multivariate
Pattern for several traits.

appear that somewhere in the central region of high frequency, mutations, and probably repeated mutations, occurred from normal dark brown hair to this depigmented variety. The pattern of distribution indicates that it was favored by selection in some totally unknown fashion. Over considerable periods of time, through gene exchange between adjacent tribes, the new mutant gene prospered and spread outward. It seems unlikely that lightly pigmented hair in childhood should in itself have any selective advantage. Rather, it is much more probable that certain effects of this mutant gene have somehow biochemically heightened the fitness of these Aborigines in their generally desert environment. Presumably the new gene mixed well with the other genes in their pools and so *new coadaptive equilibria were produced*. The equilibria seem to have attained a plateau in the region where frequencies exceed 90 percent. (See pp. 147–148 for a discussion of coadaptation.)

Professor Birdsell goes on to point out that one character cannot define a subspecies or race, and that "this example illustrates why races are scientifically undefinable." (Birdsell, 1981, p. 352). However, while this example does nothing for the definition of race, it is a good example of microevolution. "This pattern of blondness is a spectacular case of *transient polymorphism*, that is a polymorphic character changing in time, here reflected as changes in space" (Birdsell, 1981, p. 352). And Birdsell wonders whether, if British colonization had not cut the process short, all Australian aborigines might have become blond-haired.

Figure 7-4 A cline frequency of the B allele. This computer-generated map shows the frequency of the B allele of the ABO blood-group system. Note the higher frequencies in Asia, and the gradual decreasing frequencies as the clines move into Europe. (Courtesy of P. E. Schreiber, IBM Research Laboratory, San Jose, California.)

Greater than 0.160

From 0.140 to 0.160

From 0.120 to 0.140

From 0.100 to 0.120

From 0.080 to 0.100

From 0.060 to 0.080

From 0.040 to 0.060

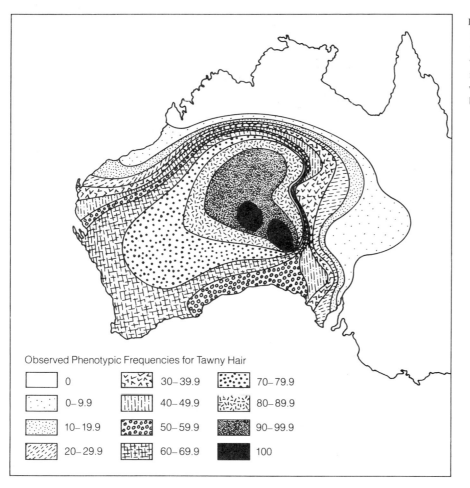

Figure 7-5   Gene distribution, tawny hair in Australia. Note the concentration of tawny hair in the center of distribution which can be traced by clines in a decreasing gradient. This pattern can thus be viewed on an evolutionary and genetic basis.

Observed Phenotypic Frequencies for Tawny Hair

0	30– 39.9	70– 79.9
0– 9.9	40– 49.9	80– 89.9
10– 19.9	50– 59.9	90– 99.9
20– 29.9	60– 69.9	100

◇ Multivariate Population Genetics

Whereas clinal studies isolate patterns of genetic variation one trait at a time, **multivariate** studies seek to describe the pattern for several traits simultaneously. Because the statistical manipulations of such analyses are exceedingly complex, high-speed computers have proven an invaluable tool.

An excellent example of this kind of approach to human diversity was undertaken by Harvard population geneticist R. D. Lewontin (1972), and his results are most informative. Lewontin measured the degree of population differences in gene frequencies for seventeen polymorphic traits, including many of those discussed in Chapter 5. In his analysis, Lewontin immediately faced the dilemma: Which groups (populations) should he contrast and how should they be weighted (all equally, or bigger groups like Arabs weighted differently than smaller ones like residents of the island, Tristan da Cunha)? After considerable deliberation, Lewontin decided to break down his sample into seven geographical areas (corresponding to the traditional concept of "major race") and included several (all equally weighted) populations within each. He then calculated how much of the total genetic variability within our species could be accounted for by these population subdivisions. (See Table 7-1.)

Surprisingly, only 6.3% of all variation can be accounted for at the level of major (geographic) race. In other words, close to 94% of human genetic diversity occurs *within* these gigantic groups. The large population units within races (generally corresponding to Garn's local races) account for an average of an additional 8.3%. Amazingly, the traditional concept of race (which isolates large human groups) explains about 15% of human genetic variation, leaving the remaining 85% unaccounted for.

Table 7-1   Inclusive List of All Populations Used in Lewontin's Population Genetics Study (1972).

Caucasians

Arabs, Armenians, Austrians, Basques, Belgians, Bulgarians, Czechs, Danes, Dutch, Egyptians, English, Estonians, Finns, French, Georgians, Germans, Greeks, Gypsies, Hungarians, Icelanders, Indians (Hindi-speaking), Italians, Irani, Norwegians, Oriental Jews, Pakistani (Urdu-speakers), Poles, Portuguese, Russians, Spaniards, Swedes, Swiss, Syrians, Tristan da Cunhans, Welsh

Black Africans

Abyssinians (Amharas), Bantu, Barundi, Batutsi, Bushmen, Congolese, Ewe, Fulani, Gambians, Ghanaians, Hobe, Hottentot, Hututu, Ibo, Iraqi, Kenyans, Kikuyu, Liberians, Luo, Madagascans, Mozambiquans, Msutu, Nigerians, Pygmies, Senegalese, Shona, Somalis, Sudanese, Tanganyikans, Tutsi, Ugandans, U.S. Blacks, "West Africans," Xosa, Zulu

Mongoloids

Ainu, Bhutanese, Bogobos, Bruneians, Buriats, Chinese, Dyaks, Filipinos, Ghashgai, Indonesians, Japanese, Javanese, Kirghiz, Koreans, Lapps, Malayans, Senoy, Siamese, Taiwanese, Tatars, Thais, Turks

South Asian Aborigines

Andamanese, Badagas, Chenchu, Irula, Marathas, Naiars, Oraons, Onge, Tamils, Todas

Amerinds

Alacaluf, Aleuts, Apache, Atacameños, "Athabascans," Aymara, Bororo, Blackfeet, Bloods, "Brazilian Indians," Chippewa, Caingang, Choco, Coushatta, Cuna, Diegueños, Eskimo, Flathead, Huasteco, Huichol, Ica, Kwakiutl, Labradors, Lacandon, Mapuche, Maya, "Mexican Indians," Navaho, Nez Percé, Paez, Pehuenches, Pueblo, Quechua, Seminole, Shoshone, Toba, Utes, "Venezuelan Indians," Xavante, Yanomama

Oceanians

Admiralty Islanders, Caroline Islanders, Easter Islanders, Ellice Islanders, Fijians, Gilbertese, Guamians, Hawaiians, Kapingas, Maori, Marshellese, Melanuans, "Melanesians," "Micronesians," New Britons, New Caledonians, New Hebrideans, Palauans, Papuans, "Polynesians," Saipanese, Samoans, Solomon Islanders, Tongans, Trukese, Yapese

Austrialian Aborigines

Source: *Evolutionary Biology*, Volume 6, ed. by Dobzhansky et al. (article by R. Lewontin), p. 387. Reprinted with permission of Plenum Publishing Corporation.

The vast majority of genetic differences among human beings is thus explicable in terms of differences from one village to another, from one family to another, and to a very significant degree, from one person to another— even within the same family. Of course, when you recall the vast amount of human polymorphism (discussed in Chapter 5) and the ways this genetic variability is rescrambled during meiosis/sexual reproduction (discussed in Chapter 3), all this individual variation should not be that amazing.

Our superficial visual perceptions tell us race does exist. But the visible phenotypic traits usually used to make racial distinctions (skin color, hair shape, nose shape, etc.) may very well be a highly biased sample, not giving an accurate picture of the actual patterns of *genetic variation*. The polymorphic traits used by Lewontin are a more objective basis for accurate biological comparisons of human groups, and they indicate that the traditional concept of race tells us very little about human variation. Indeed, Lewontin concludes with a ringing condemnation:

> Human racial classification is of no social value and is positively destructive of social and human relations. Since such racial classification is now seen to be of virtually no genetic or taxonomic significance either, no justification can be offered for its continuance (Lewontin, 1972, p. 397).

Not all population geneticists, however, are quite this critical. After all, Lewontin did find that slightly more than 6% of human variation is accounted for in the large geographic segments traditionally called major races. Whereas this is certainly a minority of all variation within *Homo sapiens*, it is not necessarily biologically insignificant. If one feels compelled to continue classifying humankind into large geographic segments, population genetics offers some aid in isolating consistent patterns of geographic variation. One such classification suggests our species can be partitioned into three major geographic groups: Africans, Caucasians, and a heterogeneous group of Easterners, including all aboriginal populations of the Pacific area (Bodmer and Cavalli-Sforza, 1976).

Whereas, to some degree, these three groups form contrasting genetic units, we must remember that the total amount of genetic variation *within* them (from one person to another, one village to another, one tribe to another, etc.) is far more than exists *between* them.

We have thus far discussed race in the abstract, as a concept, but there is a very practical aspect of race that must be considered in our modern world: the association of race and behavior, which we take up in the following section.

◇ Race and Behavior

The fact that people differ has, as we remarked at the beginning of this chapter, long been recognized, at least as far back in recorded history as the ancient Egyptians. Association of personality traits and race has also long been suggested. In his famous taxonomic scheme, Linnaeus (see p. 32), in 1758, classified humans into four groups (Box 7-1). He also assigned behavioral traits to each group: American Indians are choleric; Europeans, sanguine; Asiatics, melancholy; and Africans, phlegmatic.

One hundred years later, personality traits were still being attributed to race by, among others, Count de Gobineau, sometimes called the "Father of Racist Ideology" (Biddiss, 1970). We must point out that a *racial* classification differs from a *racist* one. The former attempts—usually unsuccessfully—to categorize humans into meaningful groups without making distinctions concerning the superiority of one versus another. Racist typologies, on the other hand, explicitly attempt—always unsuccessfully—to impute "superior" behavioral characteristics to some races and "inferior" attributes to others. Not surprisingly, whoever is doing the classifying invariably places himself or herself in the most "superior" group. Anthropologists, for the most part, have avoided the inevitable pitfalls of racist thinking. This, however, has not prevented those who exploit racist ideology from using anthropological classifications.

Gobineau claimed undesirable traits for Africans, more desirable for Asiatics, and most desirable, of course, for Europeans. Needless to say, neither psychologists nor anthropologists find any validity to the correlation of personality and race. As Professor Alexander Alland, Columbia University anthropologist, points out (1971, p. 35):

> For those who have done fieldwork in Africa, there can be little doubt that behavioral and cognitive patterns in the black community in the United States bear little resemblance to those in Africa, and that, in fact, such patterns are highly variable in Africa and dependent more upon cultural differences than shared gene pools.

RACE AND INTELLIGENCE

Belief in the relationship between race and personality is popular even today, but there is no evidence that personality or any cultural trait, or any aspect of culture, such as religion or language, is in any way racial. Very likely, most scholars today would agree with this last statement, but there is an area of disagreement still being debated with a vehemence and emotion usually uncharacteristic of the academic community. That area is the question of whether race and intelligence are associated. The overwhelming majority of academic opinion (in anthropology, biology, genetics, psychology, and sociology) cannot find valid evidence that relates the two phenomena. There are, however, scientists who *do* believe in the relationship, and perhaps the best-known advocate of the proposition that race (i.e., heritability) is the *causal* factor in intelligence is Professor Arthur R. Jensen. He estimates the heritability of intelligence at about 75% (Jensen, 1980, p. 244).

Jensen, professor of educational psychology at the University of California, Berkeley, believes that intelligence is a correlate of race, that intelligence is inherited, that IQ tests measure intelligence, that racial intelligence differences can be researched from a heritability point of view, that the uncertainty of the heredity-environment problem can be reduced, and that the lower average IQ scores of blacks (about 15 points) are a function of race (Jensen, 1969a).

Jensen's views have been criticized by scientists from various disciplines. In his recent review and analysis of the literature on testing intelligence,

Ekberg (1979, p. 55) is led to seriously question the degree to which the idea of a general intelligence can have usefulness in real-world pursuits. Instead, all the various lines of evidence indicate that behavior is too multiform to be encapsulated under the label of *intelligence,* unless what we intend by intelligence is something quite a bit different from that which is usually intended.

Much of the criticism of Jensen's, and other similar views, may be grouped under two headings: (1) inadequacy of the IQ test as a measure of intelligence; and (2) the failure to consider the influence of environment (in a broad sense) on ability and performance.

THE IQ TEST: UNITARY CHARACTER OF INTELLIGENCE

IQ tests, such as the Stanford-Binet, purport to give a single *general* rating of mental ability, known as "g," but many scientists have questioned whether intelligence is, in fact, a single variable. Geneticists refer to intelligence as polygenic, that is, a number of genes are involved in producing a phenotype (see p. 136). As Bodmer, a geneticist, says, "intelligence must be a complex characteristic under the control of many genes" (Bodmer, 1972, p. 91). William Howells, an anthropologist, echoes this view:

> First of all, intelligence is hardly a unitary character, even if forced into a single scale by IQ tests. Much work in human and animal psychology indicates that intelligence consists of differing faculties combined or substituted for one another in different ways for which the test situation may not provide an adequate measure (Howells, 1971, p. 7).

If intelligence is a complex, not unitary, characteristic and consists of a combination of differing faculties, as Bodmer and Howells suggest, then it is questionable whether intelligence consists of a single large general factor, as Jensen claims. And it is, therefore, questionable whether an intelligence test can be constructed to test the differing mental faculties.

ENVIRONMENT AND INTELLIGENCE

Those who believe that intelligence is largely genetic and can be measured by IQ tests have probably been criticized most sharply because they have failed to consider the significance of environment in the development of intelligence. The controversy over which factor is more important, nature *or* nurture, no longer applies. Both nature *and* nurture contribute, and it is probably impossible, at this point, to separate out the percentage of each contribution.

There have been attempts to sort out environmental and genetic factors, one of the best known being the study of *monozygotic* (MZ) *twins.* MZ twins share identical genotypes, and a comparison of those who have been reared together and reared apart (that is, in different environments) should prove instructive. While such studies have been done, their reliability and applicability from one population to another (often living in very different environments) are very hotly disputed. For example, Kamin (1974) analyzed studies of separated monozygotic twin pairs. In these studies, especially those performed by Sir Cyril Burt (see Issue, p. 188)—used by Jensen to support his heritability arguments—Kamin found methodological problems serious enough to throw doubt on the validity of their conclusions. After examining Kamin's analysis of Burt's figures, Jensen conceded that Burt's studies of twins were not usable for hypothesis testing (Jensen, 1974).

That average performance on IQ exams varies among groups of schoolage children is not disputed. What causes all the furor is how to *explain* these differences. If results of twin studies, etc., do not conclusively support the Jensen, et al. argument for heredity as the clearly most dominant factor, what does that leave us with? Obviously, some form of explanation that views environmental influence as significant must be considered. The following three studies reflect the view that environment must be considered as an crucial factor in IQ test results.

In 1981, Scarr reported a study, conducted by Scarr and Barker, of the cognitive differences among black and white children in Philadelphia (Scarr, 1981). These researchers found that black children performed relatively better on less culturally loaded material once the instructions were made more comprehensible to them, and also that the black environment failed to develop the skills sampled by the tests. They also noted that twins' scores were more highly correlated in the black group because family membership was more important in determining the degree to which children were exposed to the intellectual skills sampled in the tests. Their conclusion:

> The results of this study support the view that black children are being reared in circumstances that give them only marginal acquaintance with the skills and the knowledge being sampled by the tests we administered. Some families in the black community encourage the development of these skills and knowledge, whereas others do not. In general, black children do not have the same access to these skills and knowledge as white children, which explains the lower performance of black children as a group. *The hypothesis that most of the differences among the cognitive scores of black and white children are due to genetic differences between the races cannot, in our view, account for this pattern of results* (Scarr, 1981, p. 288). (Emphasis added.)

In an earlier study of genetic and environmental influences on IQ test scores, Scarr and Weinberg (1976) examined 130 black and interracial children who were adopted by advantaged white families. The authors found that the average IQ scores of these children was 106 (scores of early-adopted children were even higher). This was about 12 points higher than the score of black children with two black parents living in the same area, and compared favorably with white children's scores. The authors concluded that:

> The major findings of the study support the view that the social environment plays a dominant role in determining the average IQ level of black children and that both social and genetic variables contribute to individual variation among them (Scarr and Weinberg, 1976, p. 133).

Willerman, et al. (1970) conducted a somewhat similar test with 4-year-old black children of mixed parents—white mother and black father and black mother and white father. The results of this study indicate a difference in IQ scores if the mother is white, or if she is black. The mean score for black children with a white mother was 100.9; with a black mother, 93.7. Marital status of the mother also made a difference. The mean score of children of a white married mother was 102.3; of an unmarried mother, 98.5. Children of a black married mother, 97.6; unmarried mother, 82.6.

It seems quite clear from these studies that environment must be seriously considered as a significant influence on IQ scores. A number of environmental factors have been noted by researchers.

Scarr, in her 1981 report, suggests that many black families fail to provide the skills and knowledge sampled by the tests. Where these skills are provided in the home (black children adopted by advantaged white parents and black children of white mothers), black children scored significantly higher than black children of black parents.

Poor nutrition may be another factor that makes for lower IQ scores. Passamanick and his associates found that a deficient maternal diet associated with low income can produce pregnancy and parturition complications followed by intellectual retardation and behavioral disorders in the children (cited in Rose, 1972, p. 139). Rose also refers to a study in which nutritional supplements were added to the deficient diets of pregnant women. This resulted in significantly raised IQs in their children at the ages of 2, 3, and 4 compared with children whose mothers did not receive the supplements.

Still other factors are the attitude toward education in some socioeconomic groups, attitude toward tests, social and economic goals, and a general **weltanschauung** (world view). All of these may combine to reduce the IQ scores of blacks; it is, therefore, difficult to reconcile the glib assertions of those who promote the genetic basis of intelligence with the environmental conditions we have just reviewed.

The core of the dispute between Jensen and the majority of scientists is whether differences in black and white IQ scores are due mainly to heredity or to environment. Most scholars are agreed that it is difficult, if not impossible, to separate the two, because (as we have just discussed), the evidence is not so clearly objective that it can be easily interpreted. IQ tests, especially, are difficult to interpret because, as many investigators have emphasized, it is not possible to construct a culture-free IQ test; that is, an IQ test that eliminates completely environmental factors.

Professor Liam Hudson, professor of educational sciences at Edinburgh University, concludes a discussion of the IQ test with the observation that:

> At the moment, and probably in principle, it is impossible to design an experiment that separates out in any neat and tidy way, the influence of hereditary and environmental factors on a human being's ability to do IQ tests (Hudson, 1972, p. 15).

A similar comment is made by Professor Paul Baker, a physical anthropologist from Penn State, who has for years researched the adaptability of phenotypic traits to environmental conditions:

> Finally, I must note that popular questions such as whether race differences in intelligence exist, and if so, are they cultural or genetic in origin, are not meaningful questions at the present state of adaptational theory or evidence. At this time, we cannot even state with certainty the degree of genetic versus environmental pat-

Weltanschauung
welt: world
schauung: view
World view; a way of looking at the universe; a personal philosophy.

terning involved in the presumably adaptive variation in hand temperature: therefore, to debate seriously the genetic versus environmental patterning involved in man's total adaptive behavioral capacity (a common definition of intelligence) is inappropriate at this time as a scientific endeavor (Baker, 1966, p. 37).

Anthropologists Brace and Livingstone (1971, p. 67) suggest that *all* measured differences among major groups of humans may be explained primarily by environmental factors.

With the bulk of scientific opinion opposed to heritability as the explanation for racial intelligence, troublesome questions arise regarding the validity of IQ tests as well as the reliability of the monozygotic twin studies. We agree with Professor William Howells (1971, p. 8): "In all honesty, therefore, scientists must decline to see the existence of racial variation in mental ability at this stage."

RACISM

As a subject of inquiry, racism is not usually pursued by physical anthropologists. It may be surprising, therefore, that a discussion of racism is included in a physical anthropology textbook. Although racism, from a holistic and biosocial point of view, is a cultural phenomenon (based on attitudes, values, philosophies, economics, etc.), we believe it is not possible to divorce biological from cultural aspects in the study of humans.

Racism is the belief that one race is superior to another, and is associated with discriminatory acts and attitudes toward the "inferior" race(s). Belief in racism is usually based on the alleged inferior mental abilities of a people, and is often extended to the moral and ethical character of the "inferior" race. It is also assumed that mental abilities, ethics, and morals are hereditary.

The belief that a people are genetically inferior may be due to a number of factors, such as conquest, religion, family practices, moral and ethical systems, economic practices, and technology. Economic exploitation by imperialistic powers and competition for jobs, for example, have been suggested as reasons (or justification) for racist attitudes. European and American whites have frequently been singled out as practitioners of racism. However, there is evidence of racism in Japanese behavior toward the Eta (a lower social class in Japan) and the Ainu; in the historic attitude of the Chinese toward Mongols; and among the Bantu of South Africa toward the San (Bushmen).

From a physical anthropological point of view, racism is a cultural phenomenon that has no genetic basis. That one race is mentally or morally superior or inferior to another has yet to be demonstrated. Realistically, it is more likely that the basis of racism is rooted in economic, political, social, and psychological factors. Because it is cultural rather than genetic in character, it is difficult for physical anthropologists to address the problem. No matter what we say about the lack of evidence for mental inferiority and raise doubts about the validity of IQ scores, racism continues in many areas of the world. People point to the "strange," "immoral," and "odious" behavior of other people, and assign this to genetic factors of the "inferior" race.

We end our discussion of race and racism with a comment from the geneticist Dobzhansky:

The contention of racists is that cultural achievements of different races are so obviously unlike, their genetic capacities for achievement are just as different. It is, however, a matter of elementary genetics that the capacities of individuals, populations, or races cannot be discovered until they are given an equality of opportunity to demonstrate these capacities . . . (Dobzhansky, 1961, p. 31).

◇ Summary

This chapter is essentially divided in two parts: (1) racial classification; and (2) race and behavior.

In the past 300 years, the trend in the study of race has moved from developing typologies based on climate and geography to the use of anthropometry to the application of evolutionary and genetic principles. At the present time, many anthropologists and other scientists believe the concept of race as a research tool is futile.

Race and behavior are discussed from the point of view of IQ tests and intelligence. Jensen and others, in recent years, have emphasized the notion that race and intelligence are correlated and support their position with IQ test results. The value of IQ tests as a measure of intelligence, without considering environmental factors, is questioned. The preponderant scientific view is that the IQ test is inadequate as a measuring instrument for intelligence, and the environment is so considerable a factor, that heredity cannot be accepted as the primary reason for racial variation in intelligence.

This controversy again serves to emphasize the dual nature of humans. Human heredity/evolution is meaningless without consideration of the relevant environmental factors, and human environments have for a long time been *cultural* ones.

Racism is discussed as a cultural phenomenon, allegedly rooted in genetics, a concept for which there is no scientific evidence.

◇ Questions for Review

1. What various criteria have been used for racial classification?
2. Why is racial typology no longer considered a useful concept in the study of human diversity?
3. Why are anthropologists dissatisfied with the concept of race?
4. Trace the definition of race from Virchow to Garn. What are the objections to the criteria used in the definitions?
5. What is a cline? What is the utility of a clinal distribution?
6. What is the value of multivariate population genetics?
7. What are the problems in correlating personality with race?
8. What are the objections to the use of IQ tests as measures of intelligence?
9. How may the environment affect IQ scores?
10. Discuss intelligence in terms of "nature or nurture."

◇ Suggested Further Reading

It is possible to list only a few of the hundreds, perhaps thousands, of books and articles written on the subject of race. The books listed here (plus those in references cited) are intended to give some understanding of the seriousness and immensity of the academic attempt to cope with the concept of race, and of the social, political, and economic problems of racism.

Barzun, Jacques. *Race: A Study in Superstition*, New York: Harper and Row, 1965.
> *The author, a well-known historian, discusses beliefs about race in the recent past. Very well written and strongly recommended for its enlightened view.*

Berghe, Pierre L. van den. *Race and Racism*, New York: John Wiley and Sons, Inc., 1967.
> *A sociologist reviews the subject of race and discusses racial attitudes and problems in Mexico, South America, Brazil and the United States. For the advanced student.*

Block, N. J. and Gerald Dworkin (eds.). *The IQ Controversy*, New York: Pantheon Books (Random House), 1976.
> *Included in this volume are a number of classic articles on intelligence and heredity, some of them quite old (1915) and others more recent. The thrust of the articles by those who think otherwise (Jensen and Herrnstein) are also included. Most articles are not technical and are easily understood.*

Brues, Alice M. *People and Races*, New York: Macmillan Publishing Co., 1977.
> *An excellent summary of the somewhat more traditional anthropological view of race. Recommended for students who wish more detail than most anthropology textbooks offer.*

Garn, Stanley M. *Human Races*, Springfield, Ill.: Charles C. Thomas, 1971.
> *One of the few books by an anthropologist that includes a racial classification. Written nontechnically, and easily understood by the beginning student.*

Gould, Stephen Jay. *The Mismeasure of Man*, New York: W. W. Norton & Co., 1981.
> *A well-written argument against biological determinism by a respected paleontologist and science historian. Gould points out the fallacies in historic attempts to classify human groups on a superior/inferior basis. He also discusses the problems of testing for intelligence and attacks the belief that intelligence is a single entity. Highly recommended.*

Kennedy, Kenneth A. R. *Human Variation in Space and Time*, Dubuque, Iowa: Wm. C. Brown Co., 1976.
> *A short monograph that includes an historical view of the development of the race concept in Western thought. A good book for the beginning student.*

Klineberg, Otto. *Race Differences*, New York: Harper and Brothers, 1935.
> *Although written more than fifty years ago, this is a classic and worth reading for a psychologist's view of the evidence and significance of racial differences.*

Lawler, James M. *IQ, Heritability and Racism*, New York: International Publishers, 1978.
> *A fairly thorough review of the IQ controversy. Although definitely biased against heritability as the factor in intelligence, there is valuable information on the background of the development of the notion that heredity is a factor in IQ scores.*

Molnar, Stephen. *Human Variation*, Englewood Cliffs, New Jersey: Prentice-Hall, Inc., 1983, 1975.
> *An excellent survey of human variation, and a helpful supplement to this chapter. It is a revised edition of the author's Races, Types, and Ethnic Groups.*

Montagu, Ashley. *Race, Science and Humanity*, Princeton: D. Van Nostrand Co., Inc., 1963.
> *The author has long been interested in the concept of race and has written abundantly about it. This book is composed of a number of articles he has written on the subject. Recommended for the beginning student.*

Osborne, Richard H. (ed.). *The Biological and Social Meaning of Race*, San Francisco: W. H. Freeman and Co., 1971.

A collection of articles written by specialists in the fields of anthropology, genetics, and sociology. For the more advanced student.

Stanton, William. *The Leopard's Spots*, Chicago: The University of Chicago Press, 1960.

This is subtitled, "Scientific attitudes toward race in America. 1815–1859." It is an interesting and often anecdotal account of scientific attitudes which, from where we stand today, are strange and remarkable.

Evolutionary Record

CONTENTS

◇ ISSUE   A Cosmic Calendar

How can we possibly conceive of the awesome stretch of time that has been flowing since, scientists inform us, our universe was first formed by the cosmic explosion called the Big Bang 15 billion years ago? In *Dragons of Eden*, Carl Sagan (1977) has condensed this prodigious period into one year he calls "The Cosmic Calendar." There are three parts to the calendar.

1. A pre-December calendar. A list of a few of the significant events in the history of the universe and earth in the first 14 billion years, represented by the 334 days from January 1 through November 30

2. A month of December calendar. Events of the last 1.25 billion years represented by the month of December

3. An evening of December 31 calendar. From 10:30 P.M. (the first humans) until midnight (now), which represents the last 2.5 million years

Examine the calendar and the place of *Homo sapiens* in a time perspective. Modern humans appeared a bit more than a minute before 12:00 midnight. You may feel humble before the immensity of time of our universe, or you may feel proud of the human achievements accomplished in such a brief speck of time.

Pre-December Dates

Big Bang	January 1
Origin of the Milky Way Galaxy	May 1
Origin of the solar system	September 9
Formation of the Earth	September 14
Origin of life on Earth	~September 25
Formation of the oldest rocks known on Earth	October 2
Date of oldest fossils (bacteria and blue-green algae)	October 9
Invention of sex (by microorganisms)	~November 1
Oldest fossil photosynthetic plants	November 12
Eukaryotes (first cells with nuclei) flourish	November 15

December 31

Origin of *Proconsul* and *Ramapithecus*, probable ancestors of apes and men [?]	~ 1:30 P.M.
First humans	~10:30 P.M.
Widespread use of stone tools	11:00 P.M.
Domestication of fire by Peking man*	11:46 P.M.
Beginning of most recent glacial period	11:56 P.M.
Seafarers settle Australia	11:58 P.M.
Extensive cave painting in Europe	11:59 P.M.
Invention of agriculture	11:59:20 P.M.
Neolithic civilization; first cities	11:59:35 P.M.
First dynasties in Sumer, Ebla and Egypt; development of astronomy	11:59:50 P.M.
Invention of the alphabet; Akkadian Empire	11:59:51 P.M.
Hammurabic legal codes in Babylon; Middle Kingdom in Egypt	11:59:52 P.M.
Bronze metallurgy; Mycenaean culture; Trojan War; Olmec culture; invention of the compass	11:59:53 P.M.
Iron metallurgy; First Assyrian Empire; Kingdom of Israel; founding of Carthage by Phoenicia	11:59:54 P.M.
Asokan India; Ch'in Dynasty China; Periclean Athens; birth of Buddha	11:59:55 P.M.
Euclidean geometry; Archimedean physics; Ptolemaic astronomy; Roman Empire; birth of Christ	11:59:56 P.M.
Zero and decimals invented in Indian arithmetic; Rome falls; Moslem conquests	11:59:57 P.M.
Mayan civilization; Sung Dynasty China; Byzantine empire; Mongol invasion; Crusades	11:59:58 P.M.
Renaissance in Europe; voyages of discovery from Europe and from Ming Dynasty China; emergence of the experimental method in science	11:59:59 P.M.
Widespread development of science and technology; emergence of a global culture; acquisition of the means for self-destruction of the human species; first steps in spacecraft planetary exploration and the search for extraterrestrial intelligence	Now: The first second of New Year's Day

*See page 485 for comment on Peking man's association with fire.

1 year	=	15,000,000,000 years	1 minute	=	29,000 years
1 month	=	1,250,000,000 years	1 second	=	475 years
1 day	=	41,000,000 years	1 billion years	=	24 days

DECEMBER   COSMIC CALENDAR

SUNDAY	MONDAY	TUESDAY	WEDNESDAY	THURSDAY	FRIDAY	SATURDAY
	1 Significant oxygen atmosphere begins to develop on Earth.	2	3	4	5 Extensive vulcanism and channel formation on Mars.	6
7	8	9	10	11	12	13
14	15	16	17 Precambrian ends. Paleozoic Era and Cambrian Period begin. Invertebrates flourish.	18 First Oceanic plankton. Trilobites flourish.	19 Ordovician Period. First fish, first vertebrates	20 Silurian Period. First vascular plants. Plants begin colonization of land.
21 Devonian Period begins. First insects. Animals begin colonization of land.	22 First amphibians. First winged insects.	23 Carboniferous Period. First trees. First reptiles	24 Permian Period begins. First dinosaurs.	25 Paleozoic Era ends. Mesozoic Era begins.	26 Triassic Period. First mammals.	27 Jurassic Period. First birds.
28 Cretaceous Period. First flowers. Dinosaurs become extinct.	29 Mesozoic Era ends. Cenozoic Era and Tertiary Period begins. First cetaceans. First primates.	30 Early evolution of frontal lobes in the brains of primates. First hominids. Giant mammals flourish.	31 End of the Pliocene epoch. Quaternary (Pleistocene and Holocene Period. First humans.			

SOURCE:

Sagan, Carl, *Dragons of Eden*, New York: Random House, Inc., 1977.

Calendar reprinted by permission of the author and the author's agents, Scott Meredith Literary Agency, Inc., 845 Third Avenue, New York, New York 10022.

◇ CHAPTER EIGHT

◇ Introduction

In preceding chapters, we have discussed the mechanics of the evolutionary processes—adaptation and change through natural selection—according to concepts developed by Charles Darwin. We have also discussed the mechanisms of genetics that explain evolutionary changes between generations.

Having already dealt with the *process* of evolution, we shall now consider the *result* of that process. What actually occurred in the evolutionary record of life on earth? What were the adaptations made by living forms, and what physical changes took place in the various organisms that inhabit our globe? What evolutionary changes led to hominids, what other groups do hominids belong to, and what are the origins of these groups? We shall briefly trace invertebrate and vertebrate evolutionary history which, we believe, will help answer these questions, provide a deeper insight into evolutionary processes, and place humankind in a zoological and chronological perspective. (See Box 8-2, p. 224, Box 8-3, p. 225, and Box 8-5, p. 234 for additional views of the evolutionary processes.)

Since this book is about *Homo sapiens*, we can present only in outline the infinite number of events that occurred over the vast period of 3 billion years (Gurin, 1980), the time of life on earth. Let us then begin with the place of humans in evolutionary history.

◇ The Human Place in the Animal Kingdom

The first chapter emphasized that we are both animals and human beings. We intend, throughout the text, to discuss the relationship between both these aspects of humankind, but since we wish to trace our antecedents, we will concern ourselves first with *Homo sapiens*, the organic being.

Humans are zoologically classified as animals because they possess animal characteristics, such as:

1. Obtaining food from other organisms, not through photosynthesis
2. Mobility; most animals are mobile and can move about in one way or another at some stage of life
3. Structure and organization; tissue and organ differentiation in animals is usually more complex than in plants. Individual plant cells usually have rigid walls; animal cells usually do not
4. Nerves and muscles; most animals have nerves and muscles, which are absent in plants

This list, although incomplete, places humans in the Animal Kingdom. As multicelled animals within the Animal Kingdom, we belong to the Metazoa, a subdivision classified into more than twenty major groups called *phyla* (*sing*, phylum).

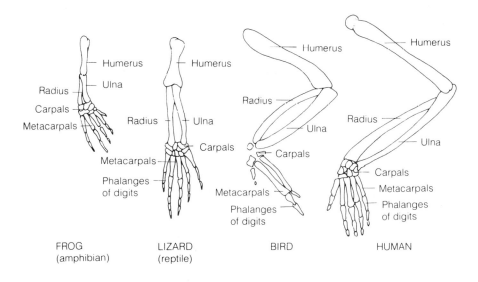

Figure 8-1 Homologies. The similarities in the bones of these air-breathing animals can be most easily explained by descent from a common ancestor.

Taxonomy

Before going further it may be useful to discuss the basis of animal classification.

Organisms are classified on the basis of evolutionary relationships; that is, the degree one group is related to another through descent from a common ancestor. The extent of the relationship is determined mainly by structural similarities based on common descent, called *homologies*. Thus, the bones of the forelimb of air-breathing vertebrates are so similar (Fig. 8-1) in arrangement and number that the simplest and best explanation for the remarkable resemblances—homologies—is that all four kinds of air-breathing vertebrates ultimately derived their forelimb from a common ancestor.

Structures that are *functionally* similar, but without genetic affinity—not derived from a common ancestor—are *analogous*. The wing of a butterfly and the wing of a bird are analogous; they perform a similar function but are without genetic affinity (Fig. 8-2).

Hominids (the group to which humans belong), prosimians, monkeys, and apes are all classified as primates. Why? When the nervous system (especially the brain), teeth, limbs, digits, and other physical traits of these animals are examined, it becomes clear they share an ancestor in common. Their homologies bring these animals into one group just as the homologies of lions, tigers, leopards, and the domestic cat bring these together into one group that evolved from a common ancestor.

The system of classification based on homologies is usually attributed to Linnaeus, although there were classificatory schemes before his. Linnaeus, it will be recalled, successfully instituted the binomial system of naming animals using two terms, genus and species. Thus, we are known as *Homo sapiens*, the domestic cat as *Felis domesticus*, the lion as *Panthera leo*, and the gorilla as *Gorilla gorilla*.

All people in the world today belong to one species, *Homo sapiens*, a form that has existed for at least the past 100,000 years.

Figure 8-3 is a classification chart arranged according to evolutionary

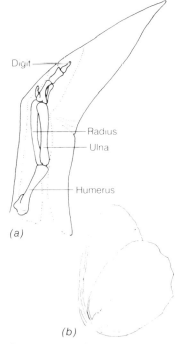

Figure 8-2 Analogies. The wings of these animals perform the same function, but their structure is quite different. Similar structure may be traced to a common ancestor; similar function represents a similar adaptive response, not necessarily a common ancestor. (*a*) Structure of bird wing; (*b*) butterfly wing.

◇ Box 8-1   Vocabulary

Analogous (ah-nal'-o-gus)   Similar in function or appearance but not in origin or development.

Homologous (hom-ol'-o-gus)   Structures that are similar in form (or function) in two or more groups of organisms related through descent from a common ancestor.

Phylum (fy'-lum; pl. phyla)   A primary division of the Animal (or Plant) Kingdom. We belong to Phylum Chordata.

Subphylum   A major division of a phylum, such as Vertebrata.

Class   A subdivision of subphylum.

Superfamily   A group of closely related families.

Family   Members of a family usually inhabit a similar environment; a category which includes genera and species.

Genus (jee'-nus; pl. genera)   A category that groups together closely related species usually inhabiting similar ecological niches.

Species (spee'shies; sing. *and* pl.)   A reproductive community; an interbreeding population (or populations) reproductively isolated from other interbreeding populations.

Dorsal (dor'-sull)   Back, pertaining to the back of an animal.

Ventral (ven'-trull)   Toward the belly; the front of an organism (as in humans) or the undersurface of an animal that does not stand erect (as a dog).

Endoskeleton (en'-doe-skeleton)   An internal bony skeleton, characteristic of vertebrates.

Exoskeleton (ex'-o-skeleton)   A hard, supporting external covering, characteristic of many invertebrates such as ants and lobsters.

Taxonomy   The theoretical study of classification, including its bases, principles, procedures, and rules (Simpson, 1961, p. 11).

Metazoa
meta: beyond
zoion: animal
Multicellular animals. A major division of the Animal Kingdom.

Kingdom
  Phylum
    Class
      Order
        Family
          Genus
            Species

The Linnaean hierarchy of zoological classification. Indentation indicates decreasing inclusiveness of the various levels (Simpson, 1961).

relationships. Observe in both Fig. 8-3 and the adjoining chart, Fig. 8-3a, that, the closer the animals resemble one another (the more homologies they share), the smaller the group to which they are assigned. The two species (in Fig. 8-3a), *H. sapiens* and *H. erectus*, belong to the genus *Homo* because they resemble each other more than either of them resembles the other three hominid species, *A. afarensis*, *A. africanus*, and *A. robustus*, which are assigned to the genus *Australopithecus*. *Homo* and *Australopithecus* resemble each other more than either one resembles apes and are, therefore, placed in the family Hominidae, and apes in Pongidae. Apes and humans resemble each other more than either resembles monkeys and are, therefore, placed in the superfamily Hominoidea, and so forth.

In summary, the more homologies two groups share, usually the more recent their descent from a common ancestor, the closer their evolutionary relationship, and the closer their position on the taxonomic chart.

To place hominids in their proper perspective in nature and to help understand human evolution, we shall glance very briefly at the evolutionary history of the Metazoa.

METAZOA

Metazoa are composed of a number of phyla, most of which are invertebrates, animals lacking a bony backbone. Invertebrates range in organization from relatively simple structures, such as sponges, to relatively complex structures,

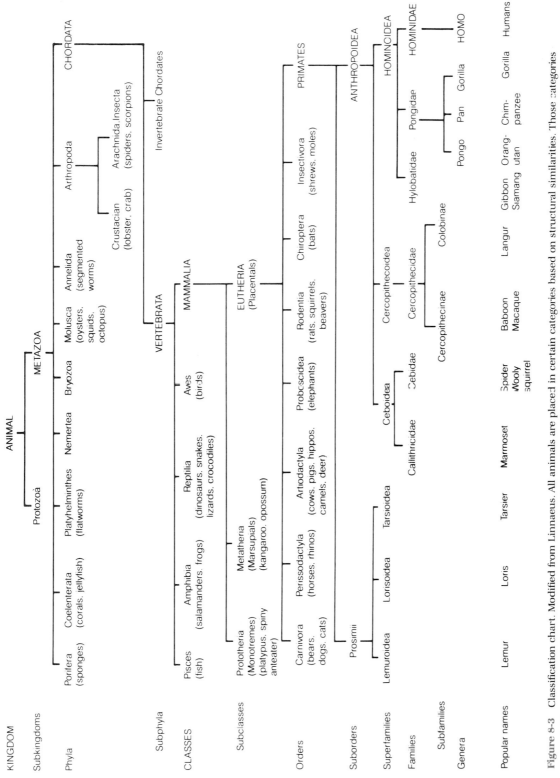

Figure 8-3 Classification chart. Modified from Linnaeus. All animals are placed in certain categories based on structural similarities. Those categories connected by a horizontal line share a common ancestor (*Pongo*, *Pan*, and *Gorilla*, for example).

Figure 8-3a   Classification of Hominoidea.

Figure 8-4   Geologic time scale. (For Cenozoic era see p. 227.)

such as chordates. Chordates are important to humans because our subphylum, Vertebrata, belongs to this category.

Vertebrates, the most numerous of the chordates, are different in certain ways from all other Metazoa. Their primary structural feature, a vertebral column, distinguishes them from invertebrates and has given them their name. Since we belong to this group, we shall discuss vertebrates later in the chapter.

With this short discussion of the human place in nature concluded, we shall return our attention to the time dimension of evolution.

◇ Early Evolutionary History

We reviewed earlier in the chapter the place of humans in nature. We now turn to their place in the time dimension of evolution. To do this, we shall briefly review the chronology of life on earth with special reference to vertebrates. Our review will follow the outline in the Geologic Time Scale (Figs. 8-4 and 8-13). The student is encouraged to refer frequently to the Time Scale as

Era	Period	Time m.y.a*	Events
		65	ROCKY MOUNTAIN REVOLUTION
MESOZOIC	Cretaceous		Appearance of placental and marsupial mammals. Dinosaurs peak and become extinct. First modern birds.
		136	
	Jurassic		Great age of dinosaurs— flying and swimming dinosaurs. First toothed birds.
		190	
	Triassic		Reptiles dominant. First dinosaurs. Egg-laying mammals.
		225	
			APPALACHIAN REVOLUTION
PALEOZOIC	Permian		Reptilian radiation. Mammal-like reptiles. Many old forms die out.
		280	
	Carbon-iferous		First reptiles. Radiation of amphibia. Modern insects evolve.
		345	
	Devonian		Age of fish. Amphibians—first air-breathing vertebrates. First forests.
		395	
	Silurian		Jawed fishes appear. First air-breathing animal—scorpionlike aurypterid. Definite land plants.
		430	
	Ordovi-cian		First fishes. Trilobites still abundant. Graptolites and corals becoming plentiful. Possible land plants.
		500	
	Cambrian		Trilobites abundant, also brachiopods, jellyfish, worms, and other invertebrates.
		570	
PRE-CAMBRIAN			Various marine protozoa, mainly algae. Toward close of era, some evidence of invertebrates.

*Million years ago.

we follow the evolutionary sequence of life on earth. (See Appendix A for the complete Time Scale.)

It is possible that the earliest evidence of life comes from Greenland sedimentary rock, perhaps 3.8 billion years old (Gurin, 1980). The earliest known structurally preserved organisms may be stromatolites found near the old mining town of North Pole, Australia. Also found in the North Pole area are "fossils—a diverse collection of long, filamentous chains of cells—[that] resemble some modern bacteria, including species that are capable of performing photosynthesis" (Gurin, 1980, p. 45). This material from North Pole has been reliably dated at 3.5 billion years. This fossil material belongs to the immense segment of geologic time called the Precambrian, which goes back to the beginning of life and ends about 600 m.y.a., with the beginning of the Paleozoic era.

Abundant fossil evidence for the Precambrian is lacking, and what does exist points to different kinds of algae as the dominant life form. Toward the end of the Precambrian, there is evidence of plants, most of which are of unknown affinity, and burrows and trails of wormlike animals. It is not until the Cambrian (the first period of the Paleozoic) is reached that the rocks contain enough fossils to give a fuller view of the life forms in existence at that time.

◇ Paleozoic Era (570–225 m.y.a.)

Beginning with the Paleozoic era, fossils become more abundant and a much fuller account of life is available. During the 345 million years of the Paleozoic, evidence for members of every phylum of animals is present. Evolution continues primarily in water, but land plants appear toward the middle, and land animals toward the end, of the era. Invertebrate fossil evidence appears in the very first period and becomes a dominant form. Vertebrates evolve fairly early to become very successful aquatic animals and, toward the end of the Paleozoic, invade land habitats as well in the form of amphibians and reptiles.

The southern continents—South America, Africa, Antarctica, Australia, and India—were all closely associated into one mass known as *Gondwanaland*. The northern continents—North America, Greeland, Europe, and Asia—were known as *Laurasia*. As the Paleozoic continued, these two great land masses united during the Carboniferous and Permian periods to form an enormous land mass known as *Pangea*.

Fish

Seventy million years after the beginning of the Paleozoic, during the Ordovician, jawless fishes—**Ostracoderms**—appeared (Romer, 1959). By the Devonian (395–345 m.y.a.) fish had multiplied so rapidly in numbers and species that they became the dominant marine animal; thus, we give the name *Age of Fish* to this period.

Not as numerous or successful as the main branch of bony fish (ray-fins) were the lobe-fins, which had diverged from the others by the middle Devonian

Ostracoderm
ostraco: hard shell
derm: skin
Shell-skin or armored.

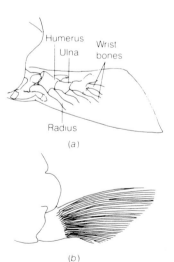

Figure 8-5 (*a*) Lobe-fin. The fin is fleshy and contains a bone structure similar to vertebrates. (*b*) Ray-fin. The fin is composed of a web of skin supported by hornlike rays.

Figure 8-6 Crossopterygian. The fish that made the transition to amphibians. Long thought to be extinct. A modern survivor is the coelacanth.

Figure 8-7 Early amphibian and lobe-finned fish. These drawings of an early amphibian and a lobe-fin illustrate the similarities of the two forms. Not a great deal of change was required to transform the fish to the air-breathing amphibian.

and went (or swam) their own way. Of importance to vertebrate evolution is the structure of their fins, which have a fleshy lobe containing bones remarkably similar to those of land vertebrates. They also possess internal nostrils (absent in ray-fins) probably useful for breathing air.

With fins containing a bony structure, nostrils, and lungs for air breathing, the lobe-finned **crossopterygians** were able to adapt to the drought conditions of the Devonian. As pools of water dried up, these fish could move across land—on their fleshy, bony fins—and, breathing air, seek a pool of water that had not yet become parched (Romer, 1959, p. 94). From this group of fish thus arose the amphibians.

AMPHIBIANS

The explosive radiation of fish in the Devonian coupled with drought conditions of that period led crossopterygians toward an amphibian body plan allowing them, as it were, to have their cake and eat it. On the one hand, they are able to spend much of their time in water; in fact, the early stages of growth have to be aquatic. On the other hand, they are able to adapt, to a certain extent, to life on land. They are, so to speak, neither fish nor land animals, but a "compromise" of both.

In terms of numbers of individuals and species, the amphibians cannot be considered as successful as other vertebrate classes. Typical amphibians are still chained to water, to which they must periodically return. As paleontologist Romer (1959, p. 101) has said: "It is, in many respects, little more than a peculiar type of fish which is capable of walking on land."

As vertebrate evolution continued, amphibians diverged into many different forms. From one of these amphibian forms another milestone in vertebrate evolution was reached with the rise of reptiles, the first true land vertebrates. These are known as *stem reptiles*, ancestors of the huge ruling reptiles of the Mesozoic and of the line leading to mammals.

Figure 8-8 Pangea. Continents at the end of the Paleozoic and during much of the Mesozoic.

(a)   (b)

REPTILES

The reptilian strategy of adaptation was more successful than the amphibian. Developing a more efficient limb structure, an improved heart, and (perhaps most important) a self-contained, self-protected, and self-feeding egg—the *amniote* egg (Fig. 8-9)—reptiles filled many of the terrestrial econiches.

One of the results of reptilian radiation was a reptilelike mammalian form (or a mammallike reptilian form) called *therapsids*. With a bony palate separating the oral and nasal cavities, teeth differentiated into **incisors**, **canines**, and **cheek teeth** (the latter cusped instead of cone-shaped) and limbs arranged in a fore-and-aft position under the body (see Fig. 8-10), therapsids were "on their way" to becoming mammals and are, in fact, considered to be the ancestors of mammals.

Therapsids appeared toward the end of the Paleozoic, and in the next era, the Mesozoic, reptiles and mammals continued to evolve.

◇ Mesozoic Era (225–65 m.y.a.)

Climatic conditions of the Mesozoic were not as extreme as they had been during the late Paleozoic. The great glaciers of the Permian Ice Age had disappeared, erosion had reduced many mountain ranges, and mountain-building produced others. The continents, which had been joined at the end of the Permian, began to drift apart and when the Mesozoic ended, the position of the continents had approached their present locations.

In the early Mesozoic, reptiles became the dominant land animal and reigned supreme for the remainder of the era, known as the *Age of Reptiles*. Reptilian radiation (see Box 8-2) proceeded at a tremendous rate and the most well-known of all reptiles—the dinosaurs—appeared in the Triassic. Not only did dinosaurs cover much of the earth, they also took to the air and water.

Dinosaurs reached their peak in the Cretaceous, but the days of these dominant beasts were numbered, and when the Cretaceous (and Mesozoic) came to a close, the enormous creatures that ruled the earth for about 150

Crossopterygians
krosso: fringe
pteryg: fins

Incisors
Front teeth used for cutting and nipping.

Canines
Usually long and pointed teeth used for piercing and grasping.

Cheek teeth
Premolars and molars used for chewing and grinding.

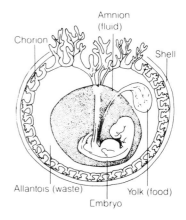

Amniote Egg

Figure 8-9　Amniote egg. Generalized diagram of the amniote egg. The embryo is surrounded by the liquid-filled amniotic chamber. The yolk sac contains food, and within the allantois enclosure (which also serves as a waste receptacle), oxygen-carbon dioxide exchange takes place.

Figure 8-10　Therapsid. Mammallike reptiles or reptilelike mammals. Mammalian characteristics include heterodont teeth, at least some chewing instead of swallowing whole, probably a coat of hair, and perhaps incipient milk glands. The limbs are more mammalian than reptilian. (Artist's rendition.)

◇ Box 8-2   Evolutionary Processes

The potential capacity of an organism to multiply is practically unlimited; its ability to increase its numbers, however, is regulated largely by the available resources of food, shelter, and space. As the size of a population increases, its food, shelter, and space decrease, and the environment will ultimately prove inadequate. Depleted resources engender pressures that will very likely drive some members of the population to seek an environment where competition is considerably reduced and the opportunity for survival and reproductive success increased. This evolutionary tendency to exploit unoccupied habitats may eventually produce an abundance of diverse species.

An instructive example of the evolutionary process known as *adaptive radiation* may be seen in the divergence of the stem reptiles to the profusion of different forms of the late Paleozoic, and especially the Mesozoic. It is a process that has taken place many times in evolutionary history when a new form of life rapidly takes advantage, so to speak, of the many now available ecological niches.

The principle of evolution illustrated by adaptive radiation is fairly simple, but important. It may be stated thus: When a new form arises, it will diverge into as many variations as two factors allow—(1) its adaptive potential and (2) the adaptive opportunities of the available zones.

In the case of reptiles, there was little divergence in the very early stages of evolution, when the ancestral type was little more than one among a variety of amphibian water-dwellers. A more efficient kind of egg had already developed and, although it had great adaptive potential, there were few zones to invade. However, once reptiles became fully terrestrial, there was a sudden opening of available zones— ecological niches—accessible to the adaptive potential of the reptilian evolutionary grade.

This new kind of egg provided the primary adaptive ingredient of the reptilian form that freed reptiles from attachment to water; strengthened limbs and skeleton for locomotion on land followed. The adaptive zones for reptiles were not limitless; nevertheless, continents were now open to them with no serious competition from any other animal. The reptiles moved into the many different econiches on land (and to some extent in the air and sea), and as they adapted to these areas, diversified into a large number of species. This spectacular radiation burst with such evolutionary rapidity, it may well be termed an adaptive explosion.

Generalized and Specialized   Another aspect of evolution closely related to that of adaptive radiation involves the transition from *generalized* to *specialized characteristics*. These two terms refer to the adaptive potential of a particular trait: one that is adapted for many functions is termed generalized whereas a trait that is limited to a narrow set of ecological functions is called specialized.

For example, a generalized mammalian limb has five fairly flexible digits adapted for many possible functions (grasping, weight support, digging). In this respect, our hands are still quite generalized. On the other hand (or foot), there have been many structural modifications in our feet suited for the ecologically specialized function of stable weight support.

These terms are also sometimes used when speaking of the adaptive potential of whole organisms. For example, the aye-aye (a curious primate living in Madagascar) is a highly specialized animal structurally adapted in its dentition for an ecologically narrow rodent/woodpecker-like niche—digging out insect larvae with prominent incisors.

The notion of adaptive potential is a relative judgment and can estimate only crudely the likelihood of one form evolving into another form or forms. Adaptive radiation is a related concept, for only a generalized ancestor can provide the flexible evolutionary basis for such rapid diversification. Only a generalized organism with potential for adaptation into varied ecological niches can lead to all the later diversification and specialization of forms into particular ecological niches.

◇ Box 8-3   Superior/Inferior, Primitive/Derived

Arthropods (see p. 219) illustrate an important point in understanding the process of evolution. It is not possible to rank organisms as better or worse. Or, if we do, our criteria must be stated. One criterion is biological success, which may be said to depend on the number of species, the number of individuals, the number of adaptations to different kinds of environments and habitats, and duration of the phylum. On all these counts, arthropods are superior to vertebrates. Arthropods are

> *from ten to a hundred times more numerous than vertebrates in species, incomparably more abundant in individuals, and divergently adapted to an even wider range of environments and habits. They easily hold their own against all the attacks of man and of other animals* (Simpson et al., 1957, p. 570).

Evolution is not the process of superior animals triumphing over inferior ones but is, rather, a series of alternative adaptive strategies that have arisen in response to inconstant environments.

In this connection it may be well to add two more terms often used in discussing evolution: *primitive* and *derived*. The same point made with the terms superior/inferior may be applied here if primitive is interpreted as somehow inferior to derived. There are no backward or advanced animals, only animals that have adapted, or extinct forms that have not. Nor can modern forms be considered advanced over fossil forms. Living species have adapted to present environmental conditions; fossil species to the environments of their day.

Sometimes the word "primitive" is used for an early form from which later (called "derived") forms have arisen. Even when terms are carefully defined in this way, their use can be misleading and confusing.

million years ended their reign. Changing geographic and climatic conditions, competition from the newly evolving mammals, plus perhaps other unknown factors (either singly or in combination) may have caused their demise. No one really knows. (See Box 8-4.)

MAMMALS

Mesozoic mammals were small animals, about the size of mice, which they resembled in appearance. Since they were so small, and many of the dinosaurs so large, the primitive mammals remained inconspicuous by dwelling

(a)   (b)   (c)

Figure 8-11 Evolution of body support in land vertebrates. The figures illustrate changes in land vertebrate limbs: (*a*) amphibian limbs project laterally from the body; (*b*) reptiles, with stronger pectoral and pelvic girdles, are more upright in an intermediate position; (*c*) in mammals, the legs project straight down.

Arboreal
Tree living.

Tertiary
Third part.

Quaternary
Fourth.

in wooded or bushy areas and may have been **arboreal**. They are not what we would consider to be very noble creatures to have as ancestors. Romer (1959) suggests the Mesozoic may be seen as a training period during which mammalian characters were being perfected and wits sharpened. The mammalian radiation of the Cenozoic (65 m.y.a. to present) saw the rise of the ancestors of all modern mammals. Mammals replaced reptiles as the dominant terrestrial vertebrate, a position they still retain.

◇ Cenozoic Era (65 m.y.a. to present)

The modern world as we know it—geologically and geographically—assumed its present configuration during the Cenozoic era. Major continental drifting slowed considerably, and interior seas on most continents were reduced. This alteration of the topography may explain the diversity of climates, patterns of seasons, water and wind currents, and the eventual onset of the Pleistocene Ice Ages. We may view life in the Cenozoic as a process of adaptation to the climatic extremes and topographic diversity, a situation for which mammals are well equipped.

The Cenozoic is divided into two periods, the **Tertiary** (about 63 million years' duration) and the **Quaternary**, from about 1.8 m.y.a. up to and including the present. Because so much evidence of living forms is available from the Cenozoic, the two periods are further subdivided into epochs. The five epochs of the Tertiary are: Paleocene, Eocene, Oligocene, Miocene, and Pliocene. The Quaternary, the final period of the Cenozoic, is divided into two epochs: the Pleistocene, well known for its *ice ages*, and the present epoch, the Holocene, which begins with the melting of the last glaciation.

Figure 8-12   Mesozoic mammal. A speculative reconstruction of what a Mesozoic mammal might have looked like. Probably no bigger than a kitten, but with mammalian teeth, these animals were capable of attacking small lizards.

MAMMALS

Conditions in the Cenozoic were nearly ideal for mammals. They radiated so rapidly and filled the available econiches so well that the Cenozoic is known as the *Age of Mammals.*

Era	Period	Epoch	Time		Glacial Sequence	
			Years ago	Scandinavian		Alpine
CENOZOIC	QUATERNARY	HOLOCENE	10,000			
		UPPER PLEISTOCENE	40,000 75,000	WEICHSEL (glacial)		WÜRM
			100,000 125,000	EEMIAN		RISS WÜRM
		MIDDLE PLEISTOCENE		Cold phase		
			175,000	Warm phase		RISS
			225,000	SAALE (glacial)		
			265,000 300,000	Warm phase		MINDEL RISS
				ELSTER (glacial)		
			380,000	HOLSTEIN		MINDEL
			400,000 430,000	ELSTER glacial		
			500,000	CROMERIAN		GÜNZ- MINDEL
			750,000	MENAPIAN glacial		GÜNZ
		LOWER PLEISTOCENE	1.8 million	Uncertain Geological Sequences		
	TERTIARY	Pliocene	5 million	Hominids (Australopithecines) present		
		Miocene	25 million	Hominoidea (apelike creatures) Dryopithecines flourish . . . Probable appearance of hominids		
		Oligocene	35 million	Anthropoidea and appearance of Hominoidea		
		Eocene	53 million	Prosimians flourish; possible appearance of Anthropoidea		
		Paleocene	65 million	Appearance of Prosimii		

Figure 8-13   Geologic time scale: Cenozoic.

CENOZOIC

Quaternary
HOLOCENE
PLEISTOCENE

Tertiary
PLIOCENE
MIOCENE
OLIGOCENE
EOCENE
PALEOCENE

Figure 8-14   The Cenozoic. The most recent era. The two epochs, Tertiary and Quaternary, and their divisions are shown. (The Precambrian, Paleozoic, and Mesozoic are shown on p. 220.)

◇ Box 8-4   Extinction

"The theories that have been propounded (to explain the extinction of dinosaurs) are legion, and one cannot do better than quote Jepsen on this topic: 'Authors, with varying competence, have suggested that the dinosaurs disappeared because the climate deteriorated (became suddenly or slowly too hot or cold or dry or wet), or that the diet did (with too much food or not enough of such substances as fern oil; from poisons in water or plants or ingested minerals; the bankruptcy of calcium or other necessary elements). Other writers have put the blame on disease, parasites, wars, anatomical or metabolic disorders (slipped vertebral discs, malfunctions or imbalance of hormone or endocrine systems, dwindling brain and consequent stupidity, heat sterilization), racial old age, evolutionary drift into senescent overspecialization, changes in the pressure or composition of the atmosphere, poison gases, volcanic dust, excessive oxygen from plants, meteorites, comets, gene pool drainage by little mammalian egg-eaters, overkill capacity by predators, fluctuation of gravitational constants, development of psychotic suicidal factors, entropy, cosmic radiation, shift of Earth's rotational poles, floods, extraction of the moon from the Pacific Basin, drainage of swamp and lake environments, sunspots, God's will, mountain building, raids by little green hunters in flying saucers, lack of even standing room in Noah's Ark, and palaeoweltschmertz' " (Jepsen, in Halstead, 1968, pp. 146–147).

Update   In 1980, four University of California, Berkeley scientists proposed an extraterrestrial cause for the extinction of many species of plants and animals, including dinosaurs, at the end of the Cretaceous.

They suggest that an asteroid struck the earth, forming an enormous crater over 100 miles across. Dust ejected from the crater reached the stratosphere and then spread around the earth. This effectively blocked sunlight from reaching the earth's surface for about two and a half years, suppressing photosynthesis. Most food chains collapsed and extinctions resulted.

The evidence for, and acceptance of, this explanation are increasing.

SOURCES:
Alvarez, Luis W., Walter Alvarez, Frank Asaro, Helen V. Michel. "Extraterrestrial Cause for the Cretaceous-Tertiary Extinction," *Science*, 208:1095–1108, June 6, 1980.

Kerr, Richard A., "Asteroid Theory of Extinctions Strengthened," *Science*, 210:514–517, October 31, 1980.

Placental Mammalian Characters   Campbell (1974, p. 39ff) has proposed that mammalian evolution was based on a single adaptive development: The ability for constant lively activity; that is, "the maintenance of a steady level of activity in the face of basic changes in the external environment." The constant and lively activity, Campbell further points out, was made possible by "the evolution of only four great complexes, all of a homeostatic nature": homoiothermy, mastication, improved reproductive efficiency, and new ways of determining behavior. (The following discussion of these complexes is summarized from Campbell, 1974.)

Homoiothermy   A constant and appropriate body temperature regardless of external conditions is a decided advantage for an active animal. **Homoiothermy** may have evolved among mammallike reptiles as early as the Permian and very probably was found later among at least some dinosaurs. It is difficult to know from fossil bones whether the warm-bloodedness of these forms was the same as that of mammals today. It would appear, however, that homoiothermy, as a basic characteristic, gave mammals the constant energy necessary for animals adapting to a highly active way of life. In addition, for the first time, vast forests of the temperate zone became available for exploitation by a vertebrate form.

Homoiothermy is so basic to the mammalian way of life that a number of physiological and behavioral adjustments have been developed to maintain a constant body temperature. To lower body temperature, mammals may perform one or more of the following activities: spread their limbs, lay their hair or fur flat against the skin, increase their respiration rate, dilate their capillaries, or sweat. To raise body temperature, they may curl into a ball, raise their hair/fur layer, constrict their capillaries, eat (metabolic action generates body heat), or shiver.

Mastication and Heterodontism   Except for extinct herbivorous forms, reptile teeth all have the same (**homodont**) structure. They curve inward with the jaw serving as a trap. Prey once caught cannot escape and is eaten whole without chewing. On the other hand, the mammalian jaw and **heterodont** dentition exploit various kinds of food more effectively. Different kinds of teeth—incisors, canines, premolars, and molars—evolved especially for trapping, nipping, chewing, cutting, crushing, and grinding, and the jaw was modified to make this dental activity possible. Mastication enables mammals to obtain more nutritive value from a wider variety of food by breaking up nuts, seeds, plant material, and meat, among other edibles. This is important to active homoiothermic animals, since they require more food intake.

Reproductive Efficiency   Reptiles changed the external method of amphibian fertilization by introducing internal fertilization. They lay eggs—**oviparity**—which, although not as vulnerable as amphibian eggs, are still easy prey for small carnivores.

Mammals evolved a new reproductive system. They retain copulation and internal fertilization, but the egg is kept within the mother, where it is protected and nourished until it achieves quite an advanced stage of growth. Birth is live—**viviparity**—and, because of the newborn's advanced stage, young mammals suffer fewer casualties than young reptiles.

Nevertheless, most mammalian young are born helpless although some, such as horses, cattle, and hares, are active within minutes or hours of birth. All newborn mammals, however, are unable to feed themselves and must be fed by special milk glands (mammae—modified sweat glands) of the mother. Suckling requires the young to remain close to the mother, a practice serving several functions. The young are fed, protected, and, through imitation, learn the behavior adaptive for their species.

Determinants of Behavior   In most animals activity and learning are motivated by the primary drives of hunger, sex, and self-preservation. Mammals developed a new determinant that does not satisfy these immediate needs; it is a drive to investigate and explore the environment and has been termed *effectance motivation*, usually called "mammalian play." This motivation can be seen in the playful activity of young mammals, the only animals that so behave. Actually, this apparent playful activity is a means of discovering and

Homoiothermy
Homo: same
therm: heat
Same temperature.

Homodontism
homo: same
dont: teeth

Heterodontism
hetero: different
dont: teeth

Oviparity
ovum: egg
parere: to bear

Viviparity
vivus: alive
parere: to bear

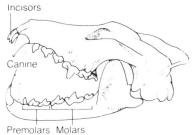

Incisors

Canine

Premolars Molars
Cheek teeth

MAMMALIAN
(heterodont)

REPTILIAN (alligator)
(homodont: no differentiation of teeth)

Figure 8-15 Reptilian and mammalian teeth.

Table 8-1   Mammalian Innovations (Distinguishing Mammals from Reptiles)*

Innovations	Complexes
Warm blood Hair/fur Sweat glands	Homoiothermy
Heterodontism Strong jaw	Mastication and heterodontism
Viviparity Suckling	Reproductive efficiency
Mammalian play	Effectance motivation

*There is some evidence that homoiothermy, fur, and viviparity are more common than once believed.

learning to interact with the environment. Effectance motivation evolved to provide the data input to maintain and supply a larger and more complex brain (Fig. 8-16) than had ever been known before in the organic world.

The four complexes summarized above explain a number of innovations that distinguish mammals from their reptilian ancestors: warm blood,* hair/fur, sweat glands, heterodontism, a stronger jaw, viviparity, suckling, and mammalian play.

A few more important distinguishing characteristics should be noted: an internal ear drum with an external ear flap; a four-chambered heart that generates greater energy; and more efficient limbs for improved locomotion.

*As noted earlier, some reptiles may have been warm-blooded.

Figure 8-16   Human brain. In humans the gray matter (cerebral cortex) is highly convoluted, which provides a greater surface for nerve connections and for eight billion brain cells. The cerebral cortex has also greatly expanded to cover most of the brain.

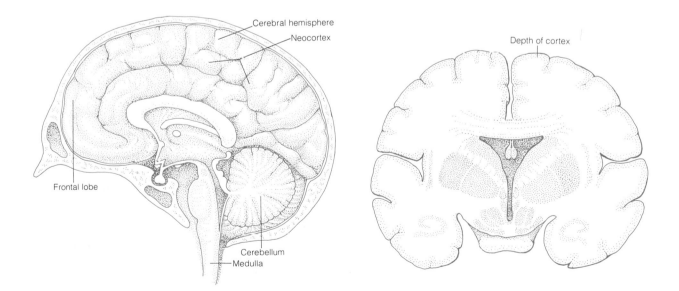

MAMMALIAN SUBCLASSES

At the present time, placental mammals comprise most of the mammalian class; however, there still survive a few monotremes (egg-laying mammals) and marsupials (pouched mammals).

Monotremes (Prototheria)   Living in the Australasian region of Australia and New Guinea are two surviving highly specialized egg-laying mammals—the duck-billed platypus and the spiny anteater.

The platypus, a semiaquatic animal about two feet long, with a beaverlike tail, a poison barb on the heel of males, and webbed toes for swimming, lives in streams and in burrows along the banks. Instead of teeth, it has developed a ducklike bill used for burrowing in the mud in search of worms and grubs. The anteater is protected by a coat of sharp spines (recalling the porcupine), a spur on the hind legs, and the jaws—also without teeth—are formed into a long, tubular snout used for probing anthills.

Monotremes are classified as mammals since the young are nursed from teatless mammary glands. However, they are very primitive mammals and retain a number of reptilian characters. They lay eggs, have but one opening for elimination, mating, and birth (hence the term **monotreme**) and display various other reptilian traits in the shoulder girdle, skull, and vertebral column. Some authorities consider monotremes as surviving mammallike reptiles.

Marsupials (Metatheria)   At the present time, **marsupials** are found only in Australia and the New World (opossums) although they were once more widely distributed in North America, South America, and Europe. Their extermination can be laid at the hands (or claws and teeth) of the brainier placental mammals whenever these two mammals have competed. Pouched animals survived in Australia because placental mammals never reached that continent before its separation from other land masses. Marsupials entered

monotreme
mono: one
treme: a hole

Marsupium
Pouch.

Figure 8-17   Mammalian classification chart.

Figure 8-18   The duck-billed platypus. Offspring licking milk from mother's fur.

Figure 8-19 Spiny anteater.

Figure 8-20 Wallaby with infant in pouch.

Australia before its separation and remained isolated, except for bats, which probably flew in early, and rodents, which island-hopped in. The marsupials, therefore, were protected from the onslaught of the more developed Cenozoic placental mammals.

Most South American marsupials were destroyed by placentals invading that continent at the end of the Tertiary when North and South America were joined. Only the opossums survive today.

Marsupials bear their young alive as a tiny embryo after a short gestation period. These tiny infants work their way into their mother's pouch by a swimming motion of the forelimbs over a pathway of dampened mother's hair. Once in the pouch they remain attached to nipples that line the pouch and are fed by the mother literally pumping milk into them. When they are old enough to move around, they live in and out of the pouch until they are surprisingly large.

Aside from the method of reproduction, marsupials differ from placentals in brain size and other details of the skull. Teeth are also somewhat different from those of placental mammals, but the post-cranial skeleton is generally comparable.

Placental Mammals (Eutheria) One of the outstanding features of placental mammals (**Eutheria**) is the placenta, which gives the subclass its name. This disclike organ furnishes oxygen and nutrients from mother to developing embryo and gets rid of waste products as well. Young are born alive, as are marsupials, but in a much more advanced stage of development.

Among the many other differences distinguishing marsupials and placentals, two stand out. First, placentals possess an expanded brain, which has been suggested as the most important reason for their superiority over the pouched mammals. It may be of interest to briefly review this development.

The evolutionary history of the brain, center of the nervous system, reflects a steady growth in size and complexity as we move from fish to mammals (Fig. 8-21). The diversification of vertebrates depends largely upon the operation of the central nervous system, and the relative success of mammals

Figure 8-21 Lateral view of brain. The illustration shows the increase in the cerebral cortex of the brain. The cerebral cortex integrates sensory information and selects responses.

over reptiles (and perhaps reptiles over amphibians) may be largely due to greater brain efficiency.

Fish reflect the basic vertebrate brain, which is composed of three sections: forebrain, midbrain, and hindbrain. The forebrain includes the **olfactory** lobes and the cerebrum; the midbrain, the largest section in fish and the center of control and coordination, is associated mainly with the optic lobe; the hindbrain combines the **cerebellum** and medulla oblongata which act as message center and source of some autonomic and reflex actions.

The trend in brain evolution has been toward an increase in the forebrain and decrease in mid- and hindbrain. The amphibian brain is not much modified from the fish; the olfactory lobe is somewhat smaller and the cerebrum slightly larger.

Significant changes appeared in the reptile brain. The **cerebrum** is greatly enlarged but much of the forebrain is still devoted to smell. A striking innovation developed in the reptilian cerebrum. The cerebral hemispheres are coated by a pallium of neurons; in the reptile a small portion of the front part of the cerebrum is covered with a new sort of nervous tract called the **neopallium** or **neocortex**. This covering in general is what we know as "gray matter," and while the reptilian neopallium was a feeble beginning, it was a most important one.

In mammals, the neopallium dramatically expanded and spread over the cerebral hemispheres. Central control, formerly in the midbrain, passed almost entirely to the neopallium of the forebrain. The cerebrum increased in size to compose most of the brain and developed convolutions making for an even greater surface area without increasing brain size.

In humans, the growth of this section of the brain reaches its ultimate development, a fact which has made the human brain, in proportion to body size, one of the largest and most complex of any animal.

The second important difference between placentals and marsupials is teeth. These clearly distinguish the two forms and have been used as a basis for classification as well as the reconstruction of mammalian evolutionary history.

Eutheria
eu: good
therion: beast

Olfactory
Smell.

Cerebellum
(sara-bell'-um)
That part of the brain concerned with co-ordination and balance. In humans, back of and below the cerebrum.

Cerebrum
(sar'-a-brum or se-ree'-brum)
Largest part of the human brain; the fore-brain and midbrain.

Neopallium
neo: new
pallium: cloak

Neocortex
neo: new
cortex: bark, covering

Herbivore   Carnivore   Human
(horse)

Figure 8-22 Canines.

Figure 8-23 Examples of specialization in herbivorous and carnivorous teeth. There is great variation in the size and shape of the canine in herbivorous animals, and canines are entirely lacking in many species.

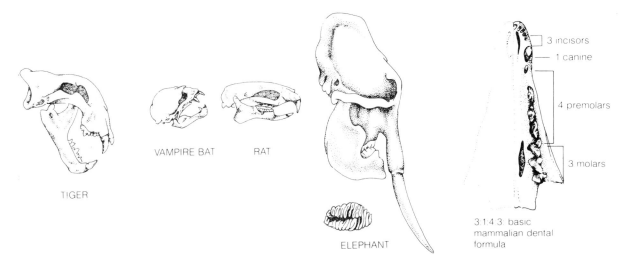

TIGER   VAMPIRE BAT   RAT   ELEPHANT

3 incisors
1 canine
4 premolars
3 molars

3.1.4.3. basic
mammalian dental
formula

◇ Box 8-5   Convergent and Parallel Evolution

Convergent Evolution   The discussion of marsupials offers an opportunity to present another evolutionary process, *convergent evolution*. We pointed out (in Box 8-2, Evolutionary Processes) that in the early stages of development, there is a tendency for newly evolved forms to become highly diversified when they invade varied environments. The diversification results from the modification of the ancestral type in adapting to new ecological niches.

Convergent evolution—a variation of adaptive radiation—is the process in which two *unrelated* groups of organisms, living in similar but separate environmental conditions, develop a similar appearance and life style. That is, similar environmental demands make for similar phenotypic responses (Mayr, 1970, p. 365). This should not be surprising since the requirements of adapting to a particular environment would require modifications of physical traits. Two similar environments would, therefore, result in similar adaptive characters.

Striking examples of convergence are the pouched mammals of Australia and placental mammals. As we have seen, Australia was isolated from South America before the great placental mammalian radiation of the Cenozoic, and marsupials survived because they were free from the competition of the more efficient placentals. When placental mammals became prominent in the Cenozoic, only a few were able to invade Australia (via island-hopping from Southeast Asia).

Without competition, the pouched mammals spread into the varied environments of the isolated continent. There were marsupials that resembled, to a lesser or greater degree, a wolf, cat, flying squirrel, groundhog, anteater, mole, and mouse. And they occupied ecological niches similar to the placental mammals they resembled (Simpson et al., 1957, p. 470).

The variety of marsupials illustrates adaptive radiation; the resemblance in form due to similarity of econiches illustrates convergent evolution.

Parallel Evolution   A variation of both adaptive radiation and convergent evolution is *parallel evolution*. This process may be illustrated as a kind of tailed U. *Related* forms diverge as in adaptive radiation, responding to different ecological niches. Then, because of the similarity of econiches, the two or more forms respond to similar selection pressures and evolve somewhat similar phenotypes, for example, the New World and Old World monkeys (see further discussion in Chapter 9).

Figure 1

(a)
Divergent evolution

Converge

+
Original form

Different forms

Convergent evolution

(b)

Figure 2

Similar phenotypes

X   X

Similar econiches

Initial divergence

+
Original form

Parallel evolution

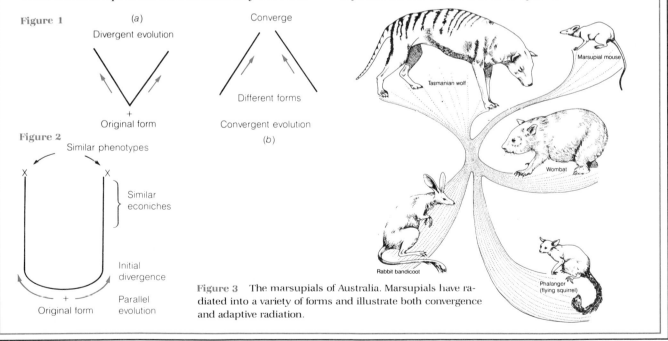

Figure 3   The marsupials of Australia. Marsupials have radiated into a variety of forms and illustrate both convergence and adaptive radiation.

The structure of teeth often informs us of their use so that it is fairly easy, for example, to distinguish between the specializations of predator and herbivore teeth. Of all the teeth, it is probably the molars that are the most specialized. They perform the powerful grinding, chewing, and crushing functions, and their structure is closely associated with diet. It is difficult to exaggerate the role of teeth in studying mammalian (and especially for our purposes, primate) evolution. The student is asked to keep this in mind when we look at primate evolution, since in many cases identification, classification, relationships, and chronological placement may be based on the structure of fossil teeth. This is particularly the case for hominids because, quite often, teeth are the only fossil evidence available.

Appearing in placentals of Cretaceous age and still persisting in many modern animals, the basic pattern of placental mammalian teeth is (on each side and in both upper and lower jaws) three incisors, one canine, four premolars, and three molars (see Box 9-2, Chapter 9). Incisors tend to be pegs or blades—adapted for nipping or cutting food, as can be seen when biting into an apple.

Canines come in a variety of forms. **Carnivore** canines are spikelike and used for stabbing, piercing, and holding. In **herbivores** canines tend to be molarlike with a grinding surface, and among humans, **omnivores**, canines are spatulate, similar to incisors and utilized in a similar manner.

Premolars (called "bicuspids" by dentists) are generally complex and used for crushing and/or grinding (as are molars, which are even more complex).

Placental mammals today are found almost everywhere on earth. With sea mammals such as dolphins and seals, we find them in water; and some placentals, the bats, have taken to the air. But placentals are essentially terrestrial animals and land is where they are found in abundant numbers and species. For example, there are the even-toed ungulates (**artiodactyls**), such as cows, deer, camels, and pigs; odd-toed ungulates (**perissodactyls**), such as the horse and rhino; carnivores, such as the bear, dog, and cat; proboscids, such as elephants; insectivores, such as shrews, moles, and hedgehogs; the incredibly successful rodents, including rats, squirrels, beavers, and gophers; and, of course, the primates, including prosimians, monkeys, apes, and humans.

Of all these groups the rodents are clearly the most successful of all mammals if number of species and individuals is our criterion. In fact, they outnumber all other species of mammals combined (Romer, 1959, p. 228). Their enormous adaptive flexibility is clearly demonstrated by their ability to cope successfully with humanmade environments.

We have traced the evolution of vertebrates from fish to mammals. Mammals, as we have seen, had come a long way from the small, insignificant, insectivorelike animals of the Mesozoic to the highly diversified and very successful vertebrates of the present. We are now prepared to take up the discussion of our own order, Primates, which, like other mammals, most likely originated as shrewlike animals in the Paleocene (or possibly the late Cretaceous). Very early, they adapted to an arboreal way of life that emphasized vision, an expanded brain, and prehensible digits, as we shall see in the next three chapters.

Carnivore
carni: meat
A flesh-eating animal.

Herbivore
herba: grass
A plant-eating animal.

Omnivore
omnis: all
Plant and meat eating.

Artiodactyl
(are-tee-o-dak'-til)
artios: even
daktylos: finger, toe
Even-toed hoof.

Perissodactyl
perissos: odd
Odd-toed hoof.

Odd-toed   Even-toed
(horse)   (hippopotamous)

Figure 8-24   Ungulates.

◇ Summary

In this chapter, we have placed humans in their natural perspective by tracing the development of evolutionary changes of invertebrates and vertebrates. We also placed humans in a temporal perspective by tracing the evolutionary development of life forms, especially vertebrates, over the immense time period of Precambrian through Tertiary.

Structural modifications of the evolutionary sequence of vertebrates—from fish to amphibians to reptiles to mammals—were included to give the very long developmental background of the hominid form. This will be continued in the chapter on primate evolution.

The basis for taxonomic classification (why animal X is placed in category Y) and several evolutionary concepts (adaptive radiation, generalized and specialized, and convergent and parallel evolution) were discussed to give a deeper understanding of "how evolution works."

◇ Questions for Review

1. What characteristics place humans in the Animal Kingdom?
2. Distinguish between homologies and analogies.
3. To what groups of the Animal Kingdom do hominids belong?
4. Explain the basis for the arrangement of the classification chart. Give several examples.
5. Outline the evolutionary history of vertebrates during the Paleozoic, Mesozoic, and Cenozoic.
6. What changes occurred in the structure of fish, amphibians, and reptiles that enables them to adapt to their econiches?
7. Define adaptive radiation and give examples.
8. Explain the evolutionary principle "generalized to specialized." Why is the reverse—"specialized to generalized"—rarely found?
9. Why are therapsids believed to be ancestors of mammals?
10. What characteristics of lobe-fins suggest they are ancestral to amphibia?
11. What "four great complexes" distinguish mammals from reptiles and contributed to mammalian success?
12. Explain the differences between convergent and parallel evolution.
13. Why are placental mammals so much more successful than marsupials?

◇ Suggested Further Reading

Augusta, Josef. *Prehistoric Reptiles and Birds*, London: Paul Hamlyn, 1961.
　　An excellent book containing beautiful illustrations of fossil reptiles, especially dinosaurs, and birds of the Mesozoic.
Barnett, Lincoln. *The World We Live In* (Vol. 1, 2), New York: Time, Inc., 1962.
　　Written for the layman; outstanding drawings and color illustrations of ancient geology and life forms.

Beerbower, James R. *Search for the Past*, Englewood Cliffs: Prentice-Hall, Inc., 1960.
   An introductory paleontology text, easy to read, with many illustrations.
Beiser, Arthur. *The Earth* (Life Nature Library), New York: Time, Inc., 1973.
   Another in the series of excellent Time-Life books.
Carrington, Richard. *The Mammals* (Life Nature Library), New York: Time, Inc., 1963.
   One of the series dealing with various life forms. The text is good and illustrations and photographs are of the high quality found in these publications.
Colbert, Edwin H. *Dinosaurs: Their Discovery and Their World*, New York: Dutton, 1962.
   Everything you want to know about dinosaurs by one of the world's experts.
Desmond, Adrian J. *The Hot-Blooded Dinosaurs*, New York: The Dial Press, 1976.
   A "hot-blooded," one-sided account written in an easily readable style. Supports Professor Bakker's view that dinosaurs were warm-blooded and the ancestors of birds.
Lewin, Roger. *Thread of Life*, New York: W. W. Norton & Co. (Smithsonian Books), 1982.
   A beautifully illustrated book by a well-known scientist presently a writer for Science *(a weekly journal published by the American Association for the Advancement of Science). Lewin covers the history of the earth and the evolution of animals from "Life Emerges from the Soup" through human evolution. Written in popular style. Highly recommended for students and nonstudents alike.*
Ommanney, Francis D. *The Fishes* (Life Nature Library), New York: Time, Inc., 1964.
   Another in the Time-Life series. Well worth reading.
Ostrom, John H. "A New Look at Dinosaurs," *National Geographic*, 154:152, August 1978.
   A fascinating article with many ideas about dinosaurs, especially endothermy. Beautiful drawings and photographs. Highly recommended. Written by one of the world's experts on dinosaurs.
Romer, Alfred S. *The Vertebrate Story* (4th Ed.), Chicago: University of Chicago Press, 1959.
   A popular account of vertebrate evolution by an outstanding paleontologist. Excellent as a reference book as well as pleasant reading.
———. *Vertebrate Paleontology* (3rd Ed.), Chicago: University of Chicago Press, 1966.
   This is Romer's authoritative work on vertebrates.
Simpson, George G. *The Meaning of Evolution*, New York: Mentor Books, 1951.
   One of the best statements on what evolution means.
Simpson, G. G., C. S. Pittendrigh, and L. H. Tiffany. *Life*, New York: Harcourt, Brace & Co., 1957.
   A biology textbook that has become a classic. Easy to read, many illustrations, authoritative.
Wood, Peter, Louis Vaczek, Dora J. Hamblin, and Jonathan N. Leonard. *Life Before Man* (Emergence of Man Series), New York: Time, Inc., 1972.
   Like other series published by Time, "Emergence of Man" fits very nicely the fossil hominid section of a physical anthropology course. Material is written for those without a technical background, illustrations are superb, and students are encouraged to examine these books.

Living Primates

CONTENTS

Today, one species of primate, *Homo sapiens*, dominates our planet. Numbering over 4 billion, we use, alter, and ultimately destroy huge hunks of the world's surface.

In the face of such an onslaught, many of the other species that share our planet are being driven to the brink of extinction. As primates ourselves, we have a special interest in the problem of preserving our primate relatives.

Even before the advent of modern technological society, primates (compared to such groups as rodents or even-toed ungulates) were not abundant. Largely restricted to forested areas in South America, Africa, and South Asia, the primates had—despite their comparative numerical inferiority—achieved a successful adaptation.

Such is no longer the case. In addition to being diminished by the dangers stemming from reduced or completely obliterated habitats, non-human primates are also easy prey for local peoples looking for food, hunters looking for scientific (mostly medical) specimens, or for poachers strictly after financial gain.

What is the future for these animals? The prospects are not hopeful. The Convention on International Trade in Endangered Species (ratified by the United States in 1973) alreadys lists *all* non-human primates as endangered or facing the prospects of soon becoming so. All of the apes—gibbons, orangutans, gorillas, and chimpanzees—are now in the convention's "most endangered" category. (All are also on the United States endangered species list: the first three as "endangered"; chimps as "threatened".)

Among the most imminently endangered of all primates is the mountain gorilla—a subspecies of the largest primate form—now restricted to an exceedingly small area of East Africa (where the borders of Rwanda, Uganda, and Zaire converge).

Mountain gorillas once ranged widely through the densely forested mountain regions bordering the great lakes of East Africa. Foraging in rough terrain, gorilla groups survived for centuries, impervious to any potential predator. In fact, the mountain gorilla was not even known to the Western world until 1903, when it was first reported by a German military expedition.

The mountain gorilla's comparative isolation from humans has been dramatically altered in recent years. It is estimated that today there are only about 220 mountain gorillas left in the wild. In the last twenty years alone, their numbers have been reduced by one-half.

Most of the deaths (perhaps as many as two-thirds) are at the hands of poachers. Gorillas are prized specimens for trophy hunters; consequently, they are often shot with high-powered rifles, after which they are decapitated, their hands cut off, and these grisly remains sold for trophies.

Gorillas also are victims of poachers in a more accidental fashion. Traps and snares are set by poachers primarily to capture antelope and buffalo, which can be sold as meat. Mountain gorillas who live in the same area step into these traps and, even if they manage to escape, usually die later from infected wounds.

Why is such reckless exploitation allowed? The answer is that, legally, it is not. Throughout the world illegal poaching of endangered species is banned, and most countries prohibit imports of products derived from such animals. Enforcement, however, is another matter. Due to political

Digit, an adult male gorilla; found after poachers had decapitated him and cut off his hands.

quently feel compelled to trap antelope and buffalo and, in the process, gorillas as well.

Despite wide publicity of the gorilla's plight in the Western world and a large influx of money from concerned conservationists, the slaughter goes on. Is there then any hope for saving the mountain gorilla? Perhaps—but time is growing dangerously short. As Dian Fossey, the leading field researcher of these primates, has ominously warned, "The mountain gorilla may become an animal which was discovered and driven extinct—in the same century."

SOURCES:

Fossey, Dian. "The Imperiled Mountain Gorilla," *National Geographic*, 159:501–523, April, 1981.

Fossey, Dian. *Gorillas in the Mist*, Boston: Houghton-Mifflin Co., 1983.

instability and periodic warfare in East Africa, central governments have been at a loss to stop the killing. In Zaire and Uganda most of the mountain gorillas are now gone. Rwanda continues to struggle with the problem, but the choices are not always easy. Among the most overcrowded and undernourished populations in Africa, Rwandans are hard-pressed to find adequate sources of animal protein. Local populations conse-

◇ CHAPTER NINE

◇ Introduction

We have seen in Chapter 8 that we are a certain kind of placental mammal, a primate. This order of rather diverse animals is characterized by a set of evolutionary trends that sets it apart from other mammals. In this chapter, we will discuss what characteristics link us to our primate cousins, and we will explore some of the fascinating and unique adaptations that the non-human primates display.

◇ Primate Evolutionary Trends

Structurally, primates are not easily distinguished as a group chiefly because of the fact that, as an order, we and our close relatives have remained quite *generalized*. Unlike the specialized dentition of rodents or the specialized limbs with great reduction of digits found in artiodactyls (cows, deer, camels, pigs), primates are characterized by their *lack* of extreme structural specializations.

For this reason, we cannot point to a single anatomical feature that can be applied exclusively and universally to the primates. On the other hand, there is a group of **evolutionary trends** (Clark, 1971) which, to a greater or lesser degree, characterize the entire order. Keep in mind, these are a set of *general* tendencies and are not equally expressed in all primates. Indeed, this situation is one that we would expect in such a diverse group of generalized animals. In addition, trends are not synonymous with *progress*. In evolutionary terms, we are using "trend" only to reflect a series of shared common characteristics (i.e., general homologies).

Following is a list of those evolutionary trends that tend to set the primates apart from other mammals. A common evolutionary history with similar adaptations to common environmental challenges is reflected in the limbs and locomotion; teeth and diet; and in the senses, brain, and behavior of the animals that make up the order.

A. Limbs and Locomotion

1. *Retention of five digits* in the hands and feet—*pentadactyly*. As in primitive mammals, this characteristic is found in all primates, though some show marked reduction of the thumb (e.g., spider monkeys, langurs) or the second digit (e.g, lorises). In no case is reduction as extreme as that seen in such animals as cows or horses.
2. *Nails instead of claws*. A consistent characteristic on at least some digits of all contemporary primates. Unlike rodents or cats, primates must climb by wrapping their hands and feet around branches and holding on by grasping. This grasping function is further aided by the presence of tactile pads at the ends of digits.

Figure 9-1　Primate (macaque) hand.

Figure 9-2　Position of the clavicle in the human skeleton.

3. *Flexible hands and feet* with a good deal of **prehensility** (grasping ability). This feature is associated directly with the lack of claws and retention of five digits.

4. *A tendency toward erectness* (particularly in the upper body). Shown to some degree in all primates, this tendency is variously associated with sitting, leaping, standing, and, occasionally, walking.

5. *Retention of the clavicle* (collarbone). Seen in all primates. The clavicle has been lost in many other quadrupedal mammals.

B. Teeth and Diet

6. *A generalized dental pattern*, particularly in the back teeth (molars). Characteristic of primates, such a pattern contrasts with the highly specialized molars seen in herbivores.

7. *A lack of specialization in diet*. This attribute is usually correlated with a lack of specialization in teeth. In other words, primates can generally be described as *omnivorous*.

C. Senses, Brain, and Behavior

8. *A reduction of the snout* and the proportionate reduction of the smell (olfactory) areas of the brain. Seen in all contemporary primates, but baboons show a secondary (coming later) increase of a *dental* muzzle.

9. *An increased emphasis on vision* with elaboration of visual areas of the brain. A trend related to the decreased dependence on smell. Binocular and stereoscopic vision is a further elaboration wherein visual fields of the two eyes overlap, transmitting both images to the brain, thus allowing depth perception. Except for some specialized nocturnal forms, color vision is most likely present in all primates.

10. *Expansion and increasing complexity of the brain*. A general trend among placental mammals and one especially true of primates. This expansion is most evident in the visual and association areas of the neopallium and to some degree in the motor cortex and cerebellum. (See p. 230.)

11. *A more efficient means of fetal nourishment*, as well as *longer periods of gestation, infancy*, and extension of the whole life span.

12. *A greater dependency on highly flexible learned behavior* is correlated with longer periods of infant and child dependency. As a result of both these trends, parental investment in each offspring is increased so that although fewer young are born, they receive more efficient rearing.

13. *Adult males often associate permanently with the group*. A behavioral trait rarely seen in other mammals, but widespread among the primates.

◇ The Arboreal Adaptation

The single most important factor influencing the evolutionary divergence of primates (with elaboration of all the trends just noted) was the adaptation to **arboreal** living. While other placental mammals were going about their business adapting to grasslands, subterranean or even marine environments,

Evolutionary trends
General structural and behavioral traits that are commonly shared by a related group of organisms.

Prehensility
Adapted for grasping.

Arboreal
Anatomy is adapted to life in the trees.

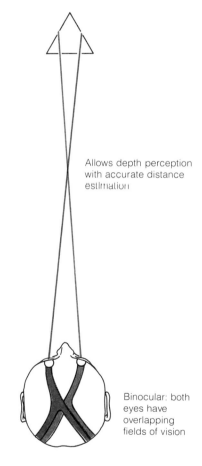

Allows depth perception with accurate distance estimation

Binocular: both eyes have overlapping fields of vision

Stereoscopic: optic nerve transmissions from each eye are relayed to *both* sides of the brain

Figure 9-3 Binocular, stereoscopic vision. Fields of vision overlap and sensory information from each eye is relayed to both sides of the brain.

Postorbital bar
The bony element that closes in the outside of the eye orbit—a characteristic of primates.

Adaptive niche
The whole way of life of an organism: where it lives, what it eats, how it gets food, and so forth.

Substrate
The surface on which an animal moves or rests.

Nocturnal
Active at night.

Diurnal
Active during daylight hours.

primates found their **adaptive niche** in the trees. Indeed, some other mammals also were adapting to arboreal living, but primates found their home (and food) mainly in the tree tops and at the ends of terminal branches. This environment—with its myriad challenges and opportunities—was the one in which our ancestors established themselves as a unique kind of animal.

Primates became primates *because* of their adaptation to arboreal living. We can see this process at work in their reliance upon vision for survival (as opposed to their depending chiefly on a sense of smell). In a complex environment with uncertain footholds, acute vision with depth perception is a necessity. Climbing can be accomplished by either digging in with claws or grasping around branches with prehensile hands and feet. Primates adopted the latter strategy, which allowed a means of progressing on the narrowest and most tenuous of **substrates**. Thus, we also see in primates pentadactyly, prehensility, and flattened nails. In addition, the varied foods found in an arboreal environment (such as fruits, leaves, berries, insects, small mammals) led to the primate omnivorous adaptation and, hence, to retention of a generalized dentition.

Finally, the long life span, increased intelligence, and more elaborated social system are primate solutions to coping with the manifold complexities of their arboreal habitat (that is, such factors as varied and seasonal food resources; and potential predators from above, below, and in the trees). This crucial development of increased behavioral flexibility may have been further stimulated by a shift from **noctural** (nighttime) to **diurnal** (daytime) activity patterns (Jerison, 1973).

A recent critique of the traditional arboreal explanation for the origin of primate structure has been proposed by Matt Cartmill (1972, 1974) of Duke University. Cartmill points out that the most significant primate trends—close-set eyes, grasping extremities, and reduced claws—may *not* have arisen from adaptive advantages in an arboreal environment.

According to this alternative theory, ancient primates may have first adapted to living in bushy forest undergrowth and only the lowest branches of the forest canopy. All these traits would have been well-suited for an animal that foraged for fruits and insects. Particularly in searching for insects, early primates are thought to have relied heavily on vision, and this theory is hence called the *visual predation hypothesis.*

The close-set eyes would have allowed these primates to judge accurately the distance from their prey without moving their heads, similar to the hunting manner of cats and owls. The regression of the olfactory sense is then viewed as a necessary result of the eye orbits coming closer together. Grasping extremities may have initially been an adaptation for pursuing insects along very narrow supports (like twigs) in the forest undergrowth. Feet, as well as hands, would be prehensile to allow the animal to maintain support while snaring its prey with both hands.

The visual predation hypothesis is as internally consistent and as likely an explanation for the early evolution of primates as the arboreal theory. In fact—given the fossil record and the morphology typical of many contemporary prosimians—it may be a better explanation for the functional developments among the *earliest* primates. In particular, the small body size and insectivorous diet seen in several living prosimians and a similar adaptation

◇ Box 9-1   Primate Cranial Anatomy

Several significant anatomical features of primate skulls help us distinguish primates from other mammals. Continuing the mammalian trend of increasing brain development, primates go even further as shown by their well-expanded brain boxes. In addition, the primate trend of increased dependence on vision is shown by the generally large eye sockets; less emphasis on smell is shown in the reduced snout; the shift to using hands for grasping (instead of using the front teeth for this purpose) is revealed in the dentition; and the tendency towards more upright posture is indicated by the relationship of the head to the spinal column.

Some of the specific anatomic details seen in all modern and most fossil primate crania are:

1. Eye sockets are enclosed circumferentially by a complete ring of bone, compared to other placental mammals where the ring is incomplete (no **postorbital bar**). This bony arrangement provides protection for the eyes.

2. The entrance into the skull for the spinal column, the *foramen magnum* (Latin: "big hole") on the base of the skull, faces more downwards instead of backwards as it does in other completely quadrupedal mammals. The position of the *foramen magnum* indicates the direction of the spinal column and is related to the posturing and balancing of the head on the trunk.

3. The face of primates is reduced (snout shortened) with the axis at the base of the skull bending, thus pulling the face more underneath the brain box. This arrangement now provides a greater vertical distance in the movable lower jaw from the point of pivot (P) to the plane of the teeth (T) allowing more biomechanical action for up-and-down crushing, grinding, etc., instead of just simple back-and-forth tearing and gnashing.

4. The ear region containing the middle ear ossicles is completely encircled by a bony encasement (bulla) whose floor is derived from a particular segment of the temporal bone. Most primate paleontologists consider this feature and the formation of a postorbital bar as the structurally best diagnostic characteristics of the primate order.

(a) Cat   (b) Lemur

Figure 1   Postorbital bar. A characteristic of primates.

(a) Dog

(b) Lemur

Figure 2   Basi-cranial flexion relative to tooth row. In primates, the skull base is more flexed, elevating the point of pivot (P) further above the tooth row and thereby increasing the force of chewing. (© 1959 by W. E. Le Gros Clark.)

Homology
Similarities between organisms based on common evolutionary descent.

inferred from the fossilized remains of many very early primates are consistent with the visual predation hypothesis.

The visual predation ("bug snatching") hypothesis and the arboreal theory are not mutually exclusive explanations. The complex of primate characteristics could have begun in nonarboreal settings, but would have become even more adaptive once the bug snatching was done *in the trees*.

At some point, in fact, the primates did take to the trees in earnest, and that is where the vast majority still live today. Whereas the basic primate structural complexes may have been initially adapted for visual predation, they became ideally suited for the arboreal adaptation that followed. We would say then that primates were "preadapted" for arboreal living.

◇ The Living Primates

When we apply the set of evolutionary trends under discussion here, we are able to classify a remarkable array of living forms as members of the same mammalian order, the Primates. We and our primate cousins, you will recall, share these characteristics due to **homology**. In other words, primates are part of a single evolutionary radiation, and the traits we all share derive from a common evolutionary descent.

PRIMATE CLASSIFICATION

While controversy on some minor points still exists, the living primates are usually categorized into subgroupings (based on increasingly similar evolutionary relationships) in the following manner:

ORDER   Primates
  SUBORDER   Prosimii
    SUPERFAMILY   Lemuroidea (lemurs of Madagascar)
    SUPERFAMILY   Lorisoidea (loris, bushbaby)
    SUPERFAMILY   Tarsiioidea (tarsier)
  SUBORDER   Anthropoidea
    SUPERFAMILY   Ceboidea (New World monkeys; e.g., spider monkey, howler monkey, capuchin)
    SUPERFAMILY   Cercopithecoidea (Old World monkeys; e.g., baboon, macaque, langur)
    SUPERFAMILY   Hominoidea
     FAMILY   Hylobatidae (gibbons)
     FAMILY   Pongidae
      GENUS   *Pan* (chimp)
      GENUS   *Gorilla*
      GENUS   *Pongo* (orangutan)
     FAMILY   Hominidae
      GENUS   *Homo* (human)

Table 9-1 shows an alternative primate classification.

Table 9-1   Alternative Classification of Living Primates—Based Upon Biochemical Data (after Dene et al., 1976)

Order Primates
  Semiorder Strepsirhini
    Suborder Lemuriformes
      Superfamily Lemuroidea
        Family Lemuridae
          Genus *Lemur*   common lemur
        Family Lepilemuridae
          Genus *Lepilemur*   sportive lemur
        Family Indriidae
          Genus *Propithecus*   sifaka
      Superfamily Cheirogaleoidea
        Family Cheirogaleidae
          Genus *Microcebus*   mouse lemur
          Cheirogaleus   dwarf lemur
      Superfamily Daubentonioidea
        Family Daubentoniidae
          Genus *Daubentonia*   aye-aye
    Suborder Lorisiformes
      Superfamily Lorisoidea
        Family Galagidae
          Subfamily Galaginae
            Genus *Galago*   bushbaby
        Family Lorisidae
          Genus *Nycticebus*   slow loris
          Loris   slender loris
        Family Perodicticidae
          Subfamily Perodicticinae
            Genus *Perodicticus*   potto
            Arctocebus   angwantibo
  Semiorder Haplorhini
    Suborder Tarsioiidea
      Family Tarsiidae
        Genus *Tarsius*   tarsier

    Suborder Anthropoidea
      Infraorder Platyrrhini   New World monkeys
        Superfamily Ceboidea
          Genus *Ateles*   spider monkey
          Logothrix   woolly monkey
          Alouatta   howler monkey
          Saguinus   tamarin
          Aotus   night monkey
          Callicebus   titi
          Chiropotes   saki
          Cebus   capuchin
          Saimiri   squirrel monkey
      Infraorder Catarrhini
        Superfamily Cercopithecoidea
          Family Cercopithecidae
           Subfamily Colobinae
            Genus *Colobus*   guerezas
            Presbytis   langur
            Pygathrix   douc langur
            Nasalis   proboscis monkey
          Subfamily Cercopithecinae
           Genus *Macaca*   macaque
            Papio   baboon
            Theropithecus   gelada
            Mandrillus   drill
            Cercocebus   mangabey
            Erythrocebus   patas
            Cercopithecus   guenon
        Superfamily Hominoidea
        Family Hylobatidae
          Subfamily Hylobatinae   gibbon
           Genus *Hylobates*   gibbon
           Symphalangus   siamang
        Family Hominidae
          Subfamily Ponginae
           Genus *Pongo*   orangutan
          Subfamily Homininae
           Genus *Gorilla*   gorilla
            Pan   chimpanzee
            Homo

◇ Grades of Primate Evolution

In terms of size, structure, and behavior, contemporary primates certainly represent a varied group of animals. What is even more remarkable about the living primates is that they still display in some form all the major grades of evolution that primates have passed through over the last 70 million years.

An evolutionary grade is, in Mayr's terms, "A group of animals similar in level of organization" (Mayr, 1970). We do not use the term, as some evolu-

Primitive
In evolutionary terms, an organism that is closer to an evolutionary divergence than a later (more derived) one.

tionary biologists have done, to imply a strict commonality of evolutionary descent and/or an equivalent adaptive response (suggesting selection above the species level). In fact, such processes are not now believed to be accurate depictions of macroevolution (Eldredge and Cracraft, 1980). (See p. 109.)

You should also note that the concept of grade does not imply any inferiority or superiority. Grades only reflect different stages of organizational levels seen during primate evolution—from more primitive to more derived. (See p. 225.)

GRADE I: TREE SHREWS (PRIMITIVE MAMMALIAN GRADE)

Tree shrews are an enigma to the taxonomist. In classifying the natural world into the higher taxonomic categories of family, order, etc., we are attempting to simplify and hopefully make sense out of the complex organic continuum that evolution has produced. Indeed, the categories are *created by us* for us. They are symbolic devices typical of the human mind's capacity to "impose arbitrary form on the environment." A tree shrew could care less whether it is classified as a primate, an insectivore (another order of placental mammals), or a whale.

It is often readily apparent that similar structural and behavioral characteristics of contemporary life forms reflect their shared evolutionary ancestry (for example, lemurs and lorises both as prosimians; humans and apes both as hominoids). There are, however, many organisms that do not fit neatly into *any* of our categories.

The tree shrew is such an animal. Some investigators, impressed by several structural similarities, regard tree shrews as primates (Simpson, 1945; Clark, 1971). However, most current researchers (Simons, 1972; Buettner-Janusch, 1973) view the primatelike characteristics of tree shrews as merely reflections of their primitive mammalian heritage. As another popular alternative, tree shrews have often been placed among the insectivores, where they do not really fit either. As a final act of taxonomic desperation, then, most experts now place tree shrews within their own order of placental mammals (Luckett, 1980a).

Given that tree shrews are an order unto themselves, what are their closest relatives among the placentals? Morphological and some biochemical data (see pp. 262–264) suggest that tree shrews, flying lemurs, and primates form an evolutionary "cluster" and could be included together within a common superorder (Luckett, 1980; Cronin and Sarich, 1980). However, other biochemical techniques suggest the tree shrew/flying lemur/primate cluster is not a natural grouping, and that tree shrews, in fact, find their nearest mammalian affinities with bats (Dene, et al., 1980) or even rabbits (Goodman, et al., 1983). What makes tree shrews intriguing and relevant to a discussion of primate evolution is that their overall anatomical structure and level of adaptation are probably very similar to the earliest primates of 70 million years ago.

Today, tree shrews live in Southeast Asia, extending from India to the islands of Indonesia. They are all generally small, squirrellike animals and may not be recognized initially as primatelike in appearance. First, they have long, projecting snouts, and their eyes do not face forward (see Fig. 9-4). Second—even more unprimatelike—they have claws (not nails) on *all* their digits. Finally, their social behavior is most unlike primates in their "absentee"

Figure 9-4 Tree shrew.

system of mothering. (On the other hand, their tendency toward grasping definitely parallels the well-developed grasping features of the primates.) It is no wonder that the tree shrews look **primitive**, since they are not much altered from the probable general appearance and adaptive level of very early placental mammals. Since the primate adaptive radiation goes back to the roots of the placental mammal radiation at the beginning of the Cenozoic (*circa* 65 m.y.a.), living tree shrews provide an excellent structural model for the earliest primates as well as for generalized placental mammals.

GRADE II: LEMURS AND LORISES

Lemurs are found today only on the island of Madagascar off the east coast of Africa. They probably reached their island sanctuary several million years ago and were able to diversify into the many ecological niches offered on this

Figure 9-5   The grades of primate evolution.

Hominoid

Monkey

Tarsier

Lemur/loris

Tree shrew

Adaptive radiation
The diversification and expansion of a life form into a number of niches.

Strepsirhini
strepsi: twisted
rhini: nose
The classificatory term used to group lemurs and lorises (either suborder or semiorder).

Haplorhini
haplo: simple
rhini: nose
The classificatory term used to group tarsiers with monkeys, apes, and humans (either suborder or semiorder).

Figure 9-6   Distribution of modern lemurs.

Figure 9-7   Ring-tailed lemur.

large island of 227,000 square miles. As the *only* primates on the island, lemurs were able to survive. In continental areas, most of their prosimian cousins perished. Thus, these surviving forms represent a kind of "living fossil," preserving an evolutionary grade that has long since vanished elsewhere.

Lemurs, however, are not uniform. Some are nocturnal, others diurnal; some are completely arboreal, others are more terrestrial. In fact, the range of forms and habitats occupied before recent human interference (in the last few hundred years) reveals a remarkable evolutionary display. One unusual lemur (called the aye-aye), still living in Madagascar, suggests a rodentlike adaptation; another (indri) resembles a small monkey; and, finally, an incredible beast with extremely short hind limbs (*Megaladapis*, now extinct) weighed more than 100 pounds (Szalay and Delson, 1979).

Some forms like the aye-aye are socially solitary, whereas others primarily associate in large permanent groups (the ring-tailed lemur). All these forms evolved in the relative sanctuary that Madagascar provided. This kind of evolution, characterized by rapid diversification and expansion into varied ecological niches, is another beautiful example of **adaptive radiation**.

Lorises, very similar to lemurs, were able to survive in *continental* areas by adopting a nocturnal activity pattern at a time when most other prosimians became extinct. In this way, they were (and are) able to avoid competition with their primate descendants, the monkeys, as well as another group— including many highly successful arboreal, diurnal forms—the rodents.

Today, the geographic range of lorises is confined to tropical areas in Africa and Southeast Asia. Their nocturnal adaptation is immediately revealed structurally by their greatly enlarged eyes. Usually quite small animals, they have elongated hindlimbs, providing an adaptation for leaping and hopping. Socially, most lorises are solitary and only occasionally form sleeping pairs.

Both lemurs and lorises represent the same general adaptive level. They both have good grasping and climbing abilities and have fairly well-developed vision that is not completely stereoscopic. They all have nails on at least one of their digits (the aye-aye has a nail only on the big toe). Most of the other varieties have only one clawed digit (on the second toe). This digit is used for grooming and is called the toilet digit. Lemurs and lorises also have prolonged life spans as compared to other small mammals, averaging about fourteen years for the lorises and nineteen years for the lemurs.

However, lorises and lemurs still show many characteristics suggesting their relatively closer relationship to early placental mammals than is true for the anthropoids (monkeys, apes, and humans). For example, their faces for the most part are still quite snouty, with a markedly projecting nose. As this feature would suggest, they still rely a great deal on the olfactory sense, and some lemurs have developed specialized scent glands for the purpose of leaving "smell" messages. Dependence on olfactory cues is also shown by the naked area of moist skin—*rhinarium*—on the nose. This area is used to conduct scent efficiently. Suggestive also of their early primate ancestry are their expressionless faces, large mobile ears, and a generally unelaborated pattern of social behavior. Finally, there are some unusual specialized aspects in their dentition, particularly the projecting lower incisors and canines forming a structure used for grooming and hence called a dental comb.

Figure 9-8 Distribution of modern lorises.

GRADE III: THE TARSIER

A once widespread prosimian form, the living tarsier is today limited to one genus (*Tarsius*) and is confined to island areas in Southeast Asia. This tiny animal (about the size of a small kitten) has avoided competition in much the same way as the lorises—by adapting to a nocturnal niche. The large forward-placed eyes which dominate the face strikingly reveal this adaptation. Another unusual feature shown by the tarsier is a greatly elongated ankle joint (tarsus), which gives the animal its name and allows it to leap great distances.

Like lemurs and lorises, tarsiers are also prosimians, as revealed by their small body size, large ears, "primitive" dental pattern, and unelaborated social behavior. However, they exhibit several physical characteristics similar to anthropoids, placing them at a different organizational level than lemurs and lorises. Indeed, like the tree shrew, tarsiers present somewhat of a taxonomic dilemma. Many primatologists, pointing to the numerous physical characteristics that tarsiers share with anthropoids (which are seen as derived states), classify tarsiers closer to anthropoids than to prosimians. Moreover, biochemically, tarsiers are more closely related to anthropoids than to lemurs or lorises (Dene et al., 1976). In order to accommodate this revised view, classification schemes and classificatory labels have been changed. For example, the suborder that includes lemurs and lorises is termed the **Strepsirhini**, while tarsiers, monkeys, apes, and humans are included within another suborder, the **Haplorhini** (Szalay and Delson, 1979). Another means of accomplishing the same goal is to retain the traditional subordinal nomenclature but to distinguish lemurs and lorises from tarsiers, monkeys, apes, and humans at a level above suborder (i.e., semiorder—see Table 9-1) (Dene et al., 1976).

As we indicated above, tarsiers show many similarities to anthropoids. Contrasted to those of other prosimians, tarsier eye orbits are completely

(a)

(b)

Figure 9-9 Two varieties of loris. (*a*) Greater galago; (*b*) a Senegal galago, or "bushbaby."

Quadrupedal
Using all four limbs relatively equally while moving.

Figure 9-10   Distribution of modern tarsiers.

Figure 9-11   Tarsier. Note the huge eyes.

Table 9-2   Numbers of Groups of Living Primates

	Genera	Species
Lemur	10	19
Loris	5	10
Tarsier	1	3
New World monkey	16	64
Old World monkey	14	74
Hominoids	6	12
Total	52	182

Source: Data abstracted from A. Jolly, 1972, pp. 16–22.

closed *in back* by bone in the manner of the anthropoids. (Lorises and lemurs are "primitive" in this respect, having an opening between the orbit and the cranial vault, or brainbox.) You will recall that all primates have orbits that are completely encircled by bone *on the outside*. In addition, tarsier skulls are more rounded and their snouts less projecting than those of other prosimians, a situation partially explained by their small size and huge eyes. Another anthropoidlike feature is their lack of a rhinarium and a more flexible upper lip, a structure allowing for more facial expression. Finally, the bony ear canal of the tarsier is also more like anthropoids than other prosimians.

In addition to those features already pointed out, several other characteristics exist that tend to distinguish monkeys, apes, and humans from the "lower" primates. These are:

1. Generally larger body size
2. Larger brain size (in absolute terms and relative to body weight)
3. More rounded skull (seen to some degree in tarsiers also)
4. Eyes completely in front of skull, full stereoscopic vision
5. Complete back wall to eye orbit (also seen in tarsiers)
6. No rhinarium (also seen in tarsiers)
7. Only two incisors (on each side) in both jaws
8. More complex social systems
9. More parental care; often by males as well as females
10. More mutual grooming

GRADE IV: MONKEYS

The monkey grade of evolution is today the most varied group of primates (see Table 9-2). Of the 180 or so living species of primates, approximately 75% (about 140 species) are classified as monkeys. These are divided into two groups separated by geographical area (New World and Old World), as well as several million years of separate evolutionary history.

New World Monkeys   The New World monkeys (Ceboidea) exhibit a wide range of size, diet, and ecological adaptation. In size, they vary from the tiny (about twelve ounces) marmosets (family: Callithricideae) to the twenty-pound howler monkey, a member of the family Cebidae (see Table 9-3). New World monkeys are almost exclusively arboreal and will usually come to the ground only to cross spaces in order to gain access to other trees. Although confined to tree environments, New World monkeys can be found in a wide range of arboreal habitats throughout most forested areas in southern Mexico, Central America, and South America.

Nose shape is one of the characteristics distinguishing New World monkeys from those found in the Old World. New World forms have broad, widely flaring noses with a thick nasal septum, with nostrils facing outward. Conversely, Old World monkeys have narrower noses with a thinner nasal septum, and the nostrils face downward. This difference in nose form has given rise to the terms *platyrrhine* (flat-nosed) and *catarrhine* (down-nosed), the latter referring to *all* Old World anthropoids (Old World monkeys, apes, and humans). Another characteristic of New World monkeys is seen in their dentition,

Figure 9-12 (*left*) A pair of golden marmosets.

Figure 9-13 (*right*) Howler monkey. Note the expanded laryngeal apparatus used in vocalization.

which has retained three premolars. All Old World anthropoids have only two (see Box 9-2). Another feature found only in the New World, though not in all forms, is the development of a prehensile (grasping) tail that can be used like a fifth limb.

In locomotion, all New World forms are basically **quadrupedal**, but some forms (for example, the spider monkey, or the howler monkey) are able to perform considerable arm-swinging suspensory locomotion (see Box 9-3).

Old World Monkeys After humans, Old World monkeys (Cercopithecoidea) are the most widely distributed of all living primates. They are seen throughout subsaharan Africa and southern Asia, ranging from tropical jungle habitats to semiarid desert and even to seasonally snow-covered areas in northern Japan.

The classification of Old World monkeys reveals how the same root with different endings designates the various levels (taxonomic categories) in a formal classification:

Table 9-3 New World Monkey Classification

SUPERFAMILY	Ceboidea
FAMILY	Callithricidae (marmosets and tamarins)
FAMILY	Cebidae (howler monkey, spider monkey, woolly monkey, capuchin, night monkey, squirrel monkey)

		Ending Indicates Level of Classification
SUPERFAMILY	Cercopithecoidea (sur-ko-pith-e-koid'-ee-uh)	oidea = superfamily
FAMILY	Cercopithecidae (sur-ko-pith-ee'-si-dee)	idae = family
SUBFAMILY	Cercopithecinae (sur-ko-pith-ee'-si-nee)	inae = subfamily
	Colobinae (kol-o-bine'-ee)	
GENUS	Colobus (kol'-o-bus)	genus endings are variable, but -us is common

Figure 9-14 Distribution of modern New World monkeys.

Figure 9-15 A New World monkey prehensile tail. Shown here in a spider monkey.

The same tooth formula, 2-1-2-3 (2 incisors, 1 canine, 2 premolars, 3 molars) found in apes and humans also characterizes Old World monkeys. They are all quadrupedal and mainly arboreal, although some (baboons, for example) are adapted primarily to life on the ground. Whether in trees or on the ground, these monkeys spend a good deal of time sleeping, feeding, and grooming while sitting with their upper bodies held erect. Associated with this universal sitting posture are usually areas of hardened skin on their rear ends called *ischial callosities* that serve as sitting pads. Old World monkeys have a good deal of manual dexterity and most have well-developed tails that are never prehensile (in adults), as is true of many New World forms; the tail, however, does serve a purpose in such functions as communication and balance.

Within the entire group of Old World monkeys (superfamily: Cercopithecoidea), there is only one taxonomically recognized family, Cercopithecidae. Within this family there are in turn two subfamilies, the cercopithecines and the colobines. The former are found mainly in Africa, but some forms (the macaques) are widely distributed in southern Asia. The colobines are found mainly in Asia, but the colobus (kol'-o-bus) monkey (from which the group is named) is widely distributed in tropical Africa.

The cercopithecines are the more generalized of the two subfamilies, showing a more omnivorous dietary adaptation. The colobines, on the other hand, are more limited dietarily, specializing more on mature leaves, a behavior that has led to their designation as "leaf-eating monkeys." As a result of this behavior, structural adaptations for digestion of cellulose (a usually indigestible plant substance) have arisen. These adaptations are reflected in the high crowned molars, sacculated (divided) stomachs, and elongated intestines.

Figure 9-16 Distribution of modern Old World monkeys.

◇ Box 9-2   Tale of the Teeth

Extremely important for interpreting the relationships of *both* living and fossil forms are the number and kinds of teeth present. There are four different kinds of teeth found in a generalized placental mammal, and primates have almost universally retained all four types: incisors, canines, premolars, and molars. A shorthand device for showing the number of each kind of tooth is called a **dental formula**. This formula indicates the teeth in one-quarter of the mouth (since the arrangement of teeth is symmetrical and usually the same in upper and lower jaws). For example, the dental formula in New World monkeys for cebids is 2-1-3-3 (2 incisors, 1 canine, 3 pre-molars, and 3 molars in each quarter of the mouth—a total of 36 teeth); and 2-1-3-2 in marmosets, which typically lose their third molars, a situation perhaps analogous to the loss of third molars, or wisdom teeth, in modern humans. The formula in *all* Old World monkeys, apes, and humans is normally 2-1-2-3—a total of 32 teeth. Most lemur and loris dental formulae are 2-1-3-3 (total of 36), but the highly specialized aye-aye shows (for a primate) remarkable reduction in numbers of teeth

$$\frac{1\text{-}0\text{-}1\text{-}3^{*}}{1\text{-}0\text{-}0\text{-}3}$$

for a total of only 18 teeth.

*When the formula differs in the lower jaw from that of the upper jaw, both are shown. For example, the tarsier has one less incisor in each half of its lower jaw than it does in its upper jaw:

$$\frac{2\text{-}1\text{-}3\text{-}3}{1\text{-}1\text{-}3\text{-}3.}$$

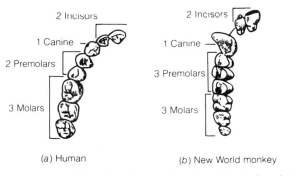

Figure 1   Dental formulae. The number of each kind of tooth is given for one-quarter of the mouth.

Relative dental formulae are extremely useful indicators of phyletic relationships because they are normally under tight genotypic control. In other words, environmental influence will usually not alter the tooth formula. In making studies of primate dental phenotypes, we are quite certain, therefore, that our comparisons are based on structural homologies. Thus, similarities in structure (relative numbers of teeth) can be used as indicators of evolutionary similarity.

Dental evidence is extremely important in the interpretation of fossils, since teeth—the hardest component of the body—are the most commonly fossilized part and comprise the vast majority of fossil primate discoveries. In addition, cusp pattern and functional wear can be used to help reconstruct dietary behavior in fossil animals. The identification of diet is of central importance in any attempt to reconstruct the nature of the ecological niche, and ultimately the whole way of life of a fossil form.

The most common forms of cercopithecines include the highly diversified arboreal guenons (genus: *Cercopithecus*); the slightly larger but still arboreal mangabeys (genus: *Cercocebus*); and the more terrestrial macaques (genus: *Macaca*), baboons—both savanna and hamadryas (genus: *Papio*), forest baboon (genus: *Mandrillus*), and the gelada baboon (genus: *Theropithecus*)—as well as the patas monkey (genus: *Erythrocebus*).

The colobus monkey of Africa (genus: *Colobus*) and the various forms of Asian langurs (genus: *Presbytis*, *Rhinopithecus*, etc.) and the proboscis monkey of Borneo (genus: *Nasalis*) make up the colobine subfamily.

Dental formula
The arrangement of teeth showing the number of each type (incisors, canines, premolars, and molars).

◇ Box 9-3   Tale of the Limbs

Besides teeth (and diet), the other major functional complex most useful in describing both extant (living) and extinct primates relates to the structure of the limbs and the form of locomotion.

A meaningful functional description of locomotion among contemporary primates should include position of the body, which limbs are used, the manner and frequency they are employed, and the nature of the substrate (such as wide tree branch, narrow branch, flat ground). By understanding the locomotory behavior of contemporary primates we can analyze their respective limb structures and form meaningful *structural-functional correlations*. With such a perspective, we can then interpret fossil primates and reconstruct their probable locomotory behavior.

A common locomotory classification of contemporary primates with their typical structural correlations is shown as (after Napier and Napier, 1967):

Category	Description of Behavior	Structural Correlates	Examples
A. Vertical clinging and leaping	leaping in trees with propulsion from hind limbs, clinging with forelimbs for vertical support	elongated hindlimbs, particularly ankle area, upper body held semi-erect	tarsier, galago
B. Quadrupedalism	using all limbs relatively equally; body horizontal	front and hindlimbs relatively equal length; spine flexible	
1. Slow climbing	slow, cautious climbing; often associated with capturing insects	widely abducted (spread) thumb, reduction of 2nd digit	potto, slow loris
2. Branch running and walking	walking or running on tops of branches, also leaping	generalized quadruped; limbs equal sized; spine flexible	ringtailed lemur, all marmosets, squirrel monkey, guenons
3. Ground running and walking	quadrupedal walking and running on ground, also tree climbing	all limbs elongated, body size usually larger than strictly arboreal species	baboons, most macaques, patas monkey
4. New World "semibrachiation"*	usually quadrupedal, some arm-swinging beneath branches with use of prehensile tail; little or no leaping	forelimbs elongated; fingers often curved, thumb reduced	howler monkey, spider monkey
5. Old World "semibrachiation"*	usually quadrupedal with arm-swinging and often considerable acrobatic leaping from branch to branch	forelimbs elongated; fingers often curved, thumb reduced	colobines (colobus, langurs)

Locomotory behavior among Old World monkeys includes arboreal quadrupedalism in the guenons and mangabeys, arm-swinging and acrobatic leaping in many of the colobines, and terrestrial quadrupedalism in the baboons, macaques, and patas monkey. In the baboons particularly, adaptation to ground living has given rise to larger body size, especially in males. Such a marked difference in body form between males and females of a species is called *sexual dimorphism*. Another striking difference in baboons is canine size, which is much larger in males.

Category	Description of Behavior	Structural Correlates	Examples
C. Ape locomotion			
1. True brachiation	acrobatic swinging arm-over-arm along (under) same branch, associated with feeding on small terminal branches	small body size, greatly elongated forelimb, curved fingers, shoulder joint oriented upward, upper body held fairly erect; spine not flexible	gibbon, siamang
2. Quadrumanual climbing	slow deliberate climbing using all four limbs for grasping	large body size, hip joint flexible like shoulder; upper body held erect, spine not flexible	orang
3. Knuckle-walking	on ground semiquadrupedal, but hands supported on knuckles; while in trees considerable arm-swinging (gorillas only as subadults)	large body size, elongated forelimbs; stable wrist joint; upper body held erect; spine shortened and inflexible	chimp, gorilla
D. Bipedalism	strictly terrestrial, standing, striding, running upright; weight alternately on single hindlimb	medium-large body size, hindlimb elongated; pelvis altered for support and muscular leverage; feet altered for stable support with little flexibility; toes shortened; upper body completely erect; head balanced on spine; spine shortened and inflexible	human**

*Semibrachiation" is a poor term, since it implies arm-over-arm suspensory locomotion. These forms are not "partial" brachiators, but are primarily quadrupedal with considerable flexibility of the upper limb.

**True bipedalism among the primates is an adaptation *only* of modern humans and our hominid ancestors. Thus the structural correlates associated with this functional complex are crucial in determining the status of our possible ancestors.

In addition, many Old World monkey females (especially baboons and many macaques) exhibit pronounced external changes, such as swelling and coloration of the genitalia, associated with the **estrous cycle**—a hormonally initiated period of sexual receptivity in female mammals correlated with ovulation.

Because of their general hardiness even under extremely trying circumstances, Old World monkeys (particularly the versatile macaques) are favorite laboratory animals for both biomedical and behavioral experiments. Indeed,

Estrous cycle
Hormonally initiated physiological changes in female primates—associated with ovulation.

Parallel evolution
The process where two life forms (that are initially related) become physically more similar through time due to adaptation to similar environments.

Hylobatidae
(Hy-lo-bat′-i-dee)

Brachiation
Arm-over-arm suspensory locomotion beneath branches.

Quadrumanual
quadru: four
manual: hand
Using all four limbs for grasping during locomotion.

Figure 9-17 A moustached guenon. An Old World monkey.

Figure 9-18 A black-and-white colobus monkey with infant.

much of what we know about the effect of infant and child deprivation has been learned from the Harlows' well-known experiments with rhesus macaques at the University of Wisconsin (Harlow, 1959). (See p. 280.)

Monkeys, Old and New World: A Striking Case of Parallel Evolution   We have mentioned several differences between monkeys in the Old World compared to those in the New World. However, the striking fact remains that they are *all* monkeys. By this statement, we mean that they all are adapted to a similar (primarily arboreal) way of life. With the exception of the South American night monkey (*Aotus*), they are diurnal and all are social, usually fairly omnivorous, and quadrupedal, though with variations of this general locomotory pattern (see Box 9-3).

These similarities are all the more striking when we consider that Old and New World monkeys have gone their separate evolutionary paths for tens of millions of years. In fact, a noted primatologist, Dr. E. L. Simons (1969), suggests the split may have occurred more than 50 m.y.a. Both forms of monkey would then have evolved independently from separate prosimian ancestors. The current consensus among researchers, however, disputes this claim (Hoffstetter, 1972; Ciochon and Chiarelli, 1980) and postulates both Old and New World monkeys arose in Africa from a common monkey ancestor and later reached South America by rafting over. (Note: South America and Africa were considerably closer together earlier in the Cenozoic. In addition, migration over water barriers may have been facilitated by "island hopping" over a chain of volcanic islands.)

In either case, what is most remarkable is that the two forms of monkey have not diverged more than they have—given the time depth of separate evolutionary history in the two hemispheres. What we see today in the diverse arboreal adaptations of monkeys is then a result of **parallel evolution** (see p. 234). Similar ecological selective forces, mainly in tropical arboreal environments, led to structural evolution in different but parallel directions. The result is that the same grade of primate we today recognize as "monkey" evolved in both New and Old Worlds.

GRADE V: HOMINOIDS

The superfamily Hominoidea includes "lesser" apes (gibbons and siamangs), great apes (orangutans, gorillas, chimpanzees), and humans. Classifying humans with the apes is not an arbitrary device, for it indicates our close structural similarities, as well as shared evolutionary history. This close similarity was noted by Tyson at the end of the seventeenth century and was forcefully restated by Huxley and Darwin in the nineteenth century. As this classification indicates, we and the apes are more closely related to each other than *either* is to an Old World monkey. In fact, many primatologists feel that the relationship between humans and great apes is so close that they are often grouped within a single family (Dene et al., 1976; Szalay and Delson, 1979). (See Table 9-1.)

The structural similarities we share with the apes are numerous but most importantly include absence of a tail, generally large body size, shortened

Figure 9-19   A female baboon in estrus. Note the sexual swelling of the genitals.

Figure 9-20   A rhesus monkey. Shown here in an isolation chamber used by NASA researchers to test the behavioral effects of long-duration space flight.

deep trunk, stable spine, and the position and musculature of the shoulder joint.

The Gibbon and Siamang   The gibbon and closely related siamang (**Hylobatidae**) are today found in the southeastern tropical areas of Asia. These animals are the smallest of the apes, with a long, slender body weighing only about thirteen pounds in the gibbon and about twenty-five pounds in the larger siamang.

The most distinctive structural feature of the hylobatids is related to their functional adaptation for **brachiation.** Consequently, they have extremely long arms, long, permanently curved fingers, and powerful shoulder muscles. This highly specialized locomotory adaptation may be related to feeding behavior while hanging beneath branches.

The Orangutan   The orang (genus: *Pongo*) is found today only in heavily forested areas on the Indonesian islands of Borneo and Sumatra. Due to poaching by humans in the past and the continuing commercial encroachment on its habitats, the orang faces imminent extinction. Such a loss would be tragic on several counts, especially because little is currently known of these mysterious red giants of the forest. Orangs are slow, cautious climbers whose whole locomotory behavior can best be described as a **quadrumanual** adaptation—a tendency to use all four limbs for grasping and support. They are large animals with pronounced sexual dimorphism (males weigh about 150 pounds and females about half that). Orangs were thought to be exclusively arboreal, but recent evidence (Galdikas, 1979) suggests they (especially males) occasionally come to the ground to traverse fairly long distances.

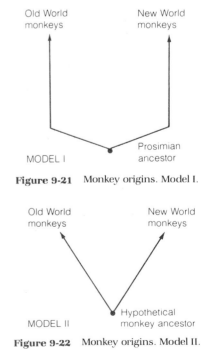

Figure 9-21   Monkey origins. Model I.

Figure 9-22   Monkey origins. Model II.

Gibbons: any area in color

Orangs: only in hatched areas

Figure 9-23 Distribution of modern Asian

The Gorilla   The largest of all living primates, the gorilla (family: Pongidae; genus: *Gorilla*) today is confined to forested areas in West Africa and the great lakes area of East Africa. This species exhibits marked sexual dimorphism, with males weighing up to 400 pounds in the wild and females around 200 pounds. Due to their very large adult weight, gorillas are almost completely terrestrial, adopting a semiquadrupedal (knuckle-walking) posture on the ground. Their forelimbs are elongated, though not so much as in gibbons, their upper bodies are normally held semierect, and their arms possess considerable mobility. Consequently, there are numerous structural modifications: a flattened (front-to-back) and broadened (side-to-side) chest; a shortened, more stable spine (compared to quadrupedal monkeys); longer clavicles; and flexible, powerful shoulders. The wrist joint is also modified to support the considerable weight of the upper body during knuckle-walking. In addition, gorillas have brains more complexly organized than monkeys or gibbons, thus allowing for more learned behavior. Once considered a wild and savage beast, the gorilla has been shown by field studies to be a shy, usually gentle vegetarian (Schaller, 1963; Fossey, 1970). Recent reports, however, have shown that—like many other primates—gorillas fairly frequently attack and kill other members of their species, particularly infants (Fossey, 1981).

The Chimpanzee   Probably the best known and most loved of all the non-human primates is the chimpanzee (family: Pongidae; genus: *Pan*). Often misunderstood because of their displays within zoos and carnival sideshows, the chimps' true nature did not come to light until long hours of field work in their natural environments provided a reliable picture. Chimps are found today in equatorial Africa stretching in a broad belt from the Atlantic Ocean in the west to Lake Tanganyika in the east.

Chimpanzees are in many ways structurally quite similar to gorillas, with corresponding limb proportions and thorax (chest) shape as well as specific features of the upper limb and wrist joint. This similarity is due to the likeness in their mode of locomotion (knuckle-walking) while on the ground. Indeed, many authorities (for example, Buettner-Janusch, 1973) consider chimps and gorillas as members of a single genus (*Pan gorilla* for the gorilla; *Pan troglodytes* for the chimp). However, the ecological adaptations of the chimp and gorilla differ, since chimps spend a great deal of time arm-swinging in the trees and feeding primarily on fruit. Conversely, gorillas are almost exclusively terrestrial vegetarians, consuming such vegetative matter as roots, shoots, and bark.

Like the brain of the gorilla, the chimpanzee brain is highly developed, and the learning capabilities of these animals are well known to visitors to animal shows as well as to scientific investigators.

Humans   Humans (family: Hominidae; genus: *Homo*) belong to the one remaining genus of the superfamily Hominoidea, a genus that today consists of only one species, *Homo sapiens*. Our primate heritage is shown again and again in the structure of our body: our dependence on vision; our lack of reliance on olfactory (smell) cues; and our flexible limbs and grasping hands are all long rooted in our primate, arboreal past. Indeed, among the primates, we show in many ways the most developed set of primate characteristics.

Figure 9-24 Gibbon.

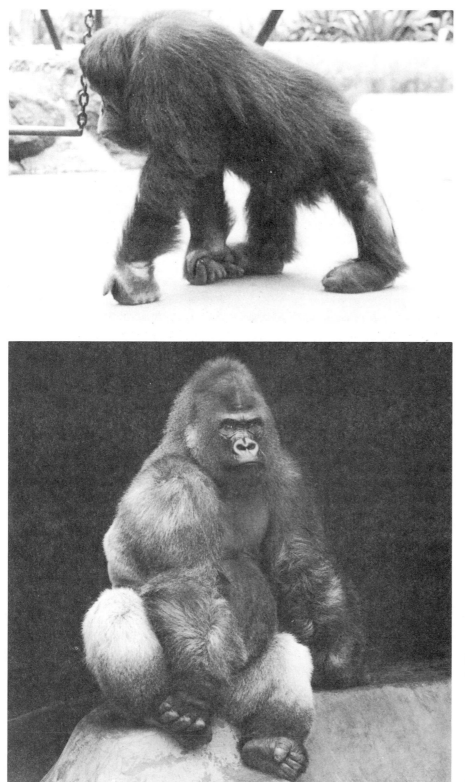

Figure 9-25 A male orangutan.

Chimpanzees: any area in color

Gorillas: only in hatched areas

Figure 9-26 Distribution of modern African apes.

Figure 9-27 A male lowland gorilla.

Figure 9-28   Chimpanzee.

For example, the development of our cerebral cortex and reliance on learned behavior with resulting complexity in social behavior are but elaborations of long-established primate trends.

The most distinct feature seen in humans is our unique manner of locomotion. The striding, bipedal gait with alternating support placed on a single hindlimb has required significant structural modifications in the pelvis and leg. By isolating similar structural modifications in the remains of fossil animals, we are able to distinguish our closely related or direct ancestors.

◇ Primate Chromosomes, Proteins, and DNA

The classification of primates used thus far in this chapter has employed the traditional approach of looking for homologies in morphological traits. However, another relatively new perspective with enormous potential for helping to clarify taxonomic problems compares **karyotypes** (chromosome numbers, shapes, banding patterns), proteins, and even roughly correlates the DNA code itself.

The usefulness of this approach is immediately obvious. When we compare outward morphology, such as limb proportions and dental formulae, we are comparing phenotypes, usually far removed from their underlying genetic basis. However, what we are really after in the construction of classification schemes are homologies, traits based on common evolutionary descent. In other words, we want to compare traits that are inherited—those coded directly in the genotype.

Direct protein products of DNA, such as hemoglobin and serum proteins (found in the blood), are excellent indicators of homologies. If two species of primates are systematically similar in their protein structure, we can infer their DNA sequences are also similar. When two species share similar DNA, that means both inherited the same blueprint (with minor revisions) from a common ancestor. Thus, we have *direct* indicators of real homologies. Two primates that superficially resemble one another (some New World and Old World monkeys, for example) may in fact not be closely related at all. Using outward morphology alone may be confusing due to unknown effects from parallel evolution. But such evidence as biochemical data and karyotype comparisons avoids these pitfalls, and indeed shows Old and New World monkeys as genetically (and evolutionarily) quite distinct.

Primatologists utilizing these techniques have, in conjunction with biochemists, in the last few years added considerable insight into our classifications of the primate order. A point worthy of mention: In most cases, biochemical evidence has reaffirmed the taxonomies constructed from comparative morphological studies (thereby supplying an extremely important independent source of data). When contradictions with traditional taxonomies have cropped up, much needed new knowledge has been gained. For example, classifying the orang with the African great apes superficially makes good sense since their outward body structures appear similar. Biochemical evidence, however, shows that both Asian apes (orangs and gibbons) are quite distinct from chimps and gorillas. Since our classifications are designed to reflect evolutionary relationships, they will have to be revised in the future to accord with this new information. (See Table 9-1.)

The way the various chromosomal and biochemical techniques are performed requires considerable technological sophistication, but their applications are straightforward. For example, two species can be compared for karotype. The more closely two species are related, the closer their karyotypes should be. When one looks at the chromosomes of the hominoids, it is readily apparent that humans and the great apes are all quite similar, with gibbons and siamangs having the most distinctive (i.e., derived) pattern (Stanyon and Chiarelli, 1982; Mai, 1983).

Among the large-bodied hominoids, the orang karyotype is the most conservative, with humans and the African apes displaying more derived features. It is interesting to note that the fossil data (which we'll take up in Chapter 12) also now suggests that orangs are probably the most conservative (i.e., primitive) of the large hominoids.

Within the human/gorilla/chimp group there are a tremendous number of similarities of the structural arrangement and banding patterns of almost all the chromosomes. A relatively small number of alterations are required to transform all three living species from a theoretical ancestor (Yunis and Prakash, 1982).

The exact sequence of evolutionary relationships among humans and the African great apes is still in some dispute. Some tentative chromosomal data have suggested that humans and chimps share a more recent ancestry after separating from gorillas (Yunis and Prakash, 1982). A more controlled study, however, with consideration of within-species variation of karyotype (Stanyon and Chiarelli, 1982), has supported the more traditional branching order, where humans and *both* African apes diverge first—followed later by a separation of chimps and gorillas.

Detailed protein structures can be compared, as between chimp and human hemoglobin, by isolating the amino acid sequences. Comparisons between humans and the African great apes for the approximately half dozen proteins analyzed in this manner show striking similarities; they are either identical or show a difference of only one or two amino acids in the entire sequence (as you will recall, the hemoglobin beta chain is 146 amino acids long).

Another method used to contrast proteins in different species is not as precise as a detailed protein analysis but is less time consuming and less costly. By measuring the strength of reaction to specially prepared antisera, similarities in proteins are calibrated on a relative scale, indicating *antigenic distance*. This approach, developed by Vincent Sarich and Allan Wilson at the University of California, Berkeley, has enabled many more proteins to be compared among a wide variety of different primate species. The results again generally tally favorably with traditional classifications (see Table 9-4).

Moreover, differences in DNA strands themselves can be compared using an elaborate technique called DNA hybridization. Scientists have recently performed some remarkable experiments in which double strands of DNA are artificially separated in two different species and then recombined into a

Karyotype
The characteristic number, size, and pattern of the chromosomes that are distinctive for particular species.

Acrocentric
A chromosome with its centromere towards one end.

Metacentric
A chromosome with its centromere near the center.

Figure 9-29 Fusion of two small chromosomes. This fusion produces one large chromosome (human chromosome number 2?).

Table 9-4 Biochemically Determined Distances between Humans and Other Animals

	Amino Acid Distance	Antigenic Distance	DNA Distance
Human—chimp	0.27	1.0	1.8
Human—gorilla	0.65	0.8	2.3
Human—orang	2.78	2.0	4.9
Human—gibbon	2.38	2.6	4.9
Human—macaque	3.89	3.6	—
Human—spider monkey	8.69	7.6	—
Human—tarsier	—*	8.8	—
Human—loris	11.36	11.2	42.0
Human—tree shrew	—	12.6	—
Primates—other placentals	—	12.11–14.91	—
Placentals—marsupials	—	15.83	—

All these figures are averages drawn from numerous individual comparisons. Each scale should be interpreted not as absolute measures, but only as *relative* ones. In addition, the scalings for each of the three sets of comparisons are independent of one another.

*Line (—) indicates data undetermined.

Source: Data abstracted from Goodman and Lasker, 1975.

new molecule, a hybrid DNA unlike anything nature ever concocted. The genetic (and evolutionary) similarity of the two species is then calculated by measuring the number of mismatched base pairs along the hybrid sequence (in other words, places where the two sides of the molecule are not complementary: A with T, G with C, etc.).

Once again, the results of this fascinating but still fairly new technique have reaffirmed our particularly close affinities with the gorilla and chimp, a definitely less direct evolutionary link with the Asian apes, and even further genetic distinctiveness from Old World monkeys.

Finally, the revolution in molecular biology brought about by recombinant DNA research has now made it possible to directly sequence the nucleotides of humans and other organisms (Goodman, et al., 1983). As a result—when this new technique has been more widely applied—we should be able to ascertain even more unambiguously the precise genetic/evolutionary relationships among the primates.

In addition, these nucleotide sequence data will inform us concerning the frequency of "neutral" mutations and (when calibrated with fossil data) may elucidate whether primate evolution has been more characterized by "gradualistic" or "punctionalistic" modes of change (see pp. 108–111).

◇ Summary

Primates are an order of placental mammals characterized by their generalized limb structure, dependence on vision, lack of reliance on smell, developed brain (particularly cerebral cortex), and complex social organizations.

All these evolutionary trends have developed, or at least have been elaborated, as a direct result of adaptation to an arboreal environment.

Living primates today represent five major grades of evolution that correspond to various stages of primate evolution over the last several million years. These grades are:

   I. Tree shrews (not really true primates)
  II. Lemurs and lorises
 III. Tarsiers
 IV. Monkeys (New World and Old World)
  V. Hominoids (apes and humans)

We are a primate and our ancestors have been primates for at least 70 million years. Only by looking at humans *as a primate* can we hope to understand the kind of animal we are and how we came to be this way.

◇ Questions for Review

1. How are primates similar to other placental mammals?
2. Discuss how binocular vision, prehensility, and an expanded cerebral cortex are adaptations for an arboreal niche.
3. What are the various superfamilies of the primate order? To which one do humans belong?
4. Discuss the geographic distribution and ecological adaptations of contemporary prosimians.
5. What are the most important differences between prosimians and anthropoids?
6. How do monkeys in the Old and New Worlds exhibit parallel evolution?
7. How do teeth reflect evolutionary relationships?
8. What are some important relationships between limb structure and locomotion in contemporary primates?
9. In what ways are humans typical primates?
10. How does biochemical evidence give indication of homologies? Why are effects due to parallel evolution more likely to cloud the picture for morphological traits than for biochemical traits?

◇ Suggested Further Reading

Buettner-Janusch, John. *Physical Anthropology: A Perspective*, New York: John Wiley and Sons, 1973.

    Chapters 4–6 (pp. 43–194) offer a superb, in-depth introduction to the anatomy, taxonomy, and biology of nonhuman primates. Written by one of today's leading authorities, this book is highly recommended for those introductory students wishing to delve further into primate studies.

Campbell, Bernard. *Human Evolution*, Chicago: Aldine Publishing Co., 1974.

    A functionally oriented review of primate dentition, locomotor systems, digestion, etc. A truly excellent source for the moderately advanced student.

Eimerl, S. and I. DeVore. *The Primates*, New York: Time, Inc., 1965.
  An excellent introduction to the primates. This beautifully illustrated work is written for the layman with many superior photos of contemporary primates, taken mainly in the wild. The first chapter is a superb summary of primate anatomical characteristics.

Le Gros Clark, W. E. *The Antecedents of Man*, Chicago: Quadrangle Books, 1971.
  An advanced analysis of primate anatomy from an evolutionary perspective. Excellent introductory chapters define primate evolutionary trends and survey contemporary forms.

Napier, J. R. and P. H. Napier. *A Handbook of Living Primates*, New York: Academic Press, 1967.
  A detailed account summarizing geographical, ecological, and morphological data for fifty-six extant genera. This book also contains an excellent introduction into primate functional anatomy and is the standard reference for classifications of locomotory behavior.

Napier, Prue. *Monkeys and Apes*, New York: Grosset and Dunlap, Inc., 1972.
  A Bantam Nature Paperback. An excellent reference for the introductory student. Outstanding illustrations.

Schultz, Adolf. *The Life of Primates*, New York: Universe Books, 1969.
  Written by the world's leading authority on comparative primate anatomy, this book provides an excellent introduction to this complex topic. Written at a level comprehensible to introductory students.

Watts, Elizabeth. *Biology of the Living Primates*, Dubuque, Iowa: Wm. C. Brown, 1975.
  A short nontechnical introduction and summary of living primates. Highly recommended for introductory students.

Models for Human Behavior

CONTENTS

For years, scholars and popular writers have discussed human aggression. One of the very basic questions has been (and still is, for that matter) whether human aggression is instinctive or learned, or a combination of both. This issue is significant because, if aggression is learned, it can be unlearned; or, the learning of aggression can be modified or replaced by other attitudes. If it is instinctive, then it may be necessary to develop quite different techniques in dealing with it. Many believe that a clue to the source of human aggression might be found in nonhuman primate behavior, especially that of

the apes. Field studies have shown monkeys—especially baboons and macaques—to be quite aggressive, but since humans are more closely related to apes, the question of ape aggression is more relevant.

Until recently, field studies of apes have been infrequent, and those that were done were not nearly as thorough as those that are contemporary. While much evidence remains to be obtained, the number of field studies since 1960 has increased manyfold and data are accumulating in great quantities on chimpanzees, gorillas, and orangutans.

Dian Fossey's early reports on go-

rillas did not mention aggression, but in her recent account, Fossey writes of two kinds of gorilla aggression. One, witnessed by a student of Fossey—Peter Veit—was a violent attack by a male on a female that resulted in the female's death. The female was ill and probably would have soon perished in any event, but the male literally stomped her to death.

Fossey also reported that infanticide accounted for the deaths of 6 out of 38 infants born over a 13-year period. The killing of the infants was perpetrated by males. Fossey believes that infanticide "is the means by which a male instinctively seeks to perpetuate his own lineage by killing another male's progeny in order to breed with the victim's mother" (Fossey, 1981, p. 512). (See Sociobiology for a discussion of this theory, p. 304).

Unlike gorillas—and, as we shall see, chimpanzees—orangutans do not appear to be aggressive. At least, observers have seen very little aggression. Biruté Galdikas (1981) reported what she believes to be a case of "rape," which, however, she did not actually witness. She heard the screams of a female, heard a good deal of thrashing about, saw the male leave shortly thereafter, and then observed bruises on the female. Whether this was an isolated incident, or whether it is a common event is still not known.

In contrast to gorillas and orangs, abundant field studies of chimpanzees show evidence of frequent aggression—including killing—among these primates. Are there killer apes—apes guilty of calculated, premeditated "murder"? The case of the male gorillas mentioned above is evidence there are. More evidence comes from chimpanzees.

In the past two decades, beginning with Jane Goodall's study of chimpanzees in Tanzania's Gombe Stream National Park, intensive research on chimpanzees, gorillas, and orangutans has been conducted in Africa and Borneo. Early reports from these studies led us to believe that apes were "gentle folk," kind to their children and playing out a more or less "live and let live" existence. The only animal that murdered its own kind, it seemed, was the human animal.

Beginning in 1974, Goodall and her colleagues at Gombe Stream observed a series of at least five unprovoked (or so it seemed to the observers) brutal, savage gang attacks by males of one group against the males of another group that had splintered off several years earlier. All seven males of the splinter group were wiped out by 1977. One attack even involved an elderly female who died as a consequence of the beating. The attackers were usually young males, using their teeth, hands, and feet, although on one occasion an older male was seen throwing a rock at a prostrate victim.

Even more disturbing, perhaps, is the cannibalism that Goodall has witnessed. She reports on a mother-daughter pair of chimps that had killed and eaten possibly up to ten newborns. Another case of cannibalism in East Africa was recently reported for the chimpanzees of the Mahale mountains. We do not know how widespread the practice is, or what its adaptive value might be.

Because of the biochemical and genetic similarity between chimpanzees and humans, chimpanzee behavior may hold clues to human origins and even present-day human behavior. The significance of the killings and the cannibalism observed among chimpanzees remains to be worked out. Meanwhile, it is distressing to find that our image of the playful, friendly chimpanzee may well be illusion rather than reality.

As Goodall observed, "It is sobering that our new awareness of chimpanzee violence compels us to acknowledge that these ape cousins of ours are even more similar to humans than we thought before."

SOURCE:

Fossey, Dian. "Imperiled Giants of the Forest," *National Geographic*, 4: 501–522, April, 1981.

Gildakas, Biruté. Public Lecture at the California Institute of Technology, May 2, 1981.

Hamburg, David A. and E. R. McCown. *The Great Apes*, Menlo Park, Ca.: The Benjamin/Cummings Publishing Co., 1979.

Goodall, Jane. "Chimp Killings: Is it the 'Man' in them?" *Science News*, 17: 276, April 29, 1978.

———, *National Geographic*, 5: 592–620, May, 1979.

Norikashi, Kohshi. "One Observed Case of Cannibalism among Wild Chimpanzees of the Mahale Mountains," *Primates*, 23 (1):66–74, January, 1982.

◇ CHAPTER TEN

◇ Introduction

How can we better understand human behavior? Observing an urbanized industrialized society such as ours will not tell us very much of our hominid heritage. After all, we have been urbanized for only a few thousand years, and the industrial revolution is merely a few centuries old, barely a flicker in evolutionary time. Consequently, to understand what behavior components may have shaped our evolution, we need a perspective broader than that which our own culture supplies. Since little is known about early hominid behavior, we study the behavior of contemporary animals adapted to environments similar to those of early hominids in the hope of gaining insight into early hominid evolution.

We shall consider as possible models for this purpose the social carnivores of the savanna (wild dogs, lions, and wolves*), as well as the nonhuman primates of the savanna (baboons) and of the forest/savanna (chimpanzees). Finally, we shall also consider modern hunting-gathering societies as a possible model for early hominid adaptation, specifically deriving detailed information from the !Kung San people of the Kalahari Desert in South Africa.

In this chapter, we place nonhuman primate behavior in the context of its possible relationship to human behavior; that is, we address the question: Does the study of nonhuman primates serve as a window on (or model for) human behavior? Or are nonhuman primates so different in behavior from hominids that the uniqueness of the former derives little from the latter?

◇ Behavior and Human Origins

What does it mean to be human? There are several *physical* characteristics, such as adaptations for bipedal locomotion and enlarged brain, that characterize humans and—to varying extents—our hominid ancestors. But from a strictly structural point of view, we are not really that unique compared to other primates, especially when compared with the great apes. In patterns of dentition, bone development, muscle structure, and so forth, we and the other hominoids are very similar, reflecting a fairly recent shared ancestry. (Probably no more than 7 or 8 m.y. at most separate us from the African great apes.) Indeed, in the nonrepeated portions of DNA, humans and chimpanzees are 99% identical. So what, precisely, is it that distinguishes the human animal?

Quite clearly, it is behavioral attributes that most dramatically set humans apart. Human culture is our strategy for coping with life's challenges. No

---

*Wolves of course are not savanna animals, but their environment—except for temperature—resembles the savanna.

other primate even comes close to the human ability to modify environments. Communication through symbolic language is yet another uniquely human characteristic (see pp. 298–302 for a discussion of "language" in great apes). In addition, several other features differentiate humans from the majority of other primates. These may be summarized as follows:

Humans are bipedal.

Humans live in permanent bisexual social groups with males often bonded to females.

Humans have large brains relative to body weight and are capable of complex learning.

Partly as a consequence of neurological reorganization, humans make highly advanced use of symbolic language.

Also related to neurological developments and bipedality, *cultural* response has become the central hominid adaptive strategy.

Humans obtain food through some male/female division of labor; moreover, food is actively transported back to a base camp (home) for purposes of sharing.

Length of dependence of young has increased in humans, resulting in greater parental investment—not only by the mother, but often by adult males as well.

With more time and energy expended on each offspring, the total number raised is low in humans compared to most mammals, but, in fact, may be higher than seen in great apes (Lovejoy, 1981).

There is a relaxation of the estrous cycle and concealed ovulation in humans, so that females can be sexually receptive at any time.

These traits are fairly characteristic of all modern humans. Moreover, much of this behavioral complex is thought to be a good *baseline* for the early stages of hominid emergence. In fact, behavioral reconstructions are often central to theories explaining how hominids came to be hominids in the first place.

A recent comprehensive reconstruction of the factors influencing human origins has been proposed by C. Owen Lovejoy (1981).* The Lovejoy model attempts to integrate the behavioral and structural modifications that prevailed during the earliest stages of hominid emergence (10–5 m.y.a.). A "prime mover," according to Lovejoy, was the selective advantage of increased male parental investment.

Lovejoy sees ecological strategies of early hominids based on some *division of labor*, where males and females exploited slightly different resources. This pattern was elaborated further as males ranged farther away (particularly in search of game), while females remained closer to a central rendezvous point, which eventually became a base camp. With females staying closer to a fixed

*Lovejoy's model is given simply as one scholar's suggestion of human origins. Many anthropologists disagree with his interpretation and organization of the data. The authors do not necessarily agree with Lovejoy's point of view.

Polygyny
(po-lyj'-y-nee)
poly: much, many
gyn: female
One male and two or more females in a
mating relationship.

Social behavior
Exhibiting gregariousness, sociability. The
behavior of animals that live together in,
and interact as, a group consisting of
adults and young of both sexes.

base, they would avoid carrying their infants long distances, thus reducing infant mortality. While females are thought to have ranged closer to camp, gathering wild plant foods and perhaps small mammals, they alone presumably could not provide sufficient subsistence for themselves and several young. The solution, Lovejoy believes, lay in male provisioning—bringing food back to the base camp for purposes of sharing. This key aspect concerning active transport of food to a central point in order to be shared is not seen in any other primate. The same idea has also been put forth by Glynn Isaac (1976, 1978) as a significant influence on early human emergence.

With males investing more, females could raise more young than would otherwise be the case. Thus, birth spacing could be reduced, and hominid males and females behaving in this way would consequently increase their reproductive success.

Several males returning to the females at the base camp might encourage male-male competition, but this could possibly be diffused by the development of one-to-one male/female bonding; i.e., a monogamous relationship (an idea championed by Desmond Morris, 1967).

Bipedality (probably the first major distinction of hominids) would have evolved because the male carrying food to his female would have to do so bipedally. Bipedality in the female would be adaptive because she could carry an infant in one hand, and provision herself with the other.

For this system to work, it would be necessary for the male to carry food to his female throughout the year. He would have to be permanently attracted to her, not just at the time of estrus. This could be arranged through the development of permanent features on the female's body, such as hair, skin, shape, and prominent breasts, which would permanently attract the male and keep him interested the year-round (also proposed by Morris). According to Lovejoy's model, distinctive human traits, such as bipedality, pair bonding, food sharing, and sexual and reproductive behavior, are thus explained.

The Lovejoy model proposes a comprehensive and internally consistent explanation of human origins. However, it is not a scientific theory, since it cannot be framed into testable hypotheses. More appropriately, Lovejoy's assertions (just as those of others before him—Desmond Morris, Robert Ardrey, and so forth) could be termed a *scenario*, a speculative reconstruction. Since social behavior does not fossilize (except for some tantalizing hints—see Chapter 12), it is unlikely that we will be able to fully reconstruct the details of early hominid biosocial evolution. If anything, the physical evidence of the early hominids themselves (Chapters 13 and 14) suggests that some of the central premises in Lovejoy's scenario are probably wrong.

However, the Lovejoy model is extremely useful in highlighting some of the major differences between humans and other primates. Sometime during the course of human evolution, the complex of features discussed in this scenario did emerge. We mainly disagree with Lovejoy, though, concerning the *sequence* and *timing* of these behavioral modifications. Unlike Lovejoy, we do not believe it likely (or even probable) that very early hominids were paired monogamously. The other developments—bipedalism, increased meat exploitation, food sharing, and greater parental investment (by males, too, but indirectly)—could very well all have proceeded in a **polygynously** mating early hominid society similar to the vast majority of living primates.

◇ Definition of Behavior: To Be or Not To Be Social

Behavior could be generally defined as "anything an organism does." As such, it is part of a phenotype (see p. 87), which in many cases bears *some* relationship to the underlying genotype. The precise mechanisms of genotype/phenotypc interaction are poorly understood—especially for the more complex animals (i.e., vertebrates). As a result, great controversies have arisen concerning the genetic contribution to behavior in such animals. (We have addressed this issue in our discussion of human intelligence on pp. 204–208.)

We are concerned, however, with those particular aspects of behavior that are most useful for informing us about human evolution. Specifically, we want to focus on **social behavior**; that is, on relationships between animals of the same species—those that associate within fairly stable groups. Most animals (such as beetles, turtles, sharks, and so forth) are not social, but pursue a solitary existence. For many species, the only social contact that occurs between individual members is when adults of the opposite sex mate.

The exceptions are what interest us. While there are many species of highly evolved colony-living social insects (termites, ants, wasps, and bees), among the vertebrates, sociality is not a blanket phenomenon. Fish, for example, are social only to a minimum, where they move together (form schools)—there is, in fish, little in the way of social differentiation (i.e., classes or castes). Nor do reptiles or amphibians exhibit much of what could be called elaborated social activity. Birds and mammals, however, *are* social, many displaying complex role development, communication, parental strategies, and learning (the latter mostly in mammals).

Of the more than 4,000 species of mammals, all are social to a degree. Most basically, there is the "bond of milk" between a mother and her dependent, unweaned young. Moreover, some contact is obviously required between adult males and females for sexual reproduction. Beyond this, however, there is not much social interaction. For example, gophers, rats, and most insectivores (moles, hedgehogs, and shrews), are solitary; that is, the mother and her unweaned young form the only longterm association. In other species, such as wild pigs, mule deer, and mountain goats, females with their young may form permanent groups, but the males remain peripheral and mostly solitary. In yet other mammals, such as sea lions, camels, and musk oxen, the males may associate with the females, but only during the breeding season.

In a few mammals, however, males associate all year long with the female groups, but it is clear that such an arrangement is the exception rather than the rule. Still, this social pattern is of great interest to us, as it is one typically seen in our own species. Some of the noteworthy mammalian examples of such integrated bisexual social grouping can be found among the social carnivores (i.e., members of the order Carnivora). Included here are lions and, most especially, the pack-hunting canids—wolves and wild dogs. Since these animals display a social structure in some ways roughly analogous to that of humans, and since they evolved in physical environments presumably similar to that of our ancestors, we will discuss the social carnivores in some detail later in this chapter.

◇ Box 10-1   Key Concepts

Agonistic   Hostile behavior (see p. 275).

Core Area   An area within the home range where the group habitually sleeps, feeds, and performs routine activities. The area within the home range of greatest regular use.

Display   Stereotyped behavior or series of behaviors that serves to communicate emotional states between individuals. Most often concerned with reproductive or agonistic behaviors.

Division of Labor   Activities performed only by members of a particular status, such as age or sex.

Dominance   Also referred to as *dominance hierarchy* and *status rank*. The physical domination of some members of a group by other members. A hierarchy of ranked statuses sustained by hostile, or threat of hostile, behavior, which results in greater access to resources, such as food, sleeping sites, and mates.

Grooming, Social   Cleaning the body of another by picking through the hair and fur with the fingers or teeth.

Home Range   The area utilized by an animal; the living area in which an animal performs its normal activities; the area the group is most familiar with, and which provides the group with food.

Mother-Infant Relationship   The attachment between mother and her offspring. One of the most basic themes running through primate social relations.

Presenting   A behavior, often indicating subordination or appeasement, in which an animal places itself on all fours and elevates its rear end toward another. (During estrus a female may present for purposes of copulation.)

Scent-Marking   Deposition of odoriferous substances, known as *pheromones*, on an animal or object, typically a tree, bush, or rock. The deposition may be through scent glands or urine or both.

Territory   That part of the home range used exclusively by one group. Neighbors (of the same species) do not enter, or else enter only on a brief foray. Also defined as the area defended by one group against another group of the same species.

The other major exception to the basic mammalian social order is the primates, especially the anthropoids. As Chapter 9 notes, monkeys and apes typically associate in permanent groups comprised of adult females, their young, *and* adult males. Among more than 150 species of anthropoids, there are only a few species that do not conform to this pattern (see Box 10-2, p. 275.) The vast majority of anthropoids could thus be seen as displaying the "nontypical" social pattern also characteristic of human societies. Surely, this is no accident, and argues for an evolutionary background to human social behavior.

◇ Nonhuman Primates

Modern apes and humans last shared an ancestor in common somewhere between 8–14 m.y.a., according to some specialists, or 4–8 m.y.a., according to others. Researchers believe that ape behavior has changed since then, but not nearly as much as the behavior of hominids, who developed culture as their strategy of adaptation. Therefore, if we are interested in what hominid behavior might have been like before culture became a significant factor in

◇Box 10-2   Types of Nonhuman Primate Social Groups

I. *Solitary Primates*   Arboreal and nocturnal, solitary in the sense that they feed alone.
EXAMPLES: mouse lemur, galago, potto, loris, aye-aye, orangutan.

II. *Family Group*   Adult male and female and their off-spring; seen only among arboreal species.
EXAMPLES: indri, titi, marmoset, gibbon.

III. *Multimale*   The most common type among primates; found in both arboreal and terrestrial forms. Several adult males and about twice as many adult females and their offspring.
EXAMPLES: ring-tailed lemur, many New World monkeys, gorilla, sifaka, chimpanzee, baboon, macaque, howler.

IV. *One-male (Harem)*   May be adaptation of multimale group to arid conditions. Since only one male is neces-

sary to procreate next generation, and since several large males would eat a disproportionate amount of scarce food, a one-male group is an efficient adaptive unit for this environment.
EXAMPLES: gelada baboon, hamadryas baboon, ground-living patas, some guenons, colobus (guereza), some langurs.

SOURCE:
After P. Napier, 1972.

ADDITIONAL SOURCES:
Bramblett, 1976 (sifaka); Jolly, 1972 (sifaka); Carpenter, 1965 (howler); Kummer, 1971 (guenon); Struhsaker and Oates, 1975 (colobus).

it, and if we wish to know what behaviors may have led hominids to become dependent on culture, we may find clues in the behavior of our closest relatives, the apes. Later in this chapter, we shall, then, explore chimpanzee behavior for such clues.

The social behavior of nonhuman primates may be viewed as a simplified model of human behavior. The shorter life span of nonhuman primates allows us to follow their behavior through developmental stages with more ease than a similar study of human behavior would provide. As intimated, nonhuman primate behavior provides clues to, or suggests ideas about, what early hominid behavior may have been like. This approach emphasizes correlating particular social structures of given animals with attributes of their habitats, since all living organisms must adapt to their environment (Figs. 10-1 and 10-2). Such observations may offer hints to the environmental pressures involved and may ultimately lead to comprehending the factors that led to human emergence.

Studies of nonhuman primates also assist with present human behavioral problems. Humans are *not* monkeys or apes, of course, but similarities do exist. For example, the way human infants learn to love and bond to mother and then family is reflected in the infant behavior patterns of monkeys and apes. It is, after all, possible that "The more we can learn about the evolutionary history and adaptations of other primate forms, the more we will know about the processes which shaped our own species" (Lancaster, 1975, p. 5).

Species of primates are numerous, and their behavior varies a good deal. Nevertheless, there are characteristics common to most, if not all, primates.

Figure 10-1 These baboons have adapted quadrupedally to a terrestrial savanna life.

Figure 10-2 Gibbons brachiating, an arboreal adaptation.

Most primates live in tropical or semitropical regions, but a few, such as the Japanese macaque and some langurs, have adapted to cold weather. Although they vary, primates are mainly *diurnal*, some are **crepuscular** and others, especially among prosimians, are *nocturnal*. Relatively few nonhuman primates are terrestrial—savanna baboons and gorillas are the best known; most others are arboreal. Intelligence, a difficult concept to define, is another characteristic common to primates, and it is generally conceded that all primates are more intelligent than most, if not all, other mammals.

Living in social groups is one of the major characteristics of primates, who solve their major adaptive problems within this social context. For other animals, "mating, feeding, sleeping, growth of the individual, and protection from pedators are usually matters for the solitary individual to solve, but for . . . primates they are most often performed in a social context" (Lancaster, 1975, p. 12).

Many different patterns of social groupings exist among the primates (see Box 10-2). Typically, the primate social group includes members of all ages and of both sexes, a composition that does not vary significantly during the annual cycle. As we pointed out, this situation differs from that of most mammals, whose adult males and females associate only during the breeding season, and whose young do not remain with the adults after reaching puberty.

Because they remain together over a long period of time, members of the specific primate group learn to know each other. They learn—as they must—how to respond to a variety of actions that may be threatening, cooperative, or indifferent. In such social groups, individuals must be able to evaluate a situation before acting. Evolutionarily speaking, this would have placed selective pressure on social intelligence which, in turn, would select for brains that could assess such situations and store the information. One of the results of such selection would be the evolution of proportionately larger and more complex brains, especially in the higher primates.

◇ Social Behavior

Since primates solve their major adaptive problems in a social context, we might expect that they participate in a number of activities to reinforce the integrity of the group for purposes of holding it together. The better known of these activities are described in the sections that follow.

Crepuscular
(kre-pus'-kew-ler)
creper: dark, dusty
Active at twilight or dawn.

Figure 10-3 Primate mothers and their infants.

ASPECTS OF SOCIAL BEHAVIOR

Grooming Almost all primates groom one another. Grooming occurs in other animal species, but social grooming is a unique primate activity and plays an important role in the life of most primates. It helps remove dirt and parasites, but "it is much more than that—it is the social cement of primates from lemur to chimpanzee" (Jolly, 1972, p. 153). Grooming is often reciprocal, with roles interchanged—the groomer may become the groomee, a process resulting in the establishment of friendly social relations among the animals in the group.

Displays A wide variety of body movements, vocalizations, olfactory signals (scent-marking, for example), and facial gestures communicate to other members of the species such emotional signals as fear, threats, greeting, danger, pain, hunger, courtship, and many other messages as well.

Animals often display when they are excited, a state that may be brought about by such situations as the presence of an outsider, a response to the

Figure 10-4 Grooming baboons. The white eyelid of the baboon is a threat display.

Figure 10-5 (a) A gorilla display. (b) A chimp display. This old male swings his arms and then throws things at the zoo spectators.

display of another member of the group, or a need for reinforcing status relationships. The gorilla is known for its magnificent display involving such activities as hooting, throwing vegetation, and chest beating.

Displays of other primates include grunting, yawning, ground slapping, branch-shaking, head bobbing and bouncing, screams, hoots, strutting, scratching, barks, scent-marking (among prosimians), and facial gestures, such as smiling and grimacing. A display primarily communicates information that "is advantageous to the individual of the species, to the social group to which he belongs, to others of the same species, and to other species" (Buettner-Janusch, 1973, p. 307).

*Dominance** Dominance rank, or status rank, may be measured by priority access to a desired object, such as food or sex, and also by the result of threat situations. A dominant individual is given priority, and in a confrontation is the one that usually does not give way. It is believed, although not all primatologists agree, that because dominant males compete more successfully for fertile females than do subordinate males, they have greater reproductive success. Also, dominant females, because they compete for food more successfully than subordinate females, are thus provided with more energy for offspring production and have greater reproductive success than subordinate females (Fedigan, 1983).

In many primate societies males are generally dominant over females of the same age, older or stronger individuals supplant weaker ones, and each

*See Fedigan, 1983, for a review of dominance theory.

(a)   (b)

group member must learn its rank in the hierarchy, at least within its own sex and age class. "Further, the length of time spent in the group, called 'residency' or male 'tenure,' also correlates significantly with rank, positively in the case of macaques . . . and negatively with the case of baboons" (Fedigan, 1983, pp. 111–112). Dominant males are sometimes responsible for protecting the troop from predators as well as for defense against other troops if that situation should arise. They may also, as in savanna baboons, act as "policemen" to break up fights among juveniles, females, and other adult males within their troop.

Dominance is adaptive because it operates to avoid conflict. When two individuals compete for the same scarce item, the dominant one assumes priority by threat behavior. Thus dominance serves to organize social interactions; individuals know where they belong and act accordingly, avoiding chaotic, unorganized social relations. The result is a smoothly functioning order of priority, which reduces endless quarrels for scarce resources.

Mother-Infant Relationship   The basic social unit among primates is the female and her infants. Adult males consort with females for mating purposes, but they may or may not participate as members of the social unit. Observations both in the field and in captivity suggest that this mother-offspring core provides the group with its stability.

Figure 10-6   Primate mothers and their infants. (In the photo depicting the human, a grandmother substitutes for the mother.)

The mother-infant attachment, one of the most basic themes running throughout primate social relations, begins at birth. A primate infant's first bond (in the anthropoids especially) is to its mother. After birth, the infant clings to its mother while she performs her daily activities, often without seeming regard for her offspring's success in holding on. Quite often, however, as she leaves for some activity, a mother will gather her infant protectively to her body. Unlike other social animals, in which the newborn are left in a nest or den, the clinging primate infant develops a closeness with the mother that

Figure 10-7 Wire mother and cloth mother.

does not end with weaning. This closeness is often maintained throughout life and is reflected in grooming behavior that continues between mother and offspring even after the children reach adulthood.

The crucial role played by primate mothers was clearly demonstrated by the Harlows, (1959), who raised some infant monkeys with surrogate mothers fashioned from cloth and other monkeys with no mothers at all. In one experiment, infants raised with surrogate mothers retained an attachment to their cloth mother, but those raised without a mother were incapable of forming a lasting affectional tie.

In another experiment (Harlow and Harlow, 1961), monkeys raised without a mother sat passively in their cages and stared vacantly into space. Some punished themselves by seizing one of their arms with the mouth and tearing the flesh until blood flowed. Those raised with a surrogate mother acted similarly, but somewhat less dramatically. None of the males or females raised without real or surrogate mothers ever achieved any semblance of normal sexual behavior. No motherless male ever successfully copulated and often violently assaulted the female he was paired with. Females (those raised without mothers as well as those raised with cloth mothers) that were successfully impregnated and bore young, paid very little attention to their infants. A mother often brushed away her baby "as if she were brushing off flies" or crushed her infant to the floor, and these mothers rarely held their infants or protected them as normal mothers do.

The Harlows conclude: "We only know that these monkeys without normal mothering and without peer affectional relationships have behaved toward their infants in a manner completely outside the range of even the least adequate of normal mothers" (1961, p. 55).

In more recent studies, Professor Suomi of the University of Wisconsin Primate Laboratory and a student of Harlow, has confirmed the importance of the mother-infant relationship. Even brief separations from the mother have lasting effects. He further points out that peer relationships suffer if the individual does not have a good relationship with its mother (Greenberg, 1977). His review of isolation studies has led Suomi to emphasize that social isolation initiated early in life can have devastating effects on subsequent development and behavior for many species of primates. The primate deprivation syndrome that results from early isolation is characterized by displays of abnormal self-directed and sterotypic behavior and by gross deficits in all aspects of social behavior (Suomi, 1982, p. 190).

Infants are mainly cared for by the mother, of course, but adult males are also known to take more than a casual interest. This phenomenon has frequently been noted among male hamadryas baboons, who sometimes "adopt" an infant. "He then carries it en route, allows it to sleep huddled against his belly at night, and prevents it from moving too far away" (Kummer, 1971, pp. 81–82).

What may be an extension of the mother-infant relationship has been called **allo**parent, or "aunt" behavior. This type of behavior occurs among many animal species but is most richly expressed in primates, and some researchers believe it is found among all social primates. No biological relationship is necessarily suggested by the term (although elder siblings often act as alloparents). It is just "that females are behaving like the maiden aunts of English turn-of-the-century middle-class families" (Jolly, 1972, p. 252). Usually, the alloparents crowd around the newborn infant and attempt to carry, cuddle, groom, hold, or just touch it. Some species, like the common langur, are well known for their aunts, and as many as eight females may hold the infant during its first day of life. Among patas monkeys, the mother may threaten a female that touches her baby, so the interested female resorts to a subtle maneuver. "A patas female may begin to groom a mother's arm and then slowly and cautiously transfer her grooming to the infant within it" (Kummer, 1971, p. 80).

Several functions are suggested for alloparenting. If the mother dies, the infant stands a chance of being adopted by an alloparent or other individual of the group. The practice may bind together the adults of the group, since it may be more convenient for the mother to leave her infant occasionally with another female. It may also assist the training of **nulliparous** females for motherhood.

Male-Female Sexual Bond   A close sexual bond between adult males and females is not common among the higher primates, although it does occur. In the one-male (harem) group, the adult male keeps his females close to him and maintains a very alert eye for any wandering adult male. Some researchers suggest that the one-male group is adaptive in arid regions where food is scarce and widely scattered, and attack by predators a constant peril. An adult male is protection for the females and offspring, and the structure of only one male to a group diminishes the consumption of scarce food resources.

Forest monkey groups, such as the black and white colobus, are also often composed of one-male groups. Here, food is no great problem and predators

Nulliparous
null: none, not any
parous: birth
Never having given birth.

Allo
Combining form indicating different or other.

hunt by stealth. The best defense is constant vigilance by all concerned. The adult male's role, therefore, is minimal, and one male is adequate for protective and reproductive functions.

The one-male/one-female family group (not found among the great apes and probably not among the early hominids) is characteristic of gibbons and some monkeys, and can be understood in terms of adaptation to their environment. A gibbon family—one adult male, one adult female, and their offspring—controls a small patch of tropical forest, which provides enough food for a small group. Gibbons jealously protect this territory from neighbors. When a young gibbon reaches maturity, it is driven out by the adult of the same sex, thus maintaining the small size of the group and its limited food supply.

Role Separation between Adults and Young   Among primates, especially the higher primates, there is a relatively long growth period spent in the protected environment of the social group. It is during this learning stage, when the young play and learn the skills needed in adulthood, that the brain develops the special intelligence characteristic of primates. This learning period is spent in physical and psychological safety because of the behavioral and psychological separation of roles between adults and young. The young play for many hours every day, learning many of the skills required by adults, free from anxiety because alert adults are always present. The separation of roles between adults and young enable the young to learn and practice the social, intellectual, and physical skills they will need as adults.

Figure 10-8   Hamadryas one-male groups.

Role Separation by Sex   Perhaps one of the most interesting points to be made about the separation of sex roles is that there is often very little separation. Except for the protective role played by males and the childbearing and nursing role of the mother, in many primate species both sexes perform similar functions. Females are expected to obtain their food, as are juveniles after they are weaned, and there is little sharing of food.

Among terrestrial primates, there is very often a sexual dimorphism in body size, weight, muscularity, distribution of hair on the body, and size of canines. Usually associated with separate roles, the larger size (as in baboons and gorillas) enables the male to play a dominant and protective function. In those species without sexual dimorphism, the females may be highly aggressive, as in gibbons, and join the males in defense of their territory.

Let us now examine two specific cases of primate social behavior: baboons and chimpanzees—baboons because of their well-developed social organization in a savanna environment, and chimpanzees because they are considered the primate most closely related to humans. These two species have been among the most extensively studied in the past, and are still being investigated by many observers.

EXAMPLES OF PRIMATE SOCIAL BEHAVIOR

Baboon Social Behavior   Baboons are diurnal, semiterrestrial, and (with some exceptions) open-country monkeys. There are several kinds of baboons, including the common or savanna, hamadryas, drill and mandrill, and gelada. The social behavior of each type varies. We shall describe the savanna baboon, the most widespread variety throughout Africa.

Group size among savanna baboons ranges from under 10 to as many as 200, with a mean somewhere around 40. The reason for this wide range is not clear, although the reproductive rate, death rate, emigrations and immigrations, and perhaps environmental conditions are likely factors. Food abundance does not seem to influence group size (Altmann and Altmann, 1970). Usually, the sex ratio in a troop is about even, although among adults, females outnumber males from about 2 to 4, to 1.

Home range (see Box 10-1) varies from 1.5 to 15 square miles, with the difference in area probably associated with proximity of neighbors, concentration of food and water resources, group size, and other factors. Within the home range, the group makes its daily round in the *core area* (see Box 10-1), which contains the crucial elements in the baboon world: sleeping trees, resting places, water holes, and food sources. There may be several core areas within one home range, and a troop may occasionally shift from one to the other.

Home ranges of neighboring groups overlap, which may or may not lead to hostility, but even where there is intergroup hostility, convincing evidence for territoriality is lacking.

Baboons sleep in trees.* In the morning they descend from their trees and move off to forage. They walk in a long file (not necessarily a single file) until

*Much of this description of baboon life is taken from the Altmann and Altmann (1970) account of baboons at the Amboseli Game Reserve in Kenya.

they reach the foraging area, where they spread out into a long, horizontal line. They continue to feed, moving forward slowly in this horizontal line and covering a total distance of roughly 3½ miles a day. By late afternoon they have reached the "sleeping" trees for that night. Some baboon troops return to the same sleeping trees on successive nights.

Baboons eat a wide variety of food. Their excellent vision, ability to climb, dig, and to cover a large area enable them to exploit many varieties of food and survive in many kinds of habitats. In the Amboseli Game Reserve in Kenya, baboon diet—grasses and acacia trees—is especially important. These baboons eat leaves, sap, cambium, blooms, seeds, seed pods, and even rotten wood. Both grass seeds and grass blades are commonly eaten. During the dry season, their special food is the rhizome and base of grass blades.

In addition to plant food, baboons eat a variety of animal food. They prey on earthworms and insects (grasshoppers, butterflies, and termites), eat bird-chicks, eggs, small frogs, lizards, and mammals (hares, young gazelles), several species of rodents, and primates (vervet monkeys and bushbabies).

The baboons at Amboseli did not share their food, although there was fighting among adult males for the meat on an infant gazelle. After the fighting ended, other baboons waited quietly, watching the one who was eating. When he finished, they walked over and picked up the scraps.

Harding and Strum (1976), observing a savanna (olive) baboon group at Kekopey, Kenya, found that, over a period of several years, the group developed rather sophisticated hunting techniques. At first their hunting was fortuitous, occasionally capturing a Thomson gazelle they happened to come across.

Figure 10-9   Baboon eating a Thomson's gazelle.

Later, they developed systematic cooperative efforts, even to the extent of pursuing the gazelles in relays. Females also began to capture prey (hares) in significant numbers. In one two-year period, 14% of all prey was caught by females and 16% by juveniles.

Adult males, females, and juveniles participated in the pursuit and capture of prey animals, but complex hunting (stalking and extended pursuit) was restricted to adult males (Strum, 1981; Hausfater, 1976).

Baboons at Kekopey also developed a form of meat-sharing and thus differed from the baboons of Amboseli. Males shared with other males and females with their young. Hausfater (1976) noted several kinds of sharing at Kekopey. Adult and juvenile baboons of both sexes all fed from a prey item, but adult males did so most frequently. Animals feeding on a carcass usually fed sequentially, but only rarely were two individuals observed to feed simultaneously from the same carcass.

While meat eating is not uncommon among baboons, and sharing of a sort occurs, it is doubtful that meat—vertebrate meat—is an important part of the diet of most baboons. As Hausfater states, "... vertebrates are probably a negligible protein source in the diet of all classes of baboons with the possible exception of adult males" (Hausfater, 1976, p. 64).

A baboon troop is organized around a male dominance hierarchy, with an *alpha male* as the most conspicuously dominant individual. In many cases, there may be several males in the central hierarchy. These co-dominants support each other in stress situations and cooperate in turning aside a threat to any one of them. Dominant males enjoy certain perquisites. They often have access to females during that time of estrus, when females are most likely to conceive. Apparently, however, this is not always the case, since recent evidence suggests that *epigamic* selection (female choice) of a mating male occurs more often than has hitherto been appreciated (Fedigan, 1983). Dominant males are less harrassed during mating, and they are assured of social space. Other less dominant animals make submissive gestures toward them, or avoid them altogether.

When predators (leopards, jackals, lions, hyenas) attack baboons, reactions are rapid, complex and variable, with a flurry of animals running in all directions. Some adult males start later and run more slowly, resulting in males interposed between the potential danger and the rest of the group. In more heavily forested areas, however, all baboons run for the trees, with the larger males usually reaching the trees first (Rowell, 1972).

There is also a female dominance hierarchy that is more stable than the male. Males change rank and groups frequently as they challenge, or are challenged by, other males. This does not occur among females, who maintain their rank for life. A baboon female infant, by observing her mother's behavior as she reacts to other female baboons, has ample opportunities to learn her mother's rank. Within a few months after birth, female infants seem to respond selectively to other individuals (J. Altmann, 1980).

High-ranking females also enjoy certain advantages. A high-ranking female can displace a low-ranking female and take over resources, such as partially dug grass corms. High-ranking females are subject to less distress interactions and have more access to newly born infants. Like less dominant males, among many privates. Ransom describes the strategy of a potential alloparent: low-ranking females make submissive gestures when approached by a high-ranking female.

Allomothering or alloparenting (p. 281) occurs among baboons as it does among many primates. Ransom (1981, p. 222) describes the strategy of a potential alloparent:

> An adult baboon may slowly approach the mother, showing various indications of friendly intent such as lip-smacking, narrowing of the eyes, and flattening of the ears, and embrace her in a variety of ways depending on the mother's posture and the sex of the other adult. During this embrace the adult will touch the infant with hand or nose several times and eventually may attempt to pull it out of the mother's arms. Such attempts for the most part appear to be intended to facilitate further investigation of the infant, but others are obviously motivated by a desire to carry it off (Ransom, 1981, p. 222).

The mother usually avoids the approach of males and will ignore or tolerate a young female. But she is permissive if the allomother is the infant's elder sibling. In an hierarchical society such as baboons, "a high-ranking female who takes an infant may refuse to return it, with the result that the infant starves to death" (Hrdy, 1981, p. 98). Sometimes a would-be allomother is insistent, even when the mother objects, and the result is a push-pull contest that may injure the infant. Among baboons, there may be a so-called nursery group composed of mothers and their infants. In such a group, a mother often interacts freely with another mother-infant pair.

Quite frequently, the most eager allomothers are nulliparous females, but because of their inexperience, they may also be incompetent. Pregnant and lactating mothers may also borrow newborns, but they tend to lose interest and, in the process of getting rid of them, may drag them along the ground or step on them. This points up the danger of allomothering, but it is useful to nulliparous females, since it provides them with the opportunity to learn mothering. Infants also gain social experience as they interact with old and young animals, both male and female. Should a mother die, the alloparent might adopt and rear her offpsirng. McKenna (1982) has noted that the attraction to infants and the female-female bonds established by alloparenting may contribute to group solidarity and cohesion. It may also hasten socialization, and possibly prepare the infant for a social life independent of its mother.

Grooming performed by both adults and young of both sexes is an important mechanism for maintaining peaceful social relationships and social bonding within the baboon troop. The most common grooming is female by female, but adult males groom females in estrus and often form a consort relationship. Females with infants are popular as groomees, and new mothers concentrate their grooming mainly on their newborn infants. Generally, the amount of grooming an individual receives reflects dominance rank.

With Lovejoy's model in mind, we raise the question, Does baboon social behavior offer clues to hominid evolution? Baboons adapted to the savanna with a tight social organization controlled by a highly structured dominance hierarchy. Although we do not know the structure of early hominid society, contemporary hunter-gatherers—such as the San—do not organize themselves in this way. Nor do hunter-gatherers display the aggression of the baboon troop. In hunting-gathering societies, meat sharing (distribution) is a very important activity, but it is rare among baboons. As Hausfater noted, animals fed on a carcass sequentially and only rarely were two individuals feeding simultaneously from the same carcass.

Is it possible, then, that studies of baboon behavior may suggest clues to early hunting behavior? Such studies have identified, as Strum (1981) has pointed out, a potential for primate predation, and it is quite likely that early hominids were also predators. Whether they next developed a scavenging or hunting stage is a moot point, and Strum believes nonhuman primate practices may help clarify the issue:

> The question left open for consideration is whether it is easier to develop technical and social innovations within a scavenging context, to gain a competitive edge on other predators, or within a hunting context, to allow the exploitation of larger prey. In either case non-human primate predatory behavior once again considerably clarifies the question we should ask about human evolution and the answers that will be acceptable. It also illustrates a complexity that predates the human experiment (Strum, 1983, p. 334).

Chimpanzees—apes that live in the forest and on the forest-savanna border—offer another possible model for early hominid behavior.

Chimpanzee Social Behavior   Although chimpanzee communities vary, observers are pretty well agreed that the basic social unit of chimpanzees is a fluid-membership group, within which exists a nucleus of strongly bonded adult males operating in a particular home range. Associated with these males are some females in their prime and even some past their prime. Also included in the group are other females whose membership is more variable, since they often transfer to other groups. Males rarely transfer from one community to another, but females do, temporarily, or—as in the case of many nulliparous females—permanently (Pusey, 1979).

The size of a community varies from one group to the next, and the same community varies from year to year. In a study at Kisoge, at the foot of the Mahale Mountains in East Africa, the researcher Nishida (1979) found that, during a seven-year study, the size of groups varied from 21 to 34 individuals; other estimates for community size range from 15 to 80. Nishida also noted that a community was divided into subgroups, which could be considered the actual living units.

Although not perhaps as finely structured as the baboon system, a definite hierarchy does exist among chimpanzee males. At the top of the hierarchy is the alpha male, followed by other less dominant males. However, the structure is highly flexible, as the following account suggests:

> Kasonta . . . had been an alpha male for a number of years when rivalry developed between him and Sobongo, the beta male. In this ongoing conflict, the gamma male, Kamemanfu, was pivotal. At times the gamma male joined alpha against beta; at other times he reversed his position and joined beta against alpha. When the latter occurred, Kasonta, the alpha male, lost confidence and the beta male, Sobonga, became the alpha male.
>
> In 1976, Sobongo, with the help of the gamma male, was threatening Kasonta and succeeded in becoming the alpha male in June. One of the rewards of the

alpha male is more frequent access to estrous females. During the months February-April, while he was still alpha, Kasonta was responsible for 85.6% of the copulations. But in months June-July, Sobongo—now the alpha male—was responsible for 87%. In May, the alpha status was unstable because gamma male Kamemanfu had switched his support to Sobongo and assisted him in attacking Kasonta. Taking advantage of the unstable situation, Kamemanfu showed the highest copulation rate.

In January, 1978, Kamemanfu threw his support back to Kasonta who reassumed his alpha status. (Nishida, 1983, p. 332).

A male's ability to dominate is related to age. As a male grows through adolescence, he becomes dominant to adolescents and then adult females. As a young adult he begins to dominante the older males, and by middle age he reaches his highest rank. At this time he can dominate most, if not all, younger and older males. As he ages and his physique deteriorates, younger individuals may begin to dominate him (Bygott, 1979).

A top-ranking male is not merely an alpha male that excels over all other males of the community. In the Kisoge study (Nishida, 1979), Kasonta, the top-ranking male of his group, was the most prominent in frequency of both aggressive behavior and threat display. Among adult males, he groomed and was groomed most frequently. Perhaps the most conspicuous characteristic of a top-ranker is the frequency with which he is followed by other adult males, and Kasonta's subgroup was usually the largest.

As we noted at Kisoge, a male's access to estrous females is directly related to his dominance rank. At Gombe, however, Goodall has not observed such a close relationship between status rank and reproductive success (personal communication). In his role as the top-ranking male, Kasonta assumed leadership in scouting and chasing, and he was the only male to defeat the male of an adjoining group without help from others.

Dominance and structural relationships are not as clearly defined among adult chimpanzee females. When a female comes into estrus, her dominance rank rises remarkably. Young adult females have been observed threatening high-ranking females, and may even snatch food from some nonconsorting adult males. Rise in dominance rank is also related to the fact that highest ranking males often monopolize estrous females. However, this high rank among estrous females is only temporary. Linear rank hierarchy may also be present, although dominance is difficult to determine because "physiological conditions of females make female relationships very complicated and unstable" (Nishida, 1979, p. 104). Generally speaking, older females are superior in rank to younger females. At Kisoge, for example, a past-prime female, Wantangwa, completely dominated all other females for the seven years of the group study (Nishida, 1979).

The relationship between a chimpanzee mother and daughter is a very close one until the daughter is at least seven years old. A newborn infant clings to the mother, holding on to her belly as she moves, and, for the first six months, the mother supports the newborn with her hand. During this time, the mother provides food, protection, transportation, and hygiene. At the end of six months, the infant begins to explore the environment without straying out of mother's sight, and eats solid food while continuing to suckle.

Figure 10-10 Flo and Flint. Flint, at the age of eight, died of "loneliness" (depression) three weeks after the death of Flo, his mother. (Baron Hugo van Lawick, © National Geographic Society.)

Weaning may begin at one year of age and continue until four or five. For the first four years, an infant is almost completely dependent on its mother. As a juvenile (ages 4–8), a daughter is still heavily dependent on her mother, but this dependency is significantly reduced during adolescence (8–10) and disappears almost completely during the daughter's subadult stage (10–12).

A similar change occurs in the close relationship between a mother and her son when he reaches about the age of ten. The young male at this time is attracted to adult males and cycling females and, again, inbreeding with female maternal kin is avoided.

Adult or adolescent females tend to disperse and form small subgroups within the home range. They travel within small areas inside the larger home range, and, where home ranges overlap, they move back and forth between the two communities.

Female-female bonds appear to be weak, and adult females usually are not seen together for any length of time. If grooming frequency is taken as an index of social bonding, we find that 46% of total grooming occurs between adult males, 39% between adult males and adult females, and 10% between adult females. Also rare among adult females are mutual greeting and sharing behavior, both of which characterize the high sociability of chimpanzees. Generally, social bonds among females may simply be due to physiologically similar activities based on similar age, maternity, and sexual receptivity.

As in baboons (see p. 286), alloparenting also occurs among chimpanzees. Mothers are often wary of females who indicate their intention of holding a neonate (newborn). Goodall observed older siblings hold a newborn with the mother's permission, but the mother rejected advances of other females (van Lawick-Goodall, 1971). Nishida (1983), however, found that among the chimpanzees of the Mahale Mountains, unrelated nulliparous females—as well as siblings, adult and adolescent males, and parous females—also took care of infants. The most frequent alloparents were nulliparous females.

The strategy of these alloparents consists of invitation, enticement, detachment from the mother, care of the infant, tickling, and rough and tumble play. The infants seem relaxed during this bout and appear at ease with any class of alloparents. Mothers, however, are often uneasy and quite solicitous of their offspring, as they carefully watch the interaction. A mother will sometimes block the advance of an alloparental candidate by drawing her infant to her chest; she may hold the hand of an alloparent and prevent contact, or she may stop the infant from leaving by placing her hand in front of it. A mother may, however, join in the playful interactions between alloparent and infant. During these bouts, mothers may sometimes rest, groom or be groomed, or supervise the alloparental care (Nishida, 1983).

Sexual attraction serves as a bond among chimpanzees, and a consort relationship frequently develops between a particular male and female. At Gombe, a male will often select a particular female as a mate, and maintain constant proximity to this female. Should another male mate with the female, the consort male interrupts the pair. The consort pair sometimes go on safari for as long as twenty-eight days. Estrous females have been observed forcing themselves between a mating pair and often present to the male.

A chimpanzee community is wary of other communities. Adult males patrol the periphery of their home range, traveling silently in close compact groups. They frequently stop to look and listen, often standing bipedally to look over the tall grass, and sometimes climb a tree to scan the area for signs of chimpanzees in the adjoining home range. When the chimpanzees return to familiar areas, they often break their remarkable silence by "an outburst of loud calling, drumming displays, and even some chasing and mild aggressive contact between individuals" (Goodall, et al., 1979).

In their patrols, chimpanzees respond to the sight or sound of neighbors with reassurance contact behavior among themselves (Fig. 10-11), such as touching, grinning, erect hair, embracing, and mounting. If the two parties are approximately of equal size, they may approach and display until one or both groups retreat. Kawanaka (1982) relates the account of an inter-unit-group encounter in which two mixed groups (adult males and females) approached each other at their territorial boundary. Although hooting from both groups could be heard, they did not meet, nor was there any agonistic behavior on either side. However, there was a good deal of stress present, evidenced by the frequent defecation of the females. If one group is outnumbered or faced with more formidable opponents, it will probably approach and then retreat. Members of different communities seldom engage in agonistic behavior because only occasionally do they come close enough for face-to-face interaction. Should a patrol party encounter a single male, however, they might attack him.

While chimpanzee males rarely cross into the home range of another community, such "trespassing" can occur. Goodall (1979) relates the account of a community at Gombe that separated, a number of adult males moving to the southern part of their home range. Over a period of three years the original group ferociously attacked and killed most of the members of the southern community by forays into their home range. Goodall could not explain this behavior except for the possibility that the northern group had

Figure 10-11 Chimp reassurance behavior. (Baron Hugo van Lawick, © National Geographic Society.)

◇ Box 10-3   Jane Goodall—Pioneer of Chimpanzee Research

It began in 1960 when a young Englishwoman, invited to visit a friend at a farm in Kenya, gave up her job and flew to Nairobi. Jane Goodall, who, at the early age of 8, had already decided to go to Africa and live with animals "when I grew up," could hardly pass up this opportunity to fulfill her childhood dream.

In Africa, a friend suggested to her that she get in touch with Louis Leakey, well-known anthropologist and, at that time, curator of what is now the National Museum of Natural History (back then, Jane had never heard of Dr. Leakey!). She sought him out and introduced herself. After they conversed, Leakey offered her a job at the museum. She accepted, and ultimately joined the Leakeys on their annual paleontological expeditions to Olduvai Gorge in Tanzania. Leakey was impressed with Jane's ability and dedication, and asked if she would like to study wild chimps in the Kigoma area on the shores of Lake Tanganyika (see map). Lacking what she felt to be the necessary academic background, Jane was surprised at the offer. Leakey himself, however, believed that university training might be a disadvantage in this case. What he wanted, he said, was someone "with a mind uncluttered and unbiased by theory," someone who had a sympathetic understanding of animals and a real desire for knowledge.

Jane happily accepted the position, and waited for the funding that Dr. Leakey set out to find. With monies eventually provided by the Wilkie Foundation (of the United States), Jane prepared to leave for Kigoma. She then learned that local officials objected to a young woman living alone in a jungle uninhabited by humans. Jane arranged for her mother to join her, which satisfied the government officials, and the two Englishwomen, along with a few African assistants, went on to undertake the now-famous research effort at the Gombe Stream Chimpanzee Reserve, today known as Gombe National Park. ·

Jane Goodall's pioneering research—now in its twenty-fifth year—is the longest continuous study of the behavior of any animal species. As a result of her work, we have come to a better understanding of humans as primates, an understanding substantially broadened by anthropologists, zoologists, and other researchers from around the world who have followed in her historic footsteps.

Figure 10-12   Two chimpanzee research sites in Tanzania. Kigoma is Jane Goodall's area; the Mahale Mountains has been the center of research for Japanese primatologists for more than fifteen years.

been prevented from using the southern part of what had once been their home range. By eliminating the southern group, this area once more became accessible to them.

Agonistic behavior occurs between adult males, reflecting a dominance-subordinance relationship, but is also directed by males against females and immature chimps. There is little agonistic behavior between adult males and infants, probably because infants are protected by the mother, although females with infants are sometimes attacked. Adult females are dominant to juveniles, but do not attack unless provoked. Adolescent males can generally intimidate young adult and adolescent females, but might be attacked by older adult females. In the rare agonistic interaction among females, the older of the two females is usually dominant.

Among males, agonistic behavior appears to occur between four groups: alpha males, high-ranking males, middle-ranking males, and low-ranking males. Agonistic interactions between these groups is frequent, and dominance-subordinance relationships are clearly defined (Bygott, 1979).

In recent years, another form of agonistic behavior has been observed. Jane Goodall (1979) reported that, in the years 1975 to 1977, a mother and her daughter had killed and eaten at least three babies. These were deliberate cases of cannibalism. Passion, an adult female, pursued a mother holding an infant, attacked her, seized and killed the baby, and then shared the flesh with her offspring. Three males in the Mahale Mountains group were also seen sharing the flesh of an infant chimp (Nishida, et al., 1979). In 1982, still another account of cannibalism was reported for the Mahale Mountains chimpanzees: A male killed an infant and consumed the flesh (Norikashi, 1982). In all these cases, the victim appeared to be male, and in most instances little interest was shown by others, including the mother of the infants, although the presence of the highest-ranking male appears to discourage cannibalism.

It is difficult to understand this practice unless perhaps it is to change an existing mother into a reproductive-ready female. That is, when a mother loses an infant, she shortly comes into estrus and is available for conception. It should be stressed that, among chimpanzees, "cannibalism is not an exceptional accident, but is deeply rooted in the chimpanzee species society . . ." (Nishida, et al., 1979, p. 19). (See Sociobiology, pp. 304–308, for a further discussion of infanticide.)

In the past, chimpanzees were considered herbivores, but recent evidence makes it clear they are capable of, and participate in, predatory behavior. More than 10 years ago, Goodall observed chimpanzees eating animals they had killed, either by fortuitous capture or deliberate hunting (van Lawick-Goodall, 1971). The chimpanzee animal diet, which supplements their predominant feeding pattern of fruits and leaves, consists mainly of the red colobus monkey and the anubis baboon, but they hunt other small mammals as well, such as bushpigs, red-tailed monkeys, and blue monkeys. In addition, chimps may gather various insects, fledgling birds, and birds' eggs. Their prey are medium to small-sized mammals and birds, always smaller than themselves. In the Mahale Mountains, chimpanzees have also been observed to kill mammals, carry away the carcasses, and eat the meat.

There is some question whether chimpanzees are cooperative hunters.

Busse (1978, p. 769) has pointed out that cooperative hunting might not be as efficient for chimpanzees as solitary hunting:

> The high level of observed competition for small kills supports the contention that over time individuals would obtain more meat by hunting alone than by hunting in groups. That chimpanzees do sometimes hunt in groups appears to be an incidental result of fortuitous encounters between chimpanzee groups and potential prey animals.

Like the baboons observed at Kekopey (p. 285), chimpanzees also share meat. Goodall observed male chimps occasionally sharing meat with other chimpanzees who begged with outstretched hands (van Lawick-Goodall, 1971). Scraps of meat left by eaters were quickly picked up by others. Some chimps attempted to take away pieces of carcass while it was being eaten by the "owner," sometimes successfully and sometimes not. Meat requesting, or begging, has several forms: by hand; peering (placing the face close to the face or meat of the meat eater); touching the meat itself, or touching the chin and lips of the meat eater; extending the hand palm up; making "soft whimper or hoo sounds while doing any of the above" (Teleki, 1973, p. 148).

Attempts to share in the meat are not always successful, and agonistic behavior during meat eating is relatively rare. Chimpanzees possessing meat portions may object to sharing and indicate this by raising the hair, waving arms, vocalizing at others, or other displays.

Other food besides meat is shared. For example, the sharing of bananas (a food provided by primatologists) occurred between all age-sex classes. Mothers pass food to their offspring regularly, and the reverse also occurs. Adult males rarely beg for bananas, and adult females seldom beg from each other (McGrew, 1979).

Chimpanzee predatory behavior has been much discussed, and indeed it is an important chimpanzee behavior. However, meat does not make up a significant portion of the chimpanzee diet, even though they appear to enjoy the taste of it. "During the many tens of thousands of hours that field researchers have observed [all] nonhuman primates, fewer than 450 sightings of vertebrate hunting and/or feeding have been reported . . ." (Butynski, 1982, p. 423). Most of these sightings have been of chimpanzees, and although they may stalk their prey, hunt cooperatively, and share meat, these behaviors are infrequent and not well developed (Butynski, 1982).

Associated with food is an interesting aspect that may be considered a sexual division of labor. Hunting by males and gathering by females have, in the past, led students of hominid evolution to assign the sexual division of labor as a uniquely hominid characteristic. However, McGrew (1979) found that male and female chimpanzees do not ingest the same kind of food. An analysis of a ten-month collection of fecal samples of chimpanzees at Gombe showed "a marked sex difference in insect eating: 45 of 81 (56%) female fecal samples contained at least one type of insect remains. Only 31 of 113 (27%) male fecal samples did so" (McGrew, 1979, p. 448). Fecal remains also showed that, in thirteen out of fourteen cases, it was the males who had eaten birds and mammals. It would appear from these data that, whereas the bulk of insects are sought and eaten by females, vertebrates are the domain of males.

Hominization
Process of becoming more human.

As a model for hominid evolution, the chimpanzees seem to be better situated than baboons. A chimpanzee community is male-dominated, but not as highly structured as the baboon community. The strongest bond is the mother-daughter relationship, and the mother never appears to become intolerant of the daughter, even after adolescence. The consort relationship—one male and one female—is quite common, and the pair may go off by themselves for as long as a month.

Behavior associated with food seems especially pertinent in this discussion. Male chimps are occasional predators, and although much of their meat is obtained fortuitously, they deliberately pursue prey, perhaps even cooperatively. What is more significant is that obtaining meat

> often involves primarily male groups roaming relatively great distances and acting cooperatively when the appropriate situation fortuitously arises—in short, *hunting*. On the other hand, female chimpanzees (predominantly) obtain ants and termites by prolonged, systematic, and repetitive manipulative sequences . . . accumulating a meal of many small units that are usually concentrated at a few known permanent sources—in short, gathering (McGrew, 1979, p. 450).

This sex difference might be considered as the basis for the hominid division of labor of female-gatherer and male-hunter that may have developed early in hominid evolution.

Food sharing is another area that was once believed to be uniquely human. There is now evidence that chimpanzees occasionally share both meat and vegetable material.

There are, of course, important differences between chimpanzee and hominid behavior: In chimpanzees, the consort relationship is not permanent, and is associated only with an estrous female; the home range is not a home base; the mother-daughter bond is not a family; chimpanzee hunting is mainly fortuitous (questions have been raised about whether this hunting is cooperative); "food sharing" may be called sharing only by stretching the meaning of the word—"distribution" is a better term (Teleki, 1973); and meat is rarely given, but it is taken, and if it is given, it is done so grudgingly and reluctantly.

Another chimpanzee activity resembling behavior once believed to be unique to hominids is the making of tools. At the present time, the evidence suggests that bipedality preceded toolmaking (stone tools) by at least a million years. Toolmaking, therefore, may not be as significant as once believed, as a factor leading to **hominization**. It is possible, however, that the object manipulation seen in chimpanzees suggests that the potential for toolmaking is primate in origin.

In additon to making simple tools, chimpanzees manipulate objects for many purposes. They throw such objects as stones, vegetation, sticks, and feces (as visitors to zoos have learned to their sorrow and their dry cleaners' profit). They also play extensively with objects, and they use leaves for cleaning the body.

The chimpanzee behavior we have described—object manipulation, food sharing, hunting, division of labor—does not mean that hominids evolved from chimpanzees. First of all, chimpanzees today evolved from an earlier form, and it is very doubtful that present-day chimp behavior is the same as that of their ancestors. Furthermore, humans developed different strategies in adapting as hunters to a savanna environment. Possibly, however, the striking morphological, biochemical, and behavioral similarities of chimpanzees and humans may point to the *kind* of ancestor that led to the hominid line.

◇ "Cultural" Behavior

At one time, anthropologists defined humans as toolmaking animals, and then modified the definition to read, "animals that make tools regularly." However, the observations of chimpanzees making and using tools by Goodall (1965) more than 20 years ago, brought such definitions into question. Many observers of chimpanzees, gorillas, orangutans, and some monkeys have verified the practice of tool manufacturing by apes and tool use by monkeys.

Probably the best-known example of nonhuman primate tool manufacture is termite fishing (Fig. 10-13). The chimpanzee inserts and probes in subterranean mounds or nests of termites with pieces of bark, vine, grass blades, or twigs. When the termites seize the probe, the chimp then withdraws the tool and eats the attached termites with its lips and teeth. Chimpanzees modify some of these objects, such as twigs, by removing the leaves—in effect manufacturing a stick from the natural material, a twig. Indeed, chimpanzees show the greatest frequency and diversity of tool using behavior of any nonhuman animal. They drag or roll branches, fallen trees, stones, cans, and camp furniture while displaying. They have been observed throwing rocks at a bushpig during predation, and throwing objects "overhead," "sidearm," and "underhand" (Beck, 1980). Chimps also make sponges from a handful of leaves, chew them for a moment, and then push them into the hollow of a tree where water has accumulated. The liquid is then sucked from this homemade sponge. Leaves are also used to dab at wounds on their bottoms, and sometimes, when a chimp has diarrhea, leaves serve as toilet paper.

At Bossou, Guinea (Africa), observers Sugiyama and Koman (1979) watched chimpanzees crack nuts with what they call a pebble tool. The striking stone weighed from 17 to 30 lb., and the platform stone on which the nut was placed weighed about 35 lb.:

> A chimpanzee who crouched in front of the platform stone chose a dry palm-seed, placed it in the cavity of the platform stone, gripped the handle side of the pebble tool, lifted it up to a height of 5-20 cm, and then struck the palm-seed. . . . When a palm-seed was broken, the chimpanzee removed the white ovule with his fingers and ate it in about 1 minute (Sugiyama and Koman, 1979, p. 515).

The authors believe this nut-cracking behavior "is highly suggestive of early man's stone-tool culture," and perhaps it is. However, it is important to note that neither the hammer stone nor the platform stone was deliberately manufactured.* Beck (1980) points out that many animals use unmodified objects

*Observers of nonhuman primates rarely distinguish *natural objects used as tools* from *modified objects deliberately manufactured* for specific purposes. The term tool is usually employed in both cases.

Figure 10-13   Chimp termiting.

as tools, but only apes—mainly chimpanzees—deliberately manufacture tools for specific purposes. However, we should be aware of the significant differences in toolmaking between chimps and humans. Chimpanzees usually select their material for a tool from a nearby item, and use it with little delay; humans collect material from a wide area, and may store it for a long time before using it. Although chimpanzees use and make tools, they do so comparatively rarely, whereas humans are utterly dependent on tools for their survival. Also, humans use tools to make other tools; other primates do not (Chalmers, 1980).

Like chimpanzees, Japanese macaques (a variety of Old World monkey) have also demonstrated a capacity for "cultural" behavior. In 1952, Japanese scientists embarked upon a provisioning procedure in which they supplied food at various places in Japan for groups of monkeys living in those areas. This method has proved eminently successful for purposes of observation, and the Japanese researchers have added significantly to our understanding of macaques.

Japanese monkeys have not been observed making tools, but one of them "invented" at least two methods of preparing food for eating. In 1952, sweet potatoes, a food new to the monkeys, were made available by scattering on the beach. The following year Imo, a young female, was observed using one hand to brush the sand off the sweet potatoes and the other hand to dip the potatoes in the water of a brook. The invention was picked up by juveniles through playmate relationships and was passed from juveniles to mothers, who then passed it on to their children. Within ten years, 90% of all troop members were washing sweet potatoes, except adults older than twelve years and infants less than one year.

Another invention, again by the "genius" Imo, was wheat washing. Wheat was distributed to the Koshima Island troop by scattering it on the sand, from which the monkeys could pick out single grains. Imo introduced the practice of scooping up sand and wheat, carrying a handful to the edge of the sea, and tossing the mixture onto the water. The sand sank, and Imo then skimmed the wheat grains off the surface and ate them! This practice also spread through the troop much as the sweet-potato washing habit: first juveniles, then adults—especially mothers—along family lines (Kawamura, 1959).

Defining the term "culture" may be useful, but so many definitions exist, there seems to be one for every cultural anthropologist. It would be much more valuable to note those characteristics of culture universally recognized by anthropologists.

Culture is learned behavior; that is, behavior acquired through learning, not through the genes. Culture includes nonmaterial attributes, such as language, art, religion, values, morals, etc., as well as material things, such as clothes, houses, tools, etc. Culture is social (not biological) heredity—it includes customs, traditions, attitudes. Culture is the behavioral patterns of a group, the "way of life" of a group. To sum up, culture is learned, not genetic, and has become so much the human way of life that we depend upon it for survival. It is the human strategy of adaptation.

Since primates (like all mammals) learn part of their behavior, then certainly primates are capable of cultural behavior. Chimpanzees, it appears,

Figure 10-14 Centers for Japanese macaque studies.

learn more than probably any other nonhuman primate, but the extent to which chimpanzees depend on culture for survival is another matter. It is clear they do not depend on culture completely, but to the extent that they learn to make and use tools, their behavior may be called cultural.

However, when we ask, "Can the chimpanzee way of life be called a culture?" we are on much less firm ground. Among chimpanzees, there is a good deal of genetically based behavior, as we have seen. Triggered by estrus, male responses are genetic, not learned. It is highly probable that dominance (that is, structuring social relationships based on rank) is also genetically based. Admittedly, though, it is difficult to know the extent of genetic influence upon chimpanzee behavior (and, sociobiologists might add, in human behavior as well). Nevertheless, the degree of human dependence on culture— for the human way of life—is total, or as total as we can determine. This is not the case with chimpanzees.

For one thing, cultural behavior is transmitted symbolically, and nonhuman primates do not transmit culture, or any kind of learned behavior as far as we can tell, symbolically. Chalmers points out that nonhuman primates can only learn from one another by direct observation; human beings suffer no

Figure 10-15   Macaque washing potatoes.

Figure 10-16   Chimpanzee facial gestures. Chimpanzees are the most facially expressive of all nonhuman primates. (From *In the Shadow of Man*, by Jane van Lawick-Goodall. Copyright © 1971 by Hugo and Jane van Lawick-Goodall. Redrawn with permission of Houghton Mifflin Company.)

such limitation. Freed from this restriction, humans can make use of experience accumulated over many generations, collected over many areas, and can develop rich and complicated traditions and cultures (Chalmers, 1980, p. 224). If culture is to have meaning as the human strategy for survival, then to refer to primate behavior as culture is to blur its meaning. We do not believe that chimpanzees have a culture, nor do we believe that terms such as "protoculture" or "incipient culture" are useful in explaining their behavior. These terms suggest that chimpanzees are on their way to developing culture, a premise which is extremely doubtful. Still, the information we gain about chimpanzees and other primates is valuable, not only because we learn more about nonhuman primates, but because we gain a fuller understanding of the possible mechanisms of early hominid evolution.

This troublesome question of culture and whether or not it can be attributed to primates must take into account language, a core element in the definition of culture.

◇ Language

Communication is common behavior among animals, from the smell and antenna signals of insects to the symbols of humans. Gestural and vocal signals have been observed among primates by a variety of investigators. Jane Goodall (1968a, 1971) documented numerous such signals among chimpanzees. She notes facial expressions, such as play-face and several grins, and vocal signals, including various kinds of hoots and grunts (Fig. 10-16). Expressions such as these are communication, of course, but can they be considered language?

Language, as distinct from communication, has been considered a uniquely human achievement, but work with apes has raised doubts about that position. Language has been defined in ways that would include insect communication on the one hand, or exclude everything except human speech on the other. While we prefer defining language in terms of symbolic communication, there is much disagreement on this subject. The assumption that *Homo sapiens* is the only organism capable of handling language has been brought into question by the success psychologists have achieved in teaching apes to communicate with symbols. Without attempting to settle the question of whether or not such ape ability should be called language, we shall briefly describe several successful experiments.

Washoe   In 1966, Beatrice and Allen Gardner, psychologists at the University of Nevada, decided to teach a two-way communication system to an eleven-month-old chimpanzee named Washoe. The gestures they selected were those of American Sign Language (ASL or Ameslan), a means of communication long used by the deaf.

Washoe's progress was slow at the beginning, but by the tenth month she possessed a vocabulary of a dozen words. At about this time, she began to combine signs such as "go in," "go out," and, later, produced combinations of three to five signs in sequence. At the end of four years, the Gardners claimed she had a vocabulary of over 130 signs, and it was possible for her and her trainer to engage in short, simple dialogues.

Washoe learned syntax—the proper order of words—as she demonstrated

Figure 10-17   Washoe signing "hat" when being questioned about a woolen hat.

in phrases like, "Roger you tickle." She occasionally signed to herself when alone and was seen signing "quiet" to herself before sneaking to a forbidden place, and "hurry" on the way to the potty chair.

The Gardners caution against evaluating chimpanzee linguistic ability on the basis of the Washoe data. If Washoe had been a preschool child, then her responses to the questions who? what? where? would place her at a relatively advanced level of linguistic competence. On the other hand, she would have been "a linguistically disadvantaged child." She was not exposed to American Sign Language until she was about one year old, and her trainers, learning Ameslan as a second language, were not fluent.

In a sequel to Project Washoe, the Gardners have instituted major improvements in teaching language to chimpanzees. Among the improvements are exposing chimpanzee subjects to sign language from birth and using research assistants who are fluent in Ameslan, being deaf themselves or raised by deaf parents. "Early results show that the first two new subjects are acquiring sign language much faster than Washoe did. It is highly likely that the marks set by Washoe will be surpassed under the more favorable conditions" (B. T. and R. A. Gardner, 1975, pp. 255–256).

When Washoe was pregnant in 1976, researchers were interested in whether she would transmit her Ameslan signs to her baby. Unfortuntely, the infant died a few hours after birth. Washoe was again "expecting" in January, 1979, when Dr. Roger Fouts, a former student of the Gardners, began research at the University of Oklahoma into the ability of chimpanzees to transmit their signs to other chimps. Washoe's second baby also died a few months later.

Dr. Fouts, who had moved to Central Washington University and taken Washoe with him, decided to present Washoe with a ten-month-old male chimp named Loulis. Washoe accepted the infant male and, after observing their interaction, Fouts stated that, by the spring of 1982, Loulis had acquired 32 signs from Washoe and other chimps (Friends of Washoe newsletter, Spring 1982). Fouts also claims that his experiments demonstrate that chimps can communicate with each other using Ameslan, and that they invent signs for objects that had no signs. Furthermore, not only do young chimpanzees learn signs from older ones, but older chimps learn from younger ones (Fouts, 1982, 1983).

Sarah Another chimpanzee language, specially devised by Professor David Premack (1971), was taught to his six-year-old simian student, Sarah, in an experiment initiated at the University of California at Santa Barbara in 1967. The symbols in this language system consisted of differently shaped and colored plastic pieces with a bit of metal on the back that adhered to a magnetized board.

Sarah was taught to recognize the plastic chips as symbols for various objects. The chips did not resemble the objects they represented; for example, the plastic chip for "apple" was not round and red. Sarah soon learned to correctly identify fruit, and was able to place two chips together in the proper sequence. Verbs were then introduced, and Sarah was able to place the chips properly to form a sentence, such as, "Mary give apple Sarah."

Sarah also learned to indicate which objects were the same and which different by removing the chip for question mark and replacing it with the correct chip for "same" or "different." After eighteen months, Premack believed Sarah had acquired a language competence comparable in many respects to a child of two or two and a half years.

Lana   There have been other experiments teaching language to chimpanzees, such as Rumbaugh's (1977) work with Lana at the Yerkes Regional Primate Center in Atlanta, Georgia. Lana worked with chips attached to keys on a specially built typewriter connected to a computer. After six months, Lana recognized symbols for thirty words, and was able to ask for food and answer questions through the machine.

In 1975, two young male chimps, Sherman and Austin, were added to the experiment. Because the experimenters were not certain Lana understood all the words she used, Sherman's and Austin's training emphasized the meaning of each word they encountered. This change in language training has led Rumbaugh and his colleagues to believe that Sherman and Austin (and, by extension, chimps in general) are capable of functional symbolic communication; that is, to these two chimps, words were representational, real symbols, understood and used by them. Sherman's and Austin's data demonstrate that chimpanzees can master referential use of learned symbols, the meanings of which have been arbitrarily assigned to lexigrams (words). In other words, apes are capable of mastering semantics! (Rumbaugh, et al., 1982, p. 379)

The training and education of chimpanzees continue. Most of the present experimenters (including Francine Patterson's work with Koko, a female gorilla, and Michael, a male) are improving their techniques in their attempts to prove that apes are indeed capable of learning language.

Not everyone, however, agrees that apes actually learn language. Sebeok (1980) compared the ape response to their trainers' signals to those of a German horse named Clever Hans. Hans, it seemed, could count by tapping with his hoof, and his owner believed he had taught Hans to solve problems. Actually, it turned out that the owner involuntarily jerked when Hans reached the correct number. Given this unconscious cue, Hans stopped tapping at the correct answer.

Nim   Dr. Herbert Terrace, who raised a chimp (named Nim Chimpsky after the well-known linguist, Noam Chomsky) almost from birth, trained him to sign using ASL. Just like Washoe, Sara, and other chimps, Nim was able to place the signs in sequence, but Terrace wondered whether Nim was actually fashioning proper sentences or reacting in the manner of Clever Hans to the trainer's signals.

After almost four years of working with Nim, Terrace analyzed videotapes of the training sessions. His conclusion:

> . . . it would be premature to conclude that a chimpanzee's combination [of words] show the same structure evident in the sentences of a child. The fact that Nim's utterances were less spontaneous and less original than those of a child, and that his utterances did not become longer, both as he learned new signs and as he acquired more experience in using sign language, suggests that much of the structure and meaning of his combinations was determined, or at least suggested, by the utterances of his teachers (Terrace, 1979, p. 221).

Terrace believes there is a tendency among the experiments to project human meaning into

> the imitative utterances of an ape who was simply trying to manipulate its teachers to feed it or engage in some kind of social activity (Terrace, 1982, p. 9).

Criticizing some experiments, Terrace writes that the use of signs in certain instances

> suggest a type of interaction between an ape and its trainer that has little to do with human language. In each instance the sole function of the ape's signing appears to be to request various rewards that can be obtained only by signing. Little, if any, evidence is available that an ape signs in order to exchange information with its trainer, as opposed to simply demanding some object or activity (Terrace, 1983, p. 38).

Other scholars have also questioned the attention given to the problem of whether apes are capable of language. Atherton and Schwartz (1983) believe more emphasis should be placed on whether apes understand what they are talking about. Whether apes learn language or whether what they do *is* language, these experiments are significant for the study of human evolution in that they demonstrate the ape capability is greater than once believed. Such demonstrations may possibly suggest clues to the origins of human language. One practical result from these experiments has been the development of successful techniques to help mentally disadvantaged children to express themselves (Rumbaugh, et al., 1982).

Although apes have shown considerable skill and intelligence in learning and using signs—and perhaps symbols—*when taught by humans*, the fact remains that, in natural settings, chimpanzees do not use language in their social intercourse or daily activities. We believe the question of language (whether or not apes are capable of it) currently does not add any meaningful resolution to the question of apes and culture.

◇ Recent Trends in Nonhuman Primate Behavioral Research

As opposed to the psychological tradition of studying animals (including primates) in laboratory settings, the anthropological tradition has concentrated on studying primates in their native habitats. While there was some initial work of this kind before World War II (e.g., Roy Carpenter's studies of howler monkeys and gibbons in the 1930s), primatology did not come of age until the late 1950s. With the pioneering work on free-ranging groups of savanna baboons (Sherwood Washburn and Irven DeVore), mountain gorillas (George Schaller), langurs (Phyllis Dolhinow), and chimpanzees (Jane Goodall), behavioral studies of nonhuman primates became an entirely new subdiscipline of physical anthropology. Since 1960 this area of research has virtually exploded, and today there are literally hundreds of primatologists worldwide investigating scores of species.

Since primatology is indeed an infant discipline, its early stages were mostly descriptive and consisted of itemizing major ecological and behavioral components of various species. It was not until the 1970s that more rigorous theoretical perspectives came into wide use. In the last decade, two major theoretical orientations have emerged—socioecology and sociobiology. Let's review each.

SOCIOECOLOGY

Around 1970, some primatologists began to look comprehensively at the relationship between specific environmental features and the social behavior of primates (Crook, 1970). This perspective emphasizes that primate behavior is *variable* (i.e., within species as well as between species). We therefore should expect behavior to differ somewhat seasonally within a single group, and to vary from group to group within the same species (particularly if they inhabit quite different environments). Moreover, there may be some general trends of socioecological relationships that can be traced independently within different categories of primates; e.g., prosimians, New World anthropoids, Old World anthropoids. (An excellent review of socioecology can be found in Jolly, 1972.)

In order to research socioecological relationships, new methodological approaches for gathering field data were developed. Rather than brief surveys of a species' behavior, it was realized that the entire annual round should be studied, preferably for a period of several years.

Secondly, it was not possible to describe *the* behavior of a primate species on the basis of a single study in one location. Of far more interest would be contrasts between populations of the same species living under different environmental conditions. For example, Thelma Rowell's study of common baboons living in forested regions (1972) reveals a markedly different behavioral pattern than research done on the same species in more open environments.

Thirdly, it was necessary to gather detailed information on environmental factors. For example, relevant factors that might influence primate social behavior include: quantity and quality of food, the distribution of food, of water, of sleeping sites, and the kinds and distribution of predators.

Finally, socioecologists quickly realized that human interference in the observed species' food supply through artificial provisioning could be expected to severely disrupt their social behavior in largely unpredictable ways. Consequently, the massive provisioning practiced at the Japanese Monkey Centers or by Jane Goodall in the early years at Gombe Stream was avoided in later research.

Some general principles socioecologists have suggested (abstracted from Jolly, 1972, pp. 100–101) are listed below. There are numerous exceptions to be found among the order, but these general tendencies have revealed some extremely interesting aspects of primate behavior.

1. *nocturnal forms*: Usually solitary and insectivorous (slow loris, dwarf lemur)
2. *diurnal, arboreal leaf eaters*: Often unimale groups; occasionally multimale; fewer than 30 individuals in group (langurs, howler monkeys)

3. *diurnal, arboreal omnivores*: Monogamous units (gibbons, marmosets); unimale groups (guenons); or small multimale groups (cebus monkey)
4. *partly terrestrial leaf eaters*: Unimale or small multimale (age-graded) groups (hanuman langur, gorilla)
5. *partly terrestrial omnivores*: Small multimale groups (ring-tailed lemur, vervets, some macaques) or large multimale groups (common baboon, some macaques)
6. *partly terrestrial and country forms*: Daytime foraging units almost always unimale (gelada baboon, hamadryas baboon, patas monkey).

SOCIOBIOLOGY

The second new (and highly controversial) perspective that has recently been enthusiastically applied by some researchers to the study of primates is called *sociobiology*. This approach (which is used for a wide variety of animal and insect species) seeks to find evolutionary explanations of animal social behavior in the hope of shedding light on the biological bases of human behavior.

First brought to popular attention in 1975 by Harvard zoologist E. O. Wilson, this approach can be traced to the pioneering works of R. A. Fisher (1930), J.B.S. Haldane (1932), W. D. Hamilton (1964), G. C. Williams (1966), and Robert Trivers (1971, 1972). Following publication of Wilson's monumental synthesis, vehement arguments exploded both inside and outside academia. What has caused all this furor, and what relevance does sociobiology have to understanding primates, particularly human primates?

Sociobiologists are basically classical Darwinists, postulating the evolution of behavior through operation of natural selection. Sociobiologists assume that, if any behavior has a genetic basis, its evolutionary impact will be directly measured by its effect on reproductive success. In other words, with behavioral phenotypes (just as with physical morphology), the success of genes underlying the phenotypes will be determined by their influence on reproduction. Individuals with genotypes coding for behaviors leading to higher reproductive success than other individuals will, by definition, be more fit. Consequently, they should pass on their genes at a differentially faster rate. Sociobiologists believe genotypes have evolved in this way, producing such phenomena as sterile worker castes in bees, courtship dances in birds, and scent marking in dogs. As a speculative model, this reasoning is all well and good. In fact, much of the theoretical way natural selection is discussed in Chapter 2 of this text utilizes terminology and concepts developed by sociobiologists.

When applied to relatively simple organisms—social insects, for example—sociobiological theory has proven of tremendous explanatory value. In fact, recent sophisticated molecular biological research with the DNA of marine snails has identified a family of genes that produce specific proteins whose combined action in turn governs the animal's egg-laying behavior (Scheller and Axel, 1984). This is of note because, for the first time, something that could be termed "complex" behavior has been traced to a specific genetic mechanism (i.e., DNA sequences that have been decoded).

Of course, neither insects nor snails are mammals (to say nothing of primates). The major dispute arises, then, when trying to postulate the actual mechanics of behavioral evolution in complex social animals like primates. Which specific behaviors among primates have a genetic basis, and how do these behaviors influence reproductive success?

In order to answer the first question, we will have to learn considerably more about genotype/phenotype interactions in complex traits. Such an understanding is probably decades away. To answer the second question, we will need accurate data on reproductive success in primate groups similar to that shown for birds in Chapter 2 (p. 42). As of yet, such data are almost completely lacking, but it is hoped this situation will be remedied in the near future. Thus, sociobiology as an *explanation* of primate behavior remains almost entirely a matter of open speculation. Application of evolutionary models specifically to explain human behavior are presently even more hypothetical.

Obtaining conclusive data for primates and other mammals, we will see, is no easy matter. A good starting point, however, is framing hypotheses concerning behavioral evolution on the basis of the evidence that does exist. A good example of such a perspective is Sarah Blaffer Hrdy's (1977) explanation of infanticide among langur monkeys of India.

Langurs typically live in social groups composed of one adult male, several females, and their offspring (sometimes called a "harem"). Other males without mates associate in bachelor groups. These peripheral males occasionally attack a harem, violently overthrow the previous harem master, and take over the group. Often following this admittedly bloody contest, even more gruesome behavior ensues. The infants, fathered by the previous harem master, are attacked and killed. The adult females in the group usually try to interfere with the males' infanticidal intentions, but to little avail. In the end, most or all the infants are killed.

Why should langurs behave so? Are they not dooming their species to ultimate extinction by such destructive actions? The answer, according to sociobiologists, is *not* in terms of the species. Male langurs do not know they are members of so-and-so species, nor, if they did, would they care what its future would be. Natural selection theory, as clarified by sociobiology, teaches us that individuals act to maximize their *own* reproductive success, no matter what its ultimate effect on the species.

Ostensibly, that is exactly what the male langur is doing. By killing the infants, he avoids a two to three year wait before the females come back into estrus. Once the infants are dead, the females stop lactating and become reproductively accessible to the newly arrived male. He can then inseminate them much earlier than would have been the case had he waited while the young (in which he had no genetic interest) were reared.

We might reasonably ask why the females should allow their infants to be slaughtered. Actually, females do attempt to resist infanticide, but their efforts in the face of large, aggressive, and determined males usually fail. Interestingly, it is not the infant's mother who assaults the attacking male, but other females in the group. Some writers suggest that these females are closely related (sisters of the mother, for example) and, if so, sociobiological theory provides an explanation for such seemingly **altruistic** behavior. Since individuals share

Altruism
Helping others without direct benefit to oneself.

Figure 10-18 Part of the large Kaukori langur group resting in mango grove.

genes with close relatives, they can contribute to their *own* reproductive success by aiding their relatives' offspring.

In diploid species (like langurs, humans, and all vertebrates) individuals share, on the average, ½ their genes with parents and, likewise, ½ with full siblings. For example, when a langur defends her sister's offspring, she is helping contribute genes to the next generation; genes she shares in common with her nieces and nephews (on the average she shares ¼ her genes in common with them). In this way, genes that underlie such cooperative behavior may spread in populations.

Of course, there are many possible strategies. Aiding a relative does not always completely inhibit one's own reproduction. The success of an individual's genes (that is, one's fitness in natural selection terms) is then measured as the sum of one's own offspring *plus* those of close relatives ("discounted" according to how closely they are related: ¼ for her nieces and nephews, half-siblings, or grandchildren, ⅛ for first cousins, etc.).

Langurs are, of course, not doing this consciously. As is true of the cooperative female defense efforts noted above, females are not making conscious choices as if they *knew* the alternatives. What occurs is simply that individuals who behave one way will have higher reproductive success than those individuals behaving in another way. Consequently, their genes (including any that underlie this behavior) are differentially passed onto the next generation, theoretically just another example of natural selection acting on variation.

The same phenomenon of infant killing has also been observed in mountain gorillas, accounting for 6 infant deaths over a 13-year period (Fossey, 1981; 1983) (see p. 00). In this example as well, the explanation offered has been sociobiological—a strategy by males to increase their own reproductive success.

Sociobiological interpretations have also been applied to a wide range of other behaviors seen in primates. For example, the extremely large testes of male chimpanzees have been explained as an adaptation to a fairly promiscuous mating pattern—where several males successfully copulate with an estrous female (a kind of "sperm competition") (Popp and DeVore, 1979). Also, the differential ranging patterns of male and female orangutans have been viewed as the result of differing reproductive strategies between sexes and maximization of food resources (Galdikas, 1979).

The Lovejoy model of human origins discussed at the beginning of the chapter is flavored with sociobiological premises. Individual reproductive success is seen as the key factor, and parental strategies were presumably shifted in hominid evolution for its greater maximization. This is all extremely interesting (and often good fun as well), but how does one go about testing such views?

In fact, all the sociobiological explanations of contemporary primate (including human) behavior, or those scenarios of hominid history, still lack the hard data on reproductive success needed to *test* such theories (in the way the value of any scientific hypothesis *must* be measured).

The difficulties in testing sociobiological theories are a major concern. To be fair, reconstruction of early hominid behavior will probably never be amenable to clear testing. In this respect, Lovejoy's theory is no weaker than many of those postulated before him. Indeed, Lovejoy does attempt to spell out some of the physical aspects of early hominids, as well as deriving specific comparisons from living primates. These points can be weighed and tested to some degree.

Testing of sociobiological theories for many living animals also poses extremely sticky methodological problems. Again, to be fair, most sociobiologists of course recognize the kinds of data that are required to establish unambiguously the validity of their claims. The obstacle is that this information is exceedingly difficult to obtain.

Mammals breed much more slowly than animals such as insects. In order to collect detailed information on individual reproductive success, life history data for entire generations would be required, perhaps for several populations. Such a pursuit would take years. In fact, to date, only one such study has been done on mammals in natural habitats—a 12-year analysis of the reproductive behavior of a red deer population on an island off Scotland (Clutton-Brock, et al., 1982). Although not in a natural setting (observations were made in a laboratory), comprehensive reproductive data have also been obtained over six years on an entire colony of mole rats (Jarvis, 1981).

What then of primate studies like that concerning langurs? Hrdy has proposed an interesting hypothesis, and we have suggested that the conclusions need more complete testing, but how could this be accomplished? Langurs can have active reproductive lives that easily span 10–15 years. We would need a minimum of two complete generations to get a handle on the reproductive dynamics and potentially variable strategies in this species (i.e., we could be in the field for 30 years!). Moreover, in order to generate an adequate sample size, we might well have to collect information on several populations simultaneously.

Even if all this could be done, we would still need to check which animals were actually reproducing. (For a recent discussion of this problem, see Fedigan, 1983). Maternity would obviously not be an issue, but paternity is another matter. Consequently, it would be necessary to capture animals (males and their suspected offspring) in order to compare genetic markers, such as red blood cell and white blood cell antigens (see pp. 136–146). In the process of removing animals from the troop, sedating them, taking blood samples, and then returning them to the troop, we might well disrupt the very behaviors we are trying to study.

Sociobiological theories have stimulated new avenues of research and have led to some interesting insights concerning primate behavior. The vast majority of efforts thus far, however, must be regarded as theoretical. Despite the many claims either defending or attacking sociobiological postulates, it is simply too early to know how well this perspective will work. Theory is, after all, only the starting point. The field applications and testing have just begun. The discipline is still barely a newborn science!

◇ Social Carnivores

Our closest relatives, the apes, are forest animals and are mainly vegetarians. Unlike apes, our early ancestors were savanna dwellers and hunters. Early on, they probably hunted mostly small game and scavenged* larger animals; however, when they did hunt, it probably was mostly in groups. To learn more about the origins of human social systems, it may be useful to look at other savanna dwellers and group hunters, the social carnivores: lions, wolves, and wild dogs. It should be noted that social carnivores and early hominids adapted in somewhat analogous ways to a similar ecological situation. Phylogenetically, hominids are homologous, of course, with primates, not with social carnivores.

Lions   Like chimpanzees, a pride of lions is loosely organized. It is centered around several related adult females which may remain together for their entire lives. Chimpanzees, on the other hand (see p. 288), are organized around a core of adult *males*. The core of the pride consists of adult lion females and their young. As male offspring reach two and one-half to three and one-half years of age, they leave the pride, or are chased off.

A definite hierarchical system appears to be lacking among lions, who do, however, show dominance and rank. That males are definitely dominant to females can easily be seen, especially at feeding time. The overwhelming majority of threat behavior is directed by males against females and cubs to prevent them from approaching too closely. There is also dominance among females, and Rudnai (1973) observed a relationship among three females in which the youngest's lower status was indicated by much of the aggressive behavior directed against her, her lack of priority in obtaining food, and the greater frequency of her performing the greeting ceremony.

*There is some disagreement among paleontologists and primatologists whether hunting, scavenging, or both were the way of life of the earliest hominids.

Males may be dominant in lions, but leadership belongs to the females. An adult female leads the pride as it moves across the savanna, but in the course of a few miles, the leadership will have alternated several times among the females. Males do not lead, but move along with the pride or tag behind, and the females and cubs pay little attention to the males' movements.

Most of the hunting by lions is done by females singly or communally, but once the prey is killed, males move in and eat their fill before allowing lionesses to feed, one of the few expressions of male dominance. Single lions tend to hunt smaller game, such as Thomson's gazelle; they may also hunt larger prey—wildebeests and zebras—but their chances of success with larger animals are twice as great if two or more lionesses cooperate.

The close mother-infant relationship so typical of primates is not found among lions. Mothering ranges between care and neglect. Mothers do nurse and protect their young and snarl at males that roam too close to their cubs. On the other hand, lionesses enjoy the conviviality of other females, and if taking care of cubs means separation from the pride, the mother may abandon them. Mothers do not bring meat from a kill to their cubs. If the cubs are at a kill, they usually obtain some meat; if they are not there, then the mother must fetch them—but only after she herself has fed. However, by the time she returns with the cubs, there may be no meat left.

When the cubs are almost two years old (about the time the mother has another litter), contact with the mother decreases and she ceases to care for them. The continuing relationship between mother and offspring so marked among chimpanzees is not present in lions. The lack of a close relationship between mother and cubs, as well as the frequent neglect of cubs by the

Figure 10-19   Lioness and cub at play.

mothers, may account for the high mortality rate of cubs, estimated to be over 60% by Schaller (1972).

The social structure of the lion pride, although loosely organized, nevertheless provides them with superior hunting techniques enabling them to catch large herbivores in open terrain. Operating as a group, lions are much more successful in hunting than solitary lions. Lack of parental care and male participation in the group structure is not a good model for what we believe early hominid behavior to be; however, the lion pride has been a successful form of adaptation to a savanna environment.

In this environment, lions have developed a strategy different from early hominids. Females are the hunters, and a close mother-offspring relationship is lacking. Lion adaptations, however, help delineate early hominid strategies. Like lions, hominids also lived in social groups and most likely were social rather than solitary hunters. Like other primates, however, early hominid females were very closely associated with their offspring, which may help explain why males were most likely the primary hunters.

Wolves   Social carnivore behavior more similar to hominid adaptations may be seen in wolves. A wolf pack and a hunter-gatherer band maintain an optimal size of the group in relation to the availability of food in regions with similar ecological characteristics. Both groups tend to control births socially—wolves through rivalry between females and humans through infanticide and contraceptive taboos. Wolves and humans live well below the carrying capacity of the environment, i.e., the environment is capable of supporting more individuals than are present. Both the pack and the band have a leader or decision maker and some form of dominance hierarchy.

Children of hunting groups and wolf cubs enjoy a great deal of freedom and are usually indulged by their elders. Food sharing exists between young and old, and rituals control much aggression within the group. Pack and band allegiance appears to be maintained through rituals involving "dancing" and "music," and during a food scarcity, both groups tend to split up, nomadic one season and sedentary when food is more abundant (Fox, 1978).

A pack of wolves is formed when a mated pair leaves its parental group to produce a litter of its own. Occasionally, several families may combine to form a large pack of 7 to 10 adults of both sexes. Packs of up to 21 wolves have been sighted. Wolves are territorial and avoid using an area through which another pack has recently traveled—probably indicated by urine-marking.

Care of young pups is basically a function of the mother who suckles them; however, there is great interest in the pups evidenced by all adult pack members. Weaning takes place at six to eight weeks, and pups eat food regurgitated by the mother or other members of the pack. When the pack hunts, the mother usually remains with the pups (although other adults and yearlings may perform this function), and the male (father) and other pack members bring back food for all. The close emotional bond of a wolf pack is believed to originate in this practice of communal feeding of pups (Mech, 1966).

Hunting is a cooperative effort and, operating as a coordinated unit, the pack stalks and chases the animal it has sighted (usually a moose). If the

Figure 10-20   Wolves attacking moose.

moose does not run, the wolves harass it from all sides, trying to make it bolt. Should the moose run, the wolves chase it and lunge at the animal, biting and tearing in order to bring it down. If the moose stands, the wolves are more cautious, and if they cannot force it to run will abandon the moose after a few minutes.

When chasing a cow moose and calf, wolves attempt to separate them. If the wolves can keep the cow busy for thirty seconds, the calf is doomed.

Wild Dogs   Wild dogs of Africa form very amiable and closely interacting groups, which average 9 to 10 members. Schaller (1972) reports that since the young tend to remain with the adults even after the birth of a new litter, it is very likely that a pack is composed of related individuals. Most observers do not believe a dominance hierarchy exists among wild dogs, but van Lawick is certain he observed dominance and submissive behavior. Submissive behavior is shown by cringing, grinning in fear, licking and nibbling the lips of the more dominant, and presenting the neck (van Lawick, 1970). Unlike wolves, no territoriality exists among wild dogs. Ranges, which average around 240 square miles and may reach over 1,000 square miles, overlap considerably without agonistic behavior between the packs. It is not uncommon for a pack that is otherwise nonterritorial to defend the area immediately around its den.

As among wolves, care of pups is a function of all pack members, but the mother retains certain prerogatives. She suckles the young, and when the den is moved, it is her task to move the pups. When there are small young, the pack remains in the vicinity of the den, leaving for hunting and returning afterward. From about the age of two and one-half months, the young accom-

Figure 10-21 Pack of wild dogs attacking zebra.

pany adults, and the den is abandoned. Once the pups become mobile, the pack ranges much more widely in its hunting activities. Both males and females hunt, but if there are small pups, usually the mother and possibly one or two others remain at the den as guards.

While pups are still at the den, returning hunters share the kill (as do wolves) by regurgitating meat to them and to the guards as well. When pups accompany adults, they take almost complete precedence at a kill and are permitted to monopolize the carcass. Wolves and dogs take much better care of the young than lions do, especially in sharing food. Schaller (1972) mentions that even a lame dog unable to keep up with the pack was able to beg meat successfully from the hunters.

Dogs start out on a hunt by trotting along at about five miles an hour with a male in the lead. When they sight a gazelle herd, they run in a broad front and scatter the herd so they can pick out a quarry which several dogs then pursue. When a dog catches up to a gazelle, it grabs a side, rump, or thigh and pulls it down. The other dogs arrive within a few seconds and tear the animal to pieces. If a gazelle should run in a circle, the dogs hunt coopera-tively. One or two dogs chase the gazelle while the rest cut across the arc and surround it.

Wild dogs hunt more successfully than lions or wolves and Schaller esti-mates a remarkable 89% success rate. For this reason, as well as their fierce-ness when attacking, they have been called "the super beasts of prey" (Wilson, 1975).

Studying social carnivores is instructive because they inhabit an ecological niche similar to that occupied by early hominids. And, like social carnivores, early hominids were also hunters. It is possible, as Schaller suggests, "that some of the same selective forces which had an influence on the social [carnivores] also had an effect on hominid societies" (1972, p. 378). Since the carnivore group, as we have seen, is superior to the solitary hunter in its success rate, there may have been selection pressures in early hominids for such cooperative methods as group hunting and encircling the prey. Living in groups makes division of labor possible as seen in the case of wild dogs, where mother guards the den while others hunt. We can conjecture that early hominids also divided their labor, shared food, and occupied a home base.

Kortlandt makes the interesting suggestion that wolves (we would include wild dogs, also) developed their cooperative hunting techniques as a result of hunting animals larger than themselves. Early hominids, he goes on, evolved similar cooperative hunting techniques since they, too, hunted game larger than themselves. Furthermore, the teamwork techniques of wolves required considerable extension of their social communication system. Kortlandt believes a similar evolutionary trend must have occurred among early hominids, but because the largely "instinctive social communication system" in hominids is poorer, they achieved an alternative evolutionary solution by extending their primarily "*noninstinctive* communication patterns," that is, speech (Kortlandt, 1965, p. 321).

◇ Hunting and Gathering Societies

We have reviewed two kinds of social animals, nonhuman primates and social carnivores, in order to gain some understanding of ourselves and our origins. Contemporary humans in an industrialized or agricultural community live far removed from ancient humans and, from an adaptive viewpoint, cannot easily be compared to nonhuman social mammals. However, there are peoples living at the present time in remote areas of the world who have maintained a way of life, to some extent at least, similar to that of early hominids. A review of these people, whom anthropologists classify as hunter-gatherers (or, as some prefer, gatherer-hunters), may give some idea of how early hominids lived 1 or 2 million years ago. We cannot claim that contemporary hunter-gatherers live identically to those ancient ones, but since adaptive problems are somewhat similar, it will be worthwhile to see how these peoples have developed adaptive strategies that enabled them to survive.

A hunting and gathering pattern (that is, hunting wild game and gathering wild plant foods) is fundamental to human behavior. More than just characteristic of early hominids, a hunting and gathering way of life has been *the* strategy used by our ancestors throughout the vast majority of human evolution.* The time span of our genus, *Homo*, has extended for about 2 million years. Of that time, our ancestors were hunter-gatherers for all but the last 10,000 years. In other words, 99.5% of the history of the genus *Homo* was spent as a hunter-gatherer.

Hunter-gatherers live today in widely divergent environments we would consider to be forbidding regions of the earth; rain forests, deserts, and the

---

*Some anthropologists believe scavenging preceded hunting and may have been the primary source of meat even for *H. erectus*.

arctic and subarctic. Such was not always the case. Before the invention of farming, hunters traversed the plains in search of food. However, with domestication, farmers pushed the hunters out of this desirable land to less hospitable areas.

Typically, hunter-gatherers live in small nomadic or seminomadic bands composed of loosely integrated families. They usually lack the more organized forms of kinship, such as clans and lineages. There are no specialized economic, religious, or political groups since the family itself is the organization that undertakes all these roles. Depending on the season and availability of food, the size of the band expands and contracts. Bands move from one area to another within their home range according to the availability of resources in different places at different times. The food resources used by the band are communal property, and all families have equal rights to them. To protect their resources, band members may defend their territory against encroachment by strangers (Service, 1966, p. 22).

A band is not a closed group; people constantly come and go, separating when food is scarce and regrouping for collective hunts, sharing a water hole, or participating in an important ceremony. Should a conflict arise, an individual may leave his band and seek to join another.

Men do most of the hunting and women the gathering, usually in small groups, but all share their food with other members of the band. Since hunter-gatherers exercise little or no control over the plants and animals upon which they depend, they have to accommodate themselves to seasonal and annual fluctuations in resources spread over wide areas.

As an example of a hunting-gathering society, let us take a brief look at the !Kung San of the Kalahari Desert in South Africa.

!KUNG SAN*

The !Kung San of the Dobe live on the border of Namibia and Botswana on the northern fringe of the Kalahari Desert of Southwest Africa. This area of hot, wet summers (October to May) and cool, dry winters (May to October) is a sparsely populated sand plain across which the hunting-gathering !Kung San occupy approximately 7,000 square miles. Within this area are 10 permanent water holes occupied by approximately 500 San. Some non-San people live here, also.

At the water holes, the !Kung live in camps or villages† of from 10 to 30 individuals. The type of village varies with the season. In the dry (summer) season, the village is fairly large. It is comprised of from 8 to 15 huts and 20 to 50 people, is located near a permanent water source, and is occupied for 3 to 6 months. In the rainy season, the village, from 3 to 20 huts, is located near a seasonal water and food source and is occupied for 3 weeks to 3

---

*The diacritical mark "!" indicates a click (something like the clucking sound made to a horse), which is part of the San phonetic system. Anthropologists have discarded the term "Bushmen" for these foragers living in the Kalahari and now refer to them as San, of which the !Kung are one group. Material on the !Kung is derived from Yellen (1977) and especially Lee (1984).

†Lee uses the words "camp" and "village" interchangeably.

months. In the spring and fall the camp is temporary, rarely occupied for more than 2 or 3 weeks, and no huts are built.

Until recently, each !Kung group moved every season, building and abandoning 3 to 6 villages each year. Eventually, these abandoned villages become buried in sand and were converted into archeological sites ". . . !Kung village sites of the 1960s strongly resemble the village sites of prehistoric foragers 100 to 500 or more years old . . ." (Lee, 1984, p. 33). A !Kung camp consists of kinspeople and affines (inlaws) who have found that they can live and work well together. Brothers, for example, may live together or apart, as may fathers and sons. The composition of the camp changes from day to day and month to month because the !Kung enjoy visiting. Each year about 30% of the population makes a permanent residential shift from one camp to another. There is a visiting network among camps, and during a given lifetime an

Figure 10-22   Map of San area.

individual may live for varying amounts of time at many different water holes. However, establishing residence with a camp does not require relinquishing a claim to any other camp.

This constant circulation might appear to cause residential instability. However, an entire camp may move together for at least part of the year. What gives the camp its stability is its core, which is composed of related older people, usually siblings and cousins. Generally, the core is considered to be the water hole owners. Surrounding each water hole is land that contains food resources. This forms the basic subsistence area for the residing group. The water hole and the land immediately around it is "owned" by the *k'ausi*, the core of related people, and the ownership is passed from generation to generation as long as the descendants continue to live there.

The core group is also recognized as the hosts, and anyone wishing to visit at the water hole is expected to approach the hosts for permission. The *k'ausi* are not owners in the sense that they can sell the land if they wish; they are simply the people who have lived there longer than any other. Both male and female kin and their spouses are included in the *k'ausi*. After a time the name of one member of the group becomes the name of the camp, but this leader is in no sense a headman.

A camp is built up over time by the addition of in-marrying spouses of the core siblings. A brother brings in his wife; and a sister may bring in her husband. These in-laws then bring in *their* siblings so that the camp has a relative—parent, child, sibling, or spouse—with links to the core group.

Settling at a water hole, the !Kung arrange their huts in a circle, with the entrances facing center. The huts are generally occupied by nuclear families, with husband, wife, and immature children sharing a single hut and hearth. Young, unmarried adults of the same sex usually live together in a separate hut, whereas widowers and co-wives have huts of their own.

Figure 10-23   A !Kung San camp.

Figure 10-24 A !Kung family works at home.

People living at a water hole—residents and visitors—all share the available resources. Members of a camp, of course, have access to the resources, and, if the sharing breaks down, it ceases to be a camp. Visitors also share, and it is understood that the residents at some future time will pay a return visit to their visitors' camp and share the resources there. A fairly complex system of obligations apply between hosts and visitors.

!Kung men are excellent hunters and devote a great deal of time and effort to their pursuit of game. While snaring game is practiced, most of the hunting consists of pursuing game either singly or in twos or threes. Outstanding trackers, !Kung hunters can deduce the following information about the animal they are tracking: species, sex, age, how fast traveling, alone or with other animals, physical condition, whether and on what it is feeding, and the time of day the animal passed this way.

Known to the !Kung are some 262 species of animals, of which about 80 are eaten. Several varieties of antelopes and game birds are eagerly sought, but the species that provide the most meat are warthogs, wildebeests, gemsboks, kudus, elands, roan antelopes, and hartebeests. Although women do not hunt, men may gather when meat is scarce, and the food thus obtained accounted for 22% of all gathered food.

When a large animal is killed, it is feasting time, and great cauldrons of meat are cooked round-the-clock. People gather from far and wide, and meat is distributed to all. The distribution is made according to a set of rules, with great care, and the arranging and rearranging of the pieces may continue for an hour to ensure that each recipient is given the right proportion. Improper meat distribution can cause bitter wrangling among close relatives. Excellent distribution will be fondly recalled for months.

As in most foraging societies, women do the gathering. As a matter of fact, the foundation of !Kung subsistence depends on the 105 species of edible

Figure 10-25   !Kung hunter returns to camp.

wild plants found in their area, especially the remarkable mongongo nut, which provides up to half the !Kung vegetable diet. The wide variety of vegetable food available to the !Kung provides a cushion against changing environmental conditions.

When the !Kung establish a campsite, they eat the more desirable plant food first. When that is consumed, young members range farther afield for less desirable species, and older members collect the food closer to home. The day's foods are pooled within families and shared with other families, so that a variety of food is available to every camp member and no one goes hungry.

In his field work, Dr. Lee investigated the question of how hard the !Kung San worked. He found that over a four-week period, the overall work week was 2.4 days of work per adult. During the month of this study, at least, the people appeared to spend less than half their days in obtaining food. They enjoyed more leisure time than members of many agricultural and industrial societies. And this was during the dry season of a year of serious drought!

On the days the Dobe people were not hunting or gathering, they were either at the water hole entertaining visitors, or themselves visiting other camps.

It is interesting to note that the men worked harder than the women. Men worked an average of 12 out of 28 days (providing about 45% of the food), while women worked about 9 (providing about 55% of the food), a work schedule that contradicts the view that women are the workhorses of a foraging society. Men appear to work one-third harder than the women. A day of gathering by the women produces about 68% more calories on the average than a day of hunting. Women, it seems, work fewer days, but produce more calories than the men.

At one time, it was believed that hunter-gatherers lived a hand-to-mouth existence, ever on the brink of starvation. Lee clearly demonstrated this is not the case by carefully measuring the caloric and protein intake of a group of !Kung. The daily intake of meat protein was 34.5 grams and 690 calories; from mongongo nuts, 58.8 grams of protein and 1,365 calories; and, from other vegetables, 3 grams of protein and 300 calories. This amounts to an average of 2,355 calories per person. Lee estimated their minimum daily energy requirements (given their size and activity) to be about 1,975 calories, which left a caloric surplus of 380. The !Kung, with a modest subsistence effort of 2.4 workdays per week, produced an adequate diet *and* a surplus. What makes this way of life possible, Lee believes, is sharing:

> If I had to point to one single feature that makes this way of life possible, I would focus on *sharing*. Each !Kung is not an island unto himself or herself; each is part of a collective. It is a small, rudimentary collective, and at times a fragile one, but it is a collective nonetheless. What I mean is that the living group pools the resources that are brought into camp so that everyone receives an equitable share. The !Kung and people like them don't do this out of nobility of soul or because they are made of better stuff than we are. In fact, they often gripe about sharing. They do it because it works for them and it enhances their survival. Without this core of sharing, life for the !Kung would be harder and infinitely less pleasant (Lee, 1984, p. 55).

Figure 10-26   Carrying her child, a !Kung woman gathers.

In summary, the !Kung San possess what is central to a foraging economy: sexual division of labor; simple technology; collective, nonexclusive ownership of land and resources; and widespread food sharing within and among local groups according to the principle of generalized reciprocity.

Attempting to reconstruct the situation in which early hominids evolved is speculative since so little evidence is available, especially for specific events. Evidence from social carnivores, especially wild dogs and wolves, points up the utility of cooperative hunting, which may be at least one of the reasons for their success. Additionally, reproductive success is enhanced by their home base, where the young are guarded from intruders and fed by returning hunters. Whether cooperative hunting is found among baboons and chimpanzees is presently not entirely certain, but, in any case, it is not the prevalent mode of obtaining meat. Furthermore, meat is not as important in their diet as is vegetable matter.

!Kung San are cooperative hunters, share both meat and vegetables according to an organized and formal plan, use a home base, pair bond, and the sexes divide their labor. A few of these characteristics, such as sharing and division of labor (and perhaps cooperative hunting) may be practiced by nonhuman primates, but to a very limited degree.

On the other hand—like all contemporary *Homo sapiens*—San people have a fully modern human brain. As such, they have highly elaborated capabilities for abstract thought, symbolic language, complex tool making, and so forth. They thus are not strictly comparable to very early hominids, whose brain sizes were much smaller, and who probably did not possess full language.

Moreover, the !Kung San were "disrupted" by outside civilization well before the first systematic anthropological studies were carried out (in the early 1950s). As a result, they use metal knives and arrowheads (the bow and arrow itself is probably a fairly recent import), wear cotton clothing, and employ many other introduced items. How much all of this has influenced their culture (from our point of view, specifically their ecological strategies) is difficult to say. Certainly the !Kung San (or, for that matter, any contemporary hunting-gathering group) do not have the same relationship with their environments that would have been true even a few generations ago.

Sadly, the degree of outside influence disrupting the traditional !Kung San culture has recently become overwhelming. Much of the wild game on which they had depended is either decimated or partially off-limits on protected game preserves. Pressure by governments (in South Africa and Botswana), as well as economic pressures to obtain cash resources, have led many San to settle on reservations. Here, many have become exposed for the first time to alcohol, tobacco, transistor radios, infant formula, and other modern items (Kolata, 1981).

Southern Africa today is a tinderbox of conflicting political and racial groups. The !Kung San have not been able to avoid these powerful forces and, in many cases, have been swept directly into the conflict. Since about 1970, the South African government has actively recruited !Kung San into the army, where they are used to fight insurgent groups in Namibia and also in neighboring Angola (Kolata, 1981).

◇ Conclusion: Fact and Fiction of Human Behavioral Evolution

As we have seen, no single behavioral model is adequate for reconstructing early hominid beginnings. They are all flawed in one way or another. What we must do, consequently, is to *select* those aspects from each model we think are most useful.

Certainly, early hominids were social. Moreover, we know that by at least 4 m.y.a. they were exploiting open environments and were adapted for bipedalism (although perhaps not completely—we'll discuss this in further detail in Chapter 15). By 2 m.y.a., some hominids were using stone tools, regularly exploiting meat resources, and carrying these and other items back to a central place (i.e., a base camp). As we will see in Chapter 13, this meat exploitation initially was limited mostly to small animals and probably the scavenging of larger kills brought down by other predators. Certainly, by 1 m.y.a., our ancestors were systematically going after very large animals.

Thus, the models provided by social carnivores, savanna baboons, and modern hunter-gatherers have something to tell us about how socially organized animals cope in a savanna environment. Moreover, from social carnivores (analogously) and from hunter-gatherers (homologously), we can glean some clues regarding the advantages of group hunting, food sharing, and base camps.

In addition, chimpanzees offer further insight concerning incipient tool use, complex (but mostly nonvocal) communication, and parental strategies for raising slowly developing offspring.

Beyond these generalizations, the record allows little in the way of more specific statements. Lovejoy points out that early hominids were bipedal *before* they began to systematically use stone implements. From this, he assumes that the earliest hominids were adapted for carrying something else other than tools—and suggests it was food. Moreover, the food was carried by males back to central places and shared with females to whom they were monogamously paired.

As we have indicated, hominids certainly were bipedal early on, and at a stage where as yet no definite stone tools have been recovered. It is quite possible—even probable—that these hominids did have tools made of perishable materials (wood, bone, fiber). Unfortunately, we probably will never know. It is also possible that early hominids did have marked sexual division of labor, monogamous pairs, concealed ovulation, and increased male parental investment. However, here, too, there is no way to know for certain.

In reading accounts of human behavioral evolution, particularly those aimed at the general public* we caution you to keep these concerns in mind. In so doing, it will be more possible to separate the hard evidence from speculation, and you can then draw your own conclusions.

◇ Summary

Since humans are primates and evolved from primates, anthropologists believe that the study of nonhuman primate behavior may offer insights into hominid origins and further the understanding of human behavior.

As an interpretive and organizational aid, we have presented the model of human behavioral origins proposed by Owen Lovejoy. In his model, Lovejoy emphasizes several key differences between human and nonhuman primates. These are helpful in highlighting how our primate cousins can be used to better understand human evolution. In addition, Lovejoy speculates about the sequence of certain behavioral innovations among our earliest hominid ancestors. We disagree with the implications of this, but controversies of this nature are helpful in demonstrating how various models can be used to illuminate our evolutionary history.

Although it varies a great deal, nonhuman primate behavior may be discussed under several categories: grooming, displays, dominance or status rank relationships, mother-infant relationships, male-female sexual bond, role separation between adults and young, and role separation by sex.

Baboon and chimpanzee social behavior, as a specific example of nonhuman primates, is briefly described and "cultural" behavior of chimpanzees and Japanese macaques discussed. The ability of apes—especially chimpanzees—to handle language raises interesting theoretical questions about the origin of language and the role language played in the evolution of early hominids. Whether chimpanzees who have been taught to sign can actually form sentences is also discussed.

*For example, Morris (1967); Ardrey (1966, 1976); Tiger and Fox (1974), and Morgan (1972).

Primatologists have recently begun to look at primate behavior from two new approaches: socioecology and sociobiology. Socioecology emphasizes the environmental factors that might bear on animal behavior, and sociobiology emphasizes the genetic basis of animal behavior.

Social carnivore adaptations to savanna ecological conditions are introduced as an analogy for the adaptation of early hominids to a similar environment. The way of life of contemporary hunter-gatherers (or gatherer-hunters), such as the !Kung, reflects the kind of adaptation that may have characterized early hominids.

◇ Questions for Review

1. List several reasons for studying nonhuman primate behavior.
2. What behavioral traits are common to all nonhuman primates?
3. Describe the primate social group.
4. What are the functions of grooming? displays? dominance?
5. Why is the mother-infant relationship an important one for primates?
6. Compare baboon and chimpanzee social behavior. What is the relationship between the social behavior and group structure of these primates?
7. Do baboons or chimpanzees serve as better models for hominid behavior? Why?
8. Discuss the learning achievements of chimpanzees. Why do the authors believe the concept of culture should not be applied to this behavior?
9. Chimpanzees have been taught to communicate symbolically; why is this significant?
10. What is the argument opposing the idea that chimpanzees are capable of learning language?
11. What is the basis for the sociobiological approach to animal behavior?
12. How does sociobiology explain altruistic behavior?
13. Describe the different adaptations of lions and wild dogs to a savanna ecological niche.
14. How does the study of social carnivores contribute to our understanding of hominid evolution?
15. What are the similarities in the adaptations of social carnivores and !Kung San?

◇ Suggested Further Reading

Barash, David, *Sociobiology and Behavior*, New York: Elsevier, 1977, 1982.
> *A recent and authoritative review of sociobiological theory by one of the leading proponents of this approach. A student with no biological background may find parts of this work difficult to comprehend; nonetheless, the ideas are highly stimulating. The reader should be cautious, for this author makes a rather one-sided presentation.*

Primate Evolution

CONTENTS

Ancient legends tell of Sasquatch, a strange, hairy, bipedal creature prowling the wilds of North America. In fact, Sasquatches, abominable snowmen, and other such creatures have been reported from at least 100 separate areas of the world. In North America, they have been reported most often from British Columbia, Washington, Oregon, and northern California. Various unexplained beasts, however, have also been "seen" from Alaska to Mexico and from the Pacific Coast to northern Michigan. Tales of these creatures, which are usually called *Bigfoot*, are today even further embellished as sightings, footprints, hair fragments, feces, and even photographs have been collected. Are we dealing with fact or fiction?

If Bigfoot lives, what could it be? Reports are consistent, detailing a very large (eight to twelve foot), upright animal. Its size, hair, and location (in the cold Northwest) all imply a mammal. Its body shape and locomotion further limit the possibilities. Possibly it is a bear, but the gait and footprints are not right. What is left then? A hominoid of some sort?

Is this possible? In any objective pursuit of knowledge we must admit that *anything* is possible, but some things are highly improbable. What kinds of hominoids are native to the New World? The only definite remains of indigenous hominoids in North, Central, or South America are those of *Homo sapiens* (and these are relatively recent—in the last 30,000–40,000 years or so).

If Bigfoot is a hominoid, where did it come from? The closest fossil primate matching the dimensions of the fleeting Sasquatches is *Gigantopithecus*. Remains of this extinct hominoid are well known from the Old World during the Pleistocene, but none has ever been found in the New World. Such a big animal has exceedingly large teeth, which generally have a fairly good chance of being preserved. From China alone there are more than 1,000 *Gigantopithecus* teeth, and this giant hominoid has not roamed the forests of China for half a million years. It seems very strange, indeed. If *Gigantopithecus* (or one of its supposed descendants) is still living, why have we not found any bones or teeth of this form? If such a large animal has existed for tens of thousands of years, where is the hard evidence?

What about the hundreds of sightings? Could they all have been faked? Probably not. Many of these people, no doubt, saw *something*. Perhaps often they were bears; the imagination can greatly influence our objectivity when primed with romantic tales of mythical beasts. What about footprints, photos, hairs, and fecal material? The prints (at least many of them) could have been faked, and so too with the photos (the primary evidence—a 16-mm film taken in northern California in 1967). Such a circumstance would suggest an elaborate, deliberate hoax, not a happy conclusion, but entirely possible (as you will see with Piltdown). The hairs and fecal materia. are from some ani-

mal, perhaps one already known, perhaps one yet to be discovered. The possibility exists that there are large terrestrial mammals in remote areas of North America unknown to science. Bigfoot may be such an animal. However, of all the possibilities, the suggestion that this creature is a hominoid is about the least likely imaginable.

The conclusion that Bigfoot is an archaic hominoid is therefore both unlikely and far from conclusively established. But it is not *completely* impossible. Perhaps descendant populations of gigantopithecines migrated from China (through thousands of miles of environments exceedingly inhospitable to such a forest-adapted form), end up in the American Northwest. In so doing, perhaps they left nary a trace all along the way. Furthering our improbable conjectures, perhaps they have existed in North America for at least 500,000 years, without leaving a single fossil remnant. Finally, perhaps they still exist today, but deliberately conceal themselves and meticulously dispose of their dead.

SOURCES:

Napier, John. *Bigfoot; the Yeti and Sasquatch in Myth and Reality*, London: Jonathan Cape, 1972.

Sanderson, Ivan T. *Abominable Snowmen: Legend Come to Life*, New York. Chilton Co., 1961.

Shuman, James B. "Is There an American Abominable Snowman?," *Reader's Digest*, January 1969, pp. 179–186.

◇ Introduction

In Chapters 8, 9, and 10, you were introduced to the time scale of evolution, placental mammals, and particularly the primate order. We now turn to the fossil history of primates over the last 70 million years. With what you now know of primate anatomy (teeth, limbs, etc.) and social behavior, you will be able to "flesh out" the bones and teeth that comprise the evolutionary record of primate origins. In this way, the ecological adaptations and evolutionary relationships of these fossil forms to each other (and to contemporary primates) will become more meaningful. Please note that when we look at primate evolution, we are looking at our own evolution as well.

◇ Time Scale

A brief review of the geological time scale will be helpful in understanding primate evolution during the Cenozoic.

Era	Epoch	Approximate Beginning (m.y.a.)
Cenozoic	Pleistocene	1.8
	Pliocene	5
	Miocene	25
	Oligocene	37
	Eocene	53
	Paleocene	65
Mesozoic	Cretaceous	135

Before discussing the fossil primates, we should caution that the formal taxonomic names for the various families and genera are horrendous to pronounce and even harder to remember. Unfortunately, there is no other adequate way to discuss the material. We must make reference to the standard nomenclature. As an aid, we suggest you refer to the marginal notes, pronunciation guide, and glossary for those names considered most significant.

◇ Earliest Primates

The first radiation of the primate order has its roots in the beginnings of the explosive adaptive radiation of placental mammals in general. Therefore, it is not surprising that the earliest suggestions of primates in the fossil record are difficult to discern from early members of other placental mammal groups, particularly the insectivores.

The earliest discovered traces suggesting the beginnings of our order come

Purgatorius
(Purg-a-tore'-ee-us)

Plesiadapis
(Please-ee-a-dap'-iss)

from the late Cretaceous and early Paleocene in the Dakota area of North America. Known only from a few teeth, this fossil form, called **Purgatorius**, exhibits the primate tendency towards a bulbous cusp pattern in the molar teeth compared to the sharper cusps seen in insectivores. Such a dental pattern apparently indicates that early primates were adapting to fruit and leaf-eating diets (Szalay, 1968), or perhaps a diet also including insects exploited in an arboreal niche (Van Valen and Sloan, 1965). Reconstructions indicate that the dental formula is still that of a generalized primitive mammal: 3-1-4-3 (Szalay and Delson, 1979). All that can be said now of this still fragmentary and mysterious animal, *Purgatorius*, is that if it was a primate, it was quite "primitive," which is not surprising considering its early date and still close ties with primitive placental mammals.

◇ Paleocene Primates (65 m.y.–53 m.y.)

During the Paleocene, the first clearly recognizable primates begin to diversify. In fact, we are able to isolate several different (at least four) families widely scattered in North America and Europe during this epoch.

One of the most widely distributed and best represented of these early primates is **Plesiadapis**, found in both North America and Europe. First known from the late Paleocene, the time range of *Plesiadapis* extends up into the early Eocene. This animal, known from a nearly complete skull plus several parts of the limb skeleton, has an estimated size range varying widely between that of a squirrel and a house cat. While these animals show definite primate tendencies, such as dependence on vision (though not completely binocular) and prehensility (though still probably with claws), they retain numerous primitive characteristics, such as lack of a postorbital bar, which serves to form a bony division between the orbit and the braincase. In addition, *Plesiadapis* and the majority of other Paleocene primates display unusual (compared to modern primates) specializations of their front teeth, which are large and procumbent (angled forward) and, in some respects, reminiscent of the specialized aye-aye.

Given these dental specializations, the possibility that any of the Paleocene forms thus far discovered are direct ancestors of later primates seems unlikely. This poses no insurmountable theoretical problem, for we must keep in mind that our meager discoveries represent only a tiny sample of the already diverse kinds of primates living at this time.

The overall anatomical plan of all these early forms could be described as prosimian or even "protoprosimian," for they are certainly more primitive than any living primate. In fact, they are more similar in evolutionary grade to the living tree shrews, which give a fairly good model of Paleocene primates (see p. 248).

◇ Ancient Landscapes and Early Primate Evolution

The distribution and the eventual fate of early primate forms is understandable only within the context of the environments in which these animals

Figure 11-1   Postorbital bar.

lived. First and foremost, we must remember that 60 m.y.a. land masses were not arranged as they are today. As we discussed on page 222, the continents have "drifted" to their present position, carried along on the shifting plates of the earth's surface.

In the late Paleozoic (*circa* 250 m.y.a.), the huge conglomerate land mass called Pangea began to break up into northern and southern continents. To the north, North America, Europe, and Asia were joined into Laurasia; to the south, Africa, South America, Australia, India, and Antarctica formed Gondwanaland (see Fig. 11-2a). Throughout the Mesozoic, the two basic land masses continued to move, with Gondwanaland breaking up into the southern continents. In the north, the continents also were separating, but North America and Europe continued to be connected through Greenland and would remain attached in this manner for several millions of years.

As we will see, this "northern connection" had a very significant influence on the geographic distribution of early primates. In fact, North America and Europe remained joined until mid-Eocene times (*circa* 45 m.y.a.) (see Fig. 11-2b). Though welded to North America, Europe was separated from Asia by a channel called the Turgai Straight. Not until the later Eocene (about 40 m.y.a.) does Europe disjoin from North America to the west and finally make contact with Asia to the east (forming an area that we today call Eurasia).

What makes all this geologic activity relevant to primate (and other paleontological) studies is that land-living animals could cross over land bridges but were effectively cut off by water barriers. Thus, we see species of *Plesiadapis* in *both* North America and Europe. On the other hand, primates are unknown in Asia until the late Eocene, when presumably they could walk in from Europe once the Turgai Strait had been closed. As far as primates go, then, from their earliest beginnings (65 m.y.a. +) up until 40 m.y.a. they were essentially limited to North America and Europe (between which free migration was still possible). With further continental movements, the "New World" and "Old World" became completely separated and thereby influenced the evolutionary histories of primates still living today (see page 333).

Figure 11-2 Continental drift. Changes in position of the continental plates from Late Paleozoic to Late Eocene. (*a*) The position of the continents at the end of the Paleozoic (*c*. 250 m.y.a.). Pangea is breaking up into a northern land mass (Laurasia) and a southern land mass (Gondwanaland). (*b*) The position of the continents during much of the Paleocene and Eocene (up to *c*. 45 m.y.a.). Note that North America and Europe are still joined but are separate from Asia.

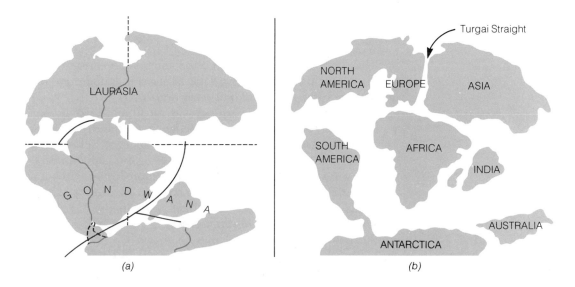

(a)　　　　　　　　　　　　(b)

Necrolemur
(Nek-roe-lee'-mur)

As the continents moved, climatic conditions changed dramatically. In the Mesozoic and into the Paleocene, the continental masses were clustered closer to the equator, and as Laurasia in particular moved north, its climate cooled. Moreover, the fragmenting of the land masses and the consequent altering of marine flow patterns (less exchange between northern and southern seas) caused the climate to cool even further.

Finally, these climatic shifts also heavily affected plant communities. Rather than the primitive, mostly tropical flora characteristic of the Mesozoic (ferns, cycads, etc.), what we see emerging in the Cenozoic is the rapid radiation of the seed plants (including flowering plants, deciduous trees, grasses, etc.). The world was never to be the same again.

Clearly, then, it is extremely important to interpret primate evolution within the context of the earth's changing environments.

◇ Eocene Primates (53 m.y.–37 m.y.)

The first primates of modern aspect appear during the Eocene. These can now clearly be called prosimians and closely resemble the loris/lemur evolutionary grade. Primate diversification accelerates during this epoch, with four new families and as many as thirty-seven genera represented during the 16-million-year span of the Eocene.

The Eocene may be characterized as the heyday of prosimians, who attained their widest geographic distribution and broadest adaptive radiation during this period. Indeed, more than twice as many genera are found in the Eocene than are known for the whole world today (sixteen living genera, with ten of these confined to Madagascar).

The most diversified and best-known Eocene primates are members of the lemurlike Adapidae, which includes some ten genera. The three best known of these are:

Adapis (Ad'-a-piss)	Europe
Notharctus (Noth-ark'-tus)	North America
Smilodectes (Smi-lo-dek'-teese)	North America

Some of these animals have been known from fossil evidence for a remarkably long time. In fact, the initial discovery of *Adapis* was made in France in 1821 and first described by Cuvier himself.

As mentioned, all these animals are fairly lemurlike in general adaptive level and show distinctive primate tendencies not seen in the Paleocene forms. For example, they all now have a complete postorbital bar and the eyes are rotated forward, allowing overlapping fields of perception and thus binocular vision. In the limb skeleton, further developments in prehensility are suggested, and some evidence points to the presence of an opposable large toe. In all these respects, we see the typical primate adaptive strategies allowing exploitation of an arboreal environment. Whereas these forms resemble lemurs in overall anatomical plan, they do not show the same specializations seen in contemporary lorises and lemurs, such as development of the dental comb (see p. 250).

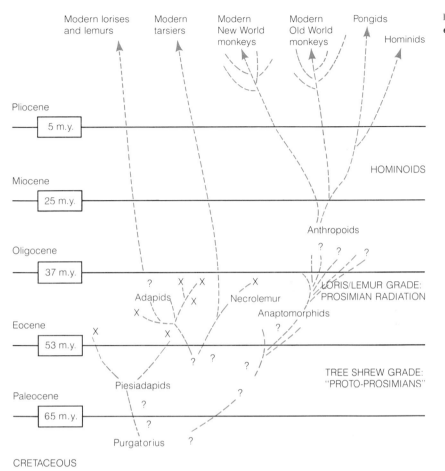

Figure 11-3 Summary, early primate evolution.

The separate evolution of the Malagasy (formerly Madagascar) lemurs may date to late Eocene times, but since this island was already isolated by a deep channel from mainland Africa, they apparently reached their island sanctuary by unintentionally floating over on drifting debris.

The evolutionary origins of the tarsiers are also indicated during the Eocene by the large-eyed and apparently noctural genus, **Necrolemur** ("dead lemur," actually a misnomer; "dead tarsier" would be more appropriate). In addition to the large size of its eyes, *Necrolemur*'s orbits are rotated completely forward, the *foramen magnum* is well forward (indicating the head was held upright over the spine), and there is some flexion in the angle at the base of the skull. All these traits reveal striking similarities with the modern tarsier. In addition, some limb bones, which may well be associated with *Necrolemur* skulls, display the distinctive tarsioid specialization of fused bones in the lower leg.

While *Necrolemur* almost certainly lies very close to the ancestral origins of the tarsioid line, it may not itself represent the actual ancestors. Specialization in the dental apparatus, shown by loss of some front teeth, indicates that this form could not have evolved into modern tarsiers. Such a circum-

Evolutionary reversal
The reacquisition of a structure previously lost in the evolution of a life form.

stance would necessitate an **evolutionary reversal**, which would involve the reacquisition of a structure already lost—an incredibly unlikely event.

The last group of Eocene primates we will discuss is the family Omomyidae (which some primatologists suggest show general affinities with the tarsiers; they include *Necrolemur* within this group) (Szalay and Delson, 1979). Although known mainly from bits of jaws and teeth, omomyids are the most widely distributed of known Eocene prosimians discovered in North America, Europe, and Asia. Indeed, they are the most widely distributed prosimian group ever! As we have just seen, primate migration into Asia was blocked until the late Eocene when the straits separating it from Europe were closed. Thus, some of these omomyids are the first Asian primates of which we have evidence.

The earlier members of this family are somewhat more generalized than the later ones, and may form the ancestral basis for all later anthropoids: New World monkeys, Old World monkeys, apes, and hominids. The affinities of these fossil omomyids with tarsiers (and inferentially with the anthropoids) have led many researchers to classify the entire group as one evolutionary unit—the Haplorhini—as opposed to the *true* prosimians (i.e., lemurs and lorises)—the Strepsirhini (see p. 251). The later forms are seemingly quite specialized, showing the highly unusual trait of incisor teeth in the upper and lower jaws to be larger than their canines.

Other evidence also argues for the emergence of anthropoids during the late Eocene. Fragmentary remains from Burma dating to about 40 m.y.a. suggest anthropoid affinities. In particular, a form referred to as *Pondaungia* shows several features of the dentition similar to that of Old World anthropoids (Maw et al, 1979). Another Burmese Eocene fossil known as *Amphipithecus* has also been proposed as a possible early anthropoid (Simons, 1972), but detailed consideration of dental anatomy suggests a more likely affinity with the prosimian adapids (Szalay and Delson, 1979).

EOCENE PROSIMIANS: SUMMARY

During the Eocene epoch, a wide and highly successful adaptive radiation of prosimian forms occurred. Some, resembling modern lorises and lemurs (Adapidae), may have given rise to direct ancestors of these modern animals by late Eocene times. Others (*Necrolemur*) resemble modern tarsiers, and still others (Omomyidae) may have been the ancestral stock for all anthropoids.

By the end of the Eocene—as the continents drifted away from the equator and caused the climate to cool—tropical areas in the northern latitudes shrank, and the range of available prosimian niches therefore also began to contract. Indeed, the end of the Eocene seems to signal an end of the prosimian radiation except for small isolated areas, where some still survive. Some prosimian forms (adapids) did manage to survive for several million years in southern Asia—where perhaps they remained isolated from the "center-stage" of primate evolution (Gingerich and Sahni, 1979). What exactly brought on this evolutionary turn of events is still not completely clear. Certainly the change in climate played a part, but competition was also coming from new fronts. The remarkably diverse and successful radiation of rodents was just beginning to accelerate rapidly during this time, no doubt

(a) (b)

Figure 11-4   Tibio-fibula. (*a*) *Necrolemur*; (*b*) modern tarsier. Note the two fused lower leg bones—a characteristic feature of tarsiers. (© 1959 by W. E. Le Gros Clark.)

bringing some of them into direct competition with prosimians. With their highly specialized teeth, large litters, short generation spans, and flexible adaptive potential, the rodents were more than a match for the prosimians.

Competition may have come from still another quarter, for some prosimians (omomyids) probably had already evolved into early monkeys by late Eocene times. Monkeys (with their larger brains, more flexible social behavior, and more varied exploitation of arboreal niches) probably also were more than a match for their prosimian cousins.

◇ New World Monkeys

The center of action for primate evolution after the close of the Eocene is confined largely to the Old World, for only on the continents of Africa and Eurasia can we trace the evolutionary development of apes and hominids.

However, the New World, while geographically separated from the Old World, was not completely devoid of anthropoid stock, for here the ceboids evolved in their own right.

Any discussion of ceboid evolution and its relation to Old World anthropoid developments must consider crucial geological events, particularly continental drift (see pp. 329–330). By late Eocene times, Europe and North America had separated, and South America and Africa, though closer together than at present, were also drifting apart.

In such a geological context, the introduction of monkeys into South America poses a certain problem. Some authorities have postulated that, because the distance between South America and Africa was still not very great, monkeys, originating in Africa, could then have rafted to the New World (Gavan, 1977; Ciochon and Chiarelli, 1980). This point, however, is disputed. Others suggest a separate origin followed by parallel evolution of monkeys in the two hemispheres (Simons, 1969).

In any case, that Old and New World primates shared any evolutionary history since at least the late Eocene (some 40 m.y.a) is unlikely. There is no trace of any ancestor of our lineage anywhere in the New World following this time until fully modern *Homo sapiens* walked in during the late Pleistocene.

While primate fossils abound in the Western Hemisphere (particularly North America) during the early Cenozoic, the record is extremely sparse later on. For the entire span of Oligocene to late Pleistocene, we have only a few bits and pieces, a jaw fragment from Bolivia, a nearly complete skull from Texas, another quite complete cranium from Argentina, and a few other small fragments from Colombia and Jamaica. Together, all the evidence comprises less than a dozen individuals. Thus, tracing the evolutionary heritage of New World monkeys with any degree of certainty is a difficult task.

◇ Old World Anthropoids

The focus of our attention will henceforth exclusively be the Old World (Europe, Asia, Africa), for this area is where our ancestors have lived for the past 40 million years. This evolutionary and geographic fact is reflected in the

Figure 11-5 Location of the Fayum, an Oligocene primate site in Egypt.

grouping of Old World anthropoids (Old World monkeys, apes, and humans) into a common infraorder (Catarrhini) as opposed to the infraorder for New World monkeys (Platyrrhini).

◇ Oligocene (37 m.y.–25 m.y.)

It is apparent that during this epoch a great deal of evolutionary action was taking place; by the end of the Oligocene, Old World monkeys and hominoids were probably evolving along their separate evolutionary pathways. No doubt, diverse species of anthropoids were adapting to varied ecological niches in Africa and probably Asia and Europe as well. Unfortunately, the fossil record for the entire period is limited to only one locality in Egypt, sixty miles southwest of Cairo. This site, called the *Fayum*, is today an extremely arid region 100 miles inland, but, in Oligocene times, it was located close to the Mediterranean shore and was traversed by meandering streams crisscrossing through areas of tropical rain forest. The upper fossil beds have been dated by potassium/argon at approximately 25–27 m.y.a., and a series of lower beds were probably deposited 33–35 m.y.a.

Much of the Fayum fossil material is quite fragmentary. Consequently, evolutionary interpretations are not as unambiguous as we would like. Given the nature of the material, the classification of the fossils into recognized genera and species (always a difficult task; see p. 351) is somewhat disputed.

Apidium (TWO SPECIES)

A well-known 30-million-year-old fossil animal from the Fayum is **Apidium**, represented by about 80 jaws or partial dentitions and over 100 postcranial elements. This animal, about the size of a squirrel, had several anthropoid-like features, but also shows quite unusual aspects in its teeth. *Apidium*'s dental formula (see p. 255) is 2-1-3-3 which, as you can easily see, reveals an extra premolar not found in any contemporary Old World anthropoid. For that matter, extremely few fossil anthropoids in the Old World have this extra premolar. Another unusual Old World anthropoid form, which has been suggested as possibly related to *Apidium*, is called *Oreopithecus* from the late Miocene (10–12 m.y.a.) of Italy. Since they are separated by some 18 million years, the *Apidium–Oreopithecus* phylogenetic relationship is a most tenuous one. The similarities between the two forms may be explained by convergence, which would account for the presence of apparently independently *derived* characteristics in both (Szalay and Delson, 1979).

Propliopithecus (TWO SPECIES)*

Among the first fossils found at the Fayum, an incomplete *Propliopithecus* mandible was recovered in 1907. Unfortunately, since detailed geological and

*Some primatologists have suggested a third species of *Propliopithecus* (*P. markrafi*) at the Fayum (Fleagle and Kay, 1983). This species, however, is also known from only a single specimen.

paleontological methods were not yet developed, the stratigraphic position of this form is not known.

Morphologically, this fossil is a quite generalized Old World anthropoid, displaying a 2-1-2-3 dental formula. In most every relevant respect, this early (?) *Propliopithecus* form is quite primitive, not showing particular derived tendencies in any direction. To date, only this one specimen represents this *Propliopithecus (haeckeli)* species.

The second *Propliopithecus* species is considerably better known, with several new specimens discovered at the Fayum between 1977 and 1979. Stratigraphically, this species (*P. chirobates*) comes from the upper beds (*circa* 27–28 m.y.a.) and is, therefore, probably later in time than the isolated *haeckeli* specimen. Consequently, it is not surprising that *chirobates* is more derived in several anatomical features. Still, this form is a remarkably primitive Old World anthropoid. Considerably more evolutionary change would be required to transform this animal into anything distinctively recognizable as either an ape or a monkey.

Earlier interpretations of fragmentary remains of this fossil suggested affinities with gibbons (Simons initially proposed a separate genus rank, "Aeolopithecus"). However, more complete recent discoveries have shown that such an evolutionary relationship is not likely (Kay et al, 1981).

Aegyptopithecus

The most complete and probably evolutionarily most significant fossil from the Fayum is **Aegyptopithecus** (*circa* 28 m.y.a.), which is known from a nearly complete skull found in 1966, as well as numerous jaw fragments and several limb bones (most of which have been found quite recently). The largest of the Fayum anthropoids, *Aegyptopithecus* is roughly the size of a modern howler monkey, 13 to 18 pounds (Fleagle, 1983). *Aegyptopithecus* is important because, better than any other fossil, it bridges the gap between the Eocene prosimians on the one hand and the Miocene hominoids on the other.

With a dental formula of 2-1-2-3, *Aegyptopithecus* shows the familiar Old World anthropoid pattern. More detailed aspects of the dentition possibly align this Oligocene form with the Miocene hominoids (which we shall discuss shortly), but the evolutionary affinities are not presently well established. In most respects, the dentition is primitive for an Old World anthropoid without specifically derived features in either the hominoid or Old World monkey direction. Recently, there has been a change in interpreting Old World monkey dental evolution. It was previously believed that the dental patterns (particularly, the molar cusp pattern) seen in Old World monkeys were the more primitive and, conversely, those seen in hominoids were more derived from the ancestral **catarrhine** condition. Reevaluation of the fossil materials now suggests that, if anything, the Old World monkey pattern is more derived, and the hominoid cusp arrangement is the more primitive.

The establishment of the "polarities" of primitive/derived characteristics is crucial to making sound evolutionary interpretations. However, the trajectories of evolutionary change are not always easy to ascertain. The determination of the ancestral catarrhine molar cusp pattern is only one example. In the subsequent section on Miocene hominoids, we will encounter several further dilemmas in sorting out such issues.

Apidium
(A-pid′-ee-um)

Catarrhine
The group (infraorder) comprising all Old World anthropoids, living and extinct.

(a)

(b)

Figure 11-6   *Aegyptopithecus* skull from the Fayum, Egypt. Oligocene, *circa* 28 m.y.a. discovered in 1966. (*a*) Front view; (*b*) side view.

Even more primitive than the teeth of *Aegyptopithecus* is the skull, which is small and resembles the skull of a monkey in some details. Brain size and relative proportions can be reconstructed from internal casts of the one well-preserved cranium thus far discovered (see Fig. 11-6). It appears that the brain was somewhat intermediate between that of prosimians and anthropoids. The visual cortex was large compared to prosimians, with concomitant reduction of the olfactory lobes, but the frontal lobes were not especially expanded. Even considering the relative small size of this animal, the brain—estimated at only 30 to 40 cm^3 (Radinsky, 1973)—was by no means large.

Evidence from the limb skeleton also revealed nothing particularly distinctive. From analysis of limb proportions and muscle insertions, primatologist John Fleagle (1983) has concluded that *Aegyptopithecus* was a short-limbed, heavily muscled, slowly moving, arboreal quadruped.

Further detailed study of *Aegyptopithecus*' anatomy has even allowed primatologists to speculate about the social behavior of this ancient primate. For instance, dental remains from different individuals vary greatly in canine size. This fact implies male/female differences (sexual dimorphism), which apparently were quite marked. Comparisons with living primates further suggest that males may have been competing for females and that the mating pattern was probably polygynous.

All in all, *Aegyptopithecus* presents somewhat of a paleontological enigma. In most respects, the dentition is primitive for an Old World anthropoid, thus be potentially an ancestor for *both* Old World monkeys and hominoids. There are some slight yet suggestive clues in the teeth that have led some researchers (most notably, E. L. Simons of Duke University) to already place *Aegyptopithecus* on the hominoid line. Primarily because of the primitive aspects of this creature, other researchers (e.g., Fleagle and Kay, 1983) are not as convinced.

There remains, then, the problem of how to classify *Aegyptopithecus*. Even though they recognize that this fossil may well have lived before the major evolutionary split between Old World monkeys and hominoids (see Fig. 11-3), John Fleagle and Richard Kay still opt to call *Aegyptopithecus* a hominoid. Accordingly, they recognize that the superfamily Hominoidea then becomes what they term a "wastebasket" category (i.e., it is used for convenience, but does not reflect phylogenetic reality). This is one solution, although it will not satisfy all researchers. Perhaps, for the moment, it would be best to regard *Aegyptopithecus* (as well as the other Fayum anthropoids) as "primitive catarrhines," without referring them to particular superfamilies.

OLIGOCENE FOSSIL ANTHROPOIDS: SUMMARY

The spectacular array of fossils from the Fayum in the period between 32 m.y. and 28 m.y. demonstrates that anthropoids were radiating along several evolutionary lines. As with the earlier primate fossil material from the Paleocene and Eocene, the fragmentary nature of the Oligocene fossil assemblage makes precise reconstruction of these evolutionary lines risky.

Given the primitive nature of these fossil forms, it is wise, for the present, not to conclude specifically how these animals relate to later primates. In earlier primatological studies (as well as earlier editions of this book), such conclusions were indeed made, but reanalysis of the fossil material from the perspective of primitive/derived evolutionary modifications has cast serious doubt on many of these interpretations. The new interpretations, however, are still far from certain. As we have mentioned, untangling the polarity of primitive versus derived evolutionary states is a most difficult task. What many paleontologists would dearly like to establish is a clear link between these Oligocene fossils (particularly *Propliopithecus* and *Aegyptopithecus*) and the unambiguously hominoid forms of the Miocene. Unfortunately, as the following quote argues, this is not yet possible:

> In light of current knowledge about the very primitive dental, cranial, and skeletal morphology of the *Oligocene* hominoids, *Propliopithecus* and *Aegyptopithecus*, there is no reason to believe that any single group of extant hominoids (either hylobatids, hominids, or pongids) can be traced back to an Oligocene divergence (Fleagle and Kay, 1983, p. 190).

◇ Miocene (25 m.y.–5 m.y.)—Hominoids Aplenty

If the Eocene was the age of prosimians and the Oligocene the time of great diversity for early anthropoids, the Miocene was certainly the epoch of hominoids.

A great abundance of hominoid fossil material has been found in the Old World from the time period 23 m.y.—7 m.y. The remarkable evolutionary success represented by this adaptive radiation is shown in the geographic range already established for hominoids during this period. Miocene hominoid fossils have been discovered in France, Germany, Spain, Czechoslovakia, Greece, Hungary, China, India, Pakistan, Turkey, Egypt, Uganda, and Kenya.

Interpretations of this vast array of fossil material (now including more than 500 individuals, and perhaps as many as 1,000) were greatly complicated

Figure 11-7 Miocene hominoid distribution—fossils thus far discovered.

for several decades due to inadequate appreciation of the range of biological variation that a single genus or species could represent. As a result, the taxonomic naming of the various fossil finds became a terrible muddle, with more than 20 genera and over 100 species proposed. The biological implications of such taxonomic enthusiasm were unfortunately not seriously considered. In such an atmosphere, it was possible for two genera to be named— one with only upper jaws represented, the other with only lower jaws, each matching the other!

It is not difficult to understand why such confusion arose if we consider that discoveries of these fossils spanned more than 100 years (the earliest find came from France in 1856) and took place on three continents. Not until the early 1960s did scientists systematically study *all* the material, the result being a considerable simplification of the earlier confusion. As a result of this research, E. L. Simons and David Pilbeam "lumped" the vast majority of Miocene forms into only two genera: one presumably quite "pongidlike" and the other "hominidlike." In just the last few years, however, a tremendous amount of new data has come to light from both new field discoveries and finds in museum collections of previously unrecognized material. Consequently, it is now apparent that the Simons-Pilbeam simplification went too far. Hominoid evolutionary radiation during the Miocene produced a whole array of diverse organisms, many of which have no living descendants (and thus no clear analog among living higher primates).

As these new discoveries are analyzed, many of the perplexing problems concerning Miocene hominoids should be solved. For the moment, it is possible to make only general interpretive statements regarding Miocene hominoid adaptive patterns.

PALEOGEOGRAPHY AND MIOCENE HOMINOID EVOLUTION

As they were to early primate evolution (see p. 328), the factors of changing geography and climates (at work as well in the Miocene) are also crucial to interpretations of the later stages of primate evolution. The Oligocene revealed a proliferation of early Old World anthropoid forms from one area in North Africa. In the Early Miocene, the evidence is also restricted to Africa, with fossils coming from rich sites in the eastern part of the continent (Kenya and Uganda). It would thus appear, on the basis of current evidence, that hominoids originated in Africa and experienced a successful adaptive radiation there before dispersing to other parts of the Old World.

The hominoids would maintain this exclusive African foothold for some time. The earliest of these East African hominoid fossils is slightly more than 20 m.y. old, and later fossil finds extend the time range up to about 14 m.y.a. For most of this period, East Africa is thought to have been more heavily forested, with much less woodlands and grasslands (savannas) than exist today (Pickford, 1983).

As in the earlier Cenozoic, the shifting of the earth's plates during the Miocene played a vital role in primate evolution. Before about 16 m.y.a., Africa was cut off from Eurasia; consequently, once hominoids had originated there in the Early Miocene, they were isolated. However, around 16 m.y.a. the African plate "docked" with Eurasia (Bernor, 1983) through the Arabian Peninsula, a contact that was to revolutionize mammalian faunas of the later Miocene. Many forms, such as proboscideans, giraffoids, and pigs, that had originated in Africa now migrated into Eurasia (van Couvering and van Couvering, 1976). Apparently, included among these mid-Miocene intercontinental pioneers were some hominoids. Since they had evolved in the mainly tropical setting of equatorial Africa, most of the earlier hominoids probably remained primarily arboreal. Accordingly, it has been suggested that a relatively continuous forest would have been necessary across the Afro-Arabian-Eurasian land bridge.

Ecological changes were, however, already afoot in Africa. By 16 m.y.a., the environment was getting drier, with less tropical rainforest and, conversely, more open woodland/bushland and savanna areas emerging (Bernor, 1983; Pickford, 1983). In other words, the environments in East Africa were being transformed more into their contemporary form. With the opportunities thus presented, some African hominoids were almost certainly radiating into these more open niches about 16 to 17 m.y.a. Part of this adaptation probably involved exploitation of different foods and more ground-living than practiced by the arboreal ancestors of these hominoids. Some partly terrestrial, more open-country adapted hominoids were probably thus on the scene and fully capable of migrating into Eurasia, even through areas that were not continuosly forested.

The environments throughout the Old World were, of course, to alter even more. Later in the Miocene, some of these environmental shifts would further influence hominoid evolution and may have played a part in the origin of our particular evolutionary lineage, the hominids. More on this later.

MIOCENE HOMINOIDS—CHANGING VIEWS AND TERMINOLOGY

So, throughout the Miocene, environmental and geographic factors imposed constraints on hominoids as well as opened new opportunities to them. Over a time span of close to 15 m.y., hominoids in the middle two-thirds of the Miocene were successful indeed. Once they migrated into Eurasia, they dispersed rapidly and diversified into a variety of species. After 14 m.y.a., we have evidence of widely distributed hominoids from Pakistan, India, Turkey, Greece, Hungary, China, and Western Europe. Much of this material has only recently been uncovered and is incredibly abundant. For example, from Lufeng in southern China alone, 5 partial skulls and more than 1,000 teeth have been found in the past decade (Wu and Oxnard, 1983). The other areas have also yielded many paleontological treasures in the last ten years. Moreover, recent searches of museum collections in East Africa, as well as resurveys of fossil sites, have uncovered yet more fossils.

Given this quantity of new information, it is not surprising that heretofore existing theories of early hominoid evolution have been reevaluated. In fact, it would not be unfair to describe the last five years as a "revolution" in paleontological views of Miocene hominoid evolution. With a great deal of this recent fossil material still unanalyzed, all the answers are not presently at hand. In fact, the more fossils found, the more complicated the situation seems to become. However, two major subgroups of Miocene hominoids have been described. These correlate nicely with the relevant ecology and geology:

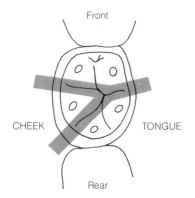

Figure 11-8   The dryopith Y-5 pattern. A characteristic feature of hominoid molars.

1. A forest living, primarily arboreal set of species, which early on are limited to Africa but later are found in Europe. This group we will call "dryopiths," a simple descriptive term and nontaxonomic (so as to avoid the pitfalls of making hasty evolutionary judgments).*

2. A more open-country (woodland or woodland/bushland/savanna mosaic) and probably more ground-living set of species. This group, mostly Eurasian in distribution, we will call "ramapiths."

DRYOPITHS

These fossil forms are best known during the earlier Miocene from East Africa, where a diverse array of species has been recognized. Some researchers also believe some dryopiths may have lived in southern Asia during the Middle-Late Miocene, but this has not been conclusively demonstrated. Certainly, in the later Miocene, there are some fragmentary dryopithlike hominoids in Western Europe, but their relationship to the earlier forms in Africa is, presently, still unclear. Our discussion will thus emphasize the more complete and better-known East African varieties.

In East Africa, the first dryopiths are the earliest hominoids we have evidence of during the Miocene. Indeed, except by broadly expanding the definition of the hominoids (see p. 336), these are the first *definite* hominoids we have from anywhere.

No doubt, these forms occupied a wide range of niches. It is therefore not surprising that they also exhibit a great deal of morphological variation, with overall sizes ranging from that of a medium-sized monkey to that of a good-sized chimp. Accurate reconstructions of overall body size are, however, quite difficult, since most of the fossil material consists only of jaws and teeth. Interpretations of this important series of fossil animals must therefore be based almost exclusively on dental criteria.

When we look at the teeth of the dryopiths, we see in all of them a definite hominoid pattern, but with a great deal of variation in specific traits. Dryopith teeth are characterized first of all by the Y-5 pattern, an arrangement of cusps in the lower molars also seen in modern hominoids (see Fig. 11-8). Most of the Miocene forms also have fairly large canines that overlap, the upper one occluding with a sectorial (cutting) first lower premolar. However, we must keep in mind that, while the features of canine size and shape of the first lower premolar are diagnostic in separating later hominids from pongids, they do not apply consistently in the Miocene; the fossil sample is too variable for the uniform application of such simplistic criteria. We also must remember that it is crucial to distinguish those characteristics that are found in a

Figure 11-9   Overlapping canines and sectorial lower first premolar. (Shown here in a macaque.)

*What to call the Miocene hominoids? A proliferation of names has been suggested for group 1: Dryopithecidae, Dryopithecinae, Dryopithecini, dryopithecines, dryomorphs, and dryopiths; and, for group 2: Sivapithecinae, Sivapithecini, sivapithecines, Ramapithecidae, Ramapithecinae, Ramapithecini, ramapithecines, ramamorphs, and ramapiths. In two earlier editions of this book, in fact, we have used two different sets of terms. Not everyone at this point is going to be completely satisfied with any of these terms. Here we follow the suggestion of Russell Ciochon (1983) and use "dryopith" and "ramapith" as descriptive, short, and taxonomically unloaded referents.

primitive state in an evolutionary lineage (and, therefore, potentially representative of common ancestral stock of forms that diverge later) from *derived* characteristics found only in particular offshoots (and, therefore, representative of forms that have already diverged).

Many of the presumed distinguishing features argued as evidence of "pongid" or "hominid" affinities for Miocene fossils are, in fact, primitive characteristics of hominoids in general. Whereas dryopith cranial remains are known from only a few discoveries, there is fortunately one splendidly preserved skull found in 1948 by Mary Leakey on an island in Lake Victoria, Kenya. Quite generalized in structure, it is monkeylike in many ways. In any case, this skull does not exhibit any of the structural specializations (such as large jaws, face, and muscle attachment areas) found in modern pongids.

A few pieces of dryopith limb skeleton have also been found, including several parts of the postcranial skeleton of an individual found in Kenya (Walker and Pickford, 1983). Including most of the limb bones, several cranial and jaw fragments, and a few vertebrae and ribs, these remains from Rusinga Island are the most complete of any Miocene hominoid individual (and among the most complete for the entire primate fossil record until fairly recent times). From that well-preserved skeleton, it is possible to accurately estimate the body size of the animal, which turns out to be about that of a male colobus monkey (i.e., around 24 pounds). Detailed analysis of the forelimb and preliminary study of other skeletal parts suggest this was a fairly generalized quadruped. Earlier interpretations have indicated that this dryopith was a brachiator, potential knuckle-walker, a ceboidlike quadruped, or a cercopithecoidlike quadruped (Greenfield, 1980). The most reasonable inference is that this small hominoid was probably an arboreal quadruped (Morbeck, 1975) with some suspensory abilities (Fleagle, 1983).

Such attempts to reconstruct the feeding or locomotory behavior of fossil animals like the dryopiths are made through comparisons with modern primates and their observed structural/functional relationships (see p. 256). However, we must be extremely cautious in applying such models too grossly to fossil animals, for they may not closely resemble the behavior of *any* contemporary primate. In our attempts to reconstruct the behavior of earlier primates, therefore, we must be careful not to obscure the uniqueness of the very animals we seek to understand.

A lack of appreciation of the structural (and presumably ecological) uniqueness found in many fossil primates has characterized recent interpretations of Miocene hominoids. It was once thought that dryopiths were clearly pongid and therefore in a direct evolutionary line leading to modern great apes and separate from that leading to hominids. While dryopiths resemble pongids in a few dental traits, they are all in all a quite varied lot, in most characteristics unlike *any* living hominoid (hominid or pongid). We should remember that using modern hominoids as models for those in the Miocene does not really provide a broad basis for comparison—only three genera of great apes (with perhaps only four species) and only one genus and one species of hominid now exist. It might well be that none of these provide a valid model for the behavior of the whole array of ecologically diverse hominoids of the Miocene. To look at these fossil animals and expect to assign them into neat categories, such as hominid and pongid, is much too simplistic. Our fossil

(a)

(b)

Figure 11-10 (a) *Proconsul africanus* skull. Discovered by Mary Leakey in 1948. (From early Miocene deposits on Rusinga Island, Kenya.) (b) A modern gorilla skull. By way of contrast, note the more projecting face, larger teeth, and more robust muscle attachments in the modern pongid.

(a) Chimpanzee   (b) P. africanus

Figure 11-11 Reconstructed upper limb of *P. africanus* compared to modern chimpanzee, (a) Chimpanzee; (b) *P. africanus*. (© 1959 by W. E. Le Gros Clark).

sample almost certainly includes members of several evolving **lineages**; some of these are probably closely related to ancestors of living primates, but most of them are probably on extinct sidebranches of hominoid evolution. The complexity of the evolutionary process demands that we not think in overly simple terms, and we should thus conceive of our evolutionary history as an intricate "bush" instead of a simple "ladder" (Gould, 1976b).

Only in terms of this more complex framework can we understand the Miocene dryopiths. For example, anthropologists once postulated that dryopiths were pongids on the basis of shape of their **dental arcade**. Unlike hominids, and resembling modern great apes, they presumably possess *parallel* tooth rows, and, in fact, some dryopiths do seem to have such a dental arcade. But most of them have tooth rows that diverge in back, unlike the parallel rows of modern great apes or the parabolic row of modern humans. The shape of the dental arcade in modern chimps and gorillas is an obvious derived characteristic seen primarily in relatively recent pongids. The same can be said of the *parabolic* row for hominids. Therefore, neither kind of tooth row tells us much about dryopith relationships.

Much of the variation seen in dryopiths can be accounted for by time (15 million years of evolution) as well as geography. The earliest and most generalized dryopiths are found in East Africa. Many primatologists, recognizing that these East African forms lack many of the derived characteristics seen in later dryopiths, have referred them to a separate genus (*Proconsul* for the early East African forms, contrasted to *Dryopithecus* for the later, more derived ones from Europe).

One general set of ecological adaptations does appear, however, to tie the dryopiths together: all are forest-adapted, primarily arboreal, and probably mostly fruit-eating (frugivorous) (Pilbeam, 1979). Given this type of adaptation, migration from area to area would require a relatively continuous forest. Ecological reconstructions of the Miocene world prior to 17 m.y.a. suggest that forests were quite widespread, thus providing the opporunity for migration within East Africa. How dryopiths were able to cross the Afro-Eurasian land bridge once climatic cooling began is still a mystery.

During the Middle Miocene, with this climatic cooling, considerable shrinkage of forested areas occurred. Consequently, further isolation of regional dryopith populations would have been promoted. The next time we pick up

Figure 11-12 Dental rows: Ape parallel arcade compared to human parabolic pattern. (a) Gorilla; (b) human.

(a) Gorilla   (b) Human

the threads of dryopith evolution is in Western Europe (Germany, Austria, France, Spain) several million years later (after 15 m.y.a.). We still do not know how these later, as-yet-fragmentary fossils are linked to the earlier, primitive dryopiths from East Africa.

On the other hand, as we have pointed out, with the shrinkage of forests, more open kinds of environments expanded, particularly woodland/forest fringe niches. Those hominoids already preadapted for exploitation of these environments would then have had considerably more evolutionary opportunities than was true previously.

Interestingly, it is at about this time (14–10 m.y.a.) that varieties of more ground-living hominoids began to diversify in several parts of the Old World. It is to this group, the ramapiths, that we now turn.

RAMAPITHS

The other major subgrouping of Miocene hominoids is the ramapiths, a highly successful and widely distributed group of species. In fact, except for later species of the genus *Homo* (in the last million years only), ramapiths were the most widely distributed hominoids that ever existed. The time range for these forms goes back at least 14 m.y. in East Africa, and they probably are also that old in Pakistan and Turkey.

The evidence for the earliest ramapith may go even further back. A newly discovered 16–18 m.y. old fossil, including pieces of the jaws and face, was uncovered in 1983 at Buluk in northern Kenya by Richard Leakey and Alan Walker (Lewin, 1983). The animal, apparently the size of a male chimp, is thought by Walker to be closely aligned with the Asian varieties of ramapiths we are about to discuss. If so, this would be the earliest representative of this group. Somewhat later (around 14 m.y.a.), again from Kenya, is another site (possibly there is a third as well) that also has some fragmentary pieces similar to ramapiths. In any case, these do not conform to the dryopith pattern we have described.

The prime evidence for the ramapith group, however, comes from Eurasia. Geographically, then, we have an interesting dichotomy: While dryopiths are mostly known from Africa, ramapiths are better known from Eurasia.

In recent years, these Eurasian ramapiths have been uncovered in several areas in remarkable abundance. As we noted on page 339, Lufeng in southern China (*circa* 8 m.y.a.) has yielded over 1,000 teeth as well as 5 partial crania. In addition, upwards of 50 individuals have been recovered from the Potwar Plateau (7–13.5 m.y.a.) in the Siwalik Hills of Pakistan (plus several more individuals recovered over several years from the Indian side of the Siwaliks). Included in the superb Pakistani collection is a multitude of mandibles (15 in all, some of which are nearly intact) many postcranial remains, and a recently discovered partial cranium, including most of the face (Pilbeam et al., 1977; Pilbeam, 1982). While not as productive as those in China and Pakistan, other sites in Western Asia and Europe have also recently added to the harvest. More than 20 individuals have been recovered from 3 sites in Turkey (12–13 + ? m.y.a.), and a similar yield has been excavated from the Rudabánya Mountains of Hungary (less than 11 m.y.a.?) (Morbeck, 1983). Finally, at least 12 or possibly 13 individuals have been found in northern Greece near Salonika (10–12 m.y.a.).

Lineage
An evolutionary line of phylogenetically related forms.

Dental arcade
The shape of the tooth row.

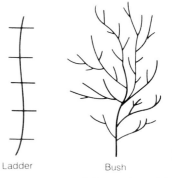

Ladder · Bush

Figure 11-13 Two phylogenetic models: A simple ladder versus a complex bush.

The earliest firmly dated ramapiths in Eurasia are from the lower beds at the Potwar Plateau, estimated minimumly at 13 m.y.a. (Raza, et al., 1983). The earliest sites in Turkey *may* also be this old, or even older (Kay and Simons, 1983). In any case, it is quite clear that no ramapiths (or any hominoid) are found anywhere in Eurasia until after the docking of the African plate with the Eurasian land mass around 16 m.y.a. (see p. 338). Once established, the ramapiths apparently lasted quite a long time, surviving in Pakistan up until about 7 m.y.a.

Dispersed over thousands of miles and over at least 7 million years of time, it is no wonder that ramapiths are quite variable. Indeed, several different species have been suggested, some in just the last year. As we'll see later in this chapter, such interpretations can be a biological minefield. Here, then, we will primarily concentrate on the more general morphological and ecological characteristics and limit our taxonomic conclusions to some genus-level considerations.

The ramapiths differ morphologically from the dryopiths in their dentition and facial anatomy. The front teeth, especially the central incisors, are often quite large, while the canine is fairly good-sized (low-crowned and robust) (Andrews, 1983). In general, the canines are large compared to what we see in humans (and earlier hominids) but are not as big as they are in the large (male) extant apes (Kay and Simons, 1983). There are, however, large discrepancies in canine size among different ramapith individuals, partly because some species were bigger overall, but also because there was apparently considerable variation (sexual dimorphism) within the same species. In fact, in body size, some ramapiths were apparently as dimorphic as modern gorillas and orangs (Andrews, 1983).

The first lower premolar is also quite variable in shape. Usually, it is fairly sectorial; that is, it shows the shearing surface typical in most catarrhines (consequently, this is most likely to be the primitive condition). In some cases, however, an accessory cusp displays enlargement, perhaps either as a precursor to the derived condition seen in hominids (Kay and Simons, 1983) or as a separate evolutionary parallelism between these ramapiths and our line (Ciochon, 1983).

The most distinctive part of the dentition of ramapiths may be seen in the back tooth row, where the molars are large, flat-wearing, and thick-enameled (in some species, the enamel is heavily wrinkled as well). The thickness of the enamel cap has played a most significant role in recent interpretations of Miocene hominoid evolution. Among living hominoids, relative to body size, humans have by far the thickest molar caps. Gorillas and chimps have thin enamel, *but* orang molars could be described as moderately thick (Ward and Pilbeam, 1983). Thick (in fact, very thick) enamel is also seen in early hominids (in the period 1–4 m.y.a.).

As a characteristic, thick enamel in the ramapiths could then be seen as a derived feature linking them specifically with either orangs or hominids. A third possibility is that thick enamel is the *primitive* condition in large-bodied hominoids, with orangs and humans maintaining a more primitive expression, while chimps and gorillas are more derived.

Again, we have a thorny problem in attempting to establish the direction (polarity) of primitive-derived character transformation. Since our evolutionary reconstructions are ultimately based on such interpretations, the conclusions are less than clearcut. More on this presently.

Probably, the most characteristic anatomical aspects of the ramapiths are seen in the face, especially the area immediately below the nose (Ward and Kimbel, 1983). Facial remains from Pakistan, Greece, and Hungary have concave profiles and projecting incisors (and, overall, remarkably resemble the modern orang). In particular, the partial cranium discovered in 1980 at the Potwar Plateau (Pakistan, *circa* 8 m.y.a.) and published two years later (Pilbeam, 1982) bears striking similarities to the orangutan (see Fig. 11-14). The published description of this specimen, with illustrations similar to those shown here, had a tremendous impact on paleoanthropology. As we have seen (p. 263), biochemical evidence demonstrates the distinctiveness of the orang from the African apes and humans; here, then, was fossil evidence suggesting some ancient Asian traces of the orang lineage. As a result, the views of biochemists and paleoanthropologists agree more closely (pp. 353–354).

Many earlier fossil-based interpretations of ramapith evolutionary affinities had, of course, to be reevaluated. As we hinted at the beginning of our discussion of Miocene hominoids (p. 338), in the 1960s E. L. Simons and David Pilbeam suggested a Middle Miocene ramapith hominoid as the first hominid (i.e., clearly diverged on our particular line and separate from that leading to

(a)

(b)

Figure 11-14 Comparison of *Sivapithecus* cranium (center) with modern chimpanzee (left) and orangutan (right). The *Sivapithecus* fossil is specimen, GSP 15000 from the Potwar Plateau, Pakistan, *c.* 8 m.y.a. (*a*) lateral view; (*b*) frontal view.

Sivapithecus
(Shiv'-ah-pith-eh-kus)

any extant ape). According to this view, this early hominid was *Ramapithecus*—known at that time mostly from India, with some bits from East Africa.

We have already illustrated some of the dramatic new discoveries of the 1970s and early 1980s. As a consequence of these new discussions, the earlier suggestion that *Ramapithecus* was a definite hominid was seriously questioned, if not rejected altogether. One primary advocate of this revised view is David Pilbeam (1977; 1982), an initial architect of the earlier widely accepted theory. Pilbeam, who has led the highly successful paleoanthropological project at the Potwar Plateau, has been swayed by the new fossils recovered there and elsewhere. These more complete specimens (like that shown in Fig. 11-14) have been placed in the genus **Sivapithecus**.

A variety of other generic terms have also been put forward for other ramapiths (see Table 11-1) but, except for *Gigantopithecus* (discussed shortly), most of these can easily be accommodated within *Sivapithecus*. What about *Ramapithecus*? The strong consensus among primatologists is that this genus is also really part of *Sivapithecus*, although most probably a separate species (Greenfield, 1979; Ward and Pilbeam, 1983; Kay and Simons, 1983; Corruccini and Ciochon, 1983).

If *Sivapithecus* can be placed in—or at least close to—the lineage of modern orangs, what becomes of the assertion that "Ramapithecus" (now part of the same evolutionary group, or "clade") is an early hominid? Many researchers, seeing distinctive oranglike derived features in these Miocene fossils, would now reject this claim (Ward and Pilbeam, 1983; Cronin, 1983; Andrews, 1983).

Paleontologists are far from unanimous in this determination. The other primary exponent of the "Ramapithecus as hominid" hypothesis, E. L. Simons (with his colleague Richard Kay), believes that *Sivapithecus*—into which they have "sunk" *Ramapithecus*—shows many derived hominid features. They point particularly to aspects of the dentition they consider hominidlike and argue that other dental/facial similarities with orangs resulted from evolutionary parallelisms. They conclude that *Sivapithecus* is already a hominid (basically, this is the same theory proposed much earlier; however, where before we had *Ramapithecus*, we now read *Sivapithecus*).

A third alternative also exists: *Sivapithecus* may not already have diverged in the orang *or* the hominid direction. Perhaps it was a common ancestor for all later large-bodied hominoids—the Asian forms (orang) and the African ones (gorilla, chimp, and human). This view would then emphasize that

Table 11-1   Some Suggested Names for Miocene Ramapith Forms

Name	Locality
Ramapithecus	India/Pakistan
Sivapithecus	India/Pakistan
Kenyapithecus (usually sunk into *Ramapithecus*)	Kenya
Bodvapithecus	Hungary
Rudapithecus	Hungary
Ouranopithecus	Greece
Gigantopithecus	India/Pakistan (Pleistocene species from China)

many features of ramapith (and probably also orang) morphology, such as enamel thickness, lower face morphology, etc., are simply primitive expressions of the ancestral hominoid condition. The African hominoids would then be seen as the more derived forms (Wolpoff, 1983; Greenfield, 1983).

We have, then, three possible alternatives for interpreting the evolutionary relationships of most of the Miocene ramapiths (i.e., *Sivapithecus*):

1. *Sivapithecus* is already on the orang line, not specifically related to any of the other hominoids. This suggests that the Asian/African hominoid divergence occurred prior to 14 m.y.a. From this assertion, no direct claim is made on when hominids originated from African hominoid stock, but the implication is considerably after 14 m.y.a. (quite comfortably, after 10 m.y.a., in fact).

2. *Sivapithecus* is specifically on the hominid line. This suggests that orangs must have diverged considerably earlier than 15 m.y.a., while hominids and African apes (gorillas and chimps) must have been diverging at about that time (or a little earlier).

3. *Sivapithecus* is a possible common ancestor of all large-bodied hominoids—orangs, chimps, gorillas, and humans. The split leading to orangs is thus seen as occurring within the ramapith "complex," somewhere between 10–15 m.y.a. The hominid/African ape split, then, is later yet (5–6 m.y.a.?).

Among knowledgeable primate paleontologists familiar with the original fossil material, one can find support for each of these three interpretations. It is thus easy to say, "more fossil material is needed to decide." However, one can *always* say that. Thanks to the spectacular successes of the last decade, we now have a wealth of hominoid fossils, including hundreds of teeth, several partial crania, dozens of jaws, etc. More fossil evidence is not likely to add substantially to the picture already emerging. In fact, more concrete interpretations of the Miocene hominoids have not come solely from additional fossils; sophistication of analysis, especially the sorting out of primitive/derived character states, has also contributed. We still have a way to go, though, in order to establish precisely which are the primitive, and which the derived, characteristics of hominoids.

For now, the first alternative on our list seems to us to be the best-supported interpretation, with the third somewhat less likely. New fossil material (especially facial remains), along with biochemical findings, indicate the second alternative to be the least probable.

Paleoecology of Sivapithecus   Of course, what *everyone* would like to know about *Sivapithecus* is: To whom is it related? We have just taken our best shot at that difficult question. Another fascinating research effort involves reconstructing the way of life of this early hominoid and speculating upon factors that influenced its evolution.

For example, what were these ramapiths eating? By referring to certain structural/functional analogs seen in modern primates, investigators have postulated a diet that correlates with ramapith dental structure. This diet is thought to chiefly include tough hard morsels, such as seeds, which some believe were exploited primarily on the ground (Jolly, 1970).

A more comprehensive comparison of a wide variety of living primates, however, reveals ramapith dental parallels (especially larger, flat-wearing, more thickly enameled molars) among several arboreal species eating nuts, seeds, and hard fruits found in the trees (Kay, 1981). Thus, ramapith dental features quite possibly could have originated in an arboreal setting. Most researchers attempting to reconstruct the paleoecology of the ramapiths, however, assume that, eventually, ramapiths did take greater advantage of terrestrial environments than their dryopith cousins. Evidence from Eurasian sites (Potwar Plateau, Lufeng, Rudabánya) suggests that ramapiths lived in environments exhibiting greater seasonality than the tropics (where most dryopiths lived). Consequently, fruits would not have been available all year long, and ramapiths could not have been primarily frugivorous (i.e., fruit-eaters) (Andrews, 1983).

Moreover, within these environments, there was less continuous forest vegetation, with more woodland/bushland mosaic niches. These changes

Figure 11-16   Two ramapith mandibles from the Potwar Plateau, Pakistan. Discovered in 1976 and 1977. Approximate age, 9 m.y.

were further stimulated by a general cooling of the earth's climate, after about 16 m.y.a. (see p. 339). Such a niche, being ecologically poor, is no place to find a primate. It is hypothesized, therefore, that ramapiths may have been environmental "opportunists," analogous to bears and pigs, exploiting below-ground resources, such as roots and tubers.

Utilization of nonarboreal resources would, of course, require some ground-living. Ramapiths are generally larger-bodied than dryopiths, a fact which could argue for greater terrestriality. Of course, body size varied greatly (some individuals may have exceeded 150 pounds) largely as a result of marked sexual dimorphism (Andrews, 1983).

Some such environmental adaptation did, indeed, prove successful for the ramapiths—witness their longevity and geographic dispersal. If ramapiths were such successful opportunists, what spelled their doom? No single answer suffices. Perhaps heightened competition from the extremely successful Old World monkeys (some of these were also becoming partly terrestrial) played a part. Also, in the later Miocene, recall that the environment continued to change. Further cooling and drying probably isolated some groups and may often have critically reduced effective breeding population size (see p. 128). As a part of this ongoing dessication process, the Mediterranean and Black Seas dried up (very late Miocene—approximately 6.5 m.y.a.) and there was further cooling in adjacent seas. To the north, in Eurasia, the challenges must have been harsh. With the exception of pockets in the more tropical areas of southern Asia, no hominoids (except *Gigantopithecus*—see the following section) apparently survived here beyond the Miocene.

To the south, in Africa, things were to be different. The African apes and hominids had diverged (or were about to), and within the still-changing (and probably more seasonal) environments of Africa, our family—the hominids— originated. The story that followed comprises the remainder of this book.

Gigantopithecus   Evidence exists for another and very distinctive ramapith that can trace its origins back into the Miocene. This highly unusual primate, called *Gigantopithecus*, came to the attention of scientists in a most unusual way. For centuries, Chinese folk medicine has prescribed the use of ground "dragon bones" in the concoction of various potions. The source of many of these bones was fossil sites and, from there, these dragon bones often found their way into Chinese apothecaries (drugstores). It was in such an establishment that the first *Gigantopithecus* teeth were recognized in 1935 by Ralph van Koenigswald, a young German paleontologist on the lookout for important fossil remains.

Since the 1930s, more than 1,000 individual teeth have been collected (largely from apothecaries). Three lower jaws were archeologically excavated in China in the 1950s, and one was recovered in northern India in 1968. The Indian specimen is clearly the oldest of the lot, falling in the late Miocene (5 m.y.–9 m.y.), while the Chinese material belongs to the Middle Pleistocene (500,000 y.a.–1 m.y.a.).

Truly an animal to titillate the imagination, *Gigantopithecus* was apparently a huge hominoid. It was named for the enormous proportions of its teeth and jaws (all that is preserved of the animal), and estimates place its weight in excess of 600 pounds and its stature somewhere between 6 and 9

Figure 11-17   A Chinese apothecary, or drugstore.

Figure 11-18 *Gigantopithecus* III mandible (left) compared to modern gorilla. This *Gigantopithecus* mandible is by far the largest hominoid jaw ever discovered.

Allometric growth
The process of differential growth whereby some parts of the body grow proportionately more than others.

Figure 11-19 *Gigantopithecus* mandible, occlusal view. Note that the canines (circled) are worn flat.

feet! (Simons and Ettel, 1970). Such estimates may, however, be somewhat exaggerated. Differential patterns of growth (called **allometric growth**) probably produced different body proportions in this extinct animal from those seen in living hominoids (Johnson, 1979). Some postcranial bones found in the Potwar Plateau (Miocene), which may belong to a *Gigantopithecus* form, support a smaller size estimate. From these data, it has been suggested that *Gigantopithecus* weighed about the same as a small female gorilla (equivalent to 150 pounds) (Pilbeam, 1979).

Numerous dental characteristics clearly establish *Gigantopithecus* as a ramapith hominoid, and some superficial features even appear hominidlike. However, these similarities are apparently functional analogies associated with heavy back tooth grinding and do not represent particularly close evolutionary relationships (that is, homologies). In fact, *Gigantopithecus* exhibits some rather unusual features, such as flat-worn canines, apparently heavily used as grinding teeth. Such a situation is unusual among primates (a similar pattern may also be present in *Sivapithecus*), and even the peglike incisors may have been used in mastication of heavy vegetation. Although some investigators have speculated that *Gigantopithecus* may be closely related to our particular evolutionary line (Weidenreich, 1946; Frayer, 1973; Gelvin, 1980), sophisticated statistical analysis has confirmed the unique status of this fossil form (Corruccini, 1975a).

Despite these findings, rather bizarre notions concerning this fossil still abound. Indeed, Soviet scientists have gone so far as to speculate the unsubstantiated "abominable snowman" as a descendant, and newspaper accounts tell of Soviet-led expeditions into the frozen heights of the Himalayas to find proof!

More conservative research has centered on reconstructions of what *Gigantopithecus* ecologically was "doing for a living." Apparently, its niche was a mixed one in China, probably consisting primarily of forest-type environments, while the earlier species lived in a more open environment in India (Simons and Ettel, 1970). Just what *Gigantopithecus* was chewing in its huge jaws is still a mystery, but apparently it consisted of enormous amounts of vegetable foods. There are many structural analogies between the teeth of

◇ Box 11-1   Timing the Hominid-Pongid Split

One of the most fundamental of all questions in human evolution is: When did the hominid line originate? Or, to put it another way: When did we last share a common ancestry with our closest living relatives, the pongids?

Scientists have taken different perspectives in attempting to answer this question. The traditional approach of paleontology is still the most common. Recent years have produced considerably more paleontological sophistication through a vast new array of fossil material, more precise chronometric dating, and more rigorous interpretation of primitive-derived characteristics. Still, the fossil record remains incomplete, and significant gaps exist for some of the most crucial intervals. So the question still persists: How old is the hominid line?

Data drawn from a completely different perspective have also been applied to this problem. Popularized by Vincent Sarich and Allan Wilson of the University of California, Berkeley (1967), this perspective utilizes comparisons of living animals. By calibrating the overall immunological reactions of proteins from different species, by sequencing the amino acids within proteins, or by doing DNA hybridization (see pp. 263–264), living species can be compared to each other.

Certainly, such data are immensely valuable in demonstrating *relative* genetic distances among contemporary organisms (as we discussed in Chapter 9). However, proponents of this view go considerably further and postulate that biochemical distance can be used directly to calculate evolutionary distance. In other words, a "molecular clock" is thought to provide unambiguous divergence dates for a host of evolutionary lineages, including hominids/pongids (Sarich, 1971).

Several hotly disputed assumptions are required, however, to perform this feat. Most importantly, the rate of molecular evolution must be constant over time. Such regularity could be accomplished if mutations were strictly *neutral* (see p. 108) or if selection pressures remained constant. Since environmental changes are decidedly not constant through time, the latter assumption is not valid. As for the first point, while neutral mutations certainly do occur (and perhaps do so quite frequently), many researchers are not convinced that most mutations are neutral (e.g., see Livingstone, 1980). Moreover, even if mutation was mostly neutral, major evolutionary shifts may still be quite nongradual in tempo—given the suggested punctuated mode of change (see p. 109).

Another possible complicating factor concerns generation length. Those species that reproduce in shorter periods of time should (according to strict application of the molecular clock) show, for the same period of time, greater amounts of molecular evolution than more slowly reproducing forms (Vogel, et al., 1976). Given the variation in generation lengths, it is not justifiable to make strict linear reconstruction for divergence times among prosimians, monkeys, and hominoids.

Another problem is that there is no certain indicator of molecular evolutionary rates; different proteins yield significantly different rates of evolution and thus greatly influence inferences about divergence times (Corruccini et al., 1980). In fact, the *greatest* margin of error would occur in attempting to calculate relatively recent evolutionary events—for example, the hominid-pongid split.

Analysis of amino acid sequences of proteins by another group of biochemists (at Wayne State University in Detroit) has confirmed that, indeed, rates of molecular evolution are not constant, but are rather characterized by periods of acceleration and deceleration (the latter being particularly true in the last few million years). Thus, these researchers conclude: "For proteins demonstrating striking shifts in rates of amino acid substitutions over time, it is not possible to calculate accurate divergence dates within Anthropoidea using the molecular clock approach. Our analysis of amino acid sequence data of several proteins by the clock model yields divergence dates, particularly within the Hominoidea, that are far too recent in view of well-established fossil evidence" (Goodman et al., 1983, p. 68).

As a result of such criticisms of the "clock," some paleontologists have been skeptical of its claimed applications. For example, Milford Wolpoff (of the University of Michigan) argues that, "Probably the best way to summarize the very disparate points raised is that the 'clock' simply *should not* work" (Wolpoff, 1983a, p. 661).

Naturally, not everyone takes so negative a view of the clock approach. Vincent Sarich continues to believe firmly in its basic accuracy (when applied correctly) and, justifiably, feels vindicated by recent recalibrations of theories derived from fossil evidence, which bring them closer to the biochemically derived hypotheses.

The fossils themselves are not going to provide the whole answer. The paleontological record is usually too

(*continued on next page*)

◇ Box 11-1   Timing the Hominid-Pongid Split, continued

incomplete to provide clearcut ancestor-descendant associations. More fossils will always help, of course, but
the way we think about them (i.e., the questions we raise
about them) is also crucial in framing workable theories.

The biochemical perspective has been important in
that it has articulated key issues for evolutionary consideration (for example, the place of the orang in relation
to other large-bodied hominoids). The interplay between
the paleontological and biochemical perspectives has
thus been most productive. In fact, these viewpoints
agree more now on several aspects of hominoid evolu-

tion than they did just a few years ago. The greatest furor has been raised from overly strong claims for the
unique validity of either approach. We have shown in
this chapter that more fossil evidence *and* more controlled analyses have forced previous views to be reconsidered. Moreover, it is equally unfair to portray the clock
approach as a complete answer. As one of the leading
advocates of this method has recently stated, "The clock
is one of an approximate, not metronomically perfect nature" (Cronin, 1983, p. 116).

Gigantopithecus and that of the bamboo-shoot-eating giant panda. An animal
having the bulk of *Gigantopithecus* would have required a huge masticatory
apparatus with large, grinding teeth and heavy jaws. And this picture is
exactly the one that we envision, even to the extreme point of including the
front teeth in this functional complex.

In addition to the apparent specialization of this animal, *Gigantopithecus*
would seem an unlikely close relative of hominids, for it survived so late—
up to the Middle Pleistocene in China. Long before this time, definite hominids had been diverging, and by the Middle Plesitocene they were already
closely approximating modern humans in such features as body size and
teeth.

Therefore, it seems likely that *Gigantopithecus* diverged from other hominoids in the middle-late Miocene, set out on a specialized evolutionary path,
and eventually became extinct in the Middle Pleistocene.

MIOCENE HOMINOIDS: SUMMARY

Firm judgments concerning the diverse array of Miocene hominoids cannot
yet be made, but it is apparent that the evolutionary picture is a good deal
more complex than previously thought. In this regard, it is interesting to note
that David Pilbeam, a proponent of the earlier simplistic view, has recently
altered his opinions. Many of his current views are reflected in the interpretations given here.

There are probably at least three distinct genera of hominoids by mid-
Miocene times, with a multitude of species. Most, if not all, of these forms
are filling niches not strictly analogous to any living hominoid, and our
interpretation must not obscure the evolutionary uniqueness these animals
no doubt possessed.

Ideally, we would like to draw conclusions concerning how these Miocene
hominoids are related to extant apes and to ourselves. The earlier, quite

uncomplicated suggestions just have not worked out, as Pilbeam has noted: "We know enough now to realize that our earlier and simple scenarios were too simple, though not enough yet to choose among a variety of more complex ones" (Pilbeam, 1977, p. 3).

Presently, we cannot trace with any certainty the hominid lineage or that of the African apes back to any of these Miocene forms. The orang, however, may well share close relationship with some of the Asian ramapiths.

It would thus be fair to say, on the basis of current evidence, that not all possible evolutionary scenarios are equally probable. The placement and frequency of question marks in Figure 11-20 reflect this fact.

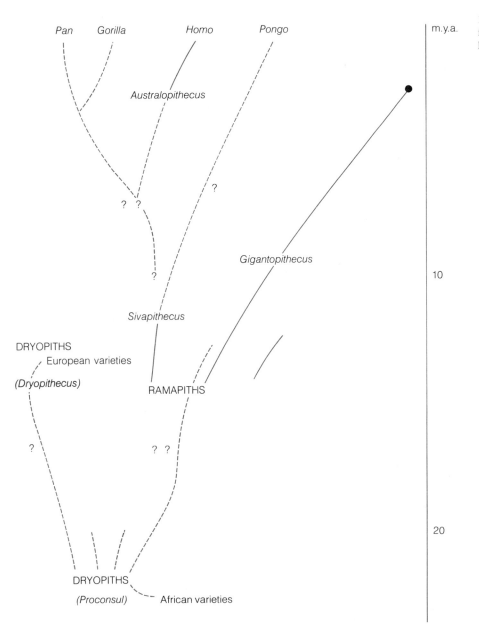

Figure 11-20 A provisional model showing possible relationships of Miocene and later hominoids.

◇ The Meaning of Genus and Species

Our discussion of fossil primates has introduced a multitude of cumbersome taxonomic names. We should pause at this point and reasonably ask: Why use so many names like *Sivapithecus*, *Ramapithecus*, and *Gigantopithecus*? What does such naming mean in evolutionary terms?

Our goal when applying genus, species, or other taxonomic labels to groups of organisms is to make meaningful biological statements about the variation that is present. When looking at populations of living or long extinct animals, we are assuredly going to see the presence of variation. This situation is true of *any* sexually reproducing organism due to the factors of recombination (as independent assortment and crossing-over—see Chapter 3). As a result of recombination, each individual organism is a unique combination of genetic material, and this uniqueness is usually reflected to some extent in the phenotype. In addition to such *individual variation*, we see other kinds of systematic variation in all biological populations. *Age changes* certainly act to alter overall body size, as well as shape, in many animals. One pertinent example for fossil hominoid studies is the great change in number, size, and shape of teeth from deciduous (milk) teeth (only twenty present) to the permanent dentition (thirty-two present). It obviously would be a great error to assign two different fossil hominoids to different species *solely* on the basis of age-dependent dental criteria. If one were represented only by milk teeth and the other only by permanent teeth, they easily could be differently aged individuals of the *same* population.

Variation due to sex also plays an important role in influencing differences among individuals observed in biological populations. Differences in structural traits between males and females of the same population are called *sexual dimorphism*, and we have seen that great variation does exist between the sexes in some primates (for example, gorillas and baboons) in such elements as overall body size and canine size.

As we have seen when looking at body size differences, as well as differences in tooth size, among the ramapiths, a reasonable assumption is that what we are really viewing is simply the variations between males and females of the same species.

Keeping in mind all the types of variation present within interbreeding groups of organisms, the minimum biological category we would like to define in fossil primate samples is the *species*. As previously defined in Chapter 4, the species is biologically described as a group of interbreeding or potentially interbreeding organisms that are reproductively isolated from other such groups. In modern organisms, this concept is theoretically testable by observations of reproductive behavior. In animals long dead, such testing is obviously impossible. Therefore, in order to get a handle on the interpretation of variation seen in fossil groups like the ramapiths we must refer to living animals.

We know without doubt that variation is present. The question is: What is its biological significance? Two immediate choices occur: Either the variation is accounted for by individual, age, and sex differences seen within every biological species—**intraspecific**—or the variation present represents differences between reproductively isolated groups—**interspecific**. How do we judge between the alterntives intra- or interspecific? We clearly must refer to already defined groups where we can observe reproductive behavior; in other words, contemporary species.

If the amount of morphological variation observed in fossil samples is comparable with that seen today *within species of closely related forms*, then we should not "split" our sample into more than one species. We must, however, be careful in choosing our modern analogs, for rates of morphological evolution vary widely among different groups of mammals. In interpreting past primates, we do best when comparing them with well-known species of modern primates.

Our evolutionary interpretations of the vast array of variable Miocene hominoids is greatly simplified by adhering to relevant biological criteria:

1. First we must look at *all* relevant material. We are not justified in splitting fossil groups into several species on the basis of only presumed differences in the sample (Simons' and Pilbeam's contribution was a major step in rectifying this situation for Miocene hominoids).
2. We must statistically reconstruct the variation observed in our often very small fossil *samples* to realistic dimensions of actual biological *populations*. Every piece of every bone found is part of an individual, who in turn was part of a variable interbreeding population of organisms.
3. We then refer to known dimensions of variation in closely related groups of living primates, keeping in mind expected effects of age, sexual dimorphism, and individual variation.
4. Our next step is to extrapolate the results to the fossil sample and make the judgment: How many species are represented?
5. Since fossil forms are widely scattered in time, we also must place the different species within a firm chronology.
6. Finally, we would like to make interpretations (at least, educated guesses) concerning which forms are related to other forms as ancestors-descendants. To do this, we must pay strict attention to primitive as opposed to derived characteristics.

Following the above steps will greatly reduce the kind of useless confusion that has characterized hominoid studies for so long. We do not, however, wish to convey the impression that the biological interpretation of fossils into taxonomic categories is simple and unambiguous. Far from it! Many complexities must be recognized. Even in living groups, sharp lines between populations representing only one species and populations representing two or more species are difficult to draw. For example, a chain of integrating subspecies in gulls exchange genes at overlapping boundaries. However, at the terminal ends of the chain, two subspecies (species?) live side-by side along the coasts of Europe with little or no hybridization. In practice, isolating exactly where species boundaries begin and end is exceptionally difficult, especially in a dynamic situation like that represented by gulls.

In contexts dealing with extinct species, the uncertainties are even greater. In addition to the overlapping patterns of variation *over space*, variation also

Intraspecific
Within one species.

Interspecific
Between two or more species.

Figure 11-21   Circular overlap in gulls. A, B, C are subspecies of *Larus argentatus*. D (*L. glaucoides*) is a separate species. All along the chain subspecies interbreed (C1 with C2; C3 with C4, etc.) but at the terminal ends A2 lives side-by-side with B3 and B4 and does *not* interbreed. Where does one then draw species designations?

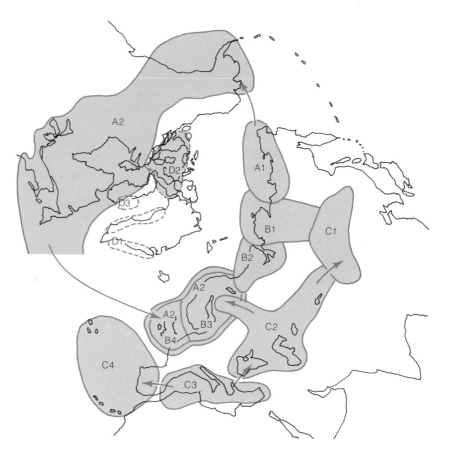

occurs *through time*. In other words, even more variation will be seen in such **paleospecies**, since individuals may be separated by thousands or even millions of years. Applying strict Linnaean taxonomy to such a situation presents an unavoidable dilemma. Standard Linnaean classification, designed to take account of the variation present at any given time, describes a static situation. However, when dealing with paleospecies we are often involved in great spans of time and thus with much additional variation.

Where do we establish meaningful species boundaries in such a dynamic situation? Often, our task is made easier because of the incompleteness of the fossil record. Quite frequently, fossil samples are separated by great gaps of time (as between A and C) and the morphological differences may therefore also be clearcut. In such a case, we feel quite comfortable calling these different species. But what about fossil populations (B, for example) that are intermediate in both time and morphology? This question has no easy answer. Any taxonomic designation in such a continuously evolving lineage is by necessity going to be arbitrary.

Such a line, which has no speciation events (see p. 107), is referred to as **monophyletic**. For such a lineage, many evolutionary biologists see no point in making separate species designations—that is, the entire line is seen as a single paleospecies (Eldredge and Cracraft, 1980). Many biologists believe, in

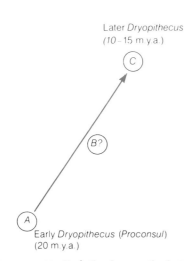

Later *Dryopithecus*
(10–15 m.y.a.)

Early *Dryopithecus* (*Proconsul*)
(20 m.y.a.)

Figure 11-22   Evolution in a continuing evolving lineage. Where does one designate the different species?

fact, that long, gradual transformations of this type are not the rule, but that branching (i.e., speciation) is much more typical of evolutionary change. (Once again, the view of the punctuationalists—see p. 109).

Moreover, it is imperative in evolutionary interpretation to understand ancestor-descendant relationships. Most paleontologists have traditionally made anatomical comparisons and then immediately constructed evolutionary trees (also called *phylogenies*). Recently, another perspective has been advanced. In this approach, a detailed interpretation of primitive versus derived states must first be explicitly stated. Only then can patterns of relationships be shown.

These are best interpreted in the form of a *cladogram* (a set of relationships shown as a hypothesis). In fact, usually several cladograms can be constructed from the same set of data. Those that are seen as most economically explaining the patterns of derived characteristics are then provisionally accepted, while less adequate ones are rejected. Such a perspective has been termed **cladistics**, and has injected a good deal more objectivity into paleontology (Eldredge and Cracraft, 1980). It must be pointed out, however, that not all paleontologists have accepted this approach. A basic assumption of cladistic analysis is that trait *patterns* are developed as the result of ancestor-descendant relationships and, conversely, that parallelism and convergence (see p. 234) have little import. In primate evolution, this assumption may not hold true; an analysis of morphological features in lemurs and lorises showed that 80% of the traits studied displayed some parallelism (Walker et al, 1981).

The next level of formal taxonomic classification, the *genus*, presents another problem. In order to have more than one genus, we obviously must have at least two species (reproductively isolated groups), and, in addition, the species must differ in a basic way. A genus is therefore defined as a group of species composed of members more closely related to each other than they are to species from another genus.

Grouping contemporary species together into genera is largely a subjective procedure wherein degree of relatedness becomes a strictly relative judgment. One possible test for contemporary animals is to check for results of hybridization between individuals of different species—rare in nature but quite common in captivity. If two normally separate species interbreed and produce live, though not necessarily fertile, offspring, this process shows genetically that they are not too distant and that they probably should be classified into a single genus. Well-known examples of such interspecific crosses within one genus are horses with donkeys (*Equus caballus* × *Equus asinus*) or lions with tigers (*Panthera leo* × *Panthera tigris*). In both these cases, the close morphological and evolutionary similarities between these species are confirmed by their occasional ability to produce live hybrids.

As mentioned, we cannot perform breeding experiments with animals that are extinct, but another definition of genus becomes highly relevant. Species that are members of one genus share the same broad adaptive zone or, in Sewall Wright's terminology (Mayr, 1962), a similar "adaptive plateau." What this represents is a general ecological life style more basic than the particular ecological niches characteristic of species. This ecological definition of genus can be an immense aid in interpreting fossil primates. Teeth are the most

Paleospecies
A group of organisms from different time periods classified within the same species.

Monophyletic
mono: one
phyletic: line of evolutionary descent

Cladistics
The school of evolutionary biology that seeks to make ancestral-descendant hypotheses through interpreting patterns of primitive/derived characteristics.

Figure 11-23 Cladograms. Three alternative statements representing ancestral-descendant relationships among three taxa. (a) C diverges earliest, with A and B sharing a more recent common ancestor; (b) B diverges earliest, with A and C sharing a more recent common ancestor; (c) A diverges earliest, with B and C sharing a more recent common ancestor.

often preserved parts, and they are usually excellent general ecological indicators.

Therefore, if among the Miocene hominoids some animals appear to inhabit different adaptive/ecological zones (for example *Proconsul* vs. *Sivapithecus* vs. *Gigantopithecus*), we are justified in postulating more than one genus present.

Operationally, then, categorization at the genus level becomes the most practical biological interpretation of fragmentary extinct forms. While species differences necessarily were also present (probably in great complexity), these are usually too intricate to recognize in incomplete material.

As a final comment, we should point out that classification by genus is also not always a clearcut business. Indeed, the argument among primate biologists over whether the chimp and gorilla represent one genus (*Pan troglodytes, Pan gorilla*) or two different genera (*Pan troglodytes, Gorilla gorilla*) demonstrate that even with living, breathing animals the choices are not always clear.

◇ Summary

In this chapter, we have traced the evolutionary history of our primate origins between 70 and 10 m.y.a. Beginning in the late Cretaceous, the earliest primate ancestors are probably little more than arboreally adapted insectivores. In the Paleocene, we begin to see more definite primate trends in such animals as *Plesiadapis*, but there are still numerous "primitive" characteristics present in these forms. In the following epoch, the Eocene, we begin to see an abundant diversification of primates of modern aspect. During this epoch, the lemurlike adapids and early ancestors of tarsiers begin their evolutionary radiation. Early anthropoid origins probably also date to sometime in the late Eocene. In addition, Old and New World primates apparently shared their last common ancestry in the Eocene or early Oligocene and have gone their separate ways ever since.

In the Old World, the Oligocene reveals a large number of possible early anthropoid ancestors at the Fayum. By and large, all these are primtive Old World anthropoids, and none of the modern lineages (Old World monkeys, gibbons, large-bodied hominoids) can definitely be traced into the Oligocene.

The Miocene reveals an abundant and complex array of hominoid forms that sort into an early African group (the dryopiths) and a later, mostly Asian group (the ramapiths). The best known of these Miocene hominoids—at least through abundance of recent discoveries—is the ramapith *Sivapithecus*. While again there is little firm evidence tying these fossil forms to extant apes or ourselves, some tentative evidence suggests that *Sivapithecus* is closely related to the ancestors of the orang. Where, then, are the ancestors of the African apes or, even more relevantly, of ourselves? In the next six chapters, we will seek to answer this question.

◇ Questions for Review

1. Why is it difficult to distinguish the earliest members of the primate order from other placental mammals? If you found a nearly complete skeleton of an early Paleocene mammal, what structural traits might lead you to believe it was a primate?

2. Compare the fossil primates of the Paleocene and Eocene with living members of the primate order.

3. Why did so many prosimians become extinct at the end of the Eocene? Discuss the alternative explanations critically.

4. If you (as an expert physical anthropologist) were brought remains of a purported 30 m.y. fossil hominoid from South America, why might you be skeptical?

5. What kinds of primates were evolving at the Fayum in Oligocene times? What is meant by saying they are primitive catarrhines?

6. Compare and contrast the anatomical features of dryopiths and ramapiths.

7. Discuss the three alternative interpretations of the evolutionary affinities of *Sivapithecus*.

8. How did the shifting of the earth's plates, as well as climatic changes, affect hominoid evolution in the Miocene?

9. What kind of primate was *Gigantopithecus*, and why is it an unlikely hominid ancestor?

10. If two fossil groups are classified as *Sivapithecus indicus* and *Sivapithecus sivalensis*, at what taxonomic level is the distinction being made? What are the biological implications of such a classification?

11. If two fossil groups are classified as *Dryopithecus* and *Sivapithecus*, at what taxonomic level is this distinction? What are the biological implications?

◇ Suggested Further Reading

Buettner-Janusch, John. *Physical Anthropology: A Perspective* (Chapter 7), New York: John Wiley and Sons, 1973.

    A comprehensive and understandable review of primate evolution covered succinctly in thirty pages.

Ciochon, Russell L. and Robert S. Corrunici (eds.). *New Interpretations of Ape and Human Ancestry*, New York: Plenum Press, 1983.

    An extremely comprehensive, up-to-date series of thirty articles on hominoid evolution, including reviews of chromosomal, biochemical, paleoenvironmental, and fossil evidence (the latter mostly covering recent Miocene discoveries, but also a couple of good analyses of Oligocene material). The vast majority of contributions are well done; the summary article by Russell Ciochon is especially recommended.

Clark, W. E. Le Gros, *History of the Primates*, Chicago: The University of Chicago Press, 1965.

    Although now out of date, still an excellent source for background information on grades of primate evolution. This work is particularly strong on comparative anatomy. Excellent illustrations.

Gavan, James. *Paleoanthropology and Primate Evolution*, Dubuque, Iowa: Wm. C. Brown Co., 1977.

> *A recent although fairly superficial treatment of primate evolution. Makes for an excellent introduction to the topic by showing the relationships between living and fossil primates.*

Simons, E. L. "Ramapithecus," *Scientific American*, **236**:28–35, 1977.

> *An up-to-date review of the crucial new evidence for hominid origins written in* Scientific American *style for the educated layman.*

———. *Primate Evolution*, New York: Macmillan, 1972.

> *A detailed treatment of the historical and anatomical facts of primate evolution. Excellent introductory chapters cover the geological and theoretical foundations of primate paleontology. Written by the leading expert on this topic, this book is recommended only for those students with a desire to learn a good deal about this complex field. Many excellent illustrations and photographs will prove useful for the introductory student.*

Simons, E. L. and P. D. Ettel. "Gigantopithecus," *Scientific American*, **222**:76–85, 1970.

> *A thorough but understandable review of* Gigantopithecus *written for popular consumption.*

Szalay, Frederick S. and Eric Delson. *Evolutionary History of the Primates*, New York: Academic Press, 1979.

> *A recent compendium of primate taxonomy, morphology, and evolutionary interpretation. Excellent photos and drawings provide a detailed look at comparative anatomy. Recommended for the advanced student. Introductory students should, however, skim this book to gain a better appreciation of the quantity and quality of fossil primate data.*

Paleoanthropology

CONTENTS

Has our evolution, both cultural and biological, been systematically and deliberately tampered with by beings from other worlds? Popularized by Erich von Däniken in a series of fantastically successful books (1968, 1970, 1973), this bizarre theory has been further promulgated in movies and television. Is it possible?

Scientific inquiry cannot "prove" *anything* impossible, but it can attempt to demonstrate what is probable. Von Däniken is correct in asserting that, given the vast number of stars (and planets) in the universe, there is a high probability of intelligent life out there *somewhere*. Of all these life forms, however, how many are capable of efficient interstellar travel (necessitating speeds approaching that of light)? Furthermore, even if some life forms possessed this technology, where would they look for other intelligent life? If they randomly sampled all "inhabitable" planets in the universe, their probability of finding us would be low indeed. Perhaps, however, they are watching or listening for signs. They might assume, as we have, that an intelligent life form with even a modest degree of technological sophistication could produce radio waves. In the hopes of hearing such an intergalactic message, we have recently turned our own ears to the heavens.

If creatures "out there" have done likewise, they may *eventually* hear our radio signals. However, we have been producing such communications for only the last fifty years or so (and these radio waves have only traveled about fifty light years). Special frequency signals aimed specifically at distant worlds have only been initiated in the last few years. Consequently, on the basis of simple logical deduction, it would seem unlikely that we have even been detected, to say nothing of actually playing host to extraterrestrial travelers.

Remember, however, that whereas such a postulation is exceedingly improbable, it is not completely impossible. What, then, of evidence?

Von Däniken has audaciously postulated that extraterrestrial beings have visited earth dozens of times. Nor did they *just* visit; they helped construct huge monuments (presumably to themselves—what a being capable of building spaceships would see in a stone edifice is a mystery). They even assisted with the writing of tablets and making of maps, and let themselves become deified by the masses of humble *H. sapiens* in the bargain.

Surely mysteries abound in the archeological record, which is incomplete and, thus, far from perfect. However, that fact does not justify postulating the unlikely, the bizarre, or the ridiculous when a much more probable (but admittedly, less exciting) explanation is easily found. Indeed, much of von Däniken's primary "hard" evidence has been debunked. The huge pyramids of Egypt and Me-soamerica, the mysterious geometric designs of Nazca, Peru, and the formidable stone monuments of Easter Island have all been demonstrated as *human* achievements using relatively simple technological principles and good old-fashioned human labor.

If, in 100,000 years, future generations of archeologists were to excavate some of the "wonders" of our world, they would (in the absence of written records) be struck by the seeming incongruities and mysteries. The incredible Gothic cathedrals of Europe, built during a period of economic and intellectual disorganization, would appear a giant paradox. Did space beings build them? Or, even closer to home, the massive vaults excavated into the Rockies housing the genealogical records of the Mormon Church might also confuse and befuddle our descendants. Yet, the architects and engineers in Utah clearly did not require or receive extraterrestrial assistance in constructing this marvel.

Human beings routinely achieve the incredible, the fantastic, the inexplicable, and they do it on their own. After all, the New York Mets did win the World Series back in 1969!

SOURCES:

von Däniken, Erich. *Chariots of the Gods?*, New York: G. P. Putnam's Sons, 1968.

———. *Gods from Outer Space*, New York: G. P. Putnam's Sons, 1970.

———. *Gold of the Gods*, New York: G. P. Putnam's Sons, 1973.

◇ Introduction

In the last three chapters, we have seen how humans are classed as primates, both structurally and behaviorally, and how our evolutionary history coincides with that of other primates. However, we are a unique kind of primate, and our ancestors have been adapted to a particular kind of life style for several million years. Some kind of ramapith may have begun this process more than 10 m.y.a., but, beginning about 5 m.y.a., evidence from Africa reveals much more definite hominid relationships. The hominid nature of these remains is revealed by more than the morphological structure of teeth and bones; we know these animals are hominids also because of the way they behaved—emphasizing once again the *biocultural* nature of human evolution. In this chapter, we will discuss the methods scientists use to explore the secrets of early hominid behavior. We will then demonstrate these through the example of the best-known early hominid site in the world: Olduvai Gorge in East Africa.

◇ Definition of Hominid

If any ramapith fossils represent the earliest stages of hominid diversification, our definition of them as hominid must then primarily be a *dental* one. Teeth and jaws are most of what we have of these Miocene forms. However, dentition is not the only way to describe the special attributes of our particular evolutionary radiation and is certainly not the most distinctive of its later stages. Modern humans and our hominid ancestors are distinguished from our closest living relatives (the great apes) by more obvious features than proportionate tooth and jaw size. For example, various scientists have pointed to other hominid characteristics, such as large brain size, bipedal locomotion, and toolmaking behavior, as being most significant in defining what makes a hominid a hominid (as opposed to a pongid, a cercopithecoid, or anything else for that matter). This last definition—humans as toolmakers—is the one that we wish to discuss in this chapter. The important structural attributes of the hominid brain, teeth, and locomotory apparatus will be discussed in the next chapter, where we investigate early hominid anatomical adaptations in greater detail.

BIOCULTURAL EVOLUTION: HUMANS AS TOOLMAKERS

Although other primates do occasionally make tools (see Chapter 10), only hominids depend on culture for their survival. We and our close hominid ancestors alone have the ability to "impose arbitrary form on the environment" (Holloway, 1969). For example, chimps who use termite sticks have a direct and immediate relationship with the raw material and purpose of the tool. Such is not the case in most human cultural behavior, which usually involves several steps often quite arbitrarily removed from a direct environmental context.

We are defining culture primarily as a mental process. The human mind—presumably the minds of our hominid ancestors as well—has the unique capacity to *create* symbols. When a chimp sees water, it probably sees only the immediate environmental setting plus any learned experiences that are directly associated. Humans, however, can introduce all kinds of additional meanings, such as "holy water," physically identical to all other water but with symbolic value. A chimp can see water and know from experience it is wet, drinkable, etc. However, the chimp will never be capable of grasping the superimposed, arbitrary ideas invented and understood only by humans.

Obviously, we cannot "get inside the head" of a chimpanzee to know exactly what it is or is not thinking. The assumptions we have made are derived from behavioral observations in natural habitats, as well as results of learning experiments. However, as discussed in Chapter 10, among scientists there is still considerable dispute concerning the behavioral capacities of chimpanzees; the assumptions expressed here reflect the views of the authors. Humans, of course, also have the capacity to manipulate their environments in infinitely more complex ways than other animals. The simple human invention of a watertight container, such as a hollowed-out gourd or an ostrich egg, is several orders of magnitude more complex than chimp or rhesus monkey "cultural" behavior.

Culture as a complex adaptive strategy has become central to human evolution and has acted as a potent selective force to mold our anatomical form over the last several million years. In the archeological record, early cultural behavior is seen in the preserved remains of stone implements, traces of a uniquely human activity. "The shaping of stone according to even the simplest plan is beyond the behavior of any ape or monkey" (Washburn, 1971, p. 105).

Thus, when we find stone tools made to a standardized pattern, we know we have found a behavior indicator of a hominid, and *only* hominid, adaptation. We are justified, then, in defining hominids as habitual toolmakers, *culturally dependent* animals, distinct in this respect from all other primates.

Figure 12-1   Early stone tools. Traces of hominid behavior, from Olduvai Gorge, East Africa, about 1.6 m.y.a.

◇ The Strategy of Paleoanthropology

In order to understand human evolution adequately, we obviously need a broad sense of information. The task of recovering and interpreting all the clues left by early hominids is the work of the paleoanthropologist. Paleoanthropology is defined as "the science of the study of ancient humans." As such, it is a diverse *multidisciplinary* pursuit seeking to reconstruct every possible bit of information concerning the dating, structure, behavior, and ecology of our hominid ancestors. In just the last few years, the study of early humans has marshalled the specialized skills of many diverse kinds of scientists. Included primarily in this growing and exciting adventure are the geologist, archeologist, physical anthropologist, and paleoecologist (Table 12-1).

Table 12-1 Subdisciplines of Paleoanthropology

Physical Sciences	Biological Sciences	Social Sciences
Geology	Physical Anthropology	Archeology
Stratigraphy	Ecology	Cultural Anthropology
Petrology	Paleontology	Ethnography
(rocks, minerals)	(fossil animals)	Psychology
Pedology	Palynology	
(soils)	(fossil pollen)	
Geophysics	Primatology	Ethnoarcheology
Chemistry		
Geomorphology		
Taphonomy*		

*Taphonomy (taphos: dead) is the study of how bones and other materials come to be buried in the earth and preserved as fossils. A taphonomist studies such phenomena as the processes of sedimentation, action of streams, preservation properties of bone, and carnivore disturbance factors.

The geologist, usually working with an anthropologist (often an archeologist) does the initial survey work in order to locate potential early hominid sites. Many sophisticated techniques can aid in this search, including aerial and satellite photography. Paleontologists may also be involved in this early search, for they can help find fossil beds containing faunal remains; where conditions are favorable for the bone preservation of such specimens as ancient pigs and elephants, conditions may also be favorable for the preservation of hominid remains. In addition, paleontologists can (through comparison with known faunal areas) give fairly quick estimates of approximate age of fossil sites without having to wait for the more expensive and time-consuming chronometric analyses. In this way, fossil beds of the "right" geologic ages (that is, where hominid finds are most likely) can be isolated.

Once potential areas of early hominid sites have been located, much more extensive surveying begins. At this point, the archeologist takes over in the search for hominid "traces." We do not necessarily have to find remains of early hominids themselves to know they consistently occupied a particular area. Behavioral clues, or **artifacts**, also inform us directly and unambiguously about early hominid occupation. Modifying rocks according to a consistent plan, or simply carrying them around from one place to another (over fairly long distances), are behaviors characteristic of no other animal but a hominid. Therefore, when we see such behavioral evidence at a site, we know absolutely that hominids were present.

No doubt, early hominids sometimes utilized implements of wood or bone, and probably began doing so several million years ago (6–4 m.y.a.?). It is not altogether clear, however, just how many of these potential tools were available without *first* processing them with stone. Naturally pointed pieces of wood could probably have been utilized as digging sticks or perhaps for puncturing an ostrich egg (to make a watertight container). Beyond this, it probably would have been quite difficult to make much use of wood resources without some modification; yet, how could this have been done without something harder with which to cut, scrape, or sharpen (i.e., stone tools)? Bone is even

Paleoecological
paleo: old
ecological: environmental setting
The study of ancient environments.

more intractable and would seem also to have been "off-limits" to hominids without some stone implement to crush, cut, etc. Probably the only bone sources available were splinters left behind at kills by large carnivores. This all remains, of course, speculative, since *direct* evidence is not available. Unfortunately, these organic materials usually are not preserved, and we thus know little about such early tool-using behavior.

On the other hand, our ancestors at some point showed a veritable fascination with stones, for these provided not only easily accessible and transportable weights (to hold down objects, such as skins and windbreaks) but also the most durable and sharpest cutting edges available at that time. Luckily for us, stone is almost indestructible, and early hominid sites are virtually strewn with thousands of stone artifacts. The earliest artifact site now documented is from the Omo region of Ethiopia, dating from at least 2.4 m.y.a. Another contender for the "earliest" stone assemblage is from the Hadar area, farther to the north in Ethiopia—dated 2.0–2.5 m.y.a.

If an area is clearly demonstrated as a hominid site, much more concentrated research will then begin. We should point out that a more mundane but very significant aspect of paleoanthropology not shown in Table 12-1 is the financial one. Just the initial survey work in usually remote areas takes many thousands of dollars, and mounting a concentrated research project takes several hundred thousand dollars. Therefore, for such work to go on, massive financial support is required from governmental agencies and/or private donations. A significant amount of the paleoanthropologist's efforts and time are necessarily devoted to writing grant proposals or to speaking on the lecture circuit to raise the required funds for this necessary work.

Once the financial hurdle has been cleared, a coordinated research project can commence. Usually headed by an archeologist or physical anthropologist, the field crew will continue to survey and map the target area in great detail. In addition, they will begin to search carefully for bones and artifacts eroding out of the soil, take pollen and soil samples for ecological analysis, and carefully recover rock samples for chronometric dating. If, in this early stage of exploration, the field crew finds a fossil hominid, they will feel very lucky indeed. The international press usually considers human fossils the most exciting kind of discovery, a situation that produces wide publicity, often working to assure future financial support. More likely, the crew will accumulate much information on geological setting, ecological data, particularly faunal remains, and, with some luck, archeological traces (hominid artifacts).

After long and arduous research in the field, even more time-consuming and detailed analysis is required back in the laboratory. The archeologist must clean, sort, label, and identify all the artifacts, and the paleontologist must do the same for all faunal remains. The kinds of animals present, whether forest browsers, woodland species, or open-country forms, will greatly help in reconstructing the local **paleoecological** settings in which early hominids lived. In addition, analysis of pollen remains by a palynologist will further aid in a detailed environmental reconstruction. All of these paleoecological analyses can assist in reconstructing the diet of early humans (see p. 386). Many complex kinds of contributions go into assembling and interpreting the relevant data in such analyses (see Table 12-2).

Table 12-2   Elements of Hominid Paleoecology

Physical Environment:

Altitude	Mean wind speed
Temperature	Degree of wind gusting
Rainfall	Mean cloud cover
Relative humidity	Surface water availability
Insolation	Surface water salinity
Soil:	
Development	
Physical composition	
Chemical composition	
Tree and shrub density	Habitat selectivity
Shade cover	Herbaceous basal cover
Degree of clumping of woody plants	Grass and forb height

Diet:

Content:	Metabolic energy requirements
Animal	Energy intake
Vegetable	Digestibility
Soil (geophagy)	Time of feeding
Manner obtained	Season of feeding
Manner eaten	
Drinking	

Population:

Numbers	Mortality
Weights	Birth spacing
Growth	Sexual maturity
Natality	

Intraspecific Relations:

Grouping	Division of labor
Group interaction	Distances between group sleeping sites
Sexual relations	Grooming
Dominance interactions	

Intraspecific Relations:

Cooperation with other species	Prey
Competition with other species	Predators
Tolerance of other species	

Other Behavior:

Extent of daily movement	Group activity at various times of the day:
Tool use and manufacture:	Feeding intensively and/or moving rapidly
material, source, use	Feeding leisurely and/or resting
Sleeping place	Resting
Vocalizations	
Diurnality/nocturnality	

Source: Reprinted by permission of the Kroeber Anthropological Society from Kroeber Anthropological Society Papers No. 50, ed., Noel T. Boaz and John E. Cronin (Berkeley: Kroeber Anthropological Society, 1977), p. 56, © 1977 by the Kroeber Anthropological Society.

Pedologist
pedon: ground, soil

Petrologist
petr: rock

More information will be provided by analysis of soil samples by a **pedologist**, and rock and mineral samples by a **petrologist**. A geomorphologist may also be asked to reconstruct the sequence of past geologic events, including volcanics, mountain building, earth movements, such as faulting, and changes in the orientation of the earth's magnetic pole.

As work progresses in later field seasons with more laboratory analyses, even more experts from other scientific specialties may be consulted. If a hominid bone or tooth is eventually recovered, a physical anthropologist will clean it, reconstruct it if necessary, describe it in minute anatomical detail, and attempt to relate it to other fossil hominid finds. The archeologist may decide that a particularly well-preserved location or the site of a hominid discovery calls for precise archeological excavation. In order to recover and record all relevant information in such an undertaking, thousands of work-hours are required to excavate even a relatively small area (a few dozen square feet). An extensively detailed *microstratigraphic analysis* may also be useful in re-creating the precise conditions of sedimentation, thus calling for the specialized skills of a taphonomist (see Table 12-1).

In the concluding stages of interpretation, the paleoanthropologist will draw together the following essentials:

1. *Dating*
   geological
   paleontological
   geophysical
2. *Paleoecology*
   paleontology
   palynology
   geomorphology
3. *Archeological traces of behavior*
4. *Anatomical evidence from hominid remains*

From all this information, the paleoanthropologist will try to "flesh out" the kind of animal that may have been our direct ancestor, or at least a very close relative. In this final analysis, still further comparative scientific information may be needed. Primatologists may assist here by showing the detailed relationships between the structure and behavior of humans and that of contemporary nonhuman primates (see Chapters 9 and 10). Cultural anthropologists may contribute ethnographic information concerning the varied nature of human behavior, particularly ecological adaptation of those groups exploiting roughly similar environmental settings as those found at our hominid site (for example, the San or Australian aborigines—see p. 314). Ethnoarcheologists can assist further by demonstrating how observed behavioral patterns (as implement manufacture and meat eating) actually end up in the ground as artifacts. Finally, neuroanatomists, psychologists, and linguists may aid physical anthropologists in the reconstruction of physiological/behavioral information suggested by the fossil hominid remains, such as brain dimensions and their relationship to language capacities.

The end result of years of research by dozens of scientists will (we hope) produce a more complete and accurate understanding of human evolution—

how we came to be the way we are. Both biological and cultural aspects of our ancestors pertain to this investigation, each process developing in relation to the other.

◇ Paleoanthropology in Action—Olduvai Gorge

Several paleoanthropological projects of the scope discussed above are now in progress in diverse places around the globe. The most important of these include: David Pilbeam's work in the Miocene beds of the Potwar Plateau of western Pakistan (*circa* 13–7 m.y.a.); Don Johanson's project in the Hadar area of Ethiopia (*circa* 3.7–1.6 m.y.a.); a now completed research project along the Omo River of southern Ethiopia (*circa* 4–1.5 m.y.a.) directed by F. Clark Howell (both the Howell and Johanson projects have sometimes been forced to cease work due to warfare in Ethiopia); Richard Leakey's fantastically successful research on the eastern side of Lake Turkana (formerly Rudolf) in northern Kenya (*circa* 2.0–1.5 m.y.a.); and Mary Leakey's famous investigations at Olduvai Gorge in northern Tanzania (*circa* 1.85 m.y.a.–present).

Of all these early hominid localities, the one that has yielded the finest quality and greatest abundance of paleoanthropological information concerning the behavior of early hominids has been Olduvai Gorge.

First "discovered" in the early twentieth century by a German butterfly collector, Olduvai was soon thereafter scientifically surveyed and its wealth of paleontological evidence recognized. In 1931, Louis Leakey made his first trip to Olduvai Gorge and almost immediately realized its significance for

Figure 12-2 Major paleoanthropological projects.

Figure 12-3 Olduvai Gorge. A sketch map showing positions of the major sites and geologic localities.

◇ BIOGRAPHY   Louis S. B. Leakey 1903–1972

Louis Leakey. Shown displaying casts of fossil hominid discoveries from East Africa. To the right is the skull of a male gorilla.

Called the "Charles Darwin of prehistory," Louis Leakey was truly a man for all seasons. Blessed with a superior intellect and an almost insatiable curiosity, Leakey untiringly quested after knowledge, which to him included everything there was to know about everything. His interests encompassed not just prehistory, archeology, and paleontology but modern African wildlife, African peoples, languages, and customs. He once stalked, killed, and butchered a gazelle with just his bare hands and stone tools he had fashioned himself. He had previously attempted to use only his teeth and hands to dismember dead animals, but found it impossible, leading him to the conclusion that early hominids also *must* have used stone tools for butchering. Leakey also was a leading authority on handwriting, a skill he put to good use as the chief of British military intelligence for Africa during World War II.

The child of British missionary parents, Louis was born in a Kikuyu village in 1903—probably one of the first white children born in East Africa. His upbringing was to be as much African as European, and he was actually initiated into the Kikuyu tribe. Sworn to a sacred oath of silence, Louis never revealed the secret rites of initiation, even to his wife Mary.

Following his early training in the African bush, Louis was dispatched to England for a more formal education, eventually receiving his degree from Cambridge. His consuming interest, however, was focused on Africa, where he returned to begin exploration of prehistoric sites—leading his first expedition in 1926 at the age of 23! In 1931, Leakey made his first trip to Olduvai Gorge with the German paleontologist Hans Reck. Louis liked to relate years later how he found the first stone tool in context at Olduvai within an hour of his arrival there!

In the next forty years, the fantastic discoveries at Olduvai by Louis and his archeologist wife, Mary, as well as their extensive work at other sites all around the Rift Valley, were to make them famous to professional and layman alike.

However, perhaps Louis' greatest contribution was not the many discoveries he made himself, but his ability to stimulate and involve others. The definitive research on all the great apes was initiated by Louis Leakey, who personally recruited Jane Goodall to work with chimpanzees, Dian Fossey to investigate the mountain gorilla, and Biruté Galdikas to learn the secrets of the orang. Louis' greatest legacy is probably that all these projects continue today, and, of course, Mary carries on the work at Olduvai and their son, Richard, at Turkana in northern Kenya.

Figure 12-4 Aerial view of Olduvai Gorge. Volcanic highlands are visible to the south.

studying early humans. Since 1935, when she first worked there, Mary Leakey has directed archeological excavations at Olduvai.

Located in the Serengeti Plain of northern Tanzania, Olduvai is a steep-sided valley resembling a miniature version of the Grand Canyon. Indeed, the geological processes that formed the gorge are similar to what happened in the formation of the Grand Canyon. Following millions of years of steady accumulation of several hundred feet of geological strata (including volcanic, lake, and river deposits), faulting occurred 70,000 years ago to the east of Olduvai. As a result, a gradient was established, causing a rapidly flowing river to cut through the previously laid strata, eventually forming a gorge 300 feet deep—similar to the way the Colorado River cut the Grand Canyon.

Olduvai today is a deep ravine cut into an almost mile high grassland plateau of East Africa, and extends more than twenty-five miles in total length. In fact, if one were to include all the side gulleys and ravines, the area of exposures would total more than seventy miles with potentially hundreds of early hominid sites. Climatically, the semiarid pattern of present day Olduvai is believed to be similar to most of the past environments preserved there over the last 2 million years. The surrounding countryside is a grassland savanna broken occasionally by scrub bushes and acacia trees. It is a note-worthy fact that this environment presently (as well as in the past) supports a vast number of large mammals (as zebra, wildebeest, and gazelle), repre-senting an enormous supply of "meat on the hoof."

Geographically, Olduvai is located on the western edge of the eastern branch of the Great Rift Valley of Africa. The geological processes associated with the formation of the Rift Valley makes Olduvai (and the other East African sites) extremely important to paleoanthropological investigation. Three re-sults of geological rifting are most significant:

1. Faulting, or earth movement, exposes geological beds near the surface that are normally hidden by hundreds of feet of accumulated overburden
2. Active volcanic processes cause rapid sedimentation and thus often yield excellent preservation of bone and artifacts that normally would be scat-tered by carnivore activity and erosion forces

Figure 12-5   The East African Rift Valley system.

3. Volcanic activity provides a wealth of radiometrically datable material

The results of these geological factors at Olduvai are the superb preservation of ancient hominids and their behavioral patterns in datable contexts, all of which are readily accessible.

The greatest contribution Olduvai has made to paleoanthropological research is the establishment of an extremely well-documented and correlated *sequence* of geological, paleontological, archeological, and hominid remains over the last 2 million years. At the very foundation of all paleoanthropological research is a well-established geological picture. At Olduvai, thanks to two decades of work by Dr. Richard Hay of Berkeley, the geological and paleogeographic situation is known in minute detail. Olduvai is today a geologist's delight, containing sediments in some places 350 feet thick accumulated from lava flows (basalts), tuffs (windblown or waterlain fine deposits from nearby volcanoes), sandstones, claystones, and limestone conglomerates, all neatly stratified. A hominid site can therefore be accurately dated relative to other sites in the Olduvai Gorge by cross-correlating known marker beds. The stratigraphic sequence at Olduvai is broken down into four major beds (Beds I–IV), with other, more recent, beds usually referred to by specific local place names (Masek, Ndutu, Naisiusiu). Moreover, careful recording of the precise context of gelogical samples also provides the basis for accurate radiometric dating.

Paleontological evidence of fossilized animal bones also has come from Olduvai in great abundance. More than 150 species of extinct animals have been recognized, including fish, turtle, crocodile, pig, giraffe, horse, and many birds, rodents, and antelopes. Careful analysis of such remains has yielded voluminous information concerning the ecological conditions of early human habitats. In addition, precise analysis of bones directly associated with artifacts can sometimes tell us about the diets and hunting capabilities of early hominids. (There are some reservations, however—see Box 12-1.)

The archeological sequence is also well documented over the last 2 million years. Beginning at the earliest hominid site in Bed I (1.85 m.y.a.), there is already a well-developed stone tool kit, including chopping tools as well as some small flake tools (Leakey, 1971). Such a tool industry is called *Oldowan* (after Olduvai) and continues into Bed II with some small modifications, after which it is called *Developed Oldowan*. In addition, around 1.6 m.y.a., the first appearance of a new tool kit, the *Acheulian*, occurs in the Olduvai archeological record. This industry is characterized by large bifacial (that is, flaked on both sides) tools commonly known as hand-axes and cleavers. For several hundred thousand years, Acheulian and Developed Oldowan are *both* found side-by-side at Olduvai, and the relationship between these parallel tool kits remains to be determined.

Finally, remains of several fossilized hominids have been found at Olduvai, ranging in time from the earliest occupation levels (*circa* 1.85 m.y.a.) to fairly recent *Homo sapiens*. Of the more than forty individuals represented, many are quite fragmentary, but a few (including four skulls and a nearly complete foot) are excellently preserved. While the center of hominid discoveries has now shifted to other areas of East Africa, it was the initial discovery by Mary Leakey of the *Zinjanthropus* skull at Olduvai in July, 1959, that focused the world's attention on this remarkably rich area. "Zinj" provides an excellent example of how financial ramifications directly result from hominid bone discoveries. Prior to 1959, the Leakeys had worked sporadically at Olduvai on

Figure 12-6 View of the Main Gorge at Olduvai. Note the clear sequence of geological beds. The discontinuity to the left is a major fault line.

◇ BIOGRAPHY   Mary Leakey 1913–

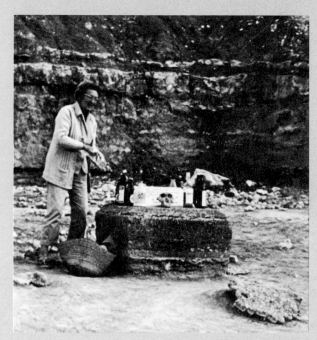

Mary Leakey. At the site of the "Zinj" find on the thirteenth anniversary of its discovery.

Mary Leakey, one of the leading prehistorians of this century, spent most of her professional life living in the shadow of her famous husband. But to a considerable degree, Louis' fame is directly attributable to Mary. Justly known for his extensive fieldwork in Miocene sites along the shores of Lake Victoria in Kenya, Louis is quite often associated with important hominoid discoveries. However, it was Mary who, in 1948, found the best-preserved dryopith skull ever discovered.

The names Louis Leakey and Olduvai Gorge are almost synonymous, but here, too, it was Mary who made the most significant single discovery—the "Zinj" skull in 1959. Mary has always been the supervisor of archeological work at Olduvai while Louis was busily engaged in traveling, lecturing, or tending to the National Museum in Nairobi.

Mary Leakey did not come upon her archeological career by chance. A direct descendant of John Frere (who, because of his discoveries in 1797, is called the father of Paleolithic archeology), Mary always had a compelling interest in prehistory. Her talent to illustrate stone tools provided her entry into African prehistory, and was the reason for her introduction to Louis in 1933. Throughout her career, she has done all the tool illustrations for her publications, and has set an extremely high standard of excellence for all would-be illustrators of Paleolithic implements.

A committed, hard-driving woman of almost inexhaustible energy, Mary conducted work at Olduvai, where she lived most of the year. Busily engaged seven days a week, she supervised ongoing excavations, as well as working on the monumental publications detailing the fieldwork already done.

Since Louis' death in 1972, Mary, to some degree, has had to assume the role of traveling lecturer and fund raiser. Today, she lives outside Nairobi, where she energetically continues her research and writing.

a financial shoestring, making marvelous paleontological and archeological discoveries. Yet, there was little support available for much needed large-scale excavations. However, following the discovery of "Zinj," the National Geographic Society funded the Leakeys' research, and within the next year, more than twice as much dirt was excavated than during the previous thirty!

◇ Dating Methods

As we have discussed, one of the key essentials of paleoanthropology is putting sites and fossils into a chronological framework. In other words, we want to know how old they are. How, then, do we date sites—or, more precisely, the geological strata in which sites are found? The question is both reasonable and important, so let us examine the dating techniques used by paleontologists, geologists, paleoanthropologists, and archeologists.

Scientists use two kinds of dating for this purpose—relative and **chronometric** (also known as *absolute dating*). Relative dating methods tell you that something is older, or younger, than something else, but not how much. If, for example, a skull were found at a depth of fifty feet, and another skull at seventy feet at the same site, we usually assume the skull discovered at seventy feet is older. We may not know the date (in years) of either one, but we would know that one is older (or younger) than the other. Whereas this may not satisfy our curiosity about the actual number of years involved, it would give some idea of the evolutionary changes in skull morphology (structure), especially if a number of skulls at different levels were found and compared.

This method of relative dating is called **stratigraphy** and was one of the first techniques to be used by scholars working with the vast period of geologic time. Stratigraphy is based upon the law of superposition, which states that a lower stratum (layer) is older than a higher stratum. Given the fact that much of the earth's crust has been laid down by layer after layer of sedimentary rock, like the layers of a cake, stratigraphy has been a valuable aid in reconstructing the history of earth and life on it.

Stratigraphic dating does, however, have a number of problems connected with it. Earth disturbances, such as volcanic activity, river activity, and mountain building, among others, may shift about strata of rock or the objects in them, and the chronology of the material may be difficult or even impossible to reconstruct. Furthermore, the time period of a particular stratum is not possible to determine with much accuracy.

Another method of relative dating is *fluorine analysis*, which applies only to bones (Oakley, 1963). Bones in the earth are exposed to the seepage of groundwater, usually containing fluorine. The longer bones lie in the earth, the more fluorine they incorporate during the fossilization process. Therefore, bones deposited at the same time in the same location should contain the same amount of fluorine. The use of this technique by Professor Oakley of the British Museum in the early 1950s exposed the Piltdown (England) hoax by demonstrating that the human skull was considerably older than the jaw found with it (Weiner, 1955). Lying in the same location, the jaw and skull should have absorbed approximately the same quantity of fluorine. But the skull contained significantly more than the jaw, which meant that it (the skull) had lain in the ground a good deal longer than the jaw. It was unlikely that the skull had met an untimely demise while the jaw lingered on for thousands of years. The discrepancy of fluorine content led Oakley and others to a closer examination of the bones, and they found that the jaw was not that of a hominid at all but of a young adult orangutan! (See p. 394.)

Unfortunately, fluorine is useful only with bones found at the same location. Because the amount of fluorine in groundwater is based upon the local river system and local conditions, it varies from place to place. Also, some groundwater may not contain any fluorine. For these reasons, comparing bones from different localities by fluorine analysis is impossible.

Chronometric
chrono: time
metric: measure
A dating technique that gives an estimate in actual numbers of years.

Stratigraphy
Sequential layering of deposits.

Figure 12-7 *Zinjanthropus* skull. Discovered by Mary Leakey at Olduvai Gorge in 1959. The skull and reconstructed jaw depicted here are casts at the National Museum of Kenya, Nairobi.

◇ GREAT MOMENTS IN PREHISTORY   Discovery of Zinjanthropus July 17, 1959

That morning I woke with a headache and a slight fever. Reluctantly I agreed to spend the day in camp.

With one of us out of commission, it was even more vital for the other to continue the work, for our precious seven-week season was running out. So Mary departed for the diggings with Sally and Toots [two of their dalmatians] in the Land-Rover, and I settled back to a restless day off.

Some time later—perhaps I dozed off—I heard the Land-Rover coming up fast to camp. I had a momentary vision of Mary stung by one of our hundreds of resident scorpions or bitten by a snake that had slipped past the dogs.

The Land-Rover rattled to a stop, and I heard Mary's voice calling over and over: "I've got him! I've got him! I've got him!"

Still groggy from the headache, I couldn't make her out.

"Got what? Are you hurt?" I asked.

"Him, the man! *Our* man," Mary said. "The one we've been looking for [for 23 years]. Come quick, I've found his teeth!"

Magically, the headache departed. I somehow fumbled into my work clothes while Mary waited.

As we bounced down the trail in the car, she described the dramatic moment of discovery. She had been searching the slope where I had found the first Oldowan tools in 1931, when suddenly her eye caught a piece of bone lodged in a rock slide. Instantly, she recognized it as part of a skull—almost certainly not that of an animal.

Her glance wandered higher, and there in the rock were two immense teeth, side by side. This time there was no question: They were undeniably human. Carefully, she marked the spot with a cairn of stones, rushed to the Land-Rover, and sped back to camp with the news.

The gorge trail ended half a mile from the site, and we left the car at a dead run. Mary led the way to the cairn, and we knelt to examine the treasure.

I saw at once that she was right. The teeth were premolars, and they had belonged to a human. I was sure they were larger than anything similar ever found, nearly twice the width of modern man's.

I turned to look at Mary, and we almost cried with sheer joy, each seized by that terrific emotion that comes rarely in life. After all our hoping and hardship and sacrifice, at last we had reached our goal—we had discovered the world's earliest known human.

From: "Finding the World's Earliest Man," by L.S.B. Leakey, *National Geographic Magazine*, 118:431, September 1960. Reprinted with permission of the publisher.

In both these methods—stratigraphy and fluorine analysis—the age of the rock stratum and the objects in it is difficult to calculate. To determine the absolute number of years of age, scientists have developed a variety of chronometric techniques based on the phenomenon of radioactive decay. The theory is quite simple: Certain radioactive isotopes of elements are unstable, disintegrate, and form an isotopic variation of another element. Since the rate of disintegration is assumed to be constant, the radioactive material forms an accurate geological time clock. By measuring the amount of disintegration in a particular sample, the number of years it took for the amount of decay is then known. Chronometric techniques have been used for dating the immense age of the earth as well as artifacts less than a thousand years old. Several techniques have been employed for a number of years and are now quite well known.

Uranium 238 (^{238}U) decays to form lead with a half-life of 4.5 billion years. That is, one-half of the original amount of ^{238}U is lost in 4.5 billion years and through various processes becomes lead. Therefore, if a chunk of rock is measured and one-half of the uranium has been converted to lead, the age of that piece of rock is 4.5 billion years. In another 4.5 billion years, half the remaining ^{238}U would have decayed. The isotope ^{238}U has proven a useful tool in dating the age of the formation of the earth.

Another chronometric technique involves potassium 40 (^{40}K)—which produces argon 40 (^{40}Ar)—with a half-life of 1.3 billion years. Known as the K/Ar, or potassium-argon method, this procedure has been extensively used by paleoanthropologists in dating materials in the 1 to 5 million year range, especially in East Africa. Organic material, such as bone, cannot be measured, but the rock matrix in which the bone is found can be. K/Ar was used to date the deposit containing the Zinjanthropus skull (it actually dated a volcanic layer above the fossil).

Rocks that provide the best samples for K/Ar are those heated to an extremely high temperature, such as that generated by volcanic activity. When the rock is in a molten state, argon 40, a gas, is driven off. As the rock cools and solidifies, potassium (^{40}K) continues to break down to ^{40}Ar, but now the gas is physically trapped in the cooled rock. In order to obtain the date of the rock, it is reheated and the escaping gas measured. Potassium-argon has been used for dating very old events, such as the age of the earth, as well as those less than 100,000 years old (Dalrymple, 1972).

A well-known chronometric method popular with archeologists is carbon 14 (^{14}C), with a half-life of 5730 years. It has been used to date material from less than 1,000 years to as much as 75,000 years,* although the probability of error rises rapidly after 40,000 years. The ^{14}C technique is based upon the following natural processes: Cosmic radiation enters the earth's atmosphere, producing neutrons, which react with nitrogen to produce a radioactive isotope of carbon, ^{14}C. As the ^{14}C is diffused around the earth, with the earth's rotation, it mixes with carbon 12 and is absorbed by plants in their life processes. It is then transferred to herbivorous animals that feed on plants and to carnivores that feed on herbivores. Thus, ^{14}C and ^{12}C are found in all living forms at a fixed ratio. When an organism dies, it no longer absorbs ^{14}C, which then decays at a constant rate to ^{14}N (and a beta particle). It takes 5370 years for half the amount of ^{14}C to become ^{14}N.

Let us say that charcoal, the remains of a campfire, is found at an archeological site and measured for the $^{14}C/^{12}C$ proportions. Suppose the findings are that the proportion of the ^{14}C to ^{12}C shows only 25% of the original ^{14}C remaining. Since it takes 5730 years for half the ^{14}C atoms to become ^{14}N, and another 5730 years for half the remaining ^{14}C to become ^{14}N, the sample must be about 11,460 years old. Half the remaining ^{14}C will become ^{14}N in the next 5730 years, leaving 12.5% of the original amount. This process continues, and as you can see, there would be very little ^{14}C left after 40,000 years, when measuring becomes difficult.

Other absolute dating techniques that do not involve radioactive elements are *dendrochronology*, or dating by tree rings, especially developed for the American Southwest, and *varve chronology* (annual glacial deposit), particu-

---

*Grootes' studies (1978) suggest 75,000 years. A new technique using ^{14}C is being worked out at the University of California's Lawrence Berkeley Lab and at the University of Rochester. Scientists involved in the project believe it will extend the dating to 100,000 years with "no trouble" (Thomsen, 1978). This technique using a cyclotron ("atom smasher") requires a much smaller sample—"as little as one thousandth of a gram"—than the conventional method.

Figure 12-8 Carbon-14 dating. Cosmic rays bombard the upper atmosphere, producing neutrons. When these collide with nitrogen, small amounts of ¹⁴C are produced. The ¹⁴C combines with oxygen to form carbon dioxide. The carbon dioxide containing ¹⁴C is absorbed by plants, and eventually animals feeding on the plants add ¹⁴C to their bodies. When the plant or animal dies, it ceases to absorb ¹⁴C and the ¹⁴C changes back to nitrogen at a regular rate.

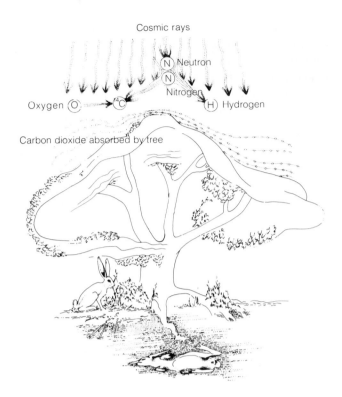

larly useful for the late Pleistocene and the post-Pleistocene in northern Europe. Although neither of the techniques has a direct bearing on dating early human fossils, they are both ingenious dating methods with important regional applications.

We should stress that none of these methods is precise, and that each method is beset with problems that must be carefully considered during laboratory measurement and in the collection of material to be measured. Because the methods are imprecise, approximate dates are given as probability statements with a plus or minus factor. For example, a date given as 1.75 ± .2 million years should be read as a 67% chance that the actual date lies somewhere between 1.55 and 1.95 million years.

There are, then, two ways in which the question of age may be answered. We can say that a particular fossil is x number of years old, a date determined usually either by K/Ar or ¹⁴C chronometric dating techniques. Or, we can say that fossil X lived before or after fossil Y, a relative dating technique.

DATING METHODS AT OLDUVAI

Olduvai has proven a rich and varied source for numerous dating techniques, and as a result it has some of the best-documented chronology for any hominid site in the Lower or Middle Pleistocene.

Potassium-argon dating had its birth as a paleoanthropological tool in the early 1960s with its application to the dating of the "Zinj" site at Olduvai. To everyone's amazement, including Louis Leakey's, the chronometric age was determined at more than 1.75 million years—more than twice the age depth previously assumed for the *whole* Pleistocene. As a result of this one monumental date (Leakey, et al., 1961), the entire history of the Pleistocene and our corresponding interpretations of hominid evolution had to be rewritten.

Potassium-argon (K/Ar) is an extremely valuable tool for dating early hominid sites and has been widely used in areas containing suitable volcanic deposits (mainly in East Africa). At Olduvai, K/Ar has given several reliable dates of the underlying basalt and several tuffs in Bed I, including the one associated with the "Zinj" find (now dated at $1.79 \pm .03$ m.y.a.). When dating relatively recent samples (from the perspective of a half-life of 1.3 billion years for K/Ar, *all* paleoanthropological material is relatively recent), the amount of radiogenic argon is going to be exceedingly small. Experimental errors in measurement can therefore occur as well as the thorny problem of distinguishing the atmospheric argon normally clinging to the outside of the sample from the radiogenic argon. In addition, the initial sample may have been contaminated or argon leakage may have occurred while it lay buried.

Due to the potential sources of error, K/Ar dating must be cross-checked using other independent methods. Once again, the sediments at Olduvai (particularly in Bed I) provide some of the best examples of the use of many of these other dating techniques.

Fission-track dating is one of the most important techniques for cross-checking K/Ar determinations. The key to fission-track dating is that ^{238}uranium (^{238}U) decays regularly by spontaneous fission so that, by counting the fraction of uranium atoms that have fissioned (shown as microscopic tracks caused by explosive fission of ^{238}U nuclei), we can ascertain the age of a mineral or natural glass sample (Fleischer and Hart, 1972). One of the earliest applications of this technique was on volcanic pumice from Bed I at Olduvai, giving a date of 2.30 ($\pm .28$ m.y.a.)—in complete accord with K/Ar dates.

Another important means of cross-checking dates is called **paleomagnetism**. This technique is based on the constantly shifting nature of the earth's magnetic pole. Of course, as anyone knows, the earth's magnetic pole is now oriented in a northerly direction, but this situation has not always been so. In fact, the orientation and intensity of the geomagnetic field have undergone numerous documented changes in the last few million years. From our present ethnocentric point of view, we call a northern orientation "normal" and a southern one "reversed." Major epochs of geomagnetic time are:

Normal
0.7 m.y.a.
Reversed
2.5 m.y.a.
Normal
3.4 m.y.a.
Reversed
,
,
,
,
?

Paleomagnetism
Dating method based on shifting magnetic poles.

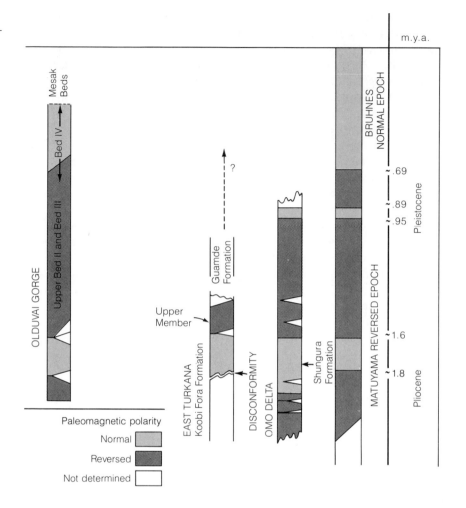

Paleomagnetic dating is accomplished by carefully taking samples of sediments that contain magnetically charged particles. Since these particles maintain the magnetic orientation they had when they were consolidated into rock (many thousands or millions of years ago), we have a kind of "fossil compass." Then the paleomagnetic *sequence* is compared against the K/Ar dates to check if they agree. Some complications can arise, for during an epoch a relatively long period of time can occur where the geomagnetic orientation is the opposite of what is expected. For example, during the reversed epoch between 2.5–1.7 m.y.a. (Matuyama Epoch) there was a time period called an *event*, lasting about 160,000 years, where orientations were normal. As this phenomenon was first conclusively demonstrated at Olduvai, it is appropriately called the *Olduvai Event*.

However, once these oscillations in the geomagnetic pole are well worked out, the sequence of paleomagnetic orientations can provide a valuable cross-check for K/Ar and fission-track age determinations.

A final dating technique employed in the Lower Pleistocene beds at Olduvai and other East African sites is based in the regular evolutionary changes in well-known groups of mammals. This technique, called faunal correlation or **biostratigraphy**, provides yet another means of cross-checking the other methods. Two groups of animals that have been widely used in biostratigraphical analysis in East Africa are fossil pigs (suids) and fossil elephants (proboscids). From areas where dates are known (by K/Ar, for instance) approximate ages can be extrapolated to other less well-known areas by noting which genera and species are present and by measuring specific evolutionary trends, such as length of the third molar in *Mesochoerus* (a giant fossil pig found at Olduvai and several other Plio-Pleistocene East African sites). In this well-documented evolutionary lineage, back teeth gradually become larger from earlier to later representatives.

All these methods, potassium-argon, fission-track, paleomagnetism, and biostratigraphy have been used in dating Beds I and II at Olduvai. So many different dating techniques are necessary because no single one is perfectly reliable by itself. Sampling error, contamination, and experimental errors can all introduce ambiguities into our so-called "absolute" dates. However, the

Biostratigraphy
Dating method based on evolutionary changes within an evolving lineage.

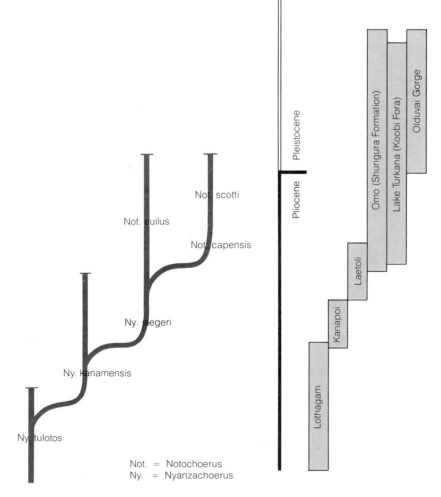

Figure 12-10 Partial biostratrigraphic sequence of pigs. Used to correlate East African sites. (After White and Harris, 1977.)

Not. scotti

Not. euilus

Not. capensis

Ny. jaegeri

Ny. kanamensis

Ny. tulotos

Not. = Notochoerus
Ny. = Nyanzachoerus

Pleistocene

Pliocene

Omo (Shungura Formation)

Lake Turkana (Koobi Fora)

Olduvai Gorge

Laetoli

Kanapoi

Lothagam

Figure 12-11 Excavations in progress at Olduvai. This site is more than one million years old. It was located when a hominid ulna (armbone) was found eroding out of the side of the gorge.

sources of error are different for each technique, and therefore cross-checking between several independent methods is the most certain way of authenticating the chronology for early hominid sites.

We should mention that still other dating techniques have been used at Olduvai in the upper beds where different methods are applicable. ¹⁴C dating has been employed to date a 17,000-year-old site in the upper part of the Gorge, and this date has been further corroborated by a relatively new dating method called *amino acid racemization* (based on regularly shifting optical properties of amino acids).

◇ Excavations at Olduvai

Because the vertical cut of the Olduvai Gorge provides a ready cross-section of 2 million years of earth history, sites can be excavated by digging "straight-in" rather than finding them by having first to remove tons of overlying dirt. In fact, sites are usually discovered by merely walking the exposures and observing what bones, stones, etc. are eroding out.

Several dozen hominid sites (at a minimum, they are bone and tool scatters) have been surveyed at Olduvai, and Mary Leakey has extensively excavated close to twenty of these. An incredible amount of paleoanthropological information has come from these excavated areas, data which can be generally grouped into three broad categories depending on implied function:

1. *Butchering sites.* Areas containing one or only a few individuals of a single species of large mammal associated with a scatter of archeological traces. An elephant butchering site and another containing a *Deinotherium* (a

large extinct relative of the elephant) have been found at levels approximately 1.7 m.y.a. Both sites contain only a single animal, and it is impossible to ascertain whether the hominids actually killed these animals or exploited them (presumably for meat resources) after they were already dead. A third butchering site dated at approximately 1.2 m.y.a. shows much more consistent and efficient hunting of large mammals by this time. Remains of 24 *Pelorovis* (a giant extinct relative of the buffalo, with horn spans more than ten feet across!), have been found here, and Louis Leakey suggested they were driven into a swamp by a band of hominids and then systematically slaughtered (Leakey, 1971).

2. *Quarry sites.* Areas where early hominids extracted their stone resources and initially fashioned their tools. At such sites, thousands of small stone fragments are found of only one type of rock usually associated with no or very little bone refuse. At Olduvai, a 1.6 m.y.–1.7 m.y. old area was apparently a chert factory site, where hominids came repeatedly to quarry this material.

3. *Living sites.* Also called campsites. General purpose areas where hominids ate, slept, and put the finishing touches on their tools. The accumulation of living debris, including broken bones of many animals of several different species and many broken stones (some complete tools, some waste flakes) is a basic human pattern. As Glynn Isaac, one of the leading prehistoric archeologists working in Africa, has noted, "The fact that discarded artifacts tend to be concentrated in restricted areas is itself highly suggestive. It seems likely that such patches of material reflect the organization of

Figure 12-12   A living floor at Olduvai. From a site approximately 1.6 m.y.a.

◇ Box 12-1   Are the Sites at Olduvai Really "Sites"?

The generally agreed-upon interpretation of the bone refuse and stone tools discovered at Olduvai has been that
most, if not all, of these materials are the result of hominid activities. Recently, however, a comprehensive reanalysis of the bone remains from Olduvai localities has
challenged this view (Binford, 1981; 1983). Archeologist
Lewis Binford criticizes those drawn too quickly to the
conclusion that these bone scatters are the remnants of
hominid behavior patterns while simultaneously ignoring
the possibility of other explanations. For example, he
forcefully states:

> All the facts gleaned from the deposits interpreted as
> living sites have served as the basis for making up
> "just-so stories" about our hominid past. No attention
> has been given to the possibility that many of the facts
> may well be referable to the behavior of nonhominids
> (Binford, 1981, p. 251).

From specifics concerning the kinds of animals present, which body parts were found, and the differences in
preservation among these skeletal elements, Binford concluded that much of what is preserved could be explained by carnivore activity. This conclusion was
reinforced by certain details observed by Binford himself
in Alaska—details on animal kills, scavenging, the transportation of elements, and preservation as the result of
wolf and dog behaviors. Binford describes his approach
thus:

> I took as 'known,' then, the structure of bone assem-
> blages produced in various settings by animal preda-
> tors and scavengers; and as 'unknown' the bone
> deposits excavated by the Leakeys at Olduvai Gorge. Us-
> ing mathematical and statistical techniques I consid-
> ered to what degree the finds from Olduvai Gorge
> could be accounted for in terms of the results of pre-
> dator behavior and how much was 'left over' (Binford,
> 1983, pp. 56–57).

In using this uniquely explicit approach, Binford arrived at quite different conclusions than those previously
suggested by other archeologists:

> For instance, the very idea of a site or living floor as-
> sumes conditions in the past for which there is no
> demonstration. In fact, it assumes the very "knowl-
> edge" we would like to obtain from the archeological
> remains. Site and living floor identifications presup-
> pose that concentrations and aggregations of archeo-
> logical and other materials are only produced by man.
> Are there not other conditions of deposition that could
> result in aggregations of considerable density found on
> old land surfaces? The answer must be a resounding
> yes.

And, later, he concludes:

> It seems to me that one major conclusion is justified
> from the foregoing analysis: The large, highly publi-

movement around a camp or home base, with recurrent dispersal and
reuniting of the group at the chosen locality. Among living primates this
pattern in its full expression is distinctive of man. The coincidence of bone
and food refuse with the artifacts strongly implies that meat was carried
back—presumably for sharing" (Isaac, 1976, pp. 27–28). (See Box 12-1 for
a different interpretation.)

Several campsites have been excavated at Olduvai, including one that is
over 1.8 m.y. old (DK I—see Box 12-2). This site has a circle of large stones
forming what may have been the base for a windbreak or, as Mary Leakey,
who dug the site, has suggested, may have been the foundation for a primitive
structure. Without the meticulous excavation and recording of modern archeological techniques, the presence of such an archeological feature would
never have been recognized. This point requires further emphasis. Many

cized sites as currently analyzed carry little specific information about hominid behavior ... arguments about base camps, hominid hunting, sharing of food, and so forth are certainly premature and most likely wildly inaccurate (Binford, 1981, pp. 281–282).

Binford is not arguing that *all* of the remains found at Olduvai have resulted from nonhominid activity. In fact, he recognized that "residual material" was consistently found on surfaces with high tool concentrations "which could *not* be explained by what we know about African animals" (Binford, 1983).

Support for the idea that at least some of the bone refuse was utilized by early hominids has come from a totally different tact. Recently, researchers have analyzed (both macroscopically and microscopically) the cutmarks left on fossilized bones. By experimenting with modern materials, they have further been able to delineate clearly the differences between marks left by stone tools as opposed to those left by animal teeth (or other factors) (Bunn, 1981; Potts and Shipman, 1981). Analysis of bones from several early localities at Olduvai showed unambiguously that these specimens were utilized by hominids, who left telltale cutmarks from stonetool usage. The sites thus far investigated reveal a somewhat haphazard cutting and chopping, apparently unrelated to deliberate disarticulation. It has thus been concluded (Shipman, 1983) that hominids scavenged carcasses (probably of carnivore kills) and did *not* hunt large animals themselves. Materials found at later sites (postdating 1 m.y.a.), on the other hand, do show deliberate disarticulation, indicating a more systematic hunting pattern, with presumably meat transport and food-sharing as well (Shipman, 1983).

If early hominids (close to 2 m.y.a.) were not hunting consistently, what did they obtain from scavenging the kills of other animals? One obvious answer is, whatever meat was left behind. However, the positioning of the cutmarks suggests that early hominids were often hacking at nonmeat-bearing portions of the skeletons. Perhaps they were simply after bone marrow, a substance not really being exploited by other predators (Binford, 1981).

The picture that emerges, then, of what hominids were doing at Olduvai around 1.8 m.y.a. hardly suggests consistent big game hunting. In Binford's words:

... this is evidence of man eating a little bit of bone marrow, a food source that must have represented an infinitesimally small component of his total diet. The signs seem clear. Earliest man, far from appearing as a mighty hunter of beasts, seems to have been the most marginal of scavengers (Binford, 1983, p. 59).

people assume archeologists derive their information simply from analysis of objects (stone tools, gold statues, or whatever). However, it is the **context** and **association** of objects (that is, precisely where the objects are found and what is found associated with them) that give the archeologist the data he requires to understand the behavioral patterns of ancient human populations. Once pot hunters or looters pilfer a site, proper archeological interpretation is never again possible.

Other living sites at Olduvai include the large occupation area at the "Zinj" site (FLK = 1.75 m.y.a.) and a very thin (perhaps occupied just a few days) living floor (HWK East = 1.7 m.y.a.). Preservation of occupational debris along one relatively narrow horizon is what is meant by a living floor, and the extraordinary conditions at Olduvai have preserved many of the bones and stones almost exactly as the hominids left them more than 1 m.y.a.

Another kind of living site is MNK (Lower Middle Bed II = 1.6 m.y.a.) where

Context
The environmental setting where an archeological trace is found.

Association
What an archeological trace is found with.

Living floor
A narrow horizon of archeological remains; corresponds to brief period of occupation.

◇ Box 12-2   Olduvai Site Names

The naming of sites at Olduvai is a marvelous wonder concocted from fascinating combinations of the English alphabet. Sites are designated with such shorthand abbreviations as FLK, MNK, LLK, etc. The 'K' stands for Korongo, Swahili for gully (Olduvai is made up of dozens of side gullies). The first initial(s) is usually, though not always, that of the individual who made an important discovery at that locality. For example, FLK stands for Frida Leakey Korongo (Louis' first wife), MNK is Mary Nicol Korongo (Mary Leakey's maiden name), and LLK is Louis Leakey Korongo (where Louis found a hominid cranium in 1961). When more than one site is found in the same gully, those discovered later are given directional orientations relative to the initial site. For example, FLK is the main site name where "Zinj" was found in 1959. FLK N (that is, "FLK North," where the elephant and *Deinotherium* butchering sites occur at slightly different levels) is just north of the main site, and FLK NN ("FLK North North," the location of yet another important hominid discovery) is just a bit farther north up the gully.

occupational debris is scattered through more than six feet of earth, suggesting hominids periodically reoccupied this area—perhaps seasonally.

The detailed excavations of all these different hominid occupation areas are of tremendous importance, since the dispersal pattern of the remains of ancient human behavior can yield great insight into the biocultural evolution of humankind.

ARTIFACTS

While context, association, and ecological information are of paramount interest to the prehistoric archeologist, detailed analysis of the stone artifacts themselves can yield much additional information about the behavior of early hominids. Mary Leakey has been the pioneer in the study of Plio-Pleistocene African artifacts, and her classification system and description of some of the artifacts found at Olduvai are discussed in Box 12-3.

◇ Diet of Early Hominids

Paleoanthropological research is concerned with more than the recovery and recording of bones and artifacts. What we are trying to obtain is a reconstruction of the kind of animal our ancestor was. Paleoanthropology must therefore be centrally concerned with interpretation of the behavioral patterns of early hominid populations.

One of the most important questions we would like to answer about early hominid behavior is: What did they eat? Scattered broken bone debris associated with artifacts *may* provide direct evidence concerning one important aspect of early human dietary behavior. However, we must not forget that modern analogs like the San of South Africa clearly show us that vegetable foods, which usually leave little trace in the archeological record, probably made up a large part (even a majority) of the caloric intake of early hominids. As Glynn Isaac has noted, reconstructing dietary behavior is like navigating around an iceberg—four-fifths of what is of interest is not visible (Isaac, 1971, p. 280).

Postulated diets available to hominids 1–2 m.y.a. with use of only a simple digging stick as a tool include: berries, fruits, nuts, buds, shoots, shallow-growing roots and tubers, most terrestrial and smaller aquatic reptiles, eggs and nesting birds, some fish, molluscs, insects, and all smaller mammals (Bartholomew and Birdsell, 1953).

Olduvai has shown that the range of postulated meat resources was indeed exploited in Beds I and II (1.85–1.0 m.y.a.). Fossils of turtles, rodents, fish, birds, pigs, horses, and small antelopes are all fairly common at many Olduvai sites. Of course, exactly how much of these remains were eaten—as opposed to having just "dropped dead" there or having been preyed upon by other animals—is still undetermined (see Box 12-1). Evidence for fish eating has also come from a comparably aged site in southern Ethiopia (the Omo), where fish bones have been found in human coprolites (fossilized feces).

Moreover, as the elephant and *Deinotherium* butchering sites indicate, occasional exploitation of large mammals also occurred more than 1.5 m.y.a. By 1 m.y.a., systematic hunting of large mammals apparently provided important meat resources, as shown by the *Pelorovis* butchering site.

Thanks to the extraordinary dedication of Louis and Mary Leakey, just one relatively small area of northern Tanzania has provided a continuous record of the development of hominids and their behavior for almost 2 million years. Without Olduvai we would know much less than we do about the emergence of human culture prior to 1 m.y.a.

◇ Summary

The biocultural nature of human evolution requires that any meaningful study of human origins examine both biological and cultural information. The multidisciplinary approach of paleoanthropology is designed to bring together varied scientific specializations in order to reconstruct the anatomy, behavior, and environments of early hominids. Such a task is centered around the skills of the geologist, paleontologist, paleoecologist, archeologist, and physical anthropologist.

Much of what we know about the origins of human culture between 1 and 2 m.y.a. comes from archeological excavations by Mary Leakey at Olduvai Gorge in East Africa. Olduvai's well-documented stratigraphic sequence, its superior preservation of remains (often as living floors), and the varied dating techniques possible there have made it an information bonanza for paleoanthropologists. Excavated sites have yielded a wealth of bones of fossil animals, as well as artifact traces of hominid behavior. Ecological reconstructions of habitat and dietary preferences are thereby possible and inform us in great detail concerning crucial evolutionary processes affecting early hominid populations.

◇ Box 12-3   Classification of Artifacts

Stone artifacts, depending on context, shape, flake scars, and inferred function, fall into four broad categories:

1. *Manuports*. Rocks that are not modified but are found out of their natural context; that is, rocks that have been manually carried, a definite hominid behavior. The stone circle at DK I perhaps consisted of manuports, and much of the occupational debris at MNK is made up of unmodified manuports. Their functions remain unknown.
2. *Utilized material*. Stones used to modify other stones but not used as tools themselves. Under this category, Mary Leakey includes hammerstones and anvils.
3. *Debitage*. Very small flakes, either waste material struck off while making tools or perhaps used themselves as very small cutting implements.
4. *Tools*. A broad category of intentionally modified stones that have been shaped according to a preset, consistent pattern. Mary Leakey classifies the stone tools found at Olduvai primarily on the basis of shape and size. As yet no definite conclusions on their functions have been reached. Tools are thus classed as spheroids, discoids, polyhedrons, bifaces, etc. Occasionally, function is inferred with such terms as chopper, scraper, burin, and awl.

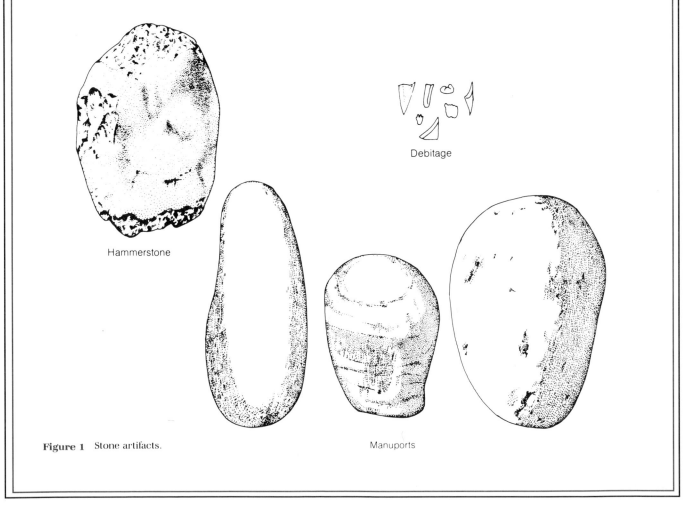

Hammerstone

Debitage

Manuports

Figure 1   Stone artifacts.

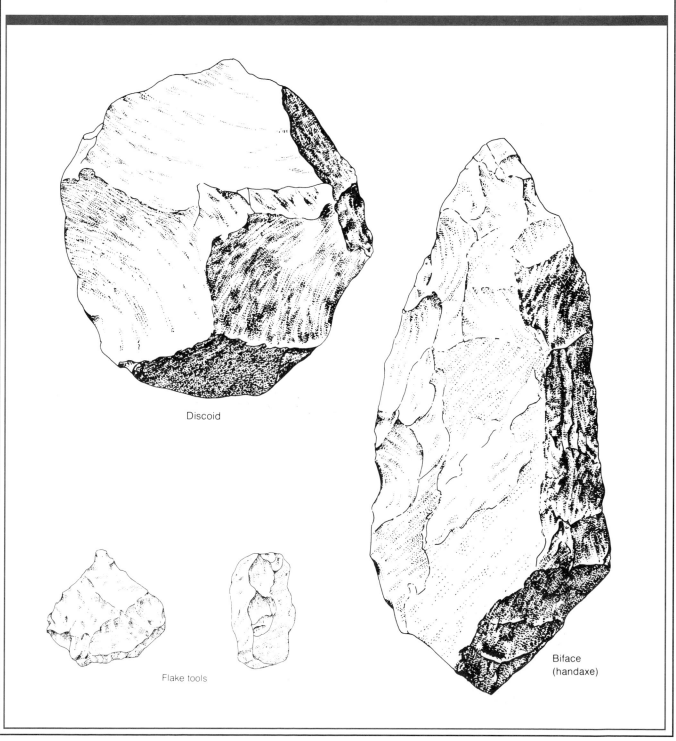

Discoid

Flake tools

Biface
(handaxe)

In the next three chapters, we will survey the fossil hominid evidence in South and East Africa that inform us directly about human origins during the Plio-Pleistocene.

◇ Questions for Review

1. Why are cultural remains so important in the interpretation of human evolution?
2. How are early hominid sites found, and what kind of specialist is involved in the excavation and analysis of paleoanthropological data?
3. What kinds of paleoanthropological information have been found at Olduvai Gorge? Why is this particular locality so rich in material?
4. What kinds of dating techniques have been used to date early hominid sites at Olduvai? Why is more than one technique necessary for accurate dating?
5. Why are context and association so important in the interpretation of archeological remains?
6. What different activities can be inferred from the different kinds of sites at Olduvai? Discuss alternative views in the interpretation of these "sites."
7. How do we infer what early hominids were eating? Give a brief list of the kinds of food that were probably exploited.

◇ Suggested Further Reading

Binford, Lewis R. *Bones. Ancient Men and Modern Myths.* New York: Academic Press, 1981.

A technical but highly stimulating discussion of how archeological inference is made. Binford applies an "ethnoarcheological" approach in which cultural behavioral evidence from the present is used to reconstruct the past. In particular, he draws upon his observations of Eskimos—their use of animal resources and the predatory scavenging behavior of wolves and dogs. Using this approach, Binford attempts to interpret the archeological sites at Olduvai, but comes to a much different conclusion than that reached by Isaac, Johanson, and the Leakeys (see references below).

Bishop, W. W. and J. A. Miller (eds.). *Calibration of Hominoid Evolution,* Edinburgh: Scottish Academic Press, 1972.

A most authoritative though highly technical series of articles on all the major dating techniques now employed at early hominid sites.

Butzer, Karl. *Environment and Archeology: An Ecological Approach* (2nd Ed.), Chicago: Aldine-Atherton, 1971.

An excellent advanced review of the paleoecological approach to understanding hominid evolution.

Campbell, Bernard. *Humankind Emerging,* Boston: Little, Brown & Co., 1976.

A general introduction to human evolution with particular emphasis on the discoveries and excavations of fossil hominids. Summarized from the Time-Life series, this book contains many beautiful illustrations.

Chard, Chester. *Man in Prehistory* (2nd Ed.), New York: McGraw-Hill, 1975.
> An excellent introduction to prehistoric archeology with discussion of archeological methods, dating techniques, and a review of culture history.

Cole, Sonia. *Leakey's Luck*, New York: Harcourt, Brace, Jovanovich, 1975.
> An entertaining account of the life of Louis Leakey with a fine summary of his and his family's discoveries, particularly those at Olduvai.

Gowlett, John. *Ascent to Civilization*. New York: Alfred A. Knopf, 1984.
> Essentially a history of archeological finds, this book also includes basic human evolutionary text. Beautifully illustrated, with many fine drawings, maps, and charts. The text is for the general public. Highly recommended—a quality work.

Isaac, Glynn and E. R. McCown (eds.). *Human Origins: Louis Leakey and the East African Evidence*, Reading, Massachussetts: W. A. Benjamin Inc., 1976.
> This up-to-date work contains several excellent not overly technical articles on the geological setting, archeological evidence, and fossil hominids from East Africa.

Johanson, Donald and Maitland Edey. *Lucy, The Beginnings of Humankind*, New York: Simon and Schuster, 1981.
> A popularized account of the discoveries at Hadar and other Plio-Pleistocene African sites. Much of the romance, controversies, strong personalities, and financial problems of paleoanthropological research is detailed. Highly recommended for the introductory student.

Leakey, M. D. *Olduvai Gorge* (Vol. 3), *Excavations in Beds I and II 1960–1963*, Cambridge: Cambridge University Press, 1971.
> A detailed analysis of the archeological evidence from Olduvai covering the time range 1.85–1.0 m.ya. Many excellent illustrations drawn by Mary Leakey beautifully depict a wide range of stone artifacts.

Leakey, Mary. *My Search for Early Man*, London: Collins, 1979.
> A personal account of many of the discoveries and excavation techniques practiced at Olduvai. Also contains useful discussions of geology, dating techniques, and artifact analysis.

Leakey, Richard E. and Roger Lewin. *People of the Lake*, New York: Anchor/Doubleday, 1978.
> A popularized account of human evolution, emphasizing the exciting discoveries in East Africa. Written by one of the leading paleoanthropologists of the day, this work presents an argument for the nonaggressive nature of human evolution. Up-to-date and highly recommended.

Reader, John. *Missing Links. The Hunt for Earliest Man*, Boston: Little, Brown and Company, 1981.
> A recent account of paleoanthropology from a historical perspective, tracing discoveries of fossil hominids over the last century. Useful as a reference for all the remaining chapters of this text. Beautifully illustrated; highly recommended.

Plio-Pleistocene Hominids: South Africa

CONTENTS

When first announed to the world in 1912, *Eoanthropus dawsoni* ("Dawson's Dawn Man") created an anthropological sensation. Found during 1911 in Sussex in the south of England by Charles Dawson, a lawyer and amateur geologist/antiquarian, this "fossil" was to confuse, bewilder, and befuddle two generations of anthropologists. "Piltdown man," as he popularly came to be called, was comprised of a fragmented skull and parts of a lower jaw. The enigma of the fossil from the very beginning was the combination of a large *sapiens*-like skull (initially estimated at 1,070 cm³, but later shown to be more like 1,400 cm³) with an apelike lower jaw.

Most tantalizing of all, Piltdown was apparently extremely ancient, associated with long extinct fauna, such as mastodon, hippo, and rhino, all suggesting a date of early Pleistocene. A puzzling feature was the presence of these early fossils mixed in with clearly late Pleistocene fauna. The prevailing consensus, however, was that Piltdown was indeed ancient, "the earliest known representative of man in Western Europe."

Despite its seeming incongruities, Piltdown was eagerly accepted by British scientists, including Keith, Elliot Smith, and Smith Woodward (all later knighted). What made the fossil such a delectable treat was that it confirmed just what had been expected, a combination of *modern* ape and *modern* human characteristics—a true "missing link." We, of course, now know that no ancestral fossil form is a fifty-fifty compromise between modern ones, but represents its own unique adaptation. In addition to mistaken enthusiasm for a missing link, the fossil also represented a "true" man as opposed to the obviously primitive beasts (Java

Figure 1   The Piltdown skull.

man, Neandertals) found elsewhere. Such a fervently biased desire to find an "ancient modern" in the human lineage has obscured evolutionary studies for decades and still causes confusion in some circles.

While generally accepted in England, experts in France, Germany, and the United States felt uneasy about Piltdown. Many critics, however, were silenced when a second fragmentary find came to light in 1917 (actually found in 1915) in an area two miles away from the original site. The matter stood in limbo for years, with some scientists as enthusiastic supporters of the Piltdown man and others remaining uneasy doubters. The uneasiness continued to fester as more hominid material accumulated in Java, China, and particularly the australopithecines in South Africa. None of these hominids showed the peculiar combination of a human cranium with an apelike jaw seen in Piltdown, but actually indicated the reverse pattern.

The final proof of the true nature of the Dawn Man came in the early 1950s, when British scientists began an intensive reexamination of the Piltdown material. In particular, fluorine analysis (see Chapter 12) performed by Kenneth Oakley showed both the skull and jaw were relatively recent. Later, more extensive tests showed the jaw to be younger than

the skull and *very* recent in date. Now a much more critical eye was turned to all the material. The teeth, looking initially as though they had been worn down flat in the typical hominid fashion, were apparently ape teeth filed down deliberately to give that impression. The mixed bag of fauna was apparently acquired from all manner of places (a fossil elephant came from Tunisia in North Africa!), and the jaw was deliberately stained with chromate to match the older fossils in color. Finally, some "tools" found at Piltdown also met the hand of a forger for the bone implements showed modifications that apparently could only have been made by a metal knife.

The "fossil" itself was probably purchased from local dealers. The skull probably came from a moderately ancient grave (a few thousand years old), and the jaw was a specially broken, filed, and stained mandible of a fairly recently deceased adolescent orang! The evidence was indisputable: a deliberate hoax. But who did it?

Just about everyone connected with the "crime" has, at one time or another, been implicated—beginning with Piltdown's discoverer: Charles Dawson. Yet, Dawson was an amateur, and, thus, may have lacked the expertise to carry out the admittedly crafty job of anatomical modification.

In addition, at various times, suspicions have been cast towards neuroanatomist Sir Grafton Elliot Smith, geologist W. J. Sollas, and French philosopher/archaeologist Father Pierre Teilhard de Chardin. Still, for none of these people has a conclusive case been made.

Recently, however, another intriguing possibility has been raised:

. . . there was another interested figure

Figure 2 The Piltdown committee. The individuals central to the "discovery" and interpretation of the Piltdown "fossil." Back row, standing, left to right: Mr. F. O. Barlow (maker of the casts), Prof. G. Elliot Smith (anatomist), Mr. C. Dawson ("discoverer"), Dr. A. Smith Woodward (zoologist). Front row, seated: Dr. A. S. Underwood (dental expert), Prof. A. Keith (anatomist), Mr. W. P. Pycraft (zoologist), Sir Ray Lankester (zoologist). From the painting by John Cook.

who haunted the Piltdown site during excavation, a doctor who knew human anatomy and chemistry, someone interested in geology and archeology, and an avid collector of fossils. He was a man who loved hoaxes, adventure and danger; a writer gifted at manipulating complex plots; and perhaps most important of all, one who bore a grudge against the British science establishment. He was none other than the creator of Sherlock Holmes, Sir Arthur Conan Doyle (Winslow and Meyer, 1983, p. 34).

Doyle, as a medical doctor, certainly possessed the anatomical knowhow to craft the forgery. His other avocations—chemistry, geology, and especially, anthropology—would have been useful to him, *if* he were the forger.

In a remarkable piece of detective work (worthy of the master sleuth Sherlock Holmes himself), John Winslow has assembled a convincing array of *circumstantial* evidence against Doyle. Doyle, first of all, is the only suspect that can be shown to have had ready access to all the elements of the forgery. He was friendly with collectors or dealers who easily could have provided him with the cranium, the orang jaw, and the stone tools. As far as the animal fossils are concerned, Doyle also could have acquired many of the local (English) fossils from collector friends, but some of the odd bits obviously are from elsewhere (most likely, Malta and Tunisia). And, interestingly enough, Doyle had traveled to Malta a few years before Piltdown came to light, and may have been in Tunisia as well. At the very least, he was closely acquainted with people who had been to this part of North Africa.

But what of motive? As rich and as successful a figure as Doyle would seem an unlikely candidate for such a ruse. Winslow, however, has also found some clues that suggest Sir Arthur *may* indeed have had a motive.

Doyle was a longtime spiritualist who believed firmly in the occult and in extrasensory powers. He bore little patience with scientific critics of such views, whom he regarded as closed-minded. In particular, he had a special rival, Edward Ray Lankester, one of the most renowned evolutionists of the early twentieth century. Perhaps, as Winslow speculates, Doyle invented the whole scheme as farce to embarrass the scientific establishment and, most especially, Lankester.

"So the case against Doyle is made. Besides the necessary skill, contacts, knowledge, and opportunity to qualify as the hoaxer, Doyle also had sufficient motive and an inviting target, Lankester" (Winslow and Meyer, 1983, p. 42).

Fascinating as it all is, we may never know whether the creator of Sherlock Holmes was also the Piltdown forger. Seventy years after the crime, the trail has grown stone cold—the forger covered his tracks very well indeed!

SOURCES:

Weiner, J. W., *The Piltdown Forgery*, London: Oxford University Press, 1955.

Winslow, John Hathaway and Alfred Meyer, "The Perpetrator at Piltdown," *Science '83*, September, 1983, pp. 33–43.

◇ CHAPTER THIRTEEN

◇ Introduction

We have seen in the last two chapters that hominids can be defined on the basis of dental adaptations and/or toolmaking behavior. In this chapter, we will review a series of remarkable discoveries in South Africa that persuaded paleoanthropologists to radically reassess their theories on human evolution.

◇ Early Hominids in the Plio-Pleistocene

The beginnings of hominid differentiation almost certainly have their roots in the late Miocene (*circa* 5–10 m.y.a.). Sometime during the period between 8 and 4 m.y.a., hominids began to adapt more fully to their peculiar ground living niche, and evolutionary evidence from this period would be most illuminating. However, scant information is presently available concerning the course of hominid evolution during this significant 4-million-year gap. But beginning around 4 m.y.a., the fossil record picks up considerably. We now have a wealth of fossil hominid material from the Pliocene and the earliest stages of the Pleistocene (5–1 m.y.a.), and this whole span is usually referred to as the Plio-Pleistocene.

◇ Earliest Discoveries

The first quarter of this century saw the discipline of paleoanthropology in its scientific infancy. Informed opinion considered the likely origins of the human family to be in Asia, where fossil forms of a primitive kind of *Homo* had been found in Indonesia in the 1890s. Europe was also considered a center of hominid evolutionary action, for spectacular discoveries there of early populations of *Homo sapiens* (including the famous Neandertals) and millions of stone tools had come to light, particularly in the early decades of this century.

Few knowledgeable scholars would have given much credence to Darwin's prediction (see Box 13-1) that the most likely place to find early relatives of humans would be on the continent of Africa. It was in such an atmosphere of preconceived biases that the discoveries of a young Australian-born anatomist were to jolt the foundations of the scientific community in the 1920s. **Raymond Dart** arrived in South Africa in 1923 at the age of 30 to take up a teaching position in anatomy at the University of Witwatersrand in Johannesburg. Fresh from his evolution-oriented training in England under some of the leading scholars of the day (especially, Sir Grafton Elliot Smith), Dart had developed a keen interest in human evolution. Consequently, he was well prepared when startling new evidence began to appear at his very doorstep.

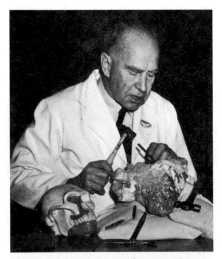

Figure 13-1 Dr. Raymond Dart working in his laboratory.

◇ Box 13-1 Hominid Origins

"In each great region of the world the living mammals are closely related to the extinct species of the same region. It is, therefore, probable that Africa was formerly inhabited by extinct apes closely allied to the gorilla and chimpanzee, and as these two species are now man's nearest allies, it is somewhat more probable that our early progenitors lived on the African continent than elsewhere."

SOURCE:
Charles Darwin. *The Descent of Man*, 1871.

The first clue came in 1924 when one of Dart's students saw an interesting baboon skull on the mantelpiece while having dinner at the home of the director of the Northern Lime Company, a commercial quarrying firm. The skull, that of a large baboon, had come from a place called Taung about 200 miles southwest of Johannesburg. When Dart saw the skull, he quickly recognized it as an extinct form and asked that any other interesting fossil material found be sent to him for his inspection.

Soon thereafter he received two boxloads of fossils and immediately recognized something that was quite unusual, a natural **endocast** of the inside of the braincase of a higher primate, but certainly no baboon. The endocast fit into another limestone block containing the fossilized front portion of skull, face, and lower jaw. However, these were difficult to see clearly, for the bone was hardened into a cemented limestone matrix called *breccia*. Dart patiently chiseled away for weeks, later describing the task: "No diamond cutter ever worked more lovingly or with such care on a priceless jewel—nor, I am sure, with such inadequate tools. But on the seventy-third day, December 23, the rock parted. I could view the face from the front, although the right side was still imbedded. . . . What emerged was a baby's face, an infant with a full set of milk teeth and its permanent molars just in the process of erupting. I doubt if there was any parent prouder of his offspring than I was of my Taung baby on that Christmas" (Dart, 1959, p. 10).

As indicated by the eruption of the first permanent molars, the Taung child was probably about 5 to 6 years of age at death. Dart's initial impression that this form was a hominoid was confirmed when he could observe the face and teeth more clearly. However, as it turned out, it took considerably more effort before the teeth could be seen completely, since Dart worked four years just to separate the upper and lower jaws.

But Dart was convinced long before he had an unimpeded view of the dentition that this discovery was a remarkable one, an early hominoid from South Africa. The question was, what kind of hominoid? Dart realized it was extremely improbable that this specimen could have been a forest ape, for South Africa has had a relatively dry climate for many millions of years. Even though the climate at Taung was not as arid as was previously believed (Butzer, 1974), it was an unlikely place to find an ape!

If not an ape, then, what was it? Features of the skull and teeth of this

Endocast
An endocast is a solid (in this case, rock) impression of the inside of the skull showing the size, shape, and some details of the surface of the brain.

(a)

(b)

Figure 13-2 (a) The Taung child discovered in 1924. The endocast is in back with the fossilized bone mandible and face in front; (b) Taung. Location of the initial australopithecine discovery.

◇ GREAT MOMENTS IN PREHISTORY
Raymond Dart and the Discovery of the Taung Child, November, 1924

On his return Young told me that at Taungs he had met an old miner, Mr. M. de Bruyn, who for many years had taken a keen interest in preserving fossils. Only the previous week he had brought quite a number of stone blocks containing bone fragments to Mr. Spiers' office. When Young mentioned my interest to Mr. Spiers, Spiers gave instructions for them to be boxed and railed to me.

I waited anxiously for their arrival, reasoning that if fossilized baboon skulls were such a common feature at Taungs many other, more interesting specimens might be found there. Of course, the packages turned up at the most inappropriate time.

I was standing by the window of my dressing room cursing softly while struggling into an unaccustomed stiff-winged collar when I noticed two men wearing the uniform of the South African Railways staggering along the driveway of our home in Johannesburg with two large wooden boxes.

My Virginia-born wife Dora, who was also donning her most formal outfit, had noticed the men with the boxes and rushed in to me in something of a panic.

"I suppose those are the fossils you've been expecting," she said. "Why on earth did they have to arrive today of all days?" She fixed me with a business-like eye. "Now Raymond," she pleaded, "the guests will start arriving shortly and you can't go delving in all that rubble until the wedding's over and everybody has left. I know how important the fossils are to you, but please leave them until tomorrow."

At the time, however, this seemed of little importance when I considered the exciting anthropological bits and pieces that the boxes from Taungs might contain. As soon as my wife had left to complete her dressing I tore the hated collar off and dashed out to take delivery of the boxes which meanwhile obstructed the entrance to the *stoep*. I was too excited to wait until my African servants carried them to the garage, and ordered them to leave the crates under the pergola while I went in search of some tools to open them.

(Later on that momentous day, my wife told me that she had twice remonstrated with me but had been ignored. I had no recollection of any interruptions.)

I wrenched the lid off the first box and my reaction was one of extreme disappointment. In the rocks I could make out traces of fossilized eggshells and turtle shells and a few fragmentary pieces of isolated bone, none of which looked to be of much interest.

Impatiently I wrestled with the lid of the second box, still hopeful but half-expecting it to be a replica of its mate. At most I anticipated baboon skulls, little guessing that from this crate was to emerge a face that would look out on the world after an age-long sleep of nearly a million years.

As soon as I removed the lid a thrill of excitement shot through me. On the very top of the rock heap was what was undoubtedly an endocranial cast or mold of the interior of the skull. Had it been only the fossilized brain cast of any species of ape it would have ranked as a great discovery, for such a thing had never before been reported. But I knew at a glance that what lay in my hands was no ordinary anthropoidal brain. Here in lime-consolidated sand was the replica of a brain three times as large as that of a baboon and considerably bigger than that of any adult chimpanzee. The startling image of the convolutions and furrows of the brain and the blood vessels of the skull was plainly visible.

I stood in the shade holding the brain as greedily as any miser hugs his gold, my mind racing ahead. Here, I was certain, was one of the most significant finds ever made in the history of anthropology.

SOURCE:
Adventures with the Missing Link by Raymond Dart, 1959. Reprinted with permission of the author.

small child held clues that Dart seized upon almost immediately. The entrance of the spinal column into the brain (the *foramen magnum* at the base of the skull) was further forward in the Taung child than in modern great apes, though not as much as in modern humans. From this fact Dart concluded that the head was balanced *above* the spine, indicating erect posture.

In addition, the slant of the forehead was not as receding as in apes, the milk canines were exceedingly small, and the newly erupted first molars were large, broad teeth. In all these respects, the Taung fossil looked more like a hominid than a pongid. There was, however, a disturbing feature that was to confuse and befuddle many scientists for several years: the brain was quite small. Recent studies have estimated the Taung's child brain size at approximately 405 cc. (cubic centimeters), which translates to a fully adult size of only 440 cc., not very large when compared to modern great apes, as the following tabulation (Tobias, 1971; 1983) shows:

	Range	Mean
Chimpanzee	282–500 cc.	394 cm³
Gorilla	340–752 cc.	506 cm³
Orang	276–540 cc.	411 cm³

As the tabulation indicates, the estimated cranial capacity for the Taung fossil falls within the range of all the modern great apes, and gorillas actually *average* about 10% greater. It must, however, be remembered that gorillas are very large animals, whereas the Taung child represents a population whose average adult size may have been less than sixty pounds. Since brain size is partially correlated with body size, comparing such differently sized animals cannot be justified. A more meaningful contrast would be with the pygmy chimpanzee (*Pan paniscus*), whose body weight is more comparable. Pygmy chimps have adult cranial capacities averaging 356 cm³ for males and 329 for females, and thus the Taung child versus a *comparably sized* pongid displays a 25% increase in cranial capacity.

Despite the relatively small size of the brain, Dart saw that it was no pongid. Details preserved on the endocast seemed to indicate that the association areas of the parietal lobes were relatively larger than in any known pongid. However, recent reexamination of the Taung specimen has shown that the sulcal (folding) pattern is actually quite pongidlike (Falk, 1980; 1983).

We must emphasize that attempts to discern the precise position of the "bumps and folds" in ancient endocasts is no easy feat. The science of "paleoneurology" is thus often marked by sharp differences of opinion. Consequently, it is not surprising that the other leading researcher in this field, Ralph Halloway (1981), disagrees with the conclusion by Falk (just cited) and suggests, alternatively, that the Taung endocast has a more hominidlike sulcal pattern.

Realizing the immense importance of his findings, Dart promptly reported them in the British scientific weekly *Nature* on February 7, 1925. A bold venture, since Dart, only 32, was presumptuously proposing a whole new view of human evolution! The small-brained Taung child was christened by Dart **Australopithecus africanus** (southern ape of Africa), which he saw as a kind of halfway "missing-link" between modern apes and humans. The concept of a single "missing link" between modern apes and humans was a fallacious one, but Dart correctly emphasized the hominidlike features of the fossil.

A storm of both popular and scholarly protest greeted Dart's article, for it ran directly counter to prevailing opinion. Despite the numerous hominid

Australopithecus
(Os-tral-oh-pith′-e-kus)

Africanus
(af-ra-kan′-us)

Figure 13-3 Pygmy chimpanzee. A modern pongid probably similar in body size to many of the australopithecines.

Figure 13-4 The human brain. Schematic diagram of surface showing major functional areas and surface features.

fossils already discovered, widespread popular skepticism of evolution still prevailed. The year 1925 was, after all, the year of the Scopes "monkey trial" in Tennessee. The biggest fly in the ointment to the leading human evolutionists of the day—Arthur Keith and Grafton Elliot Smith—was the small size of the brain compared to the relatively large proportions of the face and jaws. At that time, anthropologists generally assumed that the primary functional adaptation distinguishing the human family was an immense increase in brain size, and that dental and locomotory modifications came later. This view was seemingly confirmed by the Piltdown discovery in 1911, which displayed the combination of a large brain (estimated at 1400 cm³, well within the range of modern man) with an ape-like jaw (see pp. 394–395). Keith even went so far as to postulate a "Cerebral Rubicon" of 750 cm³ below which— by definition—no hominid could fall. Most scientists in the 1920s thus regarded this little Taung child as an interesting aberrant form of ape.

Hence, Dart's theories were received with indifference, disbelief, and scorn, often extremely caustic. Dart realized more complete remains were needed. The skeptical world would not accept the evidence of one fragmentary, immature individual no matter how highly suggestive the clues. Clearly, more fossil evidence was required, particularly more complete crania of adults. Not an experienced fossil hunter himself, Dart sought further assistance in the search for more **australopithecines** (the colloquial name referring to the members of genus *Australopithecus*).

◇ Hominids Aplenty

Soon after publication of his controversial theories, Dart found a strong ally in **Dr. Robert Broom**. A Scottish physician and part-time paleontologist, Broom's credentials as a fossil hunter had been established earlier with his highly successful paleontological work on early mammallike reptiles in South Africa.

Although interested, Broom was unable to participate actively in the search for additional australopithecines because of prior commitments and did not seriously undertake explorations until 1936. However, soon thereafter he met with incredible success. From two of Dart's students, Broom learned of

Figure 13-5 Dr. Robert Broom. Shown with one of his paleontological discoveries from South Africa. This photo was taken earlier in Dr. Broom's career; it would be almost thirty years later before he would even begin his search for australopithecines.

◇ GREAT MOMENTS IN PREHISTORY
Dr. Broom and the Discovery of the Kromdraai Ape-Man

On the forenoon of Wednesday, June 8, 1938, when I met Barlow, he said, "I've something nice for you this morning"; and he held out part of a fine palate with the first molar-tooth in position. I said, "Yes, it's quite nice. I'll give you a couple of pounds for it." He was delighted; so I wrote out a cheque, and put the specimen in my pocket. He did not seem quite willing to say where or how he had obtained it; and I did not press the matter. The specimen clearly belonged to a large ape-man, and was apparently different from the Sterkfontein being.

I was again at Sterkfontein on Saturday, when I knew Barlow would be away. I showed the specimen to the native boys in the quarry; but none of them had ever seen it before. I felt sure it had not come from the quarry, as the matrix was different. On Tuesday forenoon I was again at Sterkfontein, when I insisted on Barlow telling me how he had got the specimen. I pointed out that two teeth had been freshly broken off, and that they might be lying where the specimen had been obtained. He apologized for having misled me; and told me it was a schoolboy, Gert Terblanche, who acted as a guide in the caves on Sundays, who had picked it up and given it to him. I found where Gert lived, about two miles away; but Barlow said he was sure to be away at school. Still, I set out for his home. There I met Gert's mother and sister. They told me that the place where the specimen was picked up was near the top of a hill about half a mile away, and the sister agreed to take me up to the place. She and her mother also told me that Gert had four beautiful teeth at school with him.

The sister took us up the hill, and I picked up some fragments of the skull, and a couple of teeth; but she said she was sure Gert had some other nice pieces hidden away. Of course, I had to go to school to hunt up Gert.

The road to the school was a very bad one, and we had to leave the car, and walk about a mile over rough ground. When we got there, it was about half-past twelve, and it was play time. I found the headmaster, and told him that I wanted to see Gert Terblanche in connection with some teeth he had picked up. Gert was soon found, and drew from the pocket of his trousers four of the most wonderful teeth ever seen in the world's history. These I promptly purchased from Gert, and transferred to my pocket. I had the palate with me, and I found that two of the teeth were the second pre-molar and second molar, and that they fitted on to the palate. The two others were teeth of the other side. Gert told me about the piece he had hidden away. As the school did not break up till two o'clock, I suggested to the principal that I should give a lecture to the teachers and children about caves, how they were formed, and how bones got into them. He was delighted. So it was arranged; and I lectured to four teachers and about 120 children for over an hour, with blackboard illustrations, till it was nearly two o'clock. When I finished, the principal broke up the school, and Gert came home with me. He took us up to the hill, and brought out from his hiding place a beautiful lower jaw with two teeth in position. All the fragments that I could find at the spot I picked up.

SOURCE:
Finding the Missing Link by Robert Broom (2nd Ed.), 1951. By permission of C. A. Watts/Pitman Publishing Ltd., London.

another commercial limeworks site, called **Sterkfontein**, not far from Johannesburg. Here, as at Taung, the quarrying involved blasting out large sections with dynamite, leaving piles of debris that often contained fossilized remains. Accordingly, Broom asked the quarry manager to keep his eyes open for fossils, and when Broom returned to the site in August 1936, the manager asked, "Is this what you are looking for?" Indeed, it was, for Broom held in his hand the endocast of an adult australopithecine—exactly what he had set out to find! Looking further over the scattered debris, Broom was able to find most of the rest of the skull of the same individual.

Australopithecine
(os-tral-oh-pith'-e-seen)

Sterkfontein
(Sterk'-fon-tane)

Figure 13-6 Australopithecine sites in South Africa.

Figure 13-7 A gracile australopithecine skull from Sterkfontein (Sts. 5). This specimen is the best preserved gracile skull yet found in South Africa. Discovered in 1947.

Such remarkable success, just a few months after beginning his search, was not the end of Broom's luck, for his magical touch was to continue unabated for several more years. In 1938, he learned from a young schoolboy of another australopithecine site at **Kromdraai** about one mile from Sterkfontein, and, following World War II (1948), he found yet another australopithecine site, **Swartkrans**, in the same vicinity. A final australopithecine site, **Makapansgat**, was excavated in 1947 by Raymond Dart, who returned to the fossil-discovering bandwagon after an absence of over twenty years.

Numerous extremely important discoveries came from these five sites, discoveries that would eventually swing the tide of intellectual thought to the views Dart expressed back in 1925. Particularly important was a nearly perfect skull and a nearly complete pelvis, both found at Sterkfontein in 1947. As the number of discoveries accumulated, it became increasingly difficult to simply write them off as aberrant apes.

Although Robert Broom was an absolute wizard at finding fossils, his interpretations of them were clouded by an irresistible urge to give each new discovery a different taxonomic label. Consequently, in addition to Dart's *A. africanus* from Taung, a disconcertingly large number of other names have been used at various times for the South African australopithecines (see Table 13-1). The problem with all this taxonomic splitting was a lack of appreciation for the relevant biological principles underlying such elaborate interpretations (see Chapter 11 for a discussion of the meaning of taxonomic statements).

By 1949, at least thirty individuals were represented from the five South African sites. That year represents an important turning point, since it marks the visit to South Africa and the resulting "conversion" of W. E. Le Gros Clark. As one of the leading human evolutionists of the day, Sir Wilfrid Le Gros Clark's unequivocal support of the australopithecines as small-brained early hominids was to have wide impact. But the tides of wisdom had begun to turn even before this. Writing in 1947, **Sir Arthur Keith** courageously admitted his earlier mistake:

"When Professor Dart of the University of Witwatersrand, Johannesburg, announced in *Nature* the discovery of a juvenile *Australopithecus* and claimed for it human kinship, I was one of those who took the point of view that when the adult was discovered, it would prove to be nearer akin to the living African anthropoids—the gorilla and chimpanzee.... I am now convinced of the evidence submitted by Dr. Robert Broom that Professor Dart was right and I was wrong. The Australopi-

Table 13-1 Taxonomic Labels Applied to South African Australopithecines

	Site	Discovered and named by
Australopithecus africanus	Taung	Dart
Plesianthropus transvaalensis	Sterkfontein	Broom
Paranthropus robustus	Kromdraai	Broom
Paranthropus crassidens	Swartkrans	Broom
Australopithecus prometheus	Makapansgat	Dart
Telanthropus capensis	Swartkrans	Broom

thecinae [formal designation of the australopithecines as a subfamily of the hominids] are in or near the line which culminated in the human form" (Keith in Le Gros Clark, 1967, p. 38).

With the exposé of the Piltdown forgery in the early 1950s, the path was completely cleared for the nearly unanimous recognition of the australopithecines as early hominids. With this acceptance also came the necessary recognition that hominid brains had their greatest expansion *after* earlier changes in teeth and locomotory systems. In other words, the rates of evolution in one functional system of the body vary from other systems, thus displaying the **mosaic** nature of human **evolution**.

Even today, the evidence from South Africa continues to accumulate. The search continues at Sterkfontein, Swartkrans, and Makapansgat. An important portion of pelvis was found at Swartkrans in 1970, and a partial skull was found at Sterkfontein (west pit) in 1976. Indeed, discoveries are now coming faster than ever. In the last year alone more than 150 *new* specimens have come to light at Sterkfontein—exceeding the total for any previous year (see Table 13-2). A truly remarkable feast of early hominids, the total number of remains from South Africa exceeds 1,500 (counting all teeth as separate items), and the number of individuals is estimated to be close to 190 individuals (Tobias, 1983).

Of all the hominid remains from South Africa, less than 10% are postcranial (that is, below the head), but this evidence, nevertheless, is crucially significant in revealing the all-important locomotory function of these animals. As of 1972, this extremely informative evidence included twenty-two remains representing the shoulder girdle and upper limb, thirteen from the pelvic girdle and lower limb, and thirty-four from the rib and vertebral areas (Tobias, 1972).

From an evolutionary point of view, the most meaningful remains are those from the australopithecine pelvis, which now includes portions of nine **innominates** (Fig. 13-11). Remains of the pelvis are so important because, better than any other area of the body, this structure displays the unique requirements of a bipedal animal, such as modern humans *and* our hominid forebears. (For anatomical comparisons, see Appendix A.)

Kromdraai
(Kromm'-dry)

Swartkrans

Makapansgat
(Mak-ah-pans'-gat)

Mosaic evolution
Rate of evolution in one functional system varies from other systems.

Innominate
The fused half-portion of a pelvis; contains three bones—the ilium, ischium, and pubis.

Figure 13-8 Sir Arthur Keith.

Table 13-2 Sterkfontein Hominid Specimens, 1936–1984*

	Number in Calendar Year	Cumulative Total
1936–1979	—	145
1979	10	155
1980	5	160
1981	7	167
1982	69	236
1983	44	280
1984 (to 24 August)	164	444

*These are totals for specimens, not individuals. A single individual may be represented by several teeth in a given sample, each tooth of which counts as a different specimen. Data provided courtesy of Professor Phillip Tobias.

Figure 13-9 A partial hominid skull from Sterkfontein (Stw. 53). Discovered during recent excavations (August 1976).

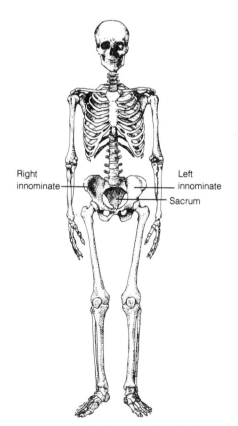

Figure 13-10 The human pelvis. Various elements shown on a modern skeleton.

◇ Hominids on Their Feet

As we discussed in Chapter 9, there is a general tendency in all primates for erect body posture and some bipedalism. However, of all living primates, efficient bipedalism as the primary form of locomotion is seen *only* in hominids. Functionally, the human mode of locomotion is most clearly shown in our striding gait, where weight is alternately placed on a single fully extended hindlimb. This specialized form of locomotion has developed to a point where energy levels are used to near peak efficiency. Such is not the case in nonhuman primates, who move bipedally with hips and knees bent and maintain balance in a clumsy and inefficient manner.

From a survey of our close primate relatives, it is apparent that, while still in the trees, our ancestors were adapted to a fair amount of upper body erectness. Prosimians, monkeys, and apes all spend considerable time sitting erect while feeding, grooming, or sleeping. Presumably, our early ancestors also displayed similar behavior. What caused these forms to come to the ground and embark on the unique way of life that would eventually lead to humans is still a mystery. Perhaps natural selection favored an animal such as *Sivapithecus* coming occasionally to the ground to forage for food on the forest floor and forest fringe. In any case, once it was on the ground and away from the immediate safety offered by trees, bipedal locomotion became a tremendous advantage.

First of all, bipedal locomotion freed the hands for carrying objects and for making and using tools. Such early cultural developments then had an even more positive effect on speeding the development of yet more efficient bipedalism—once again emphasizing the dual role of biocultural evolution. In addition, in the bipedal stance, animals have a wider view of the surrounding countryside, and, in open terrain, early spotting of predators (particularly the large cats, such as lions, leopards, and saber tooths) would be of critical importance. We know that modern ground-living primates, such as the savanna baboon and chimpanzee, will occasionally adopt this posture to "look around" when out in open country. Certainly, bipedal walking is an efficient means of covering long distances, and when large game hunting came into play (several million years after the initial adaptation to ground living), further refinements in the locomotory complex may have been favored. Finally, it has been suggested that bipedalism was initially most adaptive for carrying—particularly food brought by provisioning males to females and young (Lovejoy, 1981). (See pp. 271–272.) Exactly what initiated the process is difficult to say, but all these factors probably played a role in the adaptation of hominids to their special niche through a special form of locomotion.

Our mode of locomotion is indeed extraordinary, involving as it does a unique kind of activity in which "the body, step by step, teeters on the edge of catastrophe" (Napier, 1967, p. 56). The problem is to maintain balance on the "stance" leg while the "swing" leg is off the ground. In fact, during normal walking, both feet are simultaneously on the ground only about 25% of the time, and, as speed of locomotion increases, this figure becomes even smaller.

In order to maintain a stable center of balance in this complex form of locomotion, many drastic structural/functional alterations are demanded in the basic primate quadrupedal pattern. Functionally, the foot must be altered to act as a stable support instead of a grasping limb. When we walk, our foot is used like a prop, landing on the heel and pushing off on the toes, particularly the big toe. In addition, the leg must be elongated to increase the length of the stride and lower the center of gravity. The lower limb must also be remodeled to allow full extension of the knee and to allow the legs to be kept close together during walking, thereby maintaining the center of support directly under the body. Finally, significant changes must occur in the pelvis to permit stable weight transmission from the upper body to the legs and to maintain balance through pelvic rotation and altered proportions and orientations of several key muscles.

The major structural changes that are required for bipedalism are all seen in the australopithecines. In the pelvis, the blade (ilium—upper bone of the pelvis) is shortened top to bottom, which permits more stable weight support in the erect position by lowering the center of gravity. In addition, the pelvis is bent backwards and downwards, thus altering the position of the muscles that attach along the bone. Most importantly, the gluteus medius (glue-tee'-us meed'-ee-us) now becomes a very large muscle acting to stablize the trunk and keep it from slumping to the unsupported side while the body is supported on one leg. The gluteus maximus (glue-tee'-us max'-a-mus) also becomes important as an extensor—pulls the thigh back—during running, jumping, and climbing.

Other structural changes shown by australopithecine postcranial evidence further confirm the morphological pattern seen in the pelvis. The vertebral column, known from a beautifully preserved specimen from Sterkfontein, shows the same forward curvature as in modern hominids, bringing the center of support forward and allowing rotation of the bottom of the vertebral column (sacrum) below, thereby getting it out of the way of the birth canal. In addition, the lower limb is elongated and is apparently proportionately about as long as in modern humans. Fossil evidence of a knee fragment from Sterkfontein also shows that full extension of this joint was possible, thus allowing the leg to be completely straightened, as when a field goal kicker follows through.

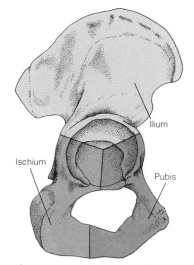

Figure 13-11   The human innominate. Composed of three bones (right side shown).

Figure 13-12   The knee in full extension.

Figure 13-13   Innominates. (*a*) *Homo sapiens*; (*b*) australopithecine (Sts. 14); (*c*) chimpanzee. Note especially the length and breadth of the iliac blade.

(a)   (b)   (c)

Figure 13-14   A nearly complete hominid foot (OH 8). From Olduvai Gorge, East Africa.

Structural evidence for the foot is not abundant in South Africa, but one ankle bone from Kromdraai shows a rather mixed pattern. This particular foot probably belonged to an animal that was a well-adapted biped but still retained considerable climbing ability. More complete evidence for evolutionary changes in the foot skeleton comes from Olduvai Gorge in East Africa, where a nearly complete hominid foot is preserved, and from the Afar region in Ethiopia, where numerous foot elements have been recovered. As in the ankle bone from Kromdraai, the East African fossils suggest a well-adapted bipedal gait. The arches are developed and the big toe is pulled in next to the other toes, but some differences in the ankle also imply that considerable flexibility was possible (for climbing?). As we will see in the next chapter, some researchers have recently concluded that the early forms of australopithecine probably spent considerable time in the trees. Moreover, they may not have been as efficient bipeds as has previously been suggested (see p. 433).

◇ Australopithecines: How Many Forms?

All the australopithecines in South Africa are clearly hominid as shown in the morphological details of their pelvis, limbs, dentition, and skull. However, a dichotomy exists among the fossils between larger, more heavily built (robust) individuals and smaller, more lightly built (gracile) ones. There is also a dichotomy in the sites of occupation of these two forms, with graciles found at Sterkfontein and Makapansgat and robusts at Swartkrans and Kromdraai (the Taung child remains somewhat of an enigma).

Accurate size and weight estimates are extremely difficult to ascertain from fragmentary evidence, but the best guess for the graciles is a stature of 4–4½ feet with a weight of about 60 pounds. Estimates by different investigators, however, vary considerably (stature, 42–57 inches; weight, 40–61 pounds). The robusts are definitely larger, standing approximately 4½–5 feet and weighing around 100 pounds. (Range of estimates: stature, 57–65 inches; weight, 70–200 pounds.)

In addition to overall size differences, gracile and robust forms may be contrasted in their respective cranial and dental anatomy. The robust skull is generally larger with a cranial capacity (sample size, or $N = 1$) estimated at 530 cm^3 compared to a mean of 450 cm^3 ($N = 7$) for the graciles. Since, of course, brain size is partially correlated with body size, we would expect larger skulls in the bigger animals. In addition to size, however, there are also differences in shape. The graciles have a more rounded braincase, which rises more vertically above the eyes, yielding a well developed forehead, as compared to the flattened-out appearance of the robust skull.

The face structure of the graciles is also more lightly built and somewhat dish-shaped compared to the more vertical configuration seen in robust specimens. In robust individuals, a raised ridge along the midline of the skull, called a **sagittal crest**, is occasionally observed. This structure provides additional attachment area for the large temporal muscle, which is the primary

Figure 13-15   A nearly complete cranium from Swartkrans (Sk. 48). The best preserved skull of a robust australopithecine from South Africa.

muscle operating the massive jaw below. Such a structure is also seen in some modern apes, especially male gorillas and orangs; however, in australopithecines, the temporal muscle acts most efficiently on the back of the mouth and is therefore not functionally equivalent to the front tooth emphasis seen in pongids (see Fig. 13-16).

The most distinctive difference observed between gracile and robust australopithecines is in the dentition. Compared to modern humans, they both have relatively large teeth, which are, however, definitely hominid in pattern. In fact, more emphasis is on the typical back-tooth grinding complex among these early forms than the forms of today; therefore, if anything, australopithecines are "hyperhominid"! Robust forms emphasize this trend to an extreme degree, showing deep jaws and much-enlarged back teeth, particularly the molars, severely crowding the front teeth (incisors and canines) together. Conversely, the graciles have proportionately larger front teeth compared to the size of their back teeth. This contrast is seen most clearly in the relative sizes of the canine compared to the first premolar: in robust individuals, the first premolar is clearly a much larger tooth than the small canine (about twice as large) whereas, in gracile specimens, it only averages about 20% larger than the fairly goodsized canine (Howells, 1973).

These differences in the relative proportions of the teeth and jaws best define a gracile, as compared to a robust, form. In fact, most of the differences in skull shape we have discussed can be directly attributed to contrasting jaw function in the two forms. Both the sagittal crest and broad vertical face of the robust form are related to the muscles and biomechanical requirements of the extremely large-tooth chewing adaptation of this animal.

◇South African Australopithecines: Interpretations

Clearly, variation among the South African Plio-Pleistocene hominids defines two fairly distinct groups: gracile and robust australopithecines. The question that now must be addressed is: How do we interpret this variation in biologically meaningful terms? In order to answer, we must keep certain biological principles clearly in mind (see Chapter 11).

We know, of course, that our australopithecine fossils are samples of what were once interbreeding populations. We also know that all such populations show variation. Our task is to interpret this variation in a biologically realistic manner, assign appropriate taxonomic labels, and, in the end, hopefully gain some insight into the nature of human evolution.

We have noted that, even in living forms, biological interpretations, such as those suggested by genus and species designations, are often a complex and risky endeavor. To assign genus and species names to long-dead fossil groups (whose adaptations must be indirectly inferred from usually small samples of fragmentary skeletal remains) is a considerably more difficult task.

As a means of reconstructing realistic dimensions of expected biological variation due to sexual dimorphism, age, and other factors, we refer to living

Sagittal crest
Raised ridge along the midline of the skull where the temporal muscle (used to move the jaw) attaches.

Temporal muscle fibers oriented towards back teeth

(a) Hominid (robust australopithecine)

Temporal muscle fibers oriented towards front teeth

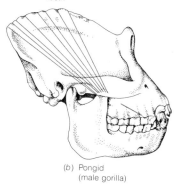

(b) Pongid (male gorilla)

Figure 13-16 Sagittal crests and temporal muscle orientations. Hominid compared to pongid.

populations of primates. Yet even this kind of analysis provides no easy, unambiguous answer to the question of how best to interpret the differences between robust and gracile australopithecines. Variation in modern primates can match the observed differences in the australopithecines either *within*

Figure 13-17 Intraspecific variation: sexual dimorphism—(*a*) male (left) and female gelada baboons. Interspecific variation: two species of macaque—(*b*) *Macaca mulatta* (Rhesus monkey); (*c*) *Macaca nemistrina*.

(a)

(b)

(c)

one species (*intraspecific*, as in gelada baboons) or *between two different species* (*interspecific*, as between some species of macaques).

Given these complexities, it is no wonder that considerable controversy surrounds the detailed interpretation of variation in australopithecine fossil material.

THE SINGLE SPECIES HYPOTHESIS

The most straightforward and economical interpretation of the australopithecines, both gracile and robust, is that they are members of one species, *A. africanus* (this name takes precedence according to the rules of the International Code of Zoological Nomenclature).

This theory—accounting for all South African australopithecine material—is usually referred to as the *single species hypothesis*. In this view, the variation among the australopithecines is explained by simple sexual dimorphism; the robust specimens are the males, and the graciles are females. Certainly, such variation is present in early hominids, and proponents of this theory point out that considerable sexual dimorphism is displayed today in other terrestrial primates, particularly baboons and gorillas (Brace, 1973). Moreover, advocates of the single species hypothesis have also correctly emphasized that it is not legitimate to describe the differences between robust and gracile on the basis of isolated individuals. Unfortunately, this has often been done using the best-preserved specimens, Sts. (Sterkfontein) 5 and Sk. (Swartkrans) 48, but these two fossils may not be representative of their respective populations. For example, Sts. 5 may be a female (therefore the popular name, "Mrs. Ples") and Sk. 48 may well be a male. To compare a male from one population with a female from the other overemphasizes the real biological differences. Clearly, what must be done then is to use *all* the relevant fossil material, and abundant samples, especially teeth, are known from both Sterkfontein and Swartkrans. When all the material is compared, it becomes apparent that considerable overlap in physical traits occurs between robust and gracile groups of australopithecines.

Whereas the single species hypothesis is attractive, and theoretically is an excellent starting point for *any* interpretation of biological variation, it does not completely explain the situation for South African australopithecines. First of all, there is the problem that robust individuals seemingly come just from Swartkrans and Kromdraai, while graciles are confined to Sterkfontein and Makapansgat. Secondly, as we will see later in the chapter (p. 413), the graciles from Sterkfontein and Makapansgat are considerably earlier in time (perhaps a million years or more) than the robusts from Swartkrans and Kromdraai. Moreover, the great amount of variation between robust and gracile australopithecines can occasionally be matched within species of some modern primates (for instance, baboons and gorillas), but are these necessarily good models for hominids? In addition, the *pattern* of variation in the teeth is not matched between sexes in any living primate.

Apparently, then, the variation among South African australopithecines is greater than can be explained by sexual dimorphism (or, for that matter, any kind of *intraspecific* variation). We are then left with the most likely conclusion

GRACILE   ROBUST

One Species

A. africanus

Figure 13-18 The single species hypothesis.

(a) Gracile

(b) Robust

Figure 13-19 Two varieties of South African australopithecines.

Table 13-3   Summary of Morphological Differences, Gracile versus Robust Australopithecines

Gracile	Robust
smaller, more lightly built	larger, more heavily built
height: 4–4½ ft.	height: 4½–5 ft.
weight: 60 lbs.	weight: 100 lbs.
skull more rounded, more vertical forehead	skull flattened out
sagittal crest never seen*	occasional sagittal crest
face usually dish-shaped and narrow	face broad and more vertical
front teeth (incisors and canines) reasonably good size; back teeth large	front teeth, quite small; back teeth, very large

*One specimen from Makapansgat may have had a sagittal crest. In many respects the Makapansgat material is transitional in nature between robust and gracile features.

that more than one species of australopithecines existed; but how do we interpret this conclusion in an evolutionarily meaningful way?

The Dietary Hypothesis

Another school of thought not only draws a species-level difference between gracile and robust australopithecines but a genus-level one as well. In this theory, usually called the *dietary hypothesis*, graciles are called *Australopithecus* and robusts, **Paranthropus**.

The central aspect of the dietary hypothesis concerns dentition and what it may tell us about diet. As we have discussed, robust australopithecines have proportionately larger back teeth and smaller front teeth than have the gracile form. From this fact, Robinson (1972) has inferred that the robust had a specialized vegetarian diet contrasted with a more omnivorous one for the graciles. All the modifications of skull and face of the robust group are then seen as directly related to the mechanical demands of chewing large amounts of vegetable foods.

Initially suggested by J. T. Robinson, once Broom's assistant and now at the University of Wisconsin, this theory has three primary biological and evolutionary implications:

1. The two groups were not interbreeding; speciation had already occurred.
2. More than speciation, genus-level differences due to variable ecological life styles had also occurred. (The direct implication here is that speciation had occurred a good deal earlier, and these two forms are thus not particularly closely related.)
3. Since only *one* species of hominid (*H. sapiens*) is now living, only *one* species at any given time could be our direct ancestor. The robust group (*Paranthropus*) is seen here as the more specialized form, whereas the gracile form (*Australopithecus*)* is usually viewed as the more likely ancestor (even this suggestion has recently come into question—see Chapter 14).

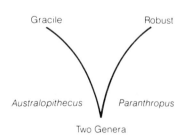

Figure 13-20   The dietary hypothesis.

While this theory explains the observed variation and the site distribution of fossil discoveries, it may be somewhat overzealous. It is often quite difficult to reconstruct diet on the basis of tooth proportions (Clark, 1967), and many of the observed dental and cranial differences may in fact be simply a function of the larger body size in the robust form (Pilbeam and Gould, 1974).

ONE GENUS, TWO SPECIES

Most anthropologists advocate a somewhat middle position between the two theories just described. They agree with points 1 and 2 of the dietary hypothesis, namely that speciation (and thus reproductive isolation) had occurred, and that the robust form was probably on an extinct sidebranch. However, advocates of this more moderate point of view (Clark, 1967; Tobias, 1967; Pilbeam, 1972) are not willing to go so far as to postulate a sufficiently major difference in ecological adaptation to justify a genus-level distinction. Moreover, they see the two species as quite closely related. Therefore, proponents of this theory postulate one genus, *Australopithecus*, with two species: gracile, *africanus*; and robust, *robustus*.

Another modification of this interpretation views the differences between graciles and robusts as the result of temporal evolution within a single evolutionary lineage (Johanson and White, 1979). In other words, gracile australopithecines simply evolved into robust ones, who then went extinct.

We feel that, on the basis of present evidence, some version of this last theory is the most probable, and explains the variation among South African australopithecines in the most biologically reasonable manner. However, as the varied opinions themselves indicate, no clear conclusion is possible given the kind and amount of evidence available.

◇ Geology and Dating Problems

The five South African australopithecine sites are extremely complex geologically. All were discovered by commercial quarrying activity, which greatly disrupted the geological picture and, in the case of Taung, completely destroyed the site.

The australopithecine remains are found with thousands of other fossilized bones embedded in limestone cliffs, caves, fissures, and sinkholes. The limestone was built by millions of generations of shells of marine organisms during the Pre-Cambrian—more than 2 billion years ago—when South Africa was submerged under a shallow sea. Once deposited, the limestones were cut through by percolating ground water from below and rain water from above, forming a maze of caves and fissures often connected to the surface by narrow shafts. Through these vertical shafts and horizontal cave openings, bones

*J. T. Robinson (1972) has included genus *Australopithecus* within *Homo*, what taxonomists call "sinking" one genus into another.

Paranthropus
(Par-an'-throw-pus)

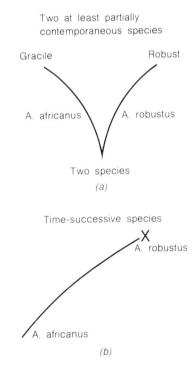

Figure 13-21 One-genus, two-species interpretation. (*a*) Two at least partially contemporaneous species. (*b*) Time-successive species: *A. africanus* evolves into *A. robustus*.

Figure 13-22 Swartkrans, geological section. The upper (reconstructed) part has been removed by erosion since the accumulation of the fossil-bearing deposit. (After Brain, 1970).

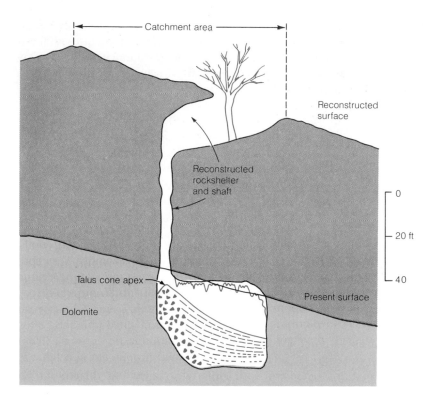

either fell or were carried in, where they conglomerated with sand, pebbles, and soil into a cementlike matrix called *breccia*.

As the cave fissures filled in, they were constantly subjected to further erosion forces from above and below, so that caves would be partially filled, then closed to the surface for a considerable time, and reopened again to commence accumulation thousands of years later. All this activity yields an incredibly complex geological situation that can only be worked out after the most detailed kind of paleoecological analysis.

Since bones accumulated in these caves and fissures largely by accidental processes, it seems likely that none of the South African australopithecine sites are *primary* hominid localities. In other words, unlike East Africa, these are not areas where hominids organized activities, scavenged food, etc.

Just how did all the fossilized bone accumulate and, most particularly, what were the australopithecines doing there? In the case of Swartkrans, Sterkfontein, and Kromdraai, the bones probably accumulated through the combined activities of carnivorous leopards, sabre-toothed cats, and hyenas. However, the unexpectedly high proportion of primate (baboon and hominid) remains suggests that these localities were the location (or very near the location) of primate sleeping sites, thus providing ready prey for the predators (Brain, 1981).

Raymond Dart has argued enthusiastically for an alternative explanation, suggesting the australopithecines camping at Makapansgat regularly used bone, tooth, and horn remains as *tools*, which he has grandly called the osteodontokeratic culture complex. Analogies with modern Hottentot food habits indicate the bone accumulation at Makapansgat may be accounted for simply by hominid and carnivore eating practices. Recent paleoecological work at Makapansgat has thrown Dart's assertions into even greater doubt. Apparently, remains accumulated here primarily in a similar fashion to Sterkfontein and Swartkrans—through a narrow shaft entrance. Therefore, large animals could have entered but not departed the deep subterranean cavern. Makapansgat, like Sterkfontein and Swartkrans, probably also represents the accumulated debris of carnivore activity (perhaps hyenas) outside the cave entrance.

So little is left of the final site, Taung, that accurate paleoanthropological reconstructions are not feasible.

Due to the complex geological picture, as well as lack of appropriate material such as volcanics for chronometric techniques, dating the South African australopithecine sites has posed tremendous problems. Without chronometric dating, the best that can be done is to correlate the faunal sequences in South Africa with areas such as East Africa where dates are better known (this approach is called "biostratigraphy"—see p. 381). Faunal sequencing of this sort on pigs, bovids such as antelopes, and baboons has provided the following tenuous chronology:

	1 m.y.	
Kromdraai		
Swartkrans		Taung?*
	2 m.y.	
Sterkfontein		
Makapansgat	3 m.y.	

Recent attempts at paleomagnetic dating (see p. 379) suggest an age of 3.3–2.8 m.y.a. for Makapansgat (Brock et al., 1977), thus pushing the estimates to the extreme limits of those provided by biostratigraphy. In fact, some researchers believe the paleomagnetic results are ambiguous and continue to "put their money" on the biostratigraphic data, especially those dates determined by analysis of pig fossils. From such considerations, they place the South African australopithecine sites as much as one-half million years later (i.e., for Makapansgat, around 2.5 m.y.a.) (White et al., 1981).

◇ Summary

Between 2 and 3 m.y.a., bipedal but small-brained hominids occupied South Africa. The fact that the tremendous expansion of the brain was a *late* development in hominid evolution came as a surprise to most scholars in the early part of this century. However, the discoveries of Raymond Dart and Robert Broom eventually were to demonstrate convincingly the mosaic nature of human evolution. Bipedal animals, the australopithecines are clearly hom-

*Some (Butzer, 1974; Tobias, 1976) have suggested Taung may be very late, even Middle Pleistocene (*circa* 700,000–800,000 y.a.), but this conclusion remains a matter of active dispute.

Osteodontokeratic
osteo: bone
dento: tooth
keratic: horn

inid, as repeatedly shown in the details of their pelvis, limbs, feet, and vertebral column. In addition, the structure of their skull and teeth also confirm the hominid affinities of these forms. While hominids, all australopithecines are not identical and fall into two major groups, robust and gracile, distinguished primarily on the basis of body size and tooth proportions.

Interpretations of the variation between these two groups have engendered several theories, three of which are discussed in this chapter: the single species hypothesis; the dietary hypothesis; and the one-genus/two-species explanation. All these theories have something to offer, but consideration of the relevant biological principles make the one-genus/two-species explanation the most reasonable at this time. Thus, there are probably at least two species of hominids in South Africa during the Plio-Pleistocene—*Australopithecus africanus* (gracile) and *Australopithecus robustus* (robust).

Just how these fossil hominids fit into a comprehensive scheme of human evolution is difficult to answer in the absence of a reliable chronology. For this kind of reliability we must turn to East Africa where discoveries in the last twenty years have demanded a total reappraisal of the earlier finds in South Africa.

◇ Questions for Review

1. Why was Raymond Dart's announcement of a small-brained bipedal hominoid greeted with such skepticism in 1925?
2. What led Dart to suggest the Taung child was *not* an ape?
3. What was Robert Broom's contribution to revealing the hominid nature of the South African australopithecines?
4. (a) Why is postcranial evidence (particularly the lower limb) so crucial in showing the australopithecines as definite hominids? (b) What particular aspects of the australopithecine pelvis and lower limb are hominidlike?
5. What are the most important morphological distinctions between gracile and robust australopithecines?
6. How might the variation between the gracile and robust forms be interpreted (in a biologically meaningful manner)? Critically evaluate:
   (a) the single species hypothesis
   (b) the dietary hypothesis
   (c) the one-genus/two-species model
7. Why is it so difficult to obtain accurate dates for the South African australopithecine sites?

◇ Suggested Further Reading

Brace, C. L., Harry Nelson, and Noel Korn. *Atlas of Fossil Man* (2nd Ed.). New York: Holt, Rinehart and Winston, 1979.

A handy reference to the fossil hominid evidence with line drawings of fossil primates and hominids listed in chronological order. Brief descriptions of the details of discoveries and dating are most useful.

Campbell, Bernard. *Human Evolution*, Chicago: Aldine Publishing Co., 1974.

A fairly advanced survey of human evolution from a functional point of view covering developments of the limb skeleton, dentition, etc. Highly recommended for the student who wishes to explore the evolution of hominid adaptive systems at a slightly higher level than presented here.

Clark, W. E. Le Gros. *Man-Apes or Ape-Men?*, New York: Holt, Rinehart, and Winston, 1967.

A fairly detailed discussion of the cranial, dental, and postcranial anatomy of the australopithecines. This work also contains some entertaining introductory chapters outlining the discoveries made by Dart and Broom.

Howell, F. Clark. *Early Man*, New York: Time-Life Books, 1965.

An excellent general introduction to fossil hominids; also contains excellent sections on archeological method and toolmaking techniques. Beautifully illustrated.

Howells, W. W. *Evolution of the Genus Homo*, Reading, Mass.: Addison-Wesley, 1973.

A short but highly informative discussion of fossil hominids. A very good discussion of the mechanics of bipedal locomotion is included.

Kennedy, G. E. *Paleoanthropology*, New York: McGraw-Hill, 1980.

A thorough introduction to the study of fossil hominids particularly and, more generally, all fossil primates. Excellent discussion of the functional trends in hominid evolution. Written for upper-division courses, but suitable as a reference book—for all remaining chapters covered in this text.

Pilbeam, David. *The Ascent of Man*, New York: Macmillan, 1972.

A comprehensive yet understandable introduction to human evolution. An excellent chapter on the South African australopithecines is a most useful reference for the material presented in this chapter.

Poirier, Frank. *Fossil Evidence. The Human Evolutionary Journey*, St. Louis: C. V. Mosby Co., 1977.

An excellent comprehensive review of hominid evolution for the moderately advanced student. This work also contains strong introductory chapters on comparative primate studies and primate paleontology. A detailed discussion of Plio-Pleistocene hominids with an up-to-date bibliography should prove most helpful for additional source material relating to this chapter.

Robinson, J. T. *Early Hominid Posture and Locomotion*, Chicago: University of Chicago Press, 1972.

Written by one of the primary participants in the discoveries of South African australopithecines, this work offers an advanced review of the functional development of bipedal locomotion and also includes a good summary of the dietary hypothesis.

Wolpoff, Milford H. *Paleoanthropology*, New York: Alfred A. Knopf, 1980.

Like the Kennedy text with the same title, this is a fairly technical overview of fossil hominids designed for upper-division students. Useful as a reference for all remaining topics in this text.

Plio-Pleistocene Hominids: East Africa

CONTENTS

◇ISSUES   Are We Instinctive Killers?

Are we preprogramed gene-machines designed to behave in an instinctively aggressive manner toward our fellow creatures? Some researchers, popular writers, and even movie producers would have us believe so. Raymond Dart, the discoverer and namer of the first australopithecine, has long advocated such a view. From fragmented fossil remains from South Africa, Dr. Dart has characterized our australopithecine forebears as a "bone-club-wielding, jaw-bone-cleaving Samsonian phase of human emergence" (Dart, 1954). Playwright-turned-popular-science-writer Robert Ardrey popularized Dart's views, proclaiming that "man is a predator whose natural instinct is to kill with a weapon" (Ardrey, 1961). Desmond Morris, a full-time zoologist, has gone even further, claiming our whole evolution has been shaped as the "naked ape" became a "killer ape" (Morris, 1967).

Such overwrought imagery has even permeated the film industry. Anyone who has seen Stanley Kubrick's *2001: A Space Odyssey* must

Reconstruction showing how the observed change to the skull of a Swartkrans australopithecine child could have been caused by a leopard. The leopard's lower canines are thought to have penetrated the skull of the dead child while it was being dragged to a feeding place. (After Brain, 1970.)

be struck (hopefully, not too hard) by the club-wielding, apish protohominid depicted as our ancestor.

In many ways, this view of ourselves is psychologically satisfying (it seems to explain so much about the inhumanity of human beings), but it

has no basis in fact. Indeed, all such reconstructions are founded solely on speculation. No evidence from the Plio-Pleistocene shows conclusively that *any* hominid met with a violent end at the hands of a fellow creature. Most, no doubt, did die violently, but large carnivores were probably the agents responsible (such as leopards at Swartkrans). At Zoudoutian (*circa* 500,000 y.a.) skull smashing seems to have been in fashion, but such evidence does not necessarily indict *Homo erectus* on several counts of murder. Similar cultural practices have been recorded among several modern groups and usually involve some sort of ritualistic cannibalism— for example, eating the brains of one's *already* dead relatives to carry on their spirit, power, etc. (Montagu, 1976). By around 100,000 y.a. (at the Krapina site in Yugoslavia) hominids were apparently systematically bashing each other's heads, but again the reasons may be more ritualistically rather than aggressively or nutritionally motivated.

Where does this leave us in terms of a comprehensive behavioral picture of *Homo sapiens*, the animal? Several relevant points can be made:
Point 1: Any animal capable of complex behavior (i.e., all vertebrates) is also capable of aggression.

Point 2: All social animals (primates in particular) must have efficient means of channeling such aggression, since they usually live in complex groups (composed of several adults— often including more than one male); therefore, we should expect aggression-mediating behavior to be deeply ingrained in our evolution (going back perhaps 60 million years).
Point 3: Observation of behavior in many "primitive" human groups shows they are patently *nonaggressive* (for example, the Tasaday—a small, isolated group discovered in the Philippines in 1971); in fact, given population densities and the frequency of interpersonal contacts in all human groups, it is obvious that the vast majority of human behavior is nonaggressive.
Point 4: While aggression is *usually* channeled, it can be and often is displayed by humans under a wide variety of circumstances—such aggressive behavior (individual fighting, but not warfare, which is usually much more ideologically motivated)

is readily mobilized using neurological equipment adapted for this function.

What is humankind? We are neither fallen angels nor risen apes; we are a complex social mammal and most of all, a primate. We retain the *capacity* for aggression, but the *social* necessities of primate life and the *cultural* necessities of hominid life have added a great deal of behavioral flexibility as well as the ability to control such behavior.

SOURCES:

Ardrey, Robert. *African Genesis*, New York: Atheneum, 1961.

Dart, Raymond. "The Predatory Transition from Apes to Man," *International Anthropological and Linguistic Review*, 1:207–208, 1954.

Montagu, Ashley. *The Nature of Human Aggression*, New York: Oxford University Press, 1976.

Morris, Desmond. *The Naked Ape*, New York: McGraw-Hill, 1967.

◇ CHAPTER FOURTEEN

◇ Introduction

For many years after their initial discovery, the South African australopithecines remained in an anthropological vacuum. Without a firm chronology, the best that anthropologists could do was to make educated guesses concerning their dates. Most scientists, therefore, placed all the South African material between 1,000,000 y.a. and 500,000 y.a. Few would have suspected the remarkable discoveries waiting to be made in East Africa, finds that would completely alter the chronology and interpretation of hominid evolution in the Plio-Pleistocene (5–1 m.y.a.)

◇ The East African Rift Valley

Stretching along a more than 1,200-mile trough extending through Ethiopia, Kenya, and Tanzania from the Red Sea in the north to the Serengeti Plain in the south is the eastern branch of the Great Rift Valley of Africa. This massive geological feature has been associated with active mountain building, faulting, and vulcanism over the last several million years.

Because of these gigantic earth movements, earlier sediments (normally buried under hundreds of feet of earth and rock) are literally thrown to the surface, where they become exposed to the trained eye of the paleoanthropologist. Such earth movements have exposed Miocene beds at sites in Kenya, along the shores of Lake Victoria, where remains of dryopiths and ramapiths have been found. In addition, Plio-Pleistocene sediments are also exposed all along the Rift Valley, and paleoanthropologists in recent years have made the most of this unique opportunity.

More than just exposing normally hidden deposits, rifting has stimulated volcanic activity, which in turn has provided a valuable means of chronometrically dating many sites in East Africa. Unlike the sites in South Africa, those along the Rift Valley are *datable* and have thus yielded much crucial information concerning the precise chronology of early hominid evolution.

Figure 14-1 East African Plio-Pleistocene hominid sites and the rift system.

◇ East African Hominid Sites

The site that focused attention on East Africa as a potential paleoanthropological gold mine was Olduvai Gorge in northern Tanzania. As discussed in great detail in Chapter 12, this site has offered unique opportunities because of the remarkable preservation of geological, paleontological, and archeological records. Following Mary Leakey's discovery of "Zinj," a robust australopithecine, in 1959 (and the subsequent dating of its find site at 1.75 m.y.a. by the K/Ar method), numerous other areas in East Africa have been surveyed and several intensively explored. We will briefly review the geological and chronological background of these important sites beginning with the earliest.

EARLIEST TRACES

For the period preceding 4 million years ago only very fragmentary remains possibly attributable to the Hominidae have been found. The earliest of these fossils comes from the Lake Baringo region of central Kenya and the Lake Turkana Basin of northernmost Kenya.

In the Lake Baringo region possible hominid fossils have been found within the following geological areas:

1. Ngorora Formation (age approximately 10 m.y.–11 m.y.)—one partial upper molar. Not much can be said about this tooth, except that it is "hominoidlike."
2. Lukeino Formation (age approximately 5.4 m.y.–7 m.y.)—one lower molar. While some authorities believe this tooth has "distinct hominid resemblances" (Howell, 1978), detailed metrical analysis indicates this tooth is clearly more pongidlike than hominidlike (Corruccini and McHenry, 1980).
3. Chemeron Formation (age approximately 4 m.y.)—one isolated temporal bone from the side of a skull (see Appendix). While not yet completely described, this bone appears quite hominidlike and has been provisionally referred to genus *Australopithecus* (Howell, 1978).
4. Tabarin (4–5? m.y.)—a newly discovered site west of Lake Baringo, where a partial hominid lower jaw was found in February 1984. The find—a small fragment containing two molar teeth—has not yet been described, and the dating for the site also is still quite provisional.

Figure 14-2 Early hominid localities in East Africa: The Baringo and Turkana Basins.

Abundant fossil-bearing beds spanning the period 10–4 m.y.a. are now known in the Lake Baringo area. Further explorations in this region may well contribute to filling that currently vexing gap in hominoid prehistory between 7 m.y.a. and 4 m.y.a.

Samburu Hills   To the north and west of Lake Baringo, some other early and potentially highly productive fossil-bearing beds have recently been explored. In the Samburu Hills of north-central Kenya, a team led by Hidemi Ishida of Osaka University discovered a partial hominoid jaw in August 1982. Consisting of the left half of an upper jaw with five teeth in place, this find has been *very* provisionally estimated as 8 million years old. Detailed descriptions are not yet available, but are eagerly awaited by paleoanthropologists.

Lothagam (Loth'-a-gum)   Located on the southwest side of Lake Turkana in northern Kenya, this site was first explored by a Harvard University team in the middle 1960s. No radiometric dates exist for this site, but faunal correlation suggests a date of around 5.5 m.y.a. While surveying the area in 1967, the Harvard team found one hominoid fossil, the back portion of a mandible with one molar in place. Although this specimen is too fragmentary for any firm decision to be based on it, the mandible does appear hominid. As such, it would be the earliest definite hominid discovery. (Some, in fact, have suggested a resemblance to *Australopithecus africanus* in South Africa.) Only surface surveys were done at Lothagam and no cultural material was found.

Kanapoi (Kan'-a-poy)   Located close to Lothagam on the southwest side of Lake Turkana, Kanapoi was also surveyed by members of the Harvard University research project. In 1965, they found one hominid bone at this site, the lower end of an upper arm bone, or humerus.

Dating of Kanapoi, also by means of faunal correlation, gives a date of approximately 4 m.y.a. Like Lothagam, the hominid material is too fragmentary to allow much elaboration, except to note that it appears hominid and resembles *A. africanus*. Also like Lothagam, surface surveys at Kanapoi revealed no archeological traces.

LAETOLI (LYE'-TOLL-EE)

Thirty miles south of Olduvai Gorge in northern Tanzania lie beds considerably older than those exposed at the Gorge. While Laetoli was first surveyed back in the 1930s, intensive work did not begin there until 1974, when Mary Leakey decided to reinvestigate the area.

With numerous volcanic sediments in the vicinity, accurate K/Ar testing is possible and provides a provisional date of 3.77–3.59 m.y.a. for this site. This date must still be considered provisional, since it has been calibrated by only one type of dating technique (K/Ar) and only on one kind of mineral (mica) (Curtis, 1981). As we will see shortly, it is crucial to corroborate dates through use of several different techniques in order to have confidence in the results.

Since systematic fossil recovery began at Laetoli in 1974, twenty-four fossil hominid specimens have been found, consisting almost exclusively of jaws and teeth with fragmentary postcranial remains of one immature individual (Johanson and White, 1979; White, 1980).

In February, 1978 Mary Leakey announced a remarkable discovery at Laetoli: fossilized footprints embossed into an ancient volcanic tuff more than 3.5 m.y.a.! Literally thousands of footprints have been found at this remarkable site, representing more than twenty different taxa (Pliocene elephants, horses, pigs, giraffes, antelopes, hyenas, and an abundance of hares). Several hominid footprints have also been found, including a trail more than 75 feet long, made by at least two—and perhaps three—individuals (Leakey and Hay, 1979) (See Fig. 14-3.)

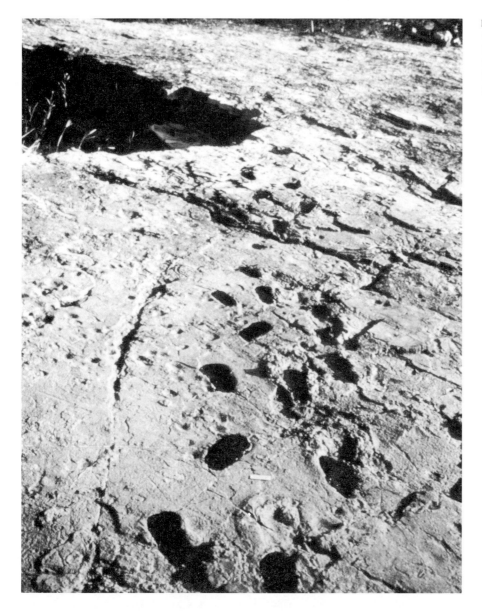

Figure 14-3 Laetoli hominid footprint trail, northern Tanzania. The trail on the left was made by one individual; the one on the right seems to have been formed by two individuals, the second stepping in the footprints of the first.

Such discoveries of well-preserved hominid footprints are extremely important to furthering our understanding of human evolution. For the first time we can make *definite* statements regarding locomotory pattern and stature of early hominids. Initial analysis of these Pliocene footprints compared to modern humans suggests a stature of about 4 feet, 9 inches for the larger individual and 4 feet 1 inch for the smaller individual, who made the trail seen in Figure 14-3 (White, 1980). Studies of these impression patterns clearly show that the mode of locomotion of these hominids was fully bipedal, and, further, *very* similar to modern humans (Day and Wickens, 1980). Some researchers, however, have concluded that these early hominids were not bipedal in quite the same way that modern humans are (see p. 433). From detailed comparisons with modern humans, estimates of step length, cadence, and speed of walking have been ascertained, indicating that the Laetoli hominids moved in a "strolling" fashion with a rather short stride (Chateris et al., 1981).

Hadar (Ha-dar´) (Afar Triangle)

Potentially one of the most exciting areas for future research in East Africa is the Afar Triangle of northeastern Ethiopia, where the Red Sea, Rift Valley, and Gulf of Aden all intersect. A joint American-French team led by Don Johanson and the French geologist Maurice Taieb began intensive field work in this area in 1973. Concentrating on a 42 km² area in the central Afar called the Hadar, paleoanthropologists have found remarkably well-preserved geological beds 400–460 feet thick. Initial K/Ar dating has suggested an age of up to 3.6 m.y.a. for the older hominid fossils and 2.5 m.y.a. for the upper artifactual-bearing beds (Johanson and Edey, 1981). These dates, too, must be considered provisional until systematically corroborated by other laboratories and other dating techniques (Curtis, 1981).

Some of the chronology at the Hadar appears clearcut. For example, there is general agreement that the Lucy skeleton (see below) is about 3 million years old. Analysis of the older beds, however, has led to some ambiguity regarding their precise dating. Study of one of the volcanic tuffs at Hadar has suggested a correlation (i.e., the result of the same volcanic eruption) with well-defined tuffs at Omo in southern Ethiopia and East Lake Turkana in northern Kenya (see below for discussion of these areas). On the basis of this chemical fingerprinting of tuffs (Brown, 1982), the paleomagnetic data, and biostratigraphic interpretations (Boaz et al., 1982), some researchers have concluded the 3.6 m.y. date for the earlier beds at Hadar is too old; accordingly, they suggest a basal date for the hominid-bearing levels of around 3.2–3.3 m.y.a.

However, opinion still varies. The proposed correlation of the volcanic tuffs across northeastern Africa is not accepted by all researchers (e.g., Aronson et al., 1983). Moreover, the biostratigraphy is also subject to differing interpretations (White, 1983).

A 300,000 to 400,000 year discrepancy may not seem all that important, but it is a most significant time period (10% of the total *known* time range of hominids). The evidence from the South African australopithecine sites has shown us the monumental problems when a sound chronology is lacking, and the dating complexities at the Hadar point up the inadequacy of even relatively accurate estimates. To form a consistent theory of exactly what was going on in the Plio-Pleistocene, we need precise chronological controls.

The chronologies, however, often take years of study to sort out. Most crucially, cross-correlations between different dating techniques (K/Ar, biostratigraphy, paleomagnetism, fission-track) must be determined. As we will see presently, it took several years of this kind of cross-checking to establish the chronology of the important hominid locality of East Lake Turkana in northern Kenya.

Due to the excellent preservation conditions in the once-lakeside environment at Hadar, an extraordinary collection of fossilized bones has been discovered—6,000 specimens in the first two seasons alone! Among the fossil remains, at least thirty-six hominid individuals (up to a maximum of as many as sixty-five) have been discovered (Johanson and Taieb, 1980).

Two extraordinary discoveries at Hadar are most noteworthy. In 1974, a partial skeleton called "Lucy" was found eroding out of a hillside. This fossil is scientifically designated as Afar Locality (AL) 288-1, but is usually just called Lucy (after a popular Beatles' song, "Lucy in the Sky with Diamonds"). Representing almost 40% of a skeleton, this is the most complete individual from anywhere in the world for the entire period before about 100,000 years ago.

The second find, a phenomenal discovery, came to light in 1975 at AL 333. Johanson and his amazed crew found dozens of hominid bones scattered along a hillside. These bones represented at least thirteen individuals including four infants. Possibly members of one social unit (a family?), this group apparently all died at the same time, perhaps during a flash flood. Considerable cultural material has been found in the Hadar area—mostly washed into stream channels, but some stone tools recently have been reported in context at a ?2.5 m.y.a. site, potentially making it the oldest cultural

Figure 14-4 Hadar deposits, northeastern Ethiopia.

◇ GREAT MOMENTS IN PREHISTORY
Discovery of the Hadar "Family," November to December, 1975

On November 1, I set out for the new area with photographer David Brill and a visiting scientist, Dr. Becky Sigmon.

Climbing into my Land Rover, David asked, "When do we find our next hominid?"

"Today," I replied.

In less than an hour, anthropology student John Kolar spotted an arm-bone fragment. From some distance away, Mike Bush, a medical student, shouted that he had found something just breaking the ground surface. It was the very first day on survey for Mike.

"Hominid teeth?" he asked, when we ran to him. There was no doubt.

We called that spot Afar Locality 333 and scheduled full excavation for the next day.

Morning found me at 333, lying on my side so that I could wield a dental pick to excavate the upper-jaw fragment Mike had found. Michèle Cavillon of our motion-picture crew called to me to look at some bones higher up the hill.

Two bone fragments lay side by side—one a partial femur and the other a fragmentary heel bone. Both were hominid.

Carefully, we started scouring the hillside. Two more leg bones—fibulae—showed up, but each from the same side. The same side? That could only indicate two individuals.

Then from high on the slope came a cry, "Look at the proximal femur—it's complete!" Turning I saw, outlined against the blue sky, the top end of a thigh bone. Even from a distance I could tell that it was not Lucy-size; it was much larger. Slowly I groped up the hillside and held the femur.

Mike wanted to come look but was distracted by finding two fragments composing a nearly complete lower jaw. The entire hillside was dotted with the bones of what were evidently at least two individuals.

We held a strategy meeting. Maurice established that the bones we found on the surface had originally been buried several yards up the slope. Mike chose a crew of seven workers to survey carefully every inch of the area and collect all bone material, sifting even the loose soil.

Time was of the essence. Rainstorms during the months of our absence could wash away fragments that would be lost forever down the ravines. I felt I was moving through a dream: Each day produced more remains.

The picture became tangled. Another upper jaw of an adult came to light. The wear pattern on the lower jaw we'd found did not match either of the uppers. At least three individuals had to be represented. More mandible fragments appeared that could not be definitely fitted to either upper jaw. Extraordinary! We had evidence of perhaps as many as five adults of the genus *Homo**

Apart from teeth and jaws, we recovered scores of hand and foot bones, leg bones, vertebrae, ribs, even a partial adult skull. A baby tooth turned up, suggesting the presence of a sixth hominid at the site. Then a nearly complete lower jaw of a baby appeared, as well as an almost intact palate with baby teeth. Not heavily worn, the teeth suggested that their possessor was only about 3 years old.

So we had evidence of young adults, old adults, and children—an entire assemblage of early hominids. All of them at one place. Nothing like this had ever been found!

SOURCE:

"Ethiopia Yields First 'Family' of Early Man" by Donald C. Johanson, *National Geographic Magazine*, Vol. 150, pp. 790–811, December 1976. Reprinted with permission of the publisher.

*Johanson and his colleagues later assigned all this material to *Australopithecus afarensis* (see p. 434).

evidence yet found. Most unfortunately, political unrest and sporadic warfare in Ethiopia forced a halt to further investigations at the Hadar in 1977. As the situation settled somewhat, hopes for further fieldwork were rekindled. In fact, initial survey work in the Afar Triangle (Middle Awash Valley) in 1981 uncovered fragments of a hominid femur and cranium (dated provisionally, 3.5–4.0 m.y.a.) (Clark et al., 1984). Plans were thus made for full-scale investigations in 1982, but Ethiopian authorities initiated a temporary moratorium on research that, for the moment, has stalled all efforts.

OMO (OH′-MOH)

The thickest and most continuous Plio-Pleistocene sequence in East Africa comes from the Omo River basin in southern Ethiopia just north of Lake Turkana. This site was also worked jointly by French and American scientists with F. Clark Howell of the University of California, Berkeley, leading the American team.

Total deposits at the Omo are more than one-half mile thick, and the area surveyed extends over more than 200 km². These exceedingly thick sediments are composed largely of lake and river deposits, but more than 100 volcanic ash deposits have also been recognized. These ash deposits provide an excellent basis for accurate K/Ar determinations. This dating technique, supported by paleomagnetic and biostratigraphic results, has placed the hominid-bearing levels at the Omo between 2.9 and 1.0 m.y.a.

A fantastically rich paleontological sample, more than 40,000 mammal specimens alone, has been collected at the Omo. This site, with its well-documented chronology and huge paleontological series, has become the basis for extrapolation to other East African and some South African sites.

Several cultural remains have come to light in the Omo area dating from around 2 m.y.a. Most of this cultural material consists of fragments of flakes struck from stone pebbles and chunks. Only one primary site, where archeological traces retain their original context, has been excavated, and it has revealed a large quantity of these rather crude-looking flakes. What hominids were doing at this location 2 m.y.a. is still somewhat of a mystery. Apparently, it was not a multi-purpose area like those at Olduvai, since no animal bones were found with the tools.

Hominid discoveries at the Omo come from 87 different localities and include more than 200 teeth, 9 lower jaws, 4 partial or fragmentary skulls, and a complete ulna (a lower-arm bone).

EAST LAKE TURKANA (TUR-CAN′-AH)

Richard Leakey, the second oldest son of Louis and Mary Leakey, has greatly benefited from the fossil-hunting training given him by his parents. In fact, in the huge, remote, arid area encompassing more than 400 square miles on the eastern side of Lake Turkana,* he and his field crew have found more

Figure 14-5 "Lucy," a partial hominid skeleton. Discovered at the Hadar in 1974.

---

*Lake Turkana was formerly called Lake Rudolf, and the naming of specimens reflects the earlier name: KNM-ER 406 = Kenya National Museum—East Rudolf specimen #406.

Figure 14-6 Excavations in progress. East Lake Turkana, northern Kenya.

than twice as many hominid remains since 1968 as his parents found at Olduvai in more than forty years of searching!

Geologically, the situation at East Lake Turkana is exceedingly complex, with deep sections of lake and river deposits crisscrossed by the effects of **tectonic movements**, stream action, and volcanic activity. While the latter is useful in providing material for radiometric dating, the geological complexities have made the precise chronology of the area a matter of dispute.

The latter sediments have been securely dated at 1.3–1.6 m.y.a., and consensus on this part of the chronology has existed for several years. However, there has been considerable dispute regarding the earlier levels, particularly a key volcanic bed called the KBS tuff.

Initially, conventional K/Ar was attempted, but frequent contamination of samples made results unreliable. Thus, a modification of this procedure[†] was performed, giving estimates of about 2.6 m.y.a. Later, on the basis of fission-track results and paleomagnetic interpretations, this date was moved down to 2.4 m.y.a.

Since, as we pointed out in Chapter 12, there are built-in errors in each of these different dating techniques, several methods must be used for cross-checking. Analysis of the faunal components at Turkana associated with the KBS tuff did not correlate with the 2.4 m.y. age when compared to fossil

[†]This technique is called the $^{40}Ar/^{39}Ar$ stepheating method and measures the steady decay of the ^{39}Ar isotope to that of ^{40}Ar.

materials from the Omo and Olduvai, but, in fact, suggested a date 600,000 years later. Further radiometric tests (using conventional K/Ar) corroborated these findings, and yet further analyses confirmed them: The lower hominid-bearing levels at Turkana are around 1.8 m.y. old.

Once again, then, as in our example of the dating of Hadar (see p. 424), the cross-correlation of different techniques is crucial to establishing a firm chronology for these ancient fossil sites. The sampling, testing, evaluation, comparison, and reconsideration of the Turkana dating materials took more than ten years before general agreement was reached.

As noted, numerous hominids have been discovered at East Lake Turkana in the last decade. The current total exceeds 150 hominid specimens, probably representing at least 100 individuals, and this fine sample includes several complete skulls, many jaws, and a fine assortment of post-cranial bones.

Next to Olduvai, Turkana has yielded the most cultural information concerning the behavior of early hominids. More than twenty archeological sites have been discovered, and excavation or testing has been done at ten localities. Two sites are of particular interest and are both directly associated with the KBS tuff (age, therefore, 1.8 m.y.a.). One is apparently a habitation site (base camp), whereas the other is the butchering site of an extinct form of hippopotamus. The stone tools from these earlier sediments at Turkana are in many ways reminiscent of the Oldowan industry in Bed I at Olduvai (with which they are contemporaneous).

OLDUVAI GORGE

The reader should by now be well acquainted with this remarkable site in northern Tanzania, particularly with its clear geological and chronological contributions. Hominid discoveries from Olduvai now total forty-eight individuals ranging in time from 1.85 m.y.a. to Upper Pleistocene times less than 50,000 years ago.

◇ East African Hominids

From the time period between 4 and 1 m.y.a., East African sites have thus far yielded close to 300 hominid individuals. This huge collection of material (much of it in well-dated contexts) has allowed paleoanthropologists to formulate (and reformulate) their interpretations of human evolution. At present, it appears that at least three groups (which we will refer to as "sets") of hominids are distinguishable in East Africa during the Plio-Pleistocene. The first of these sets was distinctly earlier and more primitive, while the other two appeared later and apparently lived contemporaneously for at least 1 million years.

SET I. EARLY PRIMITIVE AUSTRALOPITHECINES (*A. afarensis*)

Prior to 4 m.y.a. the fossil hominid (or "hominoid") remains from East Africa (which is all there is anywhere) are extremely scrappy, represented by only two molars, one cranial bone, two fragmentary jaws, and one arm bone (see

Tectonic movement
Movements of the earth—for example, along fault lines, during mountain building, and so forth.

Tuff
A solidified sediment of volcanic ash.

pp. 421–422). The best that can be said about this material is that it is hominoid, and in some cases, "hominidlike."

It is not until 4–3 m.y.a. that we get the first *definite* collection of hominid fossils. These crucial remains come from two sites explored within the last decade: Laetoli in northern Tanzania and Hadar in northeastern Ethiopia. From these two sites together several hundred hominid specimens have been recovered, representing a minimum of 60 individuals and perhaps close to 100. In addition, there are of course those fascinating hominid footprints from Laetoli.

Interpretation of fossil hominids is a laborious and highly technical undertaking. Finding the fossils is only the first step. They then have to be cleaned (often of intractable matrix), measured, described, reconstructed, and then measured again. It is thus not surprising that, although the first hominid specimens were recovered from Hadar and Laetoli in 1973 and 1974 respectively, their taxonomic affinity was not published until 1978 (Johanson et al., 1978); a systematic reappraisal of *all* hominids from the Plio-Pleistocene appeared soon thereafter in early 1979 (Johanson and White, 1979), and comprehensive descriptions were published in April, 1982, in the *American Journal of Physical Anthropology*.

Certainly, the announcement of a new species always raises considerable professional and public interest. The proposal of *A. afarensis* by Johanson and his colleagues was no exception. Predictably, not all the reaction was favorable. In science, this is a healthy attitude; hypotheses *always* need to be scrutinized and tested against further evidence.

What exactly is *A. afarensis*? Without question, it is more primitive than any of the australopithecine material from South Africa (discussed in the previous chapter) or any of the later hominid material from East Africa (discussed subsequently). In fact, *A. afarensis* is the most primitive of any definitely hominid group thus far found anywhere. By "primitive," we mean that *A. afarensis* is less evolved in any particular direction than is seen in later species of *Australopithecus* or *Homo*. That is to say, *A. afarensis* shares more primitive features with other early hominoids (such as *Dryopithecus*, *Sivapithecus*, etc.) and with living pongids than is true of later hominids, who display more derived characteristics.

For example, the teeth are quite primitive. The canines are often large, pointed teeth that slightly overlap; the first lower premolar is semisectorial, and the tooth rows are parallel or even posteriorly convergent (see Fig. 14-7a).

The pieces of crania that are preserved also display several primitive hominoid characteristics, including a compound sagittal/nuchal crest in the back (see Fig. 14-8), as well as several primitive features of the cranial base (involving the tubular appearance of the external ear canal, as well as an open-appearing articulation for the lower jaw). Cranial capacity estimates for *afarensis* show a mixed pattern when compared to later hominids. A provisional estimate for the one partially complete cranium (see Fig. 14-8b)— apparently a large individual—gives a figure of 500 cm³, but another, even more fragmentary, cranium is apparently quite a bit smaller and has been provisionally estimated at less than 400 cm³ (Holloway, 1983). Thus, for some individuals (males?), *afarensis* is well within the range of other australopithe-

(a)

(b)

Figure 14-7 Jaws of *Australopithecus afarensis*. (*a*) Maxilla, AL-200-1a, from Hadar, Ethiopia. (Note the parallel tooth rows and large canines.); (*b*) mandible, L. H. 4, from Laetoli, Tanzania. This fossil is the type specimen for the new species, *Australopithecus afarensis*.

Figure 14-8 Comparison of hominoid crania. (a) Chimpanzee; (b) *Australopithecus afarensis* composite cranium assembled from three individuals—AL 333-45, 200-1a, and 400-1a; (c) human.

cine species, but others (females?) may be significantly smaller. An overall depiction of cranial size for *A. afarensis* as a species is not possible at this time—this part of the skeleton is unfortunately too poorly represented.

A host of postcranial pieces have been found at Hadar (mostly from the partial skeleton "Lucy," and from individuals of the "family" at AL 333). Initial impressions suggest that the upper limbs are long relative to the lower ones (also a primitive hominoid condition). In addition, the wrist and hand bones show several differences from modern humans. Stature can now be confidently estimated: *A. afarensis* was a short hominid. From her partial skeleton, Lucy is figured to be only about 3½ to 4 feet tall. However, Lucy—as demonstrated by her pelvis—was a female, and at Hadar and Laetoli, there is evidence of larger individuals as well. The most economical hypothesis explaining this variation is that *A. afarensis* was quite sexually dimorphic—the larger individuals are male and the smaller ones such as Lucy are female. Estimates of male stature can be approximated from the larger footprints at Laetoli, inferring a height of about 5 feet.

Without question, *A. afarensis* was a quite sexually dimorphic form. In fact, for overall body size, this species may have been as dimorphic as *any* living primate (i.e., as much as gorillas, orangs, or baboons). The elaborate behavioral reconstruction proposed by Lovejoy (1981) (see pp. 271–272), is based upon a *lack* of dimorphism in this species. Lovejoy points particularly to the relatively small degree of canine dimorphism between presumed males and females, but, even here, there are some reasonably good-sized differences apparent. Indeed, in the original description of *A. afarensis* (Johanson et al., 1978), a feature noted to define this form was "strong variation in canine size."

Beyond the claimed lack of canine size dimorphism (which has not been presented as *quantifiable* data compared to known ranges in living primates), there are even more serious problems with the Lovejoy model. In those few nonhuman primates that are monogamous (e.g., marmosets, gibbons) there is clearly little body size dimorphism. Yet, in *A. afarensis*, males may be twice as big as females, and thus rival the amount of dimorphism in the most dimorphic living primates. Clearly, these highly dimorphic primates are uniformly polygynous, and many less dimorphic species of monkeys also follow mostly polygynous mating strategies.

In conclusion, the physical evidence of sexual dimorphism within *A. afarensis* could hardly be used to argue for monogamous mating patterns. Indeed, it could be quite forcefully used to argue against it!

Behavioral debates such as these are certainly stimulating, but what is most interesting about *A. afarensis* is the distinctive physical morphology it displays. In a majority of dental and cranial features *A. afarensis* is clearly more primitive than are later hominids. This should not come as too great a surprise, since *afarensis* is at least 1 m.y. older than other East African finds and perhaps .5–.7 m.y. older than the oldest South African hominid. In fact, from the neck up, *A. afarensis* is so primitive, that without any evidence from the limb skeleton, one would be hard-pressed to call it a hominid at all (although the back teeth are large and heavily enameled, unlike pongids). In the teeth particularly, *A. afarensis* is in some ways reminiscent of Miocene hominoids (e.g., *Sivapithecus*) (Greenfield, 1979).

What then makes *A. afarensis* a hominid? The answer is revealed by its manner of locomotion. From the abundant limb bones recovered from Hadar and those beautiful footprints from Laetoli we know unequivocally that *afarensis* walked bipedally when progressing on the ground. Whether Lucy and her contemporaries still spent considerable time in the trees, and just how efficiently they walked, have recently become topics of major dispute.

Locomotion of Australopithecus afarensis A recent comprehensive analysis of the postcranial anatomy of *A. afarensis* by Jack Stern and Randall Susman of the State University of New York at Stony Brook has challenged the view that this early hominid walked bipedally, much as you or me (Stern and Susman, 1983). Their interpretation is based upon many parts of the skeleton (limbs, hands, feet, pelvis, etc.), which they have compared with other hominids (fossil and modern), as well as with great apes.

Such features as long, curved fingers and toes, long upper limbs but short lower limbs (Jungers, 1982), the positioning of the hip and knee joints, and pelvic orientation have led these researchers to two conclusions: (1) *A. afarensis* was capable of efficient climbing and probably spent considerable time in the trees (sleeping, feeding, escaping from predators, etc.); and (2) while on the ground, *A. afarensis* was a biped, but walked with a much less efficient bent-hip, bent-knee gait than that seen in modern humans.

As might be expected, these conclusions themselves have also been challenged. While pointing out some slight differences from modern humans in postcranial anatomy, Owen Lovejoy (1983) and his associates (e.g., Latimer, 1984) see nothing that suggests these hominids were arboreal or, conversely, that precluded them from being *very* efficient bipeds. Moreover, Lucy's "little legs" may not really be that small, considering her small body size (although her arms were apparently rather long) (Wolpoff, 1983b).

Other researchers have also noted differences between the postcranium of *A. afarensis* and later hominids. Interestingly, however, in many respects the hand and pelvis of *A. afarensis* are extremely similar to *A. africanus* from South Africa (Suzman, 1982; McHenry, 1983).

From all this debate, little has yet emerged in the way of consensus, except that all agree the *A. afarensis* did exhibit some kind of bipedal locomotion while on the ground. In searching for some middle ground between the opposing viewpoints, several researchers have suggested that *A. afarensis* could have been quite at home in the trees *as well as* being an efficient terrestrial biped (Wolpoff, 1983; McHenry, 1983). As one physical anthropologist has recently put it:

> One could imagine these diminutive early hominids making maximum use of *both* terrestrial and arboreal resources in spite of their commitment to exclusive bipedalism when on the ground. The contention of a mixed arboreal and terrestrial behavioural repertoire would make adaptive sense of the Hadar australopithecine forelimb, hand, and foot morphology without contradicting the evidence of the pelvis. (Wolpoff, 1983, p. 451).

Challenges to Australopithecus afarensis Following the formal naming of *Australopithecus afarensis* in 1978 (Johanson et al., 1978) and its systematic interpretation a year later (Johanson and White, 1979), some questions have been raised concerning the status of this fossil hominid. In general, these challenges have taken two forms:

1. Is there more than one taxon represented at Hadar and Laetoli?
2. Can *afarensis* simply be included as an earlier member of *A. africanus* (i.e., the same species as at Sterkfontein and Makapansgat)?

Regarding the first question of possible multiple taxa (i.e., more than one species) at Hadar and Laetoli, some of the initial analyses by the primary researchers at Hadar did indeed suggest this possibility (Johanson and Taieb, 1976). Once *all* the Hadar material was evaluated, as well as comparisons made with the Laetoli fossils, this view was rejected (in favor of simply grouping all the fossils into one obviously variable, sexually dimorphic species).

Not all paleoanthropologists, however, are convinced of this latter interpretation. Two French paleoanthropologists, Brigett Senut and Christine Tardieu of the University of Paris, have suggested from analyses of postcranial remains (especially the elbow and knee) that early members of genus *Homo* may also have been present at Hadar and Laetoli (Senut, 1981).

While possible, of course, these claims have yet to be substantiated. Moreover, on the basis of detailed dental comparisons (White, et al., 1981), there appears to be no reason to "split" the samples into different taxa. Accordingly, *A. afarensis* is seen as a quite variable and most certainly sexually dimorphic form. As we have pointed out in Chapters 11 and 13, it is most prudent to assume a minimum number of species to be represented by any given fossil sample, unless *conclusive* evidence can be presented to suggest otherwise. For the present, anyway, most paleoanthropologists are comfortable regarding *all* the Hadar and Laetoli fossils as part of one species.

More troublesome, though, is the second question concerning the status of *A. afarensis*: Is it part of *A. africanus*? Phillip Tobias, the world's leading authority on the morphology of *A. africanus* in South Africa, believes that "the Laetoli and Hadar hominids cannot be distinguished at specific level from *A. africanus*" (Tobias, 1980, p. 1).

This assertion is also entirely possible, and, on the basis of Tobias's familiarity with the South African material, it requires serious consideration. Of all the other hominids to which *A. afarensis* could be compared, it is morphologically and chronologically closest to *A. africanus*. Yet, there are still some important differences in the face, cranial vault, mandible, and teeth, all of which consistently show *A. afarensis* to be more primitive than *A. africanus* (or, for that matter, any other known hominid) (White et al., 1981). More detailed comparisons will have to be done, but, given the overall primitive morphology of these early fossil hominids from Hadar and Laetoli, they are presently best considered within their own species, *A. afarensis*, and thus separate from *A. africanus*.

SET II. LATER AUSTRALOPITHECINES—EAST AFRICAN ROBUST FORMS (*A. boisei*, ALSO CALLED *A. robustus*)

After its discovery in 1959, the beautifully preserved cranium and upper dentition of "Zinj" was classified by Louis Leakey into a new and separate genus and species, *Zinjanthropus boisei* (boy'-see-eye). You may well ask, What biological basis was Leakey using to justify such a distinction? As it turned out, there was not much ground for postulating a totally separate genus, and most scientists (later including Leakey himself) have included this specimen in *Australopithecus*.

"Zinj" is a very robust young male australopithecine with enormous back teeth, a large broad face, and a sagittal crest atop the skull. In addition, the

Figure 14-9 *Australopithecus afarensis* reconstructed cranium—using evidence from several individuals and filling in portions for which no fossil data exist (shown in white).

skull displays considerable postorbital constriction and has a cranial capacity of 530 cm³, the same as the only South African robust australopithecine that can be measured. "Zinj's" third molars are newly erupted and unworn, suggesting his age at death was probably around 18 years.

When compared with material from South Africa, "Zinj" does show some differences in detail, but these are apparently due to one functional specialization, the massive increase in cheek tooth size. While sufficient grounds do not exist to justify assigning this East African australopithecine to a genus distinct from those in South Africa, separate specific rank may well be called for. Therefore, "Zinj" is now usually referred to as *Australopithecus boisei*, specifically distinct from *A. africanus* and *A. robustus*. The direct biological implication is that the East African variety of robust australopithecine, removed by 2,000 miles from South Africa, were reproductively isolated from their contemporaries, *A. robustus*, to the south.

We must, however, remain cautious about unnecessarily splitting these fossil populations into biologically meaningless categories. We have chastised such splitting in the early interpretations of South African australopithecines (for example, Robert Broom's classification, see p. 402), and we should not be guilty of making the same error in East Africa. In fact, many authorities believe there is not a specific difference between *A. robustus* in the south and its robust contemporary in the eastern part of the continent. Since these investigators feel there is not sufficient evidence to show that *A. boisei* falls *outside* the range of *A. robustus*, they call *both A. robustus* (the earlier name takes precedence).

In our ensuing discussion we will refer to the East African robust group as *A. boisei*, but this reference should not be interpreted as an ironclad biological conclusion. It simply provides, for the moment, a shorthand means of referring to the East African robust australopithecines.

Figure 14-10 Two mandibles discovered at East Lake Turkana. Note the difference in proportions of jaws and teeth; KNM-ER 818 (right) is one of the largest hominid mandibles ever found. KNM-ER 992 (left) is thought to be an early *Homo*. (Photographs of casts.)

Figure 14-11 A robust australopithecine mandible from East Lake Turkana (KNM-ER 729). Note the enormous proportions of the molars and premolars.

Figure 14-12 The "demicranium" discovered at East Lake Turkana (KNM-ER 732). A female robust australopithecine?

A. boisei is a well-defined group in East Africa, not only at Olduvai, but at several other sites as well. From East Turkana, particularly, several fossils have been found that are clearly members of this species, including some mandibles of gigantic proportions. In addition, a few skulls from Turkana also belong to *A boisei*. One of these, a nearly perfect skull (KNM-ER 406), is very much like "Zinj" and is also apparently a robust male australopithecine. Cranial capacity, estimated at 510 cm³, is a little smaller for the Turkana male, compared to the 530 cm³ figure for "Zinj."

Of course, *A. boisei* populations were variable, and one kind of variation we should expect to see is due to sexual dimorphism. In fact, another East Turkana fossil cranium shows this phenomenon exactly. The specimen KNM-ER 732 is a partial cranium, much like 406 and "Zinj" but smaller, particularly in the face and muscle attachment areas of the skull. Cranial capacity at around 500 cm³ for this **demicranium** is also slightly smaller than that approximated for the males. Comparison with modern populations of primates suggests that the pattern of variation seen between the larger and smaller skulls may well represent differences between males and females of one interbreeding species.

Postcranial bones at Turkana that are definitely attributable to *A. boisei* are difficult to ascertain exactly, for none has been found directly associated with a skull. However, one upper arm bone (humerus), ER 739, is very robust and quite uniquely shaped. Biomechanical reconstructions show it to be unlike *any* living hominoid. If this arm bone does indeed belong to *A. boisei*, it suggests that, postcranially, they may have been quite unusual compared to other hominids.

Further evidence along the same line comes from the Omo, where several teeth and three mandibles are, because of their size, attributed to *A. boisei*. In addition, an unusual ulna has been found which, like the Turkana humerus, also suggests that the forelimb of *A. boisei* is quite unlike other hominids.

Remains of *A. boisei* are also known from a nearly complete mandible 1 million years old from Peninj, a site near Lake Natron about seventy miles from Olduvai and also from a partial skull of about the same age (1.5–1.2 m.y.a.) from the Chesowanja site in central Kenya (in the Lake Baringo region).

Apparently, *A. boisei* does not appear anywhere in East Africa until about 2 m.y.a., and until about 1 m.y.a. lived basically unchanged. It is interesting to note that South African robust australopithecines (*A. robustus*) at Swartkrans and Kromdraai also do not appear until about this same time. Quite clearly, all varieties of robust australopithecines are much later than the more primitive *afarensis*—up to 1.0 m.y.–1.5 m.y. later. It is thus easier to understand the obviously more *derived* physical characteristics of robust australopithecines.

Many anthropologists speculate that these robust forms had a specialized vegetarian diet consisting mostly of small, hard objects (seeds, etc.). As a result of the rigorous demands of masticating these kinds of foods, robust forms gradually adopted a large back tooth chewing complex. Accompanying this change, structural modifications also occurred in the jaw and in rearrangements of cranial architecture, eventually producing that highly derived hominid form we recognize as a robust australopithecine.

First appearing at around 2 m.y.a., robust forms lived contemporaneously for 1 million years in East Africa (and perhaps South Africa also) with another, quite different, kind of hominid.

Set III. Early *Homo* (also called *Homo habilis*)

The first hint that another hominid was living contemporaneously in East Africa with *boisei* came at Olduvai Gorge in the early 1960s. Louis Leakey named a new form of hominid *Homo habilis* on the basis of remains, some a little older than "Zinj," others somewhat more recent (Leakey et al., 1964). Unfortunately, the remains at Olduvai attributable to this **taxon** are all either fragmentary or distorted in one way or another. The initial *habilis* material included a fragmentary skull with a distorted juvenile mandible (OH 7) and a partial skull with a complete upper and lower dentition (OH 13), called "Cinderella" by the Leakeys. A third *habilis* specimen, a severely fragmented skull, discovered after being trampled by local Masai cattle (OH 16), is known popularly as "Olduvai George." A final *habilis* skull, found in 1968, is a nearly complete cranium (OH 24) that was severely crushed. It required extensive restoration. This fossil, thought to be female, is called "Twiggy."

The *habilis* material at Olduvai ranges in time from 1.85 m.y.a. for the earliest to about 1.6 m.y.a. for the latest. Due to the fragmentary nature of the fossil remains, interpretations have been difficult and much disputed. The most immediately obvious feature distinguishing the *habilis* material from the australopithecines is cranial size. These six partial *habilis* skulls, although difficult to measure accurately, have an estimated average cranial capacity of 646 cm³ compared to 504 cm³ for all measurable robust australopithecines and 450 for graciles (Tobias, 1983). *Habilis*, therefore, shows a 26–42% cranial size increase respectively over both forms of australopithecine.

In their initial description of *habilis*, Leakey and his associates also pointed to differences from australopithecines in cranial shape (less postorbital con-

Demicranium
demi: half

Taxon (pl. taxa)
A population (or group of populations) that is judged to be sufficiently distinct and is assigned to a separate category (such as genus or species).

(a)

(b)

Figure 14-13 Two mandibles. Initially assigned to "*H. habilis*," from Olduvai Gorge. (*a*) OH 7; (*b*) OH 13, "Cinderella." These specimens are now usually referred to as "early *Homo*." (Photographs of casts.)

Figure 14-14 A nearly complete skull from Olduvai Gorge. Initially assigned to "*H. habilis*," OH 24, "Twiggy." This specimen may be an "early *Homo*" or perhaps, a gracile australopithecine. (Photograph of cast.)

striction) and in tooth proportions (larger front teeth relative to back teeth and narrower premolars).

The naming of this fossil material as *Homo habilis* (handy man) was meaningful from two perspectives. First of all, Leakey inferred that members of this group were the early Olduvai toolmakers. If true, how do we account for a robust australopithecine like "Zinj" lying in the middle of the largest living floor known at Olduvai? What was he doing there? Leakey has suggested he was the remains of a *habilis* meal! Excepting those instances where cutmarks are left behind (see pp. 384–386), we must point out that there is no clear way archeologically to establish the validity of such a claim. However, the debate over this assertion serves to demonstrate that cultural factors as well as physical morphology must be considered in the interpretation of hominids as biocultural organisms. Secondly, and most significantly, by calling this group *Homo*, Leakey was arguing for at least *two separate branches* of hominid evolution in the Plio-Pleistocene. Clearly only one could be on the main branch eventually leading to *Homo sapiens*. Labeling this new group *Homo* in opposition to *Australopithecus*, Leakey was guessing he had found our ancestors.

Since the initial evidence was so fragmentary, most paleoanthropologists were reluctant to accept *habilis* as a valid taxon distinct from *all* australopithecines. Differences from the hyperrobust East African variety (*A. boisei*) were certainly apparent; the difficulties arose in trying to distinguish *habilis* from *A. africanus*, particularly for dental traits that considerably overlap. Moreover, the ambiguous dating of the South African forms made it difficult to interpret the relationship between *A. africanus* and *habilis*.

Recent discoveries, especially from Lake Turkana, of better-preserved fossil material have shed new light on early *Homo* in the Plio-Pleistocene. The most important of this new *habilis* material is a nearly complete cranium (ER 1470) discovered at East Lake Turkana in 1972. With a cranial capacity of 775 cm^3, this individual is well outside the known range for australopithecines and actually overlaps the lower boundary for *Homo*. In addition, the shape of the skull vault and face are in many respects unlike that of australopithecines.

Figure 14-15 Skull profiles (seen from above).

(a)
Robust
australopithecine

(b)
Gracile
australopithecine

(c)
Early Homo

Figure 14-16 The Kenyan team at East Lake Turkana. Kamoya Kimeu (driving) is the most successful fossil hunter in East Africa. He is responsible for dozens of important discoveries.

However, the face is still quite robust (Walker, 1976), and the fragments of tooth crowns that are preserved indicate the back teeth in this individual were quite large.

Additional discoveries at Turkana also strongly suggest the presence of a hominid lineage contemporaneous with and separate from australopithecines. Another skull discovered in 1972 (ER 1590) is similar to 1470 and may even be larger! Moreover, several mandibles, including two nearly complete specimens (ER 820 and 992), have tooth proportions (relatively larger front teeth) characteristic of our genus. Finally, several postcranial remains discovered at Turkana show a taller, more gracile group than that inferred for australopithecines. The dating of all this crucial early *Homo* material from Turkana is tied to the dating of the KBS tuff. As we discussed on page 429, the dating of this key bed has recently been established at around 1.8 m.y.a. Thus, the earliest *Homo* materials at Turkana *and* Olduvai are contemporaneous (i.e., 1.8–2.0 m.y.a.).

Other Plio-Pleistocene sites also have revealed possible early members of the genus *Homo*. From the Omo in southern Ethiopia scattered remains of a few teeth and small cranial fragments are similar in pattern to other comparable early *Homo* material.

If the discussion of *Australopithecus* versus *Homo* seems confusing, do not despair. The distinction is not yet well formulated and causes much confusion even in professional ranks. It is true that the *A. boisei* group of australopithecines in East Africa is quite distinctive, characterized by an enormous backtooth grinding complex. It is equally true that another whole set of gracile fossil hominids in East Africa usually called early *Homo* does not fall into this group. The thorny problem comes in trying to distinguish these gracile individuals (*Homo sp.*) from the South African gracile variety of australopithe-

Figure 14-17 A nearly complete "early *Homo*" skull from East Lake Turkana (KNM-ER 1470). One of the most important single fossil hominid discoveries from East Africa. (*a*) Frontal view; (*b*) lateral view.

Figure 14-18 An "early *Homo*" mandible from East Lake Turkana (KNM-ER 820). Note the relatively even proportions of back teeth to front teeth.

Table 14-1 *Australopithecus* Compared to Early *Homo*

Australopithecus	*Early Homo*
Cranial:	
Face large relative to vault size	Face small relative to vault size

Absolute size of cranium smaller:
   gracile = 450 cm³ (*N* = 7)
   robust = 504 cm³ (*N* = 5)
	Cranium–larger
	   average = 646 cm³ (*N* = 6)

Cranial bone thinner	Cranial bone thicker
More postorbital construction	Less postorbital construction
Mandible large, more massive Ramus of mandible, higher	Mandible smaller, not as thick Ramus not as high
Shape of mandible: Narrow in front diverges in back, as:	Mandible more open in front, not as divergent in back; shaped more as:
-shaped	-shaped
Front teeth relatively quite small to very small compared to back teeth	Front teeth are larger relative to size of back teeth—which, in some cases (ER 1470), are still very large
Postcranial:	
Differences not yet well worked out, but some apparent differences in femur: Upper (proximal) end; smaller head, flatter, longer neck	Head larger, neck more round in cross-section and not as relatively long

After Leakey et al., 1964; Walker, 1976; Wood, 1976; Tobias, 1976; Howell, 1978; Tobias, 1983.

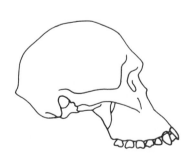

Figure 14-19 A gracile australopithecine.

cines, *A. africanus.* Since much overlap exists in physical traits (and probably chronology as well) between these two forms, this will never be an easy task. (For a summary of the current perspectives regarding the distinction between *Australopithecus* and *Homo* in the Plio-Pleistocene see Table 14-1.)

On the basis of evidence from Olduvai and particularly from Lake Turkana we can reasonably postulate that *Homo* was present in East Africa by *at least* 2 m.y.a., developing in parallel with at least one line (*A. boisei*) of australopithecines. These two hominid lines lived contemporaneously for a minimum of 1 million years, after which the australopithecine lineage apparently disappears forever. At the same time, the *habilis* line was emerging into a later form, *Homo erectus*, which, in turn, developed into *H. sapiens.*

In the next chapter, we will take up in detail several alternative theories dealing with evolutionary relationships of these fossil hominids in the Plio-Pleistocene.

◇ Summary

The East African Rift Valley contains several Plio-Pleistocene hominid sites ranging in time from slightly more than 5 m.y.a. up to about 1 m.y.a. The list that follows is a summary of these sites, their location, estimated ages, and a tentative designation of the kinds of hominids found:

Site Name	Location	Age (m.y.a.)	Hominids
Peninj	N. Tanzania	1	1 individual; australopithecine
Olduvai	N. Tanzania	1.85–1	48 specimens; australopithecines; early *Homo*
Turkana	N. Kenya (eastern side of Lake Turkana)	1.9–1.3	More than 150 specimens; many australopithecines; several early *Homo*
Omo	S. Ethiopia	2.9–1	215 specimens; several dozen individuals? australopithecines; some early *Homo*
Hadar	N.E. Ethiopia	?3.7–2.6	Minimum of 36 individuals (maximum of 65); early australopithecine (*A. afarensis*)
Laetoli	N. Tanzania	3.77–3.59	24 hominids; early australopithecine (*A. afarensis*)
Kanapoi	N. Kenya (S.W. Lake Turkana)	4	1 hominid = australopithecine??
Lothagam	N. Kenya (S.W. Lake Turkana)	5.5	1 hominid = australopithecine??

◇ Questions for Review

1. Why are the early hominid sites in East Africa so much better dated than those in South Africa (discussed in Chapter 13)?
2. In East Africa all the early hominid sites are found along the Rift Valley. Why is this significant?
3. Compare the various East African Plio-Pleistocene sites for the kinds of cultural information uncovered.
4. How does the dating problem of the KBS tuff at Lake Turkana illustrate the necessity for cross-correlation of several dating techniques?
5. What hominid sites have yielded remains of *A. afarensis*? In what ways is the fossil material more primitive than other hominids from South and East Africa?
6. What kinds of robust australopithecines have been found in East Africa? How do they compare with South African australopithecines?
7. Why are some Plio-Pleistocene hominids from East Africa called "early *Homo*"? What does this imply for the evolutionary relationships of the australopithecines?

8. What did Louis Leakey mean by using the specific name, "habilis" for a fossil hominid from Olduvai?
9. Compare the morphological features of early *Homo* with *Australopithecus*. Is it easier to draw a clear distinction between *Homo* and robust australopithecines (*A. robustus; A. boisei*) or gracile (*A. africanus*) ones? Why?

◇ Suggested Further Reading

See the following (annotated in Chapters 12 and 13) for a general introduction to Plio-Pleistocene hominids:

Howells, W. W. *Evolution of the Genus Homo*, Reading, Mass.: Addison-Wesley, 1973.

Johanson, Donald and Maitland Edey. *Lucy, The Beginnings of Humankind*, New York: Simon and Schuster, 1981.

Pilbeam, David. *The Ascent of Man*, New York: Macmillan, 1972.

Poirier, Frank. *Fossil Evidence. The Human Evolutionary Journey* (2nd Ed.), St. Louis: C. V. Mosby Co., 1977.

For more comprehensive and technical readings, see:

Coppens, Yves, F. Clark Howell, Glynn Isaac, and R.E.F. Leakey. *Earliest Man and Environments in the Lake Rudolf Basin*, Chicago: University of Chicago Press, 1975.
> *Highly technical discussion of geology, paleontology, and hominid evolution at East Turkana and the Omo basin. Reviews hominid discoveries in detail through 1974 at these sites. Contains several excellent photos of hominid discoveries.*

Isaac, G. and E. R. McCown. *Human Origins. Louis Leakey and the East African Evidence*, Menlo Park, California: W. A. Benjamin Inc., 1976.
> *A collection of recent articles on the archeology, geology, and hominids of East Africa. Especially recommended are articles on East Turkana by R. Leakey and G. Isaac, and review article on hominid evolution in the Plio-Pleistocene by P. Tobias.*

Leakey, Richard E. and Roger Lewin. *Origins*, New York: E. P. Dutton, 1977.
> *A comprehensive review of human evolution with particular emphasis on Plio-Pleistocene discoveries in East Africa. Traces primate and hominid developments up to fairly recent time and concludes with a discussion of the nature and evolution of human aggression. Highly recommended for all students.*

Walker, Alan and R.E.F. Leakey. "The Hominids of East Turkana," *Scientific American*, **239**:54–66, 1978.
> *A superb overview of the huge East Turkana collection. Walker and Leakey present somewhat more conservative interpretations than suggested earlier (by R. Leakey).*

For the ultimate in hominid descriptive analysis, see:

Tobias, P. V. *Olduvai Gorge* (Vol. II), *The Cranial and Maxillary Dentition of Australopithecus (Zinjanthropus) Boisei*, Cambridge, Cambridge University Press, 1967.
> *An incredibly thorough description of one hominid discovery (OH 5) with minute analysis of every conceivable microanatomic feature. Excellent concluding chapter contains good synthesis of Plio-Pleistocene hominids known at time of publication.*

Johanson, Donald C., et al. "Pliocene Hominid Fossils from Hadar, Ethiopia," *American Journal of Physical Anthropology*, 57(4), 1982.

The entire issue, comprising 11 articles and almost 350 pages of text, is devoted to describing the hominids from Hadar in minute detail. Articles include contributions on stratigraphy and chronology, the Lucy skeleton, cranial remains, mandibles, dental remains, dental root morphology, axial skeletal remains (ribs, vertebrae), upper limbs, hands, lower limbs, and feet.

CONTENTS

Plio-Pleistocene Hominids: Organization and Interpretation

Anthropologists have long been concerned with the behavioral evolution of our species. Accompanying changes in anatomy (locomotion, dentition, brain size and shape) were changes in mating patterns, social structure, cultural innovations, and, eventually, language. In fact, changes in these behavioral complexes are what mostly *explain* the concomitant adaptations in human biological structure.

We are, then, vitally interested in the behavioral adaptations of our early hominid ancestors. In seeking to reconstruct the behavioral patterns of these early hominids, anthropologists use inferences drawn from modern primates, social carnivores, and hunting-gathering people (see Chapter 10). In addition, they derive information directly from the paleoanthropological record (see Chapter 12).

Despite numerous detailed and serious attempts at such behavioral reconstructions, the conclusions must largely remain speculative. In point of fact, behavior does not fossilize. Accordingly, researchers must rely considerably upon their imaginations in creating scenarios of early hominid behavioral evolution. In such an atmosphere, biases often emerge; these biased renditions, in turn, stimulate heated debates and alternative scenarios—often as narrow as those being attacked.

Probably no topic has stimulated more controversy (or has been more riddled with implicit biases) than the debate concerning origins of hominid sex-role differences. Did early hominid males have characteristically different behavioral adaptations than their female counterparts? Did one sex dominate the frontier of early hominid cultural innovation? And if one sex did lead the way, which one?

A now well-known rendition of early hominid behavioral development was popularized in the 1960s and 1970s. According to this "man, the hunter" theory, the hunting of large animals by males was the central stimulus of hominid behavioral evolution. According to such widely read works as Desmond Morris' *The Naked Ape* (1967) and several books by Robert Ardrey (including *The Hunting Hypothesis*, 1976), early apish-looking forms *became* hominids as a result of a hunting way of life. As Ardrey states, "Man is man, and not a chimpanzee, because for millions upon millions of evolving years we killed for a living" (1976, p. 10).

In this reconstruction, the hunting of large, dangerous mammals by cooperating groups of males fostered the development of intelligence, language, tools, and bipedalism. Increased intelligence accompanied by the development of weapons is also blamed in this scenario for the roots of human aggressiveness, murder, and warfare. (See Issue, Chapter 14.)

This "man, the hunter" scenario further suggests that while the males are leading the vanguard in hominid evolution, females remain mostly sedentary, tied to the home base by the burden of dependent young. Females may have contributed some wild plant foods to the group's subsistence, but this is not seen as a particularly challenging (and certainly not a very noble) endeavor. In this situation of marked division of labor, sexual relationships quickly changed. Males, constantly away from the home base (and, thus, away from the females too) could not keep a watchful eye over their mates. In order to better insure fidelity (and to reduce the risk of cuckoldry), monogamy came into being. In this way, a male would be assured that the young in

which he invested was his own. This important factor of male-female bonding as a product of differential foraging patterns has recently been forcefully restated by Owen Lovejoy (1981). (See p. 271.)

From the female's point of view, it would be beneficial to maintain a close bond with a provisioning male. Consequently, she would want to appear "attractive," and thus, through time, the female breasts and buttocks would become more conspicuous. Besides rearing their young and being attractive sex objects, females were useful to males in another way. Groups of male hunters living in the same area might occasionally come into potentially dangerous competition for the same resources. As a means of solidifying political ties between groups, the males would thus routinely exchange females (by giving or "selling" their daughters to neighboring bands).

Thus, in a single stroke, this complex of features accounts for human intelligence, sexual practices, and political organization.

As might be expected, such a male-centered scenario did not go unchallenged. Ignoring females or relegating them to a definitely inferior role in human behavioral evolution drew sharp criticism from several quarters. As one anthropologist noted:

So, while the males were out hunting, developing all their skills, learning to cooperate, inventing language, inventing art, creating tools and weapons, the poor dependent females were sitting back at the home base having one child after another and waiting for the males to bring home the bacon. While this reconstruction is certainly ingenious, it gives one the decided impression that only half the species—the male half—did any evolving. In addition to containing a number of logical gaps, the argument becomes somewhat doubtful in the light of modern knowledge of genetics and primate behavior (Slocum, 1975, p. 42).

In fact, such a rigid rendering of our ancestors' behavior does not stand up to critical examination. Hunting is never defined rigorously. Does it include only large, terrestrial mammals? What of smaller mammals, sea mammals, fish, and birds? In numerous documented human societies, females actively participate in exploiting these latter resources.

Moreover, nonhuman primates do not conform to predictions derived from the "man, the hunter" model. For example, among chimpanzees, females do most of the toolmaking, not the males. Finally, in most nonhuman primates (most mammals, for that matter), it is the females—not the males—who choose with whom to mate.

Granting that the hunting hypothesis does not work, what alternatives have been proposed? As a reaction to male-centered views, Elaine Morgan (1972) advanced the "aquatic hypothesis." In this rendition, females are seen as the pioneers of hominid evolution. But rather than having the dramatic changes of hominid evolution occur on the savanna, Morgan has them take place on the seashore. As females lead the way to bipedal locomotion, cultural innovation, and intellectual development, the poor males are seen as splashing pitifully behind.

Unfortunately, this theory has less to back it up than the hunting hypothesis. Not a shred (even a watery one) of evidence has ever been discovered in the contexts predicted by the aquatic theory. Little is accom-plished by such unsubstantiated overzealous speculation. Chauvinism—whether male or female—does not elucidate our origins and only obscures the evolutionary processes that operated on the *whole* species.

Can nothing then be concluded about differential male-female sex roles? While the pattern is not as rigid as the hunting hypothesis advocates would have us believe, in the vast majority of human societies hunting of large, terrestrial mammals is almost always a male activity. In fact, a comprehensive cross-cultural survey shows that of 179 societies, males do the hunting exclusively in 166, both sexes participate in 13, and in *no* group is hunting done exclusively by females (Murdock, 1965).

In addition, as we noted in Chapter 10, there is some incipient division of labor in foraging patterns among chimpanzees. Females tend to concentrate more on termiting, while hunting (though it is only occasional) is done mostly by males. Early hominids, expanding upon such a subsistence base, eventually adapted a greater sexual division of labor than found in any other primate. Two points, however, must be kept in mind. First, both the gathering of wild plant foods and the hunting of animals would have been indispensible components of the diet. Consequently, *both* males and females always played a significant role. Secondly, the strategies must always have been somewhat flexible. With a shifting, usually unpredictable resource base, nothing else would have worked. As a result, males probably always did a considerable amount of gathering and in most foraging societies still do. Moreover, females—while not usually engaged in the stalking and killing of large prey—nonetheless contribute signifi-cantly to meat acquisition. Once large animals have been killed, there still remain the arduous tasks of butchering and transport back to the home base. In many societies, women and men participate equally in these activities.

A balanced view of human behavioral evolution must avoid simplistic and overly rigid scenarios. As recently stated by a researcher concerned with reconstructing early hominid behavior:

Both *sexes must have been able to care for young, protect themselves from predators, make and use tools, and freely move about the environment in order to exploit available resources widely distributed through space and time. It is this range of behaviors—the overall behavioral flexibility of both sexes—that may have been the* primary *ingredient of early hominids' success in the savanna environment (Zihlman, 1981, p. 97).*

SOURCES:

Ardrey, Robert. *The Hunting Hypothesis.* New York: Atheneum, 1976.

Dahlberg, Frances (ed.). *Woman the Gatherer.* New Haven: Yale University Press, 1981.

Lovejoy, C. Owen. "The Origin of Man," *Science,* 211:341–350, 1981.

Morgan, Elaine. *The Descent of Woman.* New York: Stein and Day, 1972.

Morris, Desmond. *The Naked Ape.* New York: McGraw-Hill, 1967.

Murdock, G. P. *Culture and Society,* Pittsburgh: University of Pittsburgh Press, 1965.

Slocum, Sally. "Woman the Gatherer: Male Bias in Anthropology," In: *Toward an Anthropology of Women,* R. R. Reiter, ed., New York: Monthly Review Press, pp. 36–50, 1975.

Zihlman, Adrienne L. "Women as Shapers of the Human Adaptation," In: *Woman the Gatherer, op. cit.,* pp. 75–120, 1981.

◇ CHAPTER FIFTEEN

◇ Introduction

We have seen in the last two chapters that a vast and complex array of early hominid material has been discovered in South and East Africa. In just the past few years, particularly in the eastern part of the continent, a great number of new discoveries have been made. We now have Plio-Pleistocene hominid collections totaling close to 200 individuals from South Africa and probably more than 300 from East Africa. Given the size and often fragmentary nature of the sample, along with the fact that a good deal of it is so recently discovered, we should not be surprised that many complications arise when it comes to interpretation. In addition, both popular enthusiasm and the strong personalities often connected with fossil hominid discoveries have generated even more confusion.

In this chapter, we will look at several *theories* that attempt to organize the huge amount of Plio-Pleistocene hominid material. We ask you to remember that these are only theories and must remain so, given the incomplete nature of the fossil record. Even considering the seemingly very large number of fossils there is a *great* deal of time over which they were distributed. If we estimate about 500 total individuals from all African sites recovered thus far for the period 4–1 m.y.a., we still are sampling just one individual for every 6000 years! Until much of the new material from East Africa has been properly analyzed and detailed reports published, we cannot form even reasonably secure hypotheses without extreme difficulty. At the present time, only a very few East African hominids have been thoroughly studied; all the rest are thus far described in preliminary reports.

It will no doubt appear that many opposing and conflicting theories attempt to describe exactly what is going on in human evolution during the crucial period between 5 and 1 m.y.a. And, indeed, there are many theories. Hominid fossils are intriguing to both scientists and nonscientists, for some of these ancient bones and teeth are probably those of our direct ancestors. Equally intriguing, some of these fossils are representatives of populations of our close relatives that apparently met with extinction. We would like to know how these animals lived, what kinds of adaptations (physical and cultural) they displayed, and why some continued to evolve while others died out.

◇ More Hominids—More Complications

In our review of hominid evolution in the Plio-Pleistocene, we have discussed two varieties of australopithecines in South Africa, probably representing two separate species (*A. africanus* and *A. robustus*). In East Africa, three forms are known: an early primitive australopithecine (*A. afarensis*); a later, hyperrobust form (*A. boisei*); and one smaller but brainier than any of the other forms and therefore called an early member of genus *Homo* (*H. habilis*). The vast majority

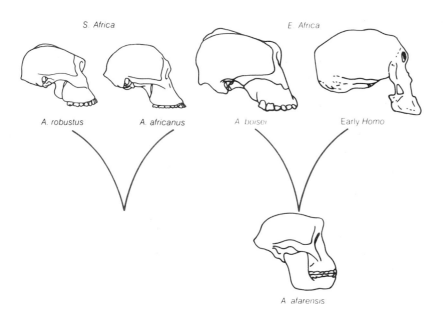

of hominid discoveries from the Plio-Pleistocene can be assigned to one of these groups. However, a few fossils do not fit neatly into this scheme. As noted, most of this material is quite new and conclusions must, therefore, remain highly speculative at this stage. Following are three more considerations drawn from this newly discovered fossil material. We will eventually work them into our interpretations of early hominid evolution.

A. africanus IN EAST AFRICA?

We have discussed in detail (Chapter 13) the gracile form of australopithecine from South Africa called *A. africanus*. This form combines small brain size and relatively small back teeth (premolars and molars, compared to the massive ones seen in the robust forms) and is well known in South Africa at about 3–2 m.y.a. But what about East Africa? From here we have after 2 m.y.a. a very robust form with massive jaws and back teeth (*A. boisei*), and a smaller form with scaled down tooth proportions and a large brain (*Homo habilis*). Until recently, a hominid with the combination of a small brain and moderately sized teeth (i.e., *africanus*) was not recognized in East Africa. As already noted, it is sometimes extremely difficult to distinguish the individuals assigned to early *H. habilis* from the smaller gracile australopithecines (*A. africanus*).

The major differences most often underscored are in brain size and tooth proportions, but these distinctions are often impossible to define in fragmentary remains. Since both gracile australopithecines and early populations of genus *Homo* have considerable within-group variation (individual, sexual dimorphism, etc.), they may also have considerable overlap of structural traits, such as tooth and brain size. Operationally, then, in East Africa it becomes a tortuous task to distinguish early members of genus *Homo* on one hand and gracile australopithecines on the other. The East African evidence of a third

Figure 15-2 A nearly complete cranium (ER 1813) discovered at East Lake Turkana, 1973. Evidence of *A. africanus* in East Africa 1.3–1.6 m.y.a.?

kind of hominid, in addition to robust *A. boisei* and *H. habilis* is tenuous, but some suggestive clues do exist.

A fossil skull found at East Turkana in 1973 (ER 1813) dated 1.6–1.3 m.y.a. led Richard Leakey (1974) to suggest the presence of *A. africanus* in East Africa contemporaneous with *A. boisei* and *Homo*. Additional finds (at the Omo) of mandibular fragments, one upper arm bone, and about twenty teeth (from around 2.5 m.y.a.) may also belong to members of *A. africanus*. Some of the remains from Olduvai initially attributed to "*habilis*," particularly the skull called "Twiggy," may again be a gracile australopithecine.

As yet, this issue is unresolved. Most researchers, for the moment, prefer to keep the evolutionary picture as uncomplicated (parsimonious) as the evidence permits. Consequently, the potential *africanus* individuals noted above are simply regarded as small representatives of *H. habilis*. In fact, within the samples used to estimate cranial capacities for *H. habilis* (cited on p. 437), both ER 1813 (513 cm^3) and OH 24 ("Twiggy"—597 cm^3) were included (following Tobias, 1983b). It should be noted, however, that if these two specimens were deleted from the *habilis* sample, the average cranial size for the species (using the four other specimens) would be significantly larger.

Homo habilis IN SOUTH AFRICA?

Some recently discovered evidence suggests that, as in East Africa, early *Homo* lived contemporaneously with australopithecines in South Africa.

The first recognition of a more advanced hominid already present in australopithecine times was made by Broom and Robinson in the early 1950s. Fossil finds from Swartkrans, the site yielding most of the remains of *A. robustus*, also contained fragments (perhaps close to 2 million years old) initially called "Telanthropus capensis" (Robinson, 1953). While suggestive, "Telanthropus" remains were too fragmentary to generate much excitement. More complete evidence came to light in a museum twenty years later by simply joining pieces of previously discovered fossils.

Ron Clarke, a physical anthropology student and expert in fossil reconstruction, was looking at hominid material in the Transvaal museum in Pretoria. While comparing fragments of two "different" individuals, one supposedly "Telanthropus" and the other a robust australopithecine, he noted they fitted together perfectly! With the additon of yet another piece, a composite cranium was asscmbled making up a good part of the face and the left side of the skull of the same individual (Clarke and Howell, 1972). Presto, a "new" find, much more complete than anything previously attributed to an advanced hominid lineage in South Africa! Thus, we can say a good deal more about it than was true for the original "Telanthropus" fossils.

The shape of the brow as well as the front part of the vault of the composite skull (SK 80/846/847) are more *Homo*-like than are australopithecine skulls. While cranial capacity cannot accurately be determined from this partial cranium, the relatively higher forehead and shallower postorbital constriction indicate a larger brain size than that of australopithecines. The key diagnostic feature of size of face relative to skull vault is apparently similar for this Swartkrans composite cranium and the East African representatives of *H. habilis*.

Figure 15-3 The composite cranium (Sk. 847) from Swartkrans. Evidence of *Homo habilis* in South Africa?

◇ Box 15-1   A Visit to the Plio-Pleistocene: East Lake Turkana, Late One Afternoon

If an observer could be transported back through time and climb a tree in the area where the Koobi Fora Formation was accumulating, what would he see?

As the upper branches are reached, the climber would find himself in a ribbon of woodland winding out through open areas. A kilometer or so away to the west would be seen the swampy shores of the lake, teeming with birds, basking crocodiles, and *Euthecodons*. Here and there are schools of hippos. Looking east, in the distance some ten or twelve kilometers away lie low, rolling hills covered with savanna vegetation. From the hills, fingers of trees and bush extend fanwise out into the deltaic plains. These would include groves of large *Acacia*, *Celtis*, and *Ficus* trees along the watercourses, fringed by shrubs and bushes. Troops of colobus move in the tree tops, while lower down are some mangabey. Scattered through the bush, the observer might see small groups of waterbuck, impala, and kudu, while out in the open areas beyond would be herds of alcelaphine antelope and some gazelle (*Megalotragus* and *Antidorcas*). Among the undergrowth little groups of *Mesochoerus* pigs rootle, munching herbiage.

Peering down through the branches of the tree, the climber would see below the clean sandy bed of a watercourse, dry here, but with a tidemark of grass and twigs caught in the fringing bushes and showing the passage of seasonal floods. Some distance away down the channel is a small residual pool.

Out beyond the bushes can be seen large open floodplains, covered with grasses and rushes, partly dry at those seasons of the year when the lake is low and when the river is not in spate. Far across the plains, a group of four or five men approach; although they are too far off for the perception of detail, the observer feels confident that they are men because they are striding along, fully upright, and in their hands they carry staves.

To continue the reconstruction in a more purely imaginative vein: as the men approach, the observer becomes aware of other primates below him. A group of creatures has been reclining on the sand in the shade of a tree while some youngsters play around them. As the men approach, these creatures rise and it becomes apparent that they too are bipedal. They seem to be female, and they whoop excitedly as some of the young run out to meet the arriving party, which can now be seen to consist mainly of males. The two groups come together in the shade of the tree, and there is excited calling, gesturing and greeting contacts. Now the observer can see them better, perhaps he begins to wonder about calling them men; they are upright and formed like men, but they are rather small, and when in groups they do not seem to engage in articulate speech. There are a wealth of vocal and gestural signals in their interaction, but no sustained sequential sound patterns.

The object being carried is the carcass of an impala, and the group congregates around this in high excitement; there is some pushing and shoving and flashes of temper and threat. Then one of the largest males takes two objects from a heap at the foot of the tree. There are sharp clacking sounds as he squats down and bangs these together repeatedly. The other creatures scramble around picking up the small sharp chips that have been detached from the stones. When there is a small scatter of flakes on the ground at his feet, the stone worker drops the two chunks, sorts through the fragments and selects two or three pieces. Turning back to the carcass, this leading male starts to make incisions. First the belly is slit open and the entrails pulled out; the guts are set on one side, but there is excited squabbling over the liver, lungs, and kidneys; these are torn apart, some individuals grab pieces and run to the periphery of the group. Then the creatures return to the carcass; one male severs skin, muscle and sinew so as to disengage them from the trunk, while some others pull at limbs. Each adult male finishes up with a segment of the carcass and withdraws to a corner of the clearing, with one or two females and juveniles congregating around him. They sit chewing and cutting at the meat, with morsels changing hands at intervals. Two adolescent males sit at the periphery with a part of the intestines. They squeeze out the dung and chew at the entrails. One of the males gets up, stretches his arms, scratches under his arm pits and then sits down. He leans against the tree, gives a loud belch and pats his belly. . . . *End of scenario.*

SOURCE:
"The Activities of Early Hominids" by Glynn Ll. Isaac. In *Human Origins. Louis Leakey and the East African Evidence*, G. Isaac and E. R. McCown, eds. The Benjamin/Cummings Publishing Company, Inc. © 1976. Reprinted with permission of the publisher.

Figure 15-4   Hominid skull from Sterkfontein (Stw. 53).

Further evidence along these same lines was found in August, 1976, at Sterkfontein. New excavations in the west pit area of Sterkfontein uncovered a partial cranium and part of an associated lower jaw. This skull is fairly complete, including a good part of the face with most of the upper dentition and parts of the cranial vault. Like the Swartkrans composite skull, this new find from Sterkfontein is also *Homo*-like, with a higher forehead and shallower postorbital constriction. The cranial capacity has not yet been approximated, but it is probably larger than that of australopithecines.

Thus it seems reasonable to postulate, at least tentatively, that *H. habilis* was living contemporaneously with australopithecines in South Africa as well as East Africa between 2 and 1.5 m.y.a. We must remember that dating in South Africa is far from clear. It seems apparent, however, that at both Swartkrans and Sterkfontein, the fossils provisionally referred to here as genus *Homo* are demonstrably younger than the australopithecines at these sites (Howell, 1978). How much younger they are nobody knows. If these fossils prove to be closer to 1 m.y.a. than to 2 m.y.a., they might most accurately be considered representatives of *Homo erectus*. (See the following section.)

Homo erectus IN THE PLIO-PLEISTOCENE

Homo habilis in East Africa and probably South Africa appears well on its way in human evolution by 2 m.y.a. Well on its way where? As we shall see in the next chapter, the fossil hominid group that succeeded early *Homo* and preceded *Homo sapiens* is called *Homo erectus*. For several years, *Homo erectus* was thought to have appeared long *after* the australopithecines, coming on the scene as late as 500,000 years ago. However, a fossil skull found at Olduvai by Louis Leakey in 1960 pushed this date back to at least 1 m.y.a., and recent calibration of dates in the upper beds at Olduvai may push this back even further—to about 1.2 m.y.a.

Yet another important fossil hominid discovery from Lake Turkana was uncovered by Richard Leakey's remarkably successful crew in September, 1975. A nearly perfectly preserved skull (ER 3733), looking much like well-known members of Asian *erectus*, was recovered from beds dating 1.6–1.3 m.y.a. What is more, from these same beds come undisputed fossils of robust australopithecines (*A. boisei*) plus perhaps members of *A. africanus*. Consequently, it appears undeniable that *Homo erectus* was living contemporaneously in East Africa with australopithecines, perhaps as much as 1.6 m.y.a.

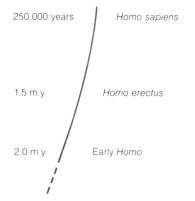

250,000 years   *Homo sapiens*

1.5 m.y.   *Homo erectus*

2.0 m.y.   Early *Homo*

Figure 15-5   The "main line" of hominid evolution over the last 2 million years.

◇ Hominids in the Plio-Pleistocene Outside Africa?

To date, the vast majority of hominid fossils and artifactual material predating 1 million years ago have been found on the African continent. There are, however, some claims (although still unconfirmed) that hominids may have dispersed from Africa earlier than had previously been believed (perhaps well before 1 m.y.a.).

JAVA

As we will see in the next chapter, there are abundant *Homo erectus* remains known from Java that are almost certainly Middle Pleistocene in date (i.e., after 700,000 B.P.*). Some fragmentary finds from earlier beds in Java are also known; their chronological placement, however, is a matter of dispute.

Initial K/Ar dates for these early Javanese hominids place them as far back as 2 million years ago, but these dates still lack confirmation by other techniques and thus are still open to question (see p. 475).

ISRAEL

A site on the western side of the Jordan River Valley in Israel, called Ùbeidiya, has been thought for some time to be quite ancient. Little has come from this site in the way of fossil hominids (just some nondiagnostic fragments), but artifacts are abundant. A recent biostratigraphic attempt at aging this site has yielded a provisional date (presumably associated with the ancient artifacts) of 2 million years (or even more!) (Repenning and Fejfar, 1982).

Obviously, the stratigraphic context at Ùbeidiya will have to be completely established, and further cross-correlation of this initial date will have to be performed. At present, it is intriguing to speculate about early hominids (*H. habilis*; very early *H. erectus*??) in southwestern Asia. We can reasonably postulate that *when* hominids first did emigrate from Africa, they passed through this region. Whether they already had done so by 2 m.y.a. remains to be seen.

FRANCE

Several sites in France (especially Vallonet Cave) have been suggested as potentially predating 1 m.y.a. No hominid fossils have been found at any of these sites, but stone tools have been discovered in what some researchers thought to be very early contexts. Systematic paleontological and geological work is still going on at several localities in south-central France, and attempts to establish a firm chronology are progressing. The most recent results (from paleomagnetic calibrations) indicate that all the potential hominid localities, in fact, postdate 1 m.y.a., although some of them perhaps not by much (Thouveny and Bonifay, 1984).

◇ Interpretations: What Does It All Mean?

By this time, it may seem anthropologists have an almost perverse fascination in finding small scraps buried in the ground and then assigning them confusing numbers and taxonomic labels impossible to remember. We must realize that the collection of all the basic fossil data is the foundation of human evolutionary research. Without fossils, our speculations would be

Figure 15-6   A nearly complete *Homo erectus* cranium (ER 3733) from East Lake Turkana. Dated approximately 1.3–1.6 m.y.a.

*B.P. indicates Before Present.

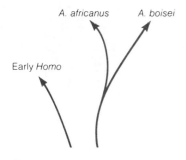

Figure 15-7 Phylogenetic interpretation. Early *Homo habilis* genetically distinct from australopithecines.

completely hollow. Several large, ongoing paleoanthropological projects discussed in Chapter 12 are now collecting additional data in an attempt to answer some of the more perplexing questions about our evolutionary history.

The numbering of specimens, which may at times seem somewhat confusing, is an attempt to keep the designations neutral and to make reference to each individual fossil as clear as possible. The formal naming of finds as *Australopithecus*, *Homo habilis*, *Homo erectus*, etc., should come much later, since it involves a lengthy series of complex interpretations. The assigning of generic and specific names to fossil finds is more than just a game, although some paleoanthropologists have acted as if it were just that. When we attach a particular label, such as *A. boisei*, on a particular fossil, we should be fully aware of the biological implications of such an interpretation (see p. 351).

Even more basic to our understanding of human evolution, the use of taxonomic nomenclature involves interpretations of fossil relationships. For example, two fossils such as "Zinj" and ER 406 are both usually called *A. boisei*. What we are saying here is they are both members of one *interbreeding* species. These two fossils can now be compared with others, like Sts. 5 from Sterkfontein, which are usually called *A. africanus*. What we are implying now is that "Zinj" and ER 406 are more closely related to each other than *either* is to Sts. 5. Furthermore, that Sts. 5 (*africanus*) populations were incapable of successfully interbreeding with *boisei* populations is a direct biological inference of this nomenclature.

We can carry the level of interpretation even further. For example, fossils such as ER 1470 are called early *Homo (Homo habilis)*. We are now making a genus-level distinction, and two basic biological implications are involved:

1. *A. africanus* (Sts. 5) and *A. boisei* ("Zinj" and ER 406) are more closely related to each other than either is to ER 1470
2. The distinction between the groups reflects a basic difference in adaptive level (see Chapter 11)

From the time that fossil sites are first located to the eventual interpretation of hominid evolutionary events, several steps are necessary. Ideally, they should follow a logical order, for if interpretations are made too hastily, they confuse important issues for many years. A reasonable sequence is:

1. Selection and surveying of sites
2. Excavation of sites; recovery of fossil hominids
3. Designating individual finds with specimen numbers for clear reference
4. Detailed study and description of fossils
5. Comparison with other fossil material—in chronological framework if possible
6. Comparison of fossil variation with known ranges of variation in closely related groups of living primates
7. Assigning taxonomic names to fossil material

The task of interpretation is still not complete, for what we really want to know in the long run is what happened to the populations represented by the fossil remains. Indeed, in looking at the fossil hominid record, we are looking for our ancestors. In the process of eventually determining those populations that are our most likely antecedents, we may conclude some hominids are on evolutionary sidebranches. If this conclusion is accurate, they necessarily must have eventually become extinct. It is both interesting and relevant to us as hominids to try to find out what caused some earlier members of our family to continue evolving while others died out.

PUTTING IT ALL TOGETHER

The interpretation of our paleontologic past in terms of which fossils are related to other fossils and how they are all related to us is usually shown diagramatically in the form of a *phylogeny*. Such a diagram is a family tree of fossil evolution. This kind of interpretation is the eventual goal of evolutionary studies, but it is the final goal, only after adequate data are available to understand what is going on. For example, the phylogeny of horse evolution for the last 60 million years is well known (see Fig. 15-8).

Whereas hominid fossil evidence has accumulated in great abundance, the fact that so much of the material has been discovered so recently makes any firm judgments concerning the route of human evolution premature. However, paleoanthropologists are certainly not deterred from making their "best guesses," and thus diverse speculative theories have abounded in recent years. The vast majority of more than 300 fossils from East Africa are still in the descriptive and early analytical stages. At this time, the construction of phylogenies of human evolution is analogous to building a house with only

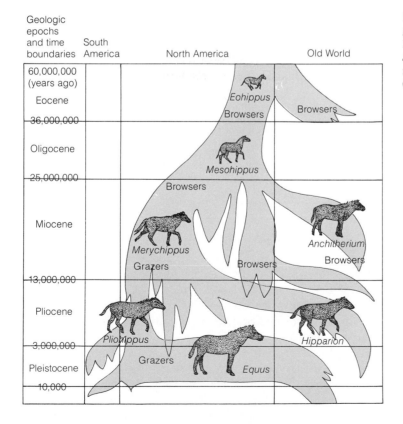

Figure 15-8 Schematic diagram (phylogeny) of horse evolution over the last 60 million years. (From *Heredity, Evolution and Society*, Second Edition, by I. Michael Lerner and William J. Libby. W. H. Freeman and Company. Copyright © 1976.)

a partial blueprint. We are not even sure how many rooms there are! Until the existing fossil evidence has been adequately studied, to say nothing about possible new finds, speculative theories must be viewed with a critical eye.

In the following pages, we will present several phylogenies representing different and opposing views of hominid evolution. We suggest you do not attempt to memorize them, for they *all* could be out of date by the time you read this book. It will prove more profitable to look at each one and assess the biological implications involved. Also, note which groups are on the main line of human evolution leading to *Homo sapiens* and which are placed on extinct sidebranches.

INTERPRETING THE INTERPRETATIONS

There are two basic interpretations of hominid evolution in the Plio-Pleistocene: the single lineage theory and the double lineage theory. The single lineage theory, derived from the single species hypothesis, states that only *one* hominid species lived at any one time. Therefore, only a single line without branching leads directly from all fossil hominid ancestors to *Homo sapiens*.

The double lineage theories postulate a major division in hominid evolution, with one main branch leading to *Homo erectus* and *sapiens* and another line with various offshoots eventually dying out.

The various double lineage theories fall into two basic categories:

1. *A. africanus-Homo* line versus *robustus-boisei* line
2. *All* later australopithecines versus *Homo*.

The first double lineage interpretation sees *A. africanus* as ancestral to *erectus* with "early *Homo*" transitional between the two. The *robustus-boisei* line diverges, ultimately becoming extinct. The second theory postulates that early *Homo* (i.e., *habilis*) and then *erectus*, forming one line, lived at the same time as australopithecines (which had already diverged) forming another line. This australopithecine sidebranch then died out during the Plio-Pleistocene.

◇ Conclusions

As we have often stated, it is still simply too early to draw firm conclusions. We can, however, suggest which possibilities seem most likely. While the single lineage theory is an economical explanation, the amount of variation during a given time—particularly in East Africa—throws doubt on this view. The finds of *H. erectus* and *A. boisei* in the same beds at East Turkana have demonstrated two very different yet contemporary forms. If we accept two or more hominid forms living contemporaneously, we are left with some double lineage explanation.

We feel that present evidence best fits a phylogeny resembling Phylogeny VI (or a more recent variation, Phylogeny IX). Such an explanation, *for the moment* at least, adequately accounts for variation in the hominid fossil record during the Plio-Pleistocene. The earliest definite hominids of which we have evidence are found in sites dating between 4 and 3 m.y.a. These fossils are

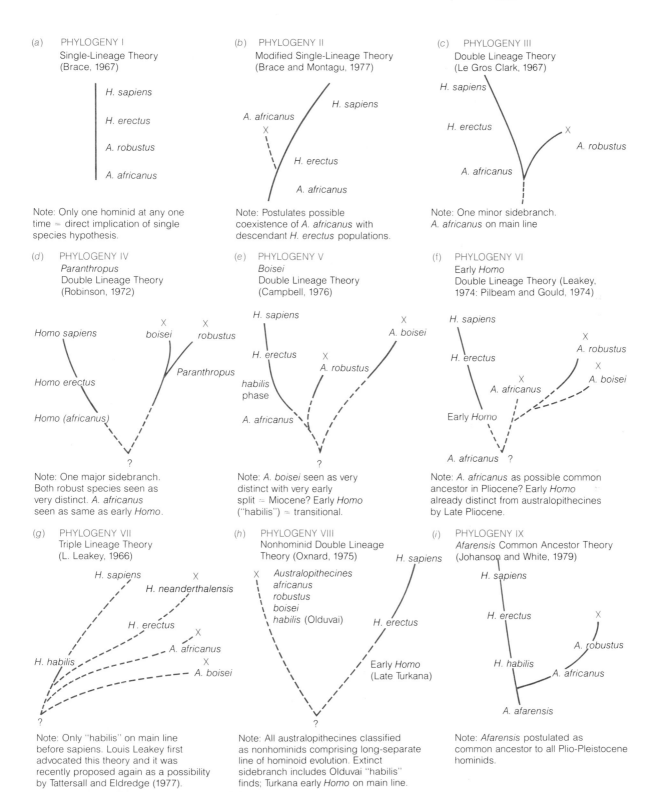

Figure 15-9 Phylogenies of hominid evolution.

Table 15-1   Dates for Early *Homo*

East Lake	
Turkana	1.8 m.y.a.
Olduvai	1.8 m.y.a.
Omo	1.85 m.y.a.
Sterkfontein	1.5–2.0 m.y.a.
Swartkrans	1.5–2.0 m.y.a.

also the most primitive of any hominid known, particularly as seen in the conformity of the cranium as well as numerous dental characteristics. Since these early forms combine a small brain with an already completely efficient bipedal adaptation, they are best considered members of the genus *Australopithecus*. However, they are not like the more specialized australopithecines seen later in both South and East Africa. Consequently, we believe the designation of these early australopithecines as a separate species (*A. afarensis*) is justified.

In addition to calling attention to a different morphology, a separate species name also can be used to make phylogenetic inferences. In this case, it appears that *afarensis*—particularly as seen in the dental complex—makes a good *potential* common ancestor for all the later australopithecines and genus *Homo*. In the later australopithecines, the relatively large front teeth are much reduced, while the back teeth become considerably larger. This trend towards a large, grinding tooth specialization is seen most dramatically in the robust australopithecines.

Meanwhile, in the evolutionary line that diverged into genus *Homo* the front teeth are also reduced, but the back teeth do not undergo the specialized development such as that of the later australopithecines. In addition, as compared to their smaller-brained australopithecine cousins, the *Homo* line displays a progressive increase in cranial capacity. Certainly, by about 2 m.y.a., the early *Homo* line is becoming larger-brained and probably more culture-dependent; these two factors obviously interact with one another as a primary determinant of human biocultural evolution. Evidence such as the 1470 skull from Turkana clearly shows us that such a large-brained lineage was evolving in East Africa in the Plio-Pleistocene. Some fragmentary remains at about the same time from South Africa suggest a similar process, since tantalizing evidence from Swartkrans and Sterkfontein implies a large-brained lineage was evolving there as well.

The other lineage (later *Australopithecus*) seems to have remained in an evolutionary backwater perfecting its already specialized adaptation, probably involving a heavy vegetarian diet with only minimal cultural dependence. By about 1.6 m.y.a., the *Homo* line—in East Africa anyway—had reached the level of *erectus*, the larger-brained, culturally more developed ancestor of our species. (For the story of *erectus*, see Chapter 16.)

A reasonable, though for now still extremely tenuous, hypothesis of the course of hominid evolution in the Plio-Pleistocene is shown in Figure 15-10.

◇ Summary

The huge amount of fossil hominid material from the Plio-Pleistocene of South and East Africa has generated a great deal of interest. As more evidence is found, more questions rather than answers seem to arise. Some possible additional complexities discussed in this chapter include: (1) the continued existence of *A. africanus* in East Africa contemporaneous with *A. boisei* and early *Homo*; (2) early *Homo* living contemporaneously with australopithecines

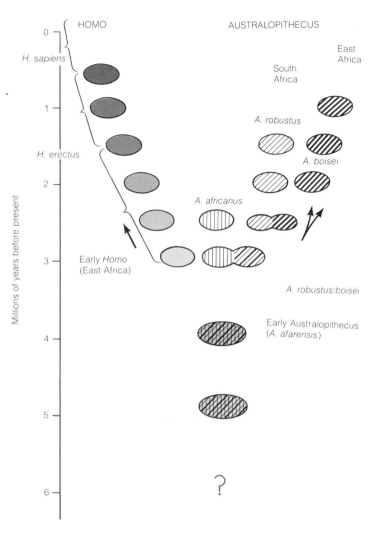

Figure 15-10   Phylogeny of hominid evolution in the Plio-Pleistocene: A provisional view.

in South Africa; (3) early appearance by 1.6 m.y.a. in East Africa of *Homo erectus*; and (4) Plio-Pleistocene hominids outside Africa?

Attempts to explain all the variation observed in fossil hominid material in the Plio-Pleistocene have yielded many alterntive theories. None of these is yet reasonably secure, and new evidence probably will force major reassessments in the next decade. What is significant in all this current debate is the way fossil hominids are utilized to make general biological inferences concerning the mechanics of human evolution.

◇ Questions for Review

1. What evidence suggests the presence of early *Homo* in South Africa in the Plio-Pleistocene?
2. What is a phylogeny?

3. Why have so many phylogenies been proposed for hominid evolution covering the last 5 million years?
4. Compare and contrast the biological implications of a single-lineage phylogeny with a double-lineage phylogeny.
5. Why is it important to be aware of within-species variation (sexual dimorphism, age, individual variation) when assessing the evolutionary relationships of fossil hominid populations?

◇ Suggested Further Reading

In the previous three chapters, several general and a few highly technical books on hominid evolution have been suggested for further study. Here, we list several readers on physical anthropology containing collections of articles by noted anthropologists. These books are excellent sources for gaining an appreciation of the original literature and the conflicting views and personalities in this rapidly growing field.

Brace, C. L. and James Metress (eds.). *Man in Evolutionary Perspective*, New York: John Wiley and Sons, 1973.
> *Articles cover topics on evolutionary principles, modern primate behavior, and hominid evolution. Contributions by Brace and Wolpoff give good synthesis of single species hypothesis.*

Dolhinow, Phyllis and Vincent Sarich (eds.). *Background for Man*, Boston: Little, Brown and Co., 1971.
> *A stimulating series of articles reflecting widely different views of hominid evolution. The contribution by Sarich on the molecular technique of reconstructing evolutionary history is a particularly good summary of this approach. Articles by J. T. Robinson and F. Clark Howell reflect the more traditional paleontological approach.*

Howell, F. Clark and F. Bourliere (eds.). *African Ecology and Human Evolution*, Chicago: Aldine Publishing Co., 1963.
> *Although this work largely precedes the explosion of paleoanthropological data from East Africa, it has several excellent examples of paleontological and paleoecological studies.*

Howells, W. W. (ed.). *Ideas on Human Evolution*, New York: Atheneum, 1967.
> *Contains several articles interesting from an historical perspective, particularly three contributions by J. T. Robinson.*

Katz, S. H. (ed.). *Biological Anthropology*, San Francisco: W. H. Freeman and Co., 1975.
> *Several superior* Scientific American *contributions on bipedal locomotion, early primates, and primate behavior. Excellent introduction to first section places hominid discoveries into historical framework. Superior illustrations throughout.*

Kennedy, W. J. (ed.). *Adventures in Anthropology*, St. Paul, Minn.: West Publishing Co., 1977.
> *A reasonably up-to-date group of articles on primate evolution, modern primate behavior and hominid evolutionary studies. This collection is particularly recommended for its strong emphasis on biocultural evolution.*

Korn, Noel (ed.). *Human Evolution* (4th Ed.), New York: Holt, Rinehart and Winston, 1978.
> *Good collection of articles on principles of evolution and interpretations of the hominid fossil record. Some interesting articles on the use of modern primates in reconstructing early hominid behavior as well as Glynn Isaac's article on paleoanthropology are worth looking at.*

Scientific American. *Human Ancestors.* (Introduction by Glynn Isaac and Richard Leakey), San Francisco: W. H. Freeman and Co., 1979.

> *While many of the contributions in this short volume are now dated, they provide an excellent background to the history of several still active paleoanthropological controversies. Recent excellent articles include those contributed by E. L. Simons (Ramapithecus), Alan Walker and Richard Leakey (summary of fossil hominids from Lake Turkana), and Larry Keeley (a provocative discussion of experimental inference regarding the use of stone tools).*

Washburn, S. L. (ed.). *The Social Life of Early Man,* Chicago: Aldine Publishing Co., 1961.

> *Although now out of date, this work contains many intriguing articles dealing with reconstruction of social behavior of early hominids.*

———— (ed.). *Classification and Human Evolution,* Chicago: Aldine Publishing Co., 1963.

> *This work contains several excellent contributions dealing with hominoid evolution and the theoretical bases of classification.*

Washburn, S. L. and Phyllis Dolhinow (eds.). *Perspectives on Human Evolution,* New York: Holt, Rinehart and Winston, 1968–1976.

> *A four-volume series dealing with human evolution largely from the perspective of modern primate studies.*

◇ CHAPTER SIXTEEN

Homo Erectus

CONTENTS

In the summer of 1941, war between the United States and Japan appeared inevitable to the officials at the Cenozoic Research Laboratory of Peking Union Medical College. To prevent the priceless Peking Man bones from falling into the hands of the Japanese, already in Peking, the officials packed them into boxes and shipped them to a warehouse at Camp Holcomb, a Marine Corps base not far from Peking. The marines, scheduled to leave China on December 8 aboard the S.S. *President Harrison*, were to take the bones with them on their return to the United States.

On December 7, 1941, Pearl Harbor was attacked, and war declared against Japan. Instead of leaving, the marines were arrested by the Japanese and interned for the duration of the war. What happened to the bones has remained a deep mystery ever since.

One account is that in the fall of 1941, Col. Ashurst, Commander of the Marine Corps Headquarters at Camp Holcomb, ordered the boxes of bones sent to Lt. Wm. E. Foley, a Marine Corps physician, who was to take the boxes with him aboard the *President Harrison*. When he received the boxes, Dr. Foley, realizing arrest and internment were imminent, distributed them to institutions and reliable Chinese friends in Tientsin, a city near Camp Holcomb. Dr. Foley has steadfastly refused ever since to divulge the names of these Chinese friends without guarantees for their safety from the Chinese government. Since he did not open the boxes when they arrived, it is not known for certain whether they even contained the bones.

In 1972, more than twenty-five years after the war ended, another chapter unfolded in the case of the missing bones. Mr. Christopher Janus, an American businessman, became interested in locating the bones after a visit to China and offered a reward of $5,000 for information leading to their recovery. Soon afterward, in New York, Janus received a telephone call from a woman who claimed her husband, a former marine now deceased, had left her a footlocker of what he believed were stolen Peking Man bones. Janus requested a meeting, which the so-called "mystery woman" insisted be held on the observation deck high atop the Empire State Building. At the meeting, the woman, who refused to give her name, showed a photograph of the footlocker's contents to Janus, who later checked the photo with Dr. Harry Shapiro, a physical anthropologist at the American Museum of Natural History. Shapiro, long interested in Peking Man and the missing bones, thought a skull in the photograph resembled that of Peking Man, and with that assurance Janus opened negotiations with the mystery woman's lawyer. The woman wanted $500,000 and guarantees that the United States government would not prosecute for possession of stolen property or confiscate the bones. Later, when these conditions were met, she raised her price to $700,000 and demanded a letter from the Chinese government stating they would not prosecute. The Chinese did not reply to the request for such a letter, and negotiations were never resumed.

Many rumors of the bones' location came to Mr. Janus, who eagerly investigated a number of them. He heard they were in Taiwan; they were not, but while there he increased the reward to $150,000. He also heard they were in Hong Kong—they were not; in Bangkok—not there, either. He was told they were in Burma, Tokyo, and Manila; but by this time he thought it was a waste of time and money to follow up these leads. Since then, 1975, Janus has not reported any further activity, and in November, 1977, withdrew his offer of reward.

The fate of the Peking bones remains unknown. The New York mystery woman might have a skull; Dr. Foley's friends in China may have all the bones; the bones might have been found in the Camp Holcomb warehouse by Japanese soldiers who, not realizing what they had, destroyed or abandoned them. They may have found their way to Burma, Bangkok, or—though very unlikely—the United States. Whoever has them—if anyone—is not telling.

The New York Times reported (May 11, 1980) that a former marine, Roger Ames, telephoned from his hospital bed in Dallas recently and told Janus the following story:

While on guard duty the night before Pearl Harbor he saw two marine officers, carrying a footlocker and shovels, dig a hole and bury the footlocker.

Urged on by the ex-marine's message, Janus decided to resume his investigation of the missing bones. He is going to attempt to locate the buried footlocker at the Peking site, where it may have been buried for safekeeping.

SOURCES:

Janus, Christopher G. with William Brashler. *The Search for Peking Man*, New York: Macmillan Publishing Co., Inc., 1975.

Shapiro, Harry L. "The Strange, Unfinished Saga of Peking Man," *Natural History,* 80:8 (No. 9), 1971.

———. *Peking Man*, New York: Simon and Schuster, 1974.

The New York Times, Sunday, May 11, 1980.

![coloured horizontal bar]

◇ Introduction

In the preceding several chapters, we introduced an early grade (see Box 16-1) of hominid evolution, the australopithecines of the Plio-Pleistocene. We discussed at some length the confusion surrounding them, confusion brought about by the various interpretations of the number of australopithecine species or lineages. Furthermore, recently discovered hominid remains in East Africa—designated as *Homo sp.* (or *H. habilis*) and apparently contemporary with australopithecines—have added to the muddle. These problems were discussed in Chapter 15, and though it is unfortunate that a clear and uncomplicated picture of early hominid evolution cannot yet be presented, we fervently hope that future discoveries will provide evidence to bring the scenario into focus.

The next grade of hominid evolution, *Homo erectus*, is much clearer, although some aspects remain murky. *H. erectus* inhabited a wider geographic area than australopithecines. We find their remains in Africa, Europe, and Asia, but not in Australia or the New World. They were taller, larger-brained, more culture-dependent, and more skillful toolmakers. Unlike australopithecines, who lived in much of the Pliocene and early Pleistocene, *H. erectus* is mainly a Pleistocene hominid. In our discussion of *H. erectus*, therefore, we must necessarily refer to the Pleistocene—its climate, **biosphere**, geological events, and dates.

Biosphere
The entire area inhabited by organisms.

Interstadial
Temperate period during the phases of a glacial period.

◇ The Pleistocene (1.8 m.y.a.–10,000 y.a.)

During much of the Pleistocene (also known as the Age of Glaciers), large areas of the northern hemisphere were covered with enormous masses of ice, which advanced and retreated as the temperature fell and rose. Until recently, European glaciers were considered to be four in number—Günz, Mindel, Riss, and Würm (to use the Alps Mountain glacial terminology). In reconstructing the history of the Pleistocene, scholars attempted to work out the dates of these glacial advances. Then they further attempted to develop the hominid history of Europe and Asia by correlating hominid fossil bones and artifacts found in association with animals indicative of the glacial advances or retreats. For example, if human bones were found with those of a warm-weather animal, the researchers assumed that this was an interglacial or **interstadial** period. This procedure may appear straightforward enough, but one of the problems was that the Alpine glaciers have not been chronometrically dated.

In addition, the glacial story has many more complications to it than had been realized (Turner, 1975). There were not four but probably eight or more glacial advances. Also, within a given major advance, there were numbers of short retreats and advances. Furthermore, the northern European (Scandi-

◇ Box 16-1   Grades of Human Evolution

1. *Australopithecus*
2. *Homo erectus*
3. *Homo sapiens* (including transitional forms, Neandertals, and modern populations)

navian) continental glaciations were found to be more suitable for study, and palynologists have arrived at what they consider to be more acceptable dates for the northern European glacial stratigraphy. However, paleonanthropologists and archeologists tend to use Alpine glacial terminology more often than Scandinavian, and we shall follow that procedure in this chapter. In Fig. 16-2 we show both schemes, so that references to one or the other can easily be reconciled.

A long-standing problem in the study of the Pleistocene involves its dating. At one time, the Plio-Pleistocene boundary was defined by the appearance of certain mammals believed to identify the beginning of the Pleistocene. Since the appearance of these mammals—modern cow, modern horse, Indian elephant—occurs at different times on different continents, this criterion

Figure 16-1 A partial listing of *Homo erectus* sites. *H. erectus* inhabited areas of Europe, Africa, and Asia, a much wider distribution than australopithecines.

1. Java
2. Peking, China
3. Lantian, China
4. Longtan, China
5. Heidelberg, Germany
6. Vérteszöllös, Hungary
7. Petralona, Greece
8. Torralba/Ambrona, Spain
9. Terra Amata, France
10. Ternifine, Algeria
11. Sidi Abd er-Rahman (Casablanca), Morocco
12. Rabat, Morocco
13. Salé Morocco
14. Olduvai Hominid 9, Tanzania
15. Olduvai Hominid 13, Tanzania
16. Olduvai Hominid 28, Tanzania
17. KNM-ER 3733, East Turkana
18. Omo, Ethiopia
19. Bodo, Ethiopia
20. Swartkrans, South Africa

	SCANDINAVIAN	ALPINE
10,000 —		
40,000 —	WEICHSEL	WÜRM
75,000 — 100,000 —	Eem	Riss-Würm
125,000 —	SAALE	
175,000 — 200,000 — 225,000 —	Warm phase	RISS
	SAALE	
265,000 —	Holstein	Mindel-Riss
300,000 —	ELSTER II	
	Warm phase	MINDEL
380,000 — 400,000 —	ELSTER I	
435,000 —	Cromerian	Günz-Mindel
500,000 —	MENAPIAN	GÜNZ
	Uncertain geological sequence	

Figure 16-2 Glacial sequence. With the exception of the Würm, dates for glacial and interglacial periods have not been well worked out yet.

could not be used on a worldwide basis. What was needed was an event that occurred everywhere on earth at the same time, and just such an event has recently been found in the reversal of the earth's magnetic field (Dalrymple, 1972).

We have known for a long time that the earth's magnetic field has frequently been reversed. During the reversal period, what we consider to be the North Pole became the South Pole, and a compass needle would have pointed south instead of north as it does now. In recent years, earth scientists have succeeded in dating these reversals, which are worldwide events. The reversals now serve as markers to correlate geophysical activity in different parts of the world.

For example, as we noted in Chapter 12, paleomagnetism has been widely applied in East Africa for the dating of early hominid sites. About 2.2 m.y.a., a "lasting" reversal occurred (except for intermittent shifts) until about 700,000 years ago. This long reversal is known as the Matuyama Reversed Epoch. Within the Matuyama Epoch are periods of "normal" magnetism, and experts agree that one of these—the Olduvai Event (occurring about 1.8 m.y.a.)—can be considered the boundary between the Pliocene and Pleistocene. The Matuyama Reversed Epoch ended about 700,000 years ago, and a "normal"

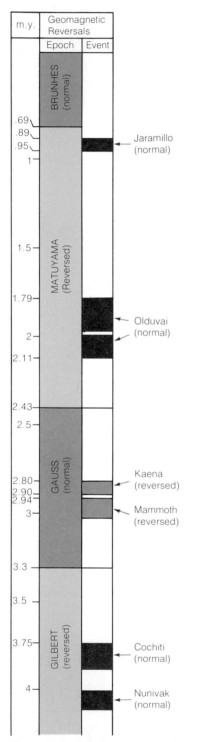

Figure 16-3 Paleomagnetic periods.

m.y.	Glacial Ages	Paleo-magnetism	Cultural Stage	Cultural Periods	Hominidae (*H. erectus*)
125,000					?Salé
200,000	R I S				
	S		L O W E R		Terra Amata (arch site)
300,000	Mindel-Riss (Holstein)	BRUHNES NORMAL EPOCH	P A L E O L I T H I C	Acheulian (hand axe)	SK 15 (date undetermined) Petralona Torralba/ Ambrona (arch site)
	Mindell II				Heidelberg
400,000	Mindel I				Vértesszöllös
430,000					? Bodo (date undetermined)
	Günz-Mindel (Cromerian)				Peking Sangiran 17 Heidelberg OH 28, OH 12 Ternifine Ndutu
500,000	Günz				
600,000	Sequence and dates uncertain				Lantian (Chenchiawo)
650,000					?Petralona *H. erectus* (Java)
700,000					Lantian (Kungwangling)

Middle Pleistocene

Figure 16-4 The Middle Pleistocene.

magnetic field period (the Brunhes Normal Epoch) was established and has continued until the present time. Professionals in the field commonly agree that the period from the beginning of the Pleistocene at 1.8 m.y.a. to 700,000 y.a. (the Matuyama-Brunhes boundary) be defined as the Lower (or Early) Pleistocene and the period beginning at 700,000 years as the Middle Pleistocene.

Although differences of opinion exist concerning the boundary between the Middle and Upper (or Late) Pleistocene, we shall use the widely accepted figure of 125,000 years, correlated with the beginning of the Riss-Würm interglacial. Figure 16-4 correlates Pleistocene, paleomagnetic periods, and Alpine glacial periods.

The Pleistocene, which lasted almost 2 million years, was an important time in hominid evolutionary history. *Homo erectus* appears. From their brain size and tools, we can clearly see that this form, using culture as their strategy of adaptation, should be called human. By the time the Pleistocene terminated, modern humans had already appeared, dependence on culture as the human way of life had dramatically increased, and domestication of plants and animals—one of the great cultural revolutions of human history—was either about to commence or had just been invented. With this background of the time span in which *H. erectus* evolved and developed, let us examine more closely the hominid to whom we owe so much.

(a)

◇ Homo Erectus

We have already observed that *H. erectus* was taller, larger-brained, and more dependent on culture than australopithecines. These statements are general, and it will therefore be necessary to discuss the characteristics of *H. erectus* in more detail. Since we are dealing with the evolution of hominids from something resembling an australopithecine stage to the modern stage, what we shall see in the modifications of hominids, for the most part, are relative changes. That is, *H. erectus* is taller than australopithecines, but shorter than *H. sapiens*; larger-brained than australopithecines, but smaller-brained than *H. sapiens*, etc. *Homo erectus*, in both physical and cultural characteristics, is intermediate between the australopithecine and *sapiens* stages.

From a time perspective, *H. erecutus* is usually associated with the Middle Pleistocene (which we have dated from 700,000 to 125,000 years ago). However, as we shall see, there are African, Javanese, and Chinese remains that may go back an additional million years. Nevertheless, the evolution of *H. erectus* proceeded most rapidly during the Middle Pleistocene.

The cranial capacity of *H. erectus* ranges widely from 775 to 1,225 cm³, with a mean of 1020 cm³. In terms of averages, this would make the skull of *H. erectus* roughly twice the size of australopithecines, 50% larger than early *Homo*, and 75% as large as *H. sapiens*.

When we look at the skull of *H. erectus* in profile, several characteristics are immediately apparent. Overhanging the orbits is a pronounced bony ledge, the supraorbital torus, and, just behind it, is a marked depression

(b)

(c)

Figure 16-5 (a) *Australopithecus* (*afarensis*); (b) *H. erectus* (Peking); (c) H. sapiens (anatomically modern). Note the changes in prognathism, ascending ramus, slope of foreheads, vault height, and development of occiput. (Not to scale.)

◇ Box 16-2   Vocabulary

Alveolar prognathism   Forward projection of the maxilla

Ascending ramus   Rear upright portion of the mandible

Callote or *calva*   Uppermost portion of the braincase

Calvarium   The skull minus the face and mandible

Cranium   The complete skull; bones of the head, face, and mandible

Cervical   Pertaining to the neck, as in cervical vertebrae

Clavicle   Collar bone

Condyle   A rounded protuberance of bone which articulates (forms a joint, moves against) with another bone. The ball in a ball and socket joint (humerus and femur)

Coronal suture   The suture running transversely across the skull joining the frontal and parietal bones

Femur   Thigh bone

Fibula   The narrow long bone on the outside of the lower leg (see tibia)

Frontal bone   The front bone of the skull including the forehead

Humerus   Upper arm bone

Lambdoid suture   The transverse suture at the back of the top of the skull joining the parietal and occipital bones

Maghreb   An area in Northwest Africa

Mandible   Lower jaw

Maxilla   Upper jaw

Occiput, occipital bone   The rear bone of the skull

Paleolithic   (Paleo: old; lithic: stone) Old Stone Age. The culture period preceding food-producing (farming, herding)

Parietal   The right and left side bones on top of the skull; joined by the sagittal suture

Platycephaly   (platy: flat; cephaly: head) Flatheadedness as opposed to dome shape of anatomically modern human beings

Sagittal suture   The suture joining the left and right parietals; bounded by coronal suture in front and lambdoidal suture behind

Scapula   Shoulder blade

Supraorbital torus   (supra: above; orbital: eye opening; torus: ridge) Ridge above the orbits on a skull, very pronounced in *H. erectus*, Neandertals, and some australopithecines

Tibia   The large long bone of the lower leg; the shin (see fibula)

Zygomatic bone   Outer portion of orbit forming parts of its floor, and the cheekbone

Zygomatic arch   The bony arch below the orbit

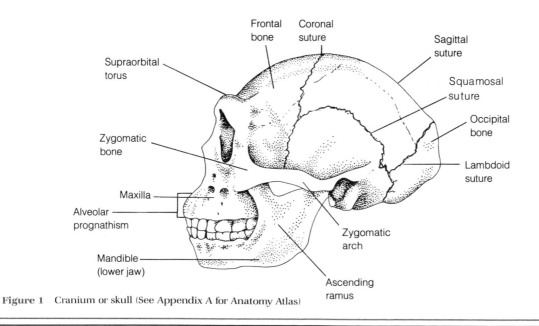

Figure 1   Cranium or skull (See Appendix A for Anatomy Atlas)

known as postorbital constriction. The forehead recedes instead of rising sharply as it does in modern humans, and the long, low skull is reminiscent of a deflated football. At the end of the skull is the occiput, a bone forming the back and part of the base of the skull. The occipital bone angles sharply down and forward, unlike the rounded profile of *H. sapiens*. The rear end of the skull profile also points up a ridge of bone—**nuchal** crest or line—for the attachment of neck muscles that hold up the head. Protruding beyond the occiput is an extension of bone called an *occipital bun*.

Returning to the front of the profile, we see the **alveolar** prognathism, receding chin, and teeth similar to but slightly larger than modern populations. Such traits reflect heavy chewing, and there is, indeed, a number of indications of well-developed **masseter** muscles. Heavy muscles require bony attachments, and these can be seen in the ridges on the mandible, the "buttresses on the facial skeleton—such as the broad nasal root, the thick supraorbital torus, the thick frontal process of the zygomatic bone—and the well-marked temporal lines" (Jacob, 1975, p. 314).

From the rear, we can see the most important feature that distinguishes an *H. erectus* skull: its pentagonal shape, with maximum breadth at or near the base. In later hominids, maximum breadth is higher up on the skull. (See Figs. 16-7, 16-13, and 16-20).

Differences in size and structure of teeth occur among the various *H. erectus* forms. In several of the Javanese upper jaws, a surprising **diastema** exists between the lateral incisor and canine, and the canine projects a bit beyond the margin of the other teeth. These are nonhominid primate characteristics that are not found among most australopithecines. What their adaptive function might have been is difficult to know. Characteristic of pongids and many australopithecines, too, is that the molar teeth increase in size from front to back. This sequence varies among *H. erectus*, but in most cases the 3rd molar is *smaller* than the second, a design that is typical of the later hominid pattern.

Two other dental traits may be mentioned. First, **shovel-shaped** incisors (Fig. 16-8). The edges of both sides of the teeth have raised ridges of enamel, and the incisors resemble a tiny scoop or coal shovel. It has been suggested that shovel-shaped incisors are an adaptive response in hunting and gathering societies, such as the Eskimo, in which a great deal of chewing takes place with the front teeth. The additional enamel may serve as structural support that enables the teeth to last longer.

The second trait is known as **taurodontism**, or enlarged pulp cavity. If roots of the molars (and sometimes premolars) should fail to grow to their adult length, a tendency of the pulp cavity in the center of the tooth to become enlarged occurs. This characteristic is an advantage among hard-chewing humans and such grazing animals as horses and cows that require high crowns on their teeth. In time, the pulp hardens and more wear is possible than in ordinary teeth.

In the past, it was believed that the locomotor skeleton of *H. erectus* was practically indistinguishable from *H. sapiens*. However, more recent analyses suggest that there are a number of morphological differences. "Nonetheless, the functional locomotor capabilities appear to have been generally similar

Alveolar
(al-vee'-lar)
Tooth-bearing portion of upper or lower jaw.

Masseter
Chewing

Nuchal
Pertaining to the neck.

Diastema
(dye-a-stee'-ma)
Gap, space.

Shoveling
Raised ridges of enamel on the tongue (lingual) side of the incisors.

Taurodontism
taurus: bull
dont: tooth
Bulltoothedness

Figure 16-6 *H. erectus* (Peking Man). From this view, the supraorbital torus, low vault of the skull, and angled occiput can be clearly seen.

Figure 16-7 *H. erectus* (Peking Man). Note that the widest part of the skull is toward the bottom, giving the skull a pentagonal form.

Figure 16-8 Shovel-shaped incisors.

Figure 16-9 Eugene Dubois.

to adaptations in *H. sapiens* for habitual erect posture and efficient striding bipedal gait" (Howell, 1978). These adaptations include a pelvic tilt mechanism, a hip extensor mechanism for raising the trunk, a pelvic rest mechanism, center of gravity behind the hip joints, transfer of body weight to the pelvis through the sacral suspensory mechanism, and powerful hip flexion and knee extension (Howell, 1978). Similarly, the forelimb morphology also diverges in distinct ways from *H. sapiens*, but, overall, *H. erectus* approximate *H. sapiens* more closely than it does *Australopithecus*.

◇Asia

JAVA

Scientific discoveries are normally the result of careful planning, hard work, and thorough knowledge of the subject. In addition, they are frequently tales of luck, adventure, and heartbreak, which brings us to the story of Eugene Dubois, a Dutch anatomist.

The latter half of the nineteenth century was a period of intellectual excitement. In England, Darwin's *Origin of Species* (published in 1859) provoked scientists and educated laymen to take opposing sides, often with great emotion. In Germany, for example, the well-known zoologist Ernst Haeckel eagerly supported Darwin's statement that man descended from apes and even suggested the name for the missing transitional link between the two: *Pithecanthropus alalus*, "the ape man without speech." He was criticized by Rudolf Virchow, one of Europe's most famous scientists and Haeckel's one-time zoology professor, who publicly and scornfully disagreed with these speculations. In 1856, a strange skull had been recovered near Dusseldorf, Germany. This specimen is what we today recognize as a Neandertal skull, but, when a description of it was published, scientific opinion was again divided and feelings ran high. "The opinions and counter-opinions about the Neandertal skull and other odd skulls, jaws, and bones that turned up in Europe kept science and the keenly interested lay public in something of an uproar for many years" (Moore, 1961, p. 235).

This stimulating intellectual climate surrounded the youthful **Eugene Dubois**, born in Holland in 1858, the year before Darwin's *Origin* and two years after the discovery of the Neandertal skull. As a young man, Dubois took up the study of medicine at the University of Amsterdam, and we can imagine how much these debates about human ancestors engaged the interest of an anatomy student. When Dubois graduated, he was appointed lecturer in anatomy at the University in 1886, but his heart was not in it. Visions of finding our fossil ancestors were more exciting than a stodgy academic career, and Dubois made up his mind to resign his university post and search for "Early Man." He was the first person ever to deliberately set out on such a venture. But where did one search in the 1880s?

Haeckel had reasoned that the missing link might be found in the Indonesian Islands under the mistaken notion that gibbons, native to that area, belonged in human ancestry. Virchow had pointed out that tropical habitats

Box 16-3   Portion of a Complete Definition of *Homo Erectus*

Homo erectus (Dubois) 1894   A species (extinct) of the genus *Homo*, known from Eurasia and Africa, distinguished by very substantial enlargement of the brain size, mean (1,020 cc) nearly twice that of large *Australopithecus* species and substantially above that of antecedent species of genus *Homo*; endocranial cast with essentially (modern) human fissuration pattern; generally low, flattened frontal region and prominent frontal keel; expanded (unilaterally) inferior frontal region, with wide separation from anterior temporal lobe; expanded precentral cortical area; exposed anterior insular area, in whole or part related to substantial development of Sylvian crest; lack of approximation between temporal lobe and cerebellum; absolutely and relatively narrow temporal lobe, tapering anteromedially, with poorly expanded inferior temporal area, salient superior temporal area, and posteriorly expanded posterior part of middle temporal convolution, expanded (unilaterally) inferior parietal region (supramarginal area); cerebellum with ipsilateral asymmetry, and cerebrum largely symmetrical, but with contralateral asymmetry expressed particularly in parieto-occipital and inferior frontal regions.

Cranial length greater than *Australopithecus*; vault bones of substantial to massive thickness, as expressed in outer and inner tables, cranial suture closure apparently earlier than in *H. sapiens*, and with coronal preceding sagittal suture closure; maximum breadth of vault at or toward the cranial base, usually coincident with biauricular breadth, with lesser bitemporal and biparietal dimensions; substantial postorbital constriction; low to more moderately arched vault, with low receding frontal (with or without notable frontal tuberosity), longitudinally flattened parietal, and occipital with marked to substantial angulation between upper (squama) and lower (nuchal) scales; usually distinct sagittal thickening, especially in bregmatic area, often associated with marked parasagittal depression; parietal smaller, more rectangular and transversely more curved than in *H. sapiens*, usually with sub-. . . .

SOURCE:
F. Clark Howell, ''Hominidae.'' In: V. J. Maglio and H.B.S. Cooke (eds.). *Evolution of African Mammals*, Cambridge: Harvard University Press, 1978.

of anthropoid apes were still totally unexplored. Indonesia seemed a judicious choice, especially since it was Dutch colonial territory. Dubois secured an appointment as a surgeon in the Royal Dutch Army and sailed for Sumatra in November, 1887, on the beginning leg of his journey to discover the first ''apeman.''

Dubois started digging in several caves in Sumatra and, except for teeth of extinct orangutan, found nothing of a hominoid nature. Hearing the digging was more favorable on Java, Dubois transferred his operations to that island. While there, he was sent a skull from a rock shelter at Wadjak, Java. Dubois then managed to be transferred to Java and immediately went to Wadjak, where, in 1889, he found a skull known as the Wadjak skull (discussed in Chapter 17).

Moving on, Dubois continued searching, and reached the small village of Trinil in August, 1891. On the banks of the Solo River near the village, he found a molar he thought might belong to a chimpanzee, and this find spurred him to even greater effort. A month later, he discovered what he had come halfway round the world to find. Lodged in the dirt was a dark, bowllike fossilized bone, which Dubois immediately recognized as the top of a skull.

Figure 16-10 The Indonesian area.

Tektite
A round, glassy body of unknown origin.

Kabuh
Middle Pleistocene geologic formation.

He worked feverishly and carefully to extract the bone "until a fine cranium emerged, a cranium like that of no living creature. Almost the whole skullcap was there, harder than marble and heavy in weight and portentiousness" (Moore, 1961, p. 237). Dubois' dream had become reality!

Or had it? The skullcap was low with a very pronounced supraorbital torus, and Dubois thought it might, like the molar, also belong to a chimpanzee. Digging stopped for the rainy season and, soon after resuming work the following year, Dubois recovered a femur fifteen yards upstream in the same level, the Trinil horizon, as the skullcap. He discerned at once that it resembled a human femur and belonged to an individual with an upright posture. But he was convinced he was dealing with a chimpanzee, or something like it, and that the molar, skullcap, and femur belonged not only to the same kind of creature, but to the same individual.

After studying his discoveries for a few years, Dubois startled the world in 1894 with a paper sensationally entitled, "*Pithecanthropus erectus*, a Human Transitional Form from Java." The name, *Pithecanthropus*, was adopted in honor of Haeckel, who had suggested the name *Pithecanthropus alalus* for the "missing link." A scientific uproar reminiscent of Darwin's time greeted Dubois' publication. Virchow, who did not seem to believe in the existence of fossil humans, rejected Dubois' views; Haeckel, of course, was overjoyed, since he believed his views had been vindicated.

The contrary opinions announced by scientists, and the outrage expressed by the public, especially the clergy, hurt and discouraged Dubois. He locked the bones in strongboxes and steadfastly refused permission to anyone, including scientists and public, to view them. Von Koenigswald, whom we shall meet shortly, gives a painful account of Dubois during this time:

> *Pithecanthropus* became Dubois' destiny. It was his discovery, his creation, his exclusive possession; on this point he was as unaccountable as a jealous lover. Anyone who disagreed with his interpretation of *Pithecanthropus* was his personal enemy. When his ideas failed to win general acceptance he sullenly withdrew, growing mistrustful, unsociable and eccentric. He showed his finds to hardly anyone, and at night he used to hear burglars prowling around the house, bent on stealing his *Pithecanthropus*. If anyone came to his door in whom he scented a colleague, he was simply not at home (von Koenigswald, 1956, p. 32).

Dubois was finally persuaded to open the strongboxes, in 1923, to the inspection of Dr. Aleš Hrdlička, an American anthropologist at the Smithsonian Institution. By 1930, the controversy had faded, especially in light of important new discoveries near Peking, China, in the late 1920s (discussed subsequently). These finds clearly demonstrated that Peking Man was human, an early form no doubt, but human nevertheless. Resemblances between the Peking skulls and Dubois' *Pithecanthropus* were obvious, and scientists pointed out that the Java form was not an apeman, as Dubois contended, but a true human.

One might expect that Dubois would welcome Peking Man and the support it provided for the human status of *Pithecanthropus*, but the eccentric Dutchman refused to recognize any connection between Peking and Java and described Peking "as a degenerate Neanderthaler" (von Koenigswald, 1956,

Figure 16-11   Skullcap (Pithecanthropus I, found by Eugene Dubois). Femur, also found by Dubois, led him to name this form *Pithecanthropus erectus*, now known as *H. erectus*. The abnormal spur of bone on the femur is known as an *exostosis*. It has no bearing on the identification of the femur. (Photograph of casts.)

◇ Box 16-4   Reference List for Important People Mentioned in Chapter 16

NAME	IDENTIFICATION	ASSOCIATED WITH
Andersson, J. Gunnar	Swedish geologist	Zhoukoudian, China
Black, Davidson	Canadian anatomist	Zhoukoudian, China
Bohlin, Birgir	Swedish geologist	Zhoukoudian, China
Dubois, Eugene	Dutch anatomist	Java
Haeckel, Ernst	Nineteenth-century German zoologist	
Howell, F. Clark	Physical anthropologist, University of California, Berkeley	Torralba/Ambrona, Spain
Isaac, Glynn	Archeologist, Harvard University	East Turkana, Kenya
Von Koenigswald, G.H.R.	German paleontologist	Java
Leakey, Louis	Physical anthropologist	Olduvai Gorge, Tanzania
Leakey, Mary D.	Archeologist	Olduvai Gorge, Tanzania
Leakey, Richard E. F.	Paleoanthropologist	East Turkana, Kenya
De Lumley, Henry	French archeologist	Terra Amata, France
Pei, W. C.	Chinese geologist and archeologist	Zhoukoudian, China
Poulianos, Ari	Greek paleoanthropologist	Petralona, Greece
Schoetensack, Otto	German paleontologist	Heidelberg, Germany
Virchow, Rudolf	Nineteenth-century German zoologist and pathologist	
Weidenreich, Franz	German, later American, anatomist and paleoanthropologist	Zhoukoudian, China

p. 55). Even more sadly, at about this time, Dubois changed his mind and declared his *Pithecanthropus* was not after all a transitional form between ape and human, but a giant gibbon, a position he tenaciously held until his death in 1940 (Wendt, 1955).

The story of *Homo erectus* does not, of course, end with the death of the beleaguered Dr. Dubois. Others, notably a younger paleontologist born in Germany, G. H. R. von Koenigswald, took up the search for ancient humans in Java in the 1930s.

Before reviewing the bone material found in Java, a cursory account of the island background will allow us to place its hominid evolutionary history in proper perspective.

The Lower Pleistocene of Java is associated with the geological Putjangan Beds and the faunal period known as Djetis. A recent K/Ar date has established the Putjangan Beds at 2.1–1.9 m.y.a. (Ninkovich and Burckle, 1978). The geological **Kabuh** Beds and Trinil fauna are associated with the Middle Pleistocene. The dating for the beginning of this period is poorly established, but there is a definite K/Ar date for **tektites** from the Kabuh Beds near Sangiran of 700,000 y.a. to 1 m.y.a. If we define the beginning of the Middle Pleistocene

Trinil fauna
Animal remains associated with the Middle Pleistocene Trinil period.

as we have, at the Matuyama-Brunhes Reversal 700,000 years ago, then the Kabuh Beds and **Trinil fauna** are somewhere in that neighborhood.

The geological strata of the Upper Pleistocene are known as the Notopuro Beds and the faunal period as the Ngandong. Again, the dating is not well established for the beginning of this period, but this need not concern us at this point, since *Homo erectus* proper probably did not survive into the Upper Pleistocene.

Most of the Javanese *H. erectus* material (summarized in Table 16-1) has been found in three areas: Modjokerto, Sangiran, and Trinil.

With this information of time, place, and stratigraphy, we are prepared for the fossil hominid material. From the Putjangan Beds of the Lower Pleistocene, dated at 1.9 m.y., von Koenigswald and his workers recovered three important finds:

1. An infant *H. erectus* skull (Perning) from the Modjokerto site
2. Portions of a heavy adult skull including occipital bone and maxilla: Sangiran 4, or *Pithecanthropus robustus*, from Sangiran
3. A mandible, Sangiran 16, from Sangiran

Another important find often referred to as *Meganthropus* (Sangiran 8) also comes from this Djetis faunal period at Sangiran. First identified by von

Table 16-1   *Homo erectus* Fossil Sites[a]

Age[b]	Name[c]	Country	Site	Material		Discovery	
				SKELETAL	CRANIAL CAPACITY (CC.)	SCIENTIST ASSOCIATED WITH FIND	YEAR
Middle Pleist. (700,000–500,000)	*H. erectus* Pithecanthropus I	Java	Sangiran	calva, femur	940[d]	Dubois	1891 1892
Middle Pleist. (700,000–500,000)	*H. erectus* Sangiran 2, 3, 10, 12	Java	Sangiran	bones of the skull	775–900	von Koenigswald, Jacob, Sartono	1937–1973
Middle Pleist. (500,000)	*H. erectus* P. VIII Sangiran 17	Java	Sangiran	almost complete cranium	1,029	Sartono	1969
Lower Pleist. (1.9–1.5 m.y.) (1.9–1.5 m.y.)	Sangiran 4	Java	Sangiran	portions of adult skull	900	von Koenigswald	1939
Lower Pleist. (1.9–1.5 m.y.)	*H. modjokertensis* Perning	Java	Modjokerto	infant calvarium	650	von Koenigswald	1936
Lower Pleist. (1.9 m.y.)	Meganthropus Sangiran 16	Java	Sangiran	mandible fragment	—	von Koenigswald	1952
Upper Pleist. (200,000)	*H. solensis* Solo Man Ngandong	Java	Ngandong	portions of eleven skulls	1,100 (avg.)	ter Haar, Oppenoorth	1931–1933

a. Only better-known fossils are included.
b. These are best estimates—authorities differ.
c. These are either the names given by the finder (or scientist associated with the find) or the name commonly used by anthropologists.
d. Holloway, 1981.

Koenigswald, and perhaps close to 2 million years old, it has been compared to robust australopithecines. However, it is most likely an early *H. erectus.*

Dubois recovered his famous skullcap, *Pithecanthropus* I, from the Trinil faunal level near the village of Trinil. Also from these Kabuh Beds, but from the productive nearby Sangiran site, came remains of Sangiran skulls 2, 3, 10, 12, and 17. These fossils are considered to be in the range of 1 million to 500,000 years.

Several fossil hominid remains have also been recovered from the Notopuro Beds containing Ngandong fauna of the Upper Pleistocene. Found along terraces of the Solo River, these hominids are called Solo Man or Ngandong. Since there is some question whether they are *H. erectus* or *H. sapiens,* we shall leave the matter for later discussion.

In summary, the material found by Dubois, von Koenigswald, Jacob, Sartono, the Geological Survey for Java, and others consist of the remains of eight skulls, several mandibles or mandible fragments, at least one complete femur and portions of others, and a number of loose teeth. The cranial capacity of those skulls suitable for measurement range from 775 to 1,029 cm³, with an average of 900 cm³. The femora found at these sites are similar (though not identical) to those of modern *H. sapiens,* and indicate the Java population was roughly the same size as (or a few inches shorter than) humans today. Java *erectus* lived, if the dates recently suggested are correct, from almost 2 million to about 500,000 years ago.

When we compare the skulls of the Lower and Middle Pleistocene of Java, we find a pattern of what Sartono (1975) has called small-brained and large-brained pithecanthropines. In the Lower Pleistocene, the evidence from Sangiran 4 suggests characteristic *H. erectus* traits, only more so. The brain is smaller, bones thicker, skull flatter, and there is that unexpected diastema in the upper jaw and the projecting canine.

By Middle Pleistocene times in Java, *H. erectus* had changed, but not a great deal. A slight increase occurred in the height of the vault (see craniograms in Fig. 16-13), and the diastema and projecting canine had disappeared. The small brain continues in the Trinil (Sangiran) 2, 3, 10, 12, and 17 specimens, which are all remarkably similar. There seems to have been very little evolutionary change within the Middle Pleistocene until the upper levels of the Kabuh Beds are reached. Here, a recent significant find, Sangiran 17, estimated at about 500,000 years, represents a decided break in the similarity of Javanese Middle Pleistocene *erectus* forms.

Although this almost complete skull retains the basic morphologic pattern of Java *erectus,* it is longer, broader, and higher. The dental arch is remarkably similar to *H. sapiens,* and the forehead is higher than any other Javanese *H. erectus* of the Middle Pleistocene. These modifications of skull size are reflected in the cranial capacity of Sangiran 17, which measures 1,029 cm³. We do not presently know what processes might have occurred in the short time represented in the 30 feet of strata separating Sangiran 12 (900 cm³) from Sangiran 17 (1,029 cm³) that could have produced this increase in cranial capacity.

Solo, or Ngandong, a problem Javanese form, should be mentioned here.

(a)

(b)

Figure 16-12   (*a*) Sangiran 12. Rear view illustrates pentagonal shape of skull. (*b*) Sangiran 17.

Figure 16-13　Craniograms.

Craniogram comparing *H. erectus* forms (note change in the cranial height of the later [P. VIII and Solo] forms)

?500,000	———	Pithecanthropus I (Dubois)
2.1–1.9	———	Sangiran 4 (Pithecanthropus IV—von Koenigswald)
?200,000	———	*H. soloensis* (Oppenoorth)
500,000	———	Sangiran 17 (Pithecanthropus VII—Sartono)

Sangiran 17

Craniogram showing outline from an occipital view: note the widest area is toward base of skull giving a pentagonal form

Sangiran 2

Figure 16-14　Craniograms.

Peking man

Pithecanthropus I, Sangiran 2, 3, 4, 12

Sangiran 17

——— Sangiran 4 (robustus)

——— Sangiran 17

Actually, there are two problems: (1) Is Ngandong *H. erectus* or *H. sapiens*? and (2) when did it live? Estimates range from 300,000 y.a.–60,000 y.a.

Similarities to *H. erectus* include the thickness of the skull bone, thick brow ridges, and sharply angled occiput. On the other hand, the vault is higher than *H. erectus*, and the forehead rises more vertically. Also, the occiput seems more filled out, the nuchal ridge for the neck muscles is lower down (a *H. sapiens* trend), and the angulation of the occiput is not as sharp. The skull is larger than *H. erectus*, ranging from 1,035 to 1,255 cm³ (the mean is 1,154 cm³) for the eleven calvaria that have been found.

Ngandong has long been considered a relative of the earlier Javanese *H. erectus* forms. This belief receives further support from a skullcap found not far from Sangiran and known by its site name, Sambungmachen. This is a larger skull than the earlier fossils from Java, probably over 1,000 cm³, and possesses some typical early *H. erectus* traits, with changes especially in the occiptal area that foreshadow the Ngandong material.

Like some of the European fossils of the Middle Pleistocene, Ngandong is difficult to place because of the mixture of *H. erectus* and *H. sapiens* traits. It is possible, of course, that like Swanscombe, Steinheim (p. 510), and some others, Ngandong is a transitional form between *H. erectus* and *H. sapiens*. Coming in the latter portion of the Middle Pleistocene, this is entirely possible.

We can say little about the hominid way of life in Java during the Lower and Middle Pleistocene. Tools have been found, but not in their original strata nor in direct association with faunal, including human, assemblages. Apparently they date from the Middle Pleistocene, and consist mainly of crudely made choppers and chopping tools similar to those found in Burma, Northwest India, and northern China.

Like other *H. erectus* populations, the Java *H. erectus* was most likely a systematic hunter, a life style made possible by the striking increase in brain size over australopithecines. The relatively large Java *H. erectus* brain may be explained by the selective pressures of a hunting society. In hunting "the abilities to learn from the past, plan for the future, and communicate one's ideas are at a premium for a creature who, alone and unarmed, is unable either to out-spring or out-fight its potential prey" (Brace and Montagu, 1977, p. 314). (For an alternative view, see p. 479.)

PEKING

The story of Peking Man is another saga filled with excitement, hard work, luck, and misfortune. It began in 1911, when J. Gunnar Andersson, a Swedish geologist, accepted an appointment as adviser to the Chinese Government to arrange a survey of its coalfields and ore resources. In his investigations, Andersson became interested in the mammals of Tertiary and Pleistocene deposits, and he and his colleagues collected many specimens. Europeans had known for a long time that the "dragon bones" (like the *Gigantopithecus* teeth mentioned in Chapter 11), so important to the Chinese for their healing and aphrodisiac power, were actually mammal bones. In 1917, the Geological Survey of China resolved to find the sites where these dragon bones were collected by local inhabitants and sold to apothecary shops. In 1921, An-

(a)

(b)

Figure 16-15 (*a*) Lateral view of Solo skull; (*b*) rear view of Solo skull.

dersson and a few other scientists were investigating a place called Chicken Bone Hill near the village of Zhoukoudian, about thirty miles southwest of Beijing.* While laying plans to excavate the hill, they were approached by a local resident who told the scientists that much larger and better dragons' bones could be obtained not far away.

The new discovery lay in an abandoned quarry 500 feet west of the railway station at Zhoukoudian. The villager showed them a fissure in the limestone wall, and in a few minutes they found the jaw of a pig, which indicated that the site was a more important one than Chicken Bone Hill. "That evening we went home with rosy dreams of great discoveries" (Andersson, 1934, pp. 97–8).

Andersson assigned a colleague, Dr. Otto Zdansky, to excavate the site, and told him, "I have a feeling that there lie here the remains of one of our ancestors and it is only a question of your finding him. Take your time and stick to it till the cave is emptied, if need be" (Andersson, 1934, p. 101). Zdansky worked the site for several summers and took the material he excavated back to Sweden. In 1926, he wrote Andersson that after carefully cleaning and preparing the material, he had found a premolar and molar, which he cautiously identified as belonging to a creature resembling *Homo* sp. Andersson, not nearly so cautious, jubilantly exclaimed, "The man I predicted has been found" (Andersson, 1934, p. 103).

Andersson's enthusiasm and the discovery of the remarkable teeth led to a more organized effort to excavate the Zhoukoudian cave under the direction of Dr. Birgir Bohlin of Sweden. Work began in April, 1927, and continued until October 18 of the same year. Two days before the season ended, Bohlin found a hominid tooth, which he immediately took to **Dr. Davidson Black**, anatomist at the Peking Union Medical College, and responsible for the study of hominid material recovered from the cave. Of this episode, Black wrote to Andersson:

*Beijing is now widely accepted as the spelling for Peking. Peking will continue to be used in the text when referring to the fossils associated with that name.

On October 19th at half-past six in the evening Bohlin came to my institution in field dress, covered with dust, but beaming with pleasure. He had finished the season's work . . . and on October 16th he had discovered the tooth. . . . Certainly I was overjoyed! Bohlin came to me before he told his wife he was in Peking. . . . (Andersson, 1934, p. 107).

After carefully examining the tooth, Black decided it belonged to the same species as the two teeth found by Dr. Zdansky. He thus set up a new genus, *Sinanthropus*, with the species name, *pekinesis*. To designate a new genus and species on the basis of three teeth was a bold move, but Black felt he was fully justified in doing so. It was an exciting discovery, and *Sinanthropus pekinensis*, which we know today as *Homo erectus pekinensis*, immediately acquired worldwide fame. Shortly after this, Black went on leave to visit America and Europe:

Figure 16-17 Dr. Davidson Black.

He had a large gold watch chain made for him in Peking with a small receptacle hanging from it, into which the tooth exactly fitted. In this way he travelled about the world with his precious fossil, showing it to colleagues and asking their opinion (von Koenigswald, 1956, p. 45).

Bohlin resumed working in 1928, and recovered more than a score of teeth, as well as parts of skulls of both young and adult individuals, but a complete skull evaded his efforts. A young Chinese geologist, W. C. Pei, took over direction of the excavation in 1929, and concentrated in what is called the lower cave. On December 1 of that year, he began digging out the sediment in one branch of the lower cave, and at 4 P.M. of the following day found one of the most remarkable fossil skulls to be recovered up to that time. One of the Chinese workers tells the story:

We had got down about 30 metres deep. . . . It was there the skull-cap was sighted, half of it embedded in loose earth, the other in hard clay. The sun had almost set. . . . The team debated whether to take it out right away or to wait until the next day when they could see better. The agonizing suspense of a whole day was felt to be too much to bear, so they decided to go on (Chia, 1975, pp. 12–13).

Pei brought the skull to Dr. Black, but because it was embedded in hard limestone, it took Black four months of hard, steady work to free it from its tough matrix. The result was worth the labor since the skull, that of a juvenile, was thick, low, and relatively small, but in Black's mind there was no doubt it belonged to early man. The response to this discovery, quite unlike that which greeted Dubois almost forty years earlier, was immediate and enthusiastically favorable. Peking Man became one of the more famous of fossil human skulls.

Work at Locality 1, as the Zhoukoudian cave is known, continued. Dr. Black maintained a killing schedule, working at night so he would not be interrupted at his desk. His health was not robust, and he probably should not have remained in Peking's harsh climate. As von Koenigswald related it:

He tried to stick it out but it was too much for him. When his secretary entered his room on March 15, 1934, she found him slumped over his desk, dead from a heart attack, with the beloved skull of Peking Man in his hand (von Koenigswald, 1956, p. 48).

◇ Box 16-5   Subspecies

Populations of a species are often designated by a sub-specific term. Here are three examples of *H. erectus* populations with their subspecific designations.

H. erectus erectus	Java, Trinil Bed
H. erectus pekinensis	China, Zhoukoudian
H. erectus heidelbergensis	Germany, Mauer

Dr. Franz Weidenreich, distinguished anatomist and well known for his work on European fossil hominids, succeeded Black. Weidenreich left his native Germany because of the academic repression and preposterous "racial" policies of the Nazi regime. He was a visiting professor of anatomy at the University of Chicago when he was appointed, in 1935, to be a visiting professor of anatomy at the Peking Union Medical College, and honorary director of the Cenozoic Research Laboratory, Geological Survey of China. Excavations at Zhoukoudian ended in 1937, with Japan's invasion of China, but the Cenozoic Research Laboratory continued.

As relations between the United States and Japan deteriorated, Weidenriech decided he had better remove the fossil material from Peking to prevent it from falling into the hands of the Japanese. Weidenreich left China in 1941, taking beautifully prepared casts, photographs, and drawings of the Peking material with him. After he left, the bones were packed in November, and arrangements made for the U.S. Marine Corps to take the bones with them when they left Peking to return to the United States. The bones never reached the United States and have never been found. No one to this day knows what happened to them, and their location remains a mystery (see p. 464).

Zhoukoudian Material   According to a recent account (Wu and Lin, 1983), the total fossil remains of Peking Man unearthed at the Zhoukoudian cave amount to:

    6 complete or almost complete skulls

  12 skull fragments

  15 pieces of mandibles

157 teeth

   3 humerus fragments

   7 femur fragments

   1 clavicle

   1 tibia fragment

   1 lunate (wrist) bone

(and over 100,000 artifacts)

Figure 16-18   Dr. Franz Weidenreich.

These belong to upwards of 40 male and female adults and children. This is a respectable amount of evidence, the most and the best of any *H. erectus* specimens, and (with the meticulous work by Dr. Weidenreich) has led to a good overall picture of the northern Chinese *H. erectus*.

Dating caves is not always a simple matter; in some cases, the roof of the cave has fallen in and not only is the stratigraphy disturbed, but fossil bones may have been washed into the cave. After a five-year comprehensive investigation of the Zhoukoudian site by more than 120 Chinese scientists (including paleoanthropologists, archeologists, geologists, climatologists, palynologists, and speleologists, who study caves), the researchers came to the following conclusions about Peking Man dates in the Zhoukoudian caves: There were three cultural stages beginning 460,000 y.a. and ending 230,000 y.a., when the people were forced out as the cave filled with rubble and sediment. These Middle Pleistocene dates place Peking Man considerably later than their conspecifics in Java, a time lapse that probably explains why the Zhoukoudian population had moved a bit further along the hominid trail than most of their Javanese relatives.

That Peking and Java hominids are related is clearly demonstrated by a comparison of the bones. The postcranial material is very similar, except that Peking's leg bones suggest he was shorter (at 5 feet 2 inches) than Java.

Peking, like Java, possesses the typical *erectus* fore and aft bulges—the supraorbital torus in front and the occipital ridge behind; the skull is keeled by a sagittal ridge, the face protrudes in alveolar prognathism, the incisors are shoveled, and molars contain large pulp cavities. Again, like the Java forms, the skull is vintage *H. erectus*, showing its greatest breadth near the bottom.

Table 16-2   *Homo erectus* Fossil Sites—China[a]

Age[b]	Name[c]	Country	Site	Material		Discovery	
				SKELETAL	CRANIAL CAPACITY (CC.)	SCIENTIST ASSOCIATED WITH FIND	YEAR
Middle Pleist. (500,000–400,000)	Peking Man, *Sinanthropus pekinensis*; *H. erectus pekinensis*	China	Zhoukoudian (Locality 1)	bones of skull, mandibles, teeth, limbs from more than forty persons	1,040 (avg.)	Bohlin Pei	1927–present
Middle Pleist. (400,000)	Longtan	China	Longtan	skull	?	Jia	1980
Lower Pleist. (800,000)	Lantian Man[d]	China	Gong Wang	calva, facial bones, teeth	780	Woo	1964
Middle Pleist. (650,000)	Lantian Man[d]	China	Chengjiawo	mandible (female)	—	Woo	1963–1965

a. Only better-known fossils are included.
b. These are best estimates—authorities differ.
c. These are either the names given by the finder (or scientist associated with the find) or the name commonly used by anthropologists.
d. See Wu, 1982.

Table 16-3 Zhoukoudian Material (Middle Pleistocene)

| Material | Discovered | | Cultural Material |
	Year	By	
Premolar, molar	1923	O. Zdansky	choppers, scrapers, points, hammerstones, anvils, worked deer skulls (?drinking cups), bone "knives," traces of fire—ash layers, charred stone and wood.
Molar	1927	B. Bohlin	
Teeth and skull fragments	1927–28	B. Bohlin	
Skullcap	1929	W. C. Pei	
Portions of skulls, mandibles, teeth, limbs, 6 complete calva, 9 skull fragments, 6 pieces of facial bone, 15 mandibles, 152 teeth, 7 fragmented limb bones; 45 persons represented.	1929–37	W. C. Pei, D. Black, F. Weidenreich	
1 calvarium, 5 teeth, 1 mandible	1960s	Pei and others	
Locality 13 (one-half mile from Peking Cave) older than Locality 1; no human skeletal material; some stone tools and traces of fire.			
Locality 15 (225 feet from Peking Cave) more recent than Locality 1; no human skeletal material, stone implements and traces of fire.			

These similarities were recognized long ago by Black and Weidenreich; at one time, in fact, it was suggested that Peking's nomen be changed from *Sinanthropus* to *Pithecanthropus pekinensis*. However, the similarities of European and African Middle Pleistocene forms to those of Asia, and the resemblance of all these to the genus *Homo*, persuaded taxonomists that the correct name was *Homo erectus*.

What mainly distinguishes Peking from Java is cranial capacity. In their recent investigation (Wu and Lin, 1983), the Chinese scientists found that the cranial capacity of the earliest Peking individuals measured "some 900 cubic centimeters." When Peking Man emerged, the average capacity had reached 1054 cubic centimeters (Wu and Lin, p. 90). Had a juvenile skull been omitted from the measurements, the average would have been larger—1088 cc. As the craniogram illustrates (Fig. 16-14), the larger Peking skull is reflected by a higher vault of the skull, a higher forehead, and a longer and broader cranium. What accounts for the larger brain? Possibly, Peking represents a later period in the evolution of *Homo erectus*. With greater dependence on culture and selective pressures associated with that dependence, brain size assuredly increased. It is probably no accident that Peking Man (460,000–230,000 years ago in China) and Sangiran 17 (500,000 years ago in Java), both late in Asiatic *H. erectus* evolution, are relatively "large-brained."

More than 100,000 artifacts were recovered from this site that was occupied for almost 250,000 years, which, according to the Chinese (Wu and Lin, p. 86) "is one of the sites with the longest history of habitation by man or his ancestors. . . ." The occupation of the site has been divided into three culture stages.

Earliest stage (460,000–420,000 y.a.)* The tools were large, close to a pound in weight, and made of soft stone, such as sandstone.

Middle Stage (370,000–350,000 y.a.) Tools become smaller and lighter (under a pound) and these smaller tools comprise 68% of the total; the large tools make up only 12%.

Final Stage (300,000–230,000 y.a.) Tools are still smaller, and the tool materials were of better quality. The coarse quartz of the earlier periods was replaced by a finer quartz, sandstone tools had almost disappeared, and flint tools increased as much as 30%.

The early tools were crude and shapeless but become more refined over time, and, toward the top of Locality 1, there are some finely made tools. Common tools at the site are choppers and chopping tools, but retouched flakes were fashioned into scrapers, points, burins, and awls. Handaxes, found in abundance in Europe and Africa, are absent from Zhoukoudian.

Stone was not the only material selected by Peking hominids; they also utilized bone and horn. Found in the cave were antler fragments, which had been hacked into pieces. Antler roots might have served as hammers and the sharp tines as digging sticks. Many skulls of sika and thick-jaw deer minus facial bones as well as antlers and crania bases leaving only the brain case were also found. Chia suggests that since the skulls show evidence of repeated whittling and over 100 specimens were discovered, all similarly shaped, "it is reasonable to infer they served as 'drinking bowls.' " He goes on to conjecture that the brain cases of Peking Man "retain similar characteristics and probably served the same purpose" (Chia, 1975, p. 31).

Animal residue—nearly ninety species of mammals—has been identified, including deer, wild boar, bison, bear, leopard, and horse, all attesting to the ability of Peking hunters. Not all the animal bones were necessarily the remains of hunting expeditions; the animals may have wandered into the cave when it was uninhabited by *H. erectus.* But many of the animals were no doubt hunted, especially the sika deer, whose remains were found in great abundance. The animal bones were scraped and split to get at the marrow, and many of them were charred, indicating they had been cooked.

Further evidence for Peking's vocation as hunter comes from the skulls themselves. We have already mentioned that the human skulls found in the cave, like many of the other mammalian skulls, were badly broken, faces removed, and the base of the skull surrounding the foramen magnum broken away. It is possible they served as "drinking bowls," but it is also possible that enlarging the foramen magnum enabled living Peking people to extract the brain. Also, the fact that relatively few postcranial bones were recovered would suggest that Peking hunted, killed, and ate his human prey elsewhere, usually bringing the skull back to the cave where he could snack at leisure.

Other suggestions for the mutilated human skulls are their use as ritual items or trophies. Eating the brains may not have been dietary, but a magical ritual to take on properties—the intelligence of the owner, for example. Pos-

---

**These dates should be considered tentative until more precise chronometric techniques are available.

(a)

(b)

(c)

Figure 16-19 Peking Man (reconstructed cranium). (*a*) Frontal view; (*b*) lateral view; (*c*) rear view. The widest part of the skull is toward the bottom.

Figure 16-20 Views of: (a) *Homo erectus erectus* and (b) *Homo erectus pekinensis*; (c) the Solo XI skull; (d) the Rhodesian skull; (e) the Saccopastore skull; and (f) the skull of La Chapelle-aux-Saints. Note the pentagonal shape of skulls in upper row compared to those of the Neandertal and Rhodesian skulls at widest point in the lower row. (From Weidenreich, 1951.)

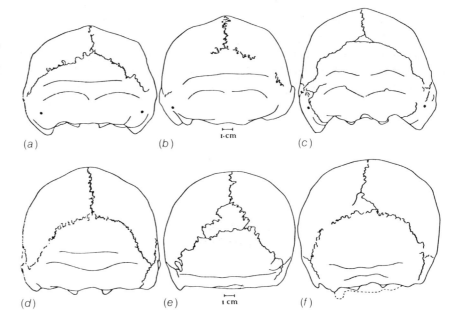

(a)   (b)   1 cm   (c)

(d)   (e)   1 cm   (f)

Chopper

Chopper

Pointed tool

Discoidal scrapper

Burin

Broken bone (note deep incision made in the bone)

Figure 16-21 Tools used by Peking Man.

sibly, the skull may have been hung about the neck as a trophy, or a symbol of the prowess of the hunter. Unfortunately, there is insufficient evidence to demonstrate any of these suggestions.

From the flourishing plant growth surrounding the cave, we can assume the inhabitants of Locality I supplemented their meat diet by gathering herbs, wild fruits, tubers, and ostrich eggs. Fragments of charred ostrich eggshells and copious deposits of hackberry seeds were unearthed in the cave.

In addition to charred eggshells and bones, charred stones and bits of charred wood have also come from the cave. All of this is evidence of fire, of course, and it is obvious that the Peking people controlled fire, although it is doubtful whether they were capable of making it themselves. The main evidence of fire comes from layers of ash over eighteen feet deep at one point. Hearths were also found, demonstrating that Peking could confine fire within a specific area and keep it burning for long periods of time.

Figure 16-22 Cannibalism at Zhoukoudian. The area around the foramen magnum has been cut out to enable Peking Man to get at the brain. Whether this was for ritual or dietary purposes is not known.

Peking Man, who seems to have lived later than *H. erectus* of Java, also enjoyed a more developed culture. With a large brain, the Zhoukoudian hominids were accomplished hunters, cooked their food, fashioned stone and bone tools, and even made ornaments. Wu and Lin (1983) state that "Peking Man was a cave dweller, a fire user, a deer hunter, a seed gatherer and a maker of specialized tools" (p. 94). This leads them to suggest three social adaptations for the Peking population:

1. Living in a group. Hunting large animals is "complicated, difficult, and hazardous," and cooperation of many individuals would be required; therefore, it is likely that Peking Man lived in a group when he began to hunt deer. (See pp. 499–502 for a discussion of this "hunting hypothesis.")
2. Sexual division of labor. Because of women's physiological constraints, it would be difficult for them to engage in hunting activities, which would then be left to the men. "The pattern of male hunters and female gatherers, which is common in hunting-and-gathering societies today, may have already been established" (p. 94).
3. Education. Tools during the more than 200,000 years that Peking Man lived in Zhoukoudian became more sophisticated. This "suggests that the earliest practice of education may have taken place in Peking Man's cave" (p. 94). Each generation could not have developed new technological skills without having learned existing ones taught by the older generation.

Could they speak? Their hunting and technological skills would suggest they possessed some kind of symbolic communication. If the skull was, in fact, used as a symbol as speculated above, then symbolic communication is even more suggestive. (See Box 16-6 for Wolpoff's neurological evidence.) Did they wear clothing? Perhaps, since they manufactured awls, and one of the bone tools may be a needle. How long did they live? Studies of the fossil remains reveal that almost 40% of the bones belong to individuals under the age of 14, and only 2.6% are estimated in the 50 to 60 age group (Chia, 1975, p. 43).

To sum up, the Zhoukoudian *H. erectus* was an excellent hunter and forager with a diet composed of a wide range of meat, vegetables, fruit, berries, and seeds. Controlling fire, they cooked their food and may also have used fire to keep marauding animals out of the cave. We can imagine that living

---

◇ Box 16-6   Speech

Human speech capacity is an extremely complicated be-havior, involving the development of tracts between the motor and associated speech areas and between the frontal and posterior parietal portions of the brain. The basis for speaking would seem to lie more in neurologi-cal structures than in morphological ones. The impor-tance of the frontal-posterior parietal tract is that it allows the frontal area to "make sense" out of the cross-modal associations of the posterior parietal area, while the motor-associational speech area tract provides a pathway for this information to reach the motor-speech area.

The evolution of language ability seems tied to the ap-pearance of hemispheric dominance and asymmetry. The marked bilateral asymmetry in size and morphology in the newly discovered Zhoukoudian cranium 5* pro-vides one of the few direct morphological correlates with the ability to speak in humans. Thus, there is every rea-son to believe that *Homo erectus* was capable of human vocal language (Wolpoff, 1980a).

*Cranial parts found in 1966 fit the temporal fragments discovered and described by Weidenreich in the 1930s.

Table 16-4   *Homo erectus* of the Lower Pleistocene

Million Years	Hominids
.9	Lantian (Gong Wang)
	Sangiran 8
1.2	OH 9
1.5	OH 13
	ER 3733
1.8 (?)	Perning (Java)
Pliocene (?)	Sangiran 4

Figure 16-23   The Longtan skull (rear view).

conditions—in a climate of very cold winters and hot summers similar to Beijing today—were harsh, and few people lived much beyond thirty years. They made tools skillfully and used them effectively. There is even a possibility of supernatural beliefs and—primitive though it may have been—of symbolic communication.

Lantian   Somewhat older than Zhoukoudian and contemporary with mate-rial from the Trinil (Kabuh levels) of Java are hominid bones from the villages of Chengjiawo and Gong Wang, near the town of Lantian, in Shaanxi province of central China. A mandible, skullcap with facial bones and teeth, stone artifacts, and some bones of other fossil vertebrates were found there in 1963–1965.

The skullcap found at Gong Wang (800,000 y.a.–750,000 y.a.) is small, with an estimated capacity of around 778 cm³, almost identical to Sangiran 4 of Java. Also, in the same manner as the early Java hominids, the vault bones are very thick and the supraorbital torus well pronounced.

The well-preserved Chengjiawo mandible (about 650,000 y.a.) possesses most of its teeth and is believed to be an old female. Interestingly, neither of the 3rd molars (wisdom teeth) had erupted; not even a tooth germ is present—the earliest known case of missing 3rd molars. This poor Lantian old woman also suffered a bad case of **periodontal** disease, not unusual among hunter-gatherers.

Longtan   On November 4, 1980, a complete skull was found in Longtan (Dragon Pool) Cave, south China. A few human teeth and a mandible fragment were also excavated, and at least twenty-five species of mammal bones. The material is presently being analyzed at the Institute of Vertebrate Paleontology and Paleoanthropology. Although a complete description is not yet available,

Chinese scientists believe it is *Homo erectus* about 400,000 years old, but somewhat different from both Zhoukoudian and Lantian. This is the first *H. erectus* skull found in south China (*China Pictorial*, 1981).

Periodontal
peri: around
dontal: teeth
Gum and jaw disease.

◇ Europe

HEIDELBERG (MAUER)

Only a jaw was found here, near the village of Mauer and not far from Heidelberg University (see Box 16-7) in 1907. The mandible is more massive than those from early (Djetis) Java, but the teeth, though not small, are not proportionate to the size of the jaw. No diastema or projecting canines are seen, and the chin recedes in the fashion of other Middle Pleistocene jaws. Dating, as in so many cases, is uncertain, and estimates range from 600,000 y.a.–250,000 y.a. Some believe Heidelberg may be the oldest human bones ever discovered in Western Europe, and that may well be the case. However, the "earliest ever" is a frequent claim for European *H. erectus* finds.

The classification of Heidelberg as an *H. erectus* has been questioned. Like the majority of European Middle Pleistocene forms, the situation is not clear-cut because the skulls possess both *H. erectus*-like traits and archaic* *sapiens* traits. As more data are made available, it is possible that classification may become clearer. However, as Wolpoff (1980b) points out, if the evolution in Europe was a continuous one, from *H. erectus* to *H. sapiens*, it is going to be difficult to draw an absolute line separating the two grades.

VÉRTESSZÖLLÖS

In 1965, at the small town of Vértesszöllös, thirty miles west of Budapest, Hungary, Dr. Laszlo Vértes unearthed an adult occiput and a few fragments of infant teeth. Extrapolating from the occiput, it is estimated that the skull may have been as large as 1,300 cm³ (Wolpoff, 1980a).

The occiput, with a well-developed nuchal torus, is noted for its thickness, greater than the *H. erectus* average. However, the bone is quite large, approximating modern size, which is remarkable for a skull that may be as much as 400,000 years old. Although it is considered to fall within *H. erectus* measurements, the large and rounded occipital bone may presage the beginnings of a *H. sapiens* trait. Overall, the occiput suggests a large-brained, heavily muscled *H. erectus* specimen. Pebble tools, recalling the Oldowan industry of Africa, were also found at the site.

The controversy surrounding the placement of Vértesszöllös is another example of the problem of classifying specimens having what appear to be both *H. erectus* and archaic *sapiens* traits. In this case, the problem is aggravated by the presence of only one adult bone—the occiput.

*"Archaic" is the term now commonly applied to early *H. sapiens*. It is not intended as a precise term or taxonomic designation. Middle Pleistocene skulls that possess *erectus*-like and *sapiens*-like traits are now often referred to as archaic *sapiens*.

Figure 16-24   Cast of the Heidelberg (Mauer) jaw.

◇ Box 16-7   Finding Heidelberg

For a number of years Professor Otto Schoetensack, a Heidelberg University paleontologist, had been observing the commercial operations at a sandpit near the village of Mauer, six miles southeast of the university town. Because of the Tertiary and Pleistocene strata, Schoetensack had arranged with the owner of the sandpit that all bones uncovered in the ancient strata during the operation be donated to the University. The sandpit had yielded hundreds of mammalian bones, but for twenty years Schoetensack waited in vain for a human fossil. It was not until October 21, 1907, that Herr Rosch, the sandpit owner, sent a thrilling message to the patient professor:

For twenty years you have been making efforts to find traces of primitive men in my sandpit in order to prove human beings lived in this district at the same time as the mammoth. Yesterday we came across this proof. Sixty-five feet below ground level at the bottom of my sandpit the lower jawbone of a prehistoric man was found, in a very good state of preservation (in Wendt, 1963, p. 442).

Schoetensack named the jaw *Homo heidelbergensis*, which raised the hackles of many European scientists who were either still opposed to the idea of evolution or did not believe the Mauer jaw belonged to the genus *Homo*. However, the furor lacked the passionate spirit of Dubois' time and may have helped justify Dubois' views.

PETRALONA

Just south of the northern Greek capital of Salonika lies Petralona where, in 1959, villagers digging for water fell into a cave that had lain sealed and unknown. Near a stalagmite, practically on the surface of the soil, they found a fossil hominid skull about 1200 cm³ in size. It is one of the largest of any *H. erectus* skulls and may be the largest of any of the European Middle Pleistocene hominids. It is an important find, since there is relatively little hominid material from Europe during the range of time when Petralona lived.

However, Petralona is a perplexing find. While almost complete (the mandible is missing) and quite well studied, one of the problems is its date, which has been estimated by various researchers from 250,000 y.a. to 750,000 y.a. Faunal remains and the geology suggest a glacial period (the Mindel) or an interglacial period, either the Cromerian (500,000 y.a. or more) or Holsteinian (around 300,000 y.a.). Furthermore, since there are differences of opinion precisely where in the cave the skull was found, the dating becomes even more difficult.

Another puzzle is determining Petralona's affiliation—to which subspecies should it be assigned? He (it is considered to be male) lived during the *H. erectus* period, if the older date is valid; if the later date is correct, then Petralona lived on the verge of *H. sapiens* origins. Dating aside, what about Petralona's morphology? What does he *look* like, or perhaps more properly, what does he *measure* like? At this point, we run into inconsistencies. In size, Petralona resembles archaic *sapiens*; the frontal bone relates him to *H. erectus* and archaic *sapiens*; the supraorbital torus is unique in some ways, in others similar to archaic *sapiens*, and in still others approximates the neandertals; the face aligns him with early neandertals; the overall facial form

Figure 16-25   The Petralona skull.

to archaic *sapiens*; and the occipital bone resembles *H. erectus* and archaic *sapiens* in some respects.

Without going into more detail, the morphology of the Petralona skull associates it here with *H. erectus*, there with archaic *sapiens*, occasionally with neandertals and even anatomically moderns, and some of its features are unique and relate the skull to no other subspecies. With Petralona's measurements, it could be considered ancestral to neandertals or to archaic *sapiens*; or to African forms, such as Broken Hill and Bodo; or to none of these. Dr. Milford Wolpoff (1980b), who examined the skull several years ago, believes it is more like *H. erectus* than some other early Europeans (e.g., Steinheim and Swanscombe, p. 508), but on the whole concludes it belongs in the *H. sapiens*, rather than *H. erectus*, grade.

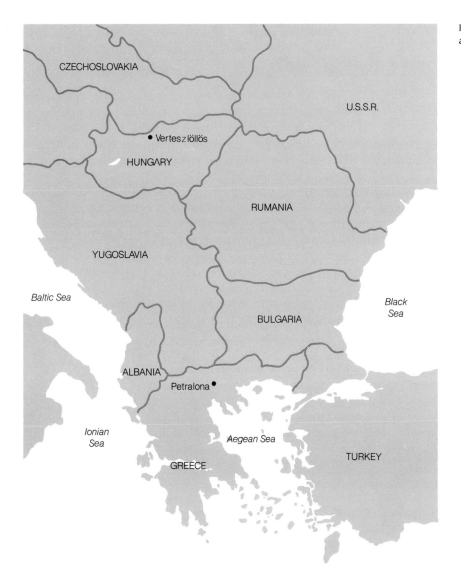

Figure 16-26   The Petralona (Greece) site and the Vértesszöllös site (Hungary).

Figure 16-27 *H. erectus* in Western Europe and North Africa.

It can be seen from the foregoing that it is difficult to assign Petralona to a definite subspecies. It has been suggested that hominids of this time period not be assigned to a subspecies, but rather to *H. sapiens* grades, without implying "that members of any grade were automatically regarded as ancestral to members of the succeeding grade" (Stringer, et al., 1977, p. 250).

For the present, because of the confusion of dates and its remarkable variation in morphology, we shall leave Petralona in this *H. erectus* chapter. However, it should be noted that it could well fit into the next chapter as a transitional form, an archaic *sapiens* ancestral (or not ancestral) to neandertals or to anatomically moderns, or to both, or neither.

From a cultural point of view, the fauna found in the cave suggest that the Petralona people were hunter/gatherers and probably led a life not too different from that described for Peking Man. Unfortunately, relatively few artifacts were found, and it would be difficult to reconstruct Petralona life on the basis of their technology.

TORRALBA/AMBRONA

Probably the best-known Middle Pleistocene site associated with *H. erectus*, but minus its bones, is in the Rio Ambrona-Masegar Valley, 100 miles northeast of Madrid, at Torralba and Ambrona, in central Spain. These sites, two miles apart, were dug by F. Clark Howell during the summers of 1961 through 1963 (Howell, 1966; 1982). Excavations were resumed in 1980 and continued in the summers of 1981, 1982, and 1983.

In this grassy valley lived a group of *H. erectus* during a mild recession of the Mindel Glaciation, sometime between 400,000 and 300,000 years ago. The evidence of their occupation comes from the remains of butchered elephants and other animals, and many tools consisting of handaxes, cleavers, and scrapers characteristic of the Middle Pleistocene industry known as Acheulian. Evidence of charcoal and worked wood and bone were also found.

Unfortunately for purposes of positive identification, no human bones or teeth have so far been discovered. Nevertheless, the number of broken animal bones, especially elephant, and the pattern of breakage and deliberate fashioning and trimming leave no doubt of humans at work. Little question remains that people were working together in a cooperative effort. Armed with wooden spears and stone tools, they evidently drove a herd of elephants along the valley into the swamps. (For vivid accounts of the Torralba/Ambrona excavations and how these populations lived and hunted, the student is encouraged to read the Time-Life books and Pfeiffer, listed at the end of the chapter. See Freeman, 1975, for a more technical discussion.)

TERRA AMATA

Another occupation site lacking human bones, dated about 300,000 y.a. during the Holstein interglacial, was located by French archeologist Henry de Lumley in the heart of the city of Nice on the opulent French Riviera. The site is now situated on a hillside, an ancient sloping sand dune, below the imposing Chateau de Rosemont, once the residence of the king of Yugoslavia, and has been recently converted into a museum of paleontology. In an alley called **Terra Amata**, not far from the port of Nice, builders, in 1966, began the construction of luxury apartments closely monitored by de Lumley, who was aware of the archeological possibilities. When bulldozers cut away several feet of earth, de Lumley spotted some pebble tools and succeeded in stopping construction for several months. Collecting a digging crew of 300, de Lumley and his archeologist wife spent 40,000 hours excavating 144 square yards 70 feet deep. They uncovered 21 separate living floors and removed 35,000 objects. (See de Lumley, 1969.)

Although this French site failed to yield human skeletal material, an imprint of a right foot 9½ inches long was found preserved in the sand. De Lumley estimated the stature of this individual at about 5 feet 1 inch.

Many of the 35,000 objects consisted of pebble tools, but there were Acheulian tools, such as cleavers, scrapers, projectile points, and choppers. Bone had also been worked. Like their Spanish neighbors, the Terra Amata people were also hunters, as indicated by the tools and remains of hunting game.

One of the most fascinating finds was evidence of huts, 21 of them at three different locations. The evidence comes from holes in the ground where stakes had been driven to form the walls, and a line of stones paralleling the stake imprints that apparently served as wall braces. The imprints suggest oval huts, and de Lumley estimated they were fairly good-sized, from 26 to 49 feet long and 13 to 20 feet wide, and may have housed ten to twenty people. The huts, he believes, were constructed of sturdy branches bent to interlock at the top. In the center of the hut was a hearth, a smoke hole above it, and an entrance at one end.

Less than fastidious, the Terra Amata hut dwellers used part of their home as a bathroom, and pollen analysis of the **coprolites** suggests the huts were occupied in spring and early summer. Since the earth of the living floors was

Terra Amata
terra: land
amata: beloved

Coprolites
Fossilized feces.

Figure 16-28 Shelter at Terra Amata. Evidence of habitation at Terra Amata enabled de Lumley to reconstruct what a hut might have looked like. (Courtesy California Academy of Sciences.)

not compacted, the occupants must have been transients, staying only for a few days at a time, much like their present-day successors who vacation at this famous resort area.

Reviewing the Middle Pleistocene, we find that remains in Europe are scarce (and Lower Pleistocene lacking) compared to Asia and Africa. The dating is presently approximate at best, but the more serious problem is the mixture of early and late physical traits.

The specimens discussed in the preceding sections are not decisively *H. erectus* or *H. sapiens*. Some of the skull bones reflect the ruggedness of *H. erectus*, while others are more subdued, tending toward a *H. sapiens* character. It is possible to argue that these hominids had already evolved beyond the *erectus* grade but were not decisively sapient. If earlier specimens are found, they may prove to belong to the *erectus* grade—in the strict sense.

Professor Howells (1980), in his survey of *H. erectus*, suggests that some evidence of earlier European inhabitants may exist. Tools found in Western Europe have been provisionally dated at almost a million years. Fossil remains associated with this material are absent, unfortunately, and it is not possible to say what hominid grade they belong to.

Homo erectus, then, as far as faunal comparison can tell us, inhabited Europe from about 700,000 (or longer) to 300,000 years ago. They hunted large game and gathered plant food, utilized caves, and may have built shelters. They may have been capable of speech, and used fire (as their Asiatic contemporaries did). Once again, though, we find it impossible to say whether they knew how to *start* a fire. Wood and bone were both worked, but their principal tools were made of stone characteristic of the Acheulian industry. The likelihood is that family units, perhaps several of them, cooperated in their economic pursuits, and from the remains at Torralba/Ambrona we may infer they were capable of deliberately planning their activities.

◇ North Africa

We have found *H. erectus* in Southeast Asia, eastern Asia, and Europe. With a more sophisticated culture than their predecessors, we might expect that *H. erectus* would spread to all the possible niches they could manage. North Africa is one of these and is represented by sites in Algeria and Morocco, all of which contain skeletal material (see Fig. 16-29).

Remains from Algeria (Ternifine) and Morocco (Rabat, Temara, and Casablanca) consist of mandibles—and a partial skull from Salé—which reflect *H. erectus* characteristics. Ternifine, the oldest North African site (?500,000 +), shows some resemblances to Asian mandibles.

A find of special interest, recovered by the French scientist Jean Jacques Jaeger, is Salé (Morocco), the only reasonably complete North African *erectus* skull. Jaeger dates the skull in the 100,000 year range and estimates the cranial capacity at 930–960 cm³, surprisingly small for this time period. According to Jaeger, the front part of the skull—teeth and frontal bone (the

Figure 16-29 The Salé skull. The most complete *erectus* skull discovered in North Africa.

face is missing)—shows the characteristics of *Homo erectus*. The occipital area, on the other hand, "gives a fairly modern impression," but all things considered, Jaeger would place the skull in the *erectus* grade of evolution (Jaeger, 1975).

The fossil evidence from North Africa appears to fit into the *erectus* stage, but the material is sadly incomplete. The recently discovered incomplete calvarium from Salé gives a provocative glimpse of what Middle Pleistocene humans in the Maghreb of North Africa looked like. But placing the fossils in their proper time period is a problem yet to be resolved. No chronometric dates are at hand, and estimates from faunal associations for the various sites range from as much as 800,000 y.a. to as late as 100,000 y.a. We have assigned the late remains to *H. erectus*, but they might also possibly be transitional to *H. sapiens*.

Table 16-5 *Homo erectus* in East Africa

Olduvai Hominid 9 (OH 9, Chellean Man)

Olduvai Hominid 13 (OH 13, Cinderella, *H. habilis*)

Olduvai Hominid 28 (OH 28)

KNM-ER 3733

Bodo

◇ East Africa

Since 1959, with the discovery of "Zinj," East Africa has become the El Dorado of the search for ancient humans. A prodigious quantity of fossil hominid remains, most of them australopithecines, have been recovered, but an increasing number of *Homo* specimens have been excavated in recent years.

It is not feasible in an introductory text to describe, or even list, all fossils from East Africa. We shall discuss a few and mention others in order to give a summary report of *H. erectus* evolution in this area.

OLDUVAI (TANZANIA)

As far back as 1960, Dr. Louis Leakey unearthed a skull at Olduvai (OH 9) that he identified as *H. erectus* (and referred to as Chellean Man). The skull OH 9 from Upper Bed II has a massive cranium; it is faceless and has the largest capacity (1,067 cm³) of all the early *H. erectus* specimens. Dated at 1.2 m.y., this is indeed a large skull for that time period. The browridge is huge, the largest known for any hominid in both thickness and projection. The cranial base is heavily buttressed where muscles attach, yet the vault bones are fairly thin, an australopithecine feature.

Another Lower Pleistocene skull recovered from Olduvai by the Leakeys is OH 13, called "Cinderella" by Louis Leakey and identified by him as a *Homo habilis*. The skull is small with thin walls (australopithecine traits), but Tobias and von Koenigswald (1965) believe the mandible resembles early *H. erectus* from Java. If their analysis is correct, OH 13—estimated to be about 1.5 m.y.— is one of the oldest African *H. erectus* forms. Is Cinderella an *A. africanus*, *H. habilis*, or *H. erectus*? Perhaps a glass slipper somewhere in the Olduvai volcanic ash may provide the answer.

Later at Olduvai, from Bed IV of the Middle Pleistocene (dated at about 500,000 years), are two finds of some significance. The skull OH 12, probably female, has a cranial capacity of 735 cm³ and resembles OH 9 from Bed II. It is interesting that similarities in skull morphology would endure for three-

Figure 16-30 *H. erectus* sites in East Africa.

quarter million years. These similarities may reflect a regional clade (see p. 357 for a discussion of clade).

The other finds are rare postcranial remains—a left femoral shaft and an innominate bone belonging to the same individual, a female found by Mary Leakey in 1970. These bones are important evidence of postcranial morphology of hominids living at this time, since they shed light on how East African *H. erectus* stood and walked (which was very much as we do). Acheulian tools were found in association with the bones.

Not far from Olduvai Gorge is Lake Ndutu, where an incomplete skull was uncovered when the lake waters receded during the 1971 dry season. Associated with the skull were spheroids, hammerstones, and a few flake tools all "rather nondescript and of an indeterminate industry" (Mturi, 1976). A date of 500,000 years has been suggested for Ndutu.

The cranium has been compared to Zhoukoudian with some advanced features, and Clarke (1976) believes Ndutu may form an evolutionary link between the Peking forms and *H. sapiens*.

LAKE TURKANA (KENYA)

Some 400 miles north of Olduvai Gorge, on the northern boundary of Kenya, is the finger lake—Lake Turkana. Excavated by Richard Leakey since 1969, the eastern shore of the lake has been a virtual gold mine for australopithecines, early *Homo*, and *H. erectus* fossil remains.

One of the oldest* of *H. erectus* forms (1.5 m.y.) is a remarkably well-preserved skull, KNM-ER 3733 (Fig. 16-32), found by Bw. Bernard Ngeneo during the 1974–1975 field program in the highly productive Koobi Fora Formation (Leakey and Walker, 1976). Consisting of an almost complete calvarium with typical *H. erectus* characteristics and resembling OH 9 on a smaller scale (Rightmire, 1979), the skull is estimated at 850 cm³, falling in the middle range of *Homo erectus* cranial measurements.

A puzzling aspect of the ER 3733 skull is that it was found in the same geological bed with robust australopithecines (*A. boisei*) and perhaps *A. africanus* as well. This raises the single- versus multiple-species question, which anthropologists have been debating for years. Is it possible for two (or more) hominid species to live side by side contemporaneously, or is there a limit of one species to one niche at one time? The evidence of the ER 3733 and australopithecine "bedmates" appears to decide the issue in favor of the multiple-species argument.

(a)

(b)

Figure 16-31 (*a*) OH 9; (*b*) OH 13 ("Cinderella" mandible—cast).

ETHIOPIA

Continuing north to Ethiopia, we find several sites that have been excavated during the past fifteen years. Just across the Kenya border, in the Lower Omo River Basin, are parietal and temporal fragments dated at 1.2–1.0 m.y.a.

In northeast Ethiopia, north of Addis Ababa, is the Afar Depression, where Lucy was found (Chapter 14). It was in the Awash River Valley area of Afar that a fairly complete skull was found, at Bodo D'Ar, during the 1976 and 1978 excavating seasons. This skull shows many typical *H. erectus* features. The vault bones are extraordinarily thick; in fact, one part of it is the thickest hominid bone ever reported. There is also some evidence of more advanced features, such as less postorbital constriction. Bodo's overall morphological pattern may be closest to the Rhodesian skull (p. 528), and may possibly be assigned to archaic *sapiens*.

The site appears to be one of butchering, where cut-up hippos and stone tools were found associated with the skull. Indeed Bodo himself appears to have been scalped—as seen in telltale cutmarks on the skull. Unfortunately, the dating is extremely ambiguous and is "estimated" somewhere between 700,000 y.a.–125,000 y.a. (Conroy et al., 1978).

A number of kill sites and butchering sites confirm that *H. erectus* was a hunter in Africa as well as in Europe and Asia. Supporting these data is the more than 1 million-year-old BK *Pelorovis* kill site at Olduvai (see Chapter 12). We also find that during this Lower Paleolithic period (Box 16-8) stone tools continued to develop, as reflected in the change from early to late Acheulian industries.

In East Africa, *Homo erectus* appeared sometime around 1.5 m.y.a. and disappeared as a species roughly 500,000 y.a. From Tanzania to Kenya to Ethiopia (and Chad, west of Ethiopia), this thick-boned, heavy brow-ridged,

Figure 16-32 ER 3733.

*In November, 1984, Richard Leakey announced the find, on the western shore of Lake Turkana, of an almost complete skeleton of a 12-year-old male: *H. erectus*, 1.6 m.y. old (the oldest African *H. erectus* known) and 5 feet 5 inches tall. As an adult, the boy would have reached a height of 6 feet.

◇ Box 16-8   The Paleolithic and Plio-Pleistocene

Pliocene and Pleistocene are geologic and zoologic epochs. Culture periods are known by other terms: Paleolithic, Mesolithic, Neolithic, Bronze Age, and so on. Beginning about 2.5 m.y.a. with the first evidence of culture, mainly stone tools, is the Paleolithic or Old Stone Age. Divided into Lower, Middle, and Upper Paleolithic, each period is assigned its own criteria based on the kinds of tools made, the style of manufacture, the material used, and other such factors. Within each period are industries that identify the types of stone tools.

The table* you see here correlates the Plio-Pleistocene and the Paleolithic.

Geologic Subdivisions	Absolute Age	Cultural Subdivisions	
		PALEOLITHIC	INDUSTRIES†
Holocene	10,000		
			Magdalenian
Upper			Solutrean
Pleistocene		Upper	Gravettian
			Aurignacian
	40,000		Chatelperronian
	125,000	Middle	Mousterian
Middle Pleistocene			
	700,000		Acheulian
Lower Pleistocene	1,000,000		
	1,800,000	Lower	
Pliocene			
			Oldowan
	5,000,000		

*Not to scale.

†These industries are not necessarily sequential and may overlap in time.

---

muscular human lived for 1 million years along rivers or streams and on the shores of the ocean or lakes.

Three kinds of sites have been found: family or multifamily living camps, kill sites, and gathering sites. Archeological material tells us that *H. erectus* hunted medium- and large-sized mammals, including giant baboons. This kind of activity suggests cooperative groups of people capable of organizing for large-game hunting.

◇ South Africa (Swartkrans)

Homo erectus is entirely lacking in South Africa except possibly for a relatively small mandible (probably female), two molars, and a radius fragment, all belonging to the same individual (SK-15), found at Swartkrans, the site of earlier australopithecine fossils. It has been dated as most likely late Middle Pleistocene, and the bones were found in association with a Developed Oldowan industry. Originally, this jaw was designated "Telanthropus" by its discoverers (Broom and Robinson). Later research has suggested it fits well into the genus *Homo*.

◇ Human Emergence: Australopithecus to Homo Erectus

Figure 16-33   SK-15 site, Swartkrans.

Hominid evolution from australopithecines to *H. erectus* is marked by: (1) The physical modifications already described—*H. erectus* is the taller, larger-brained with thick skull bones, a heavily buttressed skull evidenced by the thick and projecting supraorbital torus and nuchal torus, spongy bone toward the base of the skull that developed its greatest width along the nuchal area, reduction of the posterior teeth, and increase in the anterior teeth; (2) cultural modifications, such as more skillful toolmaking, a wider variety of tools, and a specialized tool kit, accomplished big-game hunting, organized and planning groups, regular use of fire, and perhaps speech. While these cultural modifications reflect a more sophisticated culture for *H. erectus*, it is interesting that for the hundreds of thousands of years of the Acheulian industry, there was relatively little change in the tools over time and space. There is a remarkable similarity in the tools found in Africa, Europe, and southwest Asia. Is it possible that this cultural stasis might be related to the limitations of *H. erectus'* brain size and organization and their economic adaptations?

To account for at least some of these physical and cultural changes, Wolpoff (1980a) offers a suggestive hypothesis. It should be emphasized that Wolpoff's explanation is hypothetical; direct evidence is often lacking. His hypothesis is based on the shift from the australopithecine scavenging/gathering adaptation with some small-scale hunting to a hunting/gathering adaptation characteristic of *H. erectus*.

As hunting developed into a more important source of food, it was organized and planned. Meat became a regular and dependable (rather than opportunistic) part of the diet, replacing some of the more difficult-to-chew plant foods that had been dietary staples. Improved technology produced more hunting-efficient and food-processing tools as well as more skillful manufacturing techniques. Archeological evidence shows an increasing number of tool types, such as crudely pointed chopperlike tools and small scraping tools. Spheroids, a round ball-like stone tool—usually showing evidence of battering—greatly increased in frequency, and it is thought the battering resulted from pounding foods to make them easier to chew:

> Every increase in the amount of cutting, chopping, or smashing that took place before food was chewed would have decreased the need to maintain a chewing complex that produced powerful forces (Wolpoff, 1980a, p. 168).

This combination of changes in diet and food preparation probably accounts for the reduction in the postcanine teeth.

The change in diet, from tough foods to meat and softer foods, produced further changes in the skull (Box 16-9). The load on posterior teeth decreased,

◇ Box 16-9   Forces on the Teeth and Skull

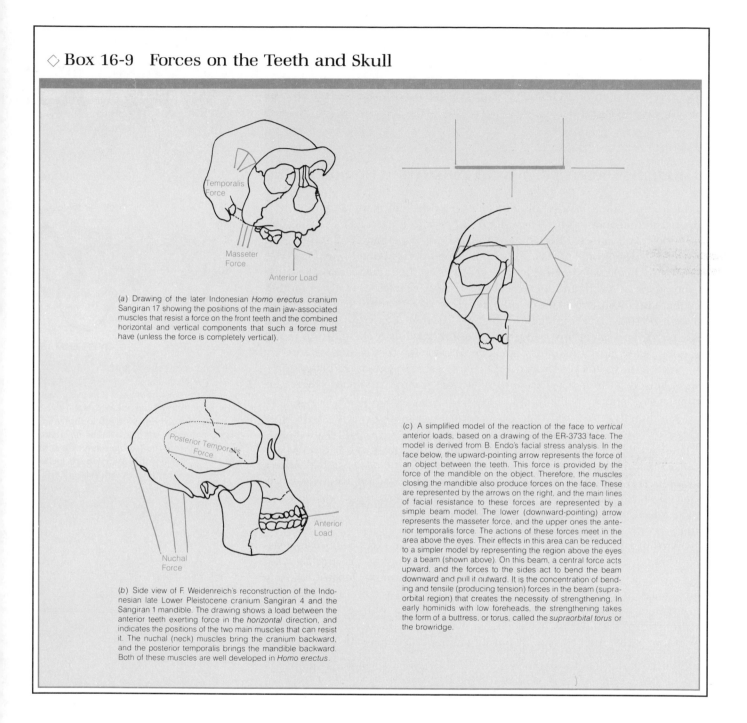

(a) Drawing of the later Indonesian *Homo erectus* cranium Sangiran 17 showing the positions of the main jaw-associated muscles that resist a force on the front teeth and the combined horizontal and vertical components that such a force must have (unless the force is completely vertical).

(b) Side view of F. Weidenreich's reconstruction of the Indonesian late Lower Pleistocene cranium Sangiran 4 and the Sangiran 1 mandible. The drawing shows a load between the anterior teeth exerting force in the *horizontal* direction, and indicates the positions of the two main muscles that can resist it. The nuchal (neck) muscles bring the cranium backward, and the posterior temporalis brings the mandible backward. Both of these muscles are well developed in *Homo erectus*.

(c) A simplified model of the reaction of the face to *vertical* anterior loads, based on a drawing of the ER-3733 face. The model is derived from B. Endo's facial stress analysis. In the face below, the upward-pointing arrow represents the force of an object between the teeth. This force is provided by the force of the mandible on the object. Therefore, the muscles closing the mandible also produce forces on the face. These are represented by the arrows on the right, and the main lines of facial resistance to these forces are represented by a simple beam model. The lower (downward-pointing) arrow represents the masseter force, and the upper ones the anterior temporalis force. The actions of these forces meet in the area above the eyes. Their effects in this area can be reduced to a simpler model by representing the region above the eyes by a beam (shown above). On this beam, a central force acts upward, and the forces to the sides act to bend the beam downward and pull it outward. It is the concentration of bending and tensile (producing tension) forces in the beam (supraorbital region) that creates the necessity of strengthening. In early hominids with low foreheads, the strengthening takes the form of a buttress, or torus, called the *supraorbital torus* or the browridge.

making for smaller back teeth, and the load on front teeth increased, resulting in their somewhat larger size. However, not only did tooth size change, but the muscles operating the jaw and the forces operating on the skull developed front and back buttressing, i.e., the supraorbital torus and the nuchal torus, where chewing and neck muscles attach. (Although the use of fire came in after hunting had become an important food source, it would also have served to make chewing easier and would have affected the load on posterior and anterior teeth.)

Unlike other carnivores (see pp. 283–295), when primates hunt they depend largely on vision, and early hominids were, therefore, diurnal (daytime) hunters. For diurnal hunting in the tropics it would be a great advantage if the hunter were heat-adapted in order to get rid of excess heat. One of the ways of doing this is by sweating, during which drops of sweat evaporate and cool the skin (see pp. 165–167). Body hair, which makes drop formation and dripping easy, reduces the amount of sweat that evaporates. Adaptation to the tropics, therefore, involved reducing the number and size of hair follicles (loss of body hair) and development of sweat glands all over the body.

Water loss through sweating makes for a thirsty hominid, and it is not surprising that most major early hominid sites are found close to water. But hunting is not always possible near water, so carrying water became very important:

> Carrying water depends on one of the most basic human inventions ... the container. The innovation of containers was one of the most important human cultural adaptations, and probably one of the critical factors that led to the development of effective organized hunting (Wolpoff, 1980a, p. 169).

It is also possible that the invention of containers may have resulted in increased body size, and to some extent, therefore, brain size. Without suffi-

---

Table 16-6 *Homo erectus* Sites

Asia	
Java	Trinil, Modjokerto, Sangiran
China	Zhoukoudian, Lantian, Longtan
Europe	Heidelberg (Mauer), Germany
	Vértesszöllös, Hungary
	Petralona, Greece
	Torralba/Ambrona, Spain
	Terra Amata, France
Africa	
North Africa	Ternifine, Algeria
	Sidi abd er-Rahman, Morocco
	Rabat, Morocco
	Salé, Morocco
	Temara, Morocco
East Africa	Olduvai Gorge, Tanzania
	East Turkana, Kenya
	Omo, Ethiopia
	Afar, Ethiopia
South Africa	Swartkrans, Republic of South Africa

cient water, a small body is advantageous since skin surface is proportionately greater and heat loss (by sweating) is improved. Carrying containers of water would remove the small-size limitation.

Another possible result of heat adaptation, suggests Wolpoff, is darker skin color as protection against ultraviolet rays of the tropical sun. However, there is currently little concrete evidence to support this. (See pp. 160–164 for a comprehensive discussion of skin pigment adaptation.)

SOCIAL CHANGES

In addition to these physical and physiological modifications, there were also social innovations. Hunting gives a group more free time, since less meat (compared to plants) is required for the same food value. Also, assuming hunting and gathering activities were planned and cooperatively executed, there was opportunity for more complex social interaction within and between populations.

With a division of labor (males hunting and females gathering), males assumed responsibility for protecting females and young. Not only was food shared within the band, but the sharing was ritualized; strategies were developed requiring cooperation between males, and attempts made at long-range planning.

Whether or not this scenario proposed by Wolpoff did, in fact, occur, when we look back at the evolution of *H. erectus*, we realize how significant were this early human's achievements toward **hominization**. It was *H. erectus* who completed striding bipedalism and erect posture; who embraced culture wholeheartedly as a strategy of adaptation; whose brain was reshaped and increased in size to within *sapiens* range; who became a proficient hunter with greater dependence on meat (which in turn reduced jaw and posterior teeth size); who apparently established more or less permanent living sites, probably some sort of social organization, such as family and band; and who used fire extensively. We salute *Homo erectus*, the first human beings.

◇ Summary

Homo erectus (also known as pithecanthropines) represents the second grade of human evolution and is usually associated with the Middle Pleistocene, although they appear much earlier. The beginning of the Middle Pleistocene has been set at the Matuyama-Brunhes paleomagnetic boundary, 700,000 years ago.

Differences from australopithecines are notable in *H. erectus*' larger and reproportioned brain, taller stature, and changes in facial structure and skull buttressing.

Remains of *H. erectus* come from three continents. In Asia, there are two locations: Java and China. Europe contains three sites that have produced hominid skeletal material: Heidelberg, Vértesszöllös, and Petralona. Two European sites with cultural material, but lacking bones, are also discussed: Torralba/Ambrona in Spain and Terra Amata in France. There are three *H. erectus* areas in Africa: North Africa, East Africa, and South Africa.

A hypothetical reconstruction of evolutionary change from australopithe-cines to pithecanthropines is presented, suggesting evolution was due to changes in diet, from plant material to greater dependence on meat. Adap-tation to tropical diurnal hunting/gathering was perhaps responsible for loss of body hair, sweat glands, and increased body size. Dependence on meat changed chewing habits and, therefore, facial and skull structure. Cultural flexibility required for hunting big game (giving rise to organized and coop-erative groups) selected for a larger and reproportioned brain and hastened the process of hominization.

◇ Questions for Review

1. Describe the Pleistocene in terms of (a) temperature and (b) the dating of fossil hominids.
2. Why is paleomagnetism more useful than other methods in dating the earth's history?
3. Describe *H. erectus*. How is *H. erectus* anatomically different from australopithecines?
4. What are the significant features of *H. erectus'* cultural life?
5. What was the intellectual climate in Europe in the latter half of the nineteenth century, especially concerning human evolution?
6. Why was there so much opposition to Dubois' interpretation of the hominid fossils he found in Java?
7. Why do you think Peking Man was enthusiastically accepted whereas Java Man was not?
8. Describe the life of Peking Man.
9. Compare the three European *H. erectus* remains. What physical and cultural characteristics justify designating them *H. erectus*?
10. What do the Torralba/Ambrona and Terra Amata sites tell us of Middle Pleistocene culture?
11. *Homo erectus* is called the first human. Why?
12. What is the *H. erectus* evidence from Africa, and what questions of human evolution does the evidence raise?
13. Summarize the evolutionary events (physical and cultural) of the Middle Pleistocene.
14. What events, according to Wolpoff, led to loss of body hair and increased body size?
15. Why do we "owe so much" to *H. erectus*?

◇ Suggested Further Reading

Bordes, François. *The Old Stone Age*, New York: McGraw-Hill Book Co., 1968.
    A thorough account of the culture of the Old Stone Age or Paleolithic based mainly on stone tools. Many excellent drawings clearly illustrate the kinds of stone tools used by Paleolithic people.

Brace, C. Loring, Harry Nelson, and Noel Korn. *Atlas of Human Evolution* (2nd Ed.), New York: Holt, Rinehart and Winston, Inc., 1979.

> *Essentially a manual of illustrations of fossil hominid carefully drawn under the supervision of Professor Brace. Background material given for each fossil illustrated.*

Howell, F. Clark. *Early Man* (Life Nature Library), New York: Time, Inc., 1965.

> *Many fine photographs and illustrations. Written under the direction of one of the leading scholars on fossil hominids.*

Leakey, Richard E. and Roger Lewin. *Origins*, New York: E. P. Dutton, 1977.

> *This work is well written and contains beautiful photographs and line drawings. Richard Leakey, son of Louis and Mary Leakey, and his co-author have written an excellent book on ancient hominids and their culture. It will serve the student well as a reference work and is an interesting book to read in the bargain.*

Moore, Ruth. *Man, Time, and Fossils.* New York: Alfred A. Knopf, 1961.

> *An excellent and readable book with fascinating background material on discoverers of fossil hominid.*

Pfeiffer, John E. *The Emergence of Man* (3rd Ed.), New York: Harper & Row, Publishers, 1978.

> *Not all anthropologists agree with Pfeiffer's view of big-game hunting, but it is an interesting hypothesis and worth reading, especially chapters VI and VII.*

Shapiro, Harry L. *Peking Man*, New York : Simon and Schuster, 1975.

> *Dr. Shapiro has been associated with the study of Peking Man for many years in his position as chairman of the Department of Anthropology at The American Museum of Natural History. In this book, he writes in detail of the discovery of Peking Man and the disappearance of the original material. A scientific whodunit.*

Wendt, Herbert. *In Search of Adam.* New York: Collier Books, 1955.

> *Chapter 11, written in Wendt's usual novellike interesting style, details Dubois' search for human ancestors.*

White, Edmund and Dale Brown. *The First Men* (The Emergence of Man Series, Time-Life Books), New York: Time, Inc., 1973.

> *A fascinating review of* Homo erectus *with excellent illustrations and photos. Very helpful for understanding* Homo erectus.

Von Koenigswald, G.H.R. *Meeting Prehistoric Man*, New York: Harper & Brothers, 1956.

> *Written for the layman by one of the foremost discoverers of fossil hominids in Java. Well worth reading.*

Homo Sapiens

CONTENTS

The world is full of wonders! Ivan T. Sanderson, a well-known writer on the subject of primates and a science editor of *Argosy*, wrote an article in the May 1969 issue of that magazine on an adventure he had recently experienced. If we take Sanderson at his word, he was completely serious.

Early in 1969, Sanderson decided to investigate a report concerning a strange-looking corpse encased in a 6,000-pound block of ice that had been placed on display at the annual Stock Fair in Chicago. Accompanying him was Dr. Bernard Heuvelmans of the Belgium Royal Academy of Sciences and a longtime student of matters like the Abominable Snowman and similar singularities.

On a remote Minnesota farm, they met the frozen Neandertal along with a Mr. Frank Hansen who owned it or rented it, or was at least in charge of it. The body was indeed encased in ice (which made examination and measurement difficult), but the two men did their best.

Sanderson described "Bozo," as they nicknamed it, as a very sturdy, approximately six-foot "human" covered with hair over almost the entire body. Its fingers and toes had nails, not claws, and it had practically no neck. Its torso was "barrel-shaped and it tapers down, not to a waist, but to rather narrow hips" (Sanderson, 1969, p. 26). And, although its legs were about the right length, its arms were longer than average. Its most outstanding characteristic was its enormous, spatulate hands, but the thumbs were surprisingly slender and long. The eyeballs were the most bizarre features of Bozo's face—both eyes had been "blown out" of their sockets, and the nose was distinctly pugged, like that of a Pekingese dog. It was also very obviously male.

"Let me say, simply," wrote Sanderson, "that one look was actually enough to convince us that this was—from our point of view, at least—'the genuine article.' This was no phony Chinese trick, or 'art' work" (1969, p. 26).

Whence cometh this Iceman? Several stories purport to explain the presence of the Iceman in the United States and on the carnival circuit. In one tale, Bozo was found floating in a block of sea ice in the Bering Sea by a Soviet whaling ship. When the Soviets put in at a Chinese port, the authorities seized the specimen, which then disappeared into Red China. It finally turned up, no one knows how, in Hong Kong, still in 6,000 pounds of ice, which had apparently not melted even one ounce worth.

An alternate story is that the original discoverers were not Soviet, but Japanese whalers, and that the find occurred somewhere off the coast of Kamchatka, not the Bering Sea. The creature was taken to Japan and then sold to a Hong Kong exporter.

Once in Hong Kong, the ice and the creature were wrapped in a sort of super plastic bag and stored in a deep freeze by an exporter who sold all kinds of curios. An agent for a wealthy American associated with the movie industry heard that the Iceman was for sale and bought it for his client. It was then rented by Mr. Hansen, who took it about, still in the ice block, from carnival to carnival, fair to fair, and sideshow to sideshow, exhibiting it to the public throughout the country.

In his book *Bigfoot*, primatologist Dr. John Napier (1973)—who had originally apparently been taken in by all of this—exposed the Iceman for what it really was. After some investigation, Napier concluded that the entire affair was a publicity stunt initiated by Mr. Hansen, who really owned the object, and not the mysterious Hollywood multimillionaire. It also appeared that the "body" was made of latex rubber and hair and had been put together on the West Coast. In 1970, Hansen "confessed" in *Saga* that the story he told Sanderson was simply a showman's spiel. What actually happened, he wrote, was that in 1960, while on a hunting trip in Minnesota, he shot a doe. When he came up to it, three hairy creatures were tearing the animal apart with their bare hands and drinking its blood. One of the creatures sprang screeching at him. Panicked, Hansen fired his rifle point blank, blowing out the creature's eyes and killing it instantly. Terrified, Hansen ran off, but returned a few days later to find the creature frozen stiff. He carried it back to his home, cautioned his wife not to say a word about it, and deposited it in their deep freeze, where it spent the next seven years until Hansen decided to take it on the road.

A different thrilling story was carried in the *National Bulletin* on June 30, 1969, under the heading, "I Was Raped by the Abominable Snowman!" A young woman, Helen Westring by name, alleged that while hunting alone in Minnesota, she met an Abominable Snowman. The monster ripped off her clothes, glared at her lustfully, and proceeded to rape her. Luckily, Helen fainted during the action, as a proper maiden should, but when she regained consciousness, she shot the brute through the right eye (which dislocated the left eye). And that was how the Iceman lost his eyes—at the hands of a heroic girl avenging her honor in the Minnesota woods!

Sanderson was convinced Bozo was real and a Neandertal (he—Sanderson—died before Napier completed his investigations). However, Sanderson and Heuvelmans are not the only believers in the presence of Neandertals living in remote areas of the world. Several Soviet paleoanthro-

pologists at the Darwin Museum in Moscow have developed a theory on the origin of *Homo sapiens*, part of which is that "relic hominoids," such as Bigfoot, Yeti, and others of native folklore, are really Neandertals or their descendants (Proshnev, 1974; Bayanov and Bourtsev, 1974, 1976).

The Soviets write persuasively of relic hominoids, but hard, convincing evidence remains surprisingly lacking. Sightings of relic hominoids (much like sightings of UFOs) have been widespread, and the evidence appears to be of about the same caliber. Why all this interest in relic hominoids that propels men to the isolated woods of the Pacific Coast, the mountaintops of Himalaya, and assorted lonely steppes and deserts? Perhaps Napier's cogent comments may help explain this strange phenomenon:

Man has an insatiable appetite for ghouls and bogles, and large sections of the entertainment business make it their concern to see that his tastes are well catered for. Horror-films, horror-comics, horror-exhibits are big business. . . . This determination of mankind to frighten itself to death can perhaps be regarded as an endearing trait, an expression of a touching, child-like naivieté in the face of the monstrous Forces of the Unknown. On the other hand, perhaps it is just a cult that owes nothing to na-

ture, religion, philosophy or the mainstream of folklore, but is simply another form of self-indulgence (Napier, 1973, p. 193).

UPDATE

Myra Shackley's archeological research in Mongolia led her to believe ("half sceptically") in the possibility of Neandertal survivals in the Altai ranges of central Asia. Local inhabitants know of people living in the Altai Mountains who are quite different from themselves and, Shackley says, may be surviving Neandertals.

Until careful studies are made, we withhold judgment.

SOURCES:

Bayanov, Dmitri and Igor Bourtsev. "Reply [to comments on Proshnev's article]," *Current Anthropology* 15(4):452–56, 1974.

———. "On Neanderthal vs. Paranthropus," *Current Anthropology* 17 (2):312–18, 1976.

Napier, John. *Bigfoot.* New York: E. P. Dutton & Co., Inc., 1973.

Proshnev, B. F. "The Troglodytidae and the Hominidae in the Taxonomy and Evolution of Higher Primates," *Current Anthropology* 15 (4):449–50, 1974.

Sanderson, Ivan T. "The Missing Link," *Argosy,* May, pp. 23–31, 1969.

Shackley, Myra. "The Case for Neanderthal Survival: Fact, Fiction or Faction?" *Antiquity* 56:31–41, 1982.

◇ Introduction

Evolution does not proceed by hops, skips, or jumps (although the rate of change may increase or decrease), but by a gradual modification that eventually produces a new species.* This period of modification may be thought of as a transition between species. We find such a transitional period somewhere in the 400,000 y.a. to 100,000 y.a. range, between the old species, *Homo erectus*, and the new, *Homo sapiens*. (See Box 17-1.)

Because the transition between species is so gradual, it is often difficult to clearly separate transitional fossil forms from the species that precede or follow them. In this chapter, several such difficult cases will be presented, such as *H. sapiens* with lingering *H. erectus* traits, or *H. erectus* with emerging sapient traits. "You pays your penny and you takes your choice."

The chapter is divided into three sections: transitional forms, Neandertal forms, and Upper Paleolithic (anatomically modern) forms. This scheme is somewhat simplistic, given the problems of gradually evolving hominids, but it will serve as an adequate device for dealing with the emergence of the *H. sapiens* grade of evolution.

◇ Transitional Forms

The term "transitional forms" as it is used in this section refers to those fossil forms that have changed too much to be definitely *H. erectus* but not enough to be considered—*without quibble*—completely *H. sapiens*. It is not necessary that a line be drawn between the two; nor is it necessary that any fossil, for that matter, be classified absolutely one way or the other.

STEINHEIM

Just as Professor Schoetensack waited so many years at the sandpit before the Mauer mandible was exposed, so Dr. F. Berchkhemer, chief curator of the Natural History Museum of Württemberg, waited with hope over twenty-five patient years for a hominid discovery at a gravel pit at Steinheim, Germany, twelve miles north of the city of Stuttgart. His patience was finally rewarded on July 24, 1933, when Herr Sigrist, owner of the gravel pit, excitedly reported the recovery of a highly petrified primitive human skull minus the jaw.

Under the heavy weight of twenty-three feet of wet earth, the Steinheim skull was warped and the left side unfortunately crushed behind the left eye. Much like the Peking skulls, the foramen magnum was cut away, allowing access to the brain, perhaps for cannibalistic or ritualistic purposes; never-

*Gould and Eldredge have recently suggested that evolution does indeed proceed by rapid "jumps," what they have called "punctuated equilibrium" (see pp. 109–111).

◇ Box 17-1   Comparison of *H. Sapiens* and *H. Erectus*

Homo sapiens differs from *H. erectus* in a number of characteristics.* In *Homo sapiens*:

1. The skull is larger with a 1,350 cm³ mean cranial capacity
2. Muscular ridges in the cranium are not strongly marked
3. The forehead is rounded and vertical
4. The supraorbital ridges are not well developed and do not form a continuous and uninterrupted torus

*For a fuller definition see Howell, 1978, p. 201ff.

5. The occipital region is rounded and the nuchal area is relatively small
6. Mastoid process is prominent and of a pyramidal shape
7. The calvaria is of maximum width, usually in the parietal region
8. Jaws and teeth are relatively small
9. Maxilla has concave surface including a canine fossa
10. The chin is distinct
11. Limb bones are relatively slender and slight

theless, much of the cranium was intact, especially the face. Unfortunately, artifacts were not found associated with the skull.

The skull is believed to be that of a young woman, who lived between 300,000 y.a.–200,000 y.a., with a cranial capacity between 1,150 and 1,175 cm³. Though the brain is small, it is larger than most *H. erectus* forms and is within the lower range of *H. sapiens*.

Figure 17-1   Sites of transitional forms and Neandertals.

Figure 17-2   Steinheim site.

(a)

(b)

Figure 17-3   Cast of Steinheim skull. (a) Basal view, showing how the foramen magnum was enlarged, apparently for removal of the brain—for dietary or ritualistic purposes; (b) frontal view showing warped skull.

Steinheim's face, except for its height, is remarkably like *H. erectus*, and the supraorbital torus is heavier than that of any Neandertal (Wolpoff, 1980b). The overall shape of the skull and its reduced bone thickness approaches *H. sapiens*. The nose is apparently broad, but the face is relatively straight (with some midfacial prognathism) and hangs nicely underneath the brows, compared to *H. erectus*. The teeth tend to be smaller than those of *H. erectus*.

This melange of *H. erectus*-like and *sapient*-like characters (Fig. 17-2) places Steinheim in the middle of the evolutionary modification, between the two hominid grades. We have, for better or worse, included Steinheim in the *H. sapiens*, rather than *H. erectus* chapter, since she seems to be definitely on her way to becoming *H. sapiens*.

SWANSCOMBE

Watching and waiting at probable sites for the appearance of human artifacts and fossil human bones are incurable pursuits for both professional and amateur archeologists. A likely site well known to a generation or more of watchers and waiters was Swanscombe, located not far from London. This site yielded remains of Pleistocene mammals and several hundred thousand Acheulian artifacts, especially handaxes, but also some flake tools.

A dentist and amateur archeologist, A. T. Marston, in June 1935, was the man who first noticed that local cement workers had uncovered an occipital bone. Marston, encouraged by his find, maintained his vigil, and in March of the following year, eight yards from where the occipital had been found, he caught sight of a left parietal which, it turned out, belonged to the same skull as the earlier bone. Like a Ripley "Believe It or Not" item, twenty years after the occipital was found, a right parietal was discovered seventy-five feet from the original find, and it fitted the other two bones exactly!

It is clear that the mammals associated with the skull, such as elephant, rhino, and red deer, were warm-weather animals and, therefore, the gravel bed in which they were found was laid down during an interglacial period. General agreement holds this period to be the second (Mindel-Riss or Holsteinian) interglacial. Dating by the uranium-thorium technique gives a date of over 300,000 years (Butzer and Isaac, 1975), which conforms with the mammals of the period. It appears, therefore, that the hominid bones belong where they were found, and are as old as the radiometric date indicates. Nevertheless, there remains considerable speculation on the age of the gravel bed deposits. Still, Swanscombe may well be honored as the first known Englishwoman.

Since the sutures joining the three bones are not obliterated,* the skull is estimated to belong to an individual twenty to twenty-five years old. The size of the bones suggests Swanscombe is female, and their morphology is surprisingly modernish. Unfortunately, the frontal bones and face are missing, and it is not known whether Swanscombe, with an occipital similar to Steinheim, also possessed Steinheim's heavy supraorbital torus. If it does, and there is some reason to believe this is the case, Swanscombe apparently is

*Sutures commence closing at about twenty years and close completely at various ages. It is possible, to some degree, to estimate age at death on the basis of the degree of suture closing.

not as modern as once believed and would fit very nicely into the Steinheim population—transitional between *H. erectus* and *H. sapiens*.

ARAGO (TAUTAVEL MAN)

Fieldwork at the Arago cave, near the village of Tautavel (which is near the Spanish border in southeastern France) began in 1964 under the supervision of the same husband and wife team who excavated Terra Amata—Henry and Marie-Antoinette de Lumley. They were attracted to the site by materials collected over the years by prehistorians and amateurs, and they believed the site to be an early one and well worth excavating (de Lumley, H. and de Lumley, M., 1973).

Abundant faunal remains reflect a cold climate, and the Mindel glaciation has been suggested for the date of Arago (Cook et al., 1982). Radiometric measurements—including several very recently developed methods—have failed to agree on a date. We are left, therefore, with a Mindel date, perhaps 400,000 y.a., but really nothing solid in numbers of years. At that time, prehistoric hunters occupied the site, and the de Lumleys located more than twenty occupation levels, each separated by two to seven feet of sterile sand. More than 100,000 Acheulian artifacts have been recovered from the site.

Over 50 cranial and postcranial remains of at least four adults and three children have been recovered. Most important of the specimens are a partial cranium, mostly face and frontal bone (Fig. 17-6), two mandibles, a parietal bone, an almost complete innominate, and various other cranial and postcranial fragments.

The cranium is apparently that of a young male, and the face is especially useful because there are so very few available from this period. It gives a pretty good idea of what these Middle Pleistocene Europeans might have looked like. The supraorbital torus is very prominent, the forehead is relatively long, flat, and narrow, and the cranial capacity is estimated to be in the 1050 to 1150 cm^3 range.

The mandibles, neither of which fit the cranium, belong to a young adult male (Arago 13) and a female of around 40 to 55 years of age (Arago 2). These are massive mandibles; the size of the female's teeth fall within the range of Neandertals and anatomically moderns, but those of the male are huge, exceeding those of Heidelberg and matching the largest of Ternifine. The mandibles display *H. erectus*, as well as archaic *sapiens*, characters.

Arago, like Swanscombe and Steinheim, is difficult to assign to a definite species. It could fit *H. erectus* or archaic *sapiens*, and scholars have classified it in both categories.

BILZINGSLEBEN

In East Germany, about twenty-five miles north of Weimar, near the village of Bilzingsleben, four hominid skull fragments and a single molar tooth were found in 1971 and over the next few years. The dating is uncertain, although it appears to be second interglacial (Mindel-Riss). The brow ridges are similar to *H. erectus*, heavy and not arched, and the skull bones are quite thick. Vlček

Figure 17-4   Cast of Swanscombe skull.

Figure 17-5   Sites for Swanscombe; Arago.

Figure 17-6   Partial Arago skull.

Figure 17-7 Sites: Gibraltar, Spy, La Naulette, Neandertal.

(1978) has pointed out the similarity to Olduvai Hominid 9 (p. 495), who lived close to a million years earlier and is assigned to *H. erectus*. However, the forehead and occipital areas of Bilzingsleben appear to be moving in a sapient direction.

It would be entirely possible to place Bilzingsleben in the preceding chapter along with Petralona and Vértesszöllös. This is the kind of problem to be expected during a period of change, when physical traits of a specimen reflect, as they do here, traces of different grades or species.

In addition to these fossil remains, there are a few other transitional forms dating from the Middle Pleistocene:

Montmaurin—Toulouse, southern France. A mandible that resembles Heidelberg in some features, and the Arago and Neandertal jaws in others.

Abri Suard—Charente, southern France. A number of skull and mandible fragments and teeth.

Cova Negra—Spain. A parietal.

Lazaret Cave—Nice, southern France. Remains of three hominids associated with Acheulian industry.

Biache-Saint-Vaast—France. Cranial fragments similar to Swanscombe.

Chang-yang—Cave of Dragons near Chang-yang, Hupei, China. A left maxilla with some teeth.

Overall during this period of transition in the second (Holsteinian) interglacial and third (Riss) glacial, there were changes in crania and postcrania that reflect the evolutionary trend from *H. erectus* to what we recognize as *H. sapiens*. While it is not always easy to attribute causes of physical modifications, it is not unreasonable to assume they were due to changing behavioral patterns.

Humans were improving their technology and intensifying their social interactions. Greater dependence on culture—more efficient technology—may have begun to reduce stress on anterior teeth with resultant changes in mandible, forehead, supraorbital torus and occipital area (see Box 16-9, p. 500). Improved technology also suggests dependence on a more efficient brain, resulting in selection for a larger brain, and/or reorganization of the brain. This may well have intensified the feedback relationship of behavior and technology that produced the physical changes.

The cranial capacity average of 1,166 cm³ for these transitional forms represents an 11% expansion in volume from the later *H. erectus* sample. The occipital region was reduced in robustness, spongy* bone at the base of the skull was reduced, and, while posterior teeth were reduced, anterior teeth continued to increase in size. There is also a tendency for the canine to be incisiform (more spatulate). Increase in anterior tooth size suggests continued use of these teeth for functions other than chewing, such as gripping, holding, or pulling. These activities may account for the prominent midfacial prognathism and the development of puffiness of the maxillary sinuses on both sides of the nose.

*Spongy (pneumatization). This refers to "a type of bone growth where air sacs or air cells are incorporated within the center of the bone tissue" (Kennedy, 1980, p. 220). If the air cells are very large, they are called *sinuses*; if very small, the bone assumes a "spongy" appearance.

Behaviorally, technological improvement suggests that these people may have had a clear mental image of the tool to be made before manufacturing it. Standardization of various tool types increased, and new shapes (ovoid and triangular) appear. A wide variety of handaxes of many different forms and sizes were probably special-purpose tools. At Bilzingsleben, East Germany, an elephant bone was set up on an anvil and smashed by using large cobbles. Also at Bilzingsleben, red deer antlers were used for axes and cleaverlike tools. Retouched bone may also have been present (Cook et al., 1982).

Although artificial structures may have been built before this period, the evidence now appears more clearly. A shelter, about 11 by 4 feet, is known from Lazaret Cave of southern France. Inside the shelter, there are remains of two hearths. Outside the cave, traces of a series of tents were found, and just inside the door of each tent was a wolf skull. The exact significance of the wolf skulls may never be known, but they were surely symbolic and possibly indicative of a ritual of some kind. At Bilzingsleben, outlines of two possible structures were recognized during recent excavations, so it is possible that artificial structures were more common than the archeological record has previously suggested.

During the Riss, it is possible that geographic differences appeared among human beings as they adapted to different environmental conditions. It was also during this time that humans first began to occupy caves extensively (seasonally, in some cases), as well as open sites. Archeological evidence makes it clear that many different food sources were being utilized, such as fruits, vegetables, seeds, nuts, and so forth, each in its own season. Marine life was exploited: from Orgnac, in southern France, comes evidence for freshwater fishing (trout, char), perch from Lazaret, and tench (carp family) from Bilzingsleben.

Although art does not become well developed until the Upper Paleolithic, beginning signs are already in evidence. At Terra Amata (p. 492) red ochre remains were found, and intentional engraving on an ox rib, dating back to the Riss glacial, is evidenced from southern France.

During the Middle Pleistocene, humans were becoming more aware of ecological opportunities, and changes in life styles appear. Shelters were becoming more common, a greater variety of food was being eaten, and changes in stone technology were made, as well as at least a beginning in the use of new materials. Not many hunting tools have been found, which suggests the possible use of wooden weapons, or perhaps the practice of netting or trapping. It is also possible that scavenging from carcasses, killed by other carnivores or natural events, has been underestimated. In any case, it does appear that the pace of change was increasing.

From an evolutionary point of view, two points should be kept in mind concerning these remains from the Holsteinian interglacial and Riss glacial: first, there is a great deal of variation in these populations, with differences in many if not all features of the skull; second, as we pointed out at the beginning of this section, some characteristics recall the preceding *H. erectus* forms and others mark a trend toward *H. sapiens*.

It should also be pointed out that chronological placement of the European hominid sample is very difficult and, at the present time, not yet possible.

Figure 17-8 Sites of Orgnac, Lazaret, Terra Amata.

Mousterian
(moo-stair'-ee-en)
A cultural tradition of the Upper Pleistocene associated with Neandertals.

Dating fossil finds is the problem and, until reliable dating is established, the course of human evolution in the latter Middle Pleistocene remains unresolved.

◇ Neandertals (125,000 y.a.–40,000 y.a.)

Despite their apparent disappearance 35,000 y.a.–40,000 y.a., Neandertals continue to haunt the best laid theories of paleoanthropologists. They fit into the general scheme of human evolution, and yet they are misfits. Classified as *H. sapiens*, they are like us and yet different, and some of those in Western Europe are even more different yet. It is not an easy task to put them in their place.

These troublesome hunters are the cave man of cartoonists, walking about with bent knees, dragging a club in one hand and a woman by her hair in the other. They are described as brutish, dwarfish, apelike, and obviously of little intelligence. This image is more than somewhat exaggerated.

While cartoonists' license is not to be denied, the fact remains that Neandertals walked as upright as any of us, and, if they dragged clubs and women, there is not the slightest evidence of it. Nor are they dwarfish or apelike, and, in the light of twentieth-century human behavior, we should be careful of whom we call brutish.

As far as intelligence is concerned, Neandertals produced excellent **Mousterian** implements and, in fact, invented a new technique, the disc-core

Figure 17-9 The Upper Pleistocene. The correlations of fossil finds with culture periods and dates are approximations and sometimes speculative. There is no intent to indicate that this depiction is validated by evidence. The culture periods of the Upper Paleolithic are not necessarily sequential as shown. This figure is simply meant to assist the student in organizing Upper Pleistocene data.

		Glacial	Paleolithic	Culture Periods		Hominidae	*Homo Sapiens*	
UPPER PLEISTOCENE	100,000 20,000 30,000 40,000 50,000 75,000 100,000 125,000	Late W Ü R M Middle Early Riss-Würm (EEM) (interglacial)	20,000 25,000 Upper Paleolithic Middle Paleolithic	Magdelenian Solutrean Gravettian Aurignacian Chatelperronian Mousterian Levalloisian Acheulian		Anatomically modern humans N E A N D E R T A L S	Florisbad Eyasi Hortus Vindija Miadeĉ Niah Qafza Border Cave Jebel Irhoud La Ferrassie Ehringsdorf Saccopastore ? Teshik-tash Krapina ? Border Cave ? Broken Hill Fontechevade Mapa	Afalou Cro-Magnon Predmosti Skhūl Fish Hoek Amud Tabun Shanidar La Chapelle Monte Circeo

technique (Campbell, 1976, p. 328). This method is a highly productive one in which a nodule of stone is trimmed around the edges to make it disc-shaped. Then flakes are removed from the core by rapping the edges, knocking off flakes until the core becomes too small and is thrown away. The flakes are then further trimmed to provide the edges necessary for whatever kind of work was needed on wood, carcasses, or hides.

Neandertals were also clever enough to cope with the cold weather of the glacial period. In addition to open sites, they lived in caves, wore clothing, built fires, gathered in settlements (some of which extended right up to the Arctic Ocean), hafted some of their tools, and hunted with a good deal of skill. They had to be skillful hunters in order to survive by subsisting off herds of reindeer, wooly rhinoceros, and mammoth. There was very little vegetable food available on the cold tundra.

Finally, the brain size of Neandertals is, on the average, at least that of *H. sapiens sapiens* and probably larger. Estimates for Neandertal skulls range from approximately 1,200 to 1,800 cm³.

For many years, the question of what to call hominids from the Middle Paleolithic (the cultural period, including the Riss-Würm or Eemian inter-glacial and the early Würm glacial) has been debated by paleoanthropologists. We shall refer to all those who more or less fit the pattern of Western Europeans and Near Easterners of this period as Neandertals. For others (in Africa and Eastern Asia) who lived at about the same time, but do not fit this pattern, we shall use the term contemporaries.

Neandertals lived from about 125,000 y.a. until roughly 40,000 y.a. Although they show considerable physical variability over this 85,000-year period, there is a characteristic morphology that includes both the earlier forms of the Eemian and the *classic* Neandertals of the early fourth glacial.

The following description (after Howells, 1973) applies more strictly to the classic Neandertals of the fourth glacial rather than those of the Eemian, who did not completely develop the extreme traits of the classical forms:

> The skull is large, long, low, and bulging at the sides. At the rear of the skull a bun protrudes, but the occiput is rounded without the angulation of *erectus*. There is less spongy bone at the base of the skull, and the greatest breadth is higher up on the skull.

> In front, the forehead rises though not as steeply as in modern *sapiens*, and the brow ridges, not quite as pronounced as *H. erectus*, arch over the orbits instead of forming the straight bar of *H. erectus*. Variability found among Neandertals may be seen in the almost complete lack of these ridges in some specimens.

> Compared to moderns, the Neandertal face stands out. Facial length is considerably greater for Neandertals than for Upper Paleolithic *sapiens* and even more so compared to ourselves. Alveolar prognathism is noticeable and, in fact, the entire face projects as if it had been pulled forward.

> Neandertal's nose was high, angled, and prominent. "Many of the unique features of Neandertal facial morphology center about the nose. A fully fleshed Neandertal nose must have been a phenomenal object" (Wolpoff, 1980a, p. 280). On both sides of the nose the maxillary sinuses expand outward, giving the maxilla a puffy look and convex shape.

Anatomically modern H. sapiens (or human beings)
Population of the Upper Paleolithic who physically resemble populations of today.

Classic Neandertals
Western Europe and Near Eastern Neandertals who lived during the early Würm.

The teeth were larger than both Upper Paleolithic and present-day populations, but posterior teeth continued to decrease in size from earlier forms. Anterior teeth in the early Würm increased then reversed growth and began to decrease in size, a process that continued with *H. sapiens sapiens*.

Our description of Neandertals has stressed the differences between them and those **anatomically modern H. sapiens** appearing in the Upper Paleolithic. Actually, the resemblances of Neandertals and anatomically moderns are significant, and Neandertals belong in the taxon, *H. sapiens*. There are probably no Neandertal traits that are totally outside the variation range of modern humans. However, taken as a group, Neandertal characteristics form a constellation of traits unlike any modern population.

NEANDERTALS AND UPPER PALEOLITHIC MODERNS

One of the many puzzling questions about human evolution is that of the ancestry of Neandertals and Upper Paleolithic *sapiens*. Upper Paleolithic humans appear in Europe about 40,000 y.a.,* at about the time Neandertal physical traits are no longer prevalent in human populations. For decades, paleoanthropologists have been vehemently arguing whether or not:

1. There are divergent lines leading to Neandertals on the one hand and Upper Paleolithic *sapiens* on the other
2. There is only one line of descent, with Neandertals evolving from transitional forms, and Upper Paleolithic *sapiens* from Neandertals
3. Neandertals disappear, to be replaced by Upper Paleolithic *sapiens*
4. These two groups represent populations isolated within their econiches or intermingled
5. *H. erectus* populations in various parts of the world evolved into separate *H. sapiens* populations (or did this occur only once, or only in a few places?)

These questions have been disputed for years, and no answers have been widely accepted; nor shall we present any. We hope, however, that the following discussion may throw some light on the matter.

Paleoanthropologists have organized the Neandertal-Upper Paleolithic *sapiens* relationship under three hypotheses:

1. Pre-*sapiens*
2. Pre-Neandertal
3. Neandertal phase of man

Pre-Sapiens Hypothesis   According to this view, the ancestors of anatomically modern humans are to be found back in the Middle Pleistocene. Neandertals are considered a side branch, too specialized to be ancestral to Upper Paleolithic *H. sapiens*; consequently they are placed in a separate species from *H. sapiens* and become extinct somewhere at the end of the early Würm. Swanscombe, of the second interglacial, and Fontechevade (discussed sub-

(a)

(b)

Figure 17-10   Cast, La Chapelle-aux-Saints. The best-known classic Neandertal. (*a*) Frontal view; (*b*) lateral view.

*Evidence appears to be accumulating that anatomically modern humans may have evolved considerably earlier than previously considered. The evidence comes especially from South Africa, and may go back more than 100,000 years. There are still questions about the dating, and the next few years may settle the matter. (See Kennedy, 1980; Rightmire, 1983.)

sequently), of the third interglacial, are believed by the adherents of the pre-*sapiens* hypothesis to display cranial morphology suggestive of the anatomically modern humans and are, therefore, proposed as the direct ancestors of Upper Paleolithic *H. sapiens*.

Unfortunately for this scheme, more recent analyses of Swanscombe and Fontechevade do not support the thesis of anatomically modern humans in the making (Sergi, 1967).

Pre-Neandertal Hypothesis   In this plan, Neandertals are said to have evolved from *H. erectus* through Swanscombe and Steinheim in the Eemian interglacial and spread throughout Europe, North Africa, and Asia. Then, at the beginning of the last (Würm) glaciation, Neandertals of Western Europe are isolated by the advance of both the Scandinavian and Alpine glaciations. Cut off from contact with other humans by glacial barriers, selection pressures of the cold environment created a breeding isolate that produced the specialized features characteristic of the **classic Neandertals** of Western Europe. At the same time, Neandertals and their contemporaries in other areas, adapting to different environmental pressures, were evolving into anatomically modern populations.

This plan presents two problems. First, the evidence is not conclusive that the physical characteristics of these specialized Neandertals (and there is general agreement they *are* specialized) are the result of adaptation to cold climate. Second, this hypothesis does not tell us what happened to the classic Neandertals. Did they also evolve into anatomically modern populations? Were they assimilated into, or destroyed by, an Upper Paleolithic population that migrated into Western Europe from Eastern Europe or Africa? (For a novelist's imaginative account of what might have happened, the reader is referred to William Golding's *The Inheritors*.)

The destruction of the Neandertals by a better-adapted contemporary population has long been suggested as an explanation for their "sudden" disappearance. This notion has received further support in recent years from two theories. First, that Neandertals were unable to speak fluently and thus would have been at a disadvantage in competition with anatomically modern humans who had appeared on the scene at about the time Neandertals "disappeared." As noted later (see p. 534), few paleoanthropologists have accepted Neandertal's inability to speak.

The second theory uses disease as the explanation for extinction. Studies of the Fore of New Guinea have shown that kuru, a severely debilitating disease often resulting in death, is associated with cannibalism (when cannibalism was prohibited in the 1950s, the incidence of this disease became rarer). It is argued that since Neandertals practiced cannibalism, they were infected with the kuru virus, which would have led to their ultimate annihilation, or to their easy destruction by a noncannibalistic population (Wolbarsht, 1975). This idea is interesting, but there is no way of proving the prevalence or absence of the disease among Neandertals. And, of course, many paleoanthropologists do not believe Neandertals "suddenly disappeared" at all. Supporters of the Pre-Neandertal hypothesis believe classic Neandertals in Europe were too specialized to have evolved into anatomically moderns (although they may have contributed genes), nor was there enough time. (See Wolpoff, 1980a, pp. 289–291, for a critique of this argument.)

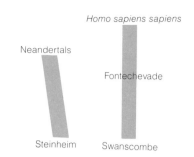

Figure 17-11   Pre-*sapiens* hypothesis. Neandertals evolve from Steinheim. They are too specialized and become extinct in the Würm. The *Homo sapiens sapiens* line originates with Swanscombe and evolves through Fontechevade to anatomically moderns of the Upper Paleolithic.

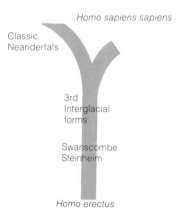

Figure 17-12   Pre-Neandertal hypothesis. The hominid line evolves from *Homo erectus* to Swanscombe/Steinheim to third interglacial forms. The fourth (Würm) glaciation isolates the population of Western Europe in a cold environment and produces specialized classic Neandertals. Third interglacial forms elsewhere evolve to anatomically modern *sapiens*.

Homo sapiens sapiens

Neandertals

Swanscombe
Steinheim

Homo erectus

Figure 17-13 Neandertal phase of man hypothesis. This is a straight-line evolutionary scheme that considers Neandertals not as a separate branch, but as the ancestors of the Upper Paleolithic anatomically modern humans.

The Neandertal Phase of Man Hypothesis   This scheme, first advanced by Hrdlička in 1927, is linear: *H. erectus* to Neandertals to *H. sapiens sapiens*. The hypothesis assumes that Neandertal populations in various parts of the world evolved into anatomically modern populations in their respective areas. No distinction is made between classic and early Neandertals, who are explained in terms of a variable population.

Such an economical hypothesis is attractive, but it does not explain what most authorities consider the specialized traits of the Western European classics. Why should these specializations be so localized? Also, whereas evidence in some areas of the world points to the evolution from Neandertals to anatomically modern human beings, no solid evidence from Western Europe suggests that classic Neandertals evolved into Upper Paleolithic *sapiens*. Perhaps they did, but the fossil remains from Western Europe supply abundant evidence of classic Neandertals, then comes a period of a few thousand years with practically no hominid remains, and then anatomically modern humans seem to suddenly appear.

This rapidly evolving change, from Neandertal to anatomically moderns in Europe—if, in fact, it did occur—might be explained in terms of punctuated equilibrium (see p. 109). However, there are several reasons why punctuation may not explain what appears to be a sudden change:

1. Forms intermediate between Neandertals and Upper Paleolithic *sapiens* have been found (see pp. 526–530)
2. Dates for Middle and Upper Pleistocene are still vague for many of the fossils; therefore, it is entirely possible that intermediate forms may fit between the time Neandertals are supposed to have disappeared and anatomically moderns appeared
3. Neandertals may not have disappeared when moderns came on the scene. The Neandertal skeleton found a few years ago at St. Cesaire (p. 523) has been dated at 32,000 years. It was found in association with tools considered to be Upper Paleolithic; therefore, it would seem that Neandertals were still living during the early Upper Paleolithic. The Middle/Upper Paleolithic transition is a hotly debated period today. (See White, 1982; Stringer, 1982.)

If we now turn to examine the evidence from the Eemian interglacial and the Würm glacial, it may help us understand the anthropological dilemma posed in the preceding discussion.

◇The Eemian (Third or Riss-Würm) Interglacial (125,000 y.a.–75,000 y.a.)

FONTECHEVADE

Archeologist Mlle. Germaine Henri-Martin broke through the cave floor at Fontechevade in southern France in 1947. Above the floor are occupation levels of people who lived there during the Upper Paleolithic. Below the floor she found evidence of a Tayacian (that is, pre-Mousterian) industry associated with warm-weather Eemian interglacial fauna. In the same deposits are portions of two human skulls, Fontechevade I and II. Fluorine analysis of the human and mammalian bones indicate they are about the same age—estimated to be about 110,000 y.a.

Fontechevade I consists of a small piece of forehead (including the critical area above the nose) belonging to an immature individual perhaps under 10 years of age. This fragment would be insignificant except that this area is where the supraorbitral torus should be, but is not. The lack of a supraorbital torus has led to much discussion about the modern look of this specimen. Did it possess a heavy brow ridge? If so, then the bone fits rather well into what might be expected at this time; if it did not, then it is possible that a smooth-forehead, modern type had evolved, and could be the ancestor of Upper Paleolithic *sapiens*. Unhappily for the argument on both sides, the bone fragment of one immature individual does not settle the matter. Neandertal children do not always possess brow ridges, and had this young person lived, he or she might have developed brow ridges—or perhaps not!

Furthermore, a more recent study (Corruccini, 1975) of the parietals of Fontechevade II, with an estimated cranial capacity of about 1,400 cm³, notes the presence of features similar to later classic Neandertals and to the much earlier Steinheim. If this is the case, then Fontechevade cannot be considered more modern than the later Neandertals and thus as *the* ancestor of Upper Paleolithic *sapiens*.

OTHERS

Other fossil remains of the Eemian interglacial are similarly inconclusive. At Ehringsdorf, near Weimar in what is now East Germany, researchers found a variety of skull bones that reflect archaic traits resembling Steinheim, and others that look quite modern. From Saccopastore, just outside Rome, come two skulls that also appear both archaic and modern. The small size of the brain, around 1,200 cm³, low vault, and prognathism of the upper face recall *erectus* traits, but the morphology of the brain, rounded occiput, and smooth area of neck muscle attachment are modern.

In Yugoslavia, from a rock shelter at Krapina, come 649 pieces of bones, many of them broken at the time of death. Evidence of charred bone, and long bones apparently split for their marrow, suggest cannibalism. The group—at least fifteen individuals have been identified and five skulls partially reconstructed—varies widely in physical traits. Krapina, like Saccopastore, Ehringsdorf, and Fontechevade, has been pointed up as possessing modern traits and, therefore, ancestral to anatomically modern humans of the Upper Paleolithic (pre-Neandertal hypothesis). However, the variable pattern of these forms raises serious questions about this evolutionary sequence.

The cultural material from these sites is essentially Mousterian, an industry usually associated with Neandertals. At Ehringsdorf, the tools include scrapers, small handaxes, drills, and **burins**, a variety that may be due to a mixture of several related populations. Over one thousand flint implements were recovered at Krapina, most of them unanalyzed. In addition to Mousterian artifacts at Krapina, there may also be Acheulian tools and possibly

Burin
A chisellike stone tool used for engraving on horn, wood, and ivory.

Figure 17-14   ontechevade II fragment. View of left side. The forehead is at the left. Courtesy of N. Vallois.

Figure 17-15 Sites of Fontechevade, Ehringsdorf, Krapina.

Pressure-flaking
A stoneworking technique in which flakes are removed from the edges by pressure rather than percussion.

In situ
(sigh'-too)
In its original or natural position.

some flakes, such as blades and microliths, similar to those from the Upper Paleolithic. This—as the Ehringsdorf assemblage—may also represent a possible mixture of different people, or cultural evolution in process, or both.

Both physical and cultural traits of the Eemian interglacial display a mixture of old and new. Physically, the population appears to be intermediate between *H. erectus* and *H. sapiens*, but tending toward the *sapient* end of the range. This is what we should expect in the course of human evolution if adaptive pressures were selecting for those traits that characterize anatomically modern humans.

The variety in technology of the Eemian may be due to adaptation to local conditions. The standardized tools of the Middle Pleistocene, especially the handaxe, were giving way to a more specialized technology. The improved technology of the Eemian may be seen in the use of flakes rather than cores, the techniques of **pressure-flaking**, and the variation in the types of tools.

◇ The Würm (Fourth) Glaciation '75,000–40,000 y.a.)

EARLY STAGES

For 300,000 years, more or less, *Homo sapiens* has been in existence and evolving from more *erectus*-like forms to Upper Paleolithic anatomically modern *sapiens* forms.

With the onset of the Würm, about 75,000 years ago, we encounter the complicated situation concerning the Neandertals in Western Europe. For the relatively short period of 30,000–35,000 years, from about 75,000 y.a.–40,000 y.a., a fairly homogeneous population lived in Western Europe. That population has engendered controversy and aroused more emotions, hypotheses, and theories than any other hominid group. As Howells has said: "Neandertal man has served to launch, to enhance, and to mar anthropological careers. Perhaps he is like the Tar Baby—each time Brer Rabbit hit him another lick, he got stuck faster" (Howells, 1975, p. 390).

It is generally accepted that fourth-glacial Neandertals are different from the *H. sapiens* preceding and following them. The question is: *How different?* Are they different enough to be considered a group apart from what was going on in Eastern Europe, the Near East, and North Africa? Or are they simply a variation of these populations? This may seem like unnecessary academic quibbling, but detailed considerations of human evolutionary theory are complicated. Most anthropologists place classic Neandertals as a side branch to the evolutionary flow from *H. erectus* to Upper Paleolithic *H. sapiens* but include the probability of gene exchange between these early fourth-glacial populations and the developing *H. sapiens sapiens* populations.

In the following section we shall describe several of these "classics" whose morphology has aroused such unprofessional emotions and academic discussion.

Neandertal Beginnings   Neandertal takes its name from the Neander Valley near Düsseldorf, Germany. In 1856, workmen quarrying limestone caves in

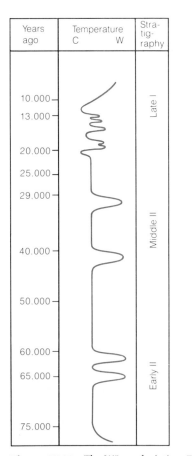

Years ago	Temperature C W	Stra-tig-raphy
10,000		Late I
13,000		
20,000		
25,000		
29,000		Middle II
40,000		
50,000		
60,000		
65,000		Early II
75,000		

Figure 17-16 The Würm glaciation. During a glacial period, such as the Würm, the temperature—and the presence of ice—varies. The 65,000 years of the Würm was not simply one long cold period.

the valley blew up the entrance to one of the caves and came across fossilized bones. The owner of the quarry believed they belonged to a bear and gave them to Johann Karl Fuhlrott, teacher of natural science in the local high school. Fuhlrott knew his subject, and when he saw the bones he realized they were not the remains of a cave bear. He believed they must be those of an ancient human, something between the gorilla (first discovered a few years earlier) and *Homo sapiens*. Exactly what the bones represented became a *cause célèbre* for many years, and the fate of Neandertal Man, as the bones were named, hung in the balance for years until later finds were made.

What swung the balance in favor of accepting the Neander Valley specimen as a genuine hominid fossil were other nineteenth-century finds similar to it. What is more important, the additional fossil remains brought home the realization that a form of human different from nineteenth-century Europeans had in fact existed.

Some of these nineteenth-century finds include a skull, which no one understood, found at Gibraltar in 1848. A decade later, the Neander Valley find placed the Gibraltar skull in a more accurate perspective as a Neandertal. In 1866, in the La Naulette Cave, Belgium, a mandible and a few odd bones were discovered and were attributed to the same species as Neandertal. In 1880, a child's mandible from Sipka, Czechoslovakia, demonstrated that large Neandertal teeth were not pathological, since this young mandible possessed large and normal teeth. Whereas there were cries of pathology and abnormality, voiced especially by Virchow (see Chapter 16), most scientists were impressed by the two skeletons recovered in 1886 from a cave at Spy, near the town of Namur, Belgium. These two skeletons were carefully observed **in situ** by scientists, and the site and excavation were carefully recorded. Similarities between these remains and those of earlier Neandertals were so extensive there could be no doubt that there really was a Neandertal Man.

In the post-Darwinian period, following the publication of *Origin* in 1859, the evolution controversy continued to rage, as we already have discussed in Chapters 2, 16, and elsewhere. Not even all scientists were persuaded that evolution was a valid concept; and more to the point, many scientists were very skeptical of the existence of hominid fossils. Cuvier's dictum, "*L'homme fossile n'existe pas*" (free translation: there is no such thing as fossil man), was still accepted by many Europeans, both laypeople and scientists. Virchow, for example, claimed to be a follower of Darwinian evolution, but was apparently unable to accept any of the hominid fossils discovered during his lifetime (he died in 1902) as honest-to-goodness hominid fossils. He described them as moderns, pathological in one way or another, and we have already alluded to the argument between Virchow and Haeckel about the evolution of hominids from pongids.

The discovery, in 1908, of La Chapelle-aux-Saints (discussed in the following section) settled the issue of the existence of fossil hominids once and for all. Unfortunately, by this time Cuvier was long since dead and, we assume, no longer in a position to change his mind. Virchow, too, had died a few years before, although the subsequent description of La Chapelle, written by Professor Marcellin Boule, seems to have followed in the footsteps of his predecessors, Cuvier and Virchow.

Figure 17-17 Sites: Gibraltar, Spy, La Naulette, Neandertal.

Figure 17-18   Cast, La Chapelle-aux-Saints.

La Chapelle-aux-Saints   One of the most important Neandertal discoveries was made in 1908 at La Chapelle-aux-Saints, near Correze in southwestern France. Found in a Mousterian cultural layer by three French priests, the Abbes A. and J. Bouysonnie and L. Bardon (already known for their archeological researches), was a nearly complete human skeleton. The body had been deliberately buried in a shallow grave and fixed in a ritual position, a bison leg placed on his chest, and the trench filled with flint tools and broken animal bones. This attitude suggests respect toward death, and the tools included with the body may very well indicate a belief in an afterlife where such implements could be used.

The skeleton was turned over for study to a famous French paleontologist, Marcellin Boule, who published his analysis in three volumes from 1911 to 1913. It was his exhaustive, and no doubt biased, publication that set the tone for the description of prehistoric man that survives to this day.

Why did Boule describe Neandertal as the slouching, brutish, apelike, unintelligent creature that became the staple of the cartoonist's prehistoric man? Professor Brace suggests the reason was that Boule, trained in France in the traditions of Cuvier's catastrophism, did not really believe in evolution. He could not deny, as Cuvier had, the existence of fossil humans, but he could reject the notion that Neandertals were ancestral to anatomical moderns, especially if Neandertal looked noticeably different. "With the over-emphasis of the nonmodern features of the La Chapelle-aux-Saints skeleton it became a much less likely candidate for the forefather of the succeeding Upper Paleolithic forms" (Brace, 1977, p. 219).

The skull of the old man, at least forty years of age—old for that time—is very large, with a cranial capacity of 1,620 cm³ (Day, 1977). The vault is low and long, the supraorbital ridges immense, with the typical Neandertal arched shape, and the forehead is low and retreating. Prognathism in the alveolar area is pronounced, and the face is long and projecting. At the rear of the skull, the occiput is protuberant and bun-shaped.

La Chapelle is not typical of classic Neandertals, but is a very robust male and "evidently represents an extreme in the Neanderthal range of variation" (Brace et al., 1979, p. 117). Unfortunately, this skeleton, which Boule claimed did not even walk completely erect (he walked as erect as any other elderly human with spinal arthritis), has been widely accepted as "Mr. Neandertal." That other classic Neandertals are not as extreme is shown by La Ferrassie, a contemporary of La Chapelle.

La Ferrassie   Between 1909 and 1912, French archeologist D. Peyrony excavated two adult skeletons and portions of skeletons of four children associated with Mousterian artifacts. Trenches had been dug for the skeletons in what has been described as a "family" cemetery. Flint flakes and bone splinters were placed in the male skeleton's grave, and over his shoulders and head was set a flat stone slab, perhaps to protect him, or could it have been to restrain him from coming back to life? (Constable, 1973, p. 98).

La Ferrassie resembles La Chapelle in the extraordinary long face and pronounced arched supraorbital ridges, but La Ferrassie's chin is relatively well marked, the forehead is not as sloping, and the occiput lacks the pro-

Figure 17-19   Sites of La Chapelle-aux-Saints, La Ferrassie, St. Césaire, Vindija.

tuberant bun. The differences between La Chapelle and La Ferrassie have led Brose and Wolpoff (1971) to define the latter as a transitional form evolving from classic Neandertals to anatomically modern *H. sapiens*, a claim denied by Professor Howells (Howells, 1974, p. 28). Whether or not La Ferrassie may be classified transitional is a matter for continued study by the experts; what is very clear, however, is that the classic Neandertal population of Western Europe is variable, as we would expect of *any* human population.

Vindija   Some thirty-five specimens from a lower level (G₃) of this Yugoslavian site are associated with a late Mousterian (Middle Paleolithic) assemblage and the Lower Würm glaciation. Although in some respects approaching anatomically moderns, the skeletal material is considered to be definitely Neandertal.

St. Cesaire   An incomplete skeleton, believed to be that of an adult woman, was found in 1979 at St. Cesaire (Charènte-Maritime, France), by Professor Bernard Vandermeersch of the University of Paris. From the evidence of limbs, and especially the skull—receding forehead, low cranial vault, supraorbital torus, midfacial prognathism—Vandermeersch defined the skeleton as Neandertal (Vandermeersch, 1981, p. 286).

St. Cesaire, the most recent Neandertal known from Europe, was recovered from a bed of discarded chipped blades, hand axes, and other stone tools of a type called "Chatelperronian."

Several questions immediately arise: Did the Neandertals really disappear at about 40,000 y.a., as we have believed for so many years, or did the Neandertals and Upper Paleolithic moderns live side by side, at some social distance (without interbreeding)? Were Neandertals relegated to an inferior status by the more sophisticated moderns? Did they become fugitives in remote areas and survive there? (Some say they still survive today—see Issue at the beginning of this chapter.) How do we explain the existence of St. Cesaire, this Middle Paleolithic individual, in the Upper Paleolithic, long after Neandertals were supposed to have become extinct? At present, there is no answer to any of these questions that is widely accepted.

Figure 17-21   Shanidar.

◇ Neandertals Outside Europe

Tabun   Neandertals very similar to those of Western Europe are found in other parts of the world. From south of Haifa, Israel, about 50,000 y.a. (Jelinek, 1982) comes Tabun, with a low vault, prognathism, heavy brow ridges, but a nicely rounded occiput. The cranial capacity of Tabun 1, a female, is estimated at 1271 cm^3.

Shanidar   A most remarkable site is Shanidar, in the Zagros Mountains in northeastern Iraq, where partial skeletons of nine male and female individuals—seven adults and two infants—were found, four of them deliberately buried. These are quite typically classic, although the nuchal torus is weak, the occiput is fairly well rounded, and an incipient chin is present on at least one of the jaws. Several skulls look deformed, as if their foreheads had been bound as children (Trinkaus, 1984). Cranial deformation is known from several areas of the world in very recent times.

One of the more interesting individuals is Shanidar 1, a male who lived to a fairly old age for his time, between 35 and 50. His stature is estimated at 5 feet 7 inches, with a cranial capacity of 1600 cm^3, a bit over the European Neandertal mean of 1510 cm^3. The right side of his body suffered a crushing injury that affected his right arm, clavicle, scapula, and lower right limb. The injury may have been due to a rockfall, or it is possible that the atrophy of the right arm was the result of nerve injury suffered from severe damage to his left eye. It is also possible that his right arm was amputated at the elbow, which, if true, is the first evidence of deliberate human surgery (See Trinkaus, 1982, 1983; Stringer and Trinkaus, 1981).

Another individual, Shanidar 4, was deliberately buried on his left side, legs drawn up against his chest in a flexed position. Pollen analysis of the soil associated with the skeleton indicates the presence of a number of spring flowers (hyacinths, daisies, hollyhocks, and bachelor's button) that had apparently been placed on the grave at the time of death (Solecki, 1971).

Neandertals must have lived dangerously, if the Shanidar evidence has been interpreted correctly. An atrophied arm, a crushing eye fracture resulting in blindness in that eye, arm and foot fractures, skull scars, and various rib injuries were found on several of the adult male skeletons. Shanidar 3 suffered a rib injury that may have been caused by a stabbing. One of his ribs was damaged by a sharp instrument that probably caused his death. If this were a deliberate stabbing, it would be the oldest known case of interpersonal violence; however, there is no way of knowing whether it was deliberate or

Figure 17-22   Sites: Tabun, Shanidar.

(a)

(b)

Figure 17-23 (*a*) The Tabun cave site, located about 15 miles south of Haifa, Israel. (*b*) A closer view of the Tabun cave.

Upper Paleolithic
Culture period noted for technological, artistic, and behavioral innovations. Also known for appearance of anatomically modern human beings. (See p. 534.)

accidental. No matter how it happened, Shanidar 3 was taken care of for at least several weeks and intentionally buried when he died (Trinkaus and Zimmerman, 1982).

Since many of the injuries were serious and the men survived for a time, some for years, it suggests that their social system was organized, that cooperation and care of the sick and disabled were an important value of their culture. Intentional burials and flowers placed on a grave are evidence of a special attitude toward death and perhaps a belief in a future life and the supernatural.

Teshik-Tash   In Soviet Uzbekistan, in a cave at Teshik-Tash, we find another deliberate burial. A nine-year-old boy, with a cranial capacity of 1,490 cm³, was buried in a shallow grave surrounded by five pairs of wild goat horns, suggesting a burial ritual or perhaps a religious cult. Like many other Neandertals, Teshik-Tash is a mixture of Neandertal traits (heavy brow ridges and occipital bun) and modern traits (high vault and definite signs of a chin).

Maba*   Finally, extending the range of Neandertals from Western Europe across Asia to southeastern China is Maba, Qujiang County, Guangdong. The characters of this middle-aged male are similar, yet different, from those of Western Europe. "The browridge is robust and protruding" and the skull bones are about the same thickness as Neandertal. "The height of the skull and the angle of the forehead are also similar to those of Neanderthal [but] obviously different from the typical Neanderthal of Western Europe" (Wu, 1982, p. 475).

◇ Contemporary Upper Pleistocene Forms

Living at about the same time as Neandertals are forms we have called contemporaries of Neandertal. These forms do not fit the physical pattern of Neandertals, nor are they quite **Upper Paleolithic** *H. sapiens* (See Box 17-2, p. 527). Contemporaries exhibit what appear to be both Neandertal and anatomically modern traits that seem to represent an evolutionary trend toward Upper Paleolithic moderns. Some of these, in fact, may well be considered transitional between Neandertals and *H. sapiens sapiens* of the Upper Paleolithic. Examples of such contemporaries who may be transitional have been found in Europe, the Near East, and Africa.

EUROPE

Hortus   Found by the de Lumleys, Hortus combines archaic and modern features, seen especially in mandibles and teeth.

Vindija   At middle levels of Vindija, in Yugoslavia, higher up in the sequence than the Neandertals from this same site, are remains dated at somewhat

Figure 17-24   Sites: Teshik-Tash, Maba.

*Formerly spelled Mapa. Chinese paleoanthropologist Wu uses Maba spelling.

◇ Box 17-2   Characteristics of Anatomically Moderns and Their Differences from Neandertals

THE CRANIUM

1. Cranial capacity, ranging from about 1,000–2,000 cm³ with a mean of 1,400 cm³, is only slightly higher than the Neandertal average
2. The forehead is more vertical, brow ridges are absent to moderate and never continuous across the orbits; ridges are slightly separated over the middle of each orbit
3. The skull vault is higher
4. There is little prognathism and the face hangs more or less vertically below the forehead
5. Alongside the nose is a canine fossa

6. A chin is always present
7. The occiput is rounded with little or no bun or strong torus
8. Maximum breadth of the skull is high on the parietals
9. Skull bones are thinner

POSTCRANIUM

1. Bone thickness throughout the entire body is reduced
2. Musculature is reduced
3. Marked curvature of long bones is lacking

---

less than 27,000 y.a. and associated with Aurignacian (Upper Paleolithic) artifacts. These later Vindija fossils have been compared to both Neandertals and Upper Paleolithic populations, and appear to indicate an evolutionary trend from Neandertals to anatomically moderns (Smith, 1982).

ISRAEL

Skhūl   Also from south of Haifa, close to the Tabun site (p. 524), comes Skhūl, dated between 35,000 and 40,000 y.a. Skhūl is represented by at least ten individuals with remarkable variability. The brow ridges are prominent on one skull, but less so on others; the chin is also variable, as is the occipital bun. The skull vault is higher and the anterior teeth a bit smaller (both of these are modern traits). The variability of this sample has been explained as a process of evolutionary change leading to anatomically moderns, although not all paleoanthropologists agree.

Qafzeh   South of Nazareth and about the same age as Skhūl, Qafzeh is quite similar to Skhūl in its combination of older and more modern traits.

Amud   Of uncertain date, Amud was found north of Lake Kinneret and, like Skhūl, also shows a mixture of Neandertal and anatomically modern traits. For example, Amud is platycephalic (flat-headed) like Neandertal, the supraorbital torus is large, the maxilla inflated, and the facial area prognathous. However, paralleling the modern features of the skulls discussed above, Amud's skull vault is high and the occiput lacks a nuchal torus. The brow ridges tend to separate into two parts above the middle of each orbit as they do in

Figure 17-25   Neandertal and contemporary sites in the Near East.

Figure 17-26 Cast, Skhūl V.

modern skulls. Amud had a very large cranial capacity, 1,740 cm³, and at 5 feet 8 inches was one of the tallest Near Eastern individuals.

NORTHWEST AFRICA

Djebel Irhoud (Morocco)   Perhaps in the range of 50,000 y.a., Skull II from this site in northwest Africa can be compared to Skhūl from Israel as a mixture of Neandertal and anatomically modern characters.

EAST AFRICA

Omo (Ethiopia)   Omo I comes from the Kibish Formation of the Omo site in southern Ethiopia, where very old hominid remains were also found (p. 427). The Kibish formation has been given a date of 130,000 years, but there are serious doubts about this. Parts of a calvarium and some postcranial fragments, including pieces of femur, were excavated. Kennedy (1984) studied the reconstructed femur and concluded that it should be classified as anatomically modern. Because of the unresolved questions about the date and the fragmentary nature of the skull, we have placed Omo in this archaic rather than fully anatomically modern, stage. Omo II, also found in the Kibish formation, is considered more archaic than Omo I.

Ndutu   This specimen was also originally assigned to *H. erectus* (see p. 496), but a recent reexamination by Rightmire (1983) notes that the occipital and temporal areas point in the direction of *H. sapiens*. Rightmire also sees similarities with Kabwe and Bodo.

Laetoli Hominid 18   In 1976, in the Ngaloba beds overlying the area where Mary Leakey found the now famous footprints of early australopithecines (p. 423), was recovered a well-preserved skull with resemblances to Omo, Kabwe, Bodo, and Ndutu. L.H. 18, like these, shows a combination of *H. erectus* and *H. sapiens* characteristics, probably more like the latter than the former. The skull is small, 1,200 cm³, and has been dated to about 120,000 y.a. (Day et al., 1980; Kennedy, 1980).

SOUTH AFRICA

Kabwe (Broken Hill)   A complete skull and some skeletal fragmentary material were recovered in 1921 from a shallow mine shaft in Kabwe, Zambia (formerly Northern Rhodesia). Kabwe has been a puzzle from the day it was found. It has been called Neandertal and neandertaloid, but conformation of the massive brow ridges (among the largest known), small brain (1,200 cm³), neck muscle attachments, and large teeth raise doubts about its affiliation with Western European Neandertals. Characteristics of the occiput, frontal bone, and parietals have led Rightmire (1976) to refer it to archaic *sapiens* and give it a formal designation as *Homo sapiens rhodesiensis*. The dating for Kabwe is uncertain, but faunal association and amino acid racemization analysis suggest it is at least 110,000 years old.

Figure 17-27 The Skhūl cave.

Elandsfontein (Hopefield, Saldanha)   Skeletal material found at Elandsfontein near Hopefield, Saldanha Bay, on the west coast of South Africa, is quite similar to Kabwe. Dating is uncertain, although a Middle Pleistocene date has been suggested.

Florisbad   In 1932, T. F. Dreyer found a partial skull near Florisbad, about thirty miles north of Bloemfontein, South Africa. The skull includes portions of parietal, frontal, and facial bones. In the past, Florisbad was considered anatomically modern and similar to the present-day San people (p. 314). However, Rightmire (1978) restudied the original fossil material and concluded that Florisbad is not as modern as once believed. Florisbad, he states, resembles archaic (*sapiens*) hominids like Kabwe and Elandsfontein, and he places it roughly intermediate between archaic *sapiens* and recent *Homo sapiens*. Dating this material has been difficult, but Rightmire gives it a date much older than 42,000 years ago.

Summarizing the evidence from the early Upper Pleistocene (third interglacial and early fourth glacial), we find two aspects of human evolution occurring at the same time. First, there is a trend toward anatomically modern *H. sapiens*, attributed to changes in diet, improved technology, or adaptations to local ecological conditions. This trend culminates in the appearance of the modern forms about 40,000 years ago. Second, there is a specialized *sapiens*, the classic Neandertals, who inhabit the Near East, central and eastern Asia, and especially Western Europe. Exactly what their relationship is to those evolving into anatomically moderns is still a matter of dispute. Finally, the specialized form of classic Neandertal has never been explained, although a number of anthropologists lean toward F. Clark Howell's theory of adaptation to cold weather.

One of the serious problems in working out the Neandertal evolution and their relationship to other hominid populations (both *H. erectus* and *H. sapiens sapiens*) is the lack of chronometric dates. Most Neandertal remains were discovered before ¹⁴C and K/Ar techniques were developed. (Also, the sites were excavated before the more rigorous archeological methods of recent years were developed, and material that might have been invaluable for dating purposes was ignored or discarded.) Furthermore, most Neandertals lived between the outer limits of both dating methods—too long ago for ¹⁴C and too recently for K/Ar; although some Neandertals have been ¹⁴C dated. Therefore, much of Neandertal dating has been based on stratigraphy and correlated with associated faunal remains. Many of these dates are uncertain, and it is not always possible to know which fossil is older and which younger. Consequently, the place of Neandertal in human phylogenetic schemes and the trends of Neandertal evolution are still frustratingly vague.

It should be emphasized that much of the discussion and research regarding Neandertals and Middle/Upper Paleolithic transitional forms has centered on Near Eastern and Western European fossils. In the past fifteen years or so, there has been a resurgence of interest in African material for this equivalent period. New finds (such as Bodo, Ndutu, Laetoli Hominid 18, and others) and restudy and reinterpretation of earlier finds (such as Kabwe, Elandsfontein, Omo, and Florisbad) have given rise to rethinking of human evolution in Africa.

Figure 17-28 Neandertal contemporary sites in Africa.

(a)

(b)

Figure 17-29 Broken Hill (Rhodesian Man). Kabwe, (a) Note very heavy supraorbital torus; (b) Photograph of cast.

Figure 17-30   Mousterian tools (after
Bordes).

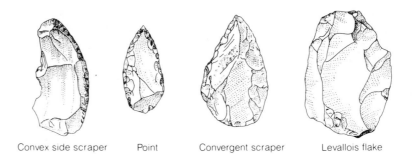

Convex side scraper   Point   Convergent scraper   Levallois flake

Similarities in East and South African skulls have suggested placing these individuals in the *H. sapiens rhodesiensis* subspecies, an evolutionary lineage separate and somewhat different from the Eurasian populations. It is also significant that dates (over 100,000 y.a.) provisionally assigned to these finds are earlier than the Neandertal and early Upper Paleolithic dates of Europe/Near East.

If these dates are found to be accurate, then it could be argued that a more sapient form evolved in Africa (probably South Africa) earlier than in Europe. Furthermore, if the early dates are valid, then there is the possibility that Neandertals in Europe were replaced by the more advanced sapient forms who immigrated from Africa. (But Smith, 1982, makes a strong case for gradual evolution from Neandertals to anatomically moderns in South-Central Europe.)

A number of paleoanthropologists have seriously considered these possibilities; however, until the nagging problem of dates, which are not at all clear, can be determined, the whole matter of human evolution in Africa for the Middle and Upper Pleistocene cannot be settled.

◇ Culture of Neandertals

Neandertals, who lived in the culture period known as the Middle Paleolithic, are usually associated with the Mousterian industry (although the Mousterian industry is not always associated with Neandertals), which had its roots in the Eemian interglacial, or even the Riss glacial. In the early Würm, Mousterian culture extended from the Atlantic Ocean across Europe and North Africa to the Soviet Union, Israel, Iran, and as far east as Uzbekistan and, perhaps, China.

Technology   Mousterian people specialized in the production of flake tools based on the Levallois method, a prepared core technique that originated perhaps as much as 200,000 y.a. A chunk of flint was chipped all the way round and on top, resembling a turtle in form, and then rapped on the side to produce a flake ready for use (Fig. 17-30).

Neandertals improved on the Levallois technique by inventing a variation. They trimmed the flint nodule around the edges to form a disc-shaped core.

Each time they struck the edge, they produced a flake until the core became too small and was discarded. Thus, the Neandertals were able to obtain more flakes per core than their predecessors. They then trimmed (retouched) the flake into various forms like scrapers, points, knives, and so on.

Neandertal craftsmen elaborated and diversified traditional methods, and there is some indication of development in the specialization of tools used in skin and meat preparation, hunting, woodworking, and perhaps hafting (attaching handles to tools). They may have made some use of new materials, such as antler and bone, but their specialization and innovation cannot be compared to the next culture period, the Upper Paleolithic. Nevertheless, the Neandertals advanced their technology, which tended to be similar in typology, over great geographic distances, far beyond that of *H. erectus*. It is quite likely that their modifications in technology laid the basis for the remarkable changes of the Upper Paleolithic.

Settlements People of Mousterian culture lived in a variety of open sites, caves, and rock shelters. Living in the open on the cold tundra suggests the erection of shelters, and there is some evidence of such structures, although the last glaciation must have destroyed many open sites. At the site of Moldova I, in the Ukraine region of the Soviet Union, archeologists found traces of an oval ring of mammoth bones, enclosing an area of about 26 by 16 feet, which may have been used to weigh down the skin walls of a temporary hut or tent. Inside the ring are traces of a number of hearths, hundreds of tools, thousands of waste flakes, and many bone fragments of animals probably brought home for comfortable dining around the fireplace.

Evidence for life in caves is abundant, and Mousterians must have occupied them extensively. Windbreaks of poles and skin were probably erected at the cave mouth for protection against the weather. Fire is in general use by this time, of course, and no doubt used for cooking, for warmth, and for keeping dangerous animals at bay.

How large were Neandertal settlements, and were they permanent or temporary? These questions are not yet answered, but Binford (1982) believes the settlements were short-term occupations used over and over again.

Religion An important innovation of the Middle Paleolithic is deliberate burial, often with indications of funerary ritual. Deliberate burials are common, as we have seen, at La Chapelle, La Ferrassie, Shanidar, and Teshik-Tash, and there are many others. At Teshik-Tash, we find an interesting ring of goat horns surrounding a child's grave, an arrangement that would certainly seem to indicate ritualism of some sort. Shanidar IV was buried with flowers, an act which may or may not suggest ritual, but which certainly does suggest a special attitude toward death. A remarkable burial occurs at the La Ferrassie rock shelter perhaps as much as 60,000 years ago. It looks like a family cemetery; the presumed parents are buried head to head and four children are interred neatly nearby. A short distance beyond, a small mound contains the bones of a newly born infant, and a bit further under a triangular stone is the grave of a six-year-old child.

Nodule

The nodule is chipped on the parameter.

Flakes are radially removed from top surface.

A final blow at one end removes a large flake.

Figure 17-31 The Levallois method.

Figure 17-32 Neandertal ritual and hunt. Neandertals are cutting up a wooly rhinoceros. The men to the left are offering pieces of meat to the rising sun. It is not known for certain whether this ritual was actually performed, but Neandertals did perform burial rituals. (Courtesy California Academy of Sciences)

Besides ritual burials, Neandertals also practiced a bear cult. At the back of the cave of Drachenloch, high up in the Swiss Alps, a stone chest was found containing seven bear skulls. Still farther back in the cave, six bear skulls had been set in niches along the walls, and limb bones placed next to them. At another site at Regourdu, in southern France, a pit covered by a heavy stone slab contained the bones of more than twenty bears, estimated to be nine feet tall and outweighing a grizzly.

From this extraordinary treatment of bear remains, Neandertals must have felt that bears were special. Perhaps they held these formidable foes in great respect, and the care taken with bear skulls and bones was an attempt to propitiate or soothe the ferocious spirits of these giant beasts. Some Siberians, Ainu of northern Japan, and a number of American Indian tribes, among others, also show a special ceremonial regard for bears.

Bears may not have been the only animals treated in a ritualistic manner. Ralph Solecki, who excavated Shanidar Cave (p. 524), found evidence of a deer ceremony in another cave in Lebanon. Neandertals had cut up a deer, placed the meat on a bed of stones, and sprinkled it with red ochre. The red ochre may have symbolized blood, and this ritual could have been a magical attempt to control deer, an animal the Neandertals hunted (Constable, 1973).

We mentioned earlier (p. 487) Peking Man's practice of cutting away the base of a human skull to remove the brain. Deep in the Guattari Cave, sixty miles south of Rome, Neandertals performed a similar ritual. Explorers found a human skull—the right side crushed and the foramen magnum area cut out—in the center of a circle of stones. Near the circle were several piles of deer, cattle, and pig bones. Apparently, the man had been killed (sacrificed?)

outside the cave, by a smashing blow to the right side of his head. His head was then taken into the cave and placed within the circle of bones.

What is the meaning of this remarkable activity? For the first time in human history, we find people who are concerned with more than the material aspects of life. Deliberately burying a corpse and depositing objects that belonged to him alongside his body reflects attitudes and values different from the ordinary. Death had meaning, perhaps mystical, something unknown, and Neandertals recognized that they had to come to terms with what they didn't understand.

Similarly with animal cults. Instead of earlier hunting practices of catch-as-catch-can, Neandertals were beginning to single out certain animals for game. Did they believe they could control their game animals? (If so, did these rituals serve as forerunners of Upper Paleolithic cave art that also may have been a form of hunting magic?) Were they attempting to help the animals multiply, improve their own hunting success, or increase the chances of their own safety? Do these rituals signify that Neandertals were becoming aware of their distinctiveness—they were something more than simply animals?

Figure 17-33   La Ferrassie burial.

(a)

(b)

Figure 17-34   Cast, Co-Magnon. (a) Lateral view; (b) frontal view.

Did the rituals reflect, as they do for many hunting peoples, that killing an animal leaves a void in the universe, and it is necessary to propitiate the animal's spirits to prevent an imbalance in the physical and spiritual universe?

No one, of course, knows the answers to these questions, and we don't even know for certain whether Neandertals believed in spirits, a future life, and the supernatural, but the evidence is irresistably suggestive.

Economy   Neandertals were successful hunters, as the abundant remains of animal bones at their sites demonstrate. As the evidence from Shanidar suggests, they probably gathered berries, nuts, and other plants. It does not appear that they sought more exotic foods, such as seafood or birds.

It is assumed that, in the freezing weather of the fourth glacial, Neandertals must have worn clothing to survive the winters—and they may have developed methods of curing skins. But since there is no evidence of sewing equipment, the clothing was probably of simple design. Nor is there evidence of personal ornaments or individual adornment, although these might be difficult to recognize.

Abstract Thought   Neandertal behavior, as deduced from the archeological and osteological evidence, is complex enough to reflect abstract ideas. Braidwood points to the "variety of combinations of the different basic habits or traditions of tool preparation" signifying "mixtures and blends of many of the other ideas and beliefs of these small groups" (Braidwood, 1975, p. 62). Therefore, there was not *one* Neandertal culture but "a great variety of loosely related cultures at about the same stage of advancement." For the first time in hominid history, we can see that humans have the ability to develop a variety of cultural adaptations to a variety of ecological conditions.

With the complexity of Neandertal life comes the question of communication, and scholars are not agreed that Middle Paleolithic people could communicate fluently on a symbolic basis (that is, via language). A controversial paper published a few years ago claims that Neandertals were unable to articulate easily because of the anatomical structure of their throats (Lieberman and Crelin, 1971). Given Neandertal brain size, their success in hunting, adaptation to severe weather, their technological improvements, and probably a well-developed social organization, most anthropologists would probably disagree.

◇ Upper Paleolithic and Homo Sapiens Sapiens

In Europe, during a warm break in the Würm glaciation, about 40,000 years ago, and elsewhere in the world at about the same time, two impressive events occurred in human evolution. Modern humans very similar to ourselves appear, and a remarkable change occurs in culture, especially in stone/bone tool technology. We shall attempt to deal later with the reason for the simultaneous appearance of these two events, but before opening that "can of worms," let us look at a sample of these early anatomically modern *sapiens*.

CRO-MAGNON

One of the first Upper Paleolithic hominids to be discovered (in 1868) comes from a rock shelter in the village of Cro-Magnon, near Les Eyzies, in the Dordogne of southern France. During the construction of a railway, workmen found the remains of five human skeletons that had been buried there between 20,000–30,000 y.a. Associated with the burials were faunal remains, worked flint, and other artifacts of the Aurignacian tradition. The best known of the five skeletons is the famous "Old Man of Cro-Magnon," who was between forty and fifty years of age when he died.

With a large brain (cranial capacity estimated at 1,590 cm³, larger than the average European today) the "Old Man" had a high forehead, protruding chin, nicely rounded occiput, and some development of the supraorbital ridges. He was an anatomically modern human being, and walking down the street dressed in modern clothes, he probably would be difficult to distinguish from a present-day European.

The term "Cro-Magnon" is often used synonymously with Upper Paleolithic moderns. However, considerable population variation was evident in Europe and elsewhere during this time. The following examples illustrate this variation.

Figure 17-35 Upper Paleolithic European Sites.

OTHERS

A neighbor of Cro-Magnon, who lived at approximately the same time, is Combe Capelle. This fossil reflects variability (which we have repeatedly emphasized) even within the same environment. Combe Capelle retains some Neandertal characteristics, such as facial prognathism, prominent brow ridges, and a considerably less developed chin than Cro-Magnon.

Some of the twenty-nine individuals of various ages and both sexes from Předmosti, Czechoslovakia, illustrate a European variation more like Combe Capelle than Cro-Magnon. A few skulls show strikingly pronounced supraorbital arches (modern), others have occipital buns, and one has a surprising amount of basal spongy bone.

Mladeč, also from Czechoslovakia, was found in association with an Aurignacian industry. Like Předmosti, the skulls possess neandertal-like traits.

During the late Pleistocene, anatomically modern *H. sapiens* appear in several regions of Africa. In North Africa, fragments of more than fifty skeletons were uncovered at Afalou-bou-Rhummel, Algeria. Except for rugged brow ridges, the skulls are completely modern. Other sites in North Africa have been found in Algeria, Morocco, the Sudan, and Egypt.

Anatomically moderns have also been found at sites in East Africa—at Lake Turkana and Olduvai, where early hominids were also found, and at Lukenya Hill in Kenya. In South Africa, remains have been found at Boskop, Fish Hoek, Springbok Flats, and Border Cave. Recently, Dr. Rightmire (1979) suggested that the Border Cave cranium is not only anatomically modern (similar to present-day Hottentots), but perhaps as much as 115,000 years old. This would mean, as discussed on p. 530, that anatomically moderns evolved earlier in Africa than in Europe or elsewhere. However, it has not been

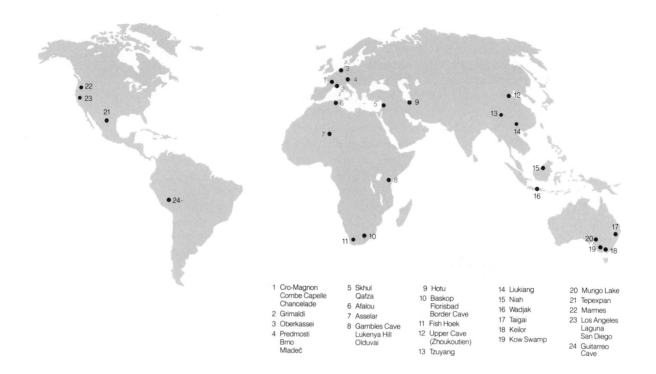

1	Cro-Magnon	5	Skhul	9	Hotu	14	Liukiang	20	Mungo Lake
	Combe Capelle		Qafza	10	Baskop	15	Niah	21	Tepexpan
	Chancelade	6	Afalou		Florisbad	16	Wadjak	22	Marmes
2	Grimaldi	7	Asselar		Border Cave	17	Taigai	23	Los Angeles
3	Oberkassei	8	Gambles Cave	11	Fish Hoek	18	Keilor		Laguna
4	Predmosti		Lukenya Hill	12	Upper Cave	19	Kow Swamp		San Diego
	Brno		Olduvai		(Zhoukoutien)			24	Guitarreo
	Mladeč			13	Tzuyang				Cave

Figure 17-36 Upper Paleolithic hominid fossil sites. Only better-known fossils are listed on the map. Note that for the first time humans lived on all continents.

an easy task to arrive at an acceptable Border Cave date, which remains debatable.

In the Far East, modern humans appeared as early as they did in Europe. In fact, the Niah Cave of North Borneo has yielded one of the earliest *H. sapiens sapiens* so far discovered. A ¹⁴C date of 40,000 years has been assigned to the skull of this teenage female. In China, from the site of Peking Man at Zhoukoudian, seven or eight individuals were found higher up in the cave, known as Upper Cave. Farther south, at Liukiang, a female cranium and postcranial material were discovered, and from Tzuyang, in Szechuan province, comes another female skull.

Modern skulls have also been found in Java and Australia. From Wadjak, Java, come two skulls excavated in the 1890s by Dubois in his search for the "missing link," and which are said to resemble (and are perhaps ancestral to) present-day Australian aborigines. A skull found at Keilor, ten miles north of Melbourne, Australia, has been carbon-dated at about 15,000 years and resembles the two modern skulls Dubois recovered from Java. From south Queensland comes the Talgai skull and, from Victoria, the Cohuna skull.

An important site recently excavated at Mungo Lake, New South Wales, may be 35,000 years old or more. This site contains tools, cremations (probably the earliest known), and anatomically modern human remains reflecting a gracile form. At Kow Swamp in Central Victoria, over 40 burials of robust, big-boned individuals, reminiscent of Java Solo Man, were excavated and dated at about 10,000 y.a. As in the manner of the Shanidar people of Iran, head deformation may have been practiced at Kow Swamp. It is interesting that the much earlier Mungo Lake people appear more modern-looking than the robust Kow Swamp population.

Studies are presently being conducted to determine where in Indonesia the early Australians came from, and when. However, native Australians are demanding the return, for reburial, of all bones and artifacts that have been excavated, and government agencies are sympathetic. Paleoanthropologists and archeologists hope they will have sufficient opportunity to complete their study of bones and artifacts before this occurs.

◇ The New World

Anthropologists generally agree that modern *H. sapiens* entered the New World across the Bering Strait some time in the past 40,000 years. Most likely this movement would have occurred during the last glaciation (Wisconsin in New World terminology) when a land bridge some 1,300 miles from north to south joined Asia to North America. The newcomers settled in central Alaska, which was free from ice, and later made their way east, into present-day Canada, and, later, into what is now the United States, Mesoamerica, and South America. The two ice sheets that covered Canada during the last (Wisconsin) glaciation must have separated to let the wanderers travel south, but geologists are not quite sure when the separation(s) occurred. A great deal of research and discussion has been going on for years by geologists, paleontologists, archeologists, and paleoanthropologists to solve the riddle of when these treks into Alaska and continental areas of the New World were made.

There are (at least) two schools of thought on the matter: (1) Those who believe that these hunters came across the Bering Strait at least 40,000 y.a. and (2) others who claim there is no *solid* evidence beyond about 12,500 y.a. Archeological evidence is abundant for the more recent date, and this evidence is quite common in the western United States, where the early projectile points known as Folsom and Clovis were found. However, there are a number of sites that may be considerably older than 12,000 years, and it is possible that human occupation in the New World may prove to be 40,000 years old or more.

The earliest people of the New World are known as big game hunters, the big game being mammoths and other large animals, which they hunted with spears or lances and also by driving them into a surround or over a cliff.

All of the excavated bone material (which is scarce) indicates these early inhabitants were anatomically modern humans. As a matter of fact, there is little acceptable osteological evidence that can be dated much more than 12,000 years or so ago. Tepexpan in Mexico and Marmes in Washington State are dated at 11,000 y.a., and Guitarrero Cave in Peru at 12,500 y.a. California specimens from Laguna, Los Angeles, and San Diego are sometimes given older dates, but these are debatable. No hard evidence at all exists for any type of human in the New World except anatomically modern *H. sapiens*— no Neandertals, no Bigfoot!

Figure 17-37   The punch blade technique.

◇ Upper Paleolithic Culture

TECHNOLOGY

About 40,000 years ago (perhaps more) anatomically modern humans begin to appear (although they may not have been present in Europe until several thousand years later). Associated with these newly evolved moderns are new technological techniques and new tools, quite different from the Mousterian of the Neandertals. The major technological difference between the earlier Mousterian and the Upper Paleolithic is the shift from flake to blade tools. A blade is a parallel-sided flake, at least twice as long as it is wide, with sharp cutting edges that make an excellent knife. The contribution of Upper Paleolithic peoples to blade manufacture was the introduction of the punch technique, in which numerous identical blades from a core of flint were punched out.

Using the blades as blanks, anatomically moderns produced a wide variety of tools, one of the characteristics of Upper Paleolithic technology. It is interesting to note that, while the variety of tools and the materials they were made from increased, Neandertals were more efficient in their use of flint. Not only did the Mousterians use fewer strokes manufacturing a tool, but they produced more cutting edges from a pound of flint, as we can see in a comparison of the following industries (the Mousterian increase is *five* times the Acheulian; the anatomically modern is *three* times the Mousterian).

	Inches Per Pound of Flint
Upper Paleolithic	120
Mousterian	40
Acheulian	8
Oldowan	2

Much regional variability existed in the Mousterian, but in the Upper Paleolithic the variation seems to be more evolutionary. That is, contemporaneous assemblages are very similar, though they change quickly over time. French archeologist F. Bordes, a specialist in Paleolithic tools, identified 62 tool types for Lower and Middle Paleolithic typologies, which together cover about 2 million years. M. Denise de Sonneville-Bordes has identified 112 types for the 30,000 years of the Upper Paleolithic, a period of much more variability among tool types.

The shaping of bone, antler, and teeth prevails in the Upper Paleolithic. In the Mousterian, bone tools were scarce, although unshaped bone fragments were probably used as tools. But even the earliest Upper Paleolithic displays large bone assemblages.

Also prominent in the Upper Paleolithic tool kit is the *burin* (or graver) used for (*a*) engraving on bone and stone and (*b*) making grooves in wood and bone that could then be used as handles or shafts for other tools. The cutting edge at the end of a burin is transverse like a chisel, and, as a matter of fact, the burin may be considered the first chisel.

A bewildering variety of rapidly changing tool types was available to these

Burin

Figure 17-38   A burin.

hunters, especially in Europe: knives, many kinds of points, notched blades used as spokeshaves (to prepare shafts for spears, for example), awls, drills, borers, scrapers of various types, spear-throwers (the first artificial propulsive devices invented by humans), throwing sticks, clubs, shaft straighteners—and this list is only a partial one. They were clearly a technologically oriented people.

Personal ornaments—pendants and decorated objects—made of antler, shell, and bone suggest that Upper Paleolithic people were developing an increasing awareness of personal, and perhaps group, identity. For whatever reason or reasons, Upper Paleolithic populations produced a culture that is noted for its rapid change, variety, artistic achievement, and comparative sophistication.

Since much of what is known about the Upper Paleolithic is based on European sites, it may be beneficial to discuss this period in Europe in more detail.

The Upper Paleolithic of Europe must focus on sites known in France. Archeological investigation began here in the 1850s, and the country produced the first Cro-Magnon and Neandertal major finds. Much of the Upper Paleolithic technology and typologies has been worked out based on the extremely rich area east of Bordeaux along the Dordogne River. In this approximately twelve-square-mile region over 200 Paleolithic sites have been found, some with 20–25 feet of deposit.

In addition to the previously mentioned shift from flakes to blades, there is also a shift in the faunal exploitation patterns. The Middle Paleolithic is characterized by a generalized exploitation, with one species (out of fifteen present), usually accounting for a maximum of 50% of the animals. In the Upper Paleolithic, a single species (reindeer) usually makes up 80% of the animals. Fishing and hunting of waterfowl and other birds become common. The fifteen to twenty large herbivores present at the time were often not hunted, since reindeer were preferred.

Middle Paleolithic (Mousterian) sites are seldom larger than 300–400 square yards and are fairly restricted. The Upper Paleolithic witnessed a population explosion of sorts, with sites of over 7,000 square yards as well as many small sites.

Not until the Upper Paleolithic does one find frequent evidence of habitation structures in France. At Pincevant, careful excavations of an occupation site were conducted so that none of the workers touched the floor but were suspended overhead. An interesting feature of these habitation structures was that they almost always faced to the south or southwest.

The Upper Paleolithic introduced many exotic raw materials into the material culture. For example, shells were present 300 miles from the Mediterranean Sea, but are never found this far inland in Mousterian sites.

In the approximately 30,000 years of the Upper Paleolithic (from roughly 40,000 y.a. to 10,000 y.a.) a sequence of cultural traditions may be traced in Europe (see Table 17-1). During this time the weather in Europe was warm, beginning with an interstadial, then fluctuating warm and cool and becoming cold around 30,000 years ago. After a brief interstadial about 20,000 years ago, the ice returns with the final Würm stage climaxing at about 18,000 years ago. Sometime around 10,000 years ago, we enter the **Holocene**, or Present.

Holocene
Entirely recent; the epoch following the Pleistocene; the Present.

Figure 17-39 Upper Paleolithic economy. A common method of hunting used in recent times in North America. This method involves driving a herd over a cliff where they could be easily killed by the hunters. (Courtesy California Academy of Sciences)

Table 17-1   Upper Paleolithic Cultures*

Glacial	Time (YEARS AGO)	Culture Periods	Hominids
	10,000		Anatomically
	17,000	Magdalenian	
LATE	20,000–	Solutrean	Modern
	25,000	Gravettian	
WÜRM	30,000–	Aurignacian	Human
	32,000	Chatelperronian	
	40,000		Beings

*Times are not necessarily precise, and culture period sequence is only suggestive.

Figure 17-40   Pincevant.

Figure 17-41   Chatelperronian tool.

The innovative Upper Paleolithic peoples developed surprisingly sophisticated cultures compared to the Neandertals. We shall briefly discuss these cultures as they developed in southwestern France, where so much archeology has been accomplished.

Chatelperronian   We may not be certain of the fate of classic Neandertals, whether they were eliminated or assimilated by, or evolved into, the ancestors of anatomically moderns, or whether they met some unimaginable end. But their Mousterian technology lingered on, at least for a time. The Chatelperronian of 32,000 years ago, the earliest of Upper Paleolithic industries, is located directly above Mousterian levels and contains numerous and varied scrapers, Mousterian points, and other evidence of Mousterian features. This period is probably a transitional one between Middle and Upper Paleolithic industries.

Aurignacian   In the Europe of 30,000 years ago, the weather becomes colder and a venturesome group of people from the central and eastern parts of Europe migrate into the culturally backward country of Western Europe. Excellent hunters (well known as Cro-Magnons), they brought with them the industry known as Aurignacian. Bone and antler, worked by splitting, sawing, and rubbing down, were the primary tool materials.

Cro-Magnons of the Aurignacian were artists and may have sculpted the female figurines, known as Venuses or mother-goddesses, which emphasize female sexual traits and could have been fertility symbols.

Aurignacian sites are more frequent and larger than those of Chatelperronians, suggesting Cro-Magnons lived in more populous groups and with good sense selected shelter in deep valleys where they would be protected from the severe cold.

Gravettian   For some reason, Aurignacian culture ebbs as another culture, the Gravettian, becomes more prominent in southern France. It begins about 25,000 years ago, a time of relatively mild climate which then becomes extremely cold.

Gravettian tools continue the Chatelperronian style. Bone becomes more common as a tool material and is used for the manufacture of awls, punches, and simple points. The great art of the Upper Paleolithic, seen in Lascaux Cave, begins during this period.

Solutrean   Both Gravettian and Aurignacian, two separate traditions, apparently disappear around 20,000 years ago to be replaced by the Solutrean. Who the Solutreans are and where they came from is another Upper Paleolithic mystery. Pfeiffer suggests their ancestors may have been Neandertals who had been isolated in the rugged mountain country of southeast France (Pfeiffer, 1978). It is possible they may be the Upper Paleolithic equivalent of Bigfoot, but rumors of surviving Neandertals have excited the imagination of credulous people for thousands of years.

In any case, this tradition did not endure for long, a few thousand years at most. It is best known for remarkable flintwork expressed in magnificent, pressure-flaked lanceheads.

Figure 17-42   Venus of Willendorf.

Magdalenian   The "brilliant Solutrean culture, which carried flintworking to one of its highest levels, suddenly disappeared in somewhat mysterious circumstances" (Bordes, 1968, p. 159). Replacing it is the Magdalenian, which directly overlies the Solutrean levels. Since the implements of the two traditions are so different, Solutrean representing one of the great achievements in stone-chipping and Magdalenian one of the poorest (at least at first), it is impossible the latter could have evolved from the former.

Although its origins are obscure, the Magdalenian is a spectacular period of technological growth that developed during the last major advance of the final Pleistocene glaciation. Large herds of reindeer that roamed the tundra of Western Europe are a major game animal, and mammoth, wild horse, bison, and a host of smaller animals are also hunted. It is a time of affluence; Magdalenians spread out over Europe, living in caves and open-air camps, and achieve a higher density of population than any of their predecessors.

They excel in the use of bone and antler in fashioning a variety of tools, weapons, and miscellaneous objects, which they often decorated beautifully. Upper Paleolithic art, already well advanced in Gravettian times, reaches its peak in the Magdalenian, and the cave art of this period in southwest France and northeast Spain is one of the world's great artistic achievements.

THE PROBLEM OF NEANDERTALS AND ANATOMICALLY MODERN HUMANS

With this review of the Upper Paleolithic, we are ready to address the question posed earlier: How is it possible to explain the sudden appearance of Upper Paleolithic (1) anatomically modern humans and (2) their sophisticated culture, especially in Western Europe? Both culture and anatomically moderns appear so suddenly (or so it seems) about 40,000 years ago that many scholars in the past have been reluctant to credit Neandertals with any part of the cultural achievements or genetic development of Upper Paleolithic peoples. (For further discussion see Brace, 1964.)

Actually, Upper Paleolithic moderns did not appear suddenly; there were

Figure 17-43   Solutrean blade. This is the best-known work of the Solutrean tradition. Solutrean stone work is considered the best of the Upper Paleolithic.

already indications of modern traits in some of the classic Neandertals of the Würm, such as La Ferrassie, and in contemporaries, such as Qafzeh and Jebel Irhoud. Furthermore, the Upper Paleolithic populations themselves display some Neandertal traits. A recent discovery at St. Césaire, France, nicely illustrates this point. An incomplete skeleton, morphologically Neandertal both in skull and limb bones, was found in a Chatelperronian level of the Upper Paleolithic. According to Vandermeersch, this find is evidence that Neandertals did not become extinct at the end of the Middle Paleolithic. "Some of them were still extant at the beginning of the Upper Paleolithic and were contemporaneous with the first European *Homo sapiens sapiens*" (Vandermeersch, 1981, p. 286).

To account for the change from Neandertal to modern, Brace suggests that Upper Paleolithic technology reduced the adaptive significance of the huge Middle Paleolithic dentition and the facial structure that supported it (Brace and Montagu, 1977, p. 335). The result was smaller teeth, smaller jaws, and less bone for the attachment of the smaller muscles of the masticatory apparatus. Thus, the Upper Paleolithic skull.

There remains the second part of the question: Why the sudden appearance of the superior Upper Paleolithic culture? Again, we find that this appearance was *not* sudden. Early Upper Paleolithic industry (Chatelperronian) included much Mousterian (Neandertal) influence, and industries that followed were influenced to some extent by the Chatelperronian. It has also been suggested that Upper Paleolithic peoples possessed a fully articulated

Figure 17-44 Magdalenian material. During this last period of the Upper Paleolithic, artistic expression reached its greatest height.

Figure 17-45 Cave painting. A fine painting of a bison bellowing.

language that would have given them a decided advantage over their predecessors, who lacked this ability. However, we have already pointed out that the claim of Neandertal inability to articulate fully has been frequently disputed. Marschack (1972) believes Upper Paleolithic superiority may have been due to the people's ability to make notational counts. Keeping track of references to past and future events would be of some advantage, and it may possibly account for the rapid development of Upper Paleolithic technology, but the connection is not an easy one to perceive.

These are not fully satisfactory answers, and the problem remains unsettled.

◇ Summary

Archaic *Homo sapiens* first appear about 300,000 years ago and, possessing both *H. erectus* and *H. sapiens* traits, is considered transitional between the two forms.

Early Neandertals are present in the Eemian interglacial, followed by transitional forms apparently evolving in the direction of anatomically modern *H. sapiens* (who are definitely present in the Upper Paleolithic by about 40,000 years ago). During the early Würm glacial, Neandertals, more specialized than other *H. sapiens*, appear in Western Europe and areas of the Near East. Hominids contemporary with Neandertals are found in northwestern, eastern, and southern Africa. Several of the African forms, according to some paleoanthropologists, are considered to be anatomically modern and considerably older than the date usually given for the appearance of anatomically moderns. Questions have been raised about both their dates and their modern morphology.

Neandertals introduced technological innovations, changes in settlement patterns, and ways of obtaining food. They may have been the first humans to practice some form of religious ceremonies. Mousterian industries, associated with Neandertals of the Middle Paleolithic, are succeeded by Upper Paleolithic industries associated with anatomically modern *sapiens*. In Europe, especially, anatomically moderns are known for the variety of new tools and toolmaking techniques, new food sources, more permanent shelters, artistic achievements, and a generally more sophisticated culture.

Recent finds in Australia suggest movements of gracile moderns from Indonesia as early as 35,000 years ago. The problem of entrance of human populations into the New World remains unsolved.

Several questions are raised in this chapter: What is the phylogenetic line from *H. erectus* to *H. sapiens sapiens*? Was this transition rapid (punctuated equilibrium) or gradual? What is the role of classic Neandertals in the evolution of anatomically modern humans? Is there a relationship between Africans believed to be anatomically modern and Upper Paleolithic populations of Europe? Did anatomically moderns migrate to Europe and displace, in some fashion, the Neandertals? How is Upper Paleolithic technology related to that of the Middle Paleolithic?

Possible solutions to most of these questions have been suggested. Unfortunately, however, entirely satisfactory answers are still unavailable.

◇ Questions for Review

1. Define "transitional forms."
2. List the physical traits that characterize *Homo sapiens*.
3. Why are Steinheim, Swanscombe, and Arago considered transitional?
4. How do Neandertals differ from *H. erectus* on the one hand and anatomically modern humans on the other?
5. What are the differences between the pre-*sapiens*, pre-Neandertal, and the Neandertal phase of man hypotheses?
6. What does the evidence of the Eemian interglacial tell us about human evolution?
7. What is the "Neandertal problem"?
8. Why is La Chapelle-aux-Saints considered an important fossil?
9. Describe Mousterian culture.
10. What does the evidence suggest for the intellectual (including communication) ability of Neandertals?
11. What is meant by contemporary forms?
12. Describe the variation of physical characteristics of Upper Paleolithic peoples.
13. What technological innovations were introduced in the Upper Paleolithic?
14. Summarize the development of culture from the Chatelperronian to the end of the Upper Paleolithic.
15. How may the "sudden" appearance of anatomically modern humans and the rich Upper Paleolithic culture be explained?

◇ Suggested Further Reading

There is an immense literature, both popular and professional, dealing with Neandertals and Upper Paleolithic *sapiens* from almost every possible point of view. The following list is not intended to be either complete or comprehensive; the books listed are readable, useful, and are directly associated with chapter material.

Brace, C. Loring, Harry Nelson and Noel Korn. *Atlas of Human Evolution* (2nd Ed.), New York: Holt, Rinehart and Winston, 1979.
>   *A handy reference for well-known fossil hominids. The large and careful drawings of skulls are considered to be very accurate.*

Braidwood, Robert J. *Prehistoric Men*, Glenview, Ill.: Scott, Foresman and Co., 1967.
>   *Professor Braidwood has written an excellent overview of the prehistory of the Paleolithic. Tool illustrations are especially well done.*

Clark, W. E. Le Gros. *History of the Primates*, Chicago: The University of Chicago Press, 1966.
>   *An introduction to the study of fossil hominids by one of the outstanding anatomists of our time. Very useful for beginning students.*

Day, Michael. *Guide to Fossil Man* (3rd Ed.), Chicago: The University of Chicago Press, 1977.
>   *A selected list of hominids arranged by geographic area. Excellent background data for each hominid with photographs.*

Hogarth, Paul and Jean-Jacques Salomon. *Prehistory*, New York: Dell Publishing Co., 1962.
>   *Imaginative illustrations portray the history of the Paleolithic. Interesting overview.*

Kuhn, Herbert. *On the Track of Prehistoric Man*, New York: Random House, 1955.
>   *Popular account of Upper Paleolithic cave art.*

Oakley, Kenneth. *Man the Tool-maker*, Chicago: The University of Chicago Press, 1966.
>   *A remarkably good reference on Paleolithic technology by a well-known British prehistorian.*

Phenice, T. W. and N. J. Sauer. *Hominid Fossils*, Dubuque: Wm. C. Brown Co., 1977.
>   *An alphabetical illustrated summary of fossil hominids. Useful as a quick reference of Pleistocene hominids, with background information for each entry.*

Pfeiffer, John E. *The Emergence of Man*, New York: Harper & Row, Publishers, 1978.
>   *In his interesting fashion, Pfeiffer discusses the rise of* H. sapiens *at some length in Chapters 8–11. Highly recommended.*

Solecki, Ralph. *Shanidar: The First Flower People*, New York: Alfred A. Knopf, 1971.
>   *Well worth reading for its popular and detailed account of the dig at Shanidar Cave under the supervision of Dr. Solecki.*

Time-Life Books have already been highly recommended. The Neandertals *and* Cro-Magnon Man *should be read by every student.*

Trinkaus, Erik and Wm. H. Howells. "The Neandertals," *Scientific American*, December, 1979:118–133.
>   *An excellent summary of Neandertals by two specialists.*

Evolution: The Human Adventure

What does it mean to be human? Certainly, part of the answer is understandable in terms of organic evolution—as it applies to any animal. Indeed, we are animals, and the evolutionary process acts similarly on humans through the combined action of the evolutionary forces: mutation, genetic drift, migration, and natural selection. Human populations have evolved and continue to do so as gene frequencies shift in response to these forces.

Thus, our origins are ultimately traceable to the roots of life on this planet, close to 3.5 billion years ago (Gurin, 1980). The last 500 million years of evolution, as told by the fossil vertebrate record, informs us more directly of our immediate precursors. Even more specifically, we can trace our roots to the placental mammal radiation and from here to the beginnings of the primate order more than 60 m.y.a.

Through comparative studies of modern primates, prosimians, monkeys, apes, and ourselves, we are able to flesh out the bits and pieces of bones and teeth that comprise the fossil record of our primate ancestors. From such comparisons we know that early anthropoids began diverging in the Old World by probably 40 m.y.a. and the first hominoid is already on the scene by 20 m.y.a.

When, however, did the unique evolutionary radiation occur that produced the first hominid? The exact timing of this evolutionary event is still disputed, but evidence suggests a date somewhere between 10–5 m.y.a. for the appearance of the first member of the human family.

The first half of hominid evolutionary history is still clouded in mystery, but ongoing research by Richard Leakey, Donald Johanson, David Pilbeam, and others is aimed at filling in this gap. We now know considerably more about the last 5 million years. Abundant evidence from the Plio-Pleistocene of South and East Africa tells of a variety of early hominid forms. The earliest definite hominid—*Australopithecus afarensis*—is an extremely small-brained, but completely bipedal, hominid. It remains to be seen if this primitive hominid consistently made tools, but to date no stone artifacts have been found in association with this fossil form. Despite its relative primitiveness, *A. afarensis* may indeed be our ancestor.

A more definitive biocultural interaction among our ancestors is indicated by 2 m.y.a. At this time, early members of our genus (*Homo*) are emerging in Africa (also possibly Asia), and they are associated with stone tool remains at several localities. Not surprisingly, then, early members of the genus *Homo* show significantly larger brains than their australopithecine cousins—whom they eventually outcompeted.

The fossil record of our ancestors continues its saga with *Homo erectus*, transitional forms, a variety of *sapiens* forms (among them, Neandertal), and finally the appearance of fully modern humans (*Homo sapiens sapiens*) around 40,000 years ago.

This then, briefly, is the human evolutionary journey. But it is told to us in more than just morphological details of tooth and bone, for we *and* our ancestors are more than just physical organisms blindly following the dictates of organic evolution. Several million years ago our early hominid ancestors began culturally to modify their environments, thus drastically altering their ecological niche and henceforth setting a new direction for human evolution.

What we are and how we came to be that way can only be answered in terms of biocultural processes. Whether we are talking about the first crude attempts to knock a flake off a lava cobble or the landing of human beings on the moon, the process is a unified one. It may well be true that "man makyth tools" but it is equally true that "tools makyth man."

The results of our unique evolutionary history are recounted in the size and the structure of our brain, our dental apparatus, and our bipedal gait (with its manifold physical requirements). We, however, can also see the imprint of our special hominid origins in our behavior: our cultural abilities to make and use tools, our symbolic language, our passion to be social.

Indeed, as we have emphasized repeatedly, the physical structure of our body has been molded by evolutionary factors relating to concomitant development of *all* these behavioral characteristics. Does our evolution, then, *explain* our behavior? Today, there are those in biology and anthropology who believe that it does.

A new emphasis in behavioral biology developed over the last decade has recently been given the name "sociobiology" (Wilson, 1975; Barash, 1982). In its more restrained pragmatic applications, this approach attempts to understand social behavior among insects and birds in terms of natural selection models. In other words, sociobiology assumes that social behavior among these animals can be best understood by relating such behavior to reproductive success of individuals. In some cases, such as sterile "altruistic" worker castes among social insects, such a perspective is most helpful (Hamilton, 1964).

What, however, can we say about human behavior? Many popular writers have argued that humankind's current behavior involving territorial nation-states, organized warfare, etc. is merely an extension of hominid behavioral propensities developed during the last several million years. Often emphasized as a primary determinant in shaping human behavior is the role of hunting (Ardrey, 1976), creating a "killer-ape" (Morris, 1967).

We have seen that systematic hunting of big game did become an important factor in *erectus* times around 1 m.y.a. The behavioral demands of such social hunting *may* have selected for more cohesive social organization, more effective means of communication, and more specialized tools. These demands in turn *may* have placed a higher selection benefit on larger brains. It makes a neat model, but even at this level it is highly speculative. Neither the fossil record nor archeological traces inform us directly concerning the exact circumstances that caused increases in hominid brain size.

Even more speculative are the postulations concerning the determining influence of hunting on human aggression, territoriality, male/female differences, and so on. Given the nature of the evidence, such wanton speculation—no matter how intellectually appealing—is to be avoided.

What then can we say about the evolution of human behavior? The development of culture most assuredly has shaped our behavioral *capacities*. The facts that *Homo sapiens* characteristically has such a complex neurological foundation and that we are all capable of symbolic language reveal our biocultural evolutionary origins. However, the development of culture also created an entirely new realm of behavioral possibilities. Our hominid ancestors, like us, were symbol-making, cognitively complex animals. Their behavior, and ours, thus has a large element of choice built in. The capacity for language and culture is inherited, but the form it will take is *learned*. As such, our behavior is subject to considerable modification even during one individual's lifetime.

Humans are not blind gene-machines simply pursuing the ultimate end of greater individual reproductive success. *Unlike any other animal on earth* we have the possibility of almost infinite behavioral creativity; what is more, we have the self-awareness that such flexibility exists. By means of cognitive devices that Richard Dawkins calls "memes," humans have forever departed from the course of gene-determined biological evolution into the sphere of a culturally and symbolically mediated development (Dawkins, 1976).

While cultural norms (as applied to the group) and biological success (as applied to the individuals within the group) may occasionally come into conflict, over the long run they should harmonize to some degree (Cavalli-Sforza and Feldman, 1981). Without a viable interaction of biocultural elements, neither human beings—nor the human groups upon which we depend for survival—could be expected to long endure.

Hominid evolutionary development has created *Homo sapiens*, an animal with behavioral flexibility. In a sense, we are products of our evolution. But unlike any other organism on this planet we can infinitely mold our own behavior through exercise of our own uniquely human creativity.

Homo sapiens groups increased the pace of cultural modification around 10,000 years ago, and since then the process of biocultural evolution has continued to accelerate. With the development of agriculture and dense permanent settlements came new selection pressures, such as infectious disease. The spread of the sickle-cell trait in response to malarial pressures is our best example of such a natural selection process acting in human populations. The differential spread of the lactose tolerant/intolerant trait is another example of selection operating in a *cultural* environment.

Does this mean we have left the realm of biological evolution completely? By no means. Mutation still occurs, and the potential mutagenic effects of artificial radiation and chemicals pose the danger of still further increasing genetic "mistakes." Natural selection is also still operating in a very powerful way; perhaps as many as 85% of all the zygotes conceived never reproduce. Moreover, results of the accelerated pace of migration in the last five centuries are visible all around us.

What we are saying is that our profound ability to modify our environments has outdistanced our biological capacity to respond. As slowly maturing mammals, our generation span is considerably longer than most other animals. Unlike the mosquitoes that have biologically (adaptively) responded to massive environmental changes such as DDT, we cannot adapt so quickly. If mosquitoes had sprayed us continually with equal amounts of insecticides (which they might call "humanicides"), we almost certainly would have been completely wiped out.

How then can we be expected to cope with the new biological pressures of the modern technological world? Clearly, the biggest dangers are the cultural ones we have created for ourselves: overcrowding, pollution, radiation, and so forth. Equally clearly, the only viable answers are also cultural ones. As human beings we possess the capability to remake our world—for better or worse. The choices are ours.

Atlas of Primate Skeletal Anatomy

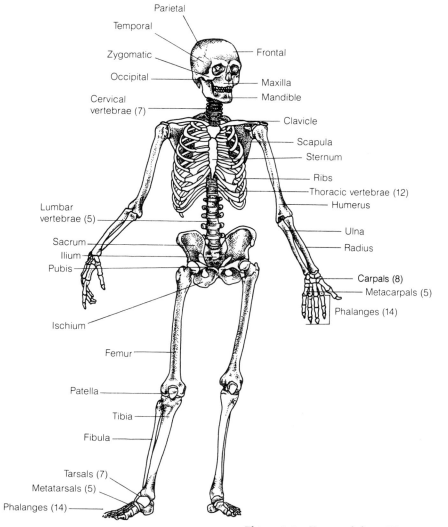

Parietal
Temporal
Zygomatic
Occipital
Cervical
vertebrae (7)
Frontal
Maxilla
Mandible
Clavicle
Scapula
Sternum
Ribs
Thoracic vertebrae (12)
Humerus
Lumbar
vertebrae (5)
Ulna
Radius
Sacrum
Ilium
Pubis
Carpals (8)
Metacarpals (5)
Phalanges (14)
Ischium
Femur
Patella
Tibia
Fibula
Tarsals (7)
Metatarsals (5)
Phalanges (14)

Figure A-1   Human skeleton (*Homo sapiens*)—bipedal hominid.

551

Figure A-2   Chimpanzee skeleton (*Pan troglodytes*) A knuckle-walking pongid.

CHIMPANZEE SKELETON

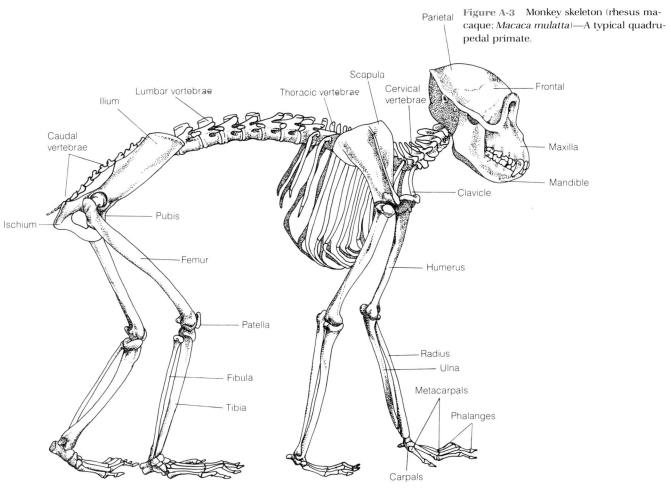

Parietal

Figure A-3   Monkey skeleton (rhesus macaque; *Macaca mulatta*)—A typical quadrupedal primate.

Scapula

Lumbar vertebrae

Thoracic vertebrae

Cervical
vertebrae

Frontal

Ilium

Caudal
vertebrae

Maxilla

Mandible

Ischium

Clavicle

Pubis

Femur

Humerus

Patella

Radius

Ulna

Fibula

Metacarpals

Tibia

Phalanges

Carpals

MONKEY SKELETON

Figure A-4   Human cranium.

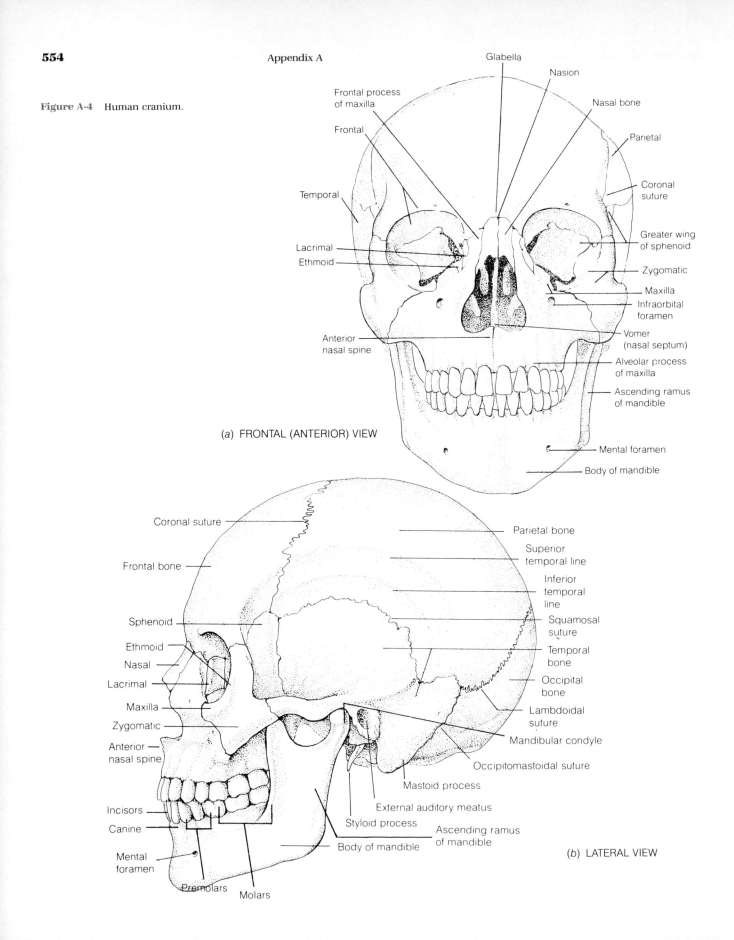

Glabella

Nasion

Nasal bone

Parietal

Frontal process
of maxilla

Frontal

Coronal
suture

Temporal

Greater wing
of sphenoid

Lacrimal

Zygomatic

Ethmoid

Maxilla

Infraorbital
foramen

Vomer
(nasal septum)

Anterior
nasal spine

Alveolar process
of maxilla

Ascending ramus
of mandible

(a) FRONTAL (ANTERIOR) VIEW

Mental foramen

Body of mandible

Coronal suture

Parietal bone

Superior
temporal line

Frontal bone

Inferior
temporal
line

Sphenoid

Squamosal
suture

Ethmoid

Temporal
bone

Nasal

Occipital
bone

Lacrimal

Maxilla

Lambdoidal
suture

Zygomatic

Mandibular condyle

Anterior
nasal spine

Occipitomastoidal suture

Mastoid process

Incisors

External auditory meatus

Canine

Styloid process

Ascending ramus
of mandible

Mental
foramen

Body of mandible

(b) LATERAL VIEW

Premolars   Molars

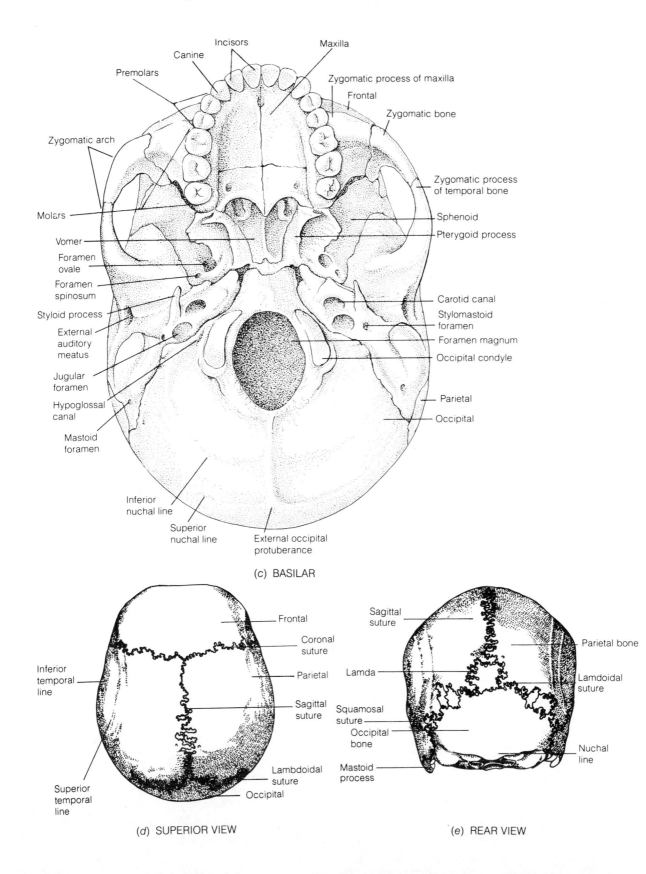

Incisors
Canine
Premolars
Maxilla
Zygomatic process of maxilla
Frontal
Zygomatic bone
Zygomatic arch
Zygomatic process
of temporal bone
Molars
Sphenoid
Pterygoid process
Vomer
Foramen
ovale
Foramen
spinosum
Styloid process
Carotid canal
Stylomastoid
foramen
Foramen magnum
External
auditory
meatus
Occipital condyle
Jugular
foramen
Parietal
Hypoglossal
canal
Occipital
Mastoid
foramen
Inferior
nuchal line
Superior
nuchal line
External occipital
protuberance

(c) BASILAR

Frontal
Coronal
suture
Inferior
temporal
line
Parietal
Sagittal
suture
Lambdoidal
suture
Superior
temporal
line
Occipital

(d) SUPERIOR VIEW

Sagittal
suture
Parietal bone
Lamda
Lamdoidal
suture
Squamosal
suture
Occipital
bone
Nuchal
line
Mastoid
process

(e) REAR VIEW

Figure A-5   Gorilla crania.

(a) MALE

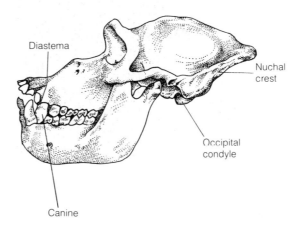

(b) FEMALE

Figure A-6   Human vertebral column.

Atlas
Axis
C3
C4
CERVICAL
CURVE
C5
C6
C7

Vertebral arch
Vertebral foramen
Superior articular facet
Transverse process

T1
T2
T3
T4
T5
T6
THORACIC
CURVE
T7
T8
T9
T10
T11
T12

Transverse costal facet
Superior articular process
Superior costal facet

Spinous process

Superior articular process
Transverse process

Intervertebral foramen and disc

L1
L2
L3
LUMBAR
CURVE
L4
L5

Pedicle

Body (centrum)

Sacrovertebral joint

PELVIC
CURVE
Sacrum (5 pieces)

Coccyx (4 pieces)

Human vertebral column (lateral view) and representative views of selected cervical, thoracic, and lumbar vertebrae (superior views).

Figure A-7 Pelvic girdles.

Figure A-8 Hand anatomy.

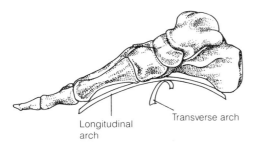

Figure A-9   Foot (pedal) anatomy.

(a) HUMAN (DORSAL VIEW)

(c) CHIMPANZEE

(b) HUMAN (MEDIAL VIEW)

Forensic Anthropology

Upon death, our so-called "soft" tissues, such as skin, hair, and muscle, deteriorate, leaving behind the "hard" tissues—bones and teeth—as human skeletal remains. The analysis of this material involves a knowledge of *skeletal biology*, a specialty practiced by some physical anthropologists.

It is a fascinating and startling fact that there are hundreds of millions of humans buried around this planet, and often their bones come to light for one reason or another. Indeed, thousands of skeletons have been excavated and are now curated in various natural history and anthropology museums. Skeletal biologists (also called *human osteologists*) are often asked to assist in unearthing these human remains and to perform various specialized analyses on them when prehistoric or, occasionally, historic burial sites are excavated. In some places (as recent controversies in Australia and Israel demonstrate), the excavation of human remains has become a highly emotional issue. Obviously, any disturbance of human burials can have profound religious implications for those people who, for cultural reasons, feel closely linked to the deceased individuals.

In the United States, ethical concerns in recent years have limited the circumstances under which Native American burials may be unearthed and studied. Quite often, such burials now are removed *only* when they are imminently threatened—for example, by construction work. Consequently, skeletal biologists are often requested to assist in the excavation of these threatened burials, to study them for a short time, and finally to supervise their reinterment in a more secure resting place.

In addition, human burials are occasionally excavated from sites that have a quite recent historical context. For example, one of the authors (R. J.) directed the removal and osteological study of the partial skeletons of four sailors who were drowned in a shipwreck in 1865 along the California coast. When the beach site where the sailors were buried began to erode and expose their graves, it was decided to remove the skeletons and to provide opportunity for their study.

Another situation that often calls for the expertise of a skeletal biologist comes about when skeletonized or partially skeletonized remains are found in what are clearly *very* recent contexts. For example, when a body with most of the soft tissue decomposed is found in a garbage bag in a wooded area outside a large city,* the coroner asks immediate questions: What is the identity of the person (actual identity, but failing that, age and sex)? What was the manner of death?

The key individuals who try to provide answers to these questions include a forensic dentist (who examines the teeth and tries to match them with

---

*The example cited here is based on an actual case, one that is not out of the ordinary. In fact, all the examples discussed in this appendix are drawn from real cases.

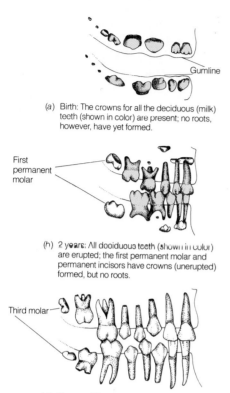

(a) Birth: The crowns for all the deciduous (milk) teeth (shown in color) are present; no roots, however, have yet formed.

First permanent molar

(b) 2 years: All deciduous teeth (shown in color) are erupted; the first permanent molar and permanent incisors have crowns (unerupted) formed, but no roots.

Third molar

(c) 12 years: All permanent teeth are erupted except the third molar (wisdom tooth).

Figure B-1 Skeletal age: dental development.

dental records) and a skeletal biologist who, from the bones, attempts to ascertain the age, sex, stature, and race of the victim, along with other information, such as the presence of any unusual injuries.

This appendix, then, serves as an introductory visual guide to the techniques used by skeletal biologists in their analysis of human skeletal remains. It is not intended as a complete summary of osteological methods, but as an illustration of some of the specialized techniques used by osteologists—especially as they pertain to forensic applications.

◇ Skeletal Age Determination

During its growth and development, the skeleton exhibits regular stages of change that allow osteologists to establish quite accurately the age of an individual at death. For example, the ages of infants and children can be determined by inspecting the degree of dental development or the regular fusion of the separate ends of long bones (called *epiphyses*) to the bone shafts.

However, once maturity is attained (by the early twenties), determining age by skeletal analysis becomes considerably more difficult. The most commonly used method for discovering the age of adults involves rating progressive

Greater tubercle fuses to head at 2 to 4 years.

Head fuses to shaft: males aged 16 to 18 females aged 15 to 17

(a) Birth

(b) 5 years

(c) 10 years

(d) 15 years

(e) 16+ years

Trochlea fuses to lower shaft: males aged 14 to 16 females aged 13 to 15

Medial epicondyle fuses: males aged 16 to 18 females aged 15 to 17

Figure B-2 Skeletal age: epiphyseal union in the humerus. Some regions of the humerus exhibit some of the earliest fusion centers in the body, while others are among the latest to complete fusion (not until late adolescence).

Pubic Symphysis

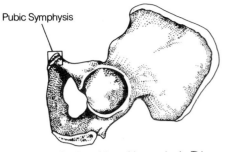

(a) Position of the pubic symphysis. This area of the pelvis shows systematic changes progressively throughout adult life. Two of these stages are shown in (b) and (c).

(b) Age: 21. The face of the symphysis shows the typical "billowed" appearance of a young joint; no rim present.

(c) Age: mid-50s. The face is mostly flat, with a distinct rim formed around most of the periphery.

changes in the area where the two halves of the pelvis join (called the *pubic symphysis*). Other areas—for example, the ends of ribs—are also sometimes used. In addition, some microscopic techniques, in which progressive cellular changes are observed, have also proven useful.

Figure B-3 Skeletal age: Remodeling of the pubic symphysis.

AGING A SKELETON: AN EXAMPLE

A forensic case requiring knowledge of age at death came about when three skeletons were discovered months after a small plane crashed in a remote region of northern California.

The identities of the three passengers, all male, were known, and the teeth of the individuals did conform to these personal identifications. However, the bones of all three were mixed together when they were received by the coroner (having been scattered at the crash site by predators, perhaps, as well as being mixed by authorities who collected the bones).

Since the crash victims were of different ages (one in his teens, one in his 30s, and one in his 40s), it was helpful to use aging criteria to separate the bones. The teenager was the easiest, since many of his epiphyses were just about to complete fusion or had just done so (leaving a telltale line). The bones of the two adults were much more difficult to distinguish, emphasizing the complexity of accurately specifying the age of mature individuals. In this case, the best that could be done was to attempt to match the bones mainly on the basis of size.

◇ Sexing the Skeleton

Ascertaining the sex of a person from skeletal remains presents a set of problems opposite to those posed by aging methodologies. While, for aging, young individuals are easiest, determining sex is achieved most accurately for mature skeletons. Like other secondary sexual characteristics, skeletal sexual dimorphism is most clearly manifested after puberty. As a result, it is relatively straightforward to find the sexual identity of teenage or older skeletons. On the other hand, for skeletons of infants and children, it is often impossible to determine their sex.

(a) FEMALE PELVIS

(b) MALE PELVIS

Figure B-4 Sexing the skeleton: the pelvis. The most diagnostic area of the body displaying skeletal sexual dimorphism is the pelvis, especially the anterior (front) aspect. The width of the pubis (A) is relatively greater in females, and the subpubic angle (B) is also more open. Both these features reflect the proportionately wider pelvic outlet in females that forms the bony birth canal.

The most consistent skeletal sexual indicators are found in the pelvis, reflecting, of course, the modifications in the female pelvis associated with childbearing.

While not as reliable, the cranium is also used (and sometimes is *all* that the osteologist has to work with). Here, differences are seen in size and especially in proportions: Males have relatively bigger and more prominent faces, larger browridges, and heavier (more robust) muscle insertions.

SEXING THE SKELETON: AN EXAMPLE

The almost completely skeletonized remains of a young individual were found rather haphazardly buried in a streambed outside a large city. To confirm more accurately the sex of this individual, the pelvis was cleaned of all remaining tissue. The osteologist was then able to see the proportions of the pelvis (wide pubis and subpubic angle, etc.) to ascertain confidently that this was a female. Interestingly, while cleaning the pelvis, the assistant coroner found a bullet lodged in the hip (smashed against the femur head).

◇ Assessing Stature

Another aspect of the skeleton that relates directly to a condition of a *living* individual is stature. Since the skeleton (especially the long bones of the lower limb) contributes directly to a person's body height, it is possible to estimate height even when only some bones remain.

The methods for stature estimation were developed from skeletal collections in which the stature of the individuals was known (for example, cadavers were measured before they were dissected in medical school anatomy labs). From such studies, standard formulae have been developed to allow stature estimates from long-bone measurements. The femur provides the most accurate estimates, but the tibia, fibula, and long bones of the upper limb can also be used. It must be noted, however, that these formulae apply most directly to *the samples from which they were drawn*. They can be reasonably extended to the *populations* these samples represent (White females, Black males, and so forth). Since the formulae differ for the two sexes and for different racial groups, it is crucial to know sex and race *beforehand* in order to select the appropriate stature estimation formula.

DETERMINING STATURE: AN EXAMPLE

Over the last few years, several skeletons have been returned to the United States by the North Vietnamese. It has been assumed that these individuals were missing American servicemen (mostly pilots whose planes were shot down).

An immediate concern, of course, was to ascertain that a returned skeleton was not simply that of a North Vietnamese. A very quick check could be done by estimating stature, since the range of variation among Vietnamese males overlaps very little with that of American servicemen.

In the case of the returned remains, stature was checked immediately by forensic anthropologists, and it was found that the skeletons almost certainly were *not* those of Vietnamese.

Confirming positive identification (exactly *which* person a particular skeleton represented) turned out, of course, to be more difficult. Dogtags were returned with given skeletons, so there were apparently clear identifications, but these had to be checked. Unfortunately, in some cases, however, no dental records existed. Consequently, less reliable indicators had to be employed. In one instance, the estimated stature from the long bones matched to within one-half inch of the missing serviceman's actual stature. Moreover, other indicators, such as a healed ankle fracture, also matched, making it extremely likely that the skeleton was, in fact, the individual identified on the dogtags.

The total length of the femur is obtained on an osteometric board. In this case, this eighteenth-century sailor's femur measured as 461 mm.

From standardized formulae (see text), tables can be constructed to obtain stature estimates from femur length. A portion of such a table is shown below:

Figure B-5 Estimating stature: measuring the length of the femur.

Femur length (mm)*	Stature	
	cm	inches
452	169	66
456	170	66
461	171	67
465	172	67
469	173	68

From these comparisons, the sailor's stature is thus estimated as 171 cm (67 inches).

*Note: Data drawn from White males with known statures at time of death.

◇ Attribution of Race

Another aspect of osteological analysis, especially relating to forensic work, is the attribution of race. For example, is a particular skeleton that of an individual who was Caucasian or Black?

Here, however, the skeletal differences are far from clearcut. Accordingly, the best that can be done is to make scientific "best guesses" on the basis of statistical inference. Techniques employed for race attribution primarily involve the use of special formulae which, like those for stature estimation, are abstracted from dissecting-room skeletal samples. Measurements taken from the cranium are the most reliable, but the pelvis, femur, and other bones can also be used.

ATTRIBUTION OF RACE: AN EXAMPLE

In mass disasters (for example, the crash of a commercial jetliner), it is obviously important to establish accurately the identity of each victim. Initially, age and sex are ascertained. Beyond this, another way to sort the remains is by race. Therefore, measurements can be taken on the cranium of each adult, applied to a formula, and a "best guess" can be made. It must be pointed out that, first, sex needs to be established (the formulae vary for males and females) and, secondly, the formula is devised to answer only a limited question. For example, Is a particular cranium from a Caucasian or from a Black individual? The mathematical statement discriminates between these two choices. If we asked the same question of an unknown individual who turned out to be Asian, the answer (telling us only whether the person was Black or White) would be meaningless.

The question of race attribution was also addressed in the preceding section concerning stature estimation. In the example concerning identification of the skeleton of an American serviceman from that of a Vietnamese, the problem was really one of race identification. In this example, stature was useful, since the ranges of variations are known to overlap very little between the two respective populations (American White—or Black, for that matter—compared to Southeast Asians).

◇ Facial Reconstruction in Human Identification*

Facial reconstruction (also termed *facial reproduction*) is a process used when other identification procedures (including fingerprints and dental matches) have been unsuccessful. Two different methods of producing a face on the skull are employed: a portrait of the individual using clues from the bones of

*Contributed by Diane L. France, Ph.D., Colorado State University, and Sandra C. Mays, Supervisor, Crime Laboratory Section, Wyoming State Crime Laboratory. Stages of reconstruction are from both authors; finished reconstruction by Sandra Mays.

the face; and a more direct, three-dimensional method of applying clay to the skull (or to a plaster cast of the skull). These techniques employ both science and art: The physical anthropologist discovers the age, sex, and race of the skull, but there is no direct evidence from bone that indicates the eye color, hair color and style, lip form, or degree of wrinkling or fleshiness in the individual. Therefore, there is a great deal of subjectivity in the rendering of the finished product; an exact reproduction is not expected, only a general likeness.

The following photographs show a facial reproduction taking shape. Erasers or blocks of clay marking tissue depths (arrived at experimentally from cadavers) are commonly glued to the skull. Clay strips, graduated to the various tissue depths, then "fill in the dots" between erasers, and the face is "fleshed out." The eyes, nose, lips, and sometimes ears are then fashioned according to various guidelines, and a wig is usually added.

Figures i and j show the reproduction of a Caucasoid female, over 60 years old. The first figure shows a nearly complete reproduction, but without the effects of aging, while Figure 5j is the finished product, including the features characteristic of a woman of that age.

Figure B-6   Facial reconstruction from a skull.

Figure a   Erasers precut to experimentally determined tissue depths are glued to skull.

Figure b   Sandra Mays applies strips of clay between erasers, graduated to eraser depths.

Figure c   Strips of clay connect erasers.

Figure d   Clay is added to ''flesh out'' the face.

Figure e and f   A nose and lips are added and refined.

Figure g and h Glass (or plastic) eyes are placed into orbits and eyelids are fashioned.

Figure i and j Completed reproduction. (i) Before adding aging features. (j) After "aging" the face to correspond with aging indicators ascertained from other parts of the skeleton.

Acclimatization Long-term physiological response within individuals to environmental pressure; usually takes a few weeks to a few months.

Acheulian The culture period, or stone tool industry, of the Middle and part of the Lower Pleistocene; characterized by the handaxe.

Acquired characteristics The notion developed by Lamarck that traits acquired during the lifetime of an organism could be passed on to offspring. Known as the theory of acquired characteristics.

Acrocentric chromosome A chromosome with its centromere towards one end.

Adaptation Genetic changes within populations in response to selection (environmental) pressure; usually takes many generations.

Adaptive niche The whole way of life of an organism: where it lives, what it eats, how it gets food, and so forth.

Adaptive radiation The rapid increase and spread of an evolving group of organisms which diversify and adapt to new niches.

Adenine One of the chemical bases (purines) found in both DNA and RNA.

Advanced In evolutionary terms, an organism further removed from an evolutionary divergence than a more primitive one; usually now termed "derived." *See* Primitive.

Aegyptopithecus An early hominoid form from the Oligocene; Fayum, Egypt.

Agonistic behavior Behavior actively related to fighting—aggression, conciliation, or retreat.

Allele Alternative form of a gene that may be present at the same locus. In the ABO blood-group system, for example, any one of these three alleles (A, B, or O) may be present at the ABO locus.

Allen's rule Within species of warm-blooded animals (birds and mammals) those populations living in colder environments will tend to have shorter appendages than populations in warmer areas.

Allo Combining form indicating different or other.

Allometric growth Differential patterns of growth whereby some parts of the body are disproportionately related to other parts.

Altruism Helping others without direct benefit to oneself. In natural selection terms: sacrificing your own reproductive success to help another.

Alveolar Tooth-bearing portion of the upper jaw.

Alveolar prognathism Forward projection of the maxilla (much reduced in anatomically modern humans).

Ameslan American sign language. AMESLAN is used among deaf humans and also for teaching language to some apes.

Amino acids Small molecules that are the building blocks of protein.

Amniote egg The developing reptilian embryo is surrounded by three sacs: one for food, one for waste matter, and one filled with liquid—amniotic fluid—for protection. This egg evolved with reptiles.

Analogous structures Similarities in parts of the anatomy not based on descent from a common ancestor (the bird wing and butterfly wing, for example), but based on common function.

Analogy Similarities between organisms based on common function, not due to evolutionary relationship. *See* Homology.

Anatomically modern *H. sapiens* (or human beings) Populations of the Upper Paleolithic who physically resemble populations of today.

Anomaly Different, irregular deviation.

Anthropoidea The suborder (of Primates) of anthropoids, including New World monkeys, Old World monkeys, and hominoids (apes and hominids).

Anthropology The study (or science) of humankind.

Anthropometry Measurement of the human body.

Anticodon A triplet of bases in tRNA which complements the triplet of bases in mRNA. The anticodon corresponds to a particular amino acid.

Arboreal Tree-living. Many prosimians and monkeys, as well as the gibbon and the orangutan, are arboreal.

Archeology The study of prehistoric culture through remains left by ancient humans.

Artifacts (archeological traces) Traces of hominid behavior. Very old artifacts are usually made of stone.

Artiodactyl Even-toed hoof (e.g., cows, pigs, camels).

Ascending ramus Rear upright portion of the mandible.

Association What an archeological trace is found with (other archeological traces, bone refuse, etc.).

Atlatl A throwing board or spearthrower.

Aurignacian A culture period (*circa* 30,000 y.a.) of the Upper Paleolithic; probable beginning of Upper Paleolithic art.

Australopithecine The common term for members of the genus, *Australopithecus*.

Australopithecus The extinct genus of Plio-Pleistocene hominids found in South and East Africa; usually divided into: *A. africanus* and *A. robustus* (S. Africa), and *A. boisei* and an early primitive representative, *A. afarensis* (E. Africa).

Autosome Any chromosome except a sex chromosome.

Balanced polymorphism The maintenance of two or more

alleles in a population due to a selective advantage of the heterozygote.

Base   One of the four chemicals attached to a sugar molecule and a phosphate to make up a nucleotide. In DNA, a base is always paired with another base.

Behavior, social   The behavior of animals that live together as a group; gregariousness, sociability.

Binomial   The binomial (two-term) system of classification developed by Linnaeus. Every organism is identified by two Latin names: the first word is the generic term; the second, the specific.

Biocultural   An approach to the study of human beings, their evolution and behavior. The biocultural approach considers both human biology and culture.

Biological adaptation   Genetic changes within populations in response to selection (environmental) pressure; usually takes many generations.

Biosphere   The entire area inhabited by organisms.

Biostratigraphy   Dating method based on evolutionary changes within an evolving lineage.

Bipedalism   Walking on two legs as the natural means of locomotion.

Blade   A parallel-sided flake at least twice as long as it is wide.

Brachiation   Arm-over-arm suspensory locomotion beneath branches.

Brachycephalic   Broad-headed. A skull in which the width of the skull is 80% or more of the length.

Breccia   Cemented conglomerate containing limestone, sand, and bone.

Breeding isolate   A population geographically and/or socially separate and, therefore, relatively easy to define.

Burin   A chisellike stone tool used for engraving on horn, wood, and ivory; characteristic of the Upper Paleolithic.

Calva (or callote)   Uppermost portion of the braincase.

Calvaria   The skull minus the face and mandible.

Calvarium   The skull minus the mandible.

Cambrian   The first period of the Paleozoic.

Canine   Usually a long and pointed (conical) tooth in front of the mouth, lateral to incisors; used for piercing and grasping.

Carbon 14 (^{14}C) dating   A method of determining the age in years of an organic specimen by measuring the loss of the radioactive isotope, ^{14}C.

Carboniferous   Fifth period of the Paleozoic. The first reptiles appear during this period.

Carnivore   A meat-eating animal. Also the common name for a member of the mammalian order, Carnivora (for example, dogs, cats, bears).

Catastrophism   The idea that there were a series of violent and sudden catastrophes which destroyed most living things.

This would explain the extinction of many species. Also part of catastrophism was the belief that after each catastrophe, a new set of creations established new species. Associated with Cuvier.

Catarrhine   The group (infraorder) comprising all Old World anthropoids, living and extinct.

Ceboidea   The anthropoid superfamily of New World monkeys, including marmosets and cebids.

Cenozoic Era (65 m.y.a.–present)   The present era; the era following the Mesozoic.

Centromere   A circular body that attaches the two arms (chromatids) of the chromosome.

Cercopithecoidea   The anthropoid superfamily of Old World monkeys including colobines and cercopithecines.

Cerebellum   Hind portion of brain. The cerebellum is the center of unconscious control of skeletal muscles.

Cerebrum   The front portion of the brain; the largest portion of the brain in placental mammals.

Cervical   Pertaining to the neck, as in cervical vertebrae.

Chatelperronian   An early culture period (*circa* 32,000 y.a.) of the Upper Paleolithic; perhaps transitional between Mousterian and later Upper Paleolithic culture.

Cheek teeth   Premolars and molars.

Chromatid   Each of the two subunits of a duplicated chromosome.

Chromosomal mutation   A rearrangement of large sections of DNA (whole pieces of chromosomes) such as deletions, translocations, inversions, and duplications.

Chromosome   A rod-shaped structure, composed of nucleic acid and protein, found in the nucleus of the cell. Chromosomes occur in pairs and contain the DNA responsible for inheritance.

Chronometric dating   Determining the age of a specimen in number of years. Potassium-argon, ^{14}C, ^{238}U, dendrochronology (and others) are used to obtain chronometric dates.

Cladistics   The school of evolutionary biology that seeks to make ancestral-descendant hypotheses through interpreting patterns of primitive/derived characteristics.

Cladogram   A diagrammatic representation of population relationships using several genetic traits simultaneously.

Class   A category of classification in the Animal (or Plant) Kingdom; a subdivision of subphylum. A class includes those animals (or plants) that have adapted to a similar way of life. Vertebrate classes are Pisces, Amphibia, Reptilia, Aves, and Mammalia.

Classic Neandertals   Western Europe and Near Eastern Neandertals who lived during the early Würm.

Clavicle   Collar bone.

Cline   A gradual distribution of gene frequencies over space.

Coadaptation (genetic coadaptation)   Interaction of genes at the genotypic level. Natural selection acts upon the complex product of such interactions rather than upon individual loci.

Codon   A triplet of bases in mRNA that codes for a specific amino acid. The triplet is matched by another triplet of bases in tRNA.

Condyle   A rounded protuberance of bone which articulates with another bone (that is, forms a joint with or moves against another bone).

Context   The environmental setting where an archeological trace is found.

Convergence (convergent evolution)   Evolution of similar adaptive traits in unrelated forms; for example, the wings of birds and wings of butterflies. *See* Parallelism.

Coprolite   Preserved dung or fecal matter which may be examined for ancient dietary evidence.

Core   Stone reduced by flake removal.

Core area   Area, within the home range, of greatest regular use.

Coronal suture   The suture running transversely across the skull joining the frontal and parietal bones.

Cosmology   The study of the creation of the universe and the laws that govern it.

Cranium   The complete skull; bone of the head, face, and mandible.

Crepuscular   Active at twilight or dawn.

Cretaceous   Final (third) period of Mesozoic. Dinosaurs become extinct. Probable appearance of first primates.

Crossing-over   The exchange of genetic material between homologous chromosomes during meiosis.

Crossopterygians   Lobe-finned fish; probably gave rise to amphibians.

Culture   The ways humans discover, invent, and develop in order to survive. Culture is the human strategy of adaptation.

Cytoplasm   That portion of the cell lying outside the nucleus.

Cytosine   One of the chemical bases (pyrimidines) found in both DNA and RNA.

Dental arcade   The shape of the tooth row: posteriorly divergent, parallel, parabolic, etc.

Dental formula   The number of each kind of tooth present. Shown usually for one-quarter of the mouth as: Incisors; Canine; Premolars; Molars.

Devonian   Fourth period of the Paleozoic. Age of Fish. Appearance of amphibians.

Diastema   Gap, space, especially between the upper lateral incisor and canine (also seen in the lower jaw between the canine and first premolar); found in many monkeys and pongids.

Diploid number (2n)   The full complement of chromosomes—46 in humans—in a somatic cell or in a sex cell before meiosis.

Display   Stereotyped behavior that serves to communicate emotional states between individuals. Display is most often associated with reproductive or agonistic behavior.

Diurnal   Active during daylight hours.

Division of Labor   Activities performed only by members of a particular status, such as age or sex.

Dizygotic   Twins derived from two zygotes, genetically related the same as any full sibs; differences between them are caused both by the environment and genetic variation.

DNA (deoxyribonucleic acid)   A large molecule composed of adenine, guanine, cytosine, and thymine plus phosphate and sugar; DNA carries the genetic code.

Dolichocephalic   Narrow or long-headed. A skull in which the width is less than 75% of the length.

Dominance (dominance hierarchy)   The physical domination of some members of a group by other members. A hierarchy of ranked statuses sustained by hostile, or threat of hostile, behavior which results in greater access to resources such as food, sleeping sites, and mates.

Dominant   A trait determined by a dominant allele. A trait that is visible or measurable and that prevents the appearance of the recessive.

Dorsal   Pertaining to the back (toward the backbone) of an animal.

Double helix   The structure of DNA, composed of a pair of matching helixes.

Dryopith   The common term for *Dryopithecus* and *Proconsul*; distributed mostly in Africa, but with some representatives in Europe.

Dryopithecus   The genus name referring to a diverse group of extinct hominoids from the Miocene.

East Lake Turkana   A Plio-Pleistocene locality in northern Kenya which has yielded dozens of fossil hominids. Hominid-bearing levels date 1.8–1.0 m.y.a.

Ecological niche (econiche)   The life-style of a particular organism (species) in a particular habitat.

Eemian   "Third" interglacial; between the Riss and Würm glaciations.

Effective breeding population   Those individuals in a population actually producing offspring; usually about one-third total population size.

Empirical   Derived from or depending on experience or experiment.

Endocast   An impression of the inside of the skull showing the size, shape, and some details of the surface of the brain.

Endogamy   Mating within the social unit (that is, the population). *See* Exogamy.

Endoskeleton   An internal bony skeleton, characteristic of vertebrates. *See* Exoskeleton.

Eocene   Second epoch of Tertiary. Radiation of prosimians. Possible appearance of anthropoids.

Estrous cycle   An hormonally initiated cycle in female mammals correlated with ovulation. Estrus may involve observable physical and behavioral changes.

Ethnography   The study of surviving, nonliterate societies.

Eutheria   The most numerous subclass of Mammalia. Embryo and fetus of these (placental) mammals are nourished by a placenta.

Evolution   A change in gene frequency in a population from one generation to the next.

Evolutionary reversal   The reacquisition of a structure previously lost in the evolution of a life form—an extremely unlikely event.

Evolutionary trend   A set of anatomical and/or behavior traits which tend to characterize a group of evolutionarily related organisms. For example: pentadactyly, retention of complete clavicle, and stereoscopic vision among the primates.

Exogamy   Mating outside the social unit (that is, the population).

Exoskeleton   A hard, supporting external covering, characteristic of many invertebrates such as ants and lobsters. *See* Endoskeleton.

F₁   First filial generation; offspring resulting from a cross of homozygous dominants and homozygous recessives. All individuals resulting from such a cross are heterozygous.

F₂   Second filial generation; offspring of a cross of F₁ individuals—a mating of two heterozygous individuals (or selfing in a species where this is possible, as in the case of Mendel's peas).

Family   Members of a family usually inhabit a similar environment; a category that includes genera and species.

Fayum   An Oligocene fossil primate site in Egypt yielding several early anthropoid forms.

Femur   Thigh bone.

Fibula   The narrow long bone of the lower leg. *See* Tibia.

Fixity of species   The belief that species, once created, never changed but remained fixed. This belief was firmly held by most scholars in the eighteenth century.

Fluorine dating   A method of relative dating by measuring the amount of fluorine in a specimen. More fluorine indicates a greater age.

Foramen magnum   Opening in the base of the skull through which the spinal cord passes.

Forensic   Pertaining to courts of law. In anthropology, the use of anthropology in questions of law.

Founder effect (Sewall Wright Effect)   A type of genetic drift in which gene frequencies are altered in small populations which are nonrandom samples of larger populations.

Frontal bone   The front bone of the skull including the forehead and the brow region over the eyes.

Gamete   A mature sex cell. A sex cell following two meiotic divisions—sperm for male; ovum for female.

Gene   That section of DNA responsible for the ultimate synthesis of a specific polypeptide chain of amino acids; that portion of DNA with a detectable function.

Gene frequency (allele frequency)   A numerical indicator of the proportion of genes (alleles) in a population. *See* Hardy-Weinberg Equilibrium.

Gene pool   The total complement of genes in a population.

Generalized   Pertains to a trait capable of several functions. The human hand is generalized because it is used for a number of functions; the human foot is specialized and is used in a very limited way. *See* Specialized.

Genetic drift (random genetic drift)   The evolutionary factor which accounts for evolutionary changes (shifts in gene frequency) due to random events. A function of population size.

Genetic screening   Testing programs to ascertain individuals with genetic diseases or carriers of potentially deleterious genes.

Genotype   The genetic makeup of a particular organism; an individual's "genetic formula"; the genes at one or more loci.

Genotypic proportion   The relative frequency of the genotypes in a population. For a two-allele system (such as A, a), there will be three genotypes (AA, Aa, aa). Hardy-Weinberg equilibrium makes idealized predictions of these genotypes according to the formula: $p^2 + 2pq + q^2 = 1$. *See* Hardy-Weinberg Equilibrium.

Genus (pl. genera)   A category of classification in the Animal (or Plant) Kingdom. Genus groups together closely related species usually inhabiting similar ecological niches; for example, *Homo, Pan, Felis, Canis.*

Geochemistry   The study of the chemical composition of the earth's crust.

Geology   The study of the history and structure of the earth as recorded in rocks.

Gracile   Small, lightly built; used to refer to smaller australopithecines. *See* Robust.

Gravettian   A culture period (*circa* 25,000 y.a.) of the Upper Paleolithic; associated with Lascaux Cave art.

Grooming   Cleaning the body of another by picking through the hair and fur with the fingers or teeth. Grooming is common among primates.

Guanine   One of the chemical bases (purines) found both in DNA and RNA.

Günz   First glacial of the Pleistocene.

Habilis   A species of genus *Homo*, first applied by Louis Leakey to Plio-Pleistocene hominids from East Africa.

Hadar   A Plio-Pleistocene hominid locality in northeastern Ethiopia. Hominid-bearing levels dated ?3.7–2.6 m.y.a.

Haploid number (n)   The number of chromosomes in the gamete after meiosis (23 in humans).

Haplorhini   The classificatory term used to group tarsiers with monkeys, apes, and humans (either suborder or semiorder).

Hardy-Weinberg Equilibrium   The mathematical relationship expressing—under ideal conditions—the predicted distribution of genes in populations; the central theorem of population genetics.

Helix A spiral or anything with a spiral form.

Helix, double The structure of DNA resembles a double helix (spiral).

Herbivore A plant-eating animal.

Heritability The relative amount of variation in a trait due to genetic causes as part of total phenotypic variation.

Heterodontism Having different teeth. Characteristic of mammals whose teeth consist of incisors, canines, premolars, and molars.

Heterozygote A cell or individual that is heterozygous. (A hybrid is heterozygous for a particular trait.)

Heterozygous Having different alleles at a given locus on a pair of homologous chromosomes.

Holistic Viewing the whole as an integrated and interdependent system. Anthropology includes as its concern all aspects of human beings—physical and behavioral.

Holocene Second (present) epoch of Quaternary; begins with end of Pleistocene glaciation.

Holstein Second interglacial between the Mindel and Riss glaciations.

Home range The area utilized by an animal; the area the group is most familiar with and which provides the group with food.

Hominid Popular form of Hominidae, the family to which humans belong. Hominids include bipedal primates such as *Australopithecus* and *Homo*.

Hominidae The family, of the order Primates, to which humans belong.

Hominization Process of becoming more human.

Hominoid Abbreviated or popular form of Hominoidea, the superfamily to which hominids, pongids, and gibbons belong.

Homo The genus to which humans belong, including *erectus* and *sapiens*.

Homodontism Having the same teeth. Refers to the situation wherein all teeth of the mouth are similar, as in fish and reptiles.

Homoiothermy Pertains to an organism that maintains the same temperature (mammals and birds, for example). Warm-blooded.

Homologous chromosomes Paired chromosomes. Chromosomes that are paired during meiosis and participate in cross-over. Homologous chromosomes contain the same loci.

Homologous structures Similarities in parts of the anatomy based upon common descent.

Homologue Occurs in meiosis when a chromosome duplicates itself. The double-stranded chromosome is a homologue.

Homology Similarities of organisms based on common evolutionary descent.

Homo sapiens The species which appeared 200,000 to 300,000 years ago; includes Neandertals and anatomically modern humans.

Homo sapiens sapiens The subspecies to which modern humans belong; beginning with the Upper Paleolithic; anatomically modern human beings.

Homozygote A cell or individual that is homozygous. (A purebred is homozygous for a particular trait.)

Homozygous Having the same allele at a given locus on a pair of homologous chromosomes.

Human A term now generally applied to *H. erectus* and *H. sapiens*.

Human evolution Biological changes over time leading to anatomically modern human beings.

Human variation Biological differences among humans.

Humerus Upper arm bone.

Hybrid Offspring of parents of mixed ancestry. A heterozygote.

Hypothesis Unproved theory. A theory is a statement with some confirmation.

Immune response system The production of specific antibodies in response to the introduction of specific foreign antigens into the body.

Immunity An organism's ability to recognize and deactivate foreign antigens very quickly as a consequence of earlier (mild) exposure (for example, through vaccination).

Inbreeding A type of nonrandom mating in which blood relatives mate more often than predicted under random mating conditions.

Incisors Front teeth, usually spatulate in primates; used for cutting and nipping.

Independent assortment Where gene pairs on one set of homologous chromosomes do not influence the distribution of gene pairs on other chromosomes—they separate independently from one another during meiosis and are randomly assorted in the gametes. Known as Mendel's second law.

Innominate The fused half-portion of a pelvis; contains three bones—the ilium, ischium, and pubis.

In situ In its original or natural position.

Interspecific variation Variation between two separate species.

Interstadial A temperate period during the phases of a glacial period.

Intraspecific variation Variation within a species due to age, sexual dimorphism, individual genetic differences, or geographic separation.

Intron Within a genetic locus, a section of DNA that is not translated.

Ischial callosities Hardened sitting pads found on the rear ends of Old World monkeys. Also seen to some degree in chimpanzees.

Jurassic   Second period of Mesozoic. Great age of dinosaurs. First appearance of birds.

Kabuh   Middle Pleistocene geologic formation.

Kanapoi   A Plio-Pleistocene hominid site in northern Kenya. Estimated age approximately 4 m.y.a.

Karyotype   The chromosome complement contained in a cell, especially the diagram of chromosomes arranged according to size and banding patterns of each chromosome.

KNM-ER   Kenya National Museum—East Rudolf (the former name for Lake Turkana). The prefix preceding paleontological discoveries from East Lake Turkana.

Kromdraai   A Plio-Pleistocene hominid site in South Africa yielding remains of robust australopithecines.

Lactose intolerance   Inability to digest milk (and other dairy products) after early childhood; characteristic of a majority of humans today. Lactose intolerance is due to the absence of the enzyme, lactase.

Laetoli   A Plio-Pleistocene hominid site in northern Tanzania. Dated 3.77–3.59 m.y.a.

Lamarckism   Lamarck's ideas about evolution. *See* Acquired characteristics.

Lambdoid suture   The horizontal or transverse suture at the back of the top of the skull joining the parietal and occipital bones.

Lemuroidea   The prosimian superfamily of lemurs, today confined to Madagascar.

Levant   Countries bordering the eastern Mediterranean.

Lineage   An evolutionary line of related forms distinct from other such lines.

Living floor   A narrow horizon of archeological remains. Corresponds to brief period of hominid occupation.

Locus (pl. loci)   The place a gene occupies on a chromosome.

Lorisoidea   The prosimian superfamily of lorises. Today all are nocturnal forms, found in Africa and southern Asia.

Lothagam   A Plio-Pleistocene hominid site in northern Kenya. Estimated age, approximately 5.5 m.y.a.

Macroevolution   Large evolutionary changes (result of long-term major shifts in gene frequencies) produced only after many generations. *See* Microevolution.

Magdalenean   Final period of the Upper Paleolithic (*circa* 15,000 y.a.) (in Europe) and a time of spectacular technological growth; associated with art from Altamira Cave in Spain.

Major histocompatibility complex (MHC)   The large genetic complex (located in humans on chromosome #6) that plays a central part in immune response—recognition of foreign antigens and production of specialized cells to deactivate them.

Makapansgat   A Plio-Pleistocene hominid site in South Africa yielding remains of gracile australopithecines.

Malnutrition   A diet insufficient in quality (i.e., lacking in some essential components) to support normal health.

Mammals   The class of animals that nurse their young from mammary glands. Primates belong to this class.

Mandible   Lower jaw.

Marsupials   A subclass of mammals—metatheria—that bear live young; infants are nursed in the mother's pouch, Marsupium pouch.

Masseter   Chewing; refers to muscles used in the operation of the jaw—originating on the zygomatic (cheek) bones and inserting on the mandible.

Mastoid process   A triangular bone behind the ear hole on a human skull; usually more pronounced in males than females.

Maxilla   Upper jaw.

Meiosis   Cell division, consisting of two divisions, in which the total complement (diploid number) of chromosomes is reduced by half (haploid number) in the gametes (sperm in males; ova in females). Also known as reduction division.

Melanin   The biochemical compound produced by specialized cells in the basal layers of the epidermis. Melanin is very important in influencing skin pigmentation.

Mendelian trait (simple trait)   An inherited trait with a straightforward pattern, controlled by one genetic locus.

Mesozoic Era (225–65 m.y.a.)   The era following the Paleozoic. Known as the Age of Reptiles.

Metacentric chromosome   A chromosome with its centromere near the center.

Metatheria   A subclass of mammals (marsupials); infants are nursed in the mother's pouch.

Metazoa   Multicellular animals. A major division of the Animal Kingdom.

Microevolution   The small-scale evolutionary changes occurring over just a few generations and involving relatively small changes in gene frequencies. What the Hardy-Weinberg formula measures. *See* Macroevolution.

Migration   Movement of individuals (and, necessarily, genes) between populations. An evolutionary factor that may cause changes in gene frequencies.

Mindel   Second glacial of the Pleistocene (correlated with the Elster).

Miocene   Fourth epoch of Tertiary. Radiation of hominoids. Possible appearance of hominids.

Mitosis   Cell division into two daughter cells in which the chromosome complement is identical to the mother cell and to each other.

Molars   Cheek teeth, following the premolars. In anthropoids these are the last three teeth of the tooth row; used for grinding and chewing.

Molecule   Smallest portion of a substance that acts like that substance and is capable of existing independently. Several to many atoms constitute a molecule.

Mongrelization   Racial mixture.

Monogenists   Term applied to those who believe that all races derived from a single pair (Adam and Eve).

Monotreme   A subclass of mammals—prototheria—that lay eggs.

Monozygotic   Twins derived from one zygote, genetically identical. Differences between the twins are caused solely by the environment.

Mosaic evolution   Term applied when the rate of evolution in one functional system varies from other systems.

Mousterian   A culture period, or stone tool industry, of the Middle Paleolithic; usually associated with Neandertals. Characterized mainly by stone flakes.

Multivariate   Pattern for several variables assessed simultaneously.

Mutation   An alteration in the genetic material (DNA). The true "creative" factor in evolution. Mutation is the only way to produce new variation and the starting point of all evolutionary change.

Natural selection   The evolutionary factor, first articulated by Charles Darwin, that causes changes in gene frequencies in populations due to differential net reproductive success of individuals. *See* Net reproductive success.

Neandertal, classic   Neandertals of the early fourth (Weichsel or Würm) glaciation, especially those of Western Europe.

Neandertals   *H. sapiens* form that preceded anatomically modern human beings (*H. sapiens sapiens*); usually associated with Mousterian culture and the Middle Paleolithic.

Negative assortative mating   A type of nonrandom mating in which individuals of unlike phenotype mate more often than predicted under random mating conditions.

Neopallium or Neocortex   A covering of the cerebral hemispheres begun in reptiles, expanded in mammals, and reaching its greatest expansion in humans. Higher mental activity is concentrated in this area.

Net reproductive success   The number of offspring successfully raised; the bottom line of natural selection.

Nocturnal   Active during nighttime. *See* Diurnal and Crepuscular.

Nuchal   Pertaining to the neck.

Nucleotide   A purine or pyrimidine base attached to a sugar and a phosphate group: a subunit of DNA and RNA.

Nulliparous   Never having given birth.

Nucleus   A body, present in most types of cells, containing chromosomes.

Occiput (occipital bone)   The rear bone of the skull. The occiput also forms most of the base, including the occipital condyles and foramen magnum.

OH   Olduvai Hominid. The prefix preceding hominid discoveries (numbered sequentially) from Olduvai Gorge.

Olduvai Gorge   A paleoanthropological site in northern Tanzania yielding remains of Plio-Pleistocene hominids and a wealth of biocultural data.

Olfactory   Smell.

Oligocene   Third epoch of Tertiary. Radiation of anthropoids.

Omnivore   An animal that will eat both plants and meat.

Omo   A Plio-Pleistocene hominid locality in southern Ethiopia. Hominid-bearing levels dated 2.9–1.0 m.y.a.

Order   A category of classification in the Animal (or Plant) Kingdom. A subdivision of Class. Members of an order usually inhabit a similar environment; for example, Carnivora, Rodentia, Primates.

Ordovician   The second period of the Paleozoic. First fishes appear.

Osteology   The study of bones.

Ostracoderm   Shell-skin or armored.

Oviparity   Egg birth, characteristic of most animals..

P$_1$ The parental generation in which homozygous dominants and recessives are crossed. Parents homozygous (pure) for round seeds and parents homozygous for wrinkled represent such a parental cross.

Paleoanthropology   The multidisciplinary approach to the study of human biocultural evolution. Includes physical anthropology, archeology, geology, ecology, and many other disciplines.

Paleocene   First epoch of Tertiary. Prosimians present.

Paleolithic   Old Stone Age. The culture period that includes the beginning of culture up to approximately the end of the Pleistocene glaciation. Usually divided into Lower, Middle, and Upper.

Paleolithic, Lower   The earliest period of the Paleolithic, characterized by Oldowan (pebble tools) and Acheulian (handaxe) industries.

Paleolithic, Middle   A stone flake industry associated with the Mousterian culture period and Neandertals.

Paleolithic, Upper   The final stage of the Paleolithic, associated with more sophisticated culture such as cave painting, sculpting, engraving, and stone tools made from blades. Appearance of anatomically modern humans.

Paleomagnetism   Dating method based on the shifting nature of the earth's geomagnetic field.

Paleontology   The study of the fossils of ancient animals.

Paleopathology   The study of ancient diseases.

Paleospecies   A group of organisms found in paleontological contexts and usually separated by large amounts of time, thus adding to the amount of variation seen in extant groups.

Paleozoic Era (570–225 m.y.a.) The era following the Proterozoic, beginning 570 million years ago. The first era in which fossils are relatively abundant.

Palynology The analysis of pollen found in the soil of archeological excavations to determine the kinds of plants present at the ancient site.

Parallelism (parallel evolution) Evolution of similar adaptive traits in forms that were once related but then diverged, developing along similar lines. *See* Convergence.

Paranthropus The genus name sometimes used to refer to robust australopithecines and, therefore, making a generic distinction between them and gracile australopithecines (*Australopithecus*).

Parietal The right and left side bones on top of the skull, joined by the sagittal suture.

Pentadactyly Having five digits. A generalized trait of mammals and primates.

Penultimate Last but one; next to last.

Peptide A compound of two or more amino acids joined by peptide bonds. Linked peptides form polypeptides which, in turn, join to form proteins.

Periodontal Gum and jaw disease.

Perissodactyl Odd-toed hoof (e.g., horse).

Permian Final period of the Paleozoic. Appearance of mammallike reptiles.

Phenotype The observable or measurable characteristic of an organism. Roundness in a seed is an observable phenotype. In blood groups, A, B, and O are measurable phenotypes.

Phenotypic ratio The ratio of phenotypes, especially from a hybrid cross. Mendel's famous F_1 hybrid cross of peas produced a 3:1 phenotypic ratio.

Phylogeny The study of evolutionary lines of descent. A "family tree."

Phylum (pl. phyla) A primary division of the Animal (or Plant) Kingdom; for example, Arthropoda, Chordata.

Piltdown A forged "fossil" hominid from England, "discovered" in 1911. Combining a fully *sapiens* cranium with a modern pongid jaw, it served to confuse anthropologists for four decades.

Pithecanthropus Name originally given to *H. erectus* by Eugene Dubois.

Placenta Tissue connected to the uterus that nourishes the fetus and absorbs its waste. This structure is characteristic of most mammals and has given its name to that form—placental mammals.

Placental mammals (eutheria) Mammals whose embryonic development is associated with a placenta.

Platycephaly Flatheadedness, as opposed to the dome shape of the skull of anatomically modern humans.

Pleistocene First epoch of the Quaternary. *H. sapiens* becomes widespread throughout Old World. *H. sapiens sapiens* evolves toward end of Pleistocene. Ice Age.

Pliocene Final (fifth) epoch of Tertiary. Hominids definitely present.

Point mutation Change in just one base in the DNA sequence. Probably the most common kind of mutation with evolutionary impact.

Polygenic Traits controlled by two or more loci; usually such traits (for example, stature, weight, IQ) are also influenced considerably by the environment.

Polygenists Term applied to those who believe in a multiple origin of races.

Polygyny One male and two or more females in a mating relationship.

Polymorphism The situation when two or more alleles at a given genetic locus occur with frequencies greater than 1% in a population.

Polypeptide A group of peptides linked together. One or more polypeptide chains make a protein.

Population Within a species, a community of individuals where mates are usually found.

Population genetics Studies in contemporary populations through measurement of gene frequencies. *See* Hardy-Weinberg Equilibrium.

Positive assortative mating A type of nonrandom mating in which individuals of like phenotype mate more often than predicted under random mating conditions.

Postcranial The skeleton behind (below) the skull.

Postorbital bar The bony element that closes in the outside of the eye orbit—a characteristic of primates.

Potassium-argon (K/Ar) dating Determining absolute age (in years) by measuring the amounts of potassium-40 (^{40}K) and argon-40 (^{40}Ar). The greater the amount of argon that has built up, the older the specimen. Used only on rocks once heated to a very high temperature, such as that generated by volcanic activity.

Prehensility Adaptation for grasping.

Premolars Cheek teeth similar in form to the molars; situated between canines and molars. Old World anthropoids possess two premolars and New World forms normally three in each quadrant. Human premolars have two cusps, compared to four or more in molars, and are known as bicuspids.

Presenting A behavior, often indicating subordination or appeasement, in which an animal places itself on all fours and elevates its rear end toward another. During estrus a female may present for purposes of copulation.

Primates The order of mammals to which humans, apes, monkeys, and prosimians belong.

Primitive In evolutionary terms, an organism that is closer to an evolutionary divergence than a later (more derived) one. *See* Advanced.

Principle of independent assortment   The distribution of one pair of genes does not influence the distribution of other pairs of genes.

Principle of segregation   Genes occur in pairs. In the production of a gamete, the pair is separated so that each gamete contains only one of the pair.

Prosimian   Common form for Prosimii; the suborder of primates, including lemurs, lorises, and tarsiers.

Protein   A macromolecule, composed of one or more polypeptide chains of amino acids. Proteins are responsible for carrying out most of the cell's metabolic activities, and are thus the basic structural and functional compounds of the cell.

Protein synthesis   The manufacture of a protein from the DNA to the final product. The process by which amino acids are linked (by a peptide bond) to form a polypeptide chain. The completed chain or chains form a protein.

Proterozoic   A geologic era immediately preceding the Paleozoic. Not much evidence of life.

Prototheria   A subclass of mammals (monotremes) that lay eggs and nurse their young.

Punctuated equilibrium   The view that evolutionary rates are not constant, but proceed slowly (equilibria) until "punctuated" by rather sudden spurts.

Purines   A class of chemical bases—adenine and guanine—found in DNA and RNA.

Pyrimidines   A class of chemical bases—cytosine, thymine, uracil—found in nucleic acids.

Quadrumanual   Using all four limbs for grasping during locomotion, as in the orang.

Quadrupedal (quadrupedalism)   Using all four limbs as weight supports while moving. Trunk typically horizontal. The basic mammalian, and primate, form of locomotion.

Quaternary   Second (present) period of Cenozoic. Period of *Homo erectus* and *Homo sapiens*.

Race   Currently defined by anthropologists as a breeding population; formerly applied to a group of people who resembled each other in physical appearance. Many anthropologists do not believe the term to be a useful one when applied to humans.

Ramapithecus   An extinct hominoid from the Miocene (13–9 m.y.a.) thought by some to be an early hominid. Now usually included within *Sivapithecus. See Sivapithecus.*

Recessive   A trait that is not phenotypically expressed in heterozygotes. A trait that is phenotypically expressed only in the homozygous state.

Recombination   The reshuffling of genetic material every generation as the result of sexual reproduction. Recombination occurs during meiosis (through crossing-over and ran-

dom assortment) and provides variation for natural selection to act upon.

Ribosomes   Small, spherical particles, composed of rRNA and proteins, found in the cytoplasm. The ribosome is the site of protein synthesis.

Rift Valley (Great Rift Valley)   A massive (1,200 mile long) geological feature in East Africa associated with mountain building, volcanoes, faulting, etc. The results of "rifting" have provided preservation and access to several superb Plio-Pleistocene sites (Olduvai, East Lake Turkana, Hadar, etc.).

RNA (ribonucleic acid)   A nucleic acid found both in the nucleus and the cytoplasm. RNA differs from DNA in that its sugar component is ribose.

  mRNA   Messenger RNA. This RNA carries genetic information from DNA in the nucleus to the ribosomes in the cytoplasm.

  rRNA   Ribosomal RNA; a major constituent of ribosomes.

  tRNA   Transfer RNA. This RNA brings amino acids together to form a polypeptide chain.

Riss   The third major glaciation of the Alpine system; equivalent to the Saale of the Scandinavian system.

Robust   Larger, more heavily built; used to refer to the larger australopithecines. *See* Gracile.

Saale   The third major glaciation of the Scandinavian system; occurred during the Pleistocene; equivalent to Riss, of the Alpine system.

Sagittal crest   Raised ridge along the midline of the skull where the temporal muscle (used to move the jaw) attaches.

Sagittal suture   The suture joining the left and right parietals; extending the length of the skull from the coronal suture in front to lambdoidal suture behind.

Savanna   A grassland with a scattering of trees, usually in the tropics or subtropics.

Scapula   Shoulder blade.

Sectorial   Compressed single-cusped tooth (1st lower premolar) seen in pongids (and many extinct hominoids); compared to the bicuspid form found in most hominids.

Segregation   Genes exist on paired chromosomes. At meiosis, the pairs are segregated so that a gamete has only one of the pair. Mendel's first law.

Sex cells   Cells that divide by meiosis and become gametes.

Sexual dimorphism   Marked physical differences between adult males and females of a species. Examples: greater size of gorilla and baboon males; sagittal and occipital crest of male gorilla.

Shovel-shaped incisors (shoveling)   Incisors with raised ridges of enamel on both sides of the teeth.

Sickle-cell anemia (sicklemia)   A severe, usually lethal disease caused by an alteration (point mutation) in adult hemoglobin. The disease is only expressed when the mutant allele is inherited in double dose.

Sickle-cell trait   An alteration (point mutation) in adult hemoglobin. This term usually refers to carrying the mutant allele in single dose (that is, a carrier).

Silurian   Third period of the Paleozoic. Jawed fishes appear. First air-breathing animals.

Sinanthropus   The name originally given by Davidson Black to hominid specimens from Zhoukoudian; now known as *H. erectus pekinensis.*

Sivapithecus   An extinct hominoid from the Miocene (*circa* 13–7 m.y.a.) found mostly in Eurasia. Some species are probably closely related to orangs.

Sociobiology   An evolutionary approach to the explanation of behavior—largely in terms of natural selection (individual reproductive success).

Solutrean   A culture period (*circa* 20,000 y.a.) of Europe; known for its magnificent flintwork.

Somatic cells   Cells that do not divide by meiosis and do not become gametes. Body cells.

Specialized   A trait that evolved for a specific function is said to be specialized. The human foot is specialized, the hand generalized. *See* Generalized.

Speciation   The evolutionary process that produces new species from previous ones.

Species   A category of classification of the Animal (or Plant) Kingdom. A population or group of populations living in the same econiche that can, or actually do, interbreed and produce fertile offspring.

Sterkfontein   A Plio-Pleistocene hominid site in South Africa yielding remains of gracile australopithecines and, perhaps, early *Homo.*

Stratigraphy   Sequential layering of deposits. The sequence of layers is used as a means of dating, relatively, the layers as well as the materials in the layers.

Strepsirhini   The classificatory term used to group lemurs and lorises (either suborder or semiorder).

Subphylum   A major division of a phylum—such as Vertebrata.

Substrate   The physical surface on which an animal moves or rests.

Superfamily   A group of closely related families.

Supraorbital torus   Ridge above the orbits on a skull. The supraorbital torus is very pronounced in *erectus*, Neandertals, and some australopithecines.

Swartkrans   A Plio-Pleistocene hominid site in South Africa yielding remains of robust australopithecines and, perhaps, early *Homo.*

Taphonomy   Study of how bones come to be buried in the earth and preserved as fossils.

Tarsiioidea   The prosimian superfamily of tarsiers, a nocturnal form found in southern Asia.

Taung   A South African Plio-Pleistocene australopithecine site. The location of the first australopithecine discovery (1924).

Taurodontism   Bulltoothedness.

Taxon   A population (or group of populations) judged to be sufficiently distinct to be assigned to a separate category (such as genus or species).

Taxonomy   The science of the classification of organisms, including the principles, procedures, and rules of classification.

Tectonic movement   Movements of the earth (along fault lines, during mountain building, and so forth).

Tektite   A round, glassy body of unknown origin.

Terrestrial   Living on the ground. Humans, gorillas, and some monkeys are terrestrial.

Territoriality   Behavior in defense of the territory of a group; establishment of exclusive right to the use of a territory. Some primates are much more territorial than others.

Territory   That part of the home range used exclusively by one group. The area defended by one group against other groups of the same species.

Tertiary   First period of the Cenozoic. Period of primate radiation. (Includes: Paleocene, Eocene, Oligocene, Miocene, and Pliocene.)

Tetrad   A structure of four chromatids of a pair of homologous chromosomes. Seen during meiosis.

Thymine   One of the chemical bases (pyrimidines) found in DNA, but not in RNA.

Tibia   The large long bone of the lower leg; the shin. *See* Fibula.

Traissic   First period of Mesozoic. First dinosaurs.

Trinil fauna   Animal remains associated with the Middle Pleistocene Trinil period in Java.

Triplet   A sequence of three bases; found in mRNA and tRNA. Codes for a specific amino acid. A codon or anticodon.

Tuff   A solidified sediment of volcanic ash.

Typology, racial   Dividing humans into discrete racial types.

Undernutrition   A diet insufficient in quantity (calories) to support normal health.

Uniformitarianism   A concept maintaining that the ancient changes in the earth's surface were caused by the same physical principles acting today. The earth's crust was formed slowly and gradually. Mountains, rivers, valleys, etc., were the result of purely natural forces such as erosion by wind, water, frost, ice, and rain. Although not originated by Charles Lyell, uniformitarianism is associated with him because he popularized it.

Upper Paleolithic   A culture period noted for technological, artistic, and behavioral innovations. Also known for the appearance of anatomically modern human beings.

Uracil One of the chemical bases (pyrimidines) found in RNA, but not in DNA.

Variation (genetic) Inherited differences between individuals. The basis of all evolutionary change.

Ventral Toward the belly; the front of an organism (as in humans) or the undersurface of an animal that does not stand erect (as a dog).

Vertebra (pl. vertebrae) A single bone of the spinal or vertebral column (backbone).

Viviparity Live birth; characteristic mainly of mammals.

World view A literal translation from the German, *Weltanschauung*. A personal or group philosophy explaining history; a way of looking at the world.

Würm The fourth glacial (corrrelated with Weichsel in the Old World).

Y-5 pattern (Dryopithecine Y-5) A pattern of cusps on the molar teeth characteristic of hominoids.

Zygomatic (or zygomatic bone) Malar or cheek bone.

Zygomatic arch The bone along the side of the skull below the orbit providing attachment for jaw muscles.

Zygote A fertilized ovum; formed by the union of a sperm and ovum.

◇ BIBLIOGRAPHY

Aigner, Jean S. and Wm. S. Laughlin
  1973   "The Dating of Lantian Man and His Significance for Analyz-
          ing Trends in Human Evolution." *American Journal of Physi-
          cal Anthropology*, 39:97–110.
Alland Jr., Alexander
  1971   *Human Diversity.* New York: Anchor Press/Doubleday.
Altman, I.
  1978   "Crowding: Historical and Contemporary Trends in Crowd-
          ing Research." *In: Human Response to Crowding*, A. Baum
          and Y. M. Epstein (eds.), New York: John Wiley and Sons.
Altmann, Jeanne
  1981   *Baboon Mothers and Infants.* Cambridge: Harvard University
          Press.
Altmann, Stuart A. and Jeanne Altmann
  1970   *Baboon Ecology.* Chicago: University of Chicago Press.
Amos, D. Bernard and D. D. Kostyu
  1980   "HLA—A Central Immunological Agency of Man." *In: Ad-
          vances in Human Genetics* (Vol. 10), H. Harris and
          K. Hirschhorn (eds.), New York: Plenum Press, pp. 137–208.
Andersson, J. Gunnar
  1934   *Children of the Yellow Earth.* New York: Macmillan.
Andrews, P. J.
  1983   "The Natural History of *Sivapithecus*." *In*: R. Ciochon and
          R. Corruccini (eds.), q.v., pp. 441–463.
Andrews, Peter and Elizabeth Evans
  1979   "The Environment of *Ramapithecus* in Africa." *Paleobiology*
          5(1):22–30.
Anthrop, Donald F.
  1973   *Noise Pollution.* Lexington, Mass.: D. C. Heath & Co.
Ardrey, Robert
  1976   *The Hunting Hypothesis.* New York: Atheneum.
Aronson, J. L., R. C. Walter, and M. Taieb
  1983   "Correlation of Tulu Boi Tuff at Koobi Fora with the Sidi
          Hakoma Tuff at Hadar." *Nature*, 306:209–210.

Baba, M. L., L. L. Darga and M. Goodman
  1981   "Maximum Parsimony Test of the Clock Model of the Molec-
          ular Change Using Amino Acid Sequence Data." Paper pre-
          sented at the Annual Meetings, American Association of
          Physical Anthropologists, April 1981.
Baker, Paul T.
  1966   "Human Biological Variation as an Adaptive Response to the
          Environment." *Eugenics Quarterly*, 13:81–91.
Baker, Paul T. and Michael A. Little
  1976   "Environmental Adaptations and Perspectives." *In: Man in
          the Andes*, P. T. Baker and M. A. Little (eds.), Stroudsburg,
          Penn.: Dowden, Hutchinson, and Ross, Inc., pp. 405–428.
Barash, David
  1982   *Sociobiology and Behavior.* 2nd Ed. New York: Elsevier.
Barzun, Jacques
  1965   *Race: A Study in Superstition.* New York: Harper and Row.

Bayanov, Dmitri and Igor Bourtsev
  1974   "Reply (to comments on Proshner's article)." *Current Anthro-
          pology*, 15(4):452–456.
  _____
  1976   "On Neanderthal vs. Paranthropus." *Current Anthropology*,
          17(2):312–318.
Beck, Benjamin B.
  1980   *Animal Tool Behavior.* New York: Garland Publishing, Inc.
Behrensmeyer, Anna K. and Andrew P. Hill
  1980   *Fossils in the Making: Vertebrate Taphonomy and Paleoecol-
          ogy.* Chicago: The University of Chicago Press.
Bennett, Kenneth A.
  1979   *Fundamentals of Biological Anthropology.* Dubuque: Wm. C.
          Brown Co. Publishers.
Biddiss, Michael D.
  1970   *Father of Racist Ideology: The Social and Political Thought of
          Count Gobineau.* New York: Weybright and Talley.
Binford, Lewis R.
  1981   *Bones. Ancient Men and Modern Myths.* New York: Academic
          Press.
  _____
  1982   Comment on White's article, "Rethinking the Middle/Upper
          Paleolithic Transition." (*See* White, 1982)
  _____
  1983   *In Pursuit of the Past.* New York: Thames and Hudson.
Birdsell, Joseph B.
  1981   *Human Evolution.* (3d Ed.), Boston: Houghton Mifflin Co.
Black, Francis L.
  1975   "Infectious Diseases in Primitive Societies." *Science*,
          187:515–518.
Boas, Franz
  1940   "Changes in the Bodily Form of Descendants of Immi-
          grants." *Reprinted In*: F. Boas (ed.), *Race, Language and Cul-
          ture.* New York: The Free Press, pp. 60–75.
  _____
  1940   "New Evidence in Regard to the Instability of Human
          Types." *Reprinted In*: F. Boas (ed.), *Race, Language and Cul-
          ture.* New York: The Free Press, pp. 76–81.
Boaz, N. T.
  1977   "Paleoecology of Early Hominidae in Africa." *Kroeber An-
          thropological Society Papers*, 50:37–62.
Boaz, N. T., F. C. Howell, and M. L. McCrossin
  1982   "Faunal Age of the Usno, Shungura B and Hadar Formation,
          Ethiopia." *Nature*, 300:633–635.
Bodmer, Walter F.
  1972   "Race and IQ: The Genetic Background." *In: Race and Intelli-
          gence*, Ken Richardson and David Speers (eds.), Baltimore:
          Penguin Books, Inc., pp. 83–113.
Bodmer, W. F. and L. L. Cavalli-Sforza
  1976   *Genetics, Evolution, and Man.* San Francisco: W. H. Freeman
          and Company.

Bogaarts, John
1980 "Does Malnutrition Affect Fecundity? A Summary of Evidence." *Science*, 208:564–569.
Bolton, Ralph
1973 "Aggression and Hypoglycemia among the Qolla; a Study in Psychological Anthropology." *Ethnology*, 12:227–257.

1984 "The Hypoglycemia–Aggression Hypothesis: Debate versus Research." *Current Anthropology*, 25:1–53.
Bonner, T. I., R. Heinemann and G. J. Todardo
1980 "Evolution of DNA Sequences Has Been Retarded in Malagasy Primates." *Nature*, 286:420–423.
Bordes, François
1968 *The Old Stone Age*. New York: McGraw-Hill Book Co.
Bowler, J. M. and A. G. Thorne (eds.)
1976 "Human Remains from Lake Mungo: Discovery and Excavation of Lake Mungo III." *In*: *The Origin of the Australians*, R. L. Kirk and A. G. Thorne (eds.), Canberra: Australian Institute of Aboriginal Studies (Humanities Press Inc., New Jersey), pp. 127–138.
Boyd, Wm. C.
1950 *Genetics and the Races of Man*. Boston: Little, Brown.
Brace, C. Loring
1964 "The Fate of the 'Classic' Neanderthals: A Consideration of Hominid Catastrophism." *Current Anthropology*, 5:3–43.

1967 *The Stages of Human Evolution*. Englewood Cliffs, N.J.: Prentice-Hall, Inc.

1973 "Sexual Dimorphism in Human Evolution." *In*: *Man in Evolutionary Perspective*, C. L. Brace and J. Metress (eds.), New York: Wiley Publishing Co., pp. 238–254.

1979 "Biological Parameters and Pleistocene Hominid Lifeways." *In*: *Primate Ecology and Human Origins*, Irwin S. Bernstein and E. O. Smith (eds.), New York: Garland Publishing Co., pp. 263–289.
Brace, C. Loring and Frank B. Livingstone
1971 "On Creeping Jensenism," *In*: *Race and Intelligence*, C. L. Brace, G. R. Gamble and J. T. Bond (eds.), Anthropological Studies, No. 8, American Anthropological Association, Washington, D.C.
Brace, C. L. and Ashley Montagu
1977 *Human Evolution* (2nd Ed.). New York: Macmillan.
Brace, C. Loring, Harry Nelson and Noel Korn
1971 *Atlas of Human Evolution*. New York: Holt, Rinehart and Winston. (2nd Ed. 1979)
Braidwood, Robert J.
1975 *Prehistoric Men* (8th Ed.). Glenview, Ill.: Scott, Foresman and Co.
Brain, C. K.
1970 "New Finds at the Swartkrans Australopithecine Site." *Nature*, 225:1112–1119.

1975 "The Bone Assemblage from the Kromdraai Australopithecine Site." *In*: *Paleoanthropology: Morphology and Paleoecol-*

ogy, R. Tuttle (ed.), World Anthropology Series, Chicago: Aldine, pp. 225–243.

1981 *The Hunters or the Hunted? An Introduction to African Cave Taphonomy*. Chicago: University of Chicago Press.
Bramblett, Claud A.
1976 *Patterns of Primate Behavior*. Palo Alto, Ca.: Mayfield Publishing Co.
Brock, A., P. L. McFadden and T. C. Partridge
1977 "Preliminary Paleomagnetic Results from Makapansgat and Swartkrans." *Nature*, 266:249–250.
Brose, David and Milford H. Wolpoff
1971 "Early Upper Paleolithic Man and Late Middle Paleolithic Tools." *American Anthropologist*, 73:1156–1194.
Buettner-Janusch, John
1973 *Physical Anthropology: A Perspective*. New York: John Wiley and Sons.
Buffon, George Louis Leclerc, Compte de
1860 "*Histoire Naturelle Generale et Particuliere*." Translated by Wm. Smellie, London. *In*: Louis L. Snyder, q.v., pp. 102–103.
Bugliarello, G., A. Alexander, J. Barnes and C. Wakstein
1976 *The Impact of Noise Pollution: A Sociotechnological Introduction*. New York: Pergamon Press.
Bunn, Henry T.
1981 "Archaeological Evidence for Meat-eating by Plio-Pleistocene Hominids from Koobi Fora and Olduvai Gorge." *Nature*, 291:574–577.
Busse, Curt D.
1978 "Do Chimpanzees Hunt Cooperatively?" *American Naturalist*, 112:767–770.
Butynski, Thomas M.
1982 "Vertebrate Predation by Primates: A Review of Hunting Patterns." *Journal of Human Evolution*, 11:421–430.
Butzer, Karl W.
1974 "Paleoecology of South African Australopithecines: Taung Revisited." *Current Anthropology*, 15:367–382.
Butzer, Karl W. and Glynn L. Isaacs, eds.
1975 *After the Australopithecines*. The Hague: Mouton Publishers and Chicago: Aldine Publishing Co.
Bygott, J. David
1979 "Agonistic Behavior, Dominance, and Social Structure in Wild Chimpanzees of the Gombe National Park." *In*: Hamburg and McCown (eds.), q.v., pp. 405–427.

Campbell, Bernard
1974 *Human Evolution*. Chicago: Aldine Publishing Co.

1976 *Humankind Emerging*. Boston: Little, Brown and Co.
Carpenter, C. R.
1965 "The Howlers of Barro Colorado Island." *In*: I. DeVore, (ed.), q.v., pp. 250–291.
Cartmill, Matt
1972 "Arboreal Adaptations and the Origin of the Order Primates." *In*: *The Functional and Evolutionary Biology of Primates*, R. H. Tuttle (ed.), Chicago: Aldine-Atherton, pp. 97–122.

1974   "Rethinking Primate Origins." *Science*, **184**:436–443.

Cavalieri, Liebe F.
1976   "New Strains of Life—or Death." *New York Times Magazine*, 22:8, August.

Cavalli-Sforza, L. L. and M. W. Feldman
1981   *Cultural Transmission and Evolution: A Quantitative Approach*. Princeton, N.J.: Princeton University Press.

Chard, Chester S.
1975   *Man in Prehistory*. New York: McGraw-Hill Book Co.

Chargaff, Ervin
1976   "On the Dangers of Genetic Meddling." *Science*, June 4.

Charteris, J., J. C. Wali, and J. W. Nottrodt
1981   "Functional Reconstruction of Gait from Pliocene Hominid Footprints at Laetoli, Northern Tanzania." *Nature*, **290**:496–498.

Chia, Lan-Po
1975   *The Cave Home of Peking Man*. Peking: Foreign Language Press.

China Pictorial
1981   "A Complete Ape-Man's Skull Unearthed at Longtan Cave." *China Pictorial*, 3:20–21, Beijing, China, March 1981 (no author).

Chopra, S.R.K.
1983   "Significance of Recent Hominoid Discoveries from the Siwalik Hills of India." *In*: R. Ciochon and R. Corruccini (eds.), q.v., pp. 539–557.

Ciochon, Russel L.
1983   "Hominoid Cladistics and the Ancestry of Modern Apes and Humans. A Summary." *In*: R. Ciochon and R. Corruccini (eds.), q.v., pp. 783–843.

Ciochon, R. L. and A. B. Chiarelli (eds.)
1980   *Evolutionary Biology of the New World Monkeys and Continental Drift*. New York: Plenum Publishing Co.

Ciochon, Russel L. and Robert S. Corruccini
1983   *New Interpretations of Ape and Human Ancestry*. New York: Plenum.

Clark, W. E. LeGros
1967   *Man-apes or Ape-men?* New York: Holt, Rinehart and Winston.

———
1959,   *The Antecedents of Man*. New York: Quadrangle/
1971   The New York Times Books (3rd Ed.).

Clarke, R. J.
1976   "New Cranium of *Homo erectus* from Lake Ndutu, Tanzania." *Nature*, **262**:485–487.

Clarke, R. J. and F. Clark Howell
1972   "Affinities of the Swartkrans 847 Hominid Cranium." *American Journal of Physical Anthropology*, **37**:319–336.

Clodd, Edward
1897   *Pioneers of Evolution from Thales to Huxley*. New York: Freeport (Reprinted 1972).

Clutton-Brock, T. H., F. E. Guiness, and S. D. Albon
1982   *Red Deer Behavior and Ecology of Two Sexes*. Chicago: University of Chicago Press.

Conroy, G., C. J. Jolly, D. Cramer and J. E. Kalb

1978   "Newly Discovered Fossil Hominid Skull from the Afar Depression." *Nature*, **276**:67–70, November 2.

Constable, George
1973   *The Neanderthals* (Emergence of Man Series, Time-Life Books). Waltham, Mass.: Little, Brown and Co.

Cook, J., C. B. Stringer, A. P. Currant, H. P. Schwarcz and A. G. Wintle
1982   "A Review of the Chronology of the European Middle Pleistocene Hominid Record." *Yearbook of Physical Anthropology*, **25**:19–64.

Cooke, H.B.S.
1978   "Faunal Evidence for the Biotic Setting of the Early African Hominids." *In*: *Early Hominids of Africa*, C. Jolly (ed.), New York: St. Martin's Press.

Coon, C. S., S. M. Garn and J. B. Birdsell
1950   *Races—A Study of the Problems of Race Formation in Man*. Springfield, Ill.: Charles C. Thomas.

Corruccini, R. S.
1975a   "Multivariate Analysis of *Gigantopithecus* Mandibles." *American Journal of Physical Anthropology*, **42**:167–170.

———
1975b   "The Interaction Between Neurocranial and Facial Shape in Hominid Evolution." *Homo*, **26**:136–139.

Corruccini, R. S. and H. M. McHenry
1980   "Cladometric Analysis of Pliocene Hominids." *Journal of Human Evolution*, **9**:209–221.

Corruccini, R. S., M. Baba, M. Goodman, R. L. Ciochon and J. E. Cronin
1980   "Non-Linear Macromolecular Evolution and the Molecular Clock." *Evolution*, **34**:1216–1219.

Count, Earl W. (ed.)
1950   *This Is Race*. New York: Henry Schuman.

Cronin, J. E.
1983   "Apes, Humans, and Molecular Clocks. A Reappraisal." *In*: R. Ciochon and R. Corruccini (eds.), q.v., pp. 115–150.

Cronin, J. E. and V. M. Sarich
1980   "Tupaiid and Archonta Phylogeny: The Macromolecular Evidence." *In*: W. P. Luckett (ed.), q.v., pp. 293–312.

Crook, J. H.
1970   "Social Organization and Environment: Aspects of Contemporary Social Ethology." *Animal Behavior*, **18**:197–209.

Curtis, Garniss
1981   "A Matter of Time: Dating Techniques and Geology of Hominid Sites." Paper delivered at the symposium, "Our Ancestors, Ourselves," Davis, Ca., May 10, 1981.

Curtis, G. H., T. Drake, R. Cerling and A. Hampel
1975   "Age of KBS Tuff in Koobi Fora Formation, East Rudolf, Kenya." *Nature*, **258**:395.

Dalrymple, G. B.
1972   "Geomagnetic Reversals and North American Glaciations." *In*: Calibration of Hominoid Evolution, W. W. Bishop and J. A. Miller (eds.), Edinburgh: Scottish Academic Press, pp. 303–329.

Damon, Albert
1977   *Human Biology and Ecology*. New York: W. W. Norton and Co.

Dart, Raymond
  1959 *Adventures with the Missing Link.* New York: Harper and Brothers.
Darwin, Charles
  1859 *On the Origin of Species.* A Facsimile of the First Edition, Cambridge, Mass.: Harvard University Press (1964).
Darwin, Francis (ed.)
  1950 *The Life and Letters of Charles Darwin.* New York: Henry Schuman.
Dawkins, Richard
  1976 *The Selfish Gene.* New York: Oxford University Press.
Day, Michael
  1965 *Guide to Fossil Man.* Cleveland: The World
  1977 Publishing Co.
Day, M. H., M. D. Leakey and C. Magori
  1980 "A New Fossil Hominid Skull from Nu Ngaloba Beds, Laetoli, Northern Tanzania." *Nature,* 289:55–56.
Day, M. H. and E. H. Wickens
  1980 "Laetoli Pliocene Hominid Footprints and Bipedalism." *Nature,* 286:385–387.
DeBonis, L.
  1983 "Phyletic Relationships of Miocene Hominoids and Higher Primate Classification." *In:* R. Ciochon and R. Corruccini (eds.), q.v., pp. 625–649.
De Luce, Judith and Hugh T. Wilder
  1983 *Language in Primates.* New York: Springer-Verlag New York Inc.
De Lumley, Henry
  1969 "A Paleolithic Camp at Nice." *Scientific American,* May, 220:42–50.
De Lumley, Henry and Marie-Antoinette
  1973 "Pre-Neanderthal Human Remains from Arago Cave in Southeastern France." *In: Yearbook of Physical Anthropology* 1973, 16:162–168.
De Lumley, Marie-Antoinette
  1975 "Ante-Neanderthals of Western Europe." *In: Paleoanthropology: Morphology and Paleoecology,* Russel H. Tuttle (ed.), The Hague: Mouton Publishers, pp. 381–387.
Dene, H. T., M. Goodman and W. Prychodko
  1976 "Immunodiffusion Evidence on the Phylogeny of the Primates." *In: Molecular Anthropology,* M. Goodman, R. E. Tashian and J. H. Tashian (eds.), New York: Plenum Press, pp. 171–195.
Dene, H., M. Goodman, W. Prychodko and G. Matsuda
  1980 "Molecular Evidence for the Affinities of Tupaiidae." *In:* W. P. Luckett (ed.), q.v., pp. 269–291.
Dingle, Herbert
  1959 "Copernicus and the Planets." *In: A Short History of Science,* Jean Lindsay (ed.), New York: Doubleday & Co., pp. 18–26.
Dobzhansky, Theodosius
  1970 *Genetics of the Evolutionary Process.* New York: Columbia University Press.
  ———
  1971 "Race Equality." *In: The Biological and Social Meaning of Race,* Richard H. Osborne (ed.), San Francisco: W. H. Freeman Co., pp. 13–24.
Drake, R. E., et al.
  1980 "KBS Tuff Dating and Geochronology of Tuffaceous Sedi-

ments in the Koobi Fora and Shungura Formations, East Africa." *Nature,* 283:368–372.
Draper, Patricia
  1973 "Crowding Among Hunter-Gatherers: The !Kung Bushmen." *Science,* 182:301–303.
Dumont, R. and B. Rosier
  1969 *The Hungry Future.* New York: F. P. Praeger.
Dunn, Frederick L.
  1968 "Epidemiological Factors: Health and Disease in Hunter-Gatherers." *In: Man the Hunter,* R. B. Lee and I. DeVore (eds.), Chicago: Aldine, pp. 221–228.
Dunn, L. C.
  1951 *Race and Biology. The Race Question in Modern Science.* UNESCO.
  ———
  1965 "Mendel, His Work, and His Place in History." *In: Proceedings of the American Philosophical Society,* Vol. 109, No. 4 (Commemoration of the publication of Gregor Mendel's pioneer experiments in genetics), August 18, Philadelphia: American Philosophical Society.
Durham, William
  1981 Paper presented to the Annual Meeting of the American Anthropological Association, Washington, D.C., Dec. 1980. Reported in *Science,* 211:40.

Eiseley, Loren
  1961 *Darwin's Century.* New York: Anchor Books.
Ekberg, Douglas R.
  1979 *Intelligence and Race.* New York: Praeger.
Eldredge, Niles and Joel Cracraft
  1980 *Phylogenetic Patterns and the Evolutionary Process.* New York: Columbia University Press.

Falk, Dean
  1980 "A Reanalysis of the South African Australopithecine Natural Endocasts." *American Journal of Physical Anthropology,* 53:525–539.
  ———
  1983 "The Taung Endocast: A Reply to Holloway." *American Journal of Physical Anthropology,* 60:479–489.
Fedigan, Linda Marie
  1983 "Dominance and Reproductive Success in Primates." *Yearbook of Physical Anthropology,* 26:91–129.
Fisher, R. A.
  1930 *The Genetical Theory of Natural Selection.* Oxford: Clarendon.
Fleagle, J. G.
  1983 "Locomotor Adaptations of Oligocene and Miocene Hominoids and their Phyletic Implications." *In:* R. Ciochon and R. Corruccini (eds.), q.v., pp. 301–324.
Fleagle, J. G. and R. F. Kay
  1983 "New Interpretations of the Phyletic Position of Oligocene Hominoids." *In:* R. Ciochon and R. Corruccini (eds.), q.v., pp. 181–210.
Fleischer, R. C. and H. R. Hart, Jr.
  1972 "Fission Track Dating, Techniques and Problems." *In: Calibration of Hominoid Evolution,* W. W. Bishop and J. A. Miller (eds.), Edinburgh: Scottish Academic Press, pp. 135–170.

Flynn, L. J. and G. Qi
1982 "Age of the Lufeng, China Hominoid Locality." *Nature*, 298:746–747.

Fobes, James L. and James E. King (eds.)
1982 *Primate Behavior.* New York: Academic Press.

Fossey, Dian
1981 "The Imperiled Mountain Gorilla." *National Geographic*, 159(4):501–523.

———
1983 *Gorillas in the Mist.* Boston: Houghton-Mifflin.

Fouts, Roger S.
1983 (See Friends of Washoe, 1983).

Fouts, Roger S. and Richard L. Budd
1979 "Artificial and Human Language Acquisition in the Chimpanzees." *In*: D. Hamburg and E. McCown (eds.), q.v., pp. 375–392.

Fox, Michael W.
1978 "Man, Wolf, and Dog." *In*: *Wolf and Man*, R. L. Halland and H. S. Sharp (eds.), New York: Academic Press, pp. 19–30.

Fox, Robin (ed.)
1975 *Biosocial Anthropology.* New York: John Wiley & Sons.

———
1971 "The Cultural Animal." *In*: *Man and Beast*, John F. Eisenberg and Wm. S. Dillon (eds.), The Smithsonian Institution Press (reprinted in Yehudi A. Cohen, *Man in Adaptation, The Biosocial Background* 2d Ed., Chicago: Aldine Publishing Co., 1974).

Francoeuer, Robert T.
1965 *Perspectives in Evolution.* Baltimore: Helicon.

Frayer, David
1973 "*Gigantopithecus* and Its Relationship to *Australopithecus*." *American Journal of Physical Anthropology*, 39:413–426.

———
1980 "Sexual Dimorphism and Cultural Evolution in the Late Pleistocene and Holocene of Europe." *Journal of Human Evolution*, 9:399–415.

Freedman, Jonathan L.
1975 *Crowding and Behavior.* New York: The Viking Press.

Freeman, L. G.
1975 "Acheulian Sites and Stratigraphy in Iberia and the Maghreb." *In*: K. W. Butzer and G. L. Isaac (eds.), q.v., pp. 661–743.

Friedman, Milton J. and William Trager
1981 "The Biochemistry of Resistance to Malaria." *Scientific American*, 244:154–164.

Friends of Washoe
1981 Central Washington University, Ellensburg, Wa.

Frisancho, A. R.
1978 "Nutritional Influences on Human Growth and Maturation." *Yearbook of Physical Anthropology*, 21:174–191.

Galdikas, Biruté M.
1979 "Orangutan Adaptation at Tanjung Puting Reserve: Mating and Ecology." *In*: *The Great Apes*, D. A. Hamburg and E. R. McCown (eds.), Menlo Park, Ca.: The Benjamin/Cummings Publishing Co., pp. 195–233.

———
1981 Public Lecture at the California Institute of Technology, May 2, 1981.

Galdikas, B.M.F. and G. Telecki
1981 "Variation in Subsistence Activities of Male and Female Pongids: New Perspectives on the Origins of Hominid Labor Division." *Current Anthropology*, 22:241–256.

Gantt, D. G.
1983 "The Enamel of Neogene Hominoids. Structural and Phyletic Implications." *In*: R. Ciochon and R. Corruccini (eds.), q.v., pp. 249–298.

Gardner, Beatrice T. and R. Allen Gardner
1975 "Evidence for Sentence Constituents in the Early Utterances of Child and Chimpanzee." *Journal of Experimental Psychology: General*, 104:244–267.

Gardner, Eldon
1965 *History of Biology.* Minneapolis: Burgess Publishing Co.

Garn, Stanley M.
1969 *Human Races.* Springfield, Ill.: Charles C. Thomas.

Gavan, James
1977 *Paleoanthropology and Primate Evolution.* Dubuque, Iowa: Wm. C. Brown Co.

Gelvin, Bruce R.
1980 "Morphometric Affinities of *Gigantopithecus*." *American Journal of Physical Anthropology*, 53:541–568.

Gerson, Donald
1977 "Radiation in the Environment." *In*: *Human Biology and Ecology*, A. Damon (ed.), New York: W. W. Norton and Co., pp. 246–265.

Gingerich, P. D. and A. Sahni
1979 "*Indraloris* and *Sivaladapis*. Miocene Adapid Primates from the Siwaliks of India and Pakistan." *Nature*, 279:415–416.

Ginger, Ray
1958 *Six Days or Forever?* Boston: Beacon Press.

Glass, Bently (ed.)
1959 *Forerunners of Darwin, 1745–1859.* Baltimore: Johns Hopkins Press.

Goldstein, M., P. Tsarong and C. M. Beall
1983 "High Altitude Hypoxia, Culture, and Human Fecundity/Fertility: A Comparative Study." *American Anthropologist*, 85:28–49.

Goodall, Jane
1965 "Chimpanzees of the Gombe Stream Reserve." *In*: *Primate Behavior*, I. DeVore (ed.), New York: Holt, Rinehart and Winston, Inc., pp. 425–473.

———
1968a "A Preliminary Report on Expressions, Movements and Communications in the Gombe Stream Chimpanzees." *In*: *Primates*, P. C. Jay (ed.), New York: Holt, Rinehart and Winston, pp. 313–374.

———
1968b "The Behavior of Free Living Chimpanzees in the Gombe Stream Reserve." *Animal Behavior Monographs*, 1:(3).

———
1971 *In the Shadow of Man.* Boston: Houghton Mifflin Co.

———
1978 Public Lecture at San Jose State University. April 26.

———
1979 "Life and Death at Gombe." *National Geographic*, 155(5):597–620.

Goodall, Jane, A. Bandora, E. Bergmann, C. Busse, H. Matama,

E. Mpongo, A. Pierce and D. Riss
1979   "Intercommunity Interactions in the Chimpanzee Popula-
        tion of the Gombe National Park." In: D. A. Hamburg and
        E. R. McCown (eds.), q.v., pp. 11–53.
Goodman, M., M. L. Baba and L. L. Darga
1983   "The Bearing of Molecular Data on the Cladogenesis and
        Times of Divergence of Hominoid Lineages." In: R. Ciochon
        and R. Corruccini (eds.), q.v., pp. 67–86.
Goodman, Morris and Gabriel W. Lasker
1975   "Molecular Evidence as to Man's Place in Nature." In: Pri-
        mate Functional Morphology and Evolution, R. H. Tuttle (ed.),
        The Hague: Mouton Publishers, pp. 71–101.
Gorcyca, Diane A., Patrick Garner and Roger Fouts
1975   "Deaf Children and Chimpanzees." Paper presented at the
        Speech Communication Association Convention, Houston,
        Texas, December.
Gossett, Thomas F.
1963   Race, the History of an Idea in America. Dallas: Southern
        Methodist University Press.
Gould, Stephen Jay
1976   "Darwin and the Captain." Natural History, January, 85:32–
        34.
Gould, S. J. and N. Eldredge
1977   "Punctuated Equilibria: the Tempo and Mode of Evolution
        Reconsidered." Paleobiology, 3:115–151.
Greenberg, Joel
1977   "Who Loves You?" Science News, 112:139–141, August 27.
Greenfield, L. O.
1979   "On the Adaptive Pattern of Ramapithecus." American Jour-
        nal of Physical Anthropology, 50:527–548.

1980   "A Late Divergence Hypothesis." American Journal of Physi-
        cal Anthropology, 52:351–365.

1983   "Toward the Resolution of Discrepancies between Phenetic
        and Paleontological Data Bearing on the Question of Human
        Origins." In: R. Ciochon and R. Corruccini (eds.), q.v., pp.
        695–703.
Grobstein, Clifford
1977   "The Recombinant DNA Debate." Scientific American,
        237:22–31, July.
Grootes, P. M.
1978   "Carbon-14 Time Scale Extended: Comparison of Chronolo-
        gies." Science, 200:11–15.
Gurin, Joel
1980   "In the Beginning." Science 80, 1(5):44–51.

Haldane, J.B.S.
1932   The Causes of Evolution. London: Longmans, Green (re-
        printed as paperback, Cornell University Press, 1966).
Hamburg, David A. and E. R. McCown
1979   The Great Apes. Menlo Park, Ca.: The Benjamin/Cummings
        Publishing Co.
Hamilton, W. D.
1964   "The Genetical Theory of Social Behavior: I and II." Journal
        of Theoretical Biology, 7:1–52.

Hanna, Joel M. and Daniel A. Brown
1979   "Human Heat Tolerance: Biological and Cultural Adapta-
        tions." Yearbook of Physical Anthropology, 22:163–186.

1983   "Human Heat Tolerance. An Anthropological Perspective."
        Annual Reviews of Anthropology, 12:259–284.
Harding, Robert and Shirley C. Strum
1976   "The Predatory Baboons of Kekopey." Natural History Maga-
        zine, 85(3):46–53.
Harlow, Harry F.
1959   "Love in Infant Monkeys." Scientific American, 200:68–74.
Harlow, Harry F. and Margaret K. Harlow
1961   "A Study of Animal Affection." Natural History, 70:48–55.
Hatley, T. and J. Kappelman
1981   "Bears, Pigs, and Pliopleistocene Hominids: A Case for the
        Exploitation of Belowground Food Resources." Human Ecol-
        ogy, 8:371–387.
Hausfater, Glenn
1976   "Predatory Behavior of Yellow Baboons." Behaviour, 56:44–68.
Heiken, A. and M. Rasmuson
1966   "Genetical Studies on the Rh Blood Group System." Heredi-
        tas Lund, 55:192–212.
Hiatt, H. H., J. D. Watson and J. A. Winsten (eds.)
1977   Origins of Human Cancer (3 volumes). Cold Spring Harbor
        Laboratory, Cold Spring Harbor, New York.
Hiernaux, Jean
1964   "The Concept of Race and the Taxonomy of Mankind." In:
        The Concept of Race, Ashley Montagu (ed.), New York: The
        Free Press, pp. 29–45.

1968   La Diversité Humaine en Afrique subsahariénne. Bruxelles:
        L'Institut de Sociologie, Université Libre de Bruxelles.
Hoffstetter, R.
1972   "Relationships, Origins, and History of the Ceboid Monkeys
        and the Caviomorph Rodents: A Modern Reinterpretation."
        In: Evolutionary Biology, Th. Dobzhansky, T.M.K. Hecht and
        W. C. Steere (eds.), Vol. 6, New York: Appleton-Century-Crofts,
        pp. 323–347.
Holloway, Ralph L.
1969   "Culture: A Human Domain." Current Anthropology, 10:395–
        407.

1981   "Revisiting the South African Taung Australopithecine En-
        docast: The Position of the Lúnate Sulcus as Determined by
        the Stereoplotting Technique." American Journal of Physical
        Anthropology, 56:43–58.

1983   "Cerebral Brain Endocast Pattern of Australopithecus Afar-
        ensis Hominid." Nature, 303:420–422.
Hooton, E. A.
1926   "Methods of Racial Analysis." Science, 63:75–81.
Howell, F. Clark
1966   "Observations on the Earlier Phases of the European Lower
        Paleolithic." American Anthropologist, 68(2):88–201.

1978   "Hominidae." In: Evolution of African Mammals, V. J. Maglio and H.B.S. Cooke (eds.), Cambridge: Harvard University Press, pp. 154–248.

1982   "Ambrona." *Leakey Foundation News*, Spring.

Howells, W. W.
1971   "The Meaning of Race." *In: The Biological and Social Meaning of Race*, Richard H. Osborne (ed.), San Francisco: W. H. Freeman and Co., pp. 3–10.

1973   *Evolution of the Genus* Homo. Reading, Mass.: Addison-Wesley.

1974   "Neanderthals: Names, Hypotheses, and Scientific Method." *American Anthropologist*, 76:24–38.

1975   "Neanderthal Man: Facts and Figures." *In: Paleoanthropology: Morphology and Paleoecology*, R. H. Tuttle (ed.), The Hague: Mouton Publishers, pp. 389–407.

1980   "*Homo erectus*—Who, When, Where: A Survey." *Yearbook of Physical Anthropology* 1980, 23:1–23.

Hrdy, Sarah Blaffer
1977   *The Langurs of Abu*. Cambridge, Mass.: Harvard University Press.

1981   *The Woman That Never Evolved*. Cambridge: Harvard University Press.

Hudson, Liam
1972   "The Context of the Debate." *In: Race and Intelligence*, K. Richardson and D. Spears, Baltimore: Penguin Books, Inc., pp. 10–16.

Iltis, Hugo
1966   *Life of Mendel*. New York: Hafner Publishing Co. (first published in Germany, 1924).

Isaac, G.
1971   "The Diet of Early Man." *World Archaeology*, 2:278–299.

1975   "Stratigraphy and Cultural Patterns in East Africa During the Middle Ranges of Pleistocene Time." *In*: K. W. Butzer and G. L. Isaac (eds.), q.v., pp. 495–542.

1976   "Early Hominids in Action: A Commentary on the Contribution of Archeology to Understanding the Fossil Record in East Africa." *Yearbook of Physical Anthropology* 1975, 19:19–35.

Iverson, Michael
1981   Public Lecture, Department of Biological Sciences Seminar, San Jose State University, February 6, 1981.

Jacob, François
1975   "Morphology and Paleoecology of Early Man in Java." *In: Paleoanthropology: Morphology and Paleoecology*, R. H. Tuttle (ed.), Chicago: Aldine Publishing Co., pp. 312–325.

Jacobs, Louis L. and David Pilbeam
1980   "Of Mice and Men: Fossil-Based Divergence Dates and Molecular 'Clocks.'" *Journal of Human Evolution*, 9:551–555.

Jarvis, J.V.M.
1981   "Eusociality in a Mammal: Cooperative Breeding in Naked Mole-Rat Colonies." *Science*, 212:571–573.

Jaeger, Jean-Jacques
1975   "The Mammalian Faunas and Hominid Fossils of the Middle Pleistocene of the Maghreb." *In*: K. W. Butzer and G. L. Isaac (eds.), q.v., pp. 399–418.

Jelinek, Arthur J.
1982   "The Tabun Cave and Paleolithic Man in the Levant." *Science*, 216:1369–1375.

Jensen, Arthur
1969   *Environment, Heredity, and Intelligence*. Cambridge, Mass.: Harvard Educational Review.

1974   "Kinship Correlations Reported by Sir Cyril Burt." *Behavior Genetics*, 4:1–28.

1980   *Bias in Mental Testing*. New York: The Free Press.

Jerison, H. J.
1973   *Evolution of the Brain and Behavior*. New York: Academic Press.

Johanson, Donald and Maitland Edey
1981   *Lucy: The Beginnings of Humankind*. New York: Simon and Schuster.

Johanson, Donald C. and Maurice Taieb
1976   "Plio-Pleistocene Hominid Discoveries in Hadar, Ethiopia." *Nature*, 260:293–297.

1980   "New Discoveries of Pliocene Hominids and Artifacts in Hadar." International Afar Research Expedition to Ethiopia (Fourth and Fifth Field Seasons, 1975–77). *Journal of Human Evolution*, 9:582.

Johanson, D. C. and T. D. White
1979   "A Systematic Assessment of Early African Hominids." *Science*, 203:321–330.

Johanson, D. C., T. D. White and Yves Coppens
1978   "A New Species of the Genus *Australopithecus* (Primates: Hominidae) from the Pliocene of Eastern Africa." *Kirtlandia*, No. 28, pp. 1–14.

Johnson, A. E., Jr.
1979   "Skeletal Estimates of *Gigantopithecus* Based on a Gorilla Analogy." *Journal of Human Evolution*, 8:585–587.

Jolly, Alison
1972   *The Evolution of Primate Behavior*. New York: Macmillan.

Jolly, C. J.
1970   "The Seed Eaters: A New Model of Hominid Differentiation Based on a Baboon Analogy." *Man*, 5:5–26.

Jungers, W. L.
1982   "Lucy's Limbs: Skeletal Allometry and Locomotion in *Australopithecus afarensis*." *Nature*, 297:676–678.

Kamin, Leon
1974   *The Science and Politics of IQ*. New York: John Wiley & Sons.

Kan, Yuet Wai and Andrée M. Dozy
  1980   "Evolution of the Hemoglobin S and C Genes in World Popu-
          lations." *Science*, 209:388–391.
Kawamura, Syunzo
  1959   "The Process of Sub-culture Propagation among Japanese
          Macaques." *In: Primate Social Behavior*, C. H. Southwick
          (ed.), Princeton: D. Van Nostrand Co. Inc., pp. 82–90 (origi-
          nally published in the *Journal of Primatology*, 2(1):43–60.)
Kawanaka, Kanji
  1982   "A Case of Inter-Unit-Group Encounter in Chimpanzees of
          the Mahale Mts." *Primates*, 23(4):558–562.
Kay, John P., et al.
  1981   "Normalization of Low-Density Lipoprotein Levels in Heter-
          ozygous Familial Hypercholesterolemia with a Combined
          Drug Regimen." *New England Journal of Medicine*, 304:251–
          258.
Kay, Richard F.
  1981   "The Nut-Crackers—A New Theory of the Adaptations of the
          Ramapithecinae." *American Journal of Physical Anthropol-
          ogy*, 55:151–156.
Kay, R. F., J. G. Fleagle and E. L. Simons
  1981   "A Revision of the Oligocene Apes of the Fayum Province,
          Egypt." *American Journal of Physical Anthropology*, 55:293–
          322.
Kay, R. F. and E. L. Simons
  1983   "A Reassessment of the Relationship Between Late Miocene
          and Subsequent Hominoidea." *In*: R. Ciochon and
          R. Corruccini (eds.), q.v., pp. 577–624.
Kelso, A. J.
  1974   *Physical Anthropology* (2nd Ed.). New York: J. B. Lippincott
          Co.
Kennedy, G. E.
  1980a   *Paleoanthropology*. New York: McGraw-Hill Book Co.
  ———
  1980b   "The Emergence of Modern Man." *Nature*, 284:11–12.
  ———
  1984   "The Emergence of *Homo sapiens*: The Post Cranial Evi-
          dence." *Man* (N.S.), 19:94–110.
King, J. L. and T. H. Jukes
  1969   "Non-Darwinian Evolution." *Science*, 164:788–798.
Klein, R. G.
  1977   "The Ecology of Early Man in Southern Africa." *Science*,
          197:115–126.
Kortland, Adriaan
  1965   "A comment on 'On the Essential Morphological Basis for
          Human Culture.'" *Current Anthropology*, 6:320–326.
Kummer, Hans
  1971   *Primate Societies*. Chicago: Aldine-Atherton, Inc.

Lack, David
  1966   *Population Studies of Birds*. Oxford: Clarendon.
Lancaster, Jane B.
  1975   *Primate Behavior and the Emergence of Human Culture*.
          New York: Holt, Rinehart and Winston, Inc.

Lasker, Gabriel W.
  1969   "Human Biological Adaptability: the Ecological Approach in
          Physical Anthropology." *Science*, 166:1480–1486.
Latimer, Bruce
  1984   "The Pedal Skeleton of *Australopithecus afarensis*." *American
          Journal of Physical Anthropology*, 63:182.
van Lawick-Goodall, Hugo and Jane
  1970   *In the Shadow of Man*. London: Wm. Collins Sons and Co.,
          Ltd.
Leakey, L.S.B.
  1966   "*Homo habilis*, *Homo erectus*, and the Australopithecinae."
          Nature, 209:1279–1281.
Leakey, L.S.B., J. F. Everden and G. H. Curtis
  1961   "Age of Bed I, Olduvai Gorge, Tanganyika." *Nature*, 191:478–
          479.
Leakey, L.S.B., P. V. Tobias and J. R. Napier
  1964   "A New Species of the Genus *Homo* from Olduvai Gorge."
          Nature, 202:7–10.
Leakey, Mary D.
  1971   "Remains of *Homo erectus* and Associated Artifacts in Bed
          IV at Olduvai Gorge, Tanzania." *Nature*, 232:380–383.
Leakey, M. D. and R. L. Hay
  1979   "Pliocene Footprints in Laetolil Beds at Laetoli, Northern
          Tanzania." *Nature*, 278:317–323.
Leakey, R.E.F.
  1974   "Further Evidence of Lower Pleistocene Hominids from East
          Rudolf, Kenya, 1973." *Nature*, 248:653–656.
  ———
  1976   "New Hominid Fossils from the Koobi Fora Formation in
          Northern Kenya." *Nature*, 261:572–574.
Leakey, R.E.F. and Alan C. Walker
  1976   "*Australopithecus*, *Homo erectus* and the Single Species Hy-
          pothesis." *Nature*, 261:572–574.
Lee, Richard B.
  1979   *The !Kung San*. Cambridge: Cambridge University Press.
  ———
  1984   *The Dobe !Kung*. New York: Holt, Rinehart and Winston.
Lerner, I. M. and W. J. Libby
  1976   *Heredity, Evolution, and Society*. San Francisco: W. H. Freeman
          and Company.
Lewellen, Ted C.
  1981   "Aggression and Hypoglycemia in the Andes: Another Look
          at the Evidence." *Current Anthropology*, 22:347–361.
Lewin, Roger
  1981   "Biggest Challenge Since the Double Helix." Research News,
          Science, 212:28–32.
  ———
  1983   "Is the Orangutan A Living Fossil?" *Science*, 222:1222–1223.
Lewontin, R. C.
  1972   "The Apportionment of Human Diversity." *In: Evolutionary
          Biology* (Vol. 6), Th. Dobzhansky et al. (eds.), New York:
          Plenum, pp. 381–398.
Lieberman, P. and E. S. Crelin
  1971   "On the Speech of Neanderthal." *Linguistic Inquiry*, 2:203–
          222.

Lindsay, Jean
1959   *A Short History of Science*. New York: Doubleday & Co.
Little, M. A., R. Brooke Thomas, Richard B. Mazess and Paul T. Baker
1971   "Populational Differences and Developmental Changes in Extremity Temperature Responses to Cold among Andean Indians." *Human Biology*, 43:70–91.
Livingstone, Frank B.
1964   "On the Nonexistence of Human Races." *In*: *Concept of Race*, A. Montagu (ed.), New York: The Free Press, pp. 46–60.

1969   "Polygenic Models for the Evolution of Human Skin Color Differences." *Human Biology*, 41:480–493.

1980   "Natural Selection and the Origin and Maintenance of Standard Genetic Marker Systems." *Yearbook of Physical Anthropology*, 1980, 23:25–42.
Lovejoy, Arthur L.
1959   "Buffon and the Problem of Species." *In*: *Forerunners of Darwin, 1745–1859*, Bentley Glass (ed.), Baltimore: Johns Hopkins Press, pp. 84–113.
Lovejoy, C. Owen
1981   "The Origin of Man." *Science*, 211:341–350.

1983   Paper presented at the Institute of Human Origins Conference on the Evolution of Human Locomotion (Berkeley).
Lovejoy, C. O., G. Kingsbury, G. Heiple and A. H. Burstein
1973   "The Gait of *Australopithecus*." *American Journal of Physical Anthropology*, 38:757–780.
Löwenberg, Bert James
1959   *Darwin, Wallace, and the Theory of Natural Selection*. Cambridge, Mass.: Arlington Books.
Luckett, W. Patrick
1980   "The Suggested Evolutionary Relationships and Classification of Tree Shrews." *In*: *Comparative Biology and Evolutionary Relationships of Tree Shrews*, W. P. Luckett (ed.), New York: Plenum Press, pp. 3–31.

Mai, L. L.
1983   "A Model of Chromosome Evolution and Its Bearing on Cladogenesis in the Hominoidea." *In*: R. Ciochon and R. Corruccini (eds.), q.v., pp. 87–114.
Maier, W.
1977   "Chronology and Biology of the South African Australopithecines." *Journal of Human Evolution*, 8:89–93.
Mann, Alan
1975   "Some Paleodemographic Aspects of the South African Australopithecines." *University of Pennsylvania Publications in Anthropology* (No. 1), Philadelphia.
Marschack, A.
1972   *The Roots of Civilization*. New York: McGraw-Hill Publishing Co.
Maw, B., R. L. Ciochon, and D. E. Savage
1979   "Late Eocene of Burma Yields Earliest Anthropoid Primate, *Pondaungia cotteri*." *Nature*, 282:65–67.

Mayr, Ernst
1962   "Taxonomic Categories in Fossil Hominids." *In*: *Ideas on Human Evolution*, W. W. Howells (ed.), New York: Atheneum, pp. 242–256.

1970   *Population, Species, and Evolution*. Cambridge: Harvard University Press.

1982   *The Growth of Biological Thought*. Cambridge: Belknap Press.
McGrew, Wm. C.
1979   "Evolutionary Implications of Sex Differences in Chimpanzee Predation and Tool Use." *In*: Hamburg and McCown (eds.), q.v., pp. 441–463.
McHenry, Henry
1975   "Fossils and the Mosaic Nature of Human Evolution." *Science*, 190:425–431.

1982   "The Pattern of Human Evolution: Studies on Behavior, Mastication, and Encephalization." *Annual Reviews of Anthropology*, 11:151–173.

1983   "The Capitate of *Australopithecus afarensis* and *A. africanus*." *American Journal of Physical Anthropology*, 62:187–198.
McKenna, James J.
1982   "The Evolution of Primate Societies, Reproduction, and Parenting." *In*: J. Fobes and J. King (eds.), q.v., pp. 87–133.
McKusick, Victor
1980   "Anatomy of the Human Genome." *Journal of Heredity*, 71:370–391.

1983   *Mendelian Inheritance in Man* (6th Ed.). Baltimore: Johns Hopkins Press.
Mech, L. David
1966   *The Wolves of Isle Royale*. Washington, D.C.: U.S. Government Printing Office.
Mendel, Gregor
1965   "Experiments in Plant Hybridisation" (A paper read before the Natural History Society of Brünn in 1865). Cambridge: Harvard University Press.
Menosky, Joseph A.
1981   "The Gene Machine." *Science 81* (July-Aug.):38–41.
Merrick, H. V. and J. P. S. Merrick
1976   "Archeological Occurrences of Earlier Pleistocene Age from the Shungura Formation." *In*: *Earliest Man and Environments in the Lake Rudolf Basin*, Y. Coppens et al. (eds.), Chicago: University of Chicago Press, pp. 574–584.
Montagu, Ashley (ed.)
1980   *Sociobiology Examined*. New York: Oxford University Press.
Moore, Lorna G. and Judith G. Regensteiner
1983   "Adaptation to High Altitude." *Annual Reviews of Anthropology*, 12:285–304.
Moore, Ruth
1961   *Man, Time and Fossils*. New York: Alfred A. Knopf.

Morbeck, M. E.
1975 "*Dryopithecus africanus* Forelimb." *Journal of Human Evolution*, 4:39–46.

——— 1983 "Miocene Hominoid Discoveries from Rudabánya. Implications from the Postcranial Skeleton." *In*: R. Ciochon and R. Corruccini (eds.), q.v., pp. 369–404.

Morris, Desmond
1967 *The Naked Ape*. New York: McGraw-Hill.

Mturi, A. A.
1976 "New Hominid from Lake Ndutu, Tanzania." *Nature*, 262:484–485.

Mueller, William H. et al.
1979 "A Multinational Andean Genetic and Health Program. VIII. Lung Function Changes with Migration between Altitudes." *American Journal of Physical Anthropology*, 51:183–196.

Murray, R. D.
1980 "The Evolution and Functional Significance of Incest Avoidance." *Journal of Human Evolution*, 9:173–178.

Napier, John
1967 "The Antiquity of Human Walking." *Scientific American*, 216:56–66.

——— 1973 *Bigfoot*. New York: E. P. Dutton & Co., Inc.

Napier, J. R. and P. H. Napier
1967 *A Handbook of Living Primates*. New York: Academic Press.

Napier, Prue
1977 *Chimpanzees*. New York: McGraw-Hill Book Co.

Newman, Marshall T.
1975 "Nutritional Adaptation in Man." *In*: *Physiological Anthropology*, Albert Damon (ed.), New York: Oxford University Press, pp. 210–259.

Newman, Russell W. and Ella H. Munro
1955 "The Relation of Climate and Body Size in U.S. Males." *American Journal of Physical Anthropology*, 13:1–17.

Newman, Russell W.
1970 "Why Man Is Such a Sweaty and Thirsty Naked Animal: A Speculative Review." *Human Biology*, 42:12–27.

Ninkovich, D. and L. H. Burcle
1978 "Absolute Age of the Base of the Hominid Bearing Beds in Eastern Java." *Nature*, 275:306–308.

Nishida, Toshisada
1979 "The Social Structure of Chimpanzees of the Mahale Mountains." *In*: *The Great Apes*, David A. Hamburg and E. R. McCown (eds.), q.v., pp. 73–121.

——— 1983 "Alloparental Behavior in Wild Chimpanzees of the Mahale Mts., Tanzania." *Folia Primatologica*, 41:1–33.

Nishida, Toshisada, S. Uehara, and R. Nyundo
1979 "Predatory Behavior among Wild Chimpanzees of the Mahale Mts." *Primates*, 20(1):1–20.

Norikoshi, Kohshi
1982 "One Observed Case of Cannibalism Among Wild Chimpanzees of the Mahale Mountains." *Primates*, 23(1):66–74.

Oakley, Kenneth
1963 "Analytical Methods of Dating Bones." *In*: *Science in Archaeology*, D. Brothwell and E. Higgs (eds.), New York: Basic Books, Inc.

Olby, Robert O.
1966 *Origins of Mendelism*. New York: Schocken Books.

Oldroyd, D. R.
1980 *Darwinian Impacts: An Introduction to the Darwinian Revolution*. Atlantic Highlands: Humanities Press.

Olson, Everett C.
1980 "Taphonomy: Its History and Role in Community Evolution." *In*: *Fossils in the Making*, K. Behrensmeyer and A. Hill (eds.), Chicago: University of Chicago Press, pp. 5–19.

Osborne, Richard (ed.)
1971 *The Biological and Social Meaning of Race*. San Francisco: W. H. Freeman Co.

Ovey, C. D. (ed.)
1964 "The Swanscombe Skull." Royal Anthropological Institute, Occasional Paper 20.

Oxnard, C. E.
1975 "The Place of the Australopithecines in Human Evolution: Grounds for Doubt?" *Nature*, 258:389–395.

Parker, Seymour
1976 "The Precultural Basis of the Incest Taboo: Toward a Biosocial Theory." *American Anthropologist*, 78:285–305.

Parks, Michael
1981 "Skulls Found in China Important in the Puzzle of Man's Evolution." *San Jose Mercury News*, Sunday, May 17, 1981.

Pauling, Linus
1974 "The Molecular Basis of Biological Specificity." *Nature*, 248:769–771.

Petit, Charles
1981 "Ancient Skull Raises New Storm." *San Francisco Chronicle*, September 26, 1981.

Pfeiffer, John E.
1978 *The Emergence of Man* (3d Ed.). New York: Harper and Row, Publishers.

Pickford, M.
1983 "Sequence and Environments of the Lower and Middle Miocene Hominoids of Western Kenya." *In*: R. Ciochon and R. Corruccini (eds.), q.v., pp. 421–439.

Pilbeam, David
1972 *The Ascent of Man*. New York: Macmillan.

——— 1975 "Middle Pleistocene Hominids." *In*: K. W. Butzer and G. L. Isaac (eds.), q.v., pp. 809–856.

——— 1977 "Beyond the Apes: Pre-*Homo* Hominids: The Ramapithecines of Africa, Asia, and Europe." Symposium Lecture, March 5, Davis, Calif.

——— 1979 "Recent Finds and Interpretations of Miocene Hominoids." *Annual Reviews of Anthropology*, 8:333–352.

1981 "New Fossil Hominoid from Pakistan." Paper presented at the Annual Meeting, American Association of Physical Anthropologists, April, 1981.

1982 "New Hominoid Skull Material From the Miocene of Pakistan." *Nature*, 295:232–234.

Pilbeam, David, G. E. Meyer, C. Badgley, et al.
1977 "New Hominoid Primates from the Siwaliks of Pakistan and Their Bearing on Hominoid Evolution." *Nature*, 270:689–695.

Popp, Joseph L. and Irven DeVore
1979 "Aggressive Competition and Social Dominance Theory." *In: The Great Apes*, David A. Hamburg and E. R. McCown (eds.), q.v., pp. 317–318.

Post, Peter W., Farrington Daniels, Jr. and Robert T. Binford, Jr.
1975 "Cold Injury and the Evolution of 'White' Skin." *Human Biology*, 47:65–80.

Potts, Richard and Pat Shipman
1981 "Cutmarks Made by Stone Tools from Olduvai Gorge, Tanzania." *Nature*, 291:577–580.

Poulianos, Aris N.
1981 "Pre-*sapiens* Man in Greece." *Current Anthropology*, 22(3):287–288.

Proshnev, B. F.
1974 "The Troglodytidae and the Hominidae in the Taxonomy and Evolution of Higher Primates." *Current Anthropology*, 15(4):449–450.

Radinsky, Leonard
1973 "*Aegyptopithecus* Endocasts: Oldest Record of a Pongid Brain." *American Journal of Physical Anthropology*, 39:239–248.

Ransom, Timothy W.
1981 *Beach Troop of the Gombe*. Lewisburg: Bucknell University Press.

Raza, S. Mahmoud, et al.
1983 "New Hominoid Primates from the Middle Miocene Chinji Formation, Potwar Plateau, Pakistan." *Nature*, 306:52–54.

Repenning, Charles A. and Oldrich Fejfar
1982 "Evidence for Earlier Date of Ubeidya, Israel, Hominid Site." *Nature*, 299:344–347.

Rightmire, G. P.
1976 "Relationships of Middle and Upper Pleistocene Hominids from Sub-Saharan Africa." *Nature*, 269:238–240.

1978 "Florisbad and Human Population Succession in Southern Africa." *American Journal of Physical Anthropology*, 48:475–486.

1979a "Cranial Remains of *Homo erectus* from Beds II and IV, Olduvai Gorge, Tanzania." *American Journal of Physical Anthropology*, 51:99–116.

1979b "Implications of the Border Cave Skeletal Remains for Later Pleistocene Human Evolution." *Current Anthropology*, 20:23–35.

1983 "Lake Ndutu Cranium and Early Homo sapiens in Africa." *American Journal of Physical Anthropology*, 61:245–254.

Roberts, D. F.
1973 *Climate and Human Variability*. An Addison-Wesley Module in Anthropology, No. 34, Reading, Mass.: Addison-Wesley.

Robinson, J. T.
1953 "Telanthropus and Its Phylogenetic Significance." *American Journal of Physical Anthropology*, 11:445–501.

1972 *Early Hominid Posture and Locomotion*. Chicago: University of Chicago Press.

Romer, Alfred S.
1959 *The Vertebrate Story*. Chicago: University of Chicago Press.

Rose, M. D.
1983 "Miocene Hominoid Postcranial Morphology. Monkey-like, Ape-like, Neither, or Both?" *In*: R. Ciochon and R. Corruccini (eds.), q.v., pp. 405–417.

Rose, Noel R.
1981 "Autoimmune Diseases." *Scientific American*, 244(2):80–103.

Rose, Steven
1972 "Environmental Effects on Brain and Behavior." *In: Race and Intelligence*, Ken Richardson and David Speers (eds.), Baltimore: Penguin Books, Inc., pp. 128–144.

Rowell, Thelma E.
1972 *The Social Behaviour of Monkeys*. Baltimore: Penguin Books.

Rudnai, Judith
1973 *The Social Life of Lions*. Wallingford, Pa.: Washington Square East.

Rumbaugh, D. M.
1977 *Language Learning by a Chimpanzee: The Lana Project*. New York: Academic Press.

Rumbaugh, Duane M., E. Sue Savage-Rumbaugh and John L. Scanlon
1982 "The Relationship Between Language in Apes and Human Beings." *In*: James E. King and James L. Fobes (eds.), q.v., pp. 361–385.

Sanderson, Ivan T.
1969 "The Missing Link." *Argosy*, May, pp. 23–31.

Sarich, Vincent
1971 "A Molecular Approach to the Question of Human Origins." *In: Background for Man*, P. Dolhinow and V. Sarich (eds.), Boston: Little, Brown & Co., pp. 60–81.

Sarich, V. M. and A. C. Wilson
1967 "Rates of Albumen Evolution in Primates." *Proceedings, National Academy of Sciences*, 58:142–148.

Sartono, S.
1975 "Implications Arising from *Pithecanthropus* VIII." *In: Paleoanthropology: Morphology and Paleoecology*, R. H. Tuttle (ed.), Chicago: Aldine Publishing Co., pp. 327–360.

Savage-Rumbaugh, E. Sue, D. M. Rumbaugh and Sally Boysen
1978 "Symbolic Communication between Two Chimpanzees (*Pan Troglodytes*)." *Science*, 201:43–56.

Scarr, Sandra
1981 "The Effects of Family Background: A Study of Cognitive Differences among Black and White Twins." *In: Race, Social*

Class, and Individual Differences in I.Q., S. Scarr (ed.), Hillsdale, N.J.: Lawrence Erlbaum Associates, Inc., pp. 261–315.

Scarr, Sandra and R. A. Weinberg
1976   "IQ Test Performances of Black Children Adopted by White Families." *In*: S. Scarr (ed.), q.v., pp. 109–159.

Schaller, George B.
1963   *The Mountain Gorilla.* Chicago: University of Chicago Press.

———
1972   *The Serengeti Lion.* Chicago: University of Chicago Press.

Scheidt, Walter
1924   "The Concept of Race in Anthropology and the Divisions into Human Races from Linnaeus to Deniker." *In*: *This Is Race*, E. W. Count (ed.), New York: Henry Schuman, pp. 354–391.

Scheller, Richard H. and Richard Axel
1984   "How Genes Control Innate Behavior." *Scientific American*, 250:54–63.

Scopes, John T. and James Presley
1967   *Center of the Storm.* New York: Holt, Rinehart and Winston.

Schull, William J., M. Otuke and J. V. Neel.
1981   "Genetic Effects of the Atomic Bombs: A Reappraisal." *Science*, 213:1220–1227.

Sebeok, Thomas A.
1980   *Speaking of Apes.* New York: Plenum Press.

Senut, Brigett
1981   "Humeral Outlines in Some Hominoid Primates and in Pliopleistocene Hominids." *American Journal of Physical Anthropology*, 56:275–283.

Sergi, Sergio
1967   "Morphological Position of the Prophaneranthropi (Swanscombe and Fontechevade)." *In*: *Ideas on Human Evolution*, Wm. Howells (ed.), Garden City, N.Y.: Doubleday and Co., pp. 507–520. (First published by Harvard University Press, 1962.)

Service, Elman R.
1966   *The Hunters.* Englewood Cliffs, N.J.: Prentice-Hall, Inc.

Shapiro, Harry
1936   *The Heritage of the Bounty.* New York: Simon and Schuster.

Shipman, P. L.
1983   "Early Hominid Lifestyle. Hunting and Gathering or Foraging and Scavenging?" Paper presented at 52nd Annual Meeting, American Association of Physical Anthropologists, Indianapolis, April, 1983.

Simons, E. L.
1969   "The Origin and Radiation of the Primates." *Annals of the New York Academy of Sciences*, 167:319–331.

———
1972   *Primate Evolution.* New York: Macmillan.

Simons, E. L. and P. C. Ettel
1970   "*Gigantopithecus.*" *Scientific American*, 222:76–85.

Simpson, G. G.
1945   "The Principles of Classification and a Classification of Mammals." *Bulletin of the American Museum of Natural History*, 85:1–350.

———
1961   *Principles of Animal Taxonomy.* New York: Columbia University Press.

Simpson, G. G., C. S. Pittendright and L. H. Tiffany
1957   *Life.* New York: Harcourt, Brace and Co., Inc.

Singer, Charles
1959   *A Short History of Scientific Ideas to 1900.* London: Oxford University Press.

Smith, Fred H.
1982   "Upper Pleistocene Hominid Evolution in South-Central Europe." *Current Anthropology*, 23:667–703.

Snyder, Louis L.
1962   *The Idea of Racialism.* New York: Van Nostrand Reinhold Co.

Solecki, Ralph
1971   *Shanidar, The First Flower People.* New York: Alfred A. Knopf.

Speth, J. D. and D. D. Davis
1976   "Seasonal Variability in Early Hominid Predation." *Science*, 192:441–445.

Stanyon, Roscoe and Brunetto Chiarelli
1982   "Phylogeny of the Hominoidea: The Chromosome Evidence." *Journal of Human Evolution*, 11:493–504.

Steegman, A. T. Jr.
1970   "Cold Adaptation and the Human Face." *American Journal of Physical Anthropology*, 32:243–250.

———
1975   "Human Adaptation to Cold." *In*: *Physiological Anthropology*, A. Damon (ed.), New York: Oxford University Press, pp. 130–166.

Stern, Curt
1973   *Principles of Human Genetics* (3rd Ed.). San Francisco: W. H. Freeman and Company.

Stern, Jack T. and Randall L. Susman
1983   "The Locomotor Anatomy of *Australopithecus afarensis.*" *American Journal of Physical Anthropology*, 60:279–317.

Stocking, George W. Jr.
1968   *Race, Culture, and Evolution.* New York: The Free Press.

Stringer, C. B. (ed.)
1981   *Aspects of Human Evolution.* London: Taylor & Francis Ltd. (Symposia of the Society for the Study of Human Biology, Vol. XXI).

———
1982   "Towards a Solution to the Neanderthal Problem." *Journal of Human Evolution*, 11(5):431–438.

Stringer, Christopher B., F. Clark Howell and John K. Melentis
1979   "The Significance of the Fossil Hominid Skull from Petralona, Greece." *Journal of Archaeological Science*, 6:235–253.

Stringer, C. B. and E. Trinkaus
1981   "The Shanidar Neanderthal Crania." *In*: *Aspects of Human Evolution*, C. B. Stringer (ed.), London: Taylor & Francis Ltd., pp. 129–165.

Struhsaker, Thomas T. and John F. Oates
1975   "Comparison of the Behavior and Ecology of Red Colobus and Black-and-White Colobus Monkeys in Uganda: A Summary." *In*: *Socioecology and Psychology of Primates*, R. H. Tuttle (ed.), Chicago: Aldine Publishing Co.

Strum, Shirley C.
1981   "Processes and Products of Change at Gilgil, Kenya." *In*: *Omnivorous Primates*, R.S.O. Harding and Geza Teleki (eds.), New York: Columbia University Press.

——— 1983   "Baboon Cues for Eating Meat." *Journal of Human Evolution*, 12:327–336.

Sugiyama, Yukimaru and Jeremy Koman
1979   "Tool-Using and -Making Behavior in Wild Chimpanzees at Bossou, Guinea." *Primates*, 20:513–524.

Suomi, Stephen J., Susan Mineka and Roberta D. DeLizio
1983   "Short- and Long-Term Effects of Repetitive Mother-Infant Separation on Social Development in Rhesus Monkeys." *Developmental Psychology*, 19:710–786.

Suzman, I. M.
1982   "A Comparative Study of the Hadar and Sterkfontein Australopithecine Innominates." *American Journal of Physical Anthropology*, 57:235.

Szalay, Frederick S.
1968   "The Beginnings of Primates." *Evolution*, 22:19–36.

Szalay, Frederick S. and Eric Delson
1979   *Evolutionary History of the Primates*. New York: Academic Press.

Tanner, J. M.
1977   "Human Growth and Constitution." *In*: *Human Biology*, G. A. Harrison, et al. (eds.), New York: Oxford University Press, pp. 299–385.

Tattersall, Ian and Niles Eldredge
1977   "Fact, Theory and Fantasy in Human Paleontology." *American Scientist*, 65:204–211.

Tauxe, Lisa
1979   "A New Date for *Ramapithecus*." *Nature*, 282:399–401.

Teleki, G.
1973   *The Predatory Behavior of Wild Chimpanzees*. Cranbrook, N.J.: Bucknell University Press.

Terrace, Herbert S.
1979   *Nim*. New York: Alfred A. Knopf.

——— 1982   "Why Koko Can't Talk." *The Sciences*, 22(9):8–10, Columbia University.

——— 1983   "Apes Who 'Talk': Language or Projection of Language by Their Teachers?" *In*: *Language in Primates*, J. de Luce and N. T. Wilder (eds.), New York: Springer-Verlag, Inc., pp. 19–42.

Thomsen, Dietrick E.
1978   "Radioisotope Dating with Accelerators." *Science News*, 113:29–30, January 14.

Thorne, A. and P. Macumber
1971   "Discoveries of Late Pleistocene Man at Kow Swamp, Australia." *Nature*, 238:316–319.

Thouveny, N. and E. Bonifay
1984   "New Chronological Data on European Plio-Pleistocene Faunas and Hominid Occupation Sites." *Nature*, 308:355–358.

Tobias, Phillip
1967   *Olduvai Gorge* (Vol. 2). *The Cranial and Maxillary Dentition of Australopithecus* (Zinjanthropus) *boisei*. Cambridge: Cambridge University Press.

——— 1971   *The Brain in Hominid Evolution*. New York: Columbia University Press.

——— 1972   "Early Man in Sub-Saharan Africa." *In*: *The Functional and Evolutionary Biology of the Primates*, R. Tuttle (ed.), Chicago: Aldine-Atherton, pp. 63–93

——— 1976   "African Hominids: Dating and Phylogeny." *In*: G. L. Isaac and E. R. McCown (eds.), q.v., pp. 377–422.

——— 1980   "*Australopithecus afarensis* and *A. africanus*. Critique and an Alternative Hypothesis." *Palaeontologica Africana*, 23:1–17.

——— 1983a   "Hominid Evolution in Africa." *Canadian Journal of Anthropology*, 3:163–185.

——— 1983b   "Recent Advances in the Evolution of the Hominids with Especial Reference to Brain and Speech." Potifical Academy of Sciences, *Scrita Varia*, 50:85–140.

Tobias, P. V. and G.H.R. von Koenigswald
1964   "A Comparison between the Olduvai Hominines and Those of Java and Some Implications for Hominid Phylogeny." *Nature*, 204:515–518.

Tomkins, Jerry R. (ed.)
1965   *D-Days at Dayton*. Baton Rouge: Louisiana State University Press.

Trigg, Roger
1982   *The Shaping of Man. Philosophical Aspects of Sociobiology*. New York: Shocken Books.

Trinkaus, Eric
1982   "The Shanidar 3 Neandertal." *American Journal of Physical Anthropology*, 57:37–60.

——— 1983   *The Shanidar Neandertals*. New York: Academic Press.

Trinkaus, E. and W. W. Howells
1900   "The Neandertals." *Scientific American*, 241(6):118–133.

Trinkaus, Eric and Marjorie LeMay
1982   "Occipital Bunning Among Later Pleistocene Hominids." *American Journal of Physical Anthropology*, 57:27–35.

Trinkaus, Eric and M. R. Zimmerman
1982   "Trauma Among the Shanidar Neandertals." *Ibid*, pp. 61–76.

Trivers, R. L.
1971   "The Evolution of Reciprocal Altruism." *Quarterly Review of Biology*, 46:35–57.

——— 1972   "Parental Investment and Sexual Selection." *In*: *Sexual Selection and the Descent of Man*, B. Campbell (ed.), Chicago: Aldine, pp. 136–179.

Turner, C.
1975   "The Correlation and Duration of Middle Pleistocene Interglacial Periods in Northwest Europe." *In*: K. W. Butzer and G. L. Isaac (eds.), q.v., pp. 259–308.

Van Couvering, A. H. and J. A. Van Covering
1976   "Early Miocene Mammal Fossils From East Africa." *In*: *Hu-*

man Origins, G. Isaac and E. R. McCown (eds.), Menlo Park, Ca.: W. A. Benjamin, pp. 155–207.

Vandermeersch, B.
1981 "A Neandertal Skeleton from a Chatelperronian Level at St. Cesaire (France)." *American Journal of Physical Anthropology*, 54:286.

Van Lawick-Goodall, Jane
1971 *In the Shadow of Man*. Boston: Houghton Mifflin Co.

Van Valen, L. and R. E. Sloan
1965 "The Earliest Primates." *Science*, 150:743–745.

Vlcek, F.
1978 "New Discovery of *Homo erectus* in Central Europe." *Journal of Human Evolution*, 7:239–252.

Vogel, F., M. Kopun and R. Rathenberg
1976 "Mutation and Molecular Evolution." *In*: *Molecular Anthropology*, M. Goodman, et al. (eds.), New York: Plenum Press, pp. 13–33.

Von Koenigswald, G.H.R.
1956 *Meeting Prehistoric Man*. New York: Harper & Brothers.

Walker, A.
1976 "Remains Attributable to *Australopithecus* from East Rudolf." *In*: *Earliest Man and Environments in the Lake Rudolf Basin*, Y. Coppens, et al. (eds.), Chicago: University of Chicago Press, pp. 484–489.

———
1981 Presentation of New Miocene Hominoid Material from East Africa. Annual Meetings, American Association of Physical Anthropologists, April, 1981.

Walker, Alan, Dean Falk, Richard Smith and M. Pickford
1983 "The Skull of *Proconsul africanus*: Reconstruction and Cranial Capacity." *Nature*, 305:525–527.

Walker, Alan and Richard E. F. Leakey
1978 "The Hominids of East Turkana." *Scientific American*, 239:54–66.

Walker, A. C. and M. Pickford
1983 "New Postcranial Fossils of *Proconsul africanus* and *Proconsul nyanzae*." *In*: R. Ciochon and R. Corruccini (eds.), q.v., pp. 325–351.

Walker, A., D. Pilbeam, and M. Cartmill
1981 "Changing Views and Interpretations of Primate Evolution." Paper presented to the Annual Meetings, American Association of Physical Anthropologists, April, 1981.

Ward, Steven and William H. Kimbel
1983 "Subnasal Alveolar Morphology and the Systematic Position of *Sivapithecus*." *American Journal of Physical Anthropology*, 61:157–171.

Ward, S. C. and D. R. Pilbeam
1983 "Maxillofacial Morphology of Miocene Hominoids From Africa and Indo-Pakistan." *In*: R. Ciochon and R. Corruccini (eds.), q.v., pp. 211–238.

Washburn, S. L.
1963 "The Study of Race." *American Anthropologist*, 65:521–531.

Watson, J. B.
1924 *Behaviorism*. New York: W. W. Norton.

Watson, James D.
1968 *The Double Helix*. New York: Atheneum.

Weidenreich, Franz
1946 *Apes, Giants, and Man*. Chicago: University of Chicago Press.

———
1951 "Morphology of Solo Man." *Anthropological Papers of the American Museum of Natural History*, Vol. 43, No. 3.

Weiner, J. S.
1954 "Nose Shape and Climate." *American Journal of Physical Anthropology*, 12:615–618.

———
1955 *The Piltdown Forgery*. London: Oxford University Press.

———
1977 "Human Ecology." *In*: *Human Biology*, G. A. Harrison et al. (eds.), New York: Oxford University Press, pp. 387–483.

Weiner, J. S. and B. G. Campbell
1964 "The Taxonomic Status of the Swanscombe Skull." *In*: *Royal Anthropological Institute of Great Britain and Ireland*, Occ. Paper 20, D. Ovey (ed.), pp. 175–215.

Weiss, Mark L. and Alan E. Mann
1981 *Human Biology and Behavior* (3rd Ed.). Boston: Little, Brown, and Co.

Wendt, Herbert
1963 *In Search of Adam*. New York: Collier Books.

White, Randall
1982 "Rethinking the Middle/Upper Paleolithic Transition." *Current Anthropology*, 23:169–192.

———
1982 "On the Middle/Upper Paleolithic Transition: A Response to Mellars." *Current Anthropology*, 23:358–359.

White, T. D.
1980 "Evolutionary Implications of Pliocene Hominid Footprints." *Science*, 208:175–176.

———
1983 Comment Made at Institute of Human Origins Conference on the Evolution of Human Locomotion (Berkeley, Ca.).

White, T. D. and J. M. Harris
1977 "Suid Evolution and Correlation of African Hominid Localities." *Science*, 198:13–21.

White, T. D., D. C. Johanson and W. H. Kimbel
1981 "*Australopithecus Africanus*: Its Phyletic Position Reconsidered." *South African Journal of Science*, 77:445–470.

Willerman, L., A. F. Naylor, and N. C. Myrianthopoulos
1970 "Intellectual Development of Children from Interracial Matings." *Science*, 170:1329–1331.

Williams, G. C.
1966 *Adaptation and Natural Selection: A Critique of Some Current Evolutionary Thought*. Princeton: Princeton University Press.

Wilson, E. O.
1975 *Sociobiology, The New Synthesis*. Cambridge: Harvard University Press.

Wolbarsht, M. L.
1975 "Letter to the editor." *Science*, 187:600.

Wolpoff, Milford H.
1980a *Paleoanthropology*. New York: Alfred A. Knopf.

———
1980b "Cranial Remains of Middle Pleistocene European Hominids." *Journal of Human Evolution*, 9:339–358.

———
1983a "*Ramapithecus* and Human Origins. An Anthropologist's

Perspective of Changing Interpretations." *In*: R. Ciochon and R. Corruccini (eds.), q.v., pp. 651–676.

———

1983b "Lucy's Little Legs." *Journal of Human Evolution*, **12**:443–453.

Wolpoff, Milford H. et al.

1981 "Upper Pleistocene Human Remains from Vindija Cave, Croatia, Yugoslavia." *American Journal of Physical Anthropology*, **54**:499–545.

Wood, B.

1976 "Remains Attributable to *Homo* in the East Rudolf Succession." *In*: *Earliest Man and Environments in the Lake Rudolf Basin*, Y. Coppens et al. (eds.), Chicago: University of Chicago Press, pp. 490–506.

Wood, C. S., G. A. Harrison, C. Dove and J. S. Weiner

1972 "Selection Feeding of *Anopheles gambiae* According to ABO Blood Group Status." *Nature*, **239**:165.

Wu, Rukang

1981 "Where Did Humankind Originate?" *China Pictoral*, No. 7, pp. 16–18.

———

1982 "Paleoanthropology in China, 1949–79." *Current Anthropology*, **23**:473–477.

Wu, Rukang and S. Lin

1983 "Peking Man." *Scientific American*, **248**(6):86–94.

Wu, Rukang and C. E. Oxnard

1983 "Ramapithecines from China: Evidence from Tooth Dimensions." *Nature*, **306**:258–260.

Yellen, John E.

1977 *Archaeological Approaches to the Present*. New York: Academic Press.

Yunis, Jorge J. and Om Prakesh

1982 "The Origin of Man: A Chromosomal Pictorial Legacy." *Science*, **215**:1525–1530.